Historical Dictionary of
American Education

HISTORICAL DICTIONARY OF AMERICAN EDUCATION

Edited by
Richard J. Altenbaugh

Greenwood Press
Westport, Connecticut • London

Library of Congress Cataloging-in-Publication Data

Historical dictionary of American education / edited by Richard J.
  Altenbaugh.
    p. cm.
  Includes bibliographical references (p.) and index.
  ISBN 0–313–28590–X (alk. paper)
   1. Education—United States—History—Dictionaries. 2.
Educators—United States—Biography—Dictionaries. I. Altenbaugh,
Richard J.
  LB15.H57   1999
  370'.9—dc21   98–51632

British Library Cataloguing in Publication Data is available.

Library of Congress Catalog Card Number: 98–51632
ISBN: 0–313–28590–X

First published in 1999

Greenwood Press, 88 Post Road West, Westport, CT 06881
An imprint of Greenwood Publishing Group, Inc.
www.greenwood.com

Printed in the United States of America

∞™ Ref LB 15 H57 1999

The paper used in this book complies with the
Permanent Paper Standard issued by the National
Information Standards Organization (Z39.48–1984).

10 9 8 7 6 5 4 3 2

To Michelle Fulton Goodall,
a dedicated educator and a dear friend.
We miss you.

CONTENTS

PREFACE

History touches all fields of education. This encompasses cognate areas as well as basic elements like school architecture, the Pledge of Allegiance, and school law. This dictionary attempts to be as inclusive as possible. It provides factual information about eminent people and important topics related to the development of American public, private, and parochial schools, covering elementary and secondary levels. In addition to major state and regional school leaders and reformers, it includes the biographies of significant national educators, philosophers, psychologists, and writers, but not necessarily limited to deceased notables. Subjects embrace significant ideas, events, institutions, agencies, and pedagogical trends that profoundly shaped this society's changing perceptions and policies regarding education. Although some items, like normal schools, cause slight overlap with higher education's philosophies and institutions, such treatments concentrate on the elementary and secondary context. Much of this factual knowledge is not unlike that in many history of education textbooks, but without contextual information and chronological structure. Further, these people and topics receive more than passing comments; albeit brief, the information is detailed enough to give the reader adequate background and a few bibliographical leads. This dictionary also contains a selected bibliography of additional educational history sources.

I attempted to rely on a methodical process to compile this list, utilizing a three-step approach. First, I stripped the indexes of leading history of education textbooks and reviewed thirty years of back issues of the *History of Education Quarterly*. Second, I sent this preliminary list to the dictionary's Advisory Committee for additions, deletions, and revisions. Their comments and suggestions greatly refined this list. Third, I accepted recommendations from authors as the articles arrived over a period of seven years. This whole project became organic, growing, changing, evolving. No matter what process I utilized, however, this project represents a no-win situation. Critics, I anticipate, will complain that I should have included some items and omitted others; such is the inherent pitfall of a reference work.

This dictionary contains 357 entries and maintains an alphabetized structure, permitting the reader to find a topic quickly and easily. I relied on this "encyclopedic" format for several reasons. A chronological approach, or even periodization, would have inhibited efficient use of this reference. Some topics, like the National Educational Association, defy easy chronological placement, since they span many decades and transcend historical periods. A topical approach, for example, curriculum or teachers, also would have been cumbersome because some items appear to overlap, like landmark court cases. In order to facilitate a chronological-periodization approach and a topical organization, these alphabetized items have been cross-referenced, and the dictionary includes an index. An asterisk within each article indicates that the topic or individual is treated in more depth as another entry. The period covered by these items begins in the colonial era and continues through the 1990s.

The authors reflect a wonderful blend. Most are established academics and scholars in the field of the history of education, curriculum and instruction, school law, educational administration, and American history; also included are promising graduate students working in specific research areas. A few of these authors work as public and private school teachers, as well as academic librarians and other professions affiliated with educational institutions. These articles reflect their rich and varied backgrounds.

Finally, although this historical dictionary attempts to be comprehensive on a national level, it omits many regional figures and rarely treats teacher-training topics, focusing instead on breadth. This is purposeful because other reference projects treat many important specific areas in the history of education. Maxine Seller has edited *Women Educators in the United States, 1820–1993* (Greenwood, 1994), relying on a biographical approach. Linda Eisenmann, editor, *Historical Dictionary of Women's Education in the United States* (Greenwood, 1998), details the contributions and experiences of female educators. Finally, Faustine Jones-Wilson et al., *Encyclopedia of African-American Education* (Greenwood, 1996), rely on a comprehensive approach. Therefore, this *Historical Dictionary of American Education* should be viewed within this broad context of supplementary reference works. Many of these editors, as well as others working on additional projects, met as a group to discuss our mutual projects at the 1994 Annual Meeting of the American Educational Research Association (AERA). Division F, History and Historiography, of AERA sponsored the panel: "A Conversation about Educational Biography: Symposium on Biography Projects Focusing on American Educators." Some overlap certainly exists among the articles included in these projects, but the reader will find, more often than not, that these reference works nicely dovetail each other.

ACKNOWLEDGMENTS

I incurred many debts as I worked on this project. Catherine V. Morsink, Dean of the College of Education at Slippery Rock University (SRU), gave a great deal of moral and financial support. In the latter case, she subsidized my presentation of this project at the 1994 annual meeting of the American Educational Research Association in New Orleans. Patti Pink and Sharon Isacco, in SRU's Word Processing Center, supplied superb skills and a genial attitude. The inimitable and indomitable Kay Wolford and Kay Castor, secretaries in the Elementary and Early Childhood and Secondary Education/Foundations of Education departments, respectively, cheerfully and tirelessly addressed countless envelopes and spent innumerable hours photocopying hundreds of articles at various stages of revision. I also want to thank Bruce Nelson, who read portions of this manuscript and offered his usual insightful comments.

I owe my greatest debt to 130 authors. Many quickly volunteered to make contributions, responding to my requests published in 1992 through professional newsletters like "The Network" and "AESA News and Comments." Others kindly accepted my invitation to write various pieces for the dictionary. I cajoled still others, who nevertheless appeared to be good natured and prompt. I was pleased throughout this process by the quality of the submissions and by everyone's professionalism. All patiently endured my nagging and persistent requests for revisions, information, and copyright agreements.

I also want to express my appreciation to a cooperative and diligent Advisory Committee, whose members possess broad scholarly backgrounds and teaching experiences and represent a wide variety of institutions, regions, and areas of expertise. They offered suggestions for the topics list, recommended authors, and wrote many articles themselves. They include Steve Aby, Ronald Butchart, Linda Eisenmann, Barbara Finkelstein, Craig Kridel, Robert A. Levin, Jeffrey Liles, Don T. Martin, Jeffrey E. Mirel, Catherine V. Morsink, Joseph Newman,

Alan Proctor, William J. Reese, Charles Russo, Peter Sola, William B. Thomas, Courtney Vaughn, and Faustine Jones-Wilson.

The good folks at Greenwood Press proved to be extremely patient as I missed countless deadlines. George Butler, series editor, should receive a special award for his guidance and tolerance.

More important, my family patiently and good-naturedly endured yet another scholarly project. The changes that occurred as I worked on this enterprise have been profound. The most vivid memory I have is that when I began working in earnest in fall 1991, Colin, my younger son, was just turning three. That was a wonderful time; I learned that young children are truly magical. I was on sabbatical from the Department of History at Northern Illinois University, and Colin and I spent many crisp autumn days playing, raking leaves, and just being plain silly. Now he has grown to be a curious, energetic, and creative boy. Ian, my older son, devolved into adolescence during this same time, becoming a young man anxious to drive the family vehicles. Buffy left our lives, replaced by the irrepressible and redoubtable Protocol Bluebonnet, another hyperactive English cocker spaniel. Finally, Marianne remained steadfast, as always. Thank you all for tolerating my blathering about new entries, word count limitations, missed deadlines, and all the other, seemingly trivial, issues involved with this dictionary.

INTRODUCTION

The history of American education represents a vital and productive field of study. Although it traces its chronological roots to the late nineteenth century, with Ellwood P. Cubberley and Paul Monroe formalizing it with their institutional, proselytizing style during the early twentieth century, it has experienced profound intellectual growth and maturation during the past forty years.[1] This stemmed from previous sharp criticism by academic historians and protracted tumult over its relationship to teacher preparation. In 1953, historian Arthur Bestor launched a blistering attack on educational historians and their work in his vitriolic *Educational Wastelands*:

Torn from its context of general historical change, the history of school systems becomes a chronicle almost devoid of meaning. Worse than that, it may easily become the kind of distorted history which presents the past as a mournful catalogue of errors, redeemed by some few feeble gropings toward that perfection of wisdom the present generation (and the instructor in particular) alone possess.[2]

Four years later the Ford Foundation's Fund for the Advancement of Education formed the Committee on the Role of Education in American History in order to move "educational" history closer to "academic" history.[3]

Bernard Bailyn eloquently initiated this trend in his 1960 historiographic classic, *Education in the Forming of American Society*, calling for a break from the staid and dominant institutional interpretation.[4] Lawrence Cremin responded five years later with an essay specifically criticizing Cubberley's ahistorical framework and generally castigating the Whig school of thought, which stressed institutional evolution and consensus. Cremin followed this with a bold proposal to study and write "educational" history rather than "school" history, to emphasize culture instead of institutions. He thus broadly defined education and its processes as "the deliberate, systematic, and sustained effort to transmit, evoke,

or acquire knowledge, attitudes, values, skills, sensibilities, as well as any outcome of that effort.'' In 1980, he expanded and refined this definition to include
''direct or indirect, intended or unintended'' learning. His comprehensive ''configuration of education'' encompassed the family, workplace, military, and media, as well as religion, colleges, libraries, museums, and, of course, schools.[5]
Even schooling now assumed a broader connotation, covering private and parochial institutions. All these historiographic efforts have fundamentally reshaped
the scope of educational history and raised its stature as a scholarly discipline,
moving it closer to social history.

Not only had educational historians moved away from a concentration on
school studies, but many began to employ a critical analysis during the late
1960s. ''Radical revisionists,'' like Michael Katz, Clarence Karier, and Joel
Spring, to name a few, dismissed the schools as sources of political, social, and
economic liberation and intellectual and personal growth; they proposed instead
a ''social control'' interpretive model.[6] As Sol Cohen observed in his 1976
survey of the field:

Historians of education are questioning stereotyped notions of the words *reform* and
progressive and are thinking in terms of the *irony* of school reform. . . . Historians of
education are now disclosing phenomena long hidden by official pieties: the maltreatment
of immigrants and ethnic groups, the discriminatory treatment of women and minority
groups, the connection between schools and politics and between education and social
stratification.[7]

The revisionist perspective introduced the concept of conflict and challenged
educational historians to reevaluate the role of public schooling in democratic
America. Throughout the 1970s, debates over the revisionist view dominated
the pages of the *History of Education Quarterly* and the annual History of
Education Society meetings. These disputes culminated in Diane Ravitch's *Revisionists Revisited*, labeling revisionism more ideological than intellectual.[8] Despite the sometimes shrill tone and raucous nature of these arguments, the
revisionist framework added yet another analytical dimension to the study of
educational history.

By the 1990s, this field had expanded its scope, analysis, and methods, revealing a mature and vibrant subject. It now studied teachers, families, and
children; treated the concepts of race, gender, ethnicity, and social class;
analyzed school curricula and classroom pedagogy; questioned the political, social, and economic functions of schooling; examined nonpublic schools; and
utilized quantitative and qualitative research tools.[9]

NOTES

1. Cubberley best illustrates this genre of educational history. See his *Public Education in the United States: A Study and Interpretation of American Education History*

(Boston: Houghton Mifflin, 1919). This work experienced several reprintings through the 1930s, and was used well into the 1950s.

2. Arthur Bestor, *Educational Wastelands: The Retreat from Learning in Our Public Schools* (Urbana: University of Illinois Press, 1953, 1985), p. 144. More important, refer to Sol Cohen's comprehensive survey of the field, "The History of the History of American Education, 1900–1976: The Uses of the Past," *Harvard Educational Review* 46 (August 1976), pp. 298–330. Bestor's same statement is quoted on p. 319. The history of education represented the theme for this issue of the *Harvard Educational Review*.

3. Refer to Cohen, p. 324, and Richard J. Storr, "The Role of Education in American History: A Memorandum for the Committee Advising the Fund for the Advancement of Education in Regard to This Subject," *Harvard Educational Review* 46 (August 1976), pp. 331–354.

4. Bernard Bailyn, *Education in the Forming of American Society: Needs and Opportunities for Study* (Chapel Hill: University of North Carolina Press, 1960).

5. Lawrence A. Cremin, *The Wonderful World of Ellwood Patterson Cubberley: An Essay on the Historiography of American Education* (New York: Teachers College Press, 1965); Lawrence A. Cremin, *Traditions of American Education* (New York: Basic Books, 1977), pp. viii, 23; Lawrence A. Cremin, *American Education: The National Experience, 1783–1876* (New York: Harper and Row, 1980), p. ix. Also refer to Cremin's *American Education: The Colonial Experience, 1607–1783* (New York: Harper and Row, 1970), and *American Education: The Metropolitan Experience, 1876–1980* (New York: Harper and Row, 1988).

6. Michael B. Katz, *The Irony of Early School Reform: Educational Innovation in Mid-Nineteenth-Century Massachusetts* (Boston: Beacon Press, 1968); Clarence J. Karier, *Shaping the American Educational State: 1900 to the Present* (New York: Free Press, 1975); Joel H. Spring, *Education and the Rise of the Corporate State* (Boston: Beacon Press, 1972). This list is illustrative and in no way exhaustive.

7. Cohen, p. 329. Also, refer to Carl F. Kaestle, "Conflict and Consensus Revisited: Notes toward a Reinterpretation of American Educational History," *Harvard Educational Review* 46 (August 1976), pp. 390–396.

8. See, for example, the responses to revisionist criticisms of John Dewey in the *History of Education Quarterly* 15 (spring 1975). Diane Ravitch, *Revisionists Revisited: A Critique of the Radical Attack on the Schools* (New York: Basic Books, 1978). Also refer to Joseph F. Kett's review of Ravitch's book, "On Revisionism," *History of Education Quarterly* 19 (summer 1979), pp. 229–236.

9. For a comprehensive overview of the field during the early 1980s, refer to John H. Best, ed., *Historical Inquiry in Education: A Research Agenda* (Washington, DC: American Educational Research Association, 1983). Representative works of the 1980s and 1990s include Larry Cuban, *How Teachers Taught: Constancy and Change in American Classrooms, 1890–1980* (New York: Teachers College Press, 1993); David J. Hogan, *Class and Reform: School and Society in Chicago, 1880–1930* (Philadelphia: University of Pennsylvania Press, 1985); N. Ray Hiner and Joseph M. Hawes, eds., *Growing up in America: Children in Historical Perspective* (Urbana: University of Illinois Press, 1985); James D. Anderson, *The Education of Blacks in the South, 1860–1935* (Chapel Hill: University of North Carolina Press, 1988); Barbara Finkelstein, *Governing the Young: Teacher Behavior in Popular Primary Schools in Nineteenth Century United States* (London: Falmer Press, 1989); Donald R. Warren, ed., *American Teachers: Histories of a Profession at Work* (New York: Macmillan, 1989); David W. Adams, *Education for*

Extinction: American Indians and the Boarding School Experience, 1875–1928 (Lawrence: University of Kansas Press, 1995); Barbara Beatty, *Preschool Education in America: The Culture of Young Children from the Colonial Era to the Present* (New Haven, CT: Yale University Press, 1995); Kate Rousmaniere, *City Teachers: Teaching and School Reform in Historical Perspective* (New York: Teachers College Press, 1997).

Historical Dictionary of
American Education

A

ABINGTON V. SCHEMPP. See BIBLE READING.

ACADEMIC FREEDOM permits instructors and students to teach and learn without reprisal for unorthodox or unpopular views. It originated as a protection from ecclesiastical and political interference in European medieval universities, which were organized and run by teachers and students and which emphasized teaching. In nineteenth-century German universities, with their emphasis on scholarship and research, academic freedom developed into the concepts of *lehr-freiheit* and *lernfreiheit*, implying freedom to examine and publicize ideas and the absence of administrative coercion in learning.

Where education is critical examination, academic freedom is important, for both the process and the results of study could challenge vested interests. In the United States, violations of academic freedom have predominated during times of political and social change. During the 1950s, the issue was communism and whether or not communist "sympathizers" should be teachers; this led to loyalty oaths. In these instances, the threats to academic freedom came from outside the schools. Today, it is said, the threats come not from outside but from within the institution, from teachers putting pressure on other teachers and students to conform to certain ways of thinking and to specific values, called "political correctness." Also, methods of inquiry have become routine; for example, the natural sciences may run less risk—except for their implications, such as the controversy about teaching evolution-creationism—than do other approaches, such as the social sciences and the humanities, that deal more directly with human values (see *SCOPES V. STATE*).

Academic freedom, however, is not self-enforcing. It requires institutional arrangements for its effectiveness. One of those arrangements is *tenure*. Tenure is the recognition that teachers earn the right, like a legal property right, to continue in their positions once they have demonstrated their competence and unless they can be proven to be no longer competent or to have neglected their duties. In elementary and secondary education, tenure is usually called "continuing contract." The tenure award is preceded by a probationary period, usually three or four years, during which the burden to demonstrate competence is on the teacher; school administrators then make a formal determination of the teacher's suitability to perform the task to which he or she is assigned, after which the burden to prove otherwise shifts to the institution. Tenure essentially operates as a form of job security and recognizes the principle of seniority. It is a bureaucratic practice. Institutions must follow rules, not only in the award of tenure but also in withholding it or whenever dismissing teachers.

Many misunderstandings occur with tenure and academic freedom. Tenure does not, as often alleged, guarantee "lifetime employment." Tenure simply requires that if the teacher's position is maintained, and the teacher has demonstrated competence to perform that duty, he or she has the right to continue in that employment. Institutions cannot dismiss instructors simply to hire less expensive or more compliant teachers. Neither is it the case that incompetent instructors, once tenured, must be retained. Ineffective teachers can be dismissed as long as institutions follow rules in doing so. Further, academic freedom does not give instructors the right to do anything they please in the classrooms. They cannot propagandize or fail to perform their assignments. The exercise of academic freedom must be relevant to the material being taught, and teachers must take the maturity of students into consideration when exercising academic freedom.

Critics wonder why a special kind of freedom—academic freedom—is necessary in the United States, where freedom of speech is protected by the Constitution. Courts have recognized, though not consistently, that academic freedom is necessary because of the educational context. Academic freedom is symbolic recognition that education is a particularly perilous, yet necessary, arena for the free discussion of ideas. Free speech in political debate seldom risks one's livelihood. Further, academic freedom does not benefit just the individual; its value is social.

Elementary and secondary teachers and students have perhaps been restricted more than those in higher education (see *TINKER V. DES MOINES*). Today, the challenge to academic freedom is the censorship of curricula materials. Not to be confused with the professional choice of teaching materials and strategies, censorship is the effort to deny access to ideas and materials, not just for one's own children but for all children, because of a dislike for those ideas and materials. It represents a fear of thinking, which is the opposite of academic freedom.

Refer to Howard K. Beale, *A History of Freedom of Teaching in American Schools* (1941); Richard Hofstadter and Walter P. Metzger, *The Development of Academic Freedom in the United States* (1955); and David Rubin, *The Rights of Teachers* (1984).

Robert R. Sherman

ACADEMIES. Between 1780 and 1860, Americans relied upon academies to satisfy much of their demand for formal education beyond elementary school. If the Latin grammar school* filled this need in the colonial era, especially for college-bound sons of the elite, the academy assumed primary responsibility for such schooling after the Revolution. However, it usually served as an alternative to college, not its precursor.

Academies came in many forms. Secular or sectarian, coeducational* or not, they taught everything from basic literacy and numeracy to military engineering. Most specialized in giving practical training of the sort that Benjamin Franklin* had in mind when he devised a plan for a public academy in Philadelphia in 1749. While not forgotten, the classical curriculum* was deemphasized. Students learned algebra, geometry, English, and modern foreign languages, along with such explicitly vocational subjects as navigation, bookkeeping, and even the principles of teaching (see VOCATIONAL EDUCATION).

Academies proliferated during the first half of the nineteenth century. By 1860, they could be found everywhere, but especially in rural areas. They were very popular in the South. In small towns, the local academy was a source of pride and ensured prosperity. It brought civic recognition, stimulated demographic growth, and provided the community with the cognitive tools for economic expansion.

By modern standards, academies operated as private institutions (see PRIVATE SCHOOLS). Although they received public support in the form of money or land grants, they were not subject to control by elected officials. Most practiced open admission, but none felt an obligation to be responsible for the common good in their community. Some charged tuition, others did not. The majority lived or died on the strength of their enrollment. Freestanding corporations, academies resisted joining with other schools to form educational systems. Such systems were the wave of the future by 1870, and in the second half of the nineteenth century the public high school* replaced the academy as the secondary school of choice because it became the capstone of progressive urban school systems (see PROGRESSIVE EDUCATION). Even the rural academy eventually fell before the relentless march of educational systematization.

By 1900, academies were no longer central to American education because they had ceased to be responsive to changes in the educational marketplace. Their memory is preserved today in name only by exclusive independent schools (see NATIONAL ASSOCIATION OF INDEPENDENT SCHOOLS) that specialize in preparing the children of the affluent for college admission.

Many local libraries and historical societies house the records of America's academies. Records are also available in the archives of some private schools. No recent or comprehensive history of the academy movement exists, but useful information can be found in Carl F. Kaestle, *The Pillars of the Republic: Common Schools and American Society, 1780–1860* (1983), and Theodore R. Sizer, ed., *The Age of Academies* (1964). For a provocative analysis of the academy's place in the development of American education, see Michael B. Katz, *Class, Bureaucracy and Schools: The Illusion of Educational Change in America* (1971).

William W. Cutler III

ACCOUNTABILITY MOVEMENT, which emerged during the early 1970s, can be traced to growing dissatisfaction with the quality of schools, a feeling that school personnel were closing ranks against public criticism, and the ever increasing pressure for tax dollars to finance education. It began as an attempt to restore power to professional educators who had been threatened by public criticism of the schools in the 1950s and by the community control* movement of the 1960s. Like the administrative progressives (see PROGRESSIVE EDUCATION) in the early twentieth century who argued for control by experts, the proponents of accountability considered education an arena for professional decision making.

Control by experts, an important theme of Leon Lessinger's book, *Every Kid a Winner* (1970), sparked the movement. Lessinger, often considered the "father" of the movement, saw community control as a threat to the quality of education. He used the hospital as his model to attack the concept of democratic control. Continuing to rely on the hospital model, he maintained that modern schooling was also based on professional knowledge gained through research and study.

Public accounting of the results of schooling represented the heart of the movement. Lessinger envisioned the creation of a national educational accounting firm operated by an educational accounting firm staffed by educational engineers who would measure educational results by the use of achievement tests and report the results to the public. He assumed that this information would provide the public with expert data that could be used to express pleasure with or criticism of the accomplishments of the school system. Accountability is a concept borrowed from business management. When applied to education, it meant that specific individuals, such as teachers, administrators, members of the board of education, the state department of education, and professional organizations, were responsible for student achievement. Prior to this, students were largely held accountable for their academic performance.

Holding teachers accountable for previously agreed-upon objectives relating to student achievement represented the most common approach to accountability. The stress was not on the *process* of teaching but on the *effects* of the teacher on student performance. The attempt was not to estimate "good" or "successful" teacher behavior but, rather, to estimate the teacher's ability to produce behavioral change in a group of students.

The concept of accountability was linked to educational reform and efficiency trends. It became a unifying theme related to management by objectives, cost effectiveness audits, systems analysis, performance contracting, voucher plans,* community participation and community control, consumer education, criterion-referenced testing, competency-based teacher education, assessment of teacher performance, bilingual and bicultural education, program evaluation, and a host of other schemes (see BILINGUAL EDUCATION; MULTICULTURAL EDUCATION).

Many educators criticized accountability. Both the National Education Association* and the National Commission on Teacher Education and Professional Standards called accountability unprofessional, inhumane, and arbitrary, especially if the profession itself did not develop the standards and methods of measurement. These organizations especially opposed laws that required the application of business and commercial instruments to education. The American Federation of Teachers* took an even stronger stand, linking accountability laws to "school-haters" who were looking for scapegoats to blame for social failures.

Lessinger's *Every Kid a Winner: Accountability in Education* (1970) represents the key source.

Don T. Martin

ACCREDITATION originated as an outgrowth of late-nineteenth-century efforts to articulate school-college relations specifically with respect to college entrance requirements. Wide variance characterized both secondary curricula and college admissions standards. In the Midwest, beginning in 1872 at the University of Michigan, college officials emphasized prescribing uniform program characteristics. University faculty evaluated high school programs, stipulated improvements, and when critieria were met, certified a school as a "diploma school." Successful graduates of diploma schools typically qualified for admission to participating colleges and universities. The Midwest practice was known as accreditation by certificate. Accreditation by examination prevailed in the East.

Accreditation practices were dominated by six regional voluntary accrediting associations, listed here with their dates of founding and of establishing accreditation standards, respectively: New England Association of Colleges and Secondary Schools (1885/1902); Middle State Association of Colleges and Secondary Schools (1887/1923); North Central Association of Colleges and Secondary Schools (1895/1902); Southern Association of Colleges and Schools (1895/1912); Northwest Association of Secondary and Higher Schools (1917/1918); and Western Association of Schools and Colleges (1924). Accreditation complemented the quantitative measure of the Carnegie unit* by focusing on the quality of a local educational program. Initially, accreditation enabled local high school* educators to lobby boards of education for program improvement; it also allowed college entrance requirements to dominate the high school curriculum.

With the founding of the College Entrance Examination Board in 1900 and the subsequent proliferation of college entrance examinations nationally, the focus of accrediting associations gradually changed. During the 1930s, the six regional accrediting associations revised their criteria to emphasize the general quality of local educational programs rather than the specialized qualifications for college entrance. Accreditation over time became regarded as a mechanism for self-study and renewal of local purposes, programs, and professional practices.

A variety of historical sources exist on this topic: Robert Kirkwood, "Accreditation" (1982); Edward A. Krug, *The Shaping of the American High School, 1880–1920* (1964); Kent W. Leach, "History and Purposes of Accreditation" (1964); John F. Nevins, *A Study of the Organization and Operation of Voluntary Accrediting Agencies* (1959); Robert Shaw, "A Backward Glance: To a Time before There Was Accreditation" (1993); Daniel Tanner and Laurel Tanner, *Curriculum Development: Theory into Practice* (1995); and John W. Vaughn, "School Evaluation and Accreditation: A Current Bibliography" (1980).

William G. Wraga

ADDAMS, JANE (September 6, 1860–May 21, 1935), a leading social reformer of the progressive period, founded Chicago's first settlement house, Hull-House, an innovative institution that pioneered progressive educational practices in non-school settings (see PROGRESSIVE EDUCATION). She was born in Cedarville, Illinois. After graduating from Rockford Female Seminary in 1877, Addams enrolled in medical school but withdrew after less than a year of study, suffering from a combination of physical disorders and psychological distress.

It was not until she encountered the desperate poverty of the streets of London that she discovered a new purpose. In 1889, with her friend, Ellen Gates Starr, she founded a settlement house, modeled on the example of London's Toynbee Hall. Hull-House, located in the heart of a crowded immigrant neighborhood, provided a place where members of the rapidly diverging classes could meet and learn from each other—the middle-class settlement workers would benefit as much from this relationship as the poor people of the Hull-House neighborhood (also, see AMERICANIZATION).

Education was an important part of the mission of settlement houses; Addams saw them as "a protest against a restricted view of education." Like John Dewey,* who frequently visited Hull-House, Addams recognized the importance of using children's native curiosity and imagination to promote an educational agenda. In settlement houses, children could do the kind of "hand work" that was not yet part of the curriculum of the public schools. In addition to supplementing the schools' traditional curriculum, settlement houses offered day care for infants, kindergartens* for preschoolers, activities and classes for older children who were no longer in school, and adult education programs.

The Labor Museum represented one example of Hull-House's innovative educational practices. Here immigrants demonstrated their crafts, such as spinning and weaving, teaching young factory workers about the basic industrial activities that were so often hidden by modern production methods. This not only allowed young workers to develop a new respect for their parents but also made "a beginning towards that education which Dr. Dewey defines as 'a continuing reconstruction of experience.' ''

Addams's commitment to improving educational opportunities led to an active interest in Chicago's public schools. She was appointed to the Chicago school board in 1905 and served as chair of the School Management Committee, responsible for teacher promotion, curriculum, and salaries. Although she was clearly bent on reform, her pragmatic approach and willingness to compromise alienated the teachers' union and other, more radical, reformers.

Addams's manuscripts can be found in the Swarthmore College Peace Collection. The best introduction to Addams and Hull-House is her *Twenty Years at Hull-House with Autobiographical Notes* (1910). Also, refer to Allen F. Davis, *American Heroine: The Life and Legend of Jane Addams* (1973); Allen F. Davis, *Spearheads for Reform: The Social Settlements and the Progressive Movement, 1890–1914* (1967); Christopher Lasch, ''Jane Addams: The College Woman and the Family Claim'' (1965); Christopher Lasch, ed., *The Social Thought of Jane Addams* (1965); and Anne Firor Scott, ''Jane Addams'' (1971).

Arthur Zilversmit

ADLER, MORTIMER. See *PAIDEIA*.

ADOLESCENCE. Every epoch of American history manifested a conscious conception of the period between childhood and adulthood. General patterns of adolescent experience in a given era were conditioned by particularities of individual circumstances. Factors such as race, class, gender, ethnicity, and place produced variations in the nature of adolescent experience at any given time. Current historical understanding of adolescence is limited by lack of availability of reliable sources documenting the adolescent experience of racial and ethnic minorities. Acknowledging these necessary variations and limitations, general patterns of adolescent experience are nevertheless apparent.

During the colonial era, the exigencies of an agricultural society largely shaped the lives of most youth. Children typically contributed to the household at an early age. Over time they assumed responsibilities commensurate with their level of maturity. Parent modeling clearly defined male and female roles for children. This setting deemphasized age distinctions. Associating with younger and older family members was the rule; mores and laws of the wider society reinforced these conditions. The journey from childhood through youth to adulthood, the latter considered to begin around thirty, was regarded as appropriate preparation for adult responsibilities.

Industrialization brought a confusion and subsequent rearrangement of expectations for youth. Whereas in traditional agricultural society adults typically made pivotal life decisions for youths regarding matters such as choice of occupation, residence, and spouse, during the nineteenth century youths increasingly made such decisions. Confronted with new choices, youths experienced new pressures; urban conditions confounded these choices and aggravated these pressures. The choices, however, had limits. During this era, gender roles became sharply delineated. The result was that expectations for the period between childhood and adulthood were more distinctly defined and, therefore, more limited for girls than for boys.

The "invention" of the concept of adolescence, principally but not exclusively in the work of G. Stanley Hall,* reflected and emerged from the confusing expectations of the nineteenth century. Hall's effort in his treatise, *Adolescence* (1904), to define and confine the "storm and stress" of adolescence was characteristic of a ubiquitous "search for order" around the turn of the century. Graded schooling, the disappearance of work opportunities outside the family setting, child labor legislation, juvenile law, a reduction in family size as a result of a declining birth rate, and a new attentive approach to parenting manifested increased organization and ordering of adolescent experience. The family, schooling, and other age-grouped institutions resulted in a relative standardization of adolescent experience. As a result, increased same-age experiences reinforced peer-group identity. A unique youth culture emerged at this time.

An unprecedented expansion of high school* offerings and enrollments accommodated the reconceptualiztion of adolescence. The purposes of secondary education shifted from a narrow focus on preparation for college to a wider focus on preparation for life (see LIFE-ADJUSTMENT EDUCATION). The comprehensive high school emerged as a unique American institution, offering a cosmopolitan program of academic, vocational, and elective courses and activities to serve the diverse backgrounds, abilities, and aspirations of a student body increasingly representative of the larger society (see VOCATIONAL EDUCATION). By midcentury, adolescence often was equated with the high school experience.

Although in earlier ages a period of youth was consciously recognized, during the twentieth century theories of adolescence appeared, evoking the myth that this recognition of adolescence as a distinct life stage was unprecedented. The difference was probably less a matter of the recognition of a new stage than the assignment of new meaning to the stage of adolescence. Although a modern concept of adolescence can be traced back at least to Rousseau, the proliferation of theories of adolescence is a particularly American phenomenon. After Hall's influential study, Margaret Mead (*Coming of Age in Samoa* [1928]), and Erik Erikson (*Childhood and Society* [1950] and *Youth: Identity and Crisis* [1968]), published works that advanced notable theories of adolescence.

Late-twentieth-century investigation of adolescence was marked by speculation that the stage had become less stressful than in the past and by renewed attention to the early-twentieth-century conception of a transition period between childhood and adolescence, later referred to as early adolescence or "transescence." Ongoing concern about adolescence reflects a heightened age consciousness in American life apparent since the mid-nineteenth century.

Numerous and rich secondary sources exist covering the history of adolescence. Refer to David Bakan, "Adolescence in America: From Idea to Social Fact" (1971); Howard Chudacoff, *How Old Are You? Age Consciousness in*

American Culture (1989); John Demos, ''The Rise and Fall of Adolescence'' (1986); Harvey J. Graff, *Conflicting Paths: Growing up in America* (1995); Nelson B. Henry, ed., *Adolescence* (1944); Mary Cover Jones, ''Adolescence'' (1950); and Joseph F. Kett, *Rites of Passage: Adolescence in America, 1790 to the Present* (1977).

William G. Wraga

ADVANCED PLACEMENT PROGRAM (AP). A Harvard-Yale-Princeton-Exeter-Andover-Lawrenceville study, begun in 1951, produced a report, *General Education in School and College*, which called for Advanced Placement. That year presidents and deans of Bowdoin, Brown, Carleton, Haverford, Kenyon, Massachusetts Institute of Technology, Middlebury, Oberlin, Swarthmore, Wabash, Wesleyan, and Williams convened a meeting that established the School and College Study of Admission with Advanced Standing. These efforts resulted in the first AP classes in the fall of 1953. After some initial subject examinations in 1954 and 1955, the first nationally administered tests took place in 1956.

The motivations for AP were complex. School-college collaboration represented the overarching theme. At the height of the Cold War, many saw the political and ideological necessity of upgrading school courses and stimulating able students and teachers to ensure victory. Professional demands for graduate work and the extension of graduate training begged for efficient use of the years available for study. Advocates argued that AP could ease the transition from school to college; colleges could avoid duplicating material taught in the top secondary schools. AP replaced the admission of gifted students at the completion of eleventh grade. Finally, proponents claimed that AP would assert a positive influence on the secondary school curriculum.

The program's growth has been dramatic. In 1954, 532 students took 929 exams in ten subject areas at eighteen secondary schools. Forty years later 458,945 students took 701,108 examinations in twenty-nine subjects at 10,860 schools. The number of colleges accepting AP scores jumped from 94 to 2,823 during that same period. Schools or colleges in fifty countries as well as the U.S. Department of Defense Schools accept or give AP credit. College Board member institutions determine the curriculum and provide the course descriptions, and Educational Testing Services conducts the testing. High school* students prepare for the annual May examinations primarily through subject courses, as well as seminars, independent study, and classes taught via computer hookups. College and secondary instructors together write the exams and evaluate them. Colleges and universities determine the scores necessary for credit or advanced placement.

See the original report *General Education in School and College* (1952) as well as articles in the *College Board Review*, 1954–1994.

Eric Rothschild

AFROCENTRICITY as a philosophy has typically been misconstrued as simply multicultural education* or a form of education that threatens to divide

American society along racial lines. Afrocentricity is instead meant to provide a vehicle for analysis relevant specifically to the African and African American experience—particularly in the areas of history and cultural studies—for African Americans. Afrocentricity is derivative of both the black studies movement that began in the late 1960s and multicultural education. The black studies movement insisted that African and African American history and culture be addressed in university curricula; it did not have the same impact on public school* curricula. Multicultural education not only concerns the African American experience but also encompasses the histories and cultures of women, Chicanos, Native Americans, Asians, and a host of other groups and has exerted a greater influence on public school curricula.

Nevertheless, Afrocentricity is a popularized conception of education for African Americans meant for consumption in all public institutions in which African Americans participate, including public schools. Although many black studies programs have maintained an Afrocentric paradigm since the early 1970s, Afrocentricity has been popular among African Americans outside the university setting only since the mid-1980s. Molefi Asante, called the ''Father of Afrocentricity,'' Leonard Jeffries, Asa Hilliard, John Henrik Clarke, and Maulana Karenga are among the growing number of African American scholars and intellectuals who have popularized this philosophy and concept. Asante's *Afrocentric Idea* (1987) played a key role in encouraging African American educators to think seriously about implementing Afrocentric curricula in the public schools.

Since 1985, school districts across the United States have adopted some Afrocentric curricula for their African American students. Portland, Oregon; Atlanta; Detroit; Baltimore; and Washington, D.C. spearheaded curricula that *center* on the experiences of African Americans. Separate African American male classrooms, justified by the argument that African American males have even more specialized needs for development and maturation than their female counterparts, have been included in this implementation process since 1989.

Beginning in the late 1980s, with California's and New York's attempts to revise the history curricula for their public schools, conservative scholars and educators like William Bennett and Thomas Sowell attacked Afrocentricity as ''unscholarly,'' ''divisive,'' and ''exclusionary.'' Other scholars, such as Diane Ravitch and Arthur Schlesinger, labeled Afrocentricity as ''multicultural education'' in order to maintain a cultural canon status quo. Liberal scholars have also criticized Afrocentricity for its almost total concern with ancient Egypt and its polemic dismissal of Eurocentric education and knowledge. Like the dialogue on multicultural education, Afrocentricity continues to draw heated debate even as it becomes increasingly popular.

For sources on Afrocentricity, see Molefi Asante, *The Afrocentric Idea* (1987); Molefi Asante, *Malcolm X as Cultural Hero: And Other Afrocentric Essays* (1993); James A. Banks, ''The Canon Debate, Knowledge Construction, and Multicultural Education'' (1993); John Henrik Clarke, *African People in World*

History (1993); John Henrik Clark, *Christopher Columbus and the Afrikan Holocaust: Slavery and the Rise of European Capitalism* (1992); Cheikh Anta Diop, *The African Origins of Civilization: Myth or Reality* (1974); Asa Hilliard, *50 Plus: Essential References on the History of African People* (1993); Asa Hilliard, "Why We Must Pluralize the Curriculum" (1992); Maulana Karenga, *Introduction to Black Studies* (1993); Maulana Karenga, ed., *Reconstructing Kemetic Culture: Papers, Perspectives, Projects* (1990); and Maulana Karenga, *The African-American Holiday of Kwanzaa: A Celebration of Family, Community and Culture* (1988). Critics include William Bennett, *Our Children and Our Country: Improving America's Schools and Affirming the Common Culture* (1988); Diane Ravitch, "Multiculturalism: E Pluribus Plures" (1990); Arthur Schlesinger, *The Disuniting of America: Reflections on a Multicultural Society* (1991); and Thomas Sowell, *Inside American Education: The Decline, the Deception, the Dogmas* (1993).

Donald E. Collins

AGE-GRADING. Perhaps no reform altered the structure of American schools so dramatically, influenced their curricular and instructional evolution down to the present day so fundamentally, and resisted counterreform efforts so successfully as the graded school. The term "graded school," or age-grading, refers to a system of schooling in which the curriculum, instruction, and grouping of children are organized in one-year increments, with children assigned to these graded classes by their age but sometimes promoted or retained in grade by their achievement. The recounted history of graded schools in the United States typically begins with the Quincy (Massachusetts) School in 1847, a common school* directed by the renowned New England educator John Philbrick. However, earlier high schools,* academies,* Latin grammar schools,* and monitorial schools* practiced some forms of graded organization or curriculum.

Philosophy and convenience spurred the evolution of age-grading. Graded elementary schools gained rapid acceptance in urban areas by 1860, though many rural schools retained their child-through-teenager one-room schoolhouses (see ONE-ROOM SCHOOLS) well into the early decades of the twentieth century. Most city and town schools in the 1850s were graded not by single age groups but by clustering such labels as infant (see INFANT SCHOOLS), primary, grammar, and high school. This multi-age classification system facilitated sorting for steadily increasing enrollment. Age-grading evolved through the mid-nineteenth century as school districts constructed new buildings to accommodate the influx of children, and as they did, they differentiated buildings and spaces for various age levels. Horace Mann* promoted age-grading in part based on his observations of German schools in 1843, whereas Henry Barnard* asserted in 1852 that the "great principle" in classifying "scholars" should be "equality of attainments, which will generally include those of the same age." Another essential and overlapping development was the publication of graded and standardized textbooks; Warren Colburn's arithmetic books (1821) and William H.

McGuffey's* *Eclectic Readers* (1836) were early examples, but as the curriculum expanded through the century, series of articulated textbooks followed both to serve and to promote graded schools. Stratifying children by age promoted efficiency, replaced cooperation with competition, and infused the schools with meritocratic principles.

Even as age-grading represented a major and fundamental reform in American educational history, vocal counterreform efforts had begun by century's end. Writing in 1899, William J. Shearer asserted that "the system of grading, which was installed to faithfully serve the children, has become their tyrannical master . . . a Procrustean bed of grades." John Dewey's* University of Chicago Laboratory School* organized instruction by grades but emphasized individualization of instruction, teaching besides and beyond the usual textbook fare, and school furniture for "working" rather than "listening" as found in most graded schools. By the time of "scientific management's" heyday in the 1920s, the National Society for the Study of Education* issued a yearbook that touted a variety of curricular and organizational alternatives to textbook-driven graded programs, such as those in Gary, Indiana, led by William Wirt,* Winnetka, Illinois, under Carleton Washburne,* and Detroit as described by Stuart Courtis (also, see GARY PLAN; WINNETKA PLAN). Often called child-centered progressive educators (see PROGRESSIVE EDUCATION), these voices decried the problem of routinization, memorization, and passive learning.

Another attack on graded schools' ability to serve young adolescents led not to calls for individualization but to the creation of a new graded institution in the 1910s and 1920s, the junior high school,* and with it came the rise of vocational education* for the secondary grades and the decline of the long-popular 1–8 or K–8 elementary school structure.

The age-graded division of children and curricula has remained perched on the fulcrum about which a whole host of reform agendas have tried to sway the system for over a hundred years. Historical as well as current debates about the role and legitimacy of standardized testing, "ability" grouping, "social promotion," and the education of the handicapped and "gifted" all owe their roots and many of their branches to the predominance of graded schools (see SPECIAL EDUCATION; TRACKING). Instructional approaches like individualized instruction, "cooperative learning,"* "higher order thinking skills," "hands-on" or activity- and project-based curricula (see PROJECT METHOD), "whole language," and thematic and interdisciplinary instruction (see INTEGRATED CURRICULUM) have attacked one or more assumptions traditionally associated with age-grading and graded textbooks. Indeed, an ongoing strand in twentieth-century reform efforts has been to seek to modify the structure of age-grading by returning to an updated version of the mid-nineteenth-century clustering of two, three, or four age cohorts of children into "flexible" learning units.

For historical background, refer to R. Freeman Butts and Lawrence A. Cremin, *A History of Education in American Culture* (1953); Lawrence A. Cremin, "What Happens to Reforms That Last? The Case of the Junior High

School'' (1992); John I. Goodlad and Robert H. Anderson, *The Non-Graded Elementary School* (1959); Carl F. Kaestle, *Pillars of the Republic* (1983); National Society for the Study of Education, *Adapting the School to Individual Differences* (1925); William J. Reese, *The Orgins of the American High School* (1995); William J. Shearer, *The Grading of Schools* (1899); and David Tyack and Larry Cuban, *Tinkering toward Utopia: A Century of Public School Reform* (1995).

Robert A. Levin

AGOSTINI V. FELTON, 117 S. Ct. (1997). The U.S. Supreme Court took the unusual step of following through on its promise to overrule its earlier decision in *Aguilar v. Felton,* 473 U.S. 402 (1985). That decision had banned the on-site delivery of remedial educational services under Title I of the Elementary and Secondary Education Act* for economically disadvantaged students in religiously affiliated nonpublic schools. Writing for a closely divided Court in another 5-to-4 decision, Justice Sandra Day O'Connor, joined by Chief Justice William Rehnquist and Justices Antonin Scalia, Anthony Kennedy, and Clarence Thomas, reasoned that the New York City Board of Education's (NYCBOE) Title I program did not violate the Establishment Clause of the Eighteenth Amendment, since there was no governmental indoctrination, there were no distinctions between recipients based on religion, and there was no excessive entanglement. Thus, Justice O'Connor ruled that as a federally funded program that offers supplemental, remedial instruction to disadvantaged children on a neutral basis, the NYCBOE's Title I program of providing services in religiously affiliated nonpublic schools did not run afoul of the Establishment Clause because it had appropriate safeguards in place. Dissenting opinions by Justices David Souter and Ruth Bader Ginsburg, joined in parts by Justices John Paul Stevens and Stephen G. Breyer, voiced fears that the Court further blurred the line between aid to religiously affiliated nonpublic schools that was ''indirect and insubstantial'' and that which was ''direct and substantial.''

Charles J. Russo and Allan G. Osborne, Jr.

ALCOTT, AMOS BRONSON (November 29, 1799–March 4, 1888), a teacher and self-educated philospher, as well as the father of *Little Women*, written by his daughter Louisa May, was known as the American Pestalozzi for his use of Pestalozzian techniques (see PESTALOZZIANISM) in the classroom and his observations on child development. He taught at numerous schools in New England, carried his educational message to England and America's West, and attempted to imbue his educational practices with his own adaptions of American transcendentalism.

Alcott's innovative teaching techniques won him acclaim from 1826 to 1839. He used an inductive aproach to teaching and learning, believed studies should follow the natural order of a child's development, condemned corporal punishment, gave books a supplemental, not primary, place in education, and thought that the school should be as homelike as possible. Alcott differed from Pestalozzi by not mentioning vocational education* and by not mechanizing the educational process. Alcott believed that education should be directed to the development of the spiritual life of the child. Education was individual, social, and spiritual, and it would bring children to recognize the divinity within themselves. Along with his cousin William Alcott, Bronson developed a new school desk that had a writing surface and seat for each individual student. Alcott also introduced the use of slates and blackboards into the classroom and physical activity in the curriculum. His schoolrooms incorporated nature into the decor in an attempt to make it a pleasing and comfortable environment for children.

Alcott taught in infant schools* in Boston and in coeducational* academies* in Philadelphia and Germantown, Pennsylvania, among other places. His most famous school was the Temple School (1834–1839) in Boston, where he was assisted by Elizabeth Peabody.* There he utilized student journal writing, for students' self-analysis and language development, and his conversational method of teaching. He based the latter approach on the idea that children were the best witnesses of the nature of God; through the teacher's dialogues with and questioning of them, God's nature and the child's divinity would be learned. The Temple School received much publicity when Peabody published her transcipts of Alcott's conversations with children in *Record of a School* (1835). In 1836 and 1837, Alcott published two volumes of his *Conversations with Children on the Gospels*. His controversial theological ideas and his enrollment of an African American girl made the school unpopular, and he closed it in 1839.

Alcott became involved with the failed utopian community Fruitlands (1840–1845); he then traveled the country on lecture tours, espousing his ideas on various social reforms and spiritual progress. Between 1855 and 1864, he served as superintendent of the Concord public schools. He visited classrooms, preached the importance of parental involvement in the neighborhood school, introduced singing, dancing, marching, and recreational periods in schools, and encouraged teachers to visit other schools as a way of learning new teaching techniques.

In 1878, the Concord School of Philosophy opened with Alcott as dean and with faculty members such as William Torrey Harris,* William Henry Channing, and Ralph Waldo Emerson. The Concord School upheld religious beliefs and values when Darwinism and naturalism were gaining credence in society. After 1882, Alcott was unable to participate in the school's lectures because of ill health.

Alcott's papers are in the Alcott-Pratt Collection, Houghton Library, Harvard University, and in Alcott's manuscripts at the Fruitlands Museum, Harvard University, Massachusetts. Biographies include Frederick C. Dahlstrand, *Amos Bronson Alcott: An Intellectual Biography* (1982); Dorothy McCuskey, *Bronson Alcott: Teacher* (1940); F. B. Sanborn, *Bronson Alcott: At Alcott House, Eng-*

land, and Fruitlands, New England (1842–1844) (1908); and Odell Shepard, *Pedler's Progress: The Life of Bronson Alcott* (1937).

Laurie Moses Hines

ALEXANDER, WILLIAM MARVIN (February 19, 1912–August 27, 1996), is recognized as the father of the middle school* movement. He was born in McKenzie, Tennessee, received his B.A. in 1934 from Bethel College, located in his hometown, and began his educational career teaching social studies in the local schools there. In 1936, he became a teaching assistant at Peabody College for Teachers in Nashville, where he earned his master's in education and history. Four years later Alexander received his Ph.D. from Teachers College, Columbia University. There he studied and associated with two of that period's most prominent and controversial figures, George Counts* and Herbert Buner. Also, at Columbia, he began his lifelong professional association with Gaylen Saylor, his classmate. This was a pivotal period regarding curriculum and American opinion regarding the purpose of the school, and Alexander was involved in the changes occurring in the Progressive Education Association.*

Alexander occupied a variety of educational positions in different parts of the country and at different levels. He served as assistant director of curriculum for Cincinnati, Ohio, schools (1939–1941); associate professor of education at the University of Tennessee (1941–1943); director of instruction and assistant superintendent for Battle Creek (Michigan) Schools (1946–1949); superintendent of schools, Winnetka, Illinois (1949–1950); and professor of education at the University of Miami (1950–1958), George Peabody College for Teachers (1958–1963), and University of Florida (1963–1977).

Alexander's concept of the middle school was his greatest contribution to educational curriculum reform, and beginning in the 1960s, he devoted much of his professional career to the promotion of middle school education. During the 1966–1967 academic year, he was awarded federal funding for a National Defense Education Act* Middle School Institute. As a result of the Institute's study, Alexander and his colleagues found that little information existed on middle school education. He subsequently coauthored publication of the *Emergent Middle School* (1968), with Emmett Williams, Vynce Haines, Mary Compton, Ronald Kealy, and Dan Prescott. This work provided the rationale and program for the establishment of middle schools across the nation. Alexander's contributions continued with his work funded by the U.S. Department of Health, Education, and Welfare,* specifically *A Survey of Organizational Patterns of Reorganized Middle Schools* (1968). Alexander authored many books and more than 150 professional articles.

Alexander received numerous awards and distinguished honors for his work. After he retired, he served as a Fulbright lecturer at the University of Tehran in Iran and as a middle school consultant across the nation.

For biographical sketches, see C. Kenneth McEwin, ''William M. Alexander:

1912–1996'' (1996) and C. Kenneth McEwin, ''William M. Alexander: Father of the American Middle School'' (1992). Among his many works, Alexander's vision for the middle school can be gleaned from his two articles ''Schools for the Middle School Years'' (1965) and ''What Educational Plan for the In-Between-Ager?'' (1966).

Jo Beth Oestreich

ALPHABET CURRICULUM IN SCIENCE. See SCIENCE EDUCATION.

ALTERNATIVE SCHOOLS, private* and public,* have been established since the 1960s to give students, parents, and teachers educational options other than traditional schooling. Members of the 1960s and 1970s counterculture wanted schools that gave students less structure and more choice and thus organized a variety of smaller, more personal, more experiential schools. Some alternative schools were consciously modeled on British open education, although others found inspiration in earlier progressive (see PROGRESSIVE EDUCATION) experiments like John Dewey's* University of Chicago Laboratory School.* Many ''free schools''* were modeled on A. S. Neill's Summerhill in England. Urban ''Freedom Schools''* provided African American students a curriculum that developed black pride. ''Schools-within-schools'' established smaller units within large public schools, often grouping students by interest rather than ability. The alternative school influence has been been mixed. Most such experiments disappeared, but a few early alternative schools survived into the 1990s. Many new ones have also been established. Some successful alternative school practices have often been incorporated into public schools and classrooms.

Timothy W. Young, *Public Alternative Education* (1990) surveys these programs and provides a useful bibliography. *Educational Leadership* 52 (September 1994) devoted an entire issue to ''The New Alternative Schools.''

James M. Wallace

AMERICAN ALLIANCE FOR HEALTH, PHYSICAL EDUCATION, RECREATION, AND DANCE (AAHPERD), represents one of the largest professional education organizations in the country with over 30,000 members. At the invitation of William G. Anderson, physical director at the Adelphi Academy, sixty leaders representing medicine, law, divinity, and education convened in Brooklyn on November 27, 1885, to discuss challenges facing the field of physical education.* From this meeting evolved the first national organization for physical education in the United States, the Association for the Advancement of Physical Education, in which forty-nine of the conference attendees elected membership. By 1903, the membership had grown to 1,000 and the name was changed to the American Physical Education Association (APEA). With the growing recognition of health education* as a separate academic discipline, the APEA became the American Association for Health and Physical Education in 1937. For similar reasons, ''Recreation'' was added to the title a year later. As a result of pressure in the 1970s to provide greater visibility to the fields represented within the organization, "Association" became "Alliance" in 1974, with "Dance" added in 1979. Because it is comprised of six associations, AAHPERD exerts wide influence and maintains considerable stature within the education community. These six associations are the Association for Research, Administration, Professional Councils and Societies; the American Association for Health Education; the American Association for Leisure and Recreation; the National Association for Girls and Women in Sport; the National Association for Sport and Physical Education; and the National Dance Association. The AAHPERD maintains its headquarters in Reston, Virginia.

Refer to AAHPERD, *The Shape of a Nation: A Survey of State Physical Education Requirements* (1987).

Michael J. Cleary

AMERICAN EDUCATION SOCIETY (AES) was organized in Boston in 1815 by Congregational clergy associated with the Andover Theological Society. The Society grew under Elias Cornelius, its first full-time executive secretary (1826–1831). As one of the national benevolent religious societies, the core of its support was Congregationalist and Presbyterian, but it extended financial support to ministerial students from evangelical Protestant denominations who pursued a thorough education—four years of college followed by three years of theological study. The Society encouraged public education in an academy and theological seminary rather than private tutorial instruction (see ACADEMIES; TUTORS). The AES exerted leadership in higher education, functioning as an embryonic accrediting agency, upholding standards and supporting the classical curriculum* in colleges. It provided the first widespread scholarship program in American education and, at its peak in the 1830s, supported significant numbers of students in academies, colleges, and theological seminaries, particularly in the Northeast. This financial support to students helped ensure the success of the institutions they attended.

The Society's insistence on a thorough education helped raise standards for the ministry and establish the theological seminary as the first graduate professional school and precursor of the university. By assisting the education of nearly 5,000 men in the antebellum years, it helped produce learned ministers who diffused education and culture, as well as religion, in the West and throughout the country. The Society had branch and auxiliary societies and inspired denominational educational societies. By 1860, it was de facto the Congregational Education Society, though its name was not changed until 1894.

The American Education Society Papers are housed at the Congregational Library, Boston. Also, refer to David F. Allmendinger, Jr., "The Strangeness of the American Education Society: Indigent Students and the New Charity, 1815–1840" (1971); Henry Barnard, "The American Education Society" (1864); Natalie A. Naylor, " 'Holding High the Standard': The Influence of the American Education Society in Ante-Bellum Education" (1984); and Natalie A.

Naylor, "Raising a Learned Ministry: The American Education Society, 1815–1860" (1971).

Natalie A. Naylor

AMERICAN FEDERATION OF TEACHERS (AFT) is the major national teachers' union in the United States. In comparison to its larger competitor, the National Education Association (NEA),* the AFT has traditionally identified itself as a trade union and focused on teachers' working conditions and collective bargaining.

Organized in 1916 as a federation of four local teacher unions from the Chicago area (see CHICAGO TEACHERS FEDERATION), the early AFT was troubled by power struggles between female elementary teachers, who constituted the bulk of the teaching force, and male high school teachers, who constituted the Federation's leadership. The union also wrestled with its identity as a professional organization versus a radical trade union. New York City Local No. 5 comprised the more militant wing of the AFT, becoming the figurehead of the national teacher union movement and a target of political persecution through the 1920s. Communist Party members took over that New York local in the 1930s, leading to an ideological civil war and eventually splitting the union into two locals.

Federation locals in the 1940s increasingly turned to the struggle for collective bargaining for improved working conditions. The postwar union also became active in civil rights issues in the urban schools that claimed the bulk of the membership. In 1951, the AFT Executive Council voted to refuse to charter segregated locals and supported other civil rights and desegregation fights.

The Federation's modern growth dates from the organization of the United Federation of Teachers (UFT)* in New York in 1960. In April 1962, half of New York City's teachers struck for improved working conditions and collective bargaining rights and won most of their demands. The national effect of the UFT strike was to encourage organized instructors in other states to challenge state no-strike laws for teachers and to fight for collective bargaining. During the 1960s and 1970s the reinvigorated AFT locals faced a power struggle with reformers over the issue of community control.* In New York City, the UFT's defense of its newly won contracts clashed with civil rights activists who promoted the development of community-run schools. The tension was heightened by the fact that over half of New York City's student population consisted of racial or ethnic minorities, whereas 90 percent of the UFT's membership was white. In 1967, in the Brooklyn school district of Ocean Hill–Brownsville,* the community board dismissed nineteen teachers and administrators, and in response the UFT struck. A similar strike in Chicago in 1969 resulted in a standoff between teachers' allegiance to collective bargaining and reformers' commitment to community control.

Early talks over an AFT-NEA merger began in 1968, leading to local mergers in some city districts, like Los Angeles. With its membership at 900,000, about half of the NEA's enrollment, the AFT continues to maintain its stronghold in urban school districts. The AFT continues to struggle with the issues of community control and the role of a teachers' union in school reform.

Collections of AFT papers are located at the Walter P. Reuther Library at Wayne State University, the Cornell University Labor Archives, and the Robert Wagner Archives at New York University. The major secondary sources on the AFT include William Eaton, *The American Federation of Teachers, 1916–1961: A History of the Movement* (1975); Marjorie Murphy, *Blackboard Unions: The AFT and the NEA, 1900–1980* (1990); and Wayne J. Urban, *Why Teachers Organized* (1982).

Kate Rousmaniere

AMERICAN INSTITUTE OF INSTRUCTION, founded in 1830, was the first national organization of educators in America. Though initially based in Boston, the organization quickly scheduled its annual meetings in outlying towns, predominantly in New England. Its membership included virtually every important nineteenth-century educator, representing all generic schools and instructional issues. Almost all states, which anticipated the creation of public school* systems, sent representatives to the institute's annual meetings during the antebellum period. Its leadership included men like Reverend Francis Wayland, the Institute's first president and president of Brown University, and welcomed some of the best-known speakers of the day, including Ralph Waldo Emerson, William Ellery Channing, Henry Ward Beecher, and Robert Winthrop. The heart of its work, however, was carried out predominantly by men, and after 1876 also by women, at the elementary and secondary levels of instruction (also, refer to HALL, SAMUEL READ).

The Institute's seventy-eight published volumes (1830–1908) and annual conferences established the earliest and longest significant discourse in nineteenth-century United States on educational matters. This voluntary organization provided much intellectual and contextual support to Horace Mann,* Henry Barnard,* and others in the creation of America's public school systems. Many other reforms and issues, debated in its four- to six-day annual conferences, included the education of women, object lessons (see OBJECT TEACHING), Pestalozzian methods (see PESTALOZZIANISM), the role of academies* and normal schools,* the professionalization of teachers, physical discipline (see CLASSROOM DISCIPLINE AND MANAGEMENT), and the centrality of character formation. The organization evinced an encompassing, quasi-evangelical brand of professionalism that was eventually supplanted by the more specialized and empirically based practices of the progressive education* movement. The Institute went out of existence in 1918, unable to compete with state-based professional associations and the broader geographical compass of the National Education Association.*

The few remaining papers of the Institute are housed at the offices of the Massachusetts State Teachers Association in Boston. Some leading secondary sources are Merle Borrowman, *The Liberal and the Technical in Teacher Education* (1956); Merle Curti, *The Social Ideas of American Educators* (1959); George B. Emerson, *History and Design of the American Institute of Instruction* (1849); Paul H. Mattingly, *The Classless Profession: American Schoolmen in the Nineteenth Century* (1975).

                                                                              Paul H. Mattingly

AMERICAN JOURNAL OF EDUCATION. See BARNARD, HENRY.

AMERICAN NORMAL SCHOOL ASSOCIATION. See NATIONAL TEACHERS ASSOCIATION; NORMAL SCHOOLS.

AMERICANIZATION is the process by which people become assimilated into the mainstream culture, economy, and polity of the United States. The label "Americans" can be claimed by all inhabitants of North and South America, but this treatment follows conventional usage in which inhabitants of the United States are called Americans. The history of Americanization deals both with the changing definition of "American" and the means by which people become Americans. Those who control major American institutions, like the public schools,* always have, of course, the dominant voice in defining both content and process.

The process of Americanization, and the issues surrounding it, predate the 1776 separation of the United States from England. During the colonial period there were disputes about whether Germans should be permitted to use their native language rather than English. In 1754, Benjamin Franklin* proposed that Germans in Pennsylvania be assimilated into British-American culture.

In 1782, Hector St. John de Crevecoeur, in an early version of the "melting pot" theory, described the process by which Europeans became Americans. Benjamin Rush* in 1786 wrote that he considered it "possible to convert men into republican machines." Noah Webster's* *American Spelling Book*, first printed in 1783 and widely used for decades in American schools, represented a conscious effort to promote an American language distinct from British English.

During much of the nineteenth century, the process of Americanization was generally taken for granted, and it was assumed that newcomers would naturally learn English, get jobs, establish families, and send their children to school. In spite of the existence of some German-language schools and Catholic parochial schools,* most children attended the compulsory common schools* which were established from midcentury on (also, see COMPULSORY EDUCATION). Part of the motivation for creating common schools was to counter the perceived disuniting impact of Catholic immigration from Ireland and other countries.

Assimilation was not always successful—or even desired—and as early as 1837 nativist groups organized to restrict the immigration of non-Anglo-Saxons and to reduce their political power. The organized Americanization movement dates from the late nineteenth century, when massive immigration from southern and eastern Europe changed the cultural, linguistic, and religious patterns of life in many of America's largest cities. The presence of large numbers of Jews, Asians, and Catholics among the newcomers generated fear among many that America would lose its assumed identity as an Anglo-Saxon society. Powerful political and social groups attempted to limit immigration, succeeding in passing restrictive laws in 1882, 1884, 1907, and 1910. Laws setting quotas favoring northern Europeans were passed in 1921 and 1924. While immigration was being restricted, people also called on the public schools to assimilate immigrants who were already here. Schools responded by consciously Americanizing immigrant children in regular school classes and, as early as 1890, by Americanizing adults through evening classes. The adult classes concentrated on teaching English and on the civic education* required as preparation for naturalization. Jane Addams's* Hull-House, opened in 1889, established programs, soon followed in other settlement houses, which assisted in assimilating immigrants and sometimes in helping them preserve elements of their original culture.

Arguments over the definition of Americanization became more intense during this period. Most people assumed that becoming an American meant abandoning one's native culture and language, but intellectuals and writers like William James, Horace Kallen, Randolph Bourne,* W.E.B. Du Bois,* and John Dewey* proposed a broader, cosmopolitan, multicultural society in which people maintained their heritages in a mosaic, rather than losing them in a social melting pot (also, see MULTICULTURAL EDUCATION).

The Americanization movement is pervaded with ironies, represented by efforts to "Americanize" former African American slaves, some of whose ancestors had been here long before the Americanizers. Even more ironic was the effort to Americanize Native Americans, who occupied the continent thousands of years before Europeans arrived here. The Carlisle Indian School in 1879 was the first of many such institutions that deliberately attempted to stamp out Indian culture and replace it with European dress, language, and social practice (see FEDERAL INDIAN BOARDING SCHOOLS).

World War I sharpened and politicized issues of Americanization, with verbal and physical attacks on "hyphenated Americans" and the imposition of narrow and nationalistic definitions of patriotism. As schools became what Lawrence Cremin called "legatee institutions," assuming tasks avoided by other institutions, they took increasing responsibility for Americanization. School districts and states taught immigrant children and their parents, and states provided financial and other assistance. The efforts were reflected at the national level as well. In 1914, the U.S. Bureau of Education* established a Division of Immigrant Education, and in 1921 the National Education Association* followed suit by creating a Department of Immigrant Education.

The movement of African Americans north and west during World War II and new waves of immigration following that war, the Vietnam War, and the collapse of the Soviet Union revived and further politicized issues of Americanization. The massive immigration of Spanish-speaking Latin Americans, and their clustering into large and somewhat separate communities, challenged old concepts of Americanization. Updating the insights of Bourne, Kallen, and others, educators and policymakers have developed programs intended to help immigrants preserve their language and culture while acquiring the language and skill needed to function in the larger economy and polity. To varying degrees such programs as multicultural education, Head Start,* Upward Bound, and English as a Second Language have succeeded in this effort (also, see BILINGUAL EDUCATION). Nonetheless, neo-nativist groups like ''English Only'' have denounced such programs and promoted the exclusive use of the English language in government and in education. As long as the United States continues to admit immigrants, struggles over the content and process of Americanization will no doubt continue.

Current controversies over immigration and Americanization show a continuum of American responses. At one end are those who wish to maintain America's imagined purity by outlawing further immigration and forcing the assimilation of current immigrants and other minorities into a narrow, nationalistic Americanism; at the other end are those who welcome continued immigration as enriching American culture and who favor helping immigrants preserve their culture while acquiring the skills and knowledge to survive in the American environment.

The Immigration History Archives, University of Minnesota, represent one of the many related collections in public, private, and university libraries. Stephen Thernstrom, ed., *The Harvard Encyclopedia of American Ethnic Groups* (1980), includes entries on over 100 ethnic groups and an excellent essay by Philip Gleason titled ''American Identity and Americanization.'' Gleason's bibliography suggests many relevant sources. John Higham, *Strangers in the Land* (1955), remains a classic. Higham's *Send These to Me: Immigrants in Urban America* (1984) updates his *Strangers* and provides extensive and useful notes. Americanization through education is dealt with in Robert A. Carlson, *The Quest for Conformity: Americanization through Education* (1975); Lawrence A. Cremin, *The Transformation of the School: Progressivism in American Education, 1876–1957* (1961); Lawrence A. Cremin, *American Education: The Metropolitan Experience, 1876–1980* (1988); and Paula Fass, *Outside In: Minorities and the Transformation of American Education* (1989). Fass's notes and Carlson's and Cremin's extensive bibliographical essays identify other sources. Key documents on Americanization are included in Sol Cohen, ed., *Education in the United States: A Documentary History* (1974), vol. 4, and in Frederick Rudolph, ed., *Essays on Education in the Early Republic* (1965).

James M. Wallace

APPRENTICESHIP, which may be formal or informal, is a system of youth education and training by which experienced practitioners teach skills to beginners. All societies maintain apprenticeship, which contains certain universal elements. The right to be an apprentice is often restricted to certain persons, and learners may have to pay a fee. Masters often train relatives but rarely take sons, and the system has seldom crossed gender lines. The individual apprentice always learns from a single master in a one-to-one relationship. In a traditional formal apprenticeship, a youth contracts with a master to learn a trade or business over an extended period, most often seven years. The apprentice is provided only with room and board or subsistence pay, and in the early years the learner is a net loss for the instructor, who calculates to gain cheap, expert labor during later years.

While theory may form part of the training, the novice learns mainly by watching and copying the boss. Gaining experience takes much time, and an apprentice's patience and commitment is tested because a master seldom comments on a youth's work. Apprenticeship ends with the learner producing a masterpiece that demonstrates, to the apprentice, master, and outsiders, full competence to practice the craft, trade, or profession. Certification is completed through an initiation that may include hazing or monetary payment, such as buying treats for fellow practitioners.

In the United States, apprenticeship has been most commonly used in skilled crafts. For centuries artisans passed on skills largely through apprenticeship, a system that English settlers brought to the American colonies. From the beginning, colonial conditions hindered the institution. The colonies suffered skilled labor shortages and, therefore, enjoyed high wages. One consequence was that mediocre artisans succeeded, and many of these masters took apprentices, who were usually trained badly. Then, too, low population density and weak government prevented the organization of the guilds that regulated both crafts and apprenticeship in England. There, many crafts could be conducted only with a guild license. Licensing was used to restrict competition, but it also kept persons who had failed to complete training from practicing.

In America, the prospect of high wages lured apprentices, including Benjamin Franklin,* to run away. Furthermore, a runaway could escape the law by moving to a different colony. The usual apprentice contracts, called indentures, were all but worthless. Lacking control, a master feared that investment in a learner's unprofitable early years would not be paid back in later years. Instead, the apprentice would seek high wages as a half-trained journeyman. As a result, American masters took few apprentices and often trained them poorly. Well-trained immigrants supplied much skilled labor.

In the early nineteenth century, the new industrial system destroyed many crafts. Even before mechanization, an emerging market economy produced powerful incentives for large-scale production. Mass production could be accomplished best by subdividing tasks into simple steps that were performed by unskilled workers, including poorly paid women and children. Thus, by 1840, apprentice shoemakers ceased to exist, since unskilled workers now performed on a vast scale the various steps in making shoes. In this new economic environment the use of written apprentice contracts generally declined.

Deskilling and industrialization affected crafts differently. For example, shoemakers and handloom weavers disappeared, but skilled printers continued to be needed. Printing also changed, however. Whereas unskilled workers operated expensive steam presses, apprentices still learned to set type by hand. No printer could ever hope to earn enough money as a skilled worker to buy a steam press and open a modern printing plant. In contrast, apprenticeship in the building trades thrived, while apprentice machinists looked forward to prosperity in a trade that benefited from industrialization. In the South, plantation slaves passed down crafts, especially blacksmithing, shoemaking, and carpentry, through informal apprenticeships.

By 1900, the United States faced a skilled labor crisis. The apprentice, keeping an eye open for a better opportunity, resisted signing any contract, while the master was unwilling to provide expensive training to an inexperienced youth who might leave before the master had recovered the expense. As a result, America trained few apprentices. A crisis occurred when skilled British and German immigrants, who had provided artisanship to the United States, gave way to less-skilled southern and eastern Europeans.

In the progressive era, educators started federal assistance for state apprenticeship systems (see SMITH-HUGHES ACT). Concentrated in the building trades, these programs were most successful in states like Wisconsin, where German immigrants had established a strong artisan tradition. Apprenticeship has thrived when contractors, labor unions, and local governments have cooperated. In areas where industrialization had led to deskilling, however, no one had an incentive for apprenticeship. Instead, youths who could not get into the building trades were sent to the progressive era's new trade schools. Industrial education, which was to teach work discipline and habits useful to factory labor as well as general principles about materials that could be applied to any number of situations, failed as a substitute for apprenticeship. Learning by watching and copying had been replaced by techniques more appropriate for liberal arts (see PROGRESSIVE EDUCATION; VOCATIONAL EDUCATION).

The building trades have continued to make good use of apprenticeship, and the United States today has about 300,000 apprentices. This represents only about 3 percent of high school* graduates, however, and it stands in contrast to Japan and, especially, Germany, which has continued to have the world's foremost apprenticeship system and highest-skilled workforce. The German government heavily subsidizes the system, and each German business willingly invests in apprentices in the expectation that these workers will remain permanently with the company. In the more mobile United States, business lacks such confidence. Even if financing could be found, a vast expansion of apprenticeship in the United States is unlikely because the number of skilled workers capable of acting as individual masters is quite limited. Today, the United States no longer imports skilled labor to overcome the lack of commitment to apprenticeship. The United States instead imports products made by other nation's skilled workers.

For a primary source, see Samuel Seabury, *Moneygripe's Apprentice: The*

Personal Narrative of Samuel Seabury III (1989). Secondary sources include Michael W. Coy, ed., *Apprenticeship: From Theory to Method and Back Again* (1989); Daniel Jacoby, ''The Transformation of Industrial Apprenticeship in the United States'' (1991); Ian M. G. Quimby, *Apprenticeship in Colonial Philadelphia* (1985); W. J. Rorabaugh, *The Craft Apprentice: From Franklin to the Machine Age in America* (1986); and U.S. Department of Labor, *Apprenticeship* (1992).

W. J. Rorabaugh

ART EDUCATION has been dominated by two objectives: personal development through art and the academic study of art. Art educators have historically emphasized one objective or the other while struggling to gain a foothold for art in schools and in academic curricula. Changes in the philosophy and methods of art education have coincided with historical movements and changes in public education.

Art education first appeared in eighteenth-century America. It existed almost exclusively in specialized art academies intended for specialized training for artists only. The emphasis was on developing precise art techniques such as perspective, color mixing, and shading, achieved through the reproduction of great works of art. Benjamin Franklin* was an early spokesperson for the introduction of art education in the general education of citizens, though his proposals had little effect at the time.

Art education shifted its emphasis with the industrial revolution. Mass reproduction technology allowed art to become a commodity that could be acquired by a mass market. With this shift from private to public consumption of art, art education abandoned the reproduction of earlier classics and focused instead on design, illustration, and the manipulation of the materials and techniques of mass production. Institutions such as Pratt Institute and Rhode Island School of Design were established to satisfy the need for industrial artists.

By the Civil War, however, under the influence of a new romanticism, institutions of higher education such as Harvard and Yale adopted art education as an element of liberal education. They stressed art's role in moral education* rather than its vocational value. Whereas most art education in the nineteenth century remained focused on art for factory production, these elite educational institutions began to emphasize art's role in personal development. Toward the end of the nineteenth century, drawing was occasionally introduced into the public school* curriculum as part of the manual training* movement, an effort to overcome the sedentary bookishness of urban common schools.*

Progressive education's* emphasis on child-centered approaches to teaching transformed art education by the beginning of the twentieth century. According to progressive educators, children should be allowed maximum self-expression. Art clearly had a central role in that process, and art education moved into public schools. The teacher's role was to nurture creativity, intervening as little as possible. Retrenchment during the Great Depression moved art education from the domain of the art teacher to the that of the classroom teacher, with significant effects on school art education. Subject-centered classroom teachers changed art education from art as free expression to art as an adjunct to the traditional school subjects.

Scientific methods began to affect art education by mid-twentieth century. On the one hand, the contemporary emphasis on presumably scientific, standardized testing created an environment for attempting to measure student artistic outcomes scientifically. On the other hand, new artistic media, techniques, and practices offered art education expanded horizons for creativity. Since 1980, Discipline Based Art Education (DBAE) has emerged. It attempts to incorporate art history, aesthetics, art creation, and art criticism into a single art program. It seeks, in other words, to merge the two historic objectives of art education. The Getty Institute, the primary patron of DBAE, has opened a national debate regarding the proportions of each component that are necessary within a successful art education program.

The most useful sources on the history of art education include Arthur D. Efland, *A History of Art Education* (1990), and Vincent Lanier, *The World of Art Education* (1991). For a valuable earlier view, see Hugo Munsterberg, *The Principles of Art Education* (1905).

Amy F. Rolleri

ASSOCIATION FOR CHILDHOOD EDUCATION INTERNATIONAL

(ACEI) originated within a committee of the National Education Association's* (NEA) Kindergarten* Department, which was planning exhibits for the 1893 World's Columbian Exposition in Chicago. Lucy Wheelock,* Patty Smith Hill,* Susan Blow,* and other leaders of this "female" department rebelled against the male-dominated NEA by founding the International Kindergarten Union* in 1892. In 1930, the name was changed to the Association for Childhood Education. The following year, the National Council of Primary Education merged with the Association. The designation "International" was added in 1946, when kits of educational materials were sent to Europe and the Near, Middle, and Far East following World War II. International exchange programs and fellowships, initiated at that time, have continued.

With a membership consisting predominately of classroom teachers, the ACEI has been a major influence in teacher professionalization. The Association's goal of helping fulfill every child's potential through education is implemented by about 150 state or provincial branches and local branches and international affiliates. Members may join divisions emphasizing infancy, early childhood, and later childhood–early adolescence. Annual study conferences have been held since 1896. The bimonthly journal *Childhood Education* has been published since 1924. Other publications include the *Journal of Research in Childhood Education*, books, newsletters, pamphlets, and position papers.

Refer to the ACEI Archives, Special Collections Division, McKeldin Library,

University of Maryland. Also, contact the ACEI Headquarters, 11501 Georgia Avenue, Suit 315, Wheaton, MD 20902–1924. For background information, see Committee of Nineteen, *Pioneers of the Kindergarten in America* (1913); Agnes Snyder, *Dauntless Women in Early Childhood Education* (1972); and Sue C. Wortham, *Childhood, 1892–1992* (1992).

Dorothy W. Hewes

ATHLETICS. American education has been distinctive in its provision for competitive athletics as a substantial part of institutional programs. Whereas most countries devoted some attention to physical culture or health instruction, American secondary schools, since the late nineteenth century, have sponsored an elaborate extracurricular array of varsity sports, especially for male students. The American version invoked some embellished examples from abroad, such as the British public school emphasis on character building, but transformed competitive sports from an essentially intramural activity, in which fellow students played on teams against one another, to a highly formalized arrangement of conferences and games with student teams from other schools; athletics became truly interscholastic. Public audiences reinforced its external nature.

Colleges, as early as 1852, pioneered the organization of formal varsity sports, creating conferences, schedules, and rules, with such policies and practices diffusing quickly to secondary education. By 1900, varsity competition enjoyed remarkable participation among students at colleges, preparatory schools, and high schools.* Crew, baseball, track and field, and most of all football captured the popular imagination. Basketball, first popular as a Young Men's Christian Association game, spread to public high schools, especially in the Midwest; colleges and universities later adopted it as a major sport.

Public support undergirded all of this. Indicative of the popularity of scholastic sports was the ascent of the student-athlete as a culture hero: In the early 1900s, "dime novels" with weekly sales of more than 2 million featured the fictional Frank Merriwell, who first gained fame as a schoolboy athlete at Fairdale Preparatory School, then as a multisport hero at Yale University. Although elite northeastern private schools* and colleges first cultivated the ethos of sportsmanship as a preparation for leadership, its lessons changed as scholastic sports spread. Urban public school administrators based their justification for elaborate athletics programs on the belief that sports provided a good source of order and discipline among a large, energetic, and not always predictable student population. Later, when colleges began to award lucrative athletic scholarships, school sports became hailed in American lore as an agent of social mobility, and most important as a symbol of local, state, religious, or ethnic pride. School boards and administrators favored sports programs as a source of institutional publicity and prestige. The 1918 *Report of the Commission on the Reform of Secondary Education** cited scholastic sports, along with student government and school assemblies, as important sources of school spirit and civic participation. After World War I, athletics cut across regions and socioeconomic classes to constitute a national theme that linked school to commuity. Football and basketball for boys dominated, with some regional variations.

In 1972, Congress extended the provision of the Civil Rights Act,* with Title IX, to preclude educational institutions from discriminating on the basis of gender. The new, increased inclusion of girls did not so much reform as extend the American institutional commitment to competitive sports to a large and previously underserved student constituency. Since the extension of athletic opportunities to female students coincided with declining educational budgets, it prompted renewed discussion of essential questions: How ought educators best integrate athletics and scholastics? The heart of the matter was that American schools were heirs to a legacy of an extracurriculum* that persistently claimed center stage with the formal course of study.

Leading secondary sources include William J. Baker and John M. Carroll, eds., *Sports in Modern America* (1981); H. G. Bissinger, *Friday Night Lights: A Town, a Team, and a Dream* (1990); J. Thomas Jable, ''The Public Schools Athletic League of New York City: Organized Athletics for City Schoolchildren, 1903–1914'' (1978); James A. Michener, *Sports in America* (1976); Jeffrey Mirel, ''From Student Control to Institutional Control of High School Athletics: Three Michigan Cities, 1883–1905'' (1982); James A. Montgomery, ''The Growth of the Interscholastic Athletics Movement in the United States, 1890–1940'' (1975).

John R. Thelin

ATKINSON, GEORGE HERBERT (May 10, 1819–February 25, 1889), a missionary, educator, and reformer, was the chief founder of the Oregon common schools* and one of the prime movers in the development of higher education in the Northwest. Born in Newburyport, Massachusetts, he graduated from Dartmouth in 1842 and from Andover Theological Seminary in 1846. In 1848, he went as a missionary to Oregon, where he organized many Congregational churches. He founded the Clackamas County Female Seminary in Oregon City, helped start Tualatin Academy in Forest Grove, which later became Pacific University, and was instrumental in the founding of Whitman College in Walla Walla, Washington.

In 1849, Atkinson drafted the educational section of Governor Joseph Lane's message to Oregon's first territorial legislature; this became the basis for the territory's first school law, passed by the legislature later that year. As the first superintendent of schools in Clackamas County, he helped to establish eighty-eight schools and promoted curricular standardization, testing, and graded schools (see AGE-GRADING). He also served as superintendent of schools in Multnomah County. In 1880, he chaired a committee that strongly supported public education against well-organized critics. Religiously and socially liberal, he defended the rights of Chinese and Native Americans and promoted industrial education* for the latter.

The Oregon Historical Center in Portland has a collection of Atkinson's papers. His widow, Nancy Bates Atkinson, compiled a volume titled *Biography of Rev. George G. H. Atkinson, D.D.* (1893). The three indices of the *Oregon Historical Quarterly* include many references to Atkinson. Two articles by David Tyack persuasively interpret Atkinson's place in educational history: "The Kingdom of God and the Common School" (1966) and "Bureaucracy and the Common School: The Example of Portland, Oregon, 1851–1913" (1967). Also, refer to David B. Tyack and Elisabeth Hansot, *Managers of Virtue: Public School Leadership in America, 1820–1980* (1982).

James M. Wallace

B

BAGLEY, WILLIAM C. See ESSENTIALISM.

BAILEY, LIBERTY HYDE (March 15, 1858–December 25, 1954), was the pivotal figure behind the Country Life Movement.* The lengthy *Report of the Commission on Country Life* (1909) is generally considered to be his work.

Bailey, born and raised on a modest Michigan farm, graduated from Michigan State University in 1882 with a bachelor's degree, and in 1886 with a master's degree. He joined the faculty at Cornell University and distinguished himself as one of the nation's leading horticulturalists. During the 1890s, Bailey became concerned with the growing trend toward city migration by American youths. He was convinced that the decontextualized curriculum and authoritarian pedagogy of rural schools directly contributed to the seduction of city life. No doubt influenced by popular Herbartian educational thought (see HERBARTARIAN MOVEMENT), Bailey began what came to be known as the Cornell Rural School Leaflet project in 1896. This represented an attempt to distribute curricular ideas to teachers in the state of New York, particularly those ideas that involved the active, hands-on study of nature. His abiding interest in the vitality of rural life led to his appointment as head of President Theodore Roosevelt's Commission on Country Life in 1908. At that point the rural school "leaflets" took on journal form and were generally available at universities and normal schools* across the country until well into the 1920s. Additionally, Bailey published many books directly or indirectly related to rural education, most notably *The State and the Farmer* (1908) and *The Country Life Movement in the United States* (1911).

For secondary sources, refer to William L. Bowers, *The Country Life Movement in America, 1900–1920* (1974); David B. Danbom, *The Resisted Revolution: Urban America and the Industrialization of Agriculture, 1900–1930* (1979); and Paul Theobald, *Call School: Rural Education in the Midwest to*

1918 (1995); Paul Theobald, "Democracy and the Origins of Rural Midwest Education: A Retrospective Essay" (1988); and Paul Theobald, "Country School Curriculum and Governance: The One-Room School Experience in the Ninteteenth-Century Midwest" (1993).

Paul Theobald

BANCROFT, GEORGE (October 3, 1800–January 17, 1891), with the assistance of Harvard colleague Joseph Cogswell, helped to bring the American boarding school* ideal to fruition. After graduating from Harvard College in 1817, Bancroft became one of the first of many Americans to study in Europe. He attended the University of Gottingen in Germany, earning a master of arts and a doctor of philosophy. Bancroft, Cogswell, Edward Everett, and George Ticknor, three Harvard colleagues, visited a variety of European educational institutions. These men concluded that their American academic training appeared inferior compared to the more rigorous intellectual standards of European scholarship. Bancroft and Cogswell, committed to improving the intellectual quality of American secondary and higher education, founded Round Hill School in Northampton, Massachusetts, in 1823, shortly after their return from Europe. They modeled Round Hill after the German *gymnasium* and Phillip Emmanuel von Fellenberg's Institute in Hofwyl, Switzerland. These European schools emphasized intellectual and moral training in a familylike atmosphere. Bancroft and Cogswell maintained that American education would greatly benefit from this European prototype. Bancroft served as schoolmaster at Round Hill from 1824 to 1831. He severed his ties with that institution because its arduous daily routine proved taxing to him. He became a preeminent U.S. historian and a high ranking Jacksonian Democratic Party official. Because of mounting financial difficulties, Round Hill closed three years after Bancroft's departure. Although short-lived, the school influenced and inspired other individuals to found boarding schools. Augustus Muhlenberg's Flushing Institute (1834) in Long Island, New York, and Dr. George C. Shattuck's St. Paul's School (1855) in Concord, New Hampshire, represented the two most notable examples.

The Massachusetts Historical Society, in Boston, houses the major collection of Bancroft's papers, including a rich assortment of material on Round Hill and Harvard. Another small collection of his papers exists at the New York City Public Library. M. A. DeWolfe Howe, *The Life and Letters of George Bancroft* (1908), 2 vols., represents an invaluable source for understanding Bancroft's role in founding Round Hill. Russell B. Nye, *George Bancroft, Brahmin Rebel* (1944; 1972), remains a definitive work, analyzing his contributions as an educator, historian, politician, and diplomat.

Mark Desjardins

BANNISTER V. PARADIS, 316 F. Supp. 185 (D.N.H. 1970). In a case reflecting judicial expansion of the concept of free speech following *Tinker v. Des Moines Independent Community School District,** a sixth-grade student, residing in Pittsfield, New Hampshire, sent home for wearing blue jeans, was granted a permanent injunction prohibiting his school from enforcing a dress code barring the wearing of "dungarees" (p. 189). In finding a violation of section 1983 of the Civil Rights Act of 1964, the federal district court ruled that "a person's right to wear clothes of his own choosing provided that, in the case of a schoolboy, they are neat and clean, is a constitutional right protected and guaranteed by the Fourteenth Amendment" (p. 188). Although the district court acknowledged that the right to wear blue jeans did not rank very high on the scale of constitutional values, the school in this case could not enforce a dress code without evidence of disruption to the educational process.

Ralph D. Mawdsley

BARNARD, HENRY (January 24, 1811–July 5, 1900), educator, historian, and editor, was born in Hartford, Connecticut, where he spent his formative years. After graduating from Yale College, he briefly taught school, studied law, and traveled in the United Staes, where he met many prominent politicians, and Europe, where he was introduced to leading reformers. He was elected to the Connecticut legislature in 1837 as a Whig and the following year was instrumental in securing the passage of a law establishing a permanent Board of Commissioners of the Common Schools, a step similar to that taken by Massachusetts. Barnard, like Horace Mann,* was appointed secretary to the Board, and, like Mann, used the position to urge the cause of school reform, tax support, and a more centralized system; he also promoted teacher professionalism and the moral aspect (see MORAL EDUCATION) of schooling. After the Board of Commissioners was abolished because of partisan wrangling in 1842, Barnard assumed a similar position in Rhode Island, where he served until 1849; there he strengthened the role of the state, sponsored teacher institutes,* and published his first significant book. He returned to Connecticut to head the newly established Normal School* and became the state superintendent of instruction and published a number of books on education; he also began the massive *American Journal of Education*, which he edited until 1880.

In 1858, now a national figure, Barnard was made chancellor of the University of Wisconsin and agent for the state's normal schools. Despite developing a comprehensive plan for higher education there, he remained in the state for a mere eighteen months and left no mark. Scholarly work occupied him for the next few years until he became principal of the newly reopened St. John's College in Maryland during the 1866–1867 academic year. He left to become the first national commissioner of education, a post he held until 1870. Barnard was no administrator and concentrated on compiling data published in two reports; his ineffectiveness led to his dismissal and the demotion of the Department of Education to a bureau (see UNITED STATES DEPARTMENT OF EDUCATION).

For the rest of his life, Barnard remained in Hartford, continuing his scholarly work and revered as the "Nestor of American Education." Throughout his career, he published extensively, editing the *Connecticut Common School Journal*, the *Journal of the Rhode Island Institute of Instruction*, and the *American Journal of Education*, a leading source for nineteenth-century history of education. His books, often repeating material previously published in the *American Journal of Education*, included *School Architecture, Normal Schools, Tribute to Gallaudet, National Education in Europe, Reformatory Education, Memoirs of Teachers, Pestalozzi and Pestalozzianism, Papers for the Teacher, English Pedagogy*, and *Armsmear*.

Barnard's extensive papers are housed in the Fales Library at the Elmer Holmes Bobst Library, New York University; the Watkinson Library, Trinity College, Hartford, Connecticut, has a sizeable collection of Barnard's personal papers and his enormous collection of textbooks. Small collections, mostly focused on Barnard's state activities, can found in the Beinecke Library, Yale University; the Special Collections in the James P. Adams Library, Rhode Island College, Providence; the Barnard Papers in the Connecticut Historical Society, Hartford; the Manuscript Collection of the Rhode Island Historical Society, Providence; and the Lyman Draper Collection, Wisconsin Historical Society. The only recent biography is Edith Nye MacMullen, *In the Cause of True Education: Henry Barnard and Nineteenth-Century School Reform* (1991). For a painstaking and conclusive analysis of the *American Journal of Education*, see Richard Emmon Thursfield, *Henry Barnard's "American Journal of Education"* (1945).

Edith Nye MacMullen

BASAL READERS. For most of the history of American reading instruction, educators have assumed that children needed special texts to introduce them to reading. The earliest of these, hornbooks* and primers, were imported into the American colonies soon after colonization. Apart from John Eliot's *Indian Primer* (1669), the *New England Primer** became the first extant "homegrown" publication of an American reading instructional text, rather than a reproduction of a British import. Combining Calvinist Christianity with five pages of syllables, it eventually sold some 3 million copies over a 150-year period. The entirely religious progression of hornbook, primer, psalter (Book of Psalms), New Testament, and Bible served as the standard reading sequence of the seventeenth century.

Beginning in the 1730s, spelling books were increasingly used for reading instruction in the colonial classroom. They differed radically from primers in organization and, often, in the secularity of their content: Only after presenting lists of spelling words, in an increasing number of syllables, did spellers offer short passages of connnected reading material. Thomas Dilworth's speller, *A New Guide to the English Tongue* (London, 1740; Philadelphia, 1747), became the favorite in the middle and New England colonies, Thomas Dyche's *A Guide to the English Tongue* (1707) in the southern colonies.

The American Revolution created a demand for indigenous American works.

By 1832, Noah Webster's* speller (1783 on) had become the nation's primary reading instructional text.

Designed for children who could already read, the "readers" published for children before the 1830s consisted of excerpts from writers of prose and poetry. The first school reader compiled by an American was Webster's *Grammatical Institute . . . Part III* (1785). It was supplanted by Lindley Murray's* *English Reader* (1799), which dominated the market between 1815 and 1836.

A movement to reform education began during the 1820s, promoted by the *American Journal of Education.** Reformers like Horace Mann* attacked rote learning and the sterile columns of words that composed the bulk of spelling books. As a result, spelling books became relegated to instruction in spelling rather than reading, and authors like Samuel Worcester, in 1826, began to write more child-centered texts. William Holmes McGuffey's* *Eclectic* series (beginning in 1836) also supplanted Murray's reader, criticized by reformers as too difficult for children. The term "reader" now designated a volume in a series designed to provide sequential reading lessons. Worcester's and McGuffey's series exemplified a further change—a reduction in overtly religious content. Readers' content, over the course of the nineteenth century, generally moved from religious and moralistic to moralistic, patriotic, historical, and informational. Until after the Civil War, the most advanced readers in each series were usually "rhetorics," providing speeches for declamation. The McGuffey series spearheaded another trend: It was one of the first to become a national series, eschewing all controversial context, and after its first edition became the creation of its publishers rather than its author.

By 1880, the classroom teaching force had been feminized, but the authors of nearly all nineteenth-century reading series had been male. Starting in 1880, women, valued as instructors, began to be sought after as authors of elementary literacy texts. Dozens of women, including Rebecca Pollard, Jenny Stickney, Ellen Cyr (the first woman to market a series under her own name), Sarah Louise Arnold, Adelaide Finch, Emma Gordon, Ella Flagg Young,* Martha Holton, and Honora Buttimer (a nun who wrote under the name "A Sister of St. Joseph"), became sole authors or senior authors of reading series.

The progressive education* movement initially had little impact on the construction of textbooks, which it preferred not to use. Methodically, several series (e.g., Lewis Monroe's readers, 1873) emphasized synthetic phonics; others added markings to the text to indicate pronunciation (e.g., Edward Ward's *Rational Method in Reading*, 1894). After about 1910, these lost ground to texts designed to encourage children to appreciate literature, which introduced nursery rhymes, folk tales, and myths. The scientific measurement movement of the 1930s ushered a switch to realistic content. While some vocabulary control had long been a feature of basals, now the movement also fostered the selection of words in readers on the basis of frequency. A "scientifically controlled vocabulary" was invoked to justify reducing the number of new words that primers offered: They dropped from an average of 406 in 1922 to 289 in 1931.

Beginning in 1930, those engaged in reading research—overwhelmingly a male enterprise—were now in demand as authors, ending the predominance of female authors. William S. Gray, University of Chicago, and Arthur Gates, colleagues of Edward Lee Thorndike,* Columbia University, Teachers College, became the leading researchers. Gray coauthored Scott, Foresman's *Elson Basic Readers* (1930); this series introduced the characters Dick and Jane, who were to define reading instruction for a generation of schoolchildren. Gates also had his own series, *The Work-Play Books* (1930).

Gray's readers and their successors and competitors up to the 1950s were remarkably uniform in content and methodology. They portrayed nuclear families in white, middle-class, suburban America, where Mother never worked outside the house. They offered few words and allowed for much repetition. Words were presented as wholes, supplemented by context clues, configuration clues, structural analysis (i.e., breaking words into affixes and roots) and "analytic" or "intrinsic" phonics, where letter-sound correspondences were induced from known words.

Criticisms of this approach (see READING INSTRUCTION) led to the publication of a few competing series based on synthetic phonics and the inclusion of more phonics in the rest. The 1960s saw more variation in the content of basal readers, whose publishers made token responses to some of the key movements of the 1960s such as the civil rights* movement and the women's movement. The renewed behaviorism* movement of the 1960s had two consequences: the composition of a few readers based on programmed learning and the creation of elaborate sets of materials that presupposed that learning to read was to master a series of discrete skills.

A handful of publishers dominated the textbook industry by the 1990s. In spite of increased costs in the production of a reading series—consisting of a kindergarten book or materials, readiness books, several preprimers, a primer, and some eight readers, often subdivided, as well as an array of supplementary workbooks—the potential profitability of a basal series grew more than any other subject-matter textbook. The continuation of state textbook adoption* guaranteed wide sales in certain states. The concomitant need to appeal to the broadest segment of potential purchasers indicates that the content of basals will continue to be noncontroversial. However, the whole language* movement of the 1980s and 1990s, which rejected basals in favor of children's books, shifted publishers' resources from basals to trade books for children.

For some historical background, see Ian Michael, *The Teaching of English from the Sixteenth Century to 1870* (1987); E. Jennifer Monaghan, "Gender and Textbooks: Women Writers of Elementary Readers, 1880–1950" (1994); Nila B. Smith, *American Reading Instruction* (1986); Richard L. Venezky, "A History of the American Reading Textbook" (1987); and Richard L. Venezky, "American Primers: Guide to the Microfiche Collection" (1990).

E. Jennifer Monaghan

BEATTY, WILLARD WALCOTT (September 17, 1891–September 29, 1961) played an important role in the progressive education* movement and became a central figure in the development of federal Native American education policy during the mid-twentieth century. Born in Berkeley, California, he graduated from the University of California-Berkeley in 1913 with a B.S. in architecture and taught at Oakland Technical High School. He served as arithmetic, history, and civics department head and director of training at San Francisco State Normal School between 1915 and 1920, where he met Frederic Burk. Burk developed a model for individualized instruction that drew admirers from all over the world. His Deweyan (see DEWEY, JOHN) progressivism influenced Beatty. The Winnetka, Illinois, school system (see WINNETKA PLAN), the first in the country to adopt Burk's scheme, hired Beatty as principal of Skokie Junior High School in 1923. At the same time, he began service as Winnetka assistant superintendent, under the leadership and influence of superintendent and noted progressive educator Carlton Washburne.* In 1926 Beatty was hired to promote the "Winnetka technique" as superintendent of schools in Bronxville, New York, an affluent suburb of New York City. He served in that capacity until 1936. In 1931, the General Education Board* asked him to survey all public and private progressive schools, and a year later he was chosen as vice-president of the Progressive Education Association,* becoming president in 1933. He resigned this position in 1937 to serve as director of education for the Indian Service.

Universally regarded as dynamic and bright, with a deep concern for the cultural individuality of Native American people, he worked comfortably with another progressive educator, John Collier,* commissioner of Indian Affairs during the New Deal. Their close working relationship allowed Beatty to overhaul the cultural assimilationist structure of Indian education (see AMERICANIZATION). He expanded the day schools, opposed the restrictive federal Indian boarding schools,* extended in-service teacher education in cultural anthropology, employing scholars from the Bureau of Ethnology as trainers, and worked, with limited but significant success, toward the development and dissemination of bilingual (see BILINGUAL EDUCATION) and bicultural curricula.

Beatty's pragmatic, progressive approach revealed itself as he shifted from a liberal, pluralist vision of Native American education during the New Deal to a more assimilationist, vocational (see VOCATIONAL EDUCATION) approach to the life adjustment* of Native American students in the postwar era. His change reflected not only some ambiguities inherent in the progressive legacy but also the way national politics, in this case, conservative, Cold War policies, were dedicated to the termination of special reservation status and exploitation of strategic resources on tribal lands. Dillon Myer, a reactionary terminationist who had served as organizer for the Japanese American internment during World War II, forced Beatty's resignation in 1952. Beatty's influence on federal Indian education remains unsurpassed.

Beatty's correspondence is held in Record Group 75, National Archives. For his shift in policy, see Willard Walcott Beatty, *Education for Action* (1944) and Willard Walcott Beatty, *Education for Cultural Change* (1953). Francis Paul

Prucha, in *The Great Father* (1984), presents the most comprehensive overview of federal–Native American relations. The most thorough treatment of Beatty and midcentury Indian education appears in Margaret Szasz, *Education and the American Indian* (1977). Also refer to George A. Boyce, *When Navajos Had Too Many Sheep: The 1940s* (1974); Donald Fixico, *Termination and Relocation in Federal Indian Policy, 1945–1960* (1986); and Lawrence C. Kelly, *Assault on Assimilation: John Collier and the Origins of Indian Policy* (1983).

                                                                         Guy Senese

BEECHER, CATHARINE ESTHER (September 6, 1800–May 12, 1878). A writer, organizer, and common school* advocate, she made significant contributions to women's education and had considerable impact on domestic economy (i.e., home economics*). Her path-breaking role as a professional woman modeled behavior for women.

Beecher was born in East Hampton, Long Island, New York, and grew up in Litchfield, Connecticut, the oldest child of Lyman Beecher, a prominent Calvinist preacher. She attended Miss Pierce's school and rose to the top of her class, displaying social and intellectual talent. She met her fiancé, Alexander Fisher, in 1821 and became formally engaged in 1822. A professor of natural philosophy at Yale, Fisher died off the Irish coast while beginning a European sabbatical. Beecher spent the winter months of 1822–1823 in Boston and Franklin, Massachusetts, visiting, reading Fisher's papers, and coming to terms with her grief. Rather than being driven into the Calvinist conversion her father earnestly entreated, she was affirmed in her womanhood and intellectual confidence.

In May 1823, Beecher founded the Hartford Female Seminary, the first of her school efforts and perhaps the most successful. When she left in 1831, it had become one of the most significant institutions for women's education in the early nineteenth century. Two years later she organized the Western Female Institute in Cincinnati, and about 1850 the Milwaukee Female College, which was ultimately absorbed by the University of Wisconsin-Milwaukee. Her Committee for Promoting National Education successfully raised funds to send over 450 female teachers to the West (see BOARD OF NATIONAL POPULAR EDUCATION). Beecher's most famous publication was *Treatise on Domestic Economy*, first published in 1841 and republished nearly every year from 1841 to 1856. She also served as an advocate for the feminization of teaching during the nineteenth century through such works as *An Essay on the Education of Female Teachers* (1835) and *Women's Profession as Mother and Educator* (1872).

Her papers are available in the Beecher-Stowe Collection, Arthur and Elizabeth Schlesinger Library on the History of Women in America, Radcliffe College, Cambridge, Massachusetts; the Alexander Metcalf Fisher Collection, Beinecke Rare Book and Manuscript Library, and the Beecher Family Papers, Sterling Memorial Library, both at Yale University, New Haven, Connecticut; the Hartford Female Seminary Papers, Connecticut Historical Society, Hartford,

Connecticut; the Milwaukee-Dawner College Papers, Area Research Center, University of Wisconsin-Milwaukee; and the Beecher Family Papers, Williston Memorial Library, Mt. Holyoke College, South Hadley, Massachusetts. Biographies include Mae Elizabeth Harveson, *Catharine Esther Beecher, Pioneer Educator* (1932); Kathryn Kish Sklar, *Catharine Beecher: A Study in American Domesticity* (1974); and Emily Nayes Vanderpoel, *Chronicles of a Pioneer School from 1792 to 1833 . . .* (1903).

David B. Ripley

BEHAVIORISM, a school of thought founded by John B. Watson in 1913, advances that the only scientifically valid subject matter for psychology is observable, measurable behavior. The underlying tenets of behaviorism are objectivism, animal psychology, and functionalism. Functionalism is concerned with the mind's function, but only as it relates to assisting the organism to adapt to its environment. Behaviorism rejects the notion that consciousness and internal mental events can be reliably studied; therefore, these phenomena are ignored.

The works of Ivan Pavlov and Edward Lee Thorndike* are fundamental to contemporary behaviorism. Pavlov gained fame for his *conditioning* procedures in 1906, using dogs as experimental subjects. In 1913, Thorndike formulated the *Law of Effect*, which asserted that rewarding a response strengthens that response, whereas punishment does not yield a comparable negative effect. Thus, positive methods are more effective than negative methods in eliciting a desired response. Thorndike's work set the tone for the work of Burrhus F. Skinner, whose contributions to behaviorism and psychology earned him an unprecedented Citation for Outstanding Lifetime Contribution to Psychology by the American Psychological Association (1990). Skinner believed that there are no eliciting stimuli for behavior and that behavior is controlled by the consequences that follow it. Formalized in the *operant conditioning* paradigm, Skinner's doctrine, developed in 1938, affirmed that a given behavior operates on the environment to produce a given consequence. If the consequence is rewarding, the behavior will increase; if not, the behavior will decrease. The implication that desired behavior should be reinforced and undesirable behavior should be ignored has served as the basis for problem solving in many contemporary subject areas, including child rearing, prison reform, practices in the workplace, and training programs for retarded and autistic individuals.

For a general work on this topic, refer to Lawrence Lipsitz, "Behaviorism Today" (1993). For an extensive review of Skinner's lifetime contributions, see Kennon A. Lattal, "Reflections on B. F. Skinner and Psychology" (1992).

Harriett H. Ford and Mary Nesbit

BELL, BERNARD IDDINGS (October 6, 1886–September 5, 1958), became known as a critic of materialism and apathy in American life, especially in the areas of religion and education. In the 1940s, he led an attack on progressive education,* its theories and practices, as a leading cause of the "unsatisfactory state of our life and culture." He proposed massive reforms in education, religion, and family life.

Educated at the University of Chicago (B.A., 1907; S.T.B., 1910), Bell focused in his early career on his work within the Episcopal Church. Following World War I, he began to focus his efforts on education. He accepted the position of warden of St. Stephen's College (later a part of Bard College) in 1919. There he encouraged students to develop their individuality and resist the standardization of education. Bell became a professor of religion at Columbia University in 1930, a post he held until 1933. He returned to the clergy in 1933, occupying the position of preaching canon of St. John's Cathedral in Providence, Rhode Island, until 1946. That year Bell assumed the post of lecturer on religious education at Seabury-Western Theological Seminary at the University of Chicago until 1954. Two years later, he resigned to devote himself to lecturing, preaching, and writing.

Bell's writing focused on criticism of education's failure to teach people to think clearly for themselves. He labeled all levels of education as materialistic, secular, and lacking high standards. He proposed better training, pay, and organization for teachers and a return of religion to the classroom. He condemned the will of majority, which encouraged individuals to accept the "standards of the crowd." His educational focus began in 1928 with such works as *Common Sense in Education* and developed through *Crisis in Education* (1949).

Bell's papers are housed at the Harper and Row Archives of Columbia University. A leading biography is by Nathaniel Wright, "The Life and Educational Thought of Bernard Iddings Bell (1886–1958)" (1964).

Charles E. Jenks

BESTOR, ARTHUR EUGENE, JR. (September 20, 1908–December 13, 1994), a leading critic of American public schools in the 1950s, attacked the excesses of education and its emphasis on "life adjustment."* He studied at Yale, where he received his A.B. (1930) and Ph.D. in history (1938). He became an expert in constitutional history, specializing in its application to separation of federal powers. Bestor's early research and writing focused on "intentional" communities or communitarian societies spanning from seventeenth-century sectarian and Owenite socialism to the nineteenth century's Oneida Community. Bestor later studied the alternative lifestyles of the 1960s and 1970s in comparison to his earlier research.

In 1953, Bestor published *Educational Wastelands: The Retreat from Learning in Our Public Schools*, which contained numerous criticisms of American public schools.* He fought against certification of teachers based upon pedagogical rather than content knowledge. Bestor's *Restoration of Learning* (1955) became the foundation for the Council for Basic Education, which he and Mortimer B. Smith,* his associate, created. Bestor continued his criticisms of the anti-intellectual nature of the life adjustment curriculum that had been produced by progressive "educationists." Bestor suggested that schools return to a previous era and provide instruction in the academic areas of a core curriculum. He felt that education was a democratic birthright but must be made intellectually demanding in order to produce citizen decision makers. These efforts catapulted him into the leadership of the anti–progressive education movement (see PROGRESSIVE EDUCATION).

Bestor's papers are housed at the University of Illinois. Biographies include Adelbert Long, "A Study of Three Contemporary Educational Critics" (1967); Etta Sellars, "A Historical Comparative Analysis of the Ideology of Selected Educational Reformers" (1994); and Marlene Wentworth, "Attitudes towards Learning: An Examination of Arthur Bestor's Educational Wastelands" (1986).

Charles E. Jenks

BIBLE READING. Calvinist Puritans, concerned about learning and piety in colonial Massachusetts, reflected that concern in the "Ould Deluder Satan Act" of 1647 (see MASSACHUSETTS EDUCATION LAWS OF 1642, 1647, 1648). A chief feature of this legislation viewed Bible reading as protection against the inroads of Satan. The statute also conveyed the necessity that Scriptures, in order to be interpreted accurately, must be under the aegis of proper authority, namely, the Puritan leaders. The Bible continued to be the major book in the district schools* of the new country, followed by Noah Webster's* *Speller.* In the early nineteenth century, the Bible was vigorously promoted by a variety of Protestant societies, for example, the American Home Missionary Society, for use in the country's institutions, including its schools.

The Bible remained the undisputed foundation of Protestantism. As such, its devotional reading was a fixture in Protestant America's schools. Indeed, Horace Mann,* termed the "Father of the Common School," defended his program of state-subsidized schooling from attacks that it was irreligious by the unique role the Bible had in the schools he proposed and supported. According to Mann, the King James version of the Bible was to be read in Massachusetts's schools without note or comment. Most Americans agreed with Mann in Protestant America and its "pan-Protestant" public schools in the mid-nineteenth century.

Challenges to Protestant hegemony of the schools, which featured the practice of devotional Bible reading, became more frequent as the century progressed. Among them were Roman Catholic protests motivated by the fact that the King James version of the Bible, a Protestant version, was used. This edition contained interpretations offensive to Catholics. Devotional Bible reading stood as the most salient evidence of Protestant domination of the mid-century common schools. Devotional Bible-reading in the public schools was subject to continuous legal challenges brought by Catholics and "free thinkers." For the most part, the Bible survived these attacks, at the very least in the sense that its reading was not adjudged to constitute sectarian instruction and hence be unconstitutional.

Bible reading in the public schools continued despite these legal challenges until 1890, when legal protests began to erode the practice. That year in Wisconsin, following a lengthy, emotion-packed struggle and overturning a circuit court decision, the State Supreme Court, in *The State ex rel. Weiss and Others, Appellant v. The District Board of School District No. Eight of the City of Edgerton* (76 Wis. 177 [1890]), declared that the devotional reading of the Bible in the public schools constituted sectarian instruction and was thus unconstitutional. The public was enraged and the outcry widespread, but the decision stood. In 1962, the U.S. Supreme Court, in *Engel v. Vitale*,* a highly controversial and largely unpopular decision, ruled that public school–sponsored prayer was unconstitutional. That year eleven states, mostly southern, required Bible reading by statute. Six states forbade the practice. As a result, some form of Bible reading occurred in 42 percent of the nation's public school districts. Finally, in 1963 the U.S. Supreme Court, in *School District of Abington v. Schempp* 374 U.S. 203 (1963), adjudged that devotional Bible reading in the public schools, although voluntary and without note or comment, violated the Establishment Clause of the First Amendment and was hence unconstitutional.

Public opposition to this decision, following but a year after the ruling on prayer, was frequent, emotional, and loud. Justice Thomas Clark, writing for the majority in the *Schempp* decision, called attention to the role religion had played in the history of humankind, describing one's education as "incomplete" without its study. He supported the development of courses *about* religion, that is, *descriptive* religion, in the public schools. A number of educational groups, among them the American Association of School Administrators (AASA), recommended that "constructive policies" about the relation of religion to the public schools be developed. Even the U.S. Congress became involved, as 111 members prepared a total of 147 constitutional amendments to permit the banned Bible reading and prayer. Nonetheless, the decision stood, as it had in Wisconsin some seventy years earlier, and protests went largely unheeded.

However, a feeling that religion had been marginalized in American life grew through the 1980s and 1990s. Thus, Bible reading did not disappear as a national issue. President Ronald Reagan declared 1983 as the "Year of the Bible." A year later cases involving religion made up 5 percent of the U.S. Supreme Court's docket. The role of religion in general and Bible reading in particular received wide media treatment that same year, and Congress passed the "Equal Access" law, which granted religious groups, such as non-school-sponsored Bible study clubs, access to public school facilities equal to that of other extracurricular bodies on school premises (see EXTRACURRICULUM). The trend has continued, with growing public pressure for the reinstatement of religion in American public life and its schools. The *Religious Freedom Restoration Act*, passed by Congress in 1993, which required government to show a "compelling interest" before it applies a neutral law in a manner that would interfere with religious practice, represented one tangible manifestation of this sentiment. Finally, a number of measures, among them a constitutional amendment to restore prayer to the schools in the form of a silent moment of meditation, have been advanced to counteract the combined efforts of *Engel* and *Schempp*.

For Mann's position on religion, see his "Twelfth Annual Report (1848)," in Lawrence A. Cremin, ed., *The Republic and the School: Horace Mann on the Education of Free Men* (1957). The AASA delineates its position in *Religion in the Public Schools* (1964). Also refer to Stephen L. Carter, *The Culture of Disbelief: How American Law and Politics Trivialize Religious Devotion* (1993); Thomas C. Hunt, *The American School in Its Social Setting* (1975); Thomas C. Hunt, "The Supreme Court, Religion, and the Temper of the Times" (1986); and Leo Pfeffer, "The *Schempp-Murray* Decision on School Prayers and Bible-Reading" (1963).

Thomas C. Hunt

BILINGUAL EDUCATION has a long history both abroad and in the United States. In 1663, at Harvard University, the Reverend John Eliot published 1,500 copies of an "Indian Bible" in the Massachusetts dialect of the Algonquian language to help teach Christianity to American Indians near Boston. Bilingual education in schools run by missionaries for Native Americans was suppressed by the U.S. government in the second half of the nineteenth century as un-American, and German-language instruction in public schools was virtually eliminated during the anti-German hysteria of World War I.

From World War I to the 1960s, most non-English-speaking students were placed in English language classes without special assistance and allowed to "sink-or-swim." The post–World War II civil rights movement helped direct the attention of Americans to the poor educational conditions and other handicaps faced by minority groups in the United States, and efforts were made to provide specialized English as a second langauge (ESL) instruction for non-English-speaking students. In 1963, a successful model of bilingual education was developed at the Coral Way School in Dade County, Florida, for the children of educated refugees from the Cuban Revolution; this model allowed the students to maintain and develop their Spanish language as they learned English.

In response to pressure by Hispanics and other groups for better education, Congress passed the Bilingual Education Act in 1968 as Title VII of the Elementary and Secondary Education Act of 1965.* The act originated as an antipoverty measure primarily to aid low-income Mexican Americans in the Southwest, and it provided, on a competitvie basis, seed money for three years to school districts to develop innovative programs to help limited-English-speaking students from low-income families learn English, with the promise that these new programs would be continued after the federal funding ceased. Programs were started without an adequate number of trained bilingual teachers and without sufficient research to support their design.

The need for more special programs for limited English proficiency (LEP) students was emphasized again in the 1974 Supreme Court decision *Lau v. Nichols.** The Court found that the historically common practice of "submersing" non-English-speaking students in a regular classroom did not give them an equal educational opportunity compared with English-speaking students as required by the Civil Rights Act of 1964.* This case concerned nearly 3,000 Chinese-speaking students in the San Francisco public school* system, of whom about two-thirds were submersed in English language classrooms. The Supreme Court mandated that the plantiffs receive some form of special bilingual or ESL instruction until they could speak English well enough to be put in a regular classroom.

The Bilingual Education Act was also reauthorized in 1974 to support teacher training and the formation of a National Clearinghouse for Bilingual Education to collect, analyze, and disseminate information about bilingual education. The amendments also barred federal support for two-way bilingual education programs such as the one at Coral Way Elementary School. The 1978 amendments to Title VII emphasized the strictly transitional nature of native language instruction and highlighted the deficit nature of the approach defining eligible students as LEP. The amendments further allowed up to 40 percent of the students served to be English speaking in order to avoid segregating LEP students and to provide them with English language role models.

A campaign to make English the official language of the country was started by Senator S. I. Hayakawa in 1981 with the introduction of a constitutional amendment in Congress to that effect. Hayakawa opposed both bilingual education and bilingual voting rights. In 1983, he helped to found U.S. English, an organization that promoted English as the official language of both states and the nation. During the administration of President Ronald Reagan, bilingual education funding was cut and officials of the U.S. Department of Education* actively opposed bilingual education. Despite the fears that the English language will be submerged by increased immigration since the Immigration and Reform and Control Act of 1986, studies show that recent immigrants are learning English faster than ever.

The Bilingual Education Act was again amended in 1984 to fund special alternative bilingual programs as well as the existing developmental and transitional programs. Developmental bilingual programs promote students' native as well as English language skills. Transitional bilingual programs teach LEP students English as quickly as possible but use their native language during the first few years to teach subjects such as math and science so that students are not held back while they are learning English. Both developmental and transitional programs use ELS teaching methodologies for the English portion of the instructional program. Special alternative programs tend to be all-English programs that immerse students in English using ESL teaching methodologies exclusively. About 80 percent of Title VII funded programs over the years were transitional. The 1988 bilingual amendments increased funding for special alternative programs and limited participation in most Title VII programs to three years despite research indicating that it takes six or seven years for a non-English-speaking child to learn enough English to be academically successful in a regular U.S. classroom. In 1994, further amendments strengthened professional development programs and increased attention to native language maintenance and research, but in 1996 and 1997 a conservative Congress appropriated money only for elementary and secondary programs.

By 1994, despite the lack of enthusiasm in Congress for bilingual education, thirty-one states had some form of bilingual certification or endorsement and forty states some form of ESL certificate or endorsement for teachers. Advocates of bilingual education such as Stephen Krashen currently promote high-quality subject matter teaching in the first language, without translation; development of literacy in the first language; and teaching using special ESL teaching methods that focus on teaching language and subject matter content together. There is also a move toward advocating two-way bilingual programs to get away from the deficit notion that speaking a non-English language is a handicap. In two-way bilingual programs, an approximately equal number of English-speaking students and students speaking another language are mixed. The English-speaking students learn the non-English language, and the non-English-speaking students learn English. The idea behind two-way programs is that bilingualism is an asset in our modern world and should be promoted in all students. It is especially important to preserve existing native language fluency. For example, kindergarten* students whose first language is Korean speak their native language more fluently than the average graduate of the intensive forty-seven-week Defense Language Institute program. It is an irony of American life that the U.S. public schools have worked to stamp out native languages of students at the same time the U.S. government has funded foreign language programs in those same schools (see AMERICANIZATION).

The continued need for special programs for LEP students is indicated by the fact that in the 1990s the Office of Bilingual Education and Minority Languages Affairs, which administers Title VII in the U.S. Department of Education, estimated that about 6 percent of American students are LEP. Two professional organizations, the National Association for Bilingual Education (NABE) and the Teachers of English to Speakers of Other Languages (TESOL), are in the forefront of promoting better instruction for non-English-speaking students. The first national conference on the teaching of English to speakers of other languages was held in 1964 in Tucson, Arizona, and TESOL was formally established in 1966. A first national bilingual conference was held in 1972 in Austin, Texas, and NABE was formally founded in 1975 "to address the educational needs of language-minority students in the U.S. and to advance the language competencies and multicultural understanding of all Americans."

Refer to James Crawford, *Language Loyalties: A Source Book on the Offical English Controversy* (1992); James Crawford, *Hold Your Tongue: Bilingualism and the Politics of "English Only"* (1992); and Rosalie Pedalino Porter, *Forked Tongue: The Politics of Bilingual Education* (1990).

Jon Reyhner

BILINGUAL EDUCATION ACT. See BILINGUAL EDUCATION.

BINET, ALFRED (July 8, 1857–October 18, 1911), along with Theodore Simon, developed the first intellegence test in France in 1905. Although formally educated in law and medicine, Binet, self-taught in the fledgling field of psychology, became arguably France's most famous experimental psychologist. In 1891, he accepted a position at the Laboratory of Physiological Psychology at the Sorbonne and became its director in 1894. The next year he founded and edited the first French psychology journal, *L'Annee Psychologique*. In 1904, the French minister of public instruction appointed Binet and three other members of the Society for the Psychological Study of the Child to serve on a commission to study the administrative and pedagogical requirements for educating retarded children. Their efforts were hampered, however, by the lack of an objective and reliable means of identifying such students. Binet and Simon consequently developed the first intelligence scales, which focused on measuring age- and grade-appropriate knowledge, behavior, or tasks rather than on underlying abilities (see INTELLIGENCE TESTING). American psychologists Lewis Terman,* Henry Goddard,* and Robert Yerkes* reinterpreted these scales as tests of innate ability and introduced them into the United States between 1908 and 1920. The public schools subsequently adopted them as a means of identifying and tracking* students of supposedly varying abilities. Intelligence tests have been the subject of intense debate over the years, and Binet's historical role in the controversy has also become the object of scrutiny. Many scholars have argued that Binet was a well-meaning diagnostician who saw the scales as a means of identifying educable students in need of remediation. More recent critics have contended that Binet's scales, rooted in a hereditarian view of intelligence (see HEREDITARIANISM), inevitably led to tracking and unequal educational opportunities.

Although *The Experimental Study of Intelligence* (1903) is considered Binet's best work, *The Development of Intelligence in Children (The Binet-Simon Scale)* (1916; 1973) best explains the intelligence scales. Theta H. Wolfe's *Alfred Binet* (1973) represents the definitive English language biography. Analyses of Binet's role in the intelligence debate appear in Stephen Jay Gould's positive treatment in *The Mismeasure of Man* (1981) and Elaine Mensh and Harry Mensh's critical appraisal in *The IQ Mythology* (1991). For the impact of Binet's scales on early-twentieth-century American schools, see Paul D. Chapman's *Schools as Sorters* (1988).

Stephen H. Aby

BLAIR EDUCATION BILL was submitted in 1882 to the U.S. Senate by New Hampshire Republican senator Henry W. Blair, chair of the Committee on Education and Labor. The bill proposed temporary federal support for common schools* through direct monetary aid to a state based on its rate of illiteracy and the ability of the state government to match the federal expenditure. The bill also prohibited the use of federal funds for sectarian schools. The fundamental principle behind the bill focused on the development of southern common schools. Public support for this bill was higher than for any other federal education bill during the nineteenth century. Although the Senate passed this bill in 1882, 1884, 1886, and 1888, House Democrats and Republicans repeatedly defeated it. They justified their opposition through arguments of constitutionality and the southern economic recovery in the 1880s. It was the last federal education bill heard on the floor of either house of Congress until the 1917 Smith-Hughes Act.*

See Gordon Canfield Lee, *The Struggle for Federal Aid: First Phase, a History of the Attempts to Obtain Federal Aid for the Common Schools, 1870–1890* (1949), and Allen J. Going, ''The South and the Blair Education Bill'' (1957).

Deanna Michael

BLOOM, BENJAMIN S. (February 21, 1913–   ) authored or coauthored this country's most widely recognized body of work on educational objectives and methodologies during the second half of the twentieth century. He earned his B.A. and M.S. degrees from Pennsylvania State University in 1935 and his Ph.D. from the University of Chicago in 1942. He began his research career in studies with the Pennsylvania State Relief Organization in 1935–1936 and the American Youth Commission in 1936–1938. His research into school- and university-based education began as a doctoral student under Ralph W. Tyler* at Chicago, where he assisted on the Cooperative Study in General Education (1939–1940) and the Board of Examinations (1940–1943). Two of his earliest works were *Teaching by Discussion* (1948), published internally at the university, and ''Examining,'' a chapter in *The Idea and Practice of General Education* (1950; reissued 1992). Bloom remained at the university until 1990, through the rank of Distinguished Service Professor of Education, interrupted only by two visiting professorships.

The core concerns of Bloom's career have been how curricular choices, teaching methods, and assessments can contribute to the development of students' intellectual capacities and nurture their talent development in both academic and artistic realms. These interests grew from Bloom's nineteen-year relationship with the Board of Examiners at Chicago. This faculty Board wrote comprehensive examinations for the university's general education, interdisciplinary core courses—often open-book exams designed in Bloom's words to emphasize ''higher mental processes.'' In 1948, informal discussions among the examiners led to the idea of a national effort to construct a hierarchical classification scheme to describe the stages of how students master academic learning: The project would also develop classifications of emotional and psychomotor development. In four years' time, blue-ribbon panels of American educators met and, under Bloom's direction and editorship, produced the *Taxonomy of Educational Objectives, Handbook I, Cognitive Domain* (1956; reissued 1984). The volume addressed how professors know when students truly understand material, what steps instructors must take to move beyond the illusory learning of rote memorization so that students can attain deeper levels of knowing, and how tests or other assessments can help. The *Taxonomy* aimed at stimulating professors to redesign curricula and assessments for introductory-level college courses. Gounded in earlier work by Bloom's mentor and collaborator, Tyler, and by Hilda Taba* at Chicago in the 1940s, the book could have survived merely as a thoughtful work on the college curriculum. But a series of dramatic turns in American educational history followed closely on the *Taxonomy*'s heels and, in the retrospective judgment of many observers, gradually promoted the *Taxonomy* and its sequels to the status of major works in elementary and secondary education. Federal and private initiatives to the Soviet Union's "first in space" *Sputnik I* satellite in 1957 and to the spread of the civil rights* movement during the late 1950s and early 1960s created a climate of intense national interest in educational objectives and outcomes for children across the spectrum of abilities, achievement, race, and class. A new, diverse professional literature, from radical social critiques to the emerging field of cognitive psychology, merged in one respect: They reinforced the ideal that more students could learn a more meaningful curriculum, at higher levels of sophistication and with a more positive impact on their quality of life and on American competitiveness, than we had previously thought possible or necessary. "Bloom's Taxonomy," as it came to be known, filled a gap in the professional literature during these pivotal discussions. Its six-stage framework provided K–12 classroom teachers, not just professors, with a vocabulary they could use to understand and apply the new notions of educational objectives and higher-order thinking skills—even as some critics found the *Taxonomy* overly formulaic and rigid. In 1971, Bloom, with coeditors J. Thomas Hastings and George F. Madaus, published a massive sequel, the *Handbook on Formative and Summative Evaluation of Student Learning*, geared specifically for elementary and secondary teachers and education majors. This book, commonly referred to by the authors as their "Handbook," marked a peak period of the *Taxonomy*'s influence in the United States as well as its growing reputation abroad. With extensive chapters on most school subjects, the authors intended that it show teachers "ways in which evaluation may be used to bring students up to mastery levels of learning." They published a condensed version, entitled *Evaluation to Improve Learning*, ten years later. The *Taxonomy* would eventually be translated in eighteen languages, and Bloom served as an educational advisor and lectured overseas. Studied, explained, or cited in hundreds of publications, the *Taxonomy* became the subject of a 1994 yearbook of the National Society for the Study of Education,* *Bloom's Taxonomy: A Forty-Year Retrospective*.

During the 1960s and 1970s, Bloom helped to define and promulgate "mastery learning," essentially an elaboration of how to apply principles of the *Taxonomy* among diverse groups of learners, emphasizing the belief that "virtually any student can learn to a high standard." In the 1980s, Bloom directed a five-year study of talent development in 120 "gifted" people in fields ranging from neurology to music to Olympic swimming. From his findings, he asserted that few were child prodigies, but that certain learning conditions, hard work, and support had enabled most to reach world-class heights. His work suggested that educators can play an active role in nurturing children's talent development, rather than viewing children's "gifts" merely as exclusively inherited or innate.

Bloom published seventeen books and dozens of articles. He also helped to found the International Association for the Evaluation of Educational Achievement.

For a brief biography, see Lorin W. Anderson, "Benjamin Bloom: His Research and Influence on Education" (1988). Also refer to Charlotte H. Cox, "Basic Skills through Mastery Learning: An Interview with Benjamin S. Bloom" (1979, 1980).

Robert A. Levin

BLOW, SUSAN ELIZABETH (June 7, 1843–March 26, 1916), kindergarten* trainer, public school kindergarten director, was a leading American advocate and interpreter of Friedrich Froebel's* German kindergarten methods. The daughter of a successful St. Louis businessman and well-to-do mother, Blow learned about the kindergarten while traveling in Germany and in 1871 asked St. Louis school superintendent William Torrey Harris* to start a public kindergarten experiment. She went to New York City in 1872 to train under German kindergartner Maria Kraus-Boelte and returned to St. Louis in 1873 to start a public kindergarten class at the Des Peres School. A powerful and charismatic lecturer, Blow began a training program in 1873 in St. Louis; she trained many influential American kindergartners, including Elizabeth Harrison and others. Like William Torrey Harris, with whom she remained in close contact, Blow was a Hegelian, much interested in philosophy, and she combined literary and cultural themes in her popular classes and lectures. She suffered from bouts of nervous exhaustion and retired in 1884 to Cazenovia, New York, to devote the rest of her career to defending pure Froebelianism and arguing against modification of German kindergarten methods. Blow wrote a series of five books, *Symbolic Education* (1894), a two-volume translation of Froebel's *Mother Play* (1895), *Letter to a Mother on the Philosophy of Froebel* (1899), *Kindergarten Education* (1899), and *Educational Issues in the Kindergarten* (1908); she lectured on the kindergarten at Teachers College, Columbia University, from 1905 to 1909 and was active in the International Kindergarten Union.* The ideas of younger kindergarten proponents, like Patty Smith Hill,* who espoused more progressive (see PROGRESSIVE EDUCATION), psychologically oriented approaches, eventually supplanted those of Blow. Nevertheless, she successfully introduced the German kindergarten to many American mothers and educators.

Blow's letters to William Torrey Harris are in the Harris Papers, Missouri Historical Society, St. Louis. Other letters reside in the archives of the Association for Childhood Education International, University of Maryland Library, College Park. Biographical entries on Blow include Laura Fisher, *Pioneers of the Kindergarten in America* (1924), and Dorothy Ross, *Notable American*

Women, 1607–1905 (1971). See also Michael Shapiro, *Child's Garden: The Kindergarten Movement from Froebel to Dewey* (1983).

Barbara Beatty

BOARD OF NATIONAL POPULAR EDUCATION was organized in Cleveland, Ohio, in April 1847 to recruit and train single Protestant evangelical women from New England and upper New York state to teach and sometimes open schools in the West. Before the National Board closed its operations in 1858, it had trained and placed nearly 600 women in schools primarily located in the Mississippi Valley, but also in Oregon and California.

Catharine Beecher,* the first general agent, prepared sixty-eight teachers in the first two classes in Albany, New York, and Hartford, Connecticut, before turning over the administration of the program to William Slade (1786–1859), former governor of Vermont. During the National Board's most active period, he helped recruit a spring and fall class of between twenty and twenty-five women teachers. Nancy Swift, the former principal of the Middlebury (Vermont) Female Seminary and a former pioneer teacher in Huntsville, Alabama, supervised their training in Hartford for six weeks and continued to correspond with the teachers after they reached their western schools. Male members of the National Board were community leaders and ministers in Ohio. They searched for communities needing teachers or desiring to start schools. The Ladies' Society for the Promotion of Education at the West in Boston merged with the National Board in 1852 after sponsoring 109 teachers of its own. The Board ceased operations after the final illness of Governor Slade.

In addition to serving as pioneer educators in developing communities of the West, two-thirds of the women sent by the National Board remained in the West. These pioneer teachers were also significant because they journeyed West as single women not only to fulfill the National Board's goals of bringing education and evangelical religious values to the West but also to seek wider opportunities for themselves at a time when women were perceived as being tied to home and family.

The papers of the Board of National Popular Education are located in the Connecticut Historical Society in Hartford, Connecticut. Also, refer to Polly Welts Kaufman, *Women Teachers on the Frontier* (1984).

Polly Welts Kaufman

BOARDING SCHOOLS can be traced to a mixture of traditions borrowed from English, German, and Swiss educational institutions. From the English public school model, American boarding school educators adopted the concept of character building; from their German counterparts they integrated the idea of the *gymnasium*; and finally from the Swiss they embraced Johann Heinrich Pestalozzi's* and Phillip Emmanuel von Fellenberg's conception of child nurture. Despite these initial European influences, by the early twentieth century American boarding schools had developed into a truly indigenous institution.

They operated as publicly incorporated nonprofit schools, run by self-perpetuating boards of trustees, and funded by philanthropic donations and tuition. Four classifications of private secondary boarding schools existed: church-affiliated, nondenominational, military, and academy. Most of these institutions offered a ninth-through-twelfth-grade college preparatory curriculum in either single-sex or coeducational* environments. Students and faculty lived on campuses located in bucolic settings, far away from the perceived nefarious influences of swelling cities. George Bancroft* and Joseph Cogswell are credited with founding the first full-fledged boarding school in 1823 with the Round Hill School, in Northampton, Massachusetts. Although several boarding schools appeared prior to the Civil War, they burgeoned between 1880 and 1910. A variety of social, economic, and cultural factors, such as the decline of the town-sponsored academy (see ACADEMIES), rise of rigid public school bureaucracies, proliferation of urban immigrants, growing concern among the wealthy for the educational and social welfare of their children, and higher admission standards of fledgling modern universities, stimulated and directed this boarding school movement. No fundamental change occurred until the widespread social and cultural changes of the 1960s forced many boarding school leaders to reexamine their elitist traditions; this resulted in the relaxation of strict conduct codes, a more inclusive curriculum, an emphasis on recruiting a more economically diverse student body, and the advent of coeducation. There currently exist approximately 300 boarding schools, which enroll about 45,000 students.

James McLachlan's *American Boarding Schools: A Historical Study* (1970) remains the definitive historical analysis of this institution. For a positive portrayal of the educational contributions of contemporary boarding schools, see Pearl Rock Kane, ed., *Independent Schools, Independent Thinkers* (1992); offering a more critical perspective is Peter Cookson and Caroline Hodges Persell's *Preparing for Power: America's Elite Boarding Schools* (1985). Institutional histories are another valuable source of information. August Heckscher's *St. Paul's: The Life of a New England School* (1980) and Frederick S. Allis, Jr.'s, *Youth from Every Quarter: A Bicentennial History of Phillips Academy, Andover* (1979) represent interesting and revealing sources.

Mark Desjardins

BOBBITT, JOHN FRANKLIN (February 16, 1876–March 7, 1956), known as the "Father of Curriculum." This reputation stemmed from his book *The Curriculum* (1918), often considered the first major modern work on curriculum, and from his application of scientific management to education as a method for developing curriculum. Bobbitt, born in southeastern Indiana, taught in rural schools from 1893 to 1902 and was graduated from Indiana University in 1901. Between 1902 and 1907, he worked at the Philippine Normal School in Manila, and in 1909 he earned a Ph.D. with G. Stanley Hall* at Clark University. He then began a thirty-two-year teaching career at the University of Chicago and earned an early reputation as a school-efficiency expert while serving as a professor of school administration. While Bobbitt's interests expanded into all as-pects of education—from scientific selection of teachers to efficient school administration—he became best known for curriculum development through school surveys. He engaged in survey fieldwork, often serving as an assistant superintendent, with school districts throughout the country. Although Bobbitt's second book, *How to Make a Curriculum* (1918), continued to maintain needs and objective analysis for curriculum making, he began to approach education as a social process. By 1926, with "Orientation of the Curriculum-Maker," in the legendary twenty-sixth yearbook of the National Society for the Study of Education,* he reversed his advocacy of education as a preparation for adult-hood. With his retirement and the publication of his last major work, *The Curriculum of Modern Education* (1941), Bobbitt had moved to an amorphous concept of "the good life" as much as he still advocated scientific analysis of needs and activities.

The Special Collections, University of Chicago Library, possesses materials pertaining to Bobbitt's career. His 1922 monograph, *Curriculum Making in Los Angeles*, proved to be a seminal work in his scientific curriculum making. Boyd H. Bode, *Modern Education Theory* (1927), represents a contemporary source. B. G. DeWulf's doctoral dissertation, "The Educational Ideas of John Franklin Bobbitt" (1962), serves as a useful biography. Other general sources include Lawrence A. Cremin, *The Transformation of the School: Progressivism in American Education, 1876–1957* (1961), and Herbert M. Kliebard, *The Struggle for the American Curriculum* (1986).

Craig Kridel

BOND, HORACE MANN (November 8, 1904–December 21, 1972), an Afri-can American college professor and administrator, was a giant in the generation of African American intellectuals that followed the Du Bois–Washington* gen-eration of the early twentieth century and preceded the civil rights activists of the 1960s. Bond finished high school at fourteen and attended Lincoln Univer-sity (Pennsylvania), graduating at age eighteen. He earned master's and doctoral degrees from the University of Chicago. His major field was education, with specializations in the history and sociology of education. Bond served on the faculties of Langston University (Oklahoma), Alabama State College (Mont-gomery), Fisk Univesity, and Dillard University. He also became chair of the Education Department at Fisk and the founding academic dean at Dillard. He was also president of the Fort Valley State College (Georgia) from 1939 until 1945, when he became president of his alma mater, Lincoln University. He remained as president there until 1957, when he resigned amid controversies over a plan to increase the number of white students at that institution, deteri-orating relations with older, white faculty, and his frequent trips away from campus. He then moved to Atlanta University, where he served as dean of the School of Education for five years and then as director of its Bureau of Edu-cational Research. He retired in 1971.

Bond authored six books and numerous articles. In the 1920s, he published articles critical of the racial bias in intelligence tests.* His two most enduring books were published in the 1930s: *The Education of the Negro in the American Social Order* (1934) and *Negro Education in Alabama: A Study of Cotton and Steel* (1939). Bond worked as a historian for the National Association for the Advancement of Colored People as it prepared a brief answering historical questions asked by the U.S. Supreme Court in deliberating the famous 1954 *Brown v. Board of Education** school desegregation case. He became particularly interested in Africa and Africans in the late 1940s, undertaking numerous trips to that continent and publishing several articles on education in Africa's emerging nations.

Bond's papers are in the Archives and Manuscripts Division, University of Massachusetts, Amherst, Library. He wrote *Education for Production* (1944), *The Search for Talent* (1959), and *Education for Freedom: A History of Lincoln University* (1976). See Wayne J. Urban, *Black Scholar: Horace Mann Bond, 1904–1972* (1992), for a complete biography.

Wayne J. Urban

BOSTON HOUSE OF REFORMATION. Dissatisfied with the Boston House of Correction, city officials opened a separate institution for juvenile offenders in 1826. The impetus came from the Massachusetts legislature, which appointed a commission to investigate the causes of pauperism. In 1821, the commission recommended that the state change the way it dealt with the poor by building a house of industry and correction. Impressed by the opening of the New York House of Refuge* in 1825, Boston civic leaders, worried about homeless and criminal children on city streets, designated an unused wing in the House of Correction as a House of Reformation, which opened under the direction of Rev. E.M.P. Wells in 1826. Wells is remembered for the classification system he introduced, a system in which privileges were granted or withheld based on conduct. This system impressed French visitors Alexis de Tocqueville and Gustave de Beaumont, who commented favorably on it in *Du systeme penitentiarie (On the Penitentiary System in the United States)* published in 1833. In 1832, Wells moved to the Boston Asylum and Farm School, a new institution for troubled youth not convicted of criminal offenses.

Gustave de Beaumont and Alexis de Tocqueville, *On the Penitentiary System in the United States and Its Application in France* (1964), can serve as a primary source. Leading secondary sources are Joseph M. Hawes, *Children in Urban Society: Juvenile Delinquency in Nineteenth-Century Society* (1971); Michael B. Katz, *The Irony of Early School Reform: Educational Innovation in Mid-Nineteenth-Century Massachusetts* (1968); Robert M. Mennel, *Thorns and Thistles: Juvenile Delinquents in the United States, 1825–1940* (1973); David J. Rothman, *The Discovery of the Asylum: Social Order and Disorder in the New Republic* (1971); Steven L. Schlossman, *Love and the American Delin-*

quent: The Theory and Practice of "Progressive" Juvenile Justice, 1825–1920 (1977).

Joseph M. Hawes

BOSTON LATIN GRAMMAR SCHOOL, the longest continuously operating secondary school in America, was founded in 1635 or 1636 as the first "public" school in the colonies. Called the most famous school in colonial America, it provided the classical education and social distinction required for admission to Harvard College. Boston Latin prepared privileged children for entry into the college and for their future positions among the religious and political elite. Partially financed by taxation since its inception, Boston Latin remained the sole tax-supported school in Boston until the 1680s. Despite this singular distinction, only a small fraction of the Boston community could benefit from its narrowly defined classical curriculum.* The school grudgingly added the more practical "English" branches of study to its catalogue by the early nineteenth century, but its monopoly of Boston's secondary education waned as more flexible models, especially the academy,* grew in prominence. Boston Latin maintains a unique place among secondary schools, owing both to its age and to its list of prominent alumni, from Cotton Mather to George Santayana. As the historic gateway to Harvard, Boston Latin retains a sense of its own history and social position uncommon among public schools.*

The primary institutional history of Boston Latin is Pauline Holmes, *A Tercentenary History of the Boston Public Latin School, 1635–1935* (1935). Also useful is Emit Duncan Grizzell, *Origin and Development of the High School in New England before 1865* (1923).

Scott Walter and William J. Reese

BOURNE, RANDOLPH SILLIMAN (May 30, 1886–December 22, 1918), was one of America's most insightful educational and cultural critics during the first decades of this century. Born in Bloomfield, New Jersey, he graduated from Columbia University in 1913. Between 1910 and 1918, he wrote many articles and reviews for such periodicals as *The Atlantic, Educational Review*, and *North American Review*. From 1914 to 1917, he contributed eighty-four articles to *The New Republic*, nearly half of which dealt with elementary, secondary, and higher education. Through this journal, Bourne interpreted John Dewey* and his ideas to political progressives (see PROGRESSIVE EDUCATION). Bourne criticized traditional education and publicized progressive ideas and experiments in *Youth and Life* (1913), *The Gary Schools* (1916), and *Education and Living* (1917). Becoming more critical of society and education, he began writing for *The Seven Arts, The Dial, The Masses*, and *The Liberator*. Near the end of his brief life, Bourne became a leading critic of Dewey and the *The New Republic* because of their support of America's entry into World War I (also, refer to the GARY PLAN).

The definitive biography is Bruce Clayton, *Forgotten Prophet: The Life of Randolph Bourne* (1984). See also Lawrence A. Cremin, *The Transformation of the School: Progressivism in American Education, 1876–1957* (1961), and James M. Wallace, *Liberal Journalism and American Education* (1991).

James M. Wallace

BOY SCOUTS OF AMERICA (BSA), founded on February 8, 1910, in New York City as an extension of the Young Men's Christian Association, was loosely based on the ideas of British scouting founder Robert S. Baden-Powell. The American scouting movement, however, developed separately from its British counterpart and created its own organizational structure. In 1916, the U.S. Congress granted the Boy Scouts a federal charter and the organization was hierarchically divided into troops in local councils within larger regions. Scouting quickly became popular, attracting over 1.6 million participants in its first decade. Eventually, the scouting movement sought to attract younger and older boys than the traditional adolescent age member by initiating the Cub Scout and Explorer programs. Scouting, in recent years, has actively recruited boys from inner city and minority areas. The current membership is approximately 5 million, and since its founding BSA has involved over 92 million youth and adult leaders.

BSA was typical of the myriad organizational reactions during the progressive era (see PROGRESSIVE EDUCATION) to counter the perceived weakening of the traditional family and community structures brought on by modern industrial society. Organized at a time when urbanization and industrialization were raising fears about the potential negative effects these developments would have on boys, BSA has always kept the inculcation of sound character traits as its main goal. The Scout Law pledges boys to be trustworthy, loyal, helpful, friendly, courteous, kind, obedient, cheerful, thrifty, brave, clean, and reverent. Through the Scout Oath, boys promise to "do my duty to God and my country . . . to help other people at all times . . . to keep myself physically strong, mentally awake, and morally straight." Scouting activities, such as camping and community service, along with individual upward advancement through the scouting ranks by acquiring merit badges and providing evidence of proficiency in a variety of areas, are all grounded in the idea of developing boys with strong character.

BSA's papers are housed at its national headquarters in Irving, Texas. The organization has also produced *Historical Highlights: A Year-by-Year Summary of the Major Events in the History of the Boy Scouts of America* (1995). Also, refer to David I. Macleod, *Building Character in the American Boy: The Boy Scouts, YMCA, and Their Forerunners, 1870–1920* (1983).

Alexander Urbiel

BOYER, ERNEST LEROY (September 13, 1928–December 8, 1995), former chief education officer of the United States and the State University of New

York (SUNY) system, became, over the last two decades of his life, one of the nation's most prolific and passionate voices for education reform. His body of work, completed principally during his fifteen-year tenure as president of the Carnegie Foundation for the Advancement of Teaching, beginning in 1981, recommended major changes in teaching and learning from kindergarten through college, including the basic curriculum, moral and civic education,* and the nature, structure, and reward system for teachers and professors. He also addressed the health and welfare of children and families and proposed new linkages among home, school, and workplace.

Boyer was born in Dayton, Ohio, and attended undergraduate school at Greenville College (Illinois) and Ohio State University. He obtained his master's and doctoral degrees in speech pathology and audiology at the University of Southern California, and held a postdoctoral fellowship in medical audiology at the University of Iowa Hospital. During the 1950s and early 1960s, Boyer built a career in college teaching (in forensics and speech) and administration in California at Loyola University, Upland College, and University of California–Santa Barbara. Boyer has been credited with introducing, at Upland, the concept of a midyear or January study term, in which colleges suspend the regular class schedule and students work in depth on a project or single course. In 1965, Boyer was appointed the first executive dean of the SUNY system; from 1970 to 1977, he served as SUNY chancellor, overseeing sixty-four campuses, 350,000 students, and 15,000 faculty. As chancellor, he established four "noncampus" SUNY sites for adult study without attending classes and instituted reward systems to recognize professors' teaching as well as research. He also held advisory positions for Presidents Richard Nixon and Gerald Ford. From 1977 to 1981, Boyer served as the twenty-third and last commissioner of education—appointed by President Jimmy Carter—the last years before Congress created the Department of Education.* Boyer maintained a ten-year consultancy in higher education with the People's Republic of China; many of his writings were translated into Chinese and Japanese. For seven years, he was a columnist for the Higher Education Supplement of the *London Times*. He also taught at the Woodrow Wilson School, Princeton University.

Under Carnegie Foundation sponsorship, Boyer gathered eminent colleagues to study and write with him on major issues confronting education. In *A Quest for Common Learning: The Aims of General Education* (1981), Boyer and Arthur Levine proposed a theme-based rather than a discipline-based reconceptualization of the first years of college, an approach Levine later implemented as president of Bradford (Massachusetts) College. Boyer and Fred Hechinger, in *Higher Learning in the Nation's Service* (1981), advocated "public policy studies for all students, especially encouraging a new program of civic education for adults." These initial publications foreshadowed two major themes of Boyer's subsequent works. First, he sought to humanize the curriculum, to make it more compelling to individual students and more likely to guide them toward a life's work that would combine individual reward with civic contribution.

Second, Boyer proposed ways to improve the conditions in which teaching and learning occur, including more planning and professional development time for teachers, smaller and non-age-graded classes in the first four years of school, better-maintained school buildings, enriched student-teacher contact through the extracurriculum,* and new partnerships with homes and businesses (also, see AGE-GRADING).

His books seem uniquely to capture both the commonalities of education from childhood through adulthood and the particular contexts that characterize and distinguish life and work at different levels of schooling. In *High School: A Report on Secondary Education in America* (1983), Boyer proposed an ambitious reform agenda based on an extensive field study of secondary education; he then provided grants to schools across the nation that sought to accept his challenges. Another national field study led to the publication of *College: The Undergraduate Experience in America* (1987), in which Boyer wrote passionately about remedying the "confusion of goals" that characterizes the most diverse, democratic system of higher education in the world. His *Scholarship Reconsidered: Priorities of the Professoriate* (1990) confronted the growing controversies over a perceived gap between distinguished senior professors who conduct research and graduate assistants or junior faculty who teach in their stead. An additional volume, reporting on a comparative study of the professoriate in twelve nations, was to be published posthumously. Finally, drawn to issues in the education of young children, he explained ways to humanize knowledge, professionalize teaching, and serve needy children in *Ready to Learn: Mandate for the Nation* (1991) and *Cornerstones for a New Century: Teacher Preparation, Early Childhood Education, a National Education Index* (1992). Boyer elaborated on a plan to create multi-age classrooms for grades K–4 in *The Basic School: A Community for Learning* (1995). (The author acknowledges the contribution of Robert Hochstein, longtime assistant to Ernest Boyer, for comments on an earlier draft of this article.)

Robert A. Levin

BRACE, CHARLES LORING. See NEW YORK CHILDREN'S AID SOCIETY.

BRADLEY, MILTON (November 8, 1836–May 30, 1911), is most well known for founding the Milton Bradley Company—a leading American manufacturer of board games. His contribution as an educator was as a promoter and publisher of kindergarten* and art materials (see ART EDUCATION). He was born in Vienna, Maine. He attended the Lawrence Scientific School from 1854 to 1856. In 1856, he obtained a job in a locomotive factory in Springfield, Massachusetts. As a young man, Bradley worked as a draftsman and made additional money in his free time by peddling stationery, pens, and inks to young women working in the mills in Lowell, Massachusetts. In 1859, he became interested in lithography and soon set up a printing business in Springfield, Massachusetts.

The Civil War brought business to a halt for Bradley. Shown an imported board game by a friend, he then conceived the idea of manufacturing board games. His first game, *The Checkered Game of Life*, sold 40,000 copies during winter 1860. He followed his success with *Games for Soldiers*—a pocketsized assortment of games for Union soldiers. In addition to games, Bradley also manufactured scientific toys such as zoetropes—one of the first motion picture devices.

In 1869, the kindergarten pioneer Elizabeth Palmer Peabody* introduced Bradley to the work of Friedrich Froebel.* Intrigued with Froebel's ideas and encouraged by Palmer Peabody, he published Edward Weibe's *Paradise of Childhood*, widely considered the first American book on the kindergarten. Bradley soon became a major promoter of the kindergarten movement and the country's main manufacturer of kindergarten materials. As part of providing supplies for kindergarteners, Bradley manufactured colored paper and developed a color system that came to be widely used in public schools throughout the country.

The main biographical source on Bradley is by the Milton Bradley Company, *Milton Bradley, a Successful Man: A Brief Sketch of His Career and the Growth of the Institution Which He Founded* (1910). Also see David Wallace Adams and Victor Edmonds, "Making Your Move: The Educational Significance of the American Board Game, 1832 to 1904" (1977).

Eugene F. Provenzo, Jr.

BRAMELD, THEODORE BURGHARD HURT (January 20, 1904–October 18, 1987), is significant for developing Cultural Reconstructionism, an educational philosophy that argues that educational institutions should lead in reforming society (also, see SOCIAL RECONSTRUCTIONISM). Integrating Reconstructionism with "anthropotherapy," planned social evolution, he emphasized that education be an agency for global reform.

Born in Neillsville, Wisconsin, Brameld attended local schools and earned a B.A. from Ripon College in 1926, with majors in English and speech. He served as field secretary for Ripon College from 1926 to 1928. He earned a Ph.D. in philosophy at the University of Chicago in 1931. His doctoral dissertation was published as *A Philosophic Approach to Communism* (1933). Brameld taught at Long Island University (1931–1935), Adelphi College (1935–1939), University of Minnesota (1939–1947), New York University (1947–1958), and Boston University (1958–1969). His books on philosophy of education include *Design for America* (1945), *Ends and Means in Education* (1950), *Patterns of Educational Philosophy* (1950), *Toward a Reconstructed Philosophy of Education* (1956), *Philosophies of Education in Cultural Perspective* (1955), *Education for the Emerging Age* (1961), *Education as Power* (1965), *The Use of Explosive Ideas in Education* (1965), and *The Climatic Decades: Mandate to Education* (1970). Later in his career Brameld developed interests in educational anthropology and international education. His books in these areas were *The Remaking of a Cul-*

ture—Life and Education in Puerto Rico (1959), *Japan: Culture, Education, and Change in Two Communities* (1968), and *The Teacher as World Citizen* (1970). He frequently contributed articles and reviews to journals, was active in the New Education Fellowship, an international organization of progressive educators, and was president of the Philosophy of Education Society (1947–1948).

For a general overview of Brameld's philosophy, see James S. Kaminsky, *A New History of Educational Philosophy* (1993), and Jonas F. Soltis, *Philosophy of Education since Mid-Century* (1981).

Gerald L. Gutek

BRECKINRIDGE, ROBERT JEFFERSON (March 8, 1780–December 27, 1871), nationally known for his work in the fields of religion, politics, and antislavery, has been also called the "Father of Public Education in Kentucky" because of his work as superintendent of public instruction from 1847 to 1853. He was born in Fayette County, Kentucky, and graduated from Union College in 1819. Following stints as an attorney, legislator, editor, minister, and moderator of the Presbyterian Church and principal of Jefferson College, Pennsylvania, Breckinridge was appointed Kentucky's sixth superintendent of public instruction in 1847. He pushed through the state legislature a property tax for educational purposes, increasing the funds devoted to public schools* from $6,000 when he began to $144,000 by midcentury. Attendance concomitantly rose from 24,000 in 1848 to 195,000 in four years. Only 10 percent of eligible children attended school when he assumed office; this figure had increased to 90 percent by the time he left office.

In 1853, Breckinridge resigned his post to become professor of theology at Danville Theological Seminary. Earlier disagreements with Governor John L. Helm hastened that action, but Breckinridge had also been disappointed that his calls for a longer school term, parental selection of textbooks, continued tuition (for financial reasons), Bible reading* in schools, and a larger salary for the superintendent had been rejected. Nevertheless, he had created a financially sound school system and given Kentucky students their first real opportunity for widespread public schooling. When Breckinridge resigned, the state's system was one of the two best in the South. His greatest contribution, he argued, was changing sentiment—now the people believed in the principle of public education, knew that knowledge led to a better life, and understood "that the work . . . can be done, and shall be done."

Breckinridge, following his career as school superintendent, continued to teach and write, but he gained considerable public attention during the Civil War when he became a leading Union proponent in Kentucky. With his own family divided by the war, he nevertheless served as temporary chair of the 1864 national Republican convention that renominated Abraham Lincoln. Breckinridge became a pariah in postwar Kentucky because of these stands.

The Library of Congress houses the Breckinridge Family Papers. For biographies, see Robert W. Hartness, "The Educational Work of Robert Jefferson Breckinridge" (1936); James C. Klotter, *The Breckinridges of Kentucky, 1760– 1981* (1986); and Willliam H. Vaughn, *Robert Jefferson Breckinridge as an Educational Administrator* (1937).

James C. Klotter

BRIGHAM, CARL CAMPBELL (May 4, 1890–January 24, 1943), is often called the "Father of the Scholastic Aptitude Test." While a student at Princeton University, where he earned his undergraduate and graduate degrees (Ph.D., psychology), Brigham studied the work of Alfred Binet* and began a lifelong study of intelligence and aptitude. During World War I, he was part of the team with Robert Yerkes,* Louis Terman,* Henry Goddard,* and Edward Boring that established the U.S. Army's testing program for officer selection (see INTEL- LIGENCE TESTING). Brigham's *Study of American Intelligence* (1923) re- sulted from his analysis of the data gathered during this program.

After the war, Brigham became a driving force behind the establishment of the Scholastic Aptitude Test and made it his life's work. A growing interest in the applications of measures of aptitude led the College Board, in 1924, to establish a Commission on Scholastic Aptitude Tests with Brigham as chair. Fearing its members would develop their own measures, the Board determined that a single instrument for use by all was necessary. Thus, in 1926 the then- revolutionary Scholastic Aptitude Test (SAT) was born under Brigham's lead- ership. It used objective test items as implemented via a multiple-choice format, contrary to academia's historic reliance on essays.

Brigham's work led to controversy because from his early analyses of mass- testing data he attributed differences found among racial and ethnic groups to genetic factors. Although he later repudiated these findings, in *A Study of Error* (1932), his initial ideas were misused by "eugenic" movements in support of racist theories. In his later years Brigham asserted that aptitude and intelligence test scores were a composite of schooling, family background, English profi- ciency, and so on, and that there was no such thing as "native intelligence." Brigham's lasting legacy is embodied in standardized multiple-choice academic instruments in all their many forms.

After Brigham's death, his wife, the former Elizabeth Duffield, destroyed the bulk of his papers; a few papers remain in the archives of Princeton University and the College Board, also in Princeton, New Jersey. Matthew Downey, *Carl Campbell Brigham: Scientist and Educator* (1961), is the chief biographical source. Leon Cronbach, "Five Decades of Public Controversy over Mental Test- ing" (1975), analyzes Brigham's work; Thomas Donlon, "Brigham's Book" (1979), and Warren Findley, "Carl C. Brigham Revisited" (1981), provide crit- ical insights into his most overlooked work and his life in the context of his time.

Catharine C. Knight

BROWN, CHARLOTTE HAWKINS (June 11, 1883–January 11, 1961), devoted her life to the building and maintaining of Palmer Memorial Institute, a rural school near Greensboro, North Carolina. She was born in Henderson, North Carolina, and attended the State Normal School at Massachusetts. In 1901, Brown accepted a teaching appointment from the American Missionary Association (AMA) in Sedalia, North Carolina. Within her first year at the school, the AMA withdrew support. However, community members convinced Brown to remain in Sedalia. During the next five decades, she took that small elementary school and developed it into a high school and junior college for male and female students from the United States, Africa, Bermuda, Central America, and Cuba. Palmer Memorial Institute became known as one of the foremost finishing schools in the country, and Brown became the "first lady of social graces." By Palmer's forty-fifth anniversary, Brown had raised more than $1.5 million.

Brown's experiences illustrate two crucial phenomena that recur in the struggle of African Americans for education. The first focuses on the building and maintaining of public education facilities for African Americans in the South during the Jim Crow period and the interconnectedness with private elementary and secondary institutions. The majority of elementary and secondary educational institutions established after the Civil War were supported and maintained by the efforts of African Americans well into the mid-twentieth century. Palmer, unlike many other institutions, provided education to a community's African American students when the state was unwilling or unable to do so.

The second issue stresses the network system Brown and other educators used to facilitate educational, social, and economic improvements for their communities. In 1913, Brown became one of the founders of the North Carolina Federation of Women's Clubs and served as president for twenty-one years. This organization was responsible for the establishment and maintenance of the Efland Home for Wayward Girls for decades until the efforts of Brown and others convinced the North Carolina General Assembly to appropriate funding for such an institute. She also organized the Girls and Young Adults Division of the Federation of Negro Women's Clubs in 1948 and spearheaded a college scholarship fund. In addition, Brown organized a home ownership association to foster African American landownership in Sedelia. Finally, Brown proved to be active as an author. She wrote *Mammy: An Appeal of the Heart of the South* (1919) and *The Correct Thing to Do, to Say, to Wear* (1941). She also aided the founding of the *Negro Braille Magazine*.

The majority of Brown's papers are housed at the Schlesinger Library, Radcliffe College; the Charlotte Hawkins Brown Collection, Division of Archives and History, North Carolina Department of Cultural Resources, Historic Sites Section, Raleigh, North Carolina; and the National Council of Negro Women's National Archives for Black Women's History, Washington, D.C. For concise biographical information, see Kathleen Thompson, "Charlotte Hawkins Brown" (1993), and Charles W. Wadelington, "Charlotte Hawkins Brown" (1996).

Valinda W. Littlefield

BROWN V. BOARD OF EDUCATION OF TOPEKA, KANSAS, 347 U.S. 483 (1954), 349 U.S. 294 (1955). This represented the most significant ruling on race and equal educational opportunities in the history of the U.S. Supreme Court. In *Brown I*, the Court held that *de jure* segregation in public schools* on the basis of race deprived minority children of equal educational opportunities in violation of the Fourteenth Ammendment's Equal Protection Clause. A year later, in *Brown II* (1955), the Court began dismantling segregated school systems.

Brown I was a consolidation of four class action law suits on behalf of African American students who had been denied admission to schools attended by white children. State laws in Clarendon County (South Carolina), Prince Edward County (Virginia), and New Castle County (Delaware) required racial segregation; it was permitted by law in Kansas. The Court heard oral arguments in *Brown I* in December 1952, but it did not reach a decision because it was divided over the constitutionality of the "separate but equal" doctrine. The Court held a second round of arguments a year later. In an opinion written by the recently appointed Chief Justice, Earl Warren, the Supreme Court unanimously struck down *de jure* segregation in public schools on May 17, 1954. Applying the principles enunciated in *Sweatt v. Painter*, 339 U.S. 629 (1950), and *McClaurin v. Oklahoma State Regents*, 339 U.S. 637 (1950), companion cases that prohibited interschool and intraschool segregation, respectively, in higher education on the basis of tangible and intangible inequities to elementary and secondary schools, the Court focused on the detrimental psychological effects of segregation on African American students. For the first time in its history, the Court relied on data from the social sciences and considered the harmful effects of racial segregation in reaching its judgment. Although it stopped short of an outright reversal, the Court unequivocally repudiated the "separate but equal" doctrine it espoused in *Plessy v. Ferguson*,* 163 U.S. 537 (1896), but which apparently originated almost fifty years earlier in the Massachusetts case of *Roberts v. City of Boston*,* 59 Mass. 198, 5 Cush. 198 (1850). As monumental as *Brown I* was, it did not address remedies.

In *Brown II*, rendered on May 31, 1955, by Chief Justice Warren, the Court neither mandated an immediate end to nor set a timetable for eliminating school segregation. However, it did offer general guidance to the lower courts, directing them to fashion their decrees on equitable principles characterized by flexibility. Moreover, aware of the far-reaching impact of its decision, involving such matters as administration, school transportation, personnel, admissions policies, and changes in local laws, the Court reasoned that once progress was underway, the lower courts could grant more time to implement its ruling.

Brown I and the limited scope of remedies ordered in *Brown II* represent a compromise that attempted to steer a middle course. On the one hand, the Court was mindful that it could not permit segregated schooling to remain in place indefinitely. Yet, on the other, it sought to avoid lecturing what it aptly perceived would be a recalcitrant and resentful South. An unfortunate consequence was that in attempting to limit conflict by easing equality in, the Court inadvertently may have strengthened the resolve of opponents who heightened their resistance. If, as opponents of *Brown* might have maintained, equal educational opportunities were as important as the Court, and others, insisted, then why did it not order an immediate end to segregated schooling? As witnessed by the struggles to implement *Brown* over the past generation, the defiance that it has spawned had yet to be overcome fully.

See Mark Tushnet and Katya Lezin, "What Really Happened in *Brown v. Board of Education*" (1991), for background analysis.

Charles J. Russo

BRUNER, JEROME SEYMOUR (October 1, 1915–   ) is one of the leading educational reformers and thinkers in cognitive psychology, learning theories, child development, and curriculum. He challenged and overcame the mindset in education that human development was primarily a function of biology. In his work, he placed emphasis on culture and the self and promoted a multidisciplinary approach to the study of the mind that included not only physiologists and neuroscientists but also historians, anthropologists, and philosophers.

He was born in New York City, attended Duke University, and completed his graduate work at Harvard University with a Ph.D. in psychology. Bruner taught at Harvard following World War II, and in 1960 he published his seminal work, *The Process of Education*. That same year Bruner, along with George Miller, founded the Centre for Cognitive Studies at Harvard, where leading figures in the field like Howard Gardner continue to work on the cognitive development of the "mind."

His work on autobiography, including *In Search of Mind* (1983) and *Acts of Meaning* (1990), is an attempt to understand the cultural processes of constructing meaning interactively. Bruner believes that the issue of "meaning making" is the center of the cognitive revolution, and his contribution to the revolution was his idea of folk psychology or the ways in which people construct views of themselves, others, and the world.

Bruner's work on curriculum and instruction can be seen in part as a precursor to William Doll's *Post-Modern Perspective on Curriculum Development* (1993), Patrick Slattery's *Curriculum Development in the Postmodern Era* (1995), and other recent attempts to construct a postmodern curriculum. In such works as *Toward a Theory of Instruction* (1966) and *The Relevance of Education* (1971), Bruner focuses on knowledge generation, construction of meaning, and recursive learning. His approach is a dramatic contrast to a scientist or positivist approach that saw knowledge as a product, the brain as a storage compartment in which knowledge could be recalled upon command, and learning as a matter of repetition and sequential ordering. For Bruner, knowledge, learning, and order are not preordained but emerge from classroom interactions. Finally, refer to

David Olson, *The Social Foundations of Language and Thought: Essays in Honor of Jerome S. Bruner* (1980).

John A. Weaver

BRYAN, ANNA E. (July, 1858–February 21, 1901), kindergarten* trainer and free kinderarten director, was instrumental in adapting German kindergarten pedagogy to American children. Daughter of a piano maker and an educated mother from Louisville, she became interested in the kindergarten while visiting Chicago and enrolled in a training school run by Alice Putnam* of the Chicago Free Kindergarten Association. In 1887, Bryan returned to Louisville, where she began a training school sponsored by the Louisville Free Kindergarten Association. Working with poor children caused Bryan to make Friedrich Froebel's* kindergarten methods more oriented to the everyday reality of city children's lives. She gave an influential speech, "The Letter Killeth," at the 1890 meeting of the Kindergarten Department of the National Education Association (NEA),* in which she urged modification of the kindergarten and emphasized spontaneous "free play," a radical departure from Froebel's rigidly sequenced artificial play activities. She trained Patty Smith Hill* and with Hill attended G. Stanley Hall's* summer school session on child study at Clark University in 1894. Bryan moved to Chicago that year and became director of kindergarten training at the Armour Institute. While in Chicago, she collaborated with Francis W. Parker,* John Dewey,* and other progressive educators (see PROGRESSIVE EDUCATION). Bryan served as chair of the International Kindergarten Union's* child study and teacher training committees from 1897 until her death. Her innovative, child-centered pedagogy helped to transform the Froebelian kindergarten into a more experimental, psychologically oriented American educational reform.

Louisville's Filson Club houses the papers of the Louisville Free Kindergarten Association. See Bryan's speech in the NEA's *Journal of Proceedings and Addresses* (1890). Also see entries on her by Barbara Beatty, *American National Biography* (in press); Patty Smith Hill, *Pioneers of the Kindergarten in America* (1924); and M. Charlotte Jammer, *Notable American Women, 1607–1950* (1971).

Barbara Beatty

BUREAU OF REFUGEES, FREEDMEN, AND ABANDONED LANDS, known popularly as the Freedman's Bureau, was established by Congress on March 3, 1865, to respond to social and economic problems created by the American Civil War and Emancipation: aid and relief for war refugees; protection and aid for freed slaves (the freedmen); and control and disposal of abandoned or confiscated property.

The Bureau was organized within the War Department and headed by General Oliver O. Howard, a career officer, who organized it along military lines. It was extensively staffed with Union officers without regard for their commitment to the Bureau's mission. Refugee aid was resolved quickly after the war. President Andrew Johnson's pardon of rebels resulted in the return of much of the abandoned and confiscated property, leaving the freedmen as the Bureau's primary concern. The Bureau redefined the freedmen's economic, legal, and intellectual place in southern society. It reorganized southern agriculutral labor, substituting contracts for slavery; it simultaneously enforced vagrancy laws against the freedmen, forcing them back onto plantations. The Bureau briefly maintained freedmen's courts to protect legal rights. It provided other legal services to the freedmen, such as civil sanction for slave marriages and assistance with bounty claims for their service in the military. The Bureau's most positive legacy was the assistance it provided freedmen and northern aid societies in securing the privileges of formal schooling for southern African Americans. It reduced rivalry among organizations, secured school buildings, provided transportation and a measure of military protection for teachers, and superintended the schools. The Bureau spent roughly $5 million on freedmen's education* over six years, providing the freedmen with an enduring educational legacy. In 1868, Congress reduced the Bureau's authority in education and bounty offices and underfunded the bureau so that even those functions began to be dismantled in 1869. The last report on freedmen's schools was issued in July 1870, and all functions ceased by 1872.

The extant papers of the Bureau of Refugees, Freedmen, and Abandoned Lands are housed in the National Archives, Washington, D.C., Record Group 105. Secondary sources include George R. Bentley, *A History of the Freedmen's Bureau* (1955); Ronald E. Butchart, *Northern Whites, Southern Blacks, and Reconstruction: Freedmen's Education, 1862–1875* (1980); William S. McFeely, *Yankee Stepfather: General O. O. Howard and the Freedmen* (1968); Donald G. Nieman, *To Set the Law in Motion: The Freedmen's Bureau and the Legal Rights of Blacks, 1865–1868* (1979). Several fine state-level studies of the Bureau exist: Martin Abbott, *The Freedmen's Bureau in South Carolina, 1865–1872* (1967); William L Richter, *Overreached on All Sides: The Freedmen's Bureau Administrators in Texas, 1865–1868* (1991); and Howard Ashley White, *The Freedmen's Bureau in Louisiana* (1970).

Ronald E. Butchart

BUSINESS EDUCATION. The early years of the American industrial revolution utilized workers with minimal skills, whereas subsequent stages required engineers, bankers, attorneys, and stockbrokers. A cadre of trained office workers was required to support these professionals. This cadre, originally men, provided the ranks of stenographers, bookkeepers, telegraphers, and clerks needed to support this later phase. By the 1850s, it was apparent that the traditional forms of schooling were not sufficient to meet the needs of this clerical sector. The common school* curriculum focused on reading,* writing, and arithmetic with a smattering of history, civics, and science (see CIVIC EDUCATION;

MATHEMATICS EDUCATION; SCIENCE EDUCATION; SOCIAL STUD-
IES). The private academy, the most prevalent form of secondary education
before 1880, offered a curriculum that was essentially college preparatory (see
ACADEMIES). The colleges and universities offered a liberal arts curriculum
dominated by the study of the classics.

Business colleges were formed primarily in metropolitan areas where the factories were located. These specialized institutions offered coursework in bookkeeping, penmanship, the elements of business law, and the forms of business
correspondence. Telegraphy, shorthand, and typing were later added. The intensive, but brief, course of study lasted about four months. Upon completion of
the educational program, students received a certificate, rather than a diploma,
which indicated proficiency in the specific skill area. The term ''college'' represented a misnomer. The entry requirement for the business college merely
consisted of the completion of eighth grade. These nonaccredited, for-profit
schools led to the formation of chains of such business colleges. The Bryant
and Stratton chain was the largest in the North, extending from Chicago to New
York City; Draughn business colleges existed throughout the South.

The passage of the Smith-Hughes Act* of 1917, which provided federal sub-
sidies for vocational education* in the public high schools,* had a negative
effect on the business colleges. Smith-Hughes gave rise to the beginnings of
high school–level business education, often referred to as the commercial course
of study. Many business colleges, as a result, closed their doors within the next
twenty years. What was once offered on a profit basis was now given for free.
Although entrepreneurial business colleges still operate in the United States today as postsecondary institutions, their numbers are greatly eclipsed by the business education programs of the public high school and the growing dominance
of the community college in the field of business education.

For historical background, refer to William E. Eaton, ''American School Penmanship: From Craft to Process'' (1985), and Ray Nash, *American Penmanship,
1800–1850: A History of Writing and a Bibliography of Copybooks from Jenkins
to Spencer* (1969).

William E. Eaton

BUSING. See *SWANN V. CHARLOTTE-MECKLENBURG.*

BUTLER, NICHOLAS MURRAY (April 2, 1862–December 7, 1947), educator, statesman, and Nobel laureate, was born in Elizabeth, New Jersey. He
became president of Columbia University in 1902 and served until 1945. In
1887, when the Industrial Education Association formed the New York College
for the Training of Teachers (now Teachers College, Columbia University), Dr.
Butler was named president. He completed three degrees at Columbia College
(now Columbia University), finishing his doctorate in 1884. After one year of
study in Paris and Berlin, he returned to Columbia and, in 1889, became dean
of the philosophy faculty. Early in his career, he often renounced traditional

practices in education and attracted large numbers of teachers for his classes on pedagogy. Butler served as president of the Paterson (New Jersey) Board of Education (1892–1893) and of the National Education Association* (1895). In 1900, he was head of the Industrial Relations Department of the National Civic Federation. He received nearly forty honorary degrees from universities around the world and was decorated by the governments of at least fifteen nations. Butler attended fourteen Republican National Conventions. Although he advised several U.S. presidents and established relationships with numerous international figures, Butler declined potential nominations for the governorship of New York, U.S. secretary of state, and ambassadorships to England, Germany, and Japan. In 1920, he made an ill-fated run for the Republican nomination for president of the United States. Butler served as president of the Carnegie Endowment for International Peace and helped promote the Kellogg-Briand Pact signed in Paris during 1927. Nicholas Murray Butler and Jane Addams* were co-recipients of the Nobel Peace Prize in 1931. Butler was a well-known and prolific public speaker on social and educational issues and world affairs. Among his many books were *The Meaning of Education* (1898), *The International Mind* (1912), and *The World Today* (1946).

Nicholas Murray Butler's Papers are housed in the Butler Library, Special Collections, Columbia University. Also, refer to Butler's *Across the Busy Years: Recollections and Reflections* (1939, 1940). Albert Marrin, *Nicholas Murray Butler* (1976), is a useful biography.

Mark J. Reid

C

CARDINAL PRINCIPLES OF SECONDARY EDUCATION. The National Educational Association's (NEA)* *Cardinal Principles* report (report of the Commission on Secondary Education), published in 1918, has been called an "archeological deposit" of the pedagogical ideas and ideologies that were taking hold in the early part of the twentieth century. Indeed, it reflected the optimism and the extraordinary faith Americans associated with the emergence of the high school* as the dominant form of secondary education in the United States. The report, saturated with the language of democracy, embraced the prospect that the American secondary school could shed its elitist past and become a truly popular institution. The centerpiece of that revitalized institution would be a curriculum tied directly to the lives of youth. In its attempt to chart a new course for American secondary education, the report also included echoes of the anti-academic bias and social efficiency that became important refrains in American educational thought.

The initiative for the report came from Clarence Darwin Kingsley, a former Brooklyn, New York, mathematics teacher, who became its principal author. Kingsley had served as the Massachusetts state high school inspector, appointed in 1912 by David Snedden,* that state's commissioner of education. Kingsley had also chaired the NEA's Committee of Nine on the Articulation of High School and College (1913) and led the New York High School Teachers' Association. Although Kingsley shared many of Snedden's ideas about using education as a means of creating a socially efficient society, he did not subscribe to the position that differentiated secondary schools should be created for various classes of students based on their probable destinations. In fact, one of the enduring legacies of the *Cardinal Principles* report remains its unequivocal endorsement of the comprehensive high school as the dominant institutional setting for American secondary education. Differentiation would be achieved not through separate kinds of secondary schools but through different kinds of curriculum within a single institution.

The best-known section of the report was its statement of the seven aims of secondary education: (1) health; (2) command of fundamental processes; (3) worthy home-membership; (4) vocation; (5) citizenship; (6) worthy use of leisure; (7) ethical character. By defining the objectives of education essentially in terms of categories of life activities, Kingsley endorsed a distinctly functional secondary education, but he stopped short of recommending the elimination of academic subjects. The report instead recommended that high school subjects like history and mathematics reorganize themselves in order to contribute directly to the achievement of at least one of the seven aims. These seven aims and the report itself became so widely accepted that in later years much of the discussion consisted not so much of debating its merits but of deploring the failure to implement many of its recommendations.

The report of the Commission on the Reorganization of Secondary Education was issued in 1918 as Bulletin No. 35 of the U.S. Bureau of Education under the title *Cardinal Principles of Secondary Education.* Kingsley's correspondence as well as other documentation relating to the report is available in the National Archives, Record Group 12. Reports from the Massachusetts commissioner of education's office from 1913 to 1918 also include much of Kingsley's work leading up to the issuance of the report. The most thorough and compelling account of the events leading up to the report, as well as consideration of the recommendations themselves, appears in Edward A. Krug's *Shaping of the American High School*, vol. 1 (1964).

Herbert M. Kliebard

CAREER EDUCATION. Sidney P. Marland, U.S. commissioner of education, spearheaded this reform movement designed to make education relate more effectively to students' lives and aspirations. Career education represents a collection of ideas expressed and tried earlier that largely stemmed from vocational education* and more specifically the vocational guidance movement (see GUIDANCE COUNSELING). Through career education, students would be introduced to various occupations in the early grades and be given the opportunity to prepare for them in later grades. Basic subjects—and all educational activities, for that matter—would directly relate to various careers.

Marland, like President Richard M. Nixon, believed career education would solve student rebellion, delinquency, and unemployment. In his first annual report to Congress in 1971, Marland argued that disenchantment among youth existed because education did not lead to career opportunities. General education programs that lacked specific goals and were not linked to the job market served as the villain. Marland argued that education should be "meaningful," that is, related to a career objective. All elements of school life had to be justified in terms of career development, resulting in complete alignment between the job market and the public school.*

Since vocational guidance was to become a part of the school's academic program, it made career education rather unique, especially in the early grades. During the elementary and junior high school* years, career education would acquaint students with the work world and a variety of occupations. After studying and preparing for an occupational choice in these early grades, the student would, upon entering high school,* prepare for entry into either a specific occupation or for higher education.

Support for career education found its way into the 1972 amendments to the Elementary and Secondary Education Act.* These amendments focused on career education and the importance of these programs for the disadvantaged. They also called for the development of career education programs that would be treated as academic subjects and be given equal status with other educational programs.

See Joel Spring, *The American School, 1642–1993* (1994), *American Education* (1994), and *The Sorting Machine Revisited: National Educational Policy since 1945* (1989).

Don T. Martin

CARLISLE INDIAN SCHOOL. See FEDERAL INDIAN BOARDING SCHOOLS.

CARNEGIE UNIT. The so-called Carnegie unit emerged from turn-of-the-century efforts to standardize college entrance requirements and secondary college preparatory programs. In 1899, the National Education Association's* Committee on College Entrance Requirements employed the term ''unit'' to designate a course of study that met at least four times per week for one school year, that was competently taught, and that conveyed subject content proposed in the Committee's report. In 1905, Andrew Carnegie established the Carnegie Foundation for the Advancement of Teaching to provide a pension fund for college and university teachers. At that time, little agreement and no formal criteria existed regarding distinctions between universities, colleges, and secondary schools. Recognizing the wide variation of characteristics among colleges and universities, the Carnegie Foundation established a definition of ''college'' that institutions were required to meet in order to qualify for Carnegie pension funds. The definition stipulated that a college require completion of ''not less than four years of academic or high school preparation'' for admission. In 1909, the Carnegie Foundation, the National Conference Committee on Standards of Colleges and Secondary Schools, and the College Entrance Examination Board refined that stipulation when they agreed on a definition of the unit: a course of study that met four or five periods per week for thirty-six to forty weeks per year over four years of high school.* The nature of content and the quality of instruction were not factors in this definition of a unit. As a means of establishing uniform college entrance requirements by accounting for high school study in terms of credits earned for seat time, the subsequently dubbed

"Carnegie unit" became, and remains, a standard measure of qualification for college admission.

Two National Education Association documents represent starting points: *Report of the Committee on College Entrance Requirements* (1899) and *The Carnegie Foundation for the Advancement of Teaching* (1919). Robert E. Roush, "The Carnegie Unit—How Did We Get It?" (1970); Howard J. Savage, "The Carnegie Foundation and the Rise of the Unit" (1948); and Ellsworth Tompkins and Walter H. Gaumintz, *The Carnegie Unit: Its Origins, Status, and Trends* (1954), provide general background. Edward A. Krug, *The Shaping of the American High School: I, 1880–1920* (1964), and Ellen Condliffe Lagemann, *Private Power for the Public Good: A History of the Carnegie Foundation for the Advancement of Teaching* (1983), provide secondary and collegiate background, respectively.

William G. Wraga

CARTER, JAMES GORDON (September 7, 1795–July 21, 1849), as a Massachusetts common school* advocate, publicized the need to improve the quality of teachers and was instrumental in establishing the Massachusetts State Board of Education. Upon graduating from Harvard (1820), he opened a private school* in Lancaster. In 1824, he published "Letters to the Honorable William Prescott, LL.D., on the Free Schools of New England, with Remarks on the Principles of Instruction." He stressed the negative effects academies* had on the free, withdrawing community support of parental affection for the common schools. He also believed that academies were prohibitive for the poor.

Carter's most fervent criticism of the free schools focused on teachers. Incompetent instructors and poor schoolbooks, he argued, represented the major defects. In *Essays upon Popular Education, Containing a Particular Examination of the Schools of Massachusetts, and an Outline of an Institution for the Education of Teachers* (1826), Carter described three types of instructors typically found in the free schools: Those who maintained teaching was easier than laboring; those who taught as temporary employment on their way to becoming doctors, lawyers, or ministers; and those who believed they could attain no other employment. He generally thought that free school teachers possessed little education, were young, inexperienced, and ill-trained, and quickly abandoned teaching.

Carter, in *Essays upon Popular Education*, proposed the teacher-training institution as a solution to the problem of incompetent teachers in the common schools. He believed that if the state instituted standards for teacher qualification, instruction in the free schools could be improved. School quality depended on teacher character, and all other school changes were subsequent to the preparation of qualified teachers. Carter's ideal teacher-training institution included a library, laboratory school,* and professors in specific subject areas. He lobbied the Massachusetts state legislature in 1827 for funds to support a teacher education seminary. The bill was defeated, but later that year Carter opened a teacher-training school at Lancaster. Although the school failed, he continued to prepare teachers on a private basis. Massachusetts ultimately established three normal schools* in 1838.

After 1835, Carter spent most of his life in politics. While a member of the state legislature, he drafted the bill establishing the Massachusetts State Board of Education in 1837. Carter also assisted in founding the American Institute of Instruction,* of which he was an officer and member.

For biographies, see Grace Taylor Brown, ''The Importance and Influence of James Gordon Carter, Pioneer Educator in Massachusetts, 1795–1849'' (1957); Grace Taylor Brown, ''James Carter'' (1858); and Thomas F. Flaherty and John J. Flaherty, ''James Carter: Champion of the Normal School Movement'' (1974).

Laurie Moses Hines

CENSORSHIP. See ACADEMIC FREEDOM.

CHARITY SCHOOLS. See PAUPER SCHOOLS.

CHICAGO TEACHERS FEDERATION (CTF), founded in 1897 and powerful through the 1930s, was the largest teachers' union of its time and the first to affiliate with organized labor. Created by and for elementary school teachers, its membership and staff consisted almost entirely of women. At its height in the early 1900s, over half of all Chicago elementary school teachers were members of the CTF. Its success was attributable primarily to its two founders and officers, former teachers Catharine Goggin* and Margaret Haley.*

The CTF was organized to defend a recently won pension law for elementary teachers and to protest a freeze on teacher salary increases. In the next two decades, it challenged corporate taxation exemptions and the centralization of city school administration and led campaigns for improved salaries and working conditions for teachers. It made unprecedented alliances with organized labor, affiliating with the Chicago Federation of Labor in 1902 to bolster its authority. In 1916, the CTF became Local 1 of the newly formed American Federation of Teachers.* A year later the CTF was forced to withdraw from both organizations under the infamous Loeb rule, which prohibited Chicago teachers from membership in any organization affiliated with trade unions.

Between 1897 and the 1920s, the CTF was known to teachers throughout the nation as the only organized advocate for female elementary teachers' rights, and it developed considerable political clout in Chicago and in the larger educational community. It challenged the National Education Association's* adminstrator-dominated politics and it promoted progressive educational reforms (see PROGRESSIVE EDUCATION), improved teacher education, and encouraged teacher participation in school management through democratic school and district councils. The CTF consistently opposed vocational education,* merit pay, and the platoon system (see GARY PLAN), and its leadership stood behind broader feminist and labor causes. Its influence declined during the Great Depression, and in 1937 the CTF amalgamated with other school employee locals into the Chicago Teachers' Union.

The CTF's papers are housed at the Chicago Historical Society. Also, see Margaret Haley's *Battleground: The Autobiography of Margaret Haley* (1982), edited by Robert L. Reid. Several monographs study the CTF's role in Chicago's educational politics at the turn of the century, including David Hogan, *Class and Reform: School and Society in Chicago, 1880–1930* (1985); Marjorie Murphy, *Blackboard Unions: The AFT and the NEA, 1900–1980* (1990); Wayne J. Urban, *Why Teachers Organized* (1982); and Julia Wrigley, *Class, Politics and the Public Schools* (1982). Doctoral dissertations include Olive O. Anderson, "The Chicago Teachers' Federation" (1908); Marjorie Murphy, "From Artisan to Semi-Professional: White Collar Unionism among Chicago Public School Teachers, 1870–1930" (1981); and Robert L. Reid, "The Professionalization of the Public School Teachers: The Chicago Experience, 1895–1920" (1968).

Kate Rousmaniere

CHILD, LYDIA MARIA FRANCIS (February 11, 1802–October 20, 1880), typified early-nineteenth-century views of childrearing, stressing the child's natural development. As a teacher, writer, and reformer, she authored numerous stories and poems, and received recognition for her abolitionist convictions, yet shunned public acclaim. Born in Medford, Massachusetts, Child spent her entire life in New England. She began her teaching career at age twenty and within three years wrote two romance novels, opened a girls' school, and began publishing *Juvenile Miscellany*, a children's magazine. Child's early writings received national acclaim. She contributed to the growing literature on childrearing with the publication of *The Mother's Book* (1831), which earned multiple printings. She emphasized the need for teachers and parents alike to nurture and draw out children's natural tendencies. Child wrote from the belief that people armed with the right knowledge could make a difference in their own lives and society. This reformist optimism permeated the literary page of *The Boston Traveler*, which she edited, and became embodied in a Dorchester Heights' girls' school, where she served as superintendent. Her intense writing and educational involvement virtually ceased when she published *An Appeal in Favor of Americans Called Africans* (1836), a powerful antislavery argument. Almost immediately after its appearance, Child's manuscripts were rejected, and her association with the girls' school and *Miscellany* ended.

Her collected correspondence has been preserved on microfiche and is available at Dickinson College, University of Delaware, Morgan State University, Princeton University, Cornell University, New York State Library (Albany), and University of Cincinnati. Child's life and works have also captured the attention of numerous biographers. Helene Bear's *The Heart Is Like Heaven* (1964) and William Osborne's *Lydia Maria Child* (1980) represent the two leading and most recent ones. Others include Bernice Lamberton, "A Biography of Lydia Maria Child" (1953).

Patrick M. Socoski

CHILD STUDY MOVEMENT became a highly visible element of the reform initiatives in the early progressive education* era. Essentially, it was a practical and assertedly scientific means used by teachers to study individual children in considerable depth with standard procedures of observation and recording. Through this careful study and thoughtful reflection about individual differences, teachers had solid evidence to adapt the curriculum to pupils rather than pitting the curriculum against pupils. Psychologist G. Stanley Hall* launched the movement in the 1890s after a decade of his own studies of individual children. In order to increase the scope of his studies of individual differences, Hall recruited teachers both to gather data for his analyses and to assist them in making curricular decisions for their pupils. Hall, with the assistance of William H. Burnham of Clark University, Earl Barnes of Stanford University, and a number of his Clark University graduate students, organized several child study organizations including the American Association for Child Study, Child Study Division of the National Education Association,* South Carolina Association for the Study of Children, and Illinois Society for Child Study. The movement flourished for a number of years, but declined after World War I due to the popularity of alternative educational concerns, including the advocacy and widespread use of intelligence testing* (see BINET, ALFRED). Even in decline, the intellectual residue of the movement included acceptance of the burgeoning educational research field, particularly in educational programs that considered a variety of individual differences, and interest in subsequent developmentalist theories of human development and learning.

Details about this movement are found in *Child Study Monthly*, vols. 1–7. For historical accounts, see Wilbur Harvey Dutton, "The Child Study Movement in American Education from Its Origin (1880) to the Organization of the Progressive Education Association (1920)" (1945); Joseph Hawes, *American Childhood: A Research Guide and Historical Handbook* (1985); and James Dale Hendricks, "The Child Study Movement in American Education, 1880–1910" (1968).

O. L. Davis, Jr.

CHILDREN-AT-RISK achieved wide usage in the late 1980s and 1990s as an inclusive label describing juveniles facing a wide range of potential threats from their external environments. As used in educational circles, "children-at-risk" refers to students who, for various reasons, seem likely to fail in school and in the transition to responsible, self-supporting adulthood. These students may be difficult to teach and manage because of learning or behavior difficulties. These youths may also be at risk because of problems at home, with their families, in their communtiies, or in the schools themselves.

The term "children-at-risk" has also been used more generally to characterize juveniles who are threatened by their social environments or who have been failed by social institutions. Parental indifference, domestic abuse, family disruption, early pregnancy, poverty, disease, the possibility of physical assault, and the availability of drugs and alchohol all present risks to young people. At the same time, the failure of schools and communities to rectify these problems has increasingly been portrayed as placing children at risk.

Some scholars have applied the concept "children-at-risk" to the history of child-welfare institutions, which were given considerable discretion in the nineteenth and early twentieth centuries to determine what factors in children's lives should be treated as risks. Juvenile courts, for example, regarded youthful status offenders (i.e., those children accused of incorrigibility or truancy), as well as criminal offenders, as being at risk and therefore equally in need of formal state intervention. For both types of children, juvenile courts attempted to address not only the behavioral problems evident in a particular case but also the environmental circumstances that contributed to the child's or family's problems (see JUVENILE DELINQUENCY).

In both contemporary and historical contexts, "children-at-risk" implies that juveniles face some threat to their well-being and that proper intervention from schools, courts, or other institutions may be capable of alleviating that threat.

For further reference, see Barry M. Franklin, *From "Backwardness" to "At-Risk"* (1994); Joan Kakebrink, ed., *Children at Risk* (1980); and Roberta Wollons, ed., *Children at Risk in America* (1993).

David Wolcott

CHILDREN'S BUREAU. Although the Bureau has gone through many reorganizations and exists in a much reduced form in the Office of Child Development, the early Children's Bureau and the women at its helm helped formulate the critical issues of federal responsibility for children's well-being and for family policies that continue to be debated to this day and are at the vortex of current social welfare reform. The Bureau was established on April 9, 1912, with a mandate to investigate and report "upon all matters pertaining to the welfare of children and child life among all classes of our people." Julia Lathrop,* first chief of the Bureau, brought her twenty years of experience at Hull-House and the settlement movement's whole-child perspective and network of reform and volunteer connections into the portals of national government (see ADDAMS, JANE). On a tiny budget of $25,640 and fifteen employees, Lathrop focused during the first year on the causes of infant mortality in the Johnstown (Pennsylvania), Study (1913), initiated a drive for uniform birth registration, educated expectant mothers through the pamphlet *Prenatal Care* (1913), and through the influential government bestseller *Infant Care* (1914) taught mothers how to care for their children. Lathrop also instructed mothers about child health through child health conferences that replaced "baby contests" of an earlier period. Over the decade, the Bureau staff increased to more than 200, and its appropriation grew sixty-fold. The Bureau expanded its scope into administration of the short-lived child labor law of 1916 and spearheaded the Sheppard-Towner Act of 1921, which promoted maternal and infant health through grant-in-aid programs to the states for seven years. Grace Abbot, Lathrop's successor, in 1921 carried out Bureau policies in the same settlement spirit. With Bureau colleagues and future Bureau chiefs Katherine Lenroot and Martha Eliot, Abbott helped to hammer out the strategy that would become Title V of the Social Security Act under President Franklin D. Roosevelt, including crippled children services, child welfare provisions, and child and maternal health programs.

The Bureau's records can be found in the National Archives. Also, see Molly Ladd-Taylor, *Raising a Baby the Government Way: Mothers' Letters to the Children's Bureau, 1915–1932* (1986); Kriste Lindenmeyer, *A Right to Childhood: The U.S. Children's Bureau and Child Welfare, 1912–1946* (1997); Jacqueline K. Parker, "Women at the Helm: Succession Politics at the Children's Bureau, 1912–1968" (1994); and Nancy Weiss, "Save the Children: A History of the Children's Bureau, 1903–1918" (1974).

Nancy Weiss

CHILDREN'S DEFENSE FUND (CDF). Marian Wright Edelman, a civil rights lawyer and the first African American woman to be admitted to practice law in Mississippi, founded this nonprofit organization in 1973 to provide a strong and effective voice for American children.

CDF has served as an advocate for all children, but especially for poor and minority children, those whose health care needs are overlooked, and children who drop out of school without acquiring the skills to enter the workforce (see DROPOUTS). CDF endeavors to create a nation in which the web of family, community, private-sector, and government support for children is so tightly woven that no child is left behind.

CDF believes that officeholders and voters of all persuasions should agree on this approach to child and national well-being. CDF has not aligned with any political party and has not supported candidates or political party platforms. To maintain its independent voice for children, CDF does not accept government funding.

The advocacy techniques CDF employs have shifted and evolved over the years as political, economic, and social circumstances have changed. Among many activities, the CDF conducts research; disseminates surveys, reports, and agendas for change; uses the mass media and other forms of public education to highlight problems, mobilize support for children, and raise children's needs higher on the national agenda; drafts, testifies about, and lobbies for legislation; provides technical assistance to states, localities, and nonprofit groups; and trains parents, service providers, youths, administrators, and other citizens to become stronger advocates for children.

The CDF's first major undertaking documented the practices of many public schools that exluded some children who were not white or did not speak English, were poor or pregnant, or needed special help to learn. Its report was a powerful catalyst for the enactment in 1975 of the Education for All Handicapped Children Act, which guaranteed for all disabled children the right to free and appropriate public education (see SPECIAL EDUCATION).

Other accomplishments for children have been many and varied. In the late 1980s, CDF advocated legislation that expanded Medicaid health insurance coverage for children and pregnant women. Also, in large part as a result of the CDF's advocacy over the past two decades, public investments in child care and Head Start* have increased significantly, improving services and allowing more poor and low-income children to participate.

CDF's large-scale community-based efforts include a five-year adolescent pregnancy prevention campaign in eighty communities nationwide during the 1980s. In 1992, the CDF initiated the annual National Observance of Children's Sabbaths, held each October to motivate congregations to advocate for and help children in their communities. Since 1993, CDF also has coordinated the Black Community Crusade for Children (BCCC) in partnership with well-established regional child-serving organizations. The BCCC seeks to reconnect the African American middle class with poor and young African Americans and to rebuild the rich fabric of community that historically has been the cornerstone for the healthy development of African American children.

Breaking new ground in child advocacy, CDF convened Stand for Children, the first-ever national day of commitment to children at the Lincoln Memorial in Washington, D.C., on June 1, 1996. Hundreds of thousands of people from across the nation gathered to demonstrate their concern for children. Stand for Children, headquartered in Washington, D.C., has evolved into a national grassroots movement with the formation of chapters nationwide. Its executive director is Jonah Edelman, son of Marian Wright Edelman.

In addition to its national headquarters in Washington, D.C., the CDF has several state affiliates.

The CDF's papers are housed at its Washington, D.C., office. For more information about CDF, visit the website: http://www.childrendefense.org

Children's Defense Fund

CHILDREN'S MUSEUMS are found in most urban centers in the United States. Their origins go back to the end of the nineteenth century. As part of his work at the University of Chicago's Laboratory School,* John Dewey* arranged regular trips for his students to the Field Columbian Museum. In addition, he proposed the establishment of small museums that could provide lessons in art, science, and industry as an integral component of schools. Dewey's ideas were not widely implemented because of cost, though a limited number of community-based children's museums were founded across the country. The Brooklyn Children's Museum, widely considered the first in the United States, opened in 1897. Part of the Brooklyn Institute of Arts and Sciences, the museum gation provisions of the 1964 Civil Rights Act. This executive inaction continued through the 1980s.

Inadequate staffing and burdensome enforcement procedures further hindered efforts to enforce the 1964 Act. HEW delegated the responsibility for investigating compliance with Title VI to the Office of Civil Rights (OCR), now in the Department of Education.* Once OCR determined that a school district failed to comply with Title VI, the Office of General Counsel (OGC) conducted a hearing to determine if federal funds should be withheld. Although OCR staffing increased during the 1970s, OGC experienced no similar increase. Limited resources largely precluded any extensive investigation of a large school district because it would monopolize an entire regional OCR office for a substantial time period. Moreover, OGC refused to accept cases unless they appeared virtually airtight. As a result, it was not unusual during the 1970s for school districts to be under investigation for over five years while continuing to receive federal funds.

The Civil Rights Act of 1964 remains available to desegregate public schools, and the Civil Rights Restoration Act of 1987 reinforced it by clarifying those programs and activities that must abide by the 1964 Act after its application had been curtailed during the previous decade. However, controversy persists over whether the 1964 Act should be limited to prohibiting discrimination in public schools or expanded to include affirmative action and compensatory programs of African Americans to overcome the effects of past discrimination. In many school districts, white exodus from urban public schools has made desegregation unfeasible because of the 1974 Supreme Court ruling in *Milliken v. Bradley*.* That decision overturned an interdistrict plan to desegregate Detroit's schools. The Restoration Act failed to nullify *Milliken*.

The original acts are the Civil Rights Act of 1866, 14 Stat. 27 (1866); Civil Rights Act of 1875, 18 Stat. 335 (1875); Civil Rights Act of 1957, Pub. L. No. 85-315, 71 Stat. 634 (1957); Civil Rights Act of 1964, Pub. L. No. 88-352, 78 Stat. 241 (1964); Civil Rights Restoration Act of 1987, Pub. L. No. 100-259, 102 Stat. 28 (1988). For the early laws, refer to James M. McPherson, ''Abolitionists and the Civil Rights Act of 1875'' (1965) and William P. Vaughn, ''Separate and Unequal: The Civil Rights Act of 1875 and Defeat of the School Integration Clause'' (1967). The 1964 Act is covered in Center for National Policy Review, *Justice Delayed and Denied: HEW and Northern School Desegregation* (1974), and Joel Spring, *The Sorting Machine Revisited: National Educational Policy since 1945* (1989).

Maureen A. Reynolds

CIVILIAN CONSERVATION CORPS (CCC),

a pet project of President Franklin D. Roosevelt, was enacted by Congress in March 1933 and enrolled approximately 2.5 million young men during its nine-year life. Designed for unmarried youths between the ages of eighteen and twenty-five, the goals of the CCC were work relief and conservation. The CCC was initially meant to be

had strong links to local teacher-training institutions including Teachers College, Columbia University; Adelphi College; and New York University. Originally conceived as a pedagogical museum where teachers could see various instructional materials displayed, the museum rapidly evolved into a center for the children of Brooklyn to learn about natural science. Early exhibits included botanical and zoological models, natural history charts, and collections of minerals, birds, insects, and shells. A library supplemented museum activities. Educators and teachers saw the museum as providing complementary but alternative instruction to the public schools. By 1911, the museum received over 160,000 visitors a year. During the late 1960s and early 1970s the idea of children's museums greatly expanded, evolving into centers for hands-on learning and experimentation. The most prominent of these museums are San Francisco's Exploratorium, the Boston Children's Museum, the Indianapolis Children's Museum, and the Brooklyn Children's Museum.

For background information on Dewey's work with school museums and field trips, see Dewey's *School and Society* and *The Child and the Curriculum* in Martin Dworkin, ed., *Dewey on Education* (1959). No formal history of children's museums in America exists. Useful information can be obtained at various museums' websites. Visit the following: The Exploratorium, http://nctra.exploratorium.edu/; Boston Children's Museum, http://www.trabalcode.com/bebimu.htm; Children's Museum of Indianapolis, http://mlc.lrde.pitt.edu/mle/Children's.html.

Eugene F. Provenzo, Jr., and Asterie Baker Provenzo

CISNEROS V. CORPUS CHRISTI INDEPENDENT SCHOOL DISTRICT,

467 F.2d 142 (5th Cir. 1972). In a class action desegregation case, the Fifth Circuit Court of Appeals found violative of equal protection Corpus Christi's practice of building schools and drawing school boundary lines that resulted in Mexican American students attending schools that were 61–90 percent Mexican American while Anglo children attended schools that were 80–90 percent Anglo. The court found that even though the segregation here was neither *de jure* nor *de facto*, it was nonetheless constitutionally impermissible under equal protection. The court rejected the school board's reliance on housing patterns to justify the segregative enrollments because the board had chosen to place new schools well within existing ethnic populations, rather than near the borders where attendance would be more diverse. To remedy this segregation, the court ordered the school board, on remand, to design student assignment plans using pairing and clustering of schools and transportation of students.

Ralph D. Mawdsley

CIVIC EDUCATION

in the United States has traditionally been taught from a mechanical and nonparticipatory approach that focuses on learning by rote the names of presidents and other federal officials, details about the U.S. Constitution and Bill of Rights, significant Supreme Court decisions, particular laws, diagrams of how government works, responsibilities of citizenship, and other routine matters. In the nineteenth century, students simply memorized passages from textbooks. Another approach made popular in the early social studies* movement (c. 1910s) was the promotion of active participatory citizenship in which students were encouraged to identify and seek solutions to actual community problems. It was argued that through active community-based civic education, young citizens would not only learn and be more accepting of democratic forms of living but also be enabled to participate more fully as adults in the governance of their communities and states, as well as nation. In both models and other variations, the cultivation of good citizenship was seen as ideal. However, what constitutes good citizenship in a free republic and what are the best means toward achieving that ideal continue to be hotly debated issues throughout the nation. Although research in the field has failed to verify a preferred or most effective model, civic education has been a cornerstone of American citizenship since the nation's founding. Leading proponents of civic education have traditionally been high-profile figures such as Presidents Woodrow Wilson, Franklin D. Roosevelt, and Ronald Reagan as well as educational leaders such John Dewey* and Harold Rugg.* Today, the leading advocates of civic education include individuals such as William Bennett and Lynn Chaney and organizations like the National Council for the Social Studies (NCSS)* and Center for Civic Education.

For historical background, refer to Richard D. Brown, *The Strength of a People: The Idea of an Informed Citizenry in America, 1650–1870* (1996); M. Stanton Evans, *The Theme Is Freedom* (1994); and Amy Gutmann, *Democratic Education* (1987). The NCSS's many publications as well as those of the Center for Civic Education are helpful for current views. See Charles N. Quigley and John H. Buchanan, Jr., *A Framework for Civic Education* (1991) and *National Standards for Civics and Government* (1995).

David Warren Saxe

CIVIL RIGHTS ACTS OF 1866, 1875, 1957, 1964. The concept of school desegregation often played a critical role in congressional maneuvering over civil rights legislation but never became a reality until the 1964 act. In 1866, when some congressmen raised concerns that the civil rights bill would be used to integrate public schools, the bill's radical Republican sponsors assured them that the proposal did not contemplate mixed schools. Shortly after the 1866 act passed, Massachusetts senator Charles Sumner, a radical Republican, began campaigning for legislation to force former Confederate states to integrate schools. Sumner first championed school desegregation in 1850, when he argued against segregated schools in *Roberts v. City of Boston,** the original ''separate but equal'' case. He successfully worked for the 1855 Massachusetts law banning segregated schools in that state.

After 1870, Sumner repeatedly presented bills prohibiting racial segregation in public schools. Few in Congress shared his passion for school desegregation.

Most Republicans joined Sumner only for pragmatic reasons, when other political agendas, such as attaching a school desegregation ri amnesty bill pardoning former Confederates to ensure that the amnesty b to pass. Although Sumner and his small group of loyal supporters saw segregation as the center of the Civil Rights Act, only a watered-dow forbidding discrimination in public transportation, inns, theaters, and places of amusement passed, and after his death. The Supreme Court in 1 declared this feeble Civil Rights Act unconstitutional.

No progress occurred with subsequent acts. During the early years of the ci rights movement, southern members of Congress deleted language from th 1957 Act which would have empowered the Justice Department to bring suit to end school segregation. The 1960 Civil Rights Act, likewise, omitted any language advancing school desegregation.

Finally, in 1964, Congress passed a Civil Rights Act that seriously addressed school desegregation. Title VI of the 1964 Act provided that no person shall be subjected to discrimination in any program receiving federal funds. At that time, the U.S. Department of Health, Education, and Welfare (HEW)* could withhold federal funds from school districts that did not comply with the law. This represented a powerful weapon, since most public school districts received federal funds for the fiscal operation of their schools. HEW, hoping to end segregated schools by 1967, required all public school districts to submit acceptable desegregation plans or risk losing all federal funds. By fall 1965, 97 percent of the southern school districts had submitted acceptable plans.

Success remained elusive, however. While 98 percent of African American children in eleven southern states attended segregated schools during the 1963–1964 school year, less than 9 percent attended them in 1972. Southern schools, on the surface, appeared to be integrated, yet 50 percent of all African American children attended majority African American public schools that same year. Seventy percent of northern African American children likewise attended majority African American public schools, with most in schools in which 80 percent of the student population was African American.

Several factors contributed to the 1964 Act's failure. The original wording created early problems. The federal government did not initially apply it to northern school districts because few of them had maintained state-mandated segregated schools. Federal courts, in the late 1960s, ruled otherwise, aiding efforts against northern and western school districts. The 1964 Act also faile to receive strong executive endorsement. President Lyndon Johnson trad southern congressional support for the Vietnam War in exchange for feel enforcement of school desegregation. Another setback occurred when Rich J. Daley, Chicago's powerful mayor, lobbied President Johnson to interver the 1965 HEW decision to cut off federal funds to that city's public sch The Department of Justice then issued guidelines prohibiting HEW from holding funds without a prior administrative hearing. President Richard exerted even less executive pressure on HEW to enforce the school educative only in the sense that hard work in rural settings under military authority was expected to build character, engender a work ethic, and tame the subversive tendencies of young unemployed people. Despite a lack of commitment to formal education within the agency by CCC director Robert Fechner and many camp commanders, an education program that offered both academic and vocational classes commenced under the auspices of the federal Office of Education during 1934 (also see UNITED STATES DEPARTMENT OF EDUCATION, VOCATIONAL EDUCATION). The CCC is credited with enabling thousands of enrollees to become literate and providing useful vocational training to many others, but the educational program was hampered by insufficient classrooms and texts, poorly trained and underpaid educational advisers, curtailed freedom of discussion, and classes that were scheduled after work hours only. For most enrollees, the education work was probably of little import. More broadly, the CCC's exclusion of females and practice of racial discrimination hardly made it a beacon of progressive social policy. Yet the CCC, more than any other New Deal program, captured the public's imagination, and it did have enduring educational value in the sense that it instructed citizens that government legitimately could be called upon to promote not only the conservation of natural resources but also the conservation of human resources through providing training and jobs. The CCC served as a precedent for Great Society youth programs, particularly the Job Corps.* Subsequently, a number of programs that have combined conservation work with jobs for youth, like the California Conservation Corps, modeled themselves after the original.

Records of the CCC are housed at the National Archives, Washington, D.C. For general treatments, see Kenneth Holland and Frank E. Hill, *Youth in the CCC* (1942); George P. Rawick, "The New Deal and Youth: The Civilian Conservation Corps, the National Youth Administration, and the American Youth Congress" (1957); and John Salmond, *The Civilian Conservation Corps: A New Deal Case Study* (1967).

Robert Lowe

CLASSICAL CURRICULUM. The earliest European colonists carried with them to America an intellectual tradition that became the staple of colonial grammar schools and colleges, would form a significant bulk of secondary and collegiate education in the nineteenth century, and would persist to the present in private academies* and specialized training (also see BOARDING SCHOOLS). Inheritors of the Renaissance, Anglo Americans based much of their educational training upon the authors of Western antiquity and expected students to read these authors in their original tongues, whether Latin, Greek, or Hebrew.

Colonial grammar schools (see BOSTON LATIN GRAMMAR SCHOOL; LATIN GRAMMAR SCHOOL), largely founded in New England, were not always able to dispense with training in basic reading and writing skills that petty and dame schools* were expected to handle. The line between petty and grammar schools was much more blurred in America than in England. Nevertheless, grammar schools were expected to train their students in the languages of the clasical authors, thus opening the repositories of knowledge that the classical texts represented.

In the nineteenth century, common and private secondary schools largely inherited the classical curriculum of colonial grammar schools, and it was not until the Committe of Ten* report of 1893 that the fate of obsolescence for the classical curriculum was sealed. The Committee of Ten, headed by Charles W. Eliot and composed of other prominent American educators, did not intend to marginalize the classical curriculum. Regardless, by recommending college preparatory tracks of secondary training that did not require training in the classical languages and texts, in addition to tracks that did, they put a formal stamp of approval on a growing tendency among secondary schools to omit the classical curriculum.

For an historical overview of the classical curriculum, see Daniel Tanner and Laurel Tanner, *History of the School Curriculum* (1990). Lawrence A. Cremin, *American Education: The Colonial Experience, 1607–1783* (1970), provides the fullest discussion of the classical curriculum during the colonial period at the grammar school level. Edward A. Krug, *The Shaping of the American High School: I, 1880–1920* (1964), gives the best detail concerning the downfall of the classical curriculum at the secondary level.

Rodney Hessinger

CLASSROOM DISCIPLINE AND MANAGEMENT. Perspectives on the best ways to educate children have been evident throughout history. Schools in this country predate the formation of the United States, as a result, many of our traditional management perspectives have their antecedents in our early religious values represented in various colonial settlements. The Puritans maintained the notion that children were inherently bad. They believed that children must be civilized through disciplinary practices designed to create fear of damnation unless they altered their behaviors and became, essentially, little adults. In other colonial settlements, the view of children was quite different. Pennsylvanian Quaker doctrines of nonviolence were mirrored in the management strategies of that colony's schoolmasters. The romanticist period of the 1700s equated children with the image of the noble savage. A child's innocence was to be treasured as an example of simplicity. The idea of taming that simplicity through harsh measures was not in keeping with the philosophy. In the early 1800s, Horace Mann* echoed a similar sentiment. In a discussion on the "Management of Disobedient Children," he described the difficult children awaiting teachers as a challenge, but he stated that it was an act of "true benevolence, Christian duty," to meet the needs of these children in order to restore them to their "Divine likeness." More recently, the progressivist movement was the first to deliberately interweave management with classroom instruction (see PROGRESSIVE EDUCATION). These various and competing perspectives about the basic nature of children have at one time or another strongly influenced management strategies. As a result, classroom discipline has changed dramatically over the years depending on the predominant viewpoint of children as being inherently bad or good.

As human psychology began to inform our common understandings of why behaviors manifested themselves, this knowledge was increasingly applied to the mangement of behaviors in the classroom and typically used to support the belief of inherent goodness or evil. The first deliberate application of psychological theory to classroom management was through the work of B. F. Skinner; the resultant methodology was broadly labeled as behavior modification (see BEHAVIORISM). This model deliberately applies external behavioral controls to achieve desired outcomes, reflecting a more Puritanical view that children, if left to their own devices, would be ill-mannered. The external controls were appropriate for the necessary redirection of their potential for bad behavior. An example of behavioral managment might be achieving a quiet classroom through the methodical applications of rewards for quiet behaviors and punishments for noisy behaviors. Students in this scheme are the passive receptors of the rewards and punishments; the theory is that they will replicate the desired behaviors for the length of time the rewards are made available or the punishement threatened. The most notable, commonly used, and widely criticized adaptation of Skinner is the ''assertive discipline'' approach. Its wide use is attributable to the ease with which it can be implemented, and its condemnation rests on the fact that this model fails to address individual student needs or cultural differences.

Cognitive psychology has more recently found its way into the lexicon of classroom management. This alternative perspective is dependent on the reasoning abilities of students and is based upon cognitive theories developed by Rudolf Dreikurs, William Glasser, Alfie Kohn, Forrest Gathercoal, and others. The models representing this perspective of classroom management put forth the premise that when fairness, honesty, respect, and other basic values are deliberately taught and modeled, students will internalize those attributes and act in ways that are mutually beneficial to themselves and others.

Although the two basic theories that give definition to the current discussion surrounding classroom management are dramatically different from each other, teachers and administrators usually combine them into a variety of eclectic strategies, or just as often, the managment practices being used reflect the personal style of a teacher with no discernible knowledge base governing the decisions being made. It is important to note that even though a teacher's practices might not be informed by pedagogical theory, they very much reflect the product of the argument concerning the inherent goodness or evil of children. The ability to manage a group of students effectively is considered to be an essential skill for teachers, yet despite the important nature of such skills, the topic is not even included in some teacher education programs. As a result, some classrooms are managed through reasoned decision-making based on an informed philosophy, whereas others follow irrational practices stemming from anger, bias, and personal favoritism.

Given this breakdown between theory and practice, many decisions are made that discourage students from active participation in their own learning and, in some cases, actually cause emotional or physical injuries. The absence of reasoned practices based on sound managment theory has resulted in a body of case law to protect students from discriminatory and unjust practices in public school classrooms. In *Tinker v. Des Moines* (1969),* the U.S. Supreme Court established First Amendment protections of free speech and expression for public school students. The Court has subsequently ruled on issues of seach and seizure, due process, equal protection, and religious freedom in schools (see *BANNISTER V. PARADIS*; *ENGEL V. VITALE*; *GOSS V. LOPEZ*; *HAZELWOOD SCHOOL DISTRICT V. KUHLMEIER*; *LAU V. NICHOLS*; *LEE V. WEISMAN*). The laws developed by state and federal court rulings give direction as to how teachers and administrators can and should implement classroom management practices. Too often, however, they are ignored, misunderstood, or completely unknown to practitioners, all of which have led to increasingly litigious educational climates.

Given the dramatic increase in the multicultural student populations represented in many of today's schools, management practices are currently changing to accommodate our new national demographics (see MULTICULTURAL EDUCATION). Democratic management strategies, a more recent focus, equally values all members of a learning community. Teachers are becoming increasingly sensitive to not demanding eye contact, knowing that some cultures view eye contact as representing disrespect or aggression. Because some cultures shun competition and value cooperation, a greater emphasis has been placed on cooperative learning.* This approach can also break down cultural misunderstandings among students and is helpful for children who do not speak English as a primary language (see BILINGUAL EDUCATION).

The recognition of classroom managment as a crucial area of study for teachers is growing in direct proportion to the incidents of violence in schools, the increasingly diverse student population, and the national statistics on school dropouts.* This continual critical examination of practices is crucial if teachers are to effectively address the broad spectrum of needs represented in today's classrooms. Classroom management decisions are interwoven throughout the school day in a complex fabric of threads representing curriculum, student-teacher interactions, and the physical arrangement of a classroom. The impact of classroom management rests in the mounting evidence that when educational decisions are consistent, equitable, and judicious, students may feel that educators are on their side and that staying in school is a viable choice.

For some historical, social, and legal background, refer to Ronald E. Butchart, "Punishments, Penalties, Prizes, and Procedures: A History of Discipline in U.S. Schools" (1996); Louis Filler, *Horace Mann on the Crisis in Education* (1965);

had strong links to local teacher-training institutions including Teachers College, Columbia University; Adelphi College; and New York University. Originally conceived as a pedagogical museum where teachers could see various instructional materials displayed, the museum rapidly evolved into a center for the children of Brooklyn to learn about natural science. Early exhibits included botanical and zoological models, natural history charts, and collections of minerals, birds, insects, and shells. A library supplemented museum activities. Educators and teachers saw the museum as providing complementary but alternative instruction to the public schools. By 1911, the museum received over 160,000 visitors a year. During the late 1960s and early 1970s the idea of children's museums greatly expanded, evolving into centers for hands-on learning and experimentation. The most prominent of these museums are San Francisco's Exploratorium, the Boston Children's Museum, the Indianapolis Children's Museum, and the Brooklyn Children's Museum.

For background information on Dewey's work with school museums and field trips, see Dewey's *School and Society* and *The Child and the Curriculum* in Martin Dworkin, ed., *Dewey on Education* (1959). No formal history of children's museums in America exists. Useful information can be obtained at various museums' websites. Visit the following: The Exploratorium, http://nctra. exploratorium.edu/; Boston Children's Museum, http://www.trabalcode.com/ bebimu.htm; Children's Museum of Indianapolis, http://mlc.lrde.pitt.edu/mle/ Children's.html.

Eugene F. Provenzo, Jr., and Asterie Baker Provenzo

CISNEROS V. CORPUS CHRISTI INDEPENDENT SCHOOL DISTRICT, 467 F.2d 142 (5th Cir. 1972). In a class action desegregation case, the Fifth Circuit Court of Appeals found violative of equal protection Corpus Christi's practice of building schools and drawing school boundary lines that resulted in Mexican American students attending schools that were 61–90 percent Mexican American while Anglo children attended schools that were 80–90 percent Anglo. The court found that even though the segregation here was neither *de jure* nor *de facto*, it was nonetheless constitutionally impermissible under equal protection. The court rejected the school board's reliance on housing patterns to justify the segregative enrollments because the board had chosen to place new schools well within existing ethnic populations, rather than near the borders where attendance would be more diverse. To remedy this segregation, the court ordered the school board, on remand, to design student assignment plans using pairing and clustering of schools and transportation of students.

Ralph D. Mawdsley

CIVIC EDUCATION in the United States has traditionally been taught from a mechanical and nonparticipatory approach that focuses on learning by rote the names of presidents and other federal officials, details about the U.S. Constitution and Bill of Rights, significant Supreme Court decisions, particular laws, diagrams of how government works, responsibilities of citizenship, and other routine matters. In the nineteenth century, students simply memorized passages from textbooks. Another approach made popular in the early social studies* movement (c. 1910s) was the promotion of active participatory citizenship in which students were encouraged to identify and seek solutions to actual community problems. It was argued that through active community-based civic education, young citizens would not only learn and be more accepting of democratic forms of living but also be enabled to participate more fully as adults in the governance of their communities and states, as well as nation. In both models and other variations, the cultivation of good citizenship was seen as ideal. However, what constitutes good citizenship in a free republic and what are the best means toward achieving that ideal continue to be hotly debated issues throughout the nation. Although research in the field has failed to verify a preferred or most effective model, civic education has been a cornerstone of American citizenship since the nation's founding. Leading proponents of civic education have traditionally been high-profile figures such as Presidents Woodrow Wilson, Franklin D. Roosevelt, and Ronald Reagan as well as educational leaders such John Dewey* and Harold Rugg.* Today, the leading advocates of civic education include individuals such as William Bennett and Lynn Chaney and organizations like the National Council for the Social Studies (NCSS)* and Center for Civic Education.

For historical background, refer to Richard D. Brown, *The Strength of a People: The Idea of an Informed Citizenry in America, 1650–1870* (1996); M. Stanton Evans, *The Theme Is Freedom* (1994); and Amy Gutmann, *Democratic Education* (1987). The NCSS's many publications as well as those of the Center for Civic Education are helpful for current views. See Charles N. Quigley and John H. Buchanan, Jr., *A Framework for Civic Education* (1991) and *National Standards for Civics and Government* (1995).

David Warren Saxe

CIVIL RIGHTS ACTS OF 1866, 1875, 1957, 1964. The concept of school desegregation often played a critical role in congressional maneuvering over civil rights legislation but never became a reality until the 1964 act. In 1866, when some congressmen raised concerns that the civil rights bill would be used to integrate public schools, the bill's radical Republican sponsors assured them that the proposal did not contemplate mixed schools. Shortly after the 1866 act passed, Massachusetts senator Charles Sumner, a radical Republican, began campaigning for legislation to force former Confederate states to integrate schools. Sumner first championed school desegregation in 1850, when he argued against segregated schools in *Roberts v. City of Boston*,* the original "separate but equal" case. He successfully worked for the 1855 Massachusetts law banning segregated schools in that state.

After 1870, Sumner repeatedly presented bills prohibiting racial segregation in public schools. Few in Congress shared his passion for school desegregation.

Most Republicans joined Sumner only for pragmatic reasons, when it suited other political agendas, such as attaching a school desegregation rider to an amnesty bill pardoning former Confederates to ensure that the amnesty bill failed to pass. Although Sumner and his small group of loyal supporters saw school segregation as the center of the Civil Rights Act, only a watered-down bill forbidding discrimination in public transportation, inns, theaters, and other places of amusement passed, and after his death. The Supreme Court in 1883 declared this feeble Civil Rights Act unconstitutional.

No progress occurred with subsequent acts. During the early years of the civil rights movement, southern members of Congress deleted language from the 1957 Act which would have empowered the Justice Department to bring suit to end school segregation. The 1960 Civil Rights Act, likewise, omitted any language advancing school desegregation.

Finally, in 1964, Congress passed a Civil Rights Act that seriously addressed school desegregation. Title VI of the 1964 Act provided that no person shall be subjected to discrimination in any program receiving federal funds. At that time, the U.S. Department of Health, Education, and Welfare (HEW)* could withhold federal funds from school districts that did not comply with the law. This represented a powerful weapon, since most public school districts received federal funds for the fiscal operation of their schools. HEW, hoping to end segregated schools by 1967, required all public school districts to submit acceptable desegregation plans or risk losing all federal funds. By fall 1965, 97 percent of the southern school districts had submitted acceptable plans.

Success remained elusive, however. While 98 percent of African American children in eleven southern states attended segregated schools during the 1963–1964 school year, less than 9 percent attended them in 1972. Southern schools, on the surface, appeared to be integrated, yet 50 percent of all African American children attended majority African American public schools that same year. Seventy percent of northern African American children likewise attended majority African American public schools, with most in schools in which 80 percent of the student population was African American.

Several factors contributed to the 1964 Act's failure. The original wording created early problems. The federal government did not initially apply it to northern school districts because few of them had maintained state-mandated segregated schools. Federal courts, in the late 1960s, ruled otherwise, aiding efforts against northern and western school districts. The 1964 Act also failed to receive strong executive endorsement. President Lyndon Johnson traded southern congressional support for the Vietnam War in exchange for feeble enforcement of school desegregation. Another setback occurred when Richard J. Daley, Chicago's powerful mayor, lobbied President Johnson to intervene in the 1965 HEW decision to cut off federal funds to that city's public schools. The Department of Justice then issued guidelines prohibiting HEW from withholding funds without a prior administrative hearing. President Richard Nixon exerted even less executive pressure on HEW to enforce the school desegregation provisions of the 1964 Civil Rights Act. This executive inaction continued through the 1980s.

Inadequate staffing and burdensome enforcement procedures further hindered efforts to enforce the 1964 Act. HEW delegated the responsibility for investigating compliance with Title VI to the Office of Civil Rights (OCR), now in the Department of Education.* Once OCR determined that a school district failed to comply with Title VI, the Office of General Counsel (OGC) conducted a hearing to determine if federal funds should be withheld. Although OCR staffing increased during the 1970s, OGC experienced no similar increase. Limited resources largely precluded any extensive investigation of a large school district because it would monopolize an entire regional OCR office for a substantial time period. Moreover, OGC refused to accept cases unless they appeared virtually airtight. As a result, it was not unusual during the 1970s for school districts to be under investigation for over five years while continuing to receive federal funds.

The Civil Rights Act of 1964 remains available to desegregate public schools, and the Civil Rights Restoration Act of 1987 reinforced it by clarifying those programs and activities that must abide by the 1964 Act after its application had been curtailed during the previous decade. However, controversy persists over whether the 1964 Act should be limited to prohibiting discrimination in public schools or expanded to include affirmative action and compensatory programs of African Americans to overcome the effects of past discrimination. In many school districts, white exodus from urban public schools has made desegregation unfeasible because of the 1974 Supreme Court ruling in *Milliken v. Bradley.** That decision overturned an interdistrict plan to desegregate Detroit's schools. The Restoration Act failed to nullify *Milliken*.

The original acts are the Civil Rights Act of 1866, 14 Stat. 27 (1866); Civil Rights Act of 1875, 18 Stat. 335 (1875); Civil Rights Act of 1957, Pub. L. No. 85-315, 71 Stat. 634 (1957); Civil Rights Act of 1964, Pub. L. No. 88-352, 78 Stat. 241 (1964); Civil Rights Restoration Act of 1987, Pub. L. No. 100-259, 102 Stat. 28 (1988). For the early laws, refer to James M. McPherson, ''Abolitionists and the Civil Rights Act of 1875'' (1965) and William P. Vaughn, ''Separate and Unequal: The Civil Rights Act of 1875 and Defeat of the School Integration Clause'' (1967). The 1964 Act is covered in Center for National Policy Review, *Justice Delayed and Denied: HEW and Northern School Desegregation* (1974), and Joel Spring, *The Sorting Machine Revisited: National Educational Policy since 1945* (1989).

Maureen A. Reynolds

CIVILIAN CONSERVATION CORPS (CCC), a pet project of President Franklin D. Roosevelt, was enacted by Congress in March 1933 and enrolled approximately 2.5 million young men during its nine-year life. Designed for unmarried youths between the ages of eighteen and twenty-five, the goals of the CCC were work relief and conservation. The CCC was initially meant to be educative only in the sense that hard work in rural settings under military authority was expected to build character, engender a work ethic, and tame the subversive tendencies of young unemployed people. Despite a lack of commitment to formal education within the agency by CCC director Robert Fechner and many camp commanders, an education program that offered both academic and vocational classes commenced under the auspices of the federal Office of Education during 1934 (also see UNITED STATES DEPARTMENT OF EDUCATION, VOCATIONAL EDUCATION). The CCC is credited with enabling thousands of enrollees to become literate and providing useful vocational training to many others, but the educational program was hampered by insufficient classrooms and texts, poorly trained and underpaid educational advisers, curtailed freedom of discussion, and classes that were scheduled after work hours only. For most enrollees, the education work was probably of little import. More broadly, the CCC's exclusion of females and practice of racial discrimination hardly made it a beacon of progressive social policy. Yet the CCC, more than any other New Deal program, captured the public's imagination, and it did have enduring educational value in the sense that it instructed citizens that government legitimately could be called upon to promote not only the conservation of natural resources but also the conservation of human resources through providing training and jobs. The CCC served as a precedent for Great Society youth programs, particularly the Job Corps.* Subsequently, a number of programs that have combined conservation work with jobs for youth, like the California Conservation Corps, modeled themselves after the original.

Records of the CCC are housed at the National Archives, Washington, D.C. For general treatments, see Kenneth Holland and Frank E. Hill, *Youth in the CCC* (1942); George P. Rawick, "The New Deal and Youth: The Civilian Conservation Corps, the National Youth Administration, and the American Youth Congress" (1957); and John Salmond, *The Civilian Conservation Corps: A New Deal Case Study* (1967).

Robert Lowe

CLASSICAL CURRICULUM. The earliest European colonists carried with them to America an intellectual tradition that became the staple of colonial grammar schools and colleges, would form a significant bulk of secondary and collegiate education in the nineteenth century, and would persist to the present in private academies* and specialized training (also see BOARDING SCHOOLS). Inheritors of the Renaissance, Anglo Americans based much of their educational training upon the authors of Western antiquity and expected students to read these authors in their original tongues, whether Latin, Greek, or Hebrew.

Colonial grammar schools (see BOSTON LATIN GRAMMAR SCHOOL; LATIN GRAMMAR SCHOOL), largely founded in New England, were not always able to dispense with training in basic reading and writing skills that petty and dame schools* were expected to handle. The line between petty and grammar schools was much more blurred in America than in England. Nevertheless, grammar schools were expected to train their students in the languages of the clasical authors, thus opening the repositories of knowledge that the classical texts represented.

In the nineteenth century, common and private secondary schools largely inherited the classical curriculum of colonial grammar schools, and it was not until the Committe of Ten* report of 1893 that the fate of obsolescence for the classical curriculum was sealed. The Committee of Ten, headed by Charles W. Eliot and composed of other prominent American educators, did not intend to marginalize the classical curriculum. Regardless, by recommending college preparatory tracks of secondary training that did not require training in the classical languages and texts, in addition to tracks that did, they put a formal stamp of approval on a growing tendency among secondary schools to omit the classical curriculum.

For an historical overview of the classical curriculum, see Daniel Tanner and Laurel Tanner, *History of the School Curriculum* (1990). Lawrence A. Cremin, *American Education: The Colonial Experience, 1607–1783* (1970), provides the fullest discussion of the classical curriculum during the colonial period at the grammar school level. Edward A. Krug, *The Shaping of the American High School: I, 1880–1920* (1964), gives the best detail concerning the downfall of the classical curriculum at the secondary level.

Rodney Hessinger

CLASSROOM DISCIPLINE AND MANAGEMENT. Perspectives on the best ways to educate children have been evident throughout history. Schools in this country predate the formation of the United States, as a result, many of our traditional management perspectives have their antecedents in our early religious values represented in various colonial settlements. The Puritans maintained the notion that children were inherently bad. They believed that children must be civilized through disciplinary practices designed to create fear of damnation unless they altered their behaviors and became, essentially, little adults. In other colonial settlements, the view of children was quite different. Pennsylvanian Quaker doctrines of nonviolence were mirrored in the management strategies of that colony's schoolmasters. The romanticist period of the 1700s equated children with the image of the noble savage. A child's innocence was to be treasured as an example of simplicity. The idea of taming that simplicity through harsh measures was not in keeping with the philosophy. In the early 1800s, Horace Mann* echoed a similar sentiment. In a discussion on the "Management of Disobedient Children," he described the difficult children awaiting teachers as a challenge, but he stated that it was an act of "true benevolence, Christian duty," to meet the needs of these children in order to restore them to their "Divine likeness." More recently, the progressivist movement was the first to deliberately interweave management with classroom instruction (see PROGRESSIVE EDUCATION). These various and competing perspectives about the basic nature of children have at one time or another strongly influenced management strategies. As a result, classroom discipline has changed dramatically over the years depending on the predominant viewpoint of children as being inherently bad or good.

As human psychology began to inform our common understandings of why behaviors manifested themselves, this knowledge was increasingly applied to the mangement of behaviors in the classroom and typically used to support the belief of inherent goodness or evil. The first deliberate application of psychological theory to classroom management was through the work of B. F. Skinner; the resultant methodology was broadly labeled as behavior modification (see BEHAVIORISM). This model deliberately applies external behavioral controls to achieve desired outcomes, reflecting a more Puritanical view that children, if left to their own devices, would be ill-mannered. The external controls were appropriate for the necessary redirection of their potential for bad behavior. An example of behavioral managment might be achieving a quiet classroom through the methodical applications of rewards for quiet behaviors and punishments for noisy behaviors. Students in this scheme are the passive receptors of the rewards and punishments; the theory is that they will replicate the desired behaviors for the length of time the rewards are made available or the punishement threatened. The most notable, commonly used, and widely criticized adaptation of Skinner is the "assertive discipline" approach. Its wide use is attributable to the ease with which it can be implemented, and its condemnation rests on the fact that this model fails to address individual student needs or cultural differences.

Cognitive psychology has more recently found its way into the lexicon of classroom management. This alternative perspective is dependent on the reasoning abilities of students and is based upon cognitive theories developed by Rudolf Dreikurs, William Glasser, Alfie Kohn, Forrest Gathercoal, and others. The models representing this perspective of classroom management put forth the premise that when fairness, honesty, respect, and other basic values are deliberately taught and modeled, students will internalize those attributes and act in ways that are mutually beneficial to themselves and others.

Although the two basic theories that give definition to the current discussion surrounding classroom management are dramatically different from each other, teachers and administrators usually combine them into a variety of eclectic strategies, or just as often, the managment practices being used reflect the personal style of a teacher with no discernible knowledge base governing the decisions being made. It is important to note that even though a teacher's practices might not be informed by pedagogical theory, they very much reflect the product of the argument concerning the inherent goodness or evil of children. The ability to manage a group of students effectively is considered to be an essential skill for teachers, yet despite the important nature of such skills, the topic is not even included in some teacher education programs. As a result, some classrooms are managed through reasoned decision-making based on an informed philosophy, whereas others follow irrational practices stemming from anger, bias, and personal favoritism.

Given this breakdown between theory and practice, many decisions are made that discourage students from active participation in their own learning and, in some cases, actually cause emotional or physical injuries. The absence of reasoned practices based on sound managment theory has resulted in a body of case law to protect students from discriminatory and unjust practices in public school classrooms. In *Tinker v. Des Moines* (1969),* the U.S. Supreme Court established First Amendment protections of free speech and expression for public school students. The Court has subsequently ruled on issues of seach and seizure, due process, equal protection, and religious freedom in schools (see *BANNISTER V. PARADIS*; *ENGEL V. VITALE*; *GOSS V. LOPEZ*; *HAZEL-WOOD SCHOOL DISTRICT V. KUHLMEIER*; *LAU V. NICHOLS*; *LEE V. WEISMAN*). The laws developed by state and federal court rulings give direction as to how teachers and administrators can and should implement classroom management practices. Too often, however, they are ignored, misunderstood, or completely unknown to practitioners, all of which have led to increasingly litigious educational climates.

Given the dramatic increase in the multicultural student populations represented in many of today's schools, management practices are currently changing to accommodate our new national demographics (see MULTICULTURAL EDUCATION). Democratic management strategies, a more recent focus, equally values all members of a learning community. Teachers are becoming increasingly sensitive to not demanding eye contact, knowing that some cultures view eye contact as representing disrespect or aggression. Because some cultures shun competition and value cooperation, a greater emphasis has been placed on cooperative learning.* This approach can also break down cultural misunderstandings among students and is helpful for children who do not speak English as a primary language (see BILINGUAL EDUCATION).

The recognition of classroom managment as a crucial area of study for teachers is growing in direct proportion to the incidents of violence in schools, the increasingly diverse student population, and the national statistics on school dropouts.* This continual critical examination of practices is crucial if teachers are to effectively address the broad spectrum of needs represented in today's classrooms. Classroom management decisions are interwoven throughout the school day in a complex fabric of threads representing curriculum, student-teacher interactions, and the physical arrangement of a classroom. The impact of classroom management rests in the mounting evidence that when educational decisions are consistent, equitable, and judicious, students may feel that educators are on their side and that staying in school is a viable choice.

For some historical, social, and legal background, refer to Ronald E. Butchart, "Punishments, Penalties, Prizes, and Procedures: A History of Discipline in U.S. Schools" (1996); Louis Filler, *Horace Mann on the Crisis in Education* (1965);

Nat Hentoff, *The First Freedom: The Tumultuous History of Free Speech in America* (1980); Michael LaMorte, *School Law: Cases and Concepts* (1992); and John Martin Rich, *Innovations in Education: Reformers and Their Critics* (1988). Specific management approaches are covered in Lee and Marilyn Canter, *Assertive Discipline: Positive Behavior Management for Today's Classroom* (1991); Rudolph Dreikurs, *Maintaining Sanity in the Classroom: Classroom Managment Techniques* (1982); Forrest Gathercoal, *Judicious Discipline* (1993); William Glasser, *Schools without Failure* (1969); Vernon Jones and Louise Jones, *Comprehensive Classroom Management: Creating Positive Learning Environments for All Students* (1995); Alfie Kohn, *Punished by Rewards* (1993); and Barbara McEwan, ed., *Practicing Judicious Discipline: An Educator's Guide to a Democratic Classroom* (1994).

Barbara McEwan

CLERC, LAURENT (December 12, 1785–July 18, 1869), indelibly shaped American deaf education and the American deaf community. Born in La Balme, France, deaf since about age one, and educated at the National Institute for the Deaf in Paris, Clerc came to the United States in 1816. He brought with him French Sign Language, the core of American Sign Language. He instructed Thomas Hopkins Gallaudet* in signs and deaf pedagogy and helped establish the American School for the Deaf (ASD), which stressed learning by sign language and reading. ASD became the model for American deaf schools before the Civil War. Clerc taught sign language to the first generation of hearing school principals, and his deaf students became teachers throughout the United States. For seven months in 1821–1822, Clerc served as interim principal of the Pennsylvania School for the Deaf, located in Philadelphia, hired its teachers, established its curriculum, and taught sign language.

Clerc's public role was crucial to deaf education's success in the United States. In 1816 and 1817, he toured New England, New Jersey, and New York raising money for ASD. His public addresses (read by Gallaudet, for Clerc did not speak) and written answers to questions stunned audiences, demonstrating abstract thinking abilities previously believed impossible for deaf persons. In 1819, Clerc met President James Monroe, befriended House Speaker Henry Clay, and conversed in written English and written French with members of Congress, leading to a federal land grant to help support ASD. Denied a permanent administrative position because of his deafness, Clerc nevertheless was so important to ASD that he was the only deaf teacher paid equally with hearing teachers and the only one allowed to vote on important faculty matters. He retired from ASD in 1858, and in 1864 received the first honorary degree given by Gallaudet University.

Clerc's personal papers and publications are in the Laurent Clerc Papers, Sterling Memorial Library, Yale University. No book-length studies of Clerc alone exist, but his life and accomplishments are well documented in Harlan Lane, *When the Mind Hears: A History of the Deaf* (1984); Phyllis Klein Valentine, "American Asylum for the Deaf: A First Experiment in Education, 1817–1880" (1993).

John Vickrey Van Cleve

COEDUCATION is now virtually universal in the United States and so much a part of American education that we do not often think of its origins. The topic of coeducation and single-sex schools is always examined from the perspective of the education of girls and women in male or patriarchal institutions, and there is seldom found any talk of adding boys to girls' schools. Hence, it is almost always an issue of equality for girls, a girl's problem that stimulates the dialogue surrounding coeducation.

It is also clear that coeducation, according to Tyack and Hansot, has a "tangled history." Nineteenth-century boys and girls who attended the newly forming common schools* and academies* sometimes found themselves segregated within the schoolhouse and classroom. In some cases, girls were assigned to special rooms; if they were in the same room, they would be on a different side of the room or in a separate corner. In other cases, boys and girls studied different subject matter. Even with these distinctions, educators never totally separated boys and girls. Although coeducation eventually became a permanent part of American schooling, however, a gender-neutral institution and a gender-free curriculum never emerged until the 1980s.

The conceptual origins of coeducation can be traced to the ideas of the American Revolution and to such men as Thomas Jefferson,* Noah Webster,* and Benjamin Rush* and to women such as Judith Sargent Murray and Susanna Rowson, who promoted the need for education for all to maintain the Republic. They called for a literate, rational, and self-reliant female. Women, who could not vote, were assigned a political role as mothers and educators of future citizens, especially their sons.

The common schools institutionalized coeducation. This process actually began during the early part of the nineteenth century and was never questioned, perhaps because in most areas the admission of girls appeared to have been gradual, natural, and totally decentralized. In the North, rural one-room schools educated boys and girls together as well as employed female teachers. Regional differences existed, however, with the South lagging behind in both the founding of public schools and in coeducation.

In urban areas, where there was a population large enough to support separate schools, coeducation, or mixed schools, was debated. Concerns arose over mixing social classes and religious groups as well as sexes. Some believed that physically bringing boys and girls together in school added a level of distraction. A real concern of parents and educators was that different studies for boys and girls were necessary because of the different lives they would eventually lead. Although William T. Harris,* school superintendent in St. Louis schools, and John Philbrick, school superintendent in Boston, both supported coeducation, no one argued that coeducation could or should eliminate all differences between men and women or that this was even desirable.

Despite some objections, the public schools became predominately coeducational. The schools that offered the same courses to boys and girls found that girls outperformed boys in their studies. In 1890, girls outnumbered boys as high school graduates.

At the turn of the century, debates dealing with coeducation again arose, only this time over secondary coeducation. A concern existed that education could actually physically harm girls and women and indeed undermine the institution of marriage as well as harm the reproductive organs. Despite the concern for women's health issues, education for girls and women grew during the first half of the nineteenth century, spurred on by economics while the argument for women's public and private roles remained tangled in "biology as destiny."

The educated women who worked were encouraged to do what they had done in the past, working in the helping fields and teaching young children. What might earlier have been an antiemulation or anticompletion movement channeled women into teaching and eventually into home economics, nursing, library science, and social work. Feminist scholars of this century are quick to note that these occupations were low-paying and held in low esteem. The were always ascribed to women, but they did result in the need for additional education for women and girls and hence led to levels of higher education.

Economic issues of the early twentieth century sent many more women to school. The schools needed both students and teachers, and women and girls were willing to engage in the needed training for the work that was a natural outgrowth of what they had done in their homes. High schools,* attended by a majority of American students after World War II, became places to educate both sexes, but with different areas of interest and different subject matter. Boys were encouraged to advance in math and science, and girls in "useful" subjects such as home economics. A hidden agenda of education might have been to provide a place for young people to meet future mates. A shift has taken place in current high schools as girls are encouraged to take courses formerly reserved for boys, but the reversal has not gone both ways. Boys have not moved into girls' classes or occupations. Because of this unidirectional move, coeducational colleges in the last quarter of the century are now predominately female. The professional schools of law and medicine are at least evenly divided between the sexes.

Coeducation has progressed unevenly based upon the issues of need and equality. Furthermore, females integrated into male schools, not vice versa. Equity meant the questioning not of gender roles but of equal access. Girls and women were invited into boys' classes, but there was no attempt to equalize future roles. In other words, education became the place to equalize opportunity, just as in the case of desegregation, schools became the place to integrate. Society remained untouched.

The single best work on coeducation is by David B. Tyack and Elisabeth Hansot, *Learning Together: A History of Coeducation in American Public Schools* (1990). Also, refer to Linda Kerber, "The Republican Mother: Women and the Enlightenment—An American Perspective" (1976); Glenna Mathews, *Just a Housewife: The Rise and Fall of Domesticity* (1987); and Sally Schwager, "Educating Women in America" (1987).

                                                                                            Rita S. Saslaw

COGSWELL, JOSEPH G. See BANCROFT, GEORGE.

COLEMAN REPORT, titled *Equality of Educational Opportunity* and issued in 1966, represented a landmark sociological analysis of public schooling.* Section 402 of the 1964 Civil Rights Act* directed the U.S. Department of Health, Education, and Welfare (HEW)* to investigate the sources of inequality of educational opportunity in the nation's schools. Francis Keppel, U.S. commissioner of education, commissioned a team of social scientists headed by sociologist James S. Coleman to conduct the study intended to describe existing conditions of educational inequality.

The team surveyed 60,000 teachers and 570,000 students in 4,000 U.S. and territorial public schools. Participants were grouped into the self-identified racial and ethnic groups of African American, Native American, Asian American, Puerto Rican, Mexican American, and white. The research study's four topics of concern included separation and segregation in the public schools; school facilities and characteristics; student achievement in the public schools; and relation of achievement to school characteristics.

This inquiry, known as the Coleman Report, concluded that most American schoolchildren attended schools segregated by race. Eighty percent of all white students in grades 1 through 12 attended schools that enrolled 90 to 100 percent white children. Sixty-five percent of all African American students in first grade attended schools that enrolled 50 percent or more African American students. A similar pattern of segregation was found for the teachers of African American and white students, with the exception of the average African American secondary student attending a school in which 59 percent of the teachers were white. Within geographic regions, African American school facilities were not found to be grossly inferior to white schools. A wide descrepancy in achievement among the six racial and ethnic groups was found. The average minority student, with the exception of Asian Americans, scored lower at every grade level on the administered reading and mathematics achievement than did the average white student.

The most prominent findings of the Coleman Report related achievement and school characteristics. Socioeconomic factors bore a strong relationship to academic achievement. Furthermore, minority pupils' achievement was strongly related to the academic background and aspirations of the other students in the school. Minority student inclusion with white students in a mixed classroom appeared to reduce achievement gaps. Perceived teacher quality appeared more important to the achievement of minority students than it did to that of white students. In particular, the vocabulary level of teachers, which Coleman construed to be an indicator of general ability, affected student achievement level.

The Coleman Report's conclusions ran counter to existing government and education policy and were given little media attention when released on July 4, 1966. After federal court judges, HEW, and some school boards used selective portions of the report in the formulation of policy, media attention increased. The U.S. Supreme Court ruling in *Swann v. Charlotte-Mecklenburg County Board of Education* (1971)* relied on the Coleman Report to justify its implementation of busing as a desegregation remedy.

Refer to the Coleman Report itself for specific findings. Criticisms of that Report included concerns about sampling, aggregated data, reliance on school administrators' reports of school facilities, stringent time constraints, insufficient analytic methods, and unsubstantiated findings. Many of these criticisms were chronicled in a collection of papers, edited by Frederick Mosteller and Daniel P. Moynihan, *On Equality of Educational Opportunity* (1972), from a Harvard University Faculty Seminar on the Coleman Report. Finally, see Gerald Unks, "Conversations: A Talk with Dr. James S. Coleman" (1979).

Rosa Maria Abreo and Elaine Clift Gore

COLLEGE ENTRANCE EXAMINATIONS. See ACCREDITATION.

COLLIER, JOHN (May 4, 1884–May 8, 1968), served as U.S. commissioner of Indian affairs from 1933 to 1945, a period characterized by historians as the "Indian New Deal." After an active career as a social worker and community organizer, mainly as director of the People's Institute in New York City, Collier became involved in Indian policy in the 1920s when he helped to spearhead a reform movement devoted to the twofold purpose of protecting Native American landholdings and the preservation of traditional culture. Appointed to the commissionership by President Franklin D. Roosevelt, Collier proposed two legislative initiatives: the Indian Reorganization Act and the Johnson O'Malley Act. As submitted to Congress, the former included a recommendation to reverse the government's long-standing policy of using Indian schools as instruments of assimilation. Congress passed an amended version of the bill that largely gutted his educational plan, but Collier, as director of the Bureau of Indian Affairs, still possessed the authority to implement his educational agenda. Over the next decade, with the assistance of two successive directors of education, Will Carson Ryan and Willard W. Beatty,* both noted advocates of progressive education*, Collier undertook several reforms: an emphasis on community day schools as opposed to boarding schools; a bicultural curriculum that built upon rather than negated native cultural ways; the production of bilingual teaching materials; and the expanded training for both Indian and non-Indian teachers (see BILINGUAL EDUCATION). Collier's educational vision, however, was eventually undermined by lack of funding, by entrenched Bureau service employees still committed to the assimilationist ideal, and finally, by the onset of World War II, which weakened still further congressional support for Collier's pluralist vision. The second major accomplishment of the Collier years was the passage, in 1934, of the Johnson-O'Malley Act, legislation that expanded federal aid, through federal-state contracts, to public schools enrolling Native American children. Although the nature of educational support and services provided by the program has changed over the years and the funding mechanisms have been periodically revised, Johnson-O'Malley funds remain an important source of federal support for Native American education to this day.

The best source of primary documents on Collier are his papers located at Beinecke Rare Book and Manuscript Library, Yale University, and the records of the Commissioner of Indian Affairs, National Archives. Also see his autobiography, *From Every Zenith: A Memoir and Some Essays on Life and Thought* (1963). For secondary sources, refer to Thomas James, "Rhetoric and Resistance: Social Science and Community Schools for Navajos in the 1930s" (1988); Lawrence C. Kelly, *The Assault on Assimilation: John Collier and the Origins of Indian Policy Reform* (1983); Donald L. Parman, *The Navajos and the New Deal* (1976); Kenneth R. Philip, *John Collier's Crusade for Indian Reform, 1920–1954* (1977); and Margaret Szasz, *Education and the American Indian: The Road to Self-Determination, 1928–1973* (1974).

David W. Adams

COMMERCIAL EDUCATION. See BUSINESS EDUCATION.

COMMITTEE OF TEN ON SECONDARY SCHOOL STUDIES. The recommendations of the Committee of Ten substantively affected the secondary curriculum for at least a generation, if not to the present day. At the July 1892 meeting of the National Education Association (NEA),* the NEA National Council formed the Committee of Ten in an effort to standardize high school* programs and college entrance requirements on a national scale. Charles W. Eliot, president of Harvard University, served as chair of and driving force behind the Committee of Ten. In its 1893 report, the Committee proposed that nine subject areas comprise the secondary college preparatory curriculum: Latin; Greek; English; other modern languages; mathematics; physics, astronomy, and chemistry; natural history (biology, including botany, zoology, and physiology); history, civil government, and political economy; and geography (physical geography, geology, and meteorology). The Committee listed these subjects to reflect their accepted order of disciplinary value but held that they were of equal utility in disciplining the mind. The Committee asserted that every subject should be taught the same way to all pupils.

The Committee of Ten recommended four programs of study for high school pupils: classical, Latin-scientific, modern languages, and English. It identified the first two programs as superior to the latter two, thus establishing a precedent for tracking* students. Despite its emphasis on standardizing college preparatory programs and admissions requirements, the Committee maintained that the primary role of secondary schools was not to prepare students for college but, rather, to prepare them for life. It considered successful completion of any of the four programs the best preparation for college and life. The Committee accepted the contemporary belief that secondary education was appropriate for only a small portion of youth.

The recommendations of the Committee of Ten were traditional insofar as they endorsed the prevailing theory of mental discipline, exalted the college preparatory curriculum over subjects such as music, art, manual training, and vocational education,* and conceded that high school should serve only small segment of the adolescent population (see ADOLESCENCE; ART EDUCATION; MUSIC EDUCATION). The recommendations were forward looking insofar as they legitimized the place of modern laboratory sciences and foreign languages in the curriculum. The report of the Committee of Ten led to the appointment in 1895 of the Committee on College Entrance requirements.

See *Report of the Committee of Ten on Secondary School Studies* (1893). For secondary sources and background, refer to Lawrence A. Cremin, "The Revolution in American Secondary Education, 1893–1913" (1955); Herbert M. Kliebard, "Constructing a History of the American Curriculum" (1992); Edward A. Krug, *The Shaping of the American High School; I, 1880–1920* (1964); Theodore R. Sizer, *Secondary Schools at the Turn of the Century* (1964); and Daniel Tanner and Laurel Tanner, *History of the School Curriculum* (1990).

William G. Wraga

COMMON SCHOOLS is a term frequently used in the same context as the more inclusive phrase "common school reform" and refers both to a form of institution and an era of intense educational activity. The antebellum period, especially between 1820 and 1850, was a time of social, economic, and demographic upheaval; the response of leading activists, ministers, lawyers, and politicians, usually Whigs, was to initiate institutions designed to fix society. Schools were a crucial target.

Legislation requiring the provision of basic schooling and establishing the role of the colonial government in the area of education originated in Massachusetts (see MASSACHUSETTS EDUCATION LAWS OF 1642, 1647, 1648) and Connecticut (1650). All states mandated rudimentary schooling by the nineteenth century, and the district school* became a familiar feature on the rural landscape. Reformers decried the quality of those schools: They were poorly constructed, ill-equiped, and often victims of the locality's stinginess; they were kept, not taught, by inexperienced and often transitory teachers; and attendance was spotty, with schools open only a few months a year and most children enrolled for only three or four years. School conditions in the growing urban centers, because of population changes and industrialization, seemed to be even more desperate.

Local organizations for the reform of schools agitated for local and state action early in the century, and national groups, like the American Institute of Instruction* and the Lyceum (see LYCEUMS), provided leadership. Horace Mann* certainly became the best-known reformer, but eminent men such as James Carter,* George Emerson, William Channing, and William Woodbridge preceded him. A list of Mann's contemporaries, Connecticut's Henry Barnard,* Michigan's John Pierce,* New York's Samuel S. Randall, Ohio's Calvin Stowe,* Rhode Island's Wilkins Updike, and North Carolina's Calvin Wiley,* among others, demonstrates the pervasiveness of school reform. The reformers maintained a clear agenda: to centralize and standardize the schools in order to promote their vision of a moral and unified nation. Specifically, they struggled for improved school buildings, pedagogical innovations, gradation of schools, better teachers and teacher training, taxation to support schools, and a modicum of systematization. The ultimate goal, according to Barnard in 1838, was to provide schools that were not "regarded as common" because they were "cheap, inferior and patronized only by the poor" but "common as the light and the air," or, as it was put so often, common because good enough for the rich and cheap enough for the poor.

The reformers employed exhortation and organization as their promotion mechanisms. As Protestant, middle-class, sometime self-righteous, they referred to their "crusade" and frequently viewed their opponents as victims or promoters of evil. They agitated locally and at the national level, promoting school reform as a kind of internal improvement. State action was their immediate objective, but the establishment of a national role was a goal until the creation of the short-lived Department of Education in 1867 (see UNITED STATES DEPARTMENT OF EDUCATION). Their opponents stressed local control and the rights of ethnic and religious dissidents. Partisan politics, Whigs against Democrats, and religious tension, mainstream Protestants against Roman Catholics and various sects, nativism against diverse ethnic groups, and even social-class hostility dominated the reform decades.

Common school reform proved to be mixed. As an effort to maintain the perceived moral and social cohesion of the rural United States in the face of a rapidly changing society and an expanding electorate, the movement was fundamentally conservative. The reformers' rhetoric was moralistic, anti-immigrant, and charged with racism. Yet through legislation and publication—all states had an educational journal, and Barnard's *American Journal of Education* served as a national forum—a number of pedagogical innovations, some child-centered, were promoted. Improved recordkeeping; some standardization of school practice, such as age-grading* and textbooks; the institution of embryonic state systems; and promotion of better teacher qualifications and professionalism, with teacher institutes,* normal schools,* and educators' associations, represented the chief successes of school reformers. Proponents focused primarily on the elementary school, but all advocated a complete system of public schools, even including higher education in the Midwest; gradation thus led to the institution of high schools* in many places. The most far-reaching accomplishment was acceptance of two principles: that schools should be supported by taxation, and that those schools should be under state supervision. More generally, the legacy of the common school reformers is the American secular religion of schooling. Common schools served as the forerunner of the modern elementary school. They were tax-supported, taught by women, divided into grades—where enrollment allowed—and governed by locally selected laypeople under the general state authority. States encouraged the inclusion of higher grades and some consolidation of districts (see CONSOLIDATION, SCHOOL), provided limited training for the teachers, and gradually instituted professional regulations; they also created fledgling bureaucracies.

The historical success of the common schools remains uneven. It is clear that the common schools provided more consistent schooling, in better schoolhouses, over a long period of time, with better prepared and paid teachers, who taught from improved texts. However, recent research indicates that vast increases in nineteenth-century enrollment cannot be documented, with the common school experience absent from the lives of many children. Few southern African Americans saw the inside of a school, while many urban working children experienced truncated schooling. Roman Catholics created their own parochial schools* after being rebuffed in their efforts to participate in the establishment of compatible common schools. Nevertheless, despite philosophical and political opposition, the common school reformers were successful in laying the foundations of the modern system of schooling because they represented the dominant consensus of republicanism, Protestantism, and capitalism and because they served the goals of individual moral development and assimilation. These goals, buttressed by the nostalgic dream of schools as they supposedly were, motivate many of the heirs of the antebellum reformers.

The standard work on common schools is Carl F. Kaestle, *Pillars of the Republic: Common Schools and American Society, 1780–1860* (1983). Frederick M. Binder, *The Age of the Common School, 1830–1856* (1974), is less critical. Somewhat dated, but still useful, is Merle Curti, *Social Ideas of American Educators* (1935, 1959). Lawrence A. Cremin, *The American Common School: An Historic Conception* (1951), is substantially improved in his *American Education: The National Experience, 1783–1876* (1980). Charles Leslie Glenn, Jr., *The Myth of the Common School* (1988), provides a highly critical analysis of the movement. David B. Tyack and Elisabeth Hansot, *Managers of Virtue* (1982), place the common school leaders along the continuum of educational leadership.

Edith Nye MacMullen

COMMUNITY CONTROL. See OCEAN HILL–BROWNSVILLE.

COMPENSATORY EDUCATION, a fairly recent school experience, is rooted in the concept of cultural deprivation. Gunnar Myrdal, in his classic *An Amer-*

ican Dilemma (1944), a comprehensive study of African Americans, contended that the cultural background of "Negroes" placed them at a disadvantage when they entered school. This work proved influential, with twenty-five reprints, and stimulated investigations into the culture of poverty. In 1964, thirty-one prominent social scientists met at the University of Chicago to discuss cultural deprivation, and agreed that culturally deprived children needed an intensive, individualized school program that provided cognitive support and affective encouragement. This group, which included James Coleman (see COLEMAN REPORT), Allison Davis, and Robert Hess, shaped prevailing attitudes and influenced pending federal legislation. The 1965 Elementary and Secondary Education Act (ESEA),* part of President Lyndon Johnson's War on Poverty program, increased federal funds for "educationally deprived" students, specifically poor students. The majority of children in this class came from African American families, causing many educators to use "culturally deprived" and "black" synonymously. Coleman and Ernest Campbell, appointed in 1965 by the U.S. Office of Education to study educational opportunities for minorities, recommended that the equalization of ghetto schools and the academic performance of poor children required even more funds. During that summer, almost 560,000 four- and five-year-olds enrolled in federal Head Start* programs in nearly 2,400 communities. The program, which was expanded in August, worked on the assumption that early intervention would stop the cycle of poverty and educational failure. Two years later, the Office of Economic Opportunity established guidelines for all Head Start programs. The Westinghouse Report, which claimed that early academic success of Head Start students was washed out in later years, gave rise to Follow Through, a variety of programs developed in the 1970s that extended Head Start into the elementary grades. Finally, ESEA's Title I programs remediated reading and language difficulties. Likewise built on cultural deprivaton assumptions, these efforts attempted to improve scholastic achievement by grouping children according to their abilities, altering the curriculum and materials, and emphasizing Standard English. By 1981, Title I programs served more than 5 million children. President Ronald Reagan that year recommended a series of sharp budget cuts in Title I, but he faced opposition from the National Coalition to Save Title I and convincing evidence that these programs produced reading gains in grades 1 through 3. As a result, Title I became incorporated into Chapter I of the 1981 Education Consolidation and Improvement Act.

Early works describing poverty, cultural deprivation, and education include writings by Benjamin S. Bloom, Allison Davis, and Robert D. Hess, *Compensatory Education for Cultural Deprivation* (1965); James S. Coleman et al., *Equality of Educational Opportunity* (1966); Myrdal (1944); and Deborah P. Wolfe, "Curriculum Adaptations for the Culturally Deprived" (1962). Frank Reissman, *The Culturally Deprived Child* (1962), takes a slightly different stance, arguing that the culture of poor children is different, but not deficient. For curriculum adaptations and studies of their effectiveness, refer to Carl Bereiter and Siegfried Englemann, *Teaching Disadvantaged Children in the Preschool* (1966); Arthur R. Jensen, "How Much Can We Boost IQ and Scholastic Achievement?" (1969); Benjamin Stickney and Virginia Plunkett, "Closing the Gap: A Historical Perspective on the Effectiveness of Compensatory Education" (1983); the Westinghouse (Report) Learning Corporation, *The Impact of Head Start* (1969); Edward Zigler and Jeanette Valentine, eds., *Project Head Start: A Legacy of the War on Poverty* (1979). Contemporary reviews can be found in Diane Ravitch, *The Troubled Crusade: American Education, 1945–1980* (1983), and Valora Washington, "Reducing the Risks to Young Black Learners" (1989).

Deborah Wells

COMPULSORY EDUCATION rests on individual state laws that require obligatory school attendance for persons of specific ages. Early historical antecedents for compulsory school attendance in the North American British colonies were poor laws, apprenticeship* laws, and those requiring instruction of children. The English poor laws provided that pauper children and orphans be apprenticed to masters to learn skills to earn a living and prevent the formation of a class of dependent poor. The English Statute of Artificers, which was transported to the colonies, required that masters teach their apprentices the skills of their particular trade and provide basic instruction in reading and writing. An early antecedent for the compulsory instruction of children occurred in Massachusetts in 1642 when its General Court required towns to oversee that children were taught reading, writing, and the laws of the Commonwealth (see MASSACHUSETTS EDUCATION LAWS OF 1642, 1647, 1648). None of these antecedents, however, required school attendance.

The reserved powers clause of the Constitution's Tenth Amendment assigned education to each of the states. The establishment of tax-supported public, or common, schools* occurred in each of the states during the nineteenth century. The establishment of public schools was necessary for the enactment and enforcement of compulsory school attendance laws, and thus legislation establishing schools was enacted prior to compulsory attendance provisions. The actual origins of compulsory school attendance legislation is generally traced to Massachusetts, which in 1837 instituted an early compulsory school attendance statute designed to limit child labor and ensure a minimum of formal education. That law required at least three months' schooling in the year that preceded a child's employment. This legislation made a rudimentary but necessary relationship between the requirement of school attendance and restrictions on child labor. Subsequent Massachusetts statutes in 1842 and 1850 further strengthened compulsory education by defining and proscribing truancy as a violation of the law. Concurrent with the Massachusetts compulsory attendance laws were those restricting child labor. Massachusetts passed a stronger compulsory attendance act in 1852, which required that every child between eight and fourteen years of age attend a public, or comparable, school for at least twelve weeks each year, six weeks of which were to be consecutive. Violators faced a $50 fine as the penalty. Mentally or physically disabled children were excluded from the provisions of the law.

Following the Massachusetts model, twelve other states passed compulsory attendance laws by 1875; by 1887, twenty-four states had enacted such legislation. These statutes, quite weak, generally required attendance for a limited number of weeks per year and imposed small fines on parents or guardians who violated the law. For example, the 1895 Pennsylvania law merely levied a $2 fine, and only after parents and guardians had been warned several times and given ample time for remediation.

Parents and employers, who regarded these laws as trespassing on parental rights and the freedom of contract, challenged compulsory attendance statutes in the courts. Cases in Ohio (1891), Indiana (1901), New Hampshire (1902), and Pennsylvania (1903) upheld the right of the states to pass compulsory education legislation under the state's police powers to promote the health and welfare of the people.

The degree to which compulsory school attendance laws were effective depended on two related conditions of legal establishment: the provision of public schooling and restrictions on child labor. By 1918, all of the states had enacted some type of compulsory school attendance law. Most of the states had also enacted legislation either restricting or severely limiting child labor, usually for children under age fourteen. By 1950, most of the statutes provided for compulsory education from age six or seven typically to sixteen, and in a few instances seventeen or eighteen. These laws generally provided for attendance for the entire school year, usually 180 days.

For historical perspectives, refer to Newton Edwards and Herman G. Richey, *The School in the American Social Order* (1963), and Edgar W. Knight, *Fifty Years of American Education: A Historical Review and Critical Appraisal* (1952). Also, see John Bender, *The Functions of Courts in Enforcing School Attendance Laws* (1972); Forest C. Ensign, *Compulsory School Attendance and Child Labor: A Study of the Historical Development of Regulations Compelling Attendance and Limiting the Labor of Children* (1921; 1969); Laurence Kotin, *Legal Foundations of Compulsory School Attendance* (1980); Patricia M. Lines, *Compulsory Education Laws and Their Impact on Public and Private Education* (1985); and August W. Steinhilber, *State Law on Compulsory Attendance* (1966).

Gerald L. Gutek

CONANT, JAMES BRYAN (March 26, 1893–February 13, 1978), during the 1950s and 1960s, published many works recommending wide-ranging educational reform. Born in Dorchester, Massachusetts, and educated at Harvard University, receiving his Ph.D. in chemistry in 1916, he became recognized for his accomplishments as a chemist, educator, and diplomat. Conant joined the faculty of the Harvard of Department Chemistry in 1919, where he played a major role in the development of physical organic chemistry with his research on hemoglobin. In 1933, he became president of the university. As president, he actively recruited a complement of young chemists who represented the best of the new chemistry. Together they made major contributions to the war efforts, during World War II, through the National Defense Research Committee. This group was founded by James Conant and Vannevar Bush. After the war, Conant became the first ambassador to West Germany.

Upon his return to private life, Conant began a series of studies of American public education. In such works as *Education in a Divided World* (1948), *The Citadel of Learning* (1956), and *The Child, the Parent, and the State* (1959), he highlighted the role of education in a democracy and attempted to unify views of education. In *Thomas Jefferson and the Development of American Public Education* (1962), Conant chronicled the continuity of reform in American education. In *The Revolutionary Transformation of the American High School* (1959) and *The American High School Today* (1959), he supported the development of large, comprehensive high schools* under the control of local communities. His *Slums and Suburbs: A Commentary on Schools in Metropolitan Areas* (1961) focused attention on the education of the underclass in urban areas. Inadequate educational and vocational guidance* for disadvantaged youth, Conant predicted, would amount to "social dynamite." Conant proposed increased funding for science education,* local control* of schools, and greater rigor in curriculum.

Conant's papers are housed at Harvard University. His *Memoirs of a Social Inventor* (1970) provides insightful autobiographical material. The leading biography is by James G. Hershberg, *Conant: Harvard to Hiroshima and the Making of the Nuclear Age* (1995).

Charles E. Jenks

CONSOLIDATION, SCHOOL. It is quite possible that school consolidation will represent a definitive characteristic of twentieth-century educational history in the United States. The 130,000 school districts existing in 1930 decreased to the approximately 15,000 remaining near the century's end. The convoluted interplay of power politics, technological innovation, and our cultural embrace of a progress-oriented public philosophy prompted this dramatic shift from local to centralized schools.

The shift to centralized control of public schooling during the first years of this century has been well documented. This shift was legitimated by an emerging industrial ethos in this country, one that held the expert manager and his role, maximizing efficiency, in high regard. It took little time to discover that larger schools with more students could dramatically increase efficiency. Added to this development was the impact of the refined internal combustion engine, something that eased the burden of getting children to and from school. Buses made their way into the American countryside as early as the 1910s, and this marked the beginning of the century-long process of taking children out of their neighborhoods and transporting them into the nearest town to attend school. Still another catalyst to consolidation lies somewhere inside the growth of a national public philosophy that is part-Lockean, part-Smithian, and part-Darwinian—a philosophy premised on possessive individualism, the unfettered pursuit of self-interest and its ostensibly concomitant robust national economy, and the assumption that "survival of the fittest" fairly applies to the human condition. This mixture produced a public philosophy committed to facilitating the "march of progress," through concerted educational effort, toward an increasingly cosmopolitan, leisure-oriented, urban future. School consolidation came to be seen as a symbol of such progess and, therefore, very nearly became synonymous with school improvement throughout the century.

See Raymond E. Callahan, *Education and the Cult of Efficiency* (1962); Paul Theobald, *Call School: Rural Education in the Midwest to 1918* (1995); and David B. Tyack and Elisabeth Hansot, *Managers of Virtue: Public School Leadership in America, 1820–1980* (1982).

Paul Theobald

CONSTRUCTIVISM is a term used to describe movements or "points of view" in several disciplines. In education, it is usually understood to be a cognitive position and a methodological orientation based on Jean Piaget's genetic epistemology, treated in his *To Understand Is to Invent*, published in 1948 and translated into English 1973. The principles or premises of constructivism are that all knowledge is constructed, or "invented"; that cognitive development and learning results from such constructions; and that such development is continually revised through reflection on and resolution of cognitive "conflict." Constructivism, in short, is the subject's organization of the experiential world. Some conceptions of constructivism appear to be based on philosphical *idealism*, particularly the ideas of Immanuel Kant, and are opposed to realism and essentialism.*

Because of the belief that *all* knowledge is actively constructed by the learner, implying rote learning as well, some advocates distinguish between "weak" and "strong" constructions, the difference appearing to be in the range the constructions achieve within their context of inquiry. Constructivism may also focus too singularly on individual learning. That concern for the social aspects of learning has led to the development of "social constructivism," based on the work of the Russian psychologist Lev Vygotsky, who was active in the 1920s and 1930s. Finally, "radical" constructivism, as defined by Ernst von Glasersfeld, forgoes argument over whether a mind-independent reality exists and can be known, since one never can give a final proof for that belief. Constructivism can thus be called a *postepistemological* hypothesis.

Constructivist teachers avoid passive educational experiences and promote active organizing and interpreting of information for one's own needs and understanding. The teacher operates as a "guide" rather than a "director." The educational implications of constructivism may be seen in the work of many theorists, particularly John Dewey,* who may never have thought of themselves in that way. Psychologists Jerome Bruner* and Lawrence Kohlberg* have been called constructivists as well. Avoiding argument over "necessary implications" for practice, Nel Noddings, one interpreter, believes that teachers can adopt constructivist practices without being committed to constructivist principles. This might encourage eclecticism in both the best and worst senses.

See Robert B. Davis, Carolyn A. Maher, and Nel Noddings, eds., *Constructivist Views on the Teaching and Learning of Mathematics* (1990); Jerome Bruner, *Acts of Meaning* (1990); and Ernst von Glaserfeld, *The Construction of Knowledge* (1987).

Robert R. Sherman

CONTINUATION SCHOOL functions as a part-time school for fourteen- to eighteen-year-old youths to extend the general education and supplement the apprenticeship* training and work experience of children who—out of necessity or inclination—do not go on to high school or college. This alternative school uses vocational motivation to interest children in pursuing occupational and cultural advancement (see VOCATIONAL EDUCATION).

At the end of the nineteenth century, some European countries conducted continuation schools during the evenings and on Sundays, and later on workdays, four to eight hours a week. In Germany a few states made attendance compulsory. The continuation school idea—adapted from the version by Georg Kerschensteiner, Munich's school superintendent—became popular in the United States through the efforts of the National Society for the Promotion of Industrial Education,* and represented an important component of the 1917 Smith-Hughes Act,* despite the opposition of John Dewey* and others to the vocationalization of secondary education. The Smith-Hughes Act gave the continuation school a leading role by stipulating that at least one-third of the federal funds spent on vocational education should go to schools that catered to working children over fourteen years of age. Enrollment steadily increased through the 1920s, to a high of 400,000, but declined with the Great Depression and the extension of compulsory education laws (see COMPULSORY ATTENDANCE). These laws and new employment practices, such as the employment of youths at least sixteen years old, led increasing numbers of students to attend comprehensive high schools.* Thus, by the 1930s, continuation schools became transformed into full-time vocational schools, integrated into adult education programs, or as in California, where the term "continuation school" is still being used, they became schools for children-at-risk with highly individualized curricula. Since the 1990s, a new movement, called "youth apprenticeship," has grown to revive the original continuation school idea and bring non-college-bound youths through work- and-school-based training into career employment.

For the early history of the continuation school, see Paul H. Douglas, *American Apprenticeship and Industrial Education* (1921), and Georg Kerschensteiner, *Three Lectures on Vocational Training* (1911). James B. Conant,* *The*

Revolutionary Transformation of the American High School (1959), and Franklin J. Keller, *Day Schools for Young Workers: The Organization and Management of Part-Time and Continuation Schools* (1924), treat later developments.
Deirdre M. Kelly, *Last Chance High: How Boys and Girls Drop in and out of
Alternative Schools* (1993), provides a sharp analysis of California's continuation schools; Steven F. Hamilton, *Apprenticeship for Adulthood: Preparing
Youth for the Future* (1990), expresses the new movement.

Michael Knoll

COOPERATIVE LEARNING is a method of instruction in which students
work together in small groups to reach a common goal. Working and learning
together is not a new idea; in the first century, Quintilian argued that students
could benefit from teaching each other. One of the first educators to advocate
cooperative learning in the United States was Colonel Francis Parker,* superintendent of the public school in Quincy, Massachusetts (1875–1880). Over
30,000 visitors a year to the Quincy schools examined Parker's instructional
methods, which included cooperative learning. Years later, John Dewey* stated,
in *Experience and Education* (1938), that cooperative learning grew out of the
new education or progressive movement, which was "of itself a product of the
discontent with traditional education." As a founding member of the progressive
education* movement, Dewey emphasized the processes of learning over curricular content and felt the social aspect of learning was vital in training students
in problem solving and democratic living. In the 1940s, Morton Deutsch built
on the theorizing of Kurt Lewin when he proposed a theory of cooperation and
competition; much modern research on cooperative learning is based on the
work of Deutsch.

Despite the work of researchers such as Deutsch, an emphasis on interpersonal
competition in public schools began the decline of cooperative learning in the
1930s and was renewed after *Sputnik* in 1957. It was not until the 1970s, when
progressive education was rediscovered, that the idea of working cooperatively
in schools resurfaced as an important part of classroom instruction.

Group responsibility, ensuring that each student learns the material being studied or researched, represents an integral part of cooperative learning. The teacher
becomes a facilitator, rather than a transmittor of information, in a cooperative
classroom. Cooperative learning includes a variety of important elements necessary to facilitate the group process: heterogeneous groups; student accountability; clear rules, established routines, and class goals; a physical environment
that encourages interaction; students skilled in cooperating with and teaching
peers; and structured cooperative activities that meet learning outcomes or objectives.

More recent proponents of cooperative learning maintain advantages for both
learners and instructors. Students experience improved self-esteem, greater understanding of the content area, improved grades, higher motivation to learn,
and improved peer relationships. Cooperative learning has been shown to be

effective with varying populations of learners, even those who have been labeled as learning disabled.* Teachers receive satisfaction from seeing students become independent learners, increased student participation, fewer papers to grade on a daily basis, less individual reteaching by the teacher, and a greater understanding of individual students facilitated by teacher observation during group work.

See John Dewey, *Experience and Education* (1938), for a classical philosophical statement. Recent perspectives include Christi Fenton, "Cooperative Learning: A View from the Inside" (1992); Mark Goor and John Schwenn, "Accommodating Diversity and Disability with Cooperative Learning" (1993); David Johnson, Roger Johnson, Edythe Holubec, and Patricia Roy, *Circles of Learning: Cooperation in the Classroom* (1984); Spencer Kagan, *Cooperative Learning* (1992); and Patricia E. Ragan, "Cooperative Learning Can Work in Residential Care Settings" (1993).

Kathleen Strickland

CORPORAL PUNISHMENT. See CLASSROOM DISCIPLINE AND MANAGEMENT; *INGRAHAM V. WRIGHT.*

COUNCIL ON BASIC EDUCATION. See ESSENTIALISM.

COUNTRY LIFE MOVEMENT evolved out of the work of a commission appointed by President Theodore Roosevelt in 1908. The task of the commission was to find solutions to what Roosevelt and leading intellectuals referred to as the "rural problem," although that problem was never clearly defined. Most historians agree, however, that the commissioners, together with their leader, Cornell professor Liberty Hyde Bailey,* were most concerned with the cityward migration of talented rural youth, a phenomenon already identified in the burgeoning social science literature and popularized by leading novelists like Hamlin Garland and Herbert Quick.

The tumultuous decade of the 1890s served as the backdrop for the country life movement. Violent clashes between labor and capital resulted in vigorous concern for the countryside because Bailey, Roosevelt, and many others considered a strong farmer class to be a necessary social buffer. The high rates of immigration from southern and eastern Europe also added to the concern for the countryside, for many felt that it was crucial to maintain a pure, appropriately Anglo-Saxon farm population. If Garland was on target when he depicted the best and brightest farm youth heading down "main-travelled roads" to the nation's cities, this could only result in an undesirable intermingling with the "lower types," to use contemporary parlance. Finally, Lincoln Steffens and other muckraking journalists called attention to the nation's growing urban slums, another reason, in the minds of many, to check the cityward migration of rural youth.

The commission issued a nationwide twelve-question survey, to which it received 115,000 responses. Additionally, the commissioners held community forums in thirty towns across the country, ostensibly to seek input on how they might work at improving conditions in the countryside. The country life movement is generally credited with providing the impetus for many lasting reforms, such as agricultural extension, postal savings banks, expansion of rural free delivery, 4-H clubs, and others. Most of the efforts of the commissioners focused on the reform of rural education; however, they were not particularly successful. Their most strenuous schooling prescriptions called for two "reforms": (1) to instill in rural yourth, through curricular change, a sense of dignity in rural living and an intellectual attachment to the countryside; and (2) to reorganize schools at the township level in an effort to equalize educational circumstances and provide the best education possible. These reforms failed to stem powerful forces, like the use of automobiles and tractors in the countryside, that seemingly worked toward rural depopulation. Whatever momentum the movement had at the outbreak of World War I in Europe disappeared before the war ended.

For references, see BAILEY, LIBERTY HYDE.

Paul Theobald

COUNTS, GEORGE SYLVESTER (December 9, 1889–November 10, 1974), a progressive educator (see PROGRESSIVE EDUCATION), in *Dare the School Build a New Social Order?* articulated social reconstructionism's* early themes.

Born and raised in Baldwin, Kansas, Counts graduated from high school in 1907. He earned an A.B. degree from Baker University in 1911, with a major in classical studies, and became a high school principal in Peabody, Kansas, from 1912 to 1913. He received a Ph.D. in education in 1916 from the University of Chicago, where his advisor was Charles H. Judd and where he studied sociology with Albion Small. Counts taught at Delaware College (1916–1917), Harris College in St. Louis, Missouri (1918–1919), Yale University (1920–1926), University of Chicago (1926–1927), Teachers College, Columbia University (1927–1956), University of Pittsburgh (1959), Michigan State University (1960), and Southern Illinois University (1962–1971).

His scholarly works on American and Soviet education emphasized relationships between schooling and society. His books on American education include: *The Selective Character of American Secondary Education* (1922); *Principles of Education* (1924); *The Social Composition of Boards of Education* (1927); *Dare the School Build a New Social Order?* (1932); *The Social Foundations of Education* (1934); *Education and American Civilization* (1952); *Decision-Making and American Values in School Administration* (1954); *Education and Human Freedom in the Age of Technology* (1958); and *Education and Foundations of Human Freedom* (1962). His interpretation positioned education in the historical, social, political, and economic contexts of American life. Counts's books on Soviet education include *The Soviet Challenge to America* (1931); *I Want to Be like Stalin* (1947); *The Country of the Blind: The Soviet System of Mind Control*, with Nucia Lodge (1949); *American Education through the Soviet Looking Glass* (1951); *The Challenge of Soviet Education* (1957); and *Khru-*

shchev and the Central Committee Speak on Education (1959). His interpretation of Soviet education changed from sympathetic commentary in the 1930s to criticism of that system's totalitarianism by the 1950s. Counts was also editor of the *Social Frontier*, research director of the Commission of the American Historical Association on the *Social Studies* (1931–1934), and member of the Educational Policies Commission of the National Education Association* (1936–1942). He was active in the Progressive Education Association,* president of the American Federation of Teachers* (1939–1942), and a member of the Educational Mission to Japan in 1946.

A political activist, Counts was New York State chair of the American Labor Party (1942–1944), and a founder of the Liberal Party, serving as chair (1954–1959) and as its candidate for senator in New York in 1952.

For the Counts Papers, see Special Collections, Morris Library, Southern Illinois University at Carbondale. Counts also wrote "A Humble Autobiography" (1971). Biographies include Lawrence J. Dennis and William E. Eaton, *George S. Counts: Educator for a New Age* (1980); Gerald L. Gutek, *The Educational Theory of George S. Counts* (1970); Gerald L. Gutek, "George Sylvester Counts (1889–1974): A Biographical Memoir" (1976); and Gerald L. Gutek, *George S. Counts and American Civilization: The Educator as Social Theorist* (1984).

Gerald L. Gutek

CRARY, ISAAC (October 2, 1804–May 8, 1854), was the architect of Michigan's public school* system. Born in Preston, Connecticut, he was educated at Bacon Academy, Colchester, and Washington (now Trinity) College, Hartford. He practiced law for two years and assisted G. D. Prentice in editing the *New England Weekly Review*. In 1832, Crary settled in Marshall, Michigan, where he commenced his law practice and edited the *Marshall Expounder*. He became a brigadier general in the Michigan militia, was a delegate to the U.S. Congress from the Territory of Michigan, and from 1837 to 1841 served as the state of Michigan's first representative to Congress.

Crary participated in the convention that drafted that state's first constitution, chaired the education committee, and wrote Article IX concerning education. He was influenced by Victor Cousin's report on the Prussian education system, and his committee's report contained a feature not found in any previous state constitution: a superintendent of public instruction. The Michigan system of schooling he crafted proved to be unique, since a separate branch of state government administered education, a state officer supervised the whole system, and the state, rather than townships, received federal land grants for school purposes.

Crary was elected to the Michigan State House of Representatives in 1842 and became speaker in 1846. He helped to found the University of Michigan and served as a regent from 1837 to 1844. As president of the State Board of Education, in 1852 he pronounced the formal dedication of the Michigan State Normal School (see NORMAL SCHOOLS) and prayed that Michigan's future teachers would "become ministering angels to the wants and necessities of humanity."

Crary's Papers and Photography Collection are housed at the Bentley Historical Library, University of Michigan. Also refer to Alan S. Brown, "The Northwest Ordinance and Michigan Education" (1987); Thomas McIntyre Cooley, *Michigan: A History of Governments* (1889); Floyd R. Dain, *Education in the Wilderness* (1968); and Willis F. Dunbar, *The Michigan Record in Higher Education* (1963). Finally, see the sources for PIERCE, JOHN DAVIS.

Laura Docter Thornburg

CUBBERLEY, ELLWOOD PATTERSON (June 6, 1868–September 15, 1941), was a pioneer professor of educational administration,* dean of the school of education at Stanford University, and author-editor of best-selling textbooks. He became one of the most influential teacher educators of his era. Cubberley used principles of science and business to define the knowledge base for teacher education and reinforce the bureaucratic hierarchy of public schools.

Born in Andrews, Indiana, Cubberley attended local schools and graduated from Indiana University in 1891. He quickly moved up the academic ladder, passing through country school teaching and college teaching on his way to the presidency of Vincennes University and the superintendency of the San Diego public schools. He received a doctorate from Teachers College, Columbia University, in 1905. During his long career at Stanford (1898–1933), Cubberley transformed a small junior college department into one of the nation's most prestigious university schools of education, the western center of the new science of education developed by psychologist Edward L. Thorndike.* Cubberley brought together at Stanford a group of faculty members with different specializations but a common belief in prescriptive behavioral science. Among the 103 volumes Cubberley edited for Houghton Mifflin's Riverside Textbooks in Education were seven books by Lewis M. Terman,* who devised the Stanford-Binet Intelligence (IQ) Test,* as well as works by other Stanford faculty members. Cubberley contributed *Public School Administration* (1916), *Public Education in the United States* (1919), and other textbooks on educational history and administration. His Riverside series sold more than 3 million copies and shaped the curriculum of teacher education programs throughout the nation. The science of education he promoted paralleled Frederick W. Taylor's science of management. Cubberley encouraged public school administrators to think of themselves as educational executives, asserting that they, like corporate managers, deserved a great deal of autonomy. Teachers, in contrast, held little autonomy in his scheme. Citing research to justify the popular belief that "school men" were naturals for administrative positions, Cubberley viewed the members of America's rapidly feminizing teaching force as subordinates who needed detailed guidelines and close supervision. Although Cubberley brought a sense of professionalism to educational administration, he relegated teachers to the bottom of the educational hierarchy.

A small collection of Cubberley's papers is housed in the Special Collections
Department, Stanford University Library. Leading biographies include Jesse B.
Sears and Adin D. Henderson, *Cubberley of Stanford and His Contribution to
American Education* (1957), and Joseph W. Newman, "Ellwood P. Cubberley:
Architect of the New Educational Hierarchy" (1992). For his influence on
school administration, see Raymond E. Callahan, *Education and the Cult of
Efficiency: A Study of the Social Forces That Have Shaped the Administration
of the Public Schools* (1962).

Joseph W. Newman

CURRY, JABEZ LAMAR MONROE (June 5, 1825–February 12, 1903), was
a southern educational reformer whose zeal for universal education in the South
reflected the spirit and convictions of Horace Mann.* Born a Georgian, Curry
moved with his family to Alabama at age thirteen. A graduate of the University
of Georgia and Harvard Law School, Curry served his adopted state, his region,
and the United States as a legislator, military officer, ambassador, and, most
significantly, as an enthusiastic champion of public education. He was president
of Howard College in Alabama (1865–1868) and professor of English at the
University of Richmond (1868–1881).

Curry was elected General Agent of the Peabody Fund* in 1881. During his
tenure, state normal schools* were established for both races in twelve southern
states, town and city systems of graded schools took root throughout the South,
and state legislatures began to assume greater responsibility for public education.
In 1890, Curry accepted the duties of agent of the Slater Fund* and in 1899
was elected president of the Capon Springs conference out of which grew the
Southern Education Board* in 1901. His adult life was devoted to the cause of
energizing public opinion on behalf of better schools for all the children of the
South. Among his memorials are a marble statue in the Hall of Statuary in the
Capitol in Washington and the naming of the Curry School of Education at the
University of Virginia.

The largest collection of Curry's papers are housed at the Library of Congress
and in the State Department of Archives and History in Montgomery, Alabama.
A smaller collection is in the library of the Virginia Baptist Historical Society
at the University of Richmond. Some Curry correspondence is in the Rutherford
B. Hayes collection in the Hayes Memorial Library in Fremont, Ohio. Additional
important materials are his reports collected in the *Proceedings* of the trustees
of the Peabody and Slater Funds. A bibliography of his most significant
publications until 1896 is in Thomas McAdory Owen, "A Bibliography of Alabama" (1898). An excellent biography and guide to sources is Jessie Pearl
Rice, *J.L.M. Curry: Southerner, Statesman and Educator* (1949). The memorial
biography by Edwin A. Alderman and Armisted C. Gordon, *J.L.M. Curry—A
Biography* (1911), is also useful.

Jennings L. Wagoner, Jr.

D

DAME SCHOOLS. In colonial New England, the rudiments of reading, writing, and ciphering were taught to young neighborhood children by a woman (a dame) in her own house. Boys were expected to be able to read before attending the village schools at about the age of seven, and girls were not expected to have additional education. Although some children were taught at home by parents or governesses, many families relied upon dame school teachers, usually widows or spinsters. The fragmentary records that are available to contemporary researchers indicate that these teachers had probably received no formal education and that little alteration was made of the home living area to accommodate the students. Household duties and income-producing activities like weaving were often carried on while children were reciting rote lessons. Both boys and girls learned knitting and sewing. Inexpensive hornbooks,* single sheets of paper attached to a wooden paddle and protected by thin sheets of cow horn, provided rudimentary instruction in letters and numbers. Essential lessons in the Scriptures were provided by the Bible and the rhyming *New England Primer.**

Parents paid fees of a few pennies or with bartered produce. By the mid-1600s, some cities and towns began paying small salaries. Following the Revolution, both salaries and public control increased, with Massachusetts requiring licensing of dame schools teachers in 1789. These informal classes dwindled away when public primary schools for both boys and girls were introduced in the early 1800s (see COMMON SCHOOLS). Although some dame school teachers were hired to teach the youngest children their alphabet and numbers, only men were considered capable of formal teaching for older children.

For general background information, see Alice M. Earle, *Child Life in Colonial Days* (1899; 1975); Nancy Hewett, *Women, Families, and Communities* (1990); and Andrea Wyman, ''The Earliest Early Childhood Teachers: Women Teachers of America's Dame Schools'' (1995).

Dorothy W. Hewes

DE GARMO, CHARLES (January 17, 1849–May 14, 1934), introduced and popularized Johann Friedrich Herbart's philosophy and pedagogy in the United States (see HERBARTARIAN MOVEMENT). A leading American Herbartian, he was noted for his emphasis on moral education and systematization of instruction.

Born in Muckwonago, Wisconsin, De Garmo graduated from Illinois State Normal University in 1873 and began his professional career as principal in the public schools in Naples, Illinois, from 1873 to 1876. He served as assistant training teacher (1876–1883) and professor of modern languages (1886–1890) at Illinois State Normal University. He received his Ph.D. degree from the University of Halle, Germany, in 1886. While in Germany, he studied Herbart's educational philosophy. He then was professor of psychology at the University of Illinois (1890–1891), president of Swarthmore College (1891–1898), and professor of the science and art of education at Cornell University (1898–1914).

De Garmo's books included *Essentials of Method* (1890); a translation of G. S. Lindner's *Manual of Empirical Psychology* (1890); *English Language Series* (1898); *Herbart and the Herbartians* (1898); *Interest and Education* (1902); *Principles of Secondary Education* (1907); and *Aesthetic Education* (1913). He was coauthor with Leon L. Winslow of *Essentials of Design in the Industrial Arts* (1923). De Garmo's article, "The Herbartian System of Pedagogics," in *The Educational Review* (1891) significantly influenced the introduction of Herbart's philosophy to Americans. In 1895, De Garmo and Charles and Frank McMurry organized the National Herbart Society.

De Garmo served as president of the Normal Department of the National Education Association* (1891), as a member of the Executive Committee of the National Herbartian Society for the Scientific Study of Teaching (1895), and as first president of the Society of Professors of Education (in 1902 and again in 1908); he was also a member of the Executive Committee of the National Society for the Scientific Study of Education* (1905).

For background on Herbartian theory, see Harold B. Dunkel, *Herbart and Education* (1969) and Harold B. Dunkel, *Herbart and Herbartianism* (1970).

Gerald L. Gutek

DE LIMA, AGNES (August 5, 1887–November 27, 1974) was a progressive educator, journalist, socialist, and feminist who wrote one of the most widely read books about progressive education*: *Our Enemy the Child* (1925). She became politically active at Vassar, from which she graduated in 1908. She lived in a settlement house* in New York City, where she worked for various progressive organizations, including the Bureau of Municipal Research, the Russell Sage Foundation, the Women's Municipal League, and the Public Education Association. After Randolph Bourne's* death in 1918, de Lima assumed part of his role as an education writer for *The New Republic*. Between 1924 and 1925, she wrote for *The New Republic* and *The Nation* a series of articles she then published as *Our Enemy the Child* (1925); it is widely cited as one of the few sources that describe actual life in progressive classrooms. An insightful observer, she was probably the first writer to identify the three strands of progressive education later described by Lawrence A. Cremin, in *The Transfor-mation of the School* (1961), as "scientists, sentimentalists, and radicals." De Lima's other influential book was *The Little Red Schoolhouse* (1942), for which John Dewey* wrote an admiring introduction. This book, written with the school staff, gave a clear picture of the inner workings of a progressive school. De Lima's association with progressive education continued during the 1930s and 1940s when she worked as a publicist for the New School for Social Research, the leading progressive experiment in higher education.

De Lima's papers are in the Special Collections at Vassar College; Alvin Saunders Johnson Collection, Sterling Memorial Library, Yale University; Special Collections, Milbank Memorial Library, Teachers College, Columbia University; Fogelman Library, New School for Social Research; and in the possession of James Wallace, who is writing de Lima's biography. His chapter on de Lima in *Liberal Journalism and American Education, 1914–1941* (1991) places her in the context of political and educational progressivism; the notes to that chapter identify other sources.

James M. Wallace

DEAF EDUCATION. The education of most American deaf children has oc-curred outside the context of the public school system. Residential schools, governed either by autonomous boards or by state agencies for prisons and hospitals, were the placement of choice for deaf pupils for nearly 200 years.

American deaf education formally began in the second decade of the nine-teenth century. In 1815 John Braidwood, whose family operated private deaf schools in Scotland and England, opened a small oral school for deaf students on a plantation near Richmond, Virginia. Braidwood's school failed in 1817, for Braidwood and his sponsor, William Bolling, had neglected to develop a base of political and financial support. In the same year, however, the American School for the Deaf (ASD) opened in Hartford, Connecticut, founded by Mason Cogswell, Thomas Hopkins Gallaudet,* and Laurent Clerc.*

ASD established patterns that dominated American deaf education into the late nineteenth century. These included the placement of deaf pupils in publicly supported residential institutions that used sign language for instructional pur-poses, employed primarily male deaf and hearing teachers, emphasized voca-tional training (see VOCATIONAL EDUCATION), and generally did not accept pupils younger than ten years of age. Schools on the ASD model proliferated by midcentury, and in 1864 the world's first college for deaf students opened in Washington, D.C. Today's Gallaudet University, the college fit the ASD mold: Only deaf students attended; it was residential and privately owned but publicly supported; and sign language was the core medium of instruction.

The relative homogeneity of early American deaf education gave way to bitter acrimony in the late nineteenth century as the major issues confronting deaf education, then and today, were debated. Reformers, led by Alexander Graham Bell, insisted that the true purpose of deaf education was socialization of deviants. Bell agreed that sign language was adequate for intellectual development and for teaching vocational skills, but he argued that its use prevented deaf children from learning to speak, speechread, and master the use of English. The result, reformers said, was that deaf people were becoming a class apart in American society, forming their own clubs and churches, launching their own newspapers, and marrying each other, raising eugenic fears.

Although there was no evidence that sign language use interfered with the learning of speech, speechreading, or English, and despite the opposition of deaf adults, American deaf education underwent radical changes in the late nineteenth and early twentieth centuries. The first pure oral schools, those that forbid use of formal signs or of a fingerspelled alphabet, opened in New York and Massachusetts in 1867. Under public pressure, residential schools began teaching speech, then commenced instruction by means of speech, and finally, by the 1920s, had nearly eliminated instruction in sign language except for a minority of students deemed intellectually deficient. Deaf teachers were fired. Younger students were admitted, and the teaching force, once entirely male, was overwhelmingly female by the twentieth century. Some states, particularly Wisconsin, went one step farther and attempted to educate deaf children in classrooms with hearing children, rather than among other deaf children in residential institutions.

The new orthodoxy of speech and speechreading–based instruction predominated in deaf education (except at Gallaudet College) from about 1900 until the late 1960s. Then growing tolerance of cultural diversity, awareness of minority rights, and disappointment with the failure of deaf students to achieve academically led to a reintroduction of sign language in nearly all deaf classrooms. By the 1980s, communication debates had shifted focus from oral versus manual methods to the merits of various kinds of signed language.

The communication skills necessary to teach deaf children and the low incidence of deafness in the general population, as well as limited expectations for those who were deaf, largely explain the appeal of separate residential institutions. Urbanization, the legal and financial inducements of the Education of All Handicapped Children Act of 1975 (see SPECIAL EDUCATION), new attitudes toward disability, and the availability of sign language interpreters, however, have changed this situation. By the mid-1990s, about 70 percent of all deaf children attended classes with their hearing peers. Nevertheless, the issues that have most animated discussions of deaf education have been distinct from those that confront public schools.

The most persistent of these focuses on communication: What is the best medium of instruction for deaf pupils? Proposed answers usually take the form of an endorsement of either a speech and speechreading–based approach (termed oralism) or a sign language–based approach (termed manualism), but considerable variations exist within these overall categories. Manualism, for example, can mean many things, from an English-based invented sign system that uses one sign for each word in English, adds English grammatical markers to signs, follows English word order, and is accompanied by spoken or mouthed English words, to American Sign Language (ASL). ASL substitutes conceptual equivalence for a word-for-word translation of English, uses the signed language's natural grammatical markers, does not follow English word order, and cannot be employed simultaneously with spoken or mouthed English.

In addition to the persistence of the communication issue, four other factors have characterized the history of American deaf education and help explain why communication questions remained unanswered. First, deaf education's primary function is contentious. The relative value of socialization into an English-speaking culture versus the development of intellectual skills and acquisition of knowledge has not been settled. Second, few educational decisions have been research-driven. Communications arguments and policy decisions have relied on anecdotes and reasoning from analogies rather than research studies. Third, although deaf Americans have made huge strides professionally and socially, deaf education is still not successful by the usual measures. Studies demonstrate consistently that most deaf children do not achieve skills in English or mathematics commensurate with their years of schooling or their intellectual ability. Finally, despite headway in the administration of residential schools and Gallaudet University since the 1980s, deaf education is still dominated by hearing people, as it always has been.

The future of deaf education in America is ambiguous. Legal and budgetary pressure and the ideology of inclusion have combined to reduce enrollment at residential institutions, and proponents of cochlear implants and gene therapy argue that deafness as a human condition will be eliminated in the future. Yet most leaders of the deaf community are skeptical about these trends and claims. Placement of deaf students in hearing classrooms with an interpreter to mediate between the deaf child and the teacher and other pupils creates an artificial situation and denies deaf students the social and intellectual stimulation of informal interaction with peers, teachers, and school staff. Deaf children in this environment may go through school without meeting a deaf adult and without being exposed to the equality and acceptance offered by deaf culture and the deaf community. Technology and medicine have long claimed to end deafness, yet they have not done so. Deaf educators and community leaders believe it is better to assume that signed visual communication will continue to characterize deaf education and that research and policy should be driven by attempts to make this communication more effective rather than to eliminate it (also, refer to *HENDRICK HUDSON CENTRAL SCHOOL DISTRICT V. ROWLEY*).

The most important sources of documentation for the early history of American deaf education are the articles and statistics published in the *American Annals of the Deaf*, particularly from its inception in 1847 until about 1920. An excellent general introduction to deaf education is Donald F. Moores, *Educating the Deaf: Psychology, Principles, and Practices* (1996). For historical studies of the nineteenth century, see Harlan Lane, *When the Mind Hears: A History of the Deaf* (1984); Phyllis Klein Valentine, ''American Asylum for the Deaf:

A First Experiment in Education, 1817–1880'' (1993); and John Vickrey Van Cleve and Barry A. Crouch, *A Place of Their Own: Creating the Deaf Community in America* (1989). The historical and social context of the communications debates are treated most carefully in Richard Winefield, *Never the Twain Shall Meet: Bell, Gallaudet, and the Communications Debate* (1987), and particularly Douglas C. Baynton, *Forbidden Signs: American Culture and the Campaign against American Sign Language* (1996). Deaf education in the twentieth century has been little examined, but a good starting point is Robert M. Buchanan, ''Deaf Students and Workers in the United States: 1800–1950'' (1995). For a provocative, if ultimately unconvincing, interpretation of American deaf education, see Harlan Lane, *The Mask of Benevolence: Disabling the Deaf Community* (1992).

John Vickrey Van Cleve

DEWEY, JOHN (October 20, 1859–June 1, 1952), one of America's preeminent philosophers, made significant contributions to such areas as social philosophy, logic, aesthetics, social psychology, and ethics; but in an autobiographical essay, he asserted that it is in his work on education, particularly as expressed in *Democracy and Education* (1916), that his philosophy is ''most fully expounded.'' Dewey's identification with philosophy of education is so strong that his name has become virtually synonymous with American education in general and with the progressive education* movement in particular. However, so much of Dewey's philosophy of education has been reduced to slogans and his work so poorly understood that his actual influence on American education is marginal at best. Nevertheless, his powerful arguments about the role of education in a democracy and his remarkable insights into the nature of teaching and learning continue to be studied and admired.

Born in Burlington, Vermont, Dewey enrolled at the University of Vermont in 1875. After Dewey graduated, his cousin, who was principal of a high school in Oil City, Pennsylvania, offered him a teaching position. He taught Latin, algebra, and science there for two and a half years before returning to the Burlington area, teaching for a short time in a rural school in Charlotte, Vermont. While in Oil City, Dewey wrote some philosohical articles, and after receiving encouragement from William Torrey Harris,* he decided to pursue his philosophical studies and in 1882 enrolled at Johns Hopkins University. There he came under the influence of George Sylvester Morris, an idealist philosopher, and also studied with G. Stanley Hall,* a rising star in the field of psychology.

Dewey received his Ph.D. in 1884 and accepted an instructorship at the University of Michigan, where he taught philosophy and psychology and was active in the Student Christian Association. He taught at the University of Minnesota for a year beginning in 1888, returning to Michigan as a professor. Taking his first tentative steps in the direction of serious involvement with education, Dewey became a founding member, in 1892, of the National Herbart Society (see HERBARTARIAN MOVEMENT). In 1894, with his reputation as a philosopher growing, Dewey was offered the position of head of the Department of Philosophy, Psychology, and Pedagogy at the University of Chicago, where did his most creative work in pedagogy. In 1896, he established the University of Chicago Laboratory School* as a way to test his ideas in education. The school's curriculum initially reflected a Herbartian influence, but then developed a distinctively Deweyan cast. After he published *School and Society* (1899) as part of an effort to explain the theory behind his school, the fame of the Dewey School, as it became known, grew rapidly.

Dewey's position in curriculum matters is sometimes crudely described as "child-centered," though he was actually trying to achieve a creative synthesis of the child's spontaneous interests and tendencies on the one hand and the refined intellectual resources of the culture on the other. This effort is reflected in *The Child and the Curriculum* (1902). In it, he argues that the apparent dichotomy between the child and the curriculum (i.e., the subjects of study) can be dissolved by seeing each as a form of experience—the spontaneous but often chaotic experience of the child leading eventually to the logically organized and abstracted experience of the human race as embodied in the disciplines of knowledge. At the Laboratory School, Dewey sought to achieve a synthesis in part through the introduction of what he called "occupations." These represented fundamental social activities, such as growing food, raising animals, and building shelters, out of which emerged the knowledge required by the human race to perform those activities successfully and from which emerged the logically organized disciplines. By introducing active occupations into the life of the school, Dewey hoped to engage students in the performance of tasks that required the instrumental use of knowledge, leading children to appreciate the relationship between organized knowledge and the successful accomplishment of human purpose. As children matured, the curriculum would more closely reflect the disciplines of knowledge themselves, a process Dewey was later to call "the progressive organization of subject matter." At the same time, children would be developing their social sense and moral judgment.

Dewey suddenly resigned his position in 1904 in a dispute with Chicago's president, William Rainey Harper, over the running of the Laboratory School. He then accepted a professorship in the Philosophy Department at Columbia University, where he remained until his retirement in 1930. During his Columbia period, he published some of his most widely acclaimed books, including *Essays in Experimental Logic* (1916), *Reconstruction in Philosophy* (1920), *Human Nature and Conduct* (1922), *Experience and Nature* (1929), and *The Quest for Certainty* (1929). He also wrote his magnus opus in education, *Democracy and Education* (1916), in which he sought to define democracy not simply as a political system but as a way of life and undertook to explore what this implied for an education consistent with the nature of democracy. In the case of vocational education,* he tried to redirect its emphasis on "trade education" and "securing technical efficiency," arguing that as typically practiced, vocational education merely becomes an instrument for perpetuating abuses in the industrial order rather than operating to transform it. Always concerned with people's day-to-day experiences, Dewey felt that work was not simply a way of earning a living and sought to explore the possibility of making the workplace a more democratic and fulfilling environment. Finally, during this period, Dewey lectured in Japan (1919) and China (1919–1921) and conducted educational surveys in Turkey (1924), Mexico (1926), and the Soviet Union (1928).

After his retirement from Columbia, Dewey remained active in political and social affairs and maintained a busy writing schedule. His last book on education, *Experience and Education* (1938), represented in part a critique of progressive education. He coauthored his last book, *Knowing and the Known* (1949), with Arthur F. Bentley.

Dewey's papers are stored in the Morris Library at Southern Illinois University-Carbondale, which also hosts the Center for Dewey Studies. Dewey's *Collected Works* in thirty-seven volumes was edited by Jo Ann Boydston. Among the best biographies are Richard Bernstein, *John Dewey* (1966); Neil Coughlin, *Young John Dewey* (1975); and George Dykhuizen, *The Life and Mind of John Dewey* (1973). Three excellent recent studies of Dewey's life and thought are Steven Rockefeller, *John Dewey* (1991); Alan Ryan, *John Dewey and the High Tide of American Liberalism* (1995); and Robert Westbrook, *John Dewey and American Democracy* (1991). An invaluable guide to Dewey's published writing as well as secondary sources about him is Milton Halsey Thomas, *John Dewey* (1962). Jo Ann Boydston and Robert L. Andresen edited and compiled *John Dewey: Checklist of Translations, 1900–1967* (1969); Jo Ann Boydston and Kathleen Poulos edited *A Checklist of Writings about John Dewey* (1974).

Herbert M. Kliebard

DISTRIBUTIVE EDUCATION. See VOCATIONAL EDUCATION.

DISTRICT SCHOOLS generally refers to the small one- and two-room schools that dotted the American countryside until well into the twentieth century. Educational "districts" were created under the auspices of state or territorial legislation dealing with the establishment of free, or partially free, schools. The criteria for the creation of districts varied from state to state, but it often required little more than a petition signed by the majority of the residents in a particular vicinity, asking to be declared an official school district complete with the power to levy a school tax. Once this request was granted, an election was held to determine three school board officers, usually a president, clerk, and treasurer. The board, together with the tax-paying residents of the new district, then began to plan for the construction of a schoolhouse large enough for the children in that new district. Each year the board had to attend to such matters as schoolhouse maintenance, fuel, instructional materials (such as maps and a globe), and hiring the teacher. Supplying textbooks was a pivotal school board duty as early as the 1880s and 1890s in many of the states of the trans-Mississippi west.

Other areas dismissed the call for free textbooks until well into the 1910s and 1920s.

Because of the loose criteria for establishing school districts, they sometimes assumed unusual configurations. As residents moved in and out of the district, these configurations frequently caused hard feelings, since many families found themselves closer to the school in a neighboring district than they were to their own. As a consequence, one of the duties of the county superintendent of schools was to field requests asking if a particular family might leave one school district to become part of another. If the attempt to place a farm in another school district failed, the parents could still petition the neighboring school board asking that their children be admitted as "outside scholars." This circumstance appeared so common that almost every rural school board had to determine a policy stating whether they would admit outside scholars free, with a tuition charge, or not at all (also, refer to OLD-FIELD SCHOOLS).

Refer to David B. Tyack, "The Tribe and the Common School: Community Control in Rural Education" (1972).

Paul Theobald

DOUGLAS COMMISSION. See MASSACHUSETTS COMMISSION ON INDUSTRIAL AND TECHNICAL EDUCATION.

DOUGLASS, FREDERICK (February 14, 1817–February 20, 1895), one of the great nineteenth-century African American leaders, possesses a legacy that continues to inspire African Americans in the arenas of history and education today. He was, among other things, a prominent leader in the abolitionist movement in the 1840s and 1850s, the black and women's suffrage movement in the 1860s, and after 1880 an advocate for the internal migration of blacks in the United States. Douglass throughout his career always opposed the external migration of blacks to Africa and the Caribbean, as he believed that the contributions of African Americans to the founding and development of the United States made them as American as any white person. Indeed, some scholars have argued that Douglass's stance on the contributions of African Americans to the United States was a nineteenth-century precursor to the development of both black history and multicultural education* in the twentieth century.

Douglass's educational philosophy is best understood in his emphasis on literacy in the nineteenth-century African American community. The fact that Douglass, as a young slave, secretly learned how to read and write, since southern laws typically prohibited slave literacy, played a huge role in his advocacy for African American education. This personal struggle with the institution of slavery also led Douglass to realize that, as a result of forced illiteracy, few African Americans, free or enslaved, would be prepared for a post-Emancipation America.

During his final years, Douglass also addressed the issue of segregated school systems, which were being implemented throughout the South from the late

1870s through the end of the nineteenth century. In an 1879 speech in Baltimore, titled "Black Teachers for Black Pupils," he suggested to the African American crowd that their rights to "freedom and equality" were being violated by the city's school board, which had refused to hire qualified African American teachers for the segregated school system. Douglass's speech suggests not that he was against segregation but, rather, that he wished to ensure that a level of equality was maintained within this segregated arrangement; he was perhaps more concerned with preventing African American exclusion from public education than with advocating an integrated educational system (see PUBLIC SCHOOLS). Thus, Douglass's major contribution to education was his determination to ensure the development and success of African American schools on all educational levels, enabling African Americans to achieve a high level of literacy.

See John W. Blassingame and John R. McKivigan, eds., *The Frederick Douglass Papers, Series One: Speeches, Debates, and Interviews, Vols. 1–5* (1979–1985). Douglass's own accounts can be found in *Narrative of the Life of Frederick Douglass, an American Slave, Written by Himself* (1845); *My Bondage and My Freedom* (1855); and *Life and Times of Frederick Douglass: His Early Life as a Slave, His Escape from Bondage, and His Complete History* (1881). Biographies include William L. Andrews, *Critical Essays on Frederick Douglass* (1991); Nathan I. Huggins, *Slave and Citizen: The Life of Frederick Douglass* (1980); Waldo E. Martin, Jr., *The Mind of Frederick Douglass* (1984); Waldo E. Martin, Jr., "Frederick Douglass: Humanist as Race Leader" (1988); and Benjamin Quarles, *Frederick Douglass* (1948).

Donald E. Collins

DROPOUT. This concept has experienced a dramatic transformation over the past century. Grounded in a functionalist worldview and supported by a psychometric ideology, "dropout" was originally a mark to label what was perceived as deviant behavior or a deficient disposition. By the early part of the twentieth century, dropouts were viewed in terms of possessing low IQs, displaying improper moral and ethical codes, lacking family guidance, and engaging in delinquent behavior (see INTELLIGENCE TESTING; JUVENILE DELINQUENCY). Although no official date marks when the term "dropout" was first used, the period between 1890 and 1920 was when education scholars like Leonard Ayres and Edward L. Thorndike* began to address issues of "student elimination." However, dropouts were not seen as a widespread problem, since not until the 1950s did more students begin to graduate than drop out. The 1950s and 1960s mark the era in which the issue of dropouts became a focal point for school officials and education scholars.

By the late 1950s and early 1960s, studies such as S. M. Miller, Betty Saleem, and Herrington Bryce's *School Dropouts* (1964) demonstrated that many dropouts actually possessed high IQs, were discriminated against, and experienced a generally hostile atmosphere in schools. Still couched in a functionalist and positivist framework, the focus of research at this time began to shift from the deviance of the individual to institutional racism, teacher attitudes, and irrelevant curriculum.

Recently, two dominant paradigms to explain the current concern of dropouts have emerged. First, there is a group of thinkers centered around the efforts of Michelle Fine and her work *Framing Dropouts: Notes on the Politics of an Urban High School* (1991). Fine suggests that the issues of dropouts is complex, but the responsibility for the recent rise in the dropout rate is the school system. Students see schooling as irrelevant to their needs and experiences, and teachers and administrators refuse to address issues students face. Fine argues that this atmosphere promotes the silencing of students who then seek out alternative ways to claim their voices.

The second paradigm is the "at-risk" discourse that emerged in the middle of the 1980s. Concerned with economic competitiveness and the global market place proponents of the "at-risk" approach, like former Secretary of Education William Bennett, argue that the best strategy to prevent dropouts is a preemptive move. Educational officials, it is believed, should target "at-risk" school populations that more than likely will drop out for a variety of economic, social, and cultural reasons. Once these groups are targeted preventive programs should be created. Opponents to the "at-risk" approach argue that it is a return to the functionalist worldview that stigmatizes the students and constructs a school that devalues the students.

For a historical perspective, see Sherman Dorn, *Creating the Dropout: An Institutional and Social History of School Failure* (1996). Gary Natriello, ed., *School Dropouts: Patterns and Policies* (1986), provides a fine review of the literature and recent scholarship. Deirdre M. Kelly and Jane Gaskell, *Debating Dropouts: Critical Policy and Research Perspectives on School Leaving* (1996), provides an additional overview. In addition to Miller, Saleem, and Bryce (1964) and Fine (1991), specialized fields within the study of dropouts have recently emerged. Deirdre M. Kelly, *Last Chance High* (1993), focuses on creating alternative schools; Kofi Lomotey, *Going to School: The African-American Experience* (1990), on race and dropouts; Martin Carnoy and Henry Levin, *Schooling and Work in the Democratic State* (1985), on broader economic trends such as the increase of economic inequality; and Gloria Ladson-Billings, *Dreamkeepers* (1994), on innovative curriculum development.

John A. Weaver

DU BOIS, WILLIAM EDWARD BURGHARDT (February 23, 1868–August 27, 1963), considered one of the great African American scholars of the twentieth century, underwent a number of changes in educational philosophy between the turn of the century and the end of the 1930s. At the time of Booker T. Washington's* "Atlanta Compromise" (1895), Du Bois generally supported Washington's program of industrial education.* Four years later, when Du Bois published his classical urban sociological study, *The Philadelphia Negro*, he suggested an educational program similar in nature to Washington's recommendations for African American uplift.

By the time Du Bois published *Souls of Black Folk* (1903), he had begun to diverge from Washington's industrial education philosophy, recommending instead a classical* (or liberal arts) education program for African Americans. Indeed, Du Bois's pivotal polemic was where he first outlined his concept "Talented Tenth," in which the most intellectually talented of the African American community would absorb classical education and utilize that training to uplift black masses. According to some scholars, there were signs even in 1903 that Du Bois's ideas would eventually lend themselves to the notion of cultural pluralism.

This notion did not manifest itself in Du Bois's speeches and writings, though, before the late 1920s and early 1930s. At this point, Du Bois argued that neither industrial nor classical education alone would lead to solving African American problems. Du Bois, at the same time, suggested an educational program that dealt with the "dual consciousness" of African Americans, that is, both their "African" heritage and their "American" heritage, necessary for blacks to address the obstacles of segregation and racial discrimination. Over a forty-year period, Du Bois's educational philosophy moved dramatically toward what is today called multicultural education.*

The W.E.B. Du Bois papers are available at the Library of Congress Manuscript Division (in NAACP Papers); the Moorland-Springarn Research Center, Howard University; the Schomburg Center for Research in Black Culture, New York City Public Library; and the W.E.B Du Bois Institute, Harvard University. Also refer to his autobiography, *The Autobiography of W.E.B. Du Bois: A Soliloquy on Viewing My Life from the Last Decade of Its First Century* (1968). Du Bois's many works include those listed above as well as *The Education of Black People: Ten Critiques, 1906–1960* (1973). A recent biography is by David Levering Lewis, *W.E.B. Du Bois: Biography of a Race, 1868–1919* (1993). Other sources are Frederick D. Dunn, "The Educational Philosophies of Washington, Du Bois, and Houston: Laying the Foundations for Afrocentrism and Multiculturalism" (1993), and August Meier, *Negro Thought in America, 1880–1915: Racial Ideologies in the Life of Booker T. Washington* (1963).

Donald E. Collins

E

EARLY CHILDHOOD EDUCATION. See ASSOCIATION FOR CHILD-HOOD EDUCATION INTERNATIONAL; DAME SCHOOLS; INFANT SCHOOLS; MONTESSORI, MARIA; NATIONAL ASSOCIATION FOR THE EDUCATION OF YOUNG CHILDREN; NURSERY SCHOOLS.

EDUCATIONAL ADMINISTRATION as a profession has been shaped by social and historical forces beyond and within the school setting. The roles of educational administrators and the expectations held for individuals in these roles have evolved as a result of society's changing expectations of schools and students. Educational administrators have shaped their roles as they interacted with these forces within the context of their settings. As a result, role expectations for superintendents as well as supervisors have been and are continuing to be defined.

The state superintendency emerged before school superintendency, with New York naming the first state superintendent in 1821. Early school superintendents were primarily found within urban settings, and by 1870 thirty city school districts had employed superintendents. The county superintendency developed as a result of the county officials' realization that as a governmental body, they were not adequately prepared to perform such duties as the examination of schools or the testing of teachers necessary for determining teaching qualifications. As early as 1854, New York employed assistant superintendents, who aided the superintendent in the examination and inspection of schools. As this role developed, assistant superintendents became specialists in specific areas of school district management.

The role of the principal evolved from its earliest form as head teacher whose primary role involved teaching and managing the schoolhouse. By 1870, increasing numbers of principals no longer taught; rather, they devoted full-time attention to the management of the school and the supervision of teachers. After

1900, as the number of students and schools increased, the principal's power grew. The need to exercise increased supervisory behavior created yet another level of educational administration—the assistant principal. Expectations for the principalship and the assistant principalship shifted, giving both positions more bureaucratic power and authority.

A distinct gender pattern also emerged. The number of female instructors increased throughout the nineteenth century, but the line separating educational administration from teaching was distinct. Without Henry Barnard's* support, Emma Willard* would not have become superintendent of schools in Bensington, Connecticut, in 1840. Other women served as principals of female seminaries,* operating as ministers to promulgate belief in women's roles as nurturers and mothers.

Women were selected as common school* principals in rural areas. Because women were readily availability and would be asked to supervise only other female teachers, coupled with the difficulty of attracting male candidates to the area, rural communities often hired female administrators. Urban school districts usually hired male principals, based on a view that male teachers were natural candidates for administrative positions. Urban districts placed advertisements for principals in educational journals specifying male candidates. Because women were perceived as subordinate to men and incapable of handling male students, they were not considered viable choices for high school principalships. Age-grading* and the debate over coeducation* further perpetuated separateness of opportunity for women in educational administration.

Principals typically operated as clerks, maintaining school records. Women usually served as assistant principals, assuming this recordkeeping responsibility. Women were also appointed as principal of primary departments, with a male principal controlling the entire school building. Another indication of early administrative responsibility was the occurence of females operating as preceptresses to the male principal; they assisted the male principal by assuming teaching responsibilities.

By the late nineteenth and early twentieth centuries, as the number of schools and the school bureaucracy escalated, superintendents assumed greater authority and gave building principals increased responsibility for the supervision of schools. They, in turn, were charged with oversight responsibilities intended to assure the achievement of maximum efficiency in school operations. Age-grading and student classification became important to the smooth operation of the schools, with principals assuming primary authority for coordinating the process and graded courses of study. Educational administration became identified with school management.

As educational administrators began to view themselves as professionals, communities expected that they become more than just managers of schools or educational experts. School superintendents and principals had to operate as public relations experts. At the same time, the distance between the role of the principal and the teacher was growing because of increased emphasis on supervision of teacher performance. The move to professional status resulted in the establishment of national and state organizations for principals during the 1920s.

By 1890, despite the fact that 92 percent of the teachers were female, males continued to dominate principal and superintendent positions. However, the number of women becoming elementary principals began to increase, with 66 percent by the end of the century. Between 1900 and 1930, females became superintendents of small county school districts in rural areas, where few male candidates applied for such low-status positions. Women also assumed leadership roles in state and national educational organizations. Ella Flagg Young,* superintendent of the Chicago schools, was elected president of the National Education Association (NEA)* in 1910.

Between 1930 and 1950, educational administrators placed increasing faith in business principles. Superintendents and principals, as middle management, preserved and expanded the bureaucracy. Training programs presented administrative work as technical and mechanistic; they also emphasized uniformity and standardization. Expectations also changed for school administrators. As the progressive movement (see PROGRESSIVE EDUCATION) expanded with its demands that schools become examples of "Democracy in Action," educational administrators were expected to be responsive to the needs of societies and families, provide firsthand learning experiences for students by using the community as laboratory, construct coordinated, integrated curricula, and provide supervision that supported changed teaching strategies. As a result, the roles of educational administrators, particularly the principal, grew beyond that of a business executive to include that of a social agent who practiced democratic administration.

Educational administration established itself as a discipline during the 1950s. Colleges of education hosted administrative degree and certification programs, dictated by state laws. Without a unique knowledge base, programs borrowed theory and research from applied behavioral sciences. The emphasis in administrative thinking shifted from duty analysis to the examination of superior-subordinate relationships, leadership theories, and administrative behavior. Administrators recognized that leadership should be an element of their roles, particularly community leadership, which created broader relationships between the school and its setting. Administrators also adopted greater "professionalization," with the break of the National Association of Secondary School Principals and the American Association of School Administrators from the NEA symbolizing this trend.

The concept of instructional leadership extended the view of educational administration in the 1970s. Research illustrated that instructional leaders attended to the learning needs of students and served as stewards of resources, a process that was critical for assuring school accountability for student performance. The importance of the role educational administrators could play in implementing educational policies and instituting change became clearer. Administrators had to take more humanistic and socially relevant action in order to ensure that the schools achieved the expectations held by the public. With dwindling student populations, more numerous court rulings, the introduction of state-mandated testing, and increased costs, accountability demands began to push administrators to devise educational programs that could be clearly evaluated. Schools and schooling became political footballs as a result of community access to accountability information (see ACCOUNTABILITY MOVEMENT). As a result, administrators again extended their roles and became politicians.

Since the beginning of the twentieth century, the majority of female educational administrators became elementary principals. As school districts became multileveled bureaucracies after 1930, women began to abandon that position for supervisory positions focused on curriculum programing. Although inroads have been made in the number of females entering educational administration positions, males continue to hold the majority of positions as superintendent, assistant superintendent, and high school principal. The fastest growth area in educational administration for women has been middle school–junior high* principalships.

Educational administrators in the 1990s faced dramatic and multiple changes driven by state mandates for educational reform that included "high stakes" accountability. They could no longer be expected to be only school managers; instead, they were to act as leaders who could deal with constant change and diversity. They became transformational leaders, supporting the development of learning communities. Administrators operated as organizational architects, executive directors, social architects, and moral agents as they managed complexity, solved ambiguous problems in unstable environments, and ethically made sense of challenging problems.

Refer to some original administrative textbooks, such as Elmer E. Brown, *The Making of Our Middle Schools* (1905); Ellwood P. Cubberley,* *Public School Administration* (1916); and Paul R. Pierce, *The Origin and Development of the Public School Principalship* (1935). Lynn G. Beck and Joseph Murphy, *Understanding the Principalship: Metaphorical Themes, 1920s–1990s* (1993), and J. Glanz, *Bureaucracy and Professionalism: The Evolution of Public School Supervision* (1991), supply a broad historical development of school administrators. Raymond E. Callahan, *Education and the Cult of Efficiency: A Study of the Social Forces That Have Shaped the Administration of the Public Schools* (1962), provides a classic and critical historical treatment; in contrast, William J. Reese, *The Origins of the American High School* (1995), places administrative development in a secondary context. Charol Shakeshaft, *Women in Educational Administration* (1989); David B. Tyack and Elisabeth Hansot, *Learning Together: A History of Coeducation in American Public Schools* (1990); and David B. Tyack and Elisabeth Hansot, *Managers of Virtue: Public School Leadership in America, 1820–1890* (1982), provide a general background of gender issues. More contemporary administrative pieces include Daniel E. Griffiths, Robert T.

Stout, and Patricia B. Forsyth, eds., *Leaders for America's Schools* (1988), and Phillip Hallinger, Keith Leithwood, and Joseph Murphy, eds., *Cognitive Perspectives on Educational Leadership* (1993).

Reene A. Alley

EDUCATIONAL OBJECTIVES. See BLOOM, BENJAMIN.

EDUCATIONAL TECHNOLOGY can be traced back to the Ancient Romans and their use of wax tablets and styluses for writing. In the Middle Ages, stained-glass windows provided viewers with visual instruction, as did illuminated manuscripts. During the Renaissance and early modern period illustrated instructional texts came into widespread use. Of particular note is John Amos Comenius's *Orbis Sensualium Pictus* (1659). Combining texts in Latin and various vernacular languages with highly detailed pictures, Comenius's work clearly had an important influence on early textbooks such as *The New England Primer.**

The introduction of educational manipulables seems to have corresponded with the modern discovery of childhood. In 1692, the English philosopher John Locke published *Some Thoughts on Education*, in which he described a set of simple alphabet dice intended to help children learn words. Educational devices of this type did not come into widespread use in England and Germany until the first half of the nineteenth century. In 1825, John Ayerton Paris developed the first scientific toy, the *thaumatrope* (meaning "wonder turner" in Greek), which demonstrated the phenomenon of the persistence of vision. The *thaumatrope*, along with other scientific toys such as *zoetropes, phatascopkes, phenektascopes*, and *kaleidoscopes*, became part of a tradition of "philosophical toys," which played an important role in popularizing scientific principles for the masses. Probably the most well known scientific toy was *The Magic Lantern*, which was a primitive slide projection system.

After the blackboard, which was probably first used in the United States in the 1820s, the most important innovation in educational technology that was adopted and used in American schools were the German kindergarten* educator Frederick Froebel's* *Gifts* and *Occupations*. These consisted of twenty educational toys and exercises that focused on areas such as shape discrimination, structured block building, paper weaving, and construction of skeletal and structural forms. A closely related system of educational manipulables was developed by the Italian physician Maria Montessori* at the beginning of the twentieth century.

Examples of different educational technologies can be seen in architectural and pattern books published in the nineteenth century. Henry Barnard* in his 1848 book *School Architecture*, for example, includes extensive illustration of different learning devices ranging from geographical globes to counting boards and blackboards.

Increasingly, new scientific discoveries brought with them new educational technologies. The introduction of the phonograph saw its application and use in schools around the turn of the century—its first large-scale demonstration being at the 1893 World's Columbian Exposition in Chicago. At the 1904 Louisiana Purchase Exposition in St. Louis, materials left over from foreign exhibits at the fair were purchased by the St. Louis school system to create an extensive educational museum, which included not only hands-on materials but also collections of lantern slides that could be sent to individual schools (see INTERNATIONAL EXPOSITIONS). The Educational Museum of the St. Louis public schools is widely considered to be the first audiovisual program established in conjunction with a school system in the United States (also, refer to CHILDREN'S MUSEUMS).

The development of audiovisual programs like that of the St. Louis public schools, complimented the efforts of theorists like John Dewey* who called for hands-on education and the creation of school museums. Films, by bringing the world to the child, were seen as part of this movement. In 1913, Thomas Edison made clear the perceived promise of film for learning when he explained that "scholars will soon be instructed through the eyes. It is possible to touch every branch of human knowledge with the motion picture."

In fact, educational technologies like film and in turn radio and television have largely failed to meet much of their promise for the schools. Historian Larry Cuban argues that the educational technologies teachers have most consistently used—chalkboards and textbooks—have been easy to use, reliable, and responsive to teacher needs. Whether film, radio, television or computers, technologies fail because teachers are inadequately trained to make effective use of them in their instructional strategies, because they are expensive, and because they are often unreliable.

Emerging educational technologies such as hypermedia and the Internet have the potential to radically redefine educational delivery systems in the future. Their potential as a shaping force in education, by providing virtually universal access to information, represents a revolution comparable to the introduction of the printed book during the early Renaissance. Whether or not this will indeed be the case will depend upon how these new educational technologies are adapted and used by teachers.

For an excellent overview of technology and its impact on teachers in the twentieth century, see Larry Cuban, *Teachers and Machines: The Classroom Use of Technology since 1920* (1986). Background on educational technologies such as blocks can be found in Eugene F. Provenzo, Jr., and Arlene Brett, *The Complete Block Book* (1983). The origins of the Educational Museum of the St. Louis Public Schools is detailed in Eugene F. Provenzo, Jr., *Culture as Curriculum: Education and the International Expositions, 1876–1904* (in press).

Eugene F. Provenzo, Jr.

EIGHT-YEAR STUDY. This thirty-school study constituted the activities of the Commission on the Relation of School and College of the Progressive Education Association (PEA).* By the late 1920s, the PEA recognized that only one out of six high school* students continued to college, yet conventional college preparation still dominated the basic course of study at the high school level. At the 1930 PEA meeting, members wanted to address the needs of non-college-bound high school students, and they formed the Commission on the Relation of School and College to foster close, working relationships between school and college in order to foster secondary "reconstruction" and "experimentation."

The Commission project selected approximately thirty schools that wished to revise their secondary curriculum. The final list included ten public schools, six university laboratory schools,* and thirteen private schools.* The selection process balanced public and private, as well as urban and rural, with large and small schools. The participating schools had already, or were about to, become some of the most progressive schools in the country, including Denver's public high schools, Chicago's Francis W. Parker School (see PARKER, FRANCIS W.), New York's Lincoln School, Ohio State's University Laboratory School, Des Moines's Theodore Roosevelt High School, and Tulsa's Central High School.

After three years of planning, each school developed its own curricular program. The three general types of curricular structures included a broad-fields course, core curriculum based on social demands, and core curriculum based on adolescent needs. An Evaluation Staff was formed in 1934, and curriculum associates began visiting and working with the schools' staffs in 1936. The Commission designed a follow-up study and selected 1,475 students (30–40 from each school) who had been admitted to college beginning in 1936. They matched these with graduates from traditional secondary school programs and evaluated the pairs as they proceeded through college. These groups of students appeared comparable in terms of educational background and family circumstances. The work officially closed in 1942 with a five-volume report.

To correct a general misconception, the follow-up design was not the sole purpose of the Commission's project. Perhaps most important, the thirty-school study displayed innovative and creative methods of testing, student advisement, instruction, administration, and staff development as well as curriculum design. The study also concluded that graduates from these thirty experimental schools did not experience any impairment in their college preparation. In spite of criticisms aimed at the research design, the thirty-school study proved, beyond a doubt, that many different forms of secondary curricular design can ensure college success. In fact, students from the most experimental schools earned markedly higher achievement rates than their traditionally and progressively prepared counterparts. Fate obscured what might still be considered one of the most important educational experiments in American education, since the report was released two months after the United States entered World War II. The Eight-Year Study continues to be legendary for the list of individuals who participated in the project—Ralph Tyler,* Hilda Taba,* James Michener, Paul Dietrich, Bruno Bettleheim, and Robert Havighurst, to name just a few.

The Commission's 1942 report, "Adventure in American Education," included five volumes: Wilford M. Aikin, *The Story of the Eight-Year Study*; H. H. Giles, S. P. McCutchen, and A. N. Zechiel, *Exploring the Curriculum*; Eugene R. Smith, Ralph W. Tyler, and the Evaluation Staff, *Appraising and Recording Student Progress*; Dean Chamberlin, E. S. Chamberlin, N. E. Draught, and William E. Schott, *Did They Succeed in College?*; and, with each chapter prepared by the staff of the participating schools, *Thirty Schools Tell Their Story*. Also refer to Harold Alberty, *Reorganizing the High School Curriculum* (1957), and Craig Kridel, "The Eight-Year Study Reconsidered" (1994).

Craig Kridel

ELEMENTARY AND SECONDARY EDUCATION ACT (ESEA) initially passed the U.S. Congress as Public Law 89-10 on April 11, 1965, as part of President Lyndon Johnson's "Great Society" programs of legal and social reform enacted at the height of the civil rights movement. ESEA became best known for its "Title I"—compensatory education* for the poor. Between 1968 and 1994, Congress passed eight major amendment-reauthorization packages that will maintain ESEA at least through 1999 as the major federal funding for public schools.*

ESEA stands as landmark legislation in several respects. Politically, it represents Congress's first success, after decades of attempts, to provide large-scale general aid to education that overcame the traditional opposition from religious minority groups and states' rights advocates. These longstanding barriers fell when legislators developed a plan of state- and locally administered aid that would flow, at least theoretically, to private* and parochial* as well as public school children to neighborhoods heavily affected by poverty—though public schools have received the overwhelming share. In addition, ESEA created a large new pool of federal funds that could be withheld under the nondiscrimination compliance provisions of the Civil Rights Act of 1964. This placed ESEA funding, and the debates over its reauthorizations under subsequent presidents, at the heart of the nationwide controversy over local compliance with federal court-ordered busing of children to reduce racial segregation in schools. In addition, requiring gender equity in programs receiving federal education funds became a new feature of ESEA under Title IX of the Education Amendments of 1972. Also, ESEA designated state education agencies to implement its provisions and monitor compliance; and, as part of the law, it funded substantial increases in their staffs and authority. This contributed to an evolving, enlarged role for state departments of education in overseeing local school district activities.

Educationally, and as social policy, ESEA also established watersheds. It institutionalized a "cultural deprivation" model of thinking about why low-income children often performed poorly in school—a model that, though debatable, meshed with the prevailing liberal social reformism of the 1960s and 1970s in its focus on individual families and neighborhoods as the principal sources of restricted student opportunity. ESEA fueled remedial education bureaucracies in the more than 15,000 U.S. school districts. This created a large cadre of teacher specialists helping needy students—often in "pull-out" programs outside the regular classroom—and often relying on traditional and marginally productive teaching strategies while letting the mainstream school program off the hook regarding accountability for student learning. This "separatist" staffing and bureaucracy for remedial education arose, in part, from ESEA's increasingly stringent requirements during the 1970s that Title I funding "supplement" rather than "supplant" existing educational programs (see, for example, P.L. 91-230, 1970, Title I) in order to avoid the growing practice of school districts simply substituting federal for local dollars in their general operating budgets. However, ESEA's most recent amendments—the Improving America's Schools Act of 1994 (P.L. 103-382)—extended earlier efforts from 1978 and 1988 that loosened bureaucratic strings on Title I funds and encouraged greater integration of remedial with regular education services. Furthermore, Title I's newest provisions and name ("Helping Disadvantaged Children Meet High Standards") reflect a growing trend in education and in federal policy toward setting loftier academic goals for all American children, a movement that recalls the pre-ESEA days of the National Defense Education Act (1958).*

ESEA also asserted other significant education and policy principles, especially in areas related to the expanding movement for civil rights. Title VI of the original legislation, Education of Handicapped Children, served as the precursor to P.L. 94-142, the landmark Education for All Handicapped Children Act* (1975, passed as separate legislation apart from ESEA and later as IDEA, the Individuals with Disabilities Education Act of 1990). This law, modeled after earlier legislation in Massachusetts and elsewhere, provided that "special education"* children—those identified with specific physical or mental deficits who were previously relegated to segregated programs—would gain new legal protections and greater opportunities to be more fully integrated into regular classrooms. Title IX, Prohibition of Sex Discrimination (1972), continues to stimulate legal, professional, and civic controversy over appropriate ways to protect the rights of females and males in academic, athletic, and other school extracurricular programs (see EXTRACURRICULUM) receiving federal funds. Title VII (P.L. 90-247, 1968), the Bilingual Education Act,* began a series of federal initiatives to mandate instruction in immigrant students' native tongues rather than English only, responding to the nation's increased attention to the perceived rights and needs of immigrant Americans as well as to the evolution of a multicultural curriculum (see MULTICULTURAL EDUCATION) in elementary, secondary, and higher education. ESEA, from the outset, also addressed remedial education for Native American children served by separate Bureau of Indian Affairs schools—though not in ways that mirrored the civil rights and integrationist policies prevailing elsewhere in the law and in society. ESEA also provided funds for educating the children of migrant workers.

Several smaller provisions of ESEA addressed educational programs and policies outside the specific realm of civil rights. One notable initiative provided funding for locally organized "teacher centers" that would identify, endorse, disseminate, and provide peer training for teachers in exemplary curricula and methodologies. ESEA-funded teacher centers played a significant role in teacher innovations and curriculum development, especially during the legislation's first two decades. Libraries (see SCHOOL LIBRARIES) and community-based adult education programs also received new funding throughout ESEA's early years.

Policy analysts and scholars have studied ESEA's outcomes over the years, particularly with regard to the effectiveness of compensatory "remedial" education for children of the poor, and the question of whether "achievement gaps" between "disadvantaged" and "regular" learners are narrowed by Title I services. (Indeed, historian Ellen Condliffe Lagemann states that U.S. educational research itself grew and became much more policy-studies oriented in the wake of ESEA's passage.) A wide assortment of studies seem to establish that remedial education, as typically delivered through ESEA Title I programs (known as Chapter I from 1981 to 1993), provided only marginal academic gains over several years of children's enrollment. Such modest results have been attributed to several causes, including overly conservative, low-expectations teaching methodologies in remedial programs; excessive segregation of remediation from the regular classroom, thus permitting the regular teachers to give insufficient attention to lower-achieving students; a blame-the-victim philosophy that identifies children on lower rungs of the social class system, rather than the system itself, as needing to be fixed. Despite these factors and outcomes—and although ESEA and other federal aid programs have never funded more than 10 percent of total public school spending (with the remainder paid through state and local revenues)—ESEA retains its prominence and its popularity as the cornerstone of federal aid to education. ESEA's historic legacies and present roles and impact remain complex and controversial.

See the Subcommittee on Elementary, Secondary, and Vocational Education of the Committee on Education and Labor, U.S. House of Representatives, "A Compilation of Papers on the Twentieth Anniversary of the Elementary and Secondary Education Act of 1965" (1985). Also, refer to the Center for Research on the Education of Students at Risk, Johns Hopkins University. This is an internet site containing complete texts of current research articles related to ESEA/IASA: http://scov.csos.juh.edu/Crespar/. Selected secondary analysis includes Julie Roy Jeffrey, *Education for Children of the Poor: A Study of the Origins and Implementation of the Elementary and Secondary Education Act of 1965* (1978); John F. Jennings, ed., *National Issues in Education: ESEA* (1995); Carl F. Kaestle and Marshall S. Smith, "The Federal Role in Elementary and Secondary Education, 1940–1980" (1982); Francis Keppel, *The Necessary Revolution in American Education* (1966); Michael Kirst and Richard Jung, "The Utility of a Longitudinal Approach in Assessing Implementation: A Thirteen-Year View of Title I, ESEA" (1982); Ellen Condliffe Lagemann, "Contested Terrain: A History of Education Research in the United States, 1890–1990" (1997); Milbrey Wallin McLaughlin, *Evaluation and Reform: The Elementary and Secondary Education Act of 1965/Title I* (1975); Diane Ravitch, *The Troubled Crusade: American Education, 1945–1980* (1983); Richard W. Riley, ''The Improving of America's Schools Act and Elementary and Secondary Education Reform'' (1995); Joel H. Spring, *The Sorting Machine Revisited: National Educational Policy since 1945* (1989); and Kenneth K. Wong and Margaret C. Wang, eds., *Rethinking Policy for At-Risk Students* (1994).

Robert A. Levin

ELIOT, CHARLES WILLIAM. See COMMITTEE OF TEN ON SECONDARY SCHOOL STUDIES.

ENGEL V. VITALE, 370 U.S. 421 (1962). The U.S. Supreme Court in this case decided whether an authorized New York State Regents' prayer, to be recited in all school classrooms, with the provision that it be voluntary, was a violation of the establishment clause of the First Amendment. The composed prayer read: ''Almightly God, we acknowledge our dependence upon Thee, and we beg Thy blessings upon us, our parents, our teachers and our Country.'' The Court ruled that having schoolchildren recite even a voluntary prayer violated the establishment clause. The Court reached this decision by referring to the historical background at the time the establishment clause was adopted. History had shown that alliance between church and state incurred hatred and disrespect of those individuals who held contrary beliefs, often resulting in outright religious persecution. Church and state alliance was present in the Regents' prayer; consequently, the element of coercion existed because the state's power and prestige was behind the prayer's recitation that manifested a particular religious belief.

Tony Eastland, *Religious Liberty in the Supreme Court: The Cases That Define the Debate over Church and State* (1993), focuses on legal reasoning and effect; while David A. J. Richards, *Toleration and the Constitution* (1986), maintains an intellectual history approach.

Bruce Beezer

ENGLISH AS A SECOND LANGUAGE. See BILINGUAL EDUCATION.

ENGLISH CLASSICAL SCHOOL opened in Boston in 1821 and, after some name changes, became the English High School, the nation's first such publicly funded institution. Conceived by a special subcommittee headed by Samuel Adams Wells of the Boston School Committee, the school easily won voter approval at the annual town meeting. The subcommittee consisted of Federalists who supported centralized authority exemplified by the high school,* which accepted only highly qualified boys through a competitive entrance test. Its founders sought to expand the city's public school* system beyond the grammar-level instruction in nonclassical subjects. In contrast to the venerable Boston Latin Grammar School,* a college preparatory institution for boys, English High provided advanced studies for business, mercantile life, and the professions.

English High School achieved significance because it promoted the notion of free secondary education in a nonclassical curriculum. As commerce and trade expanded during the period, new types of learning seemed appropriate for particular children. Advanced nonclassical education, since the mid-eighteenth century, had largely been provided in tuition academies,* in pay schools, or through private tutors.* To compete with academies that often received public funding, mostly through land grants, and various pay schools that lacked such resources, English High offered an English or modern curriculum, including algebra, geography, history, advanced science, and a modern foreign language. Such classes became common in most high schools in the nineteenth century. English High remained an unusual place, since most public high schools were coeducational and often offered Latin and other college preparatory courses.

See William J. Reese, *The Origins of the American High School* (1995).

William J. Reese and Scott Walter

ENGLISH LANGUAGE ARTS. Although English as an organized field of study emerged only in the late nineteenth century when the great universities of England and America so defined the academic discipline focusing on the study of literature written in English, certain studies in the field actually date back to ancient Greek civilization with its concern with poetics and to the medieval trivium of grammer, rhetoric, and logic. All these studies became integrated into English in the American high school* during the first decade of the century.

The elementary school curriculum in language arts emerged separately. The earliest beginning occurred with the use of the primers of New England designed to teach beginning reading and morality (see *NEW ENGLAND PRIMER*). Noah Webster's* *Speller* (1787) followed by the McGuffey* *Readers* (1836) further defined the focus of the early grades. Because so many of the classrooms involved children at various levels of development, a graded series of readers became an imperative. This focus on reading and spelling at the earliest levels taught by use of graded readers continued throughout the nineteenth century. Revised editions of the McGuffeys and competitve readers increasingly included literature of various genres appropriate for children as the moralistic bias declined. However, few attempts to unify the elementary school and secondary school curriculum occurred until the mid-twentieth century.

To guard against college domination of the school curriculum, the National Council of Teachers of English (NCTE),* organized in 1911, stressed free, or independent, reading, as well as more formal study of literature and composition, frequently taught in alternate semesters. Given an overemphasis on the formal qualities of literature, and undoubtedly influenced by the student-oriented Progressive Education Association,* the NCTE tried to define literature as experience for students—experience in literature as well as experience through literature.

Language arts as a term seems first to have been utilized by NCTE leaders in the late 1940s to refer to the four major skill areas receiving attention: reading, writing, speaking, and listening. Influential reports of the 1950s, such as *The*

English Language Arts, dealt with ways of integrating classroom efforts in relation to children's needs then receiving extensive attention in the teaching profession. For the most part, this effort marked the end of separate courses in composition in the high school and the use of thematic and topical units of classwork as a unifying focus at both secondary and elementary grades. The research of Arthur Gates in 1922 and the publication of William S. Gray's formal readers beginning in 1930 stressed the reading of selections, followed by related skill instruction and workbook practice, and enhanced the primary-level stress on basic reading at the elementary grades. The elementary years continued to emphasize the teaching of reading skills; at the secondary level, on literature (see READING INSTRUCTION). Indeed, a national high school survey in 1969, by Squire and Appleby, reported that high school classrooms devoted more than 80 percent of time to literature, and as late as 1980, data indicated that 80 percent of elementary schools used basic readers. The emergence of "process writing" in the mid-1970s, followed by the National Writing Project of the 1980s, with its workshops on writing for K–12 teachers, helped to refocus attention on writing in addition to reading and literature as central in language arts. The influential whole language movement that followed stressed integrating all "skills" and "arts" (see INTEGRATED CURRICULUM).

Literature for children and young people continues to be emphasized, supported by attention to arts and skills. "English" remains the most widely accepted term used to refer to the high school and college curriculum; "language arts," for the primary and intermediate grades. The emergence of a hybrid term, "English language arts," became necessary as a way of referring to the total K–12 curriculum.

For general historical background, see Arthur Applebee, *Tradition and Reform in the Teaching of English* (1974); John Dixon, "Historical Considerations: An International Perspective" (1991); James Gray, *The Bay Area Writing Project Model of University-School Collaboration* (1987); Wilbur Hatfield, *The Experience Curriculum in English* (1935); J. N. Hook, *A Long Way Together* (1979); P. David Pearson, Rebecca Barr, Michael Kamil, and Peter Mosenthal, eds., *Handbook on Research on Reading* (1984); Dora V. Smith, *The English Language Arts* (1952); Nila B. Smith, *American Reading Instruction* (1934; 1986); James R. Squire, "The History of the Profession" (1991); and James R. Squire and Robert Applebee, *High School English Instruction Today* (1969).

James R. Squire

ESSENTIALISM, although claiming ancient roots, is associated primarily with twentieth-century American education. Not rightly called a doctrine or a theory, nor is it a philosophical term, though philosophy has debated "essences," the term characterizes an educational point of view if not a philosophy. It has two strains or contributors: philosophical idealism (Plato) and realism (Aristotle). Some scholars see it more as a product of the Renaissance.

From idealism, essentialism takes the belief that the world represents the cosmic mind and that knowledge is symbolic, not material. Because inquiry begins with sensation, however, essentialism adopts a realist perspective, a nature ruled by laws and principles that form the basis for truth and morality. The function of education is to ascertain these principles or ideas.

These beliefs imply conservativism. Essentialism may be contrasted with progressivism's emphasis on activity, tentativeness, flexibility, and reconstruction (see PROGRESSIVE EDUCATION; SOCIAL RECONSTRUCTIONISM). Essentialism instead stresses tradition, order, universal principles, and discipline. Education is used to strengthen and refine, rather than to change, habits, values, beliefs, and practices. It seeks to "anchor" the present in the truth of the past. Education must introduce students to "fundamentals" or the "basics" derived from their social heritage. Symbolic studies (language and mathematics), humanities (literature, history, and philosophy), morality (community tradition, including religion), and physical and biological studies would dominate the curriculum. Because of the different emphases of idealism and realism, instruction might be focused on books (symbolic experience) or directly on sense experience itself and might, more or less, promote vocational preparation.

Essentialism has waxed and waned in the history of American education. It has been suggested that its influence has been more pronounced during culturally conservative times and in opposition to progressive movements. Each of these periods could be characterized as "back to basics," that term being synonymous with essentialism. The psychologist and teacher educator William C. Bagley stressed essentialism in the 1930s. Schools, he argued, should provide stability in the midst of change and ensure that students are equipped with basic skills, primarily academic, needed to cope with changing conditions and ensure the future. Schools should conserve and transmit the dominant cultural heritage. Periodic revivals of essentialist concerns have occurred since that time. In the 1950s, Arthur Bestor* criticized schooling and teacher education; in the 1980s the National Commission on Excellence in Education's *A Nation at Risk* (1983) articulated essentialist ideas. The Council for Basic Education, organized in 1956, continues to monitor American education, especially elementary and secondary education, and press the essentialist agenda.

See Bagley's *Education and Emergent Man* (1934) and "An Essentialist's Platform for the Advancement of American Education" (1938). For a biography of Bagley, refer to I. L. Kandel, *William Chandler Bagley* (1961). Theodore Brameld,* *Philosophies of Education in Cultural Perspective* (1955), includes extensive treatment of essentialist ideas.

Robert R. Sherman

ETHNIC HERITAGE STUDIES ACT. See MULTICULTURAL EDUCATION.

EUGENICS. See HEREDITARIANISM.

EXCEPTIONAL CHILDREN. See SPECIAL EDUCATION.

EXISTENTIALISM is a philosophical position whose main concerns are metaphysical (the nature of human subjectivity) and ethical. Existential themes can be found in Greek philosophy, in Socratic inquiry and Stoic ethics, and in the modern era can be traced to the Danish theologian Søren Kierkegaard, in the first half of the nineteenth century, who believed that cultural conditions, primarily science and schematic philosophy, alienated the individual and that religion had become complacent and conformist rather than liberating. The French philosopher and playwright Jean-Paul Sartre turned to existentialism in response to the distress created by the two world wars in the first half of the twentieth century. Both philosophers, and others, sought to strengthen individual choice and responsibility.

Existentialism rejects essentialism.* Turning much of philosophical thought on its head, Sartre argues that ''existence precedes essence,'' meaning that individuals do not conform to a conception of human nature but define themselves by their own choices and actions. All things are possible for the existentialist. The German philosopher Friedrich Nietzsche said that ''God is dead''; Sartre said that even if he wasn't, it would make no difference. What each philosopher had in mind was that humans cannot escape responsibility by relying on others. Humans create their own meanings and values. Thus, Sartre called existentialism a form of humanism.

The study of existentialism came into American education after World War II. The philosophy rejects other-directed prescriptions, so an educational program is paradoxical at best. Nevertheless, some educational suggestions may be given. Awareness of subjectivity, the reality of freedom, the necessity of choice and action, and anguish over the possibility that one could lose everything are dominant existential themes that an education would seek to develop. Studies that emphasize subjectivity, such as the arts and humanities, and values (particularly freedom and responsibility), to be found in philosophy, history, and literature, would have a large role in an existential education.

Some interpreters believe that an existential education should begin in secondary and higher education, but others advise it should be whenever the child has an urge to know him- or herself. Morris has suggested that there is an ''existential moment'' in the life of every child. The aim of education should be to develop the child's subjective sense of being and to emphasize individual responsibility for choosing and acting on one's own values. Vocational and professional aims of education would be secondary to experiences that are intrinsic and that have humanizing and liberalizing effects. Most important is that education cannot provide cures or easy compromises.

Direct interest in existential education appears to be mute in recent years. Some existentialist concerns are shared by progressive education,* though the existentialist would reject the progressive focus on the social- and problem-centered methods. Because the existentialist believes that individuals construct their own knowledge and values, rather than being "objective" or prescribed by authority, existentialism also has something in common with "constructivism."*

For a historical overview, see Jean Wahl, *A Short History of Existentialism* (1949). George F. Kneller, *Existentialism and Education* (1958); Van Cleve Morris, *Existentialism in Education: What It Means* (1966); Robert G. Olson, *An Introduction to Existentialism* (1962); and Jean-Paul Sartre, *Existentialism* (1957), provide a general philosophical background.

Robert R. Sherman

EXTRACURRICULUM. Student activities conducted outside of the formal curriculum of colleges and secondary schools existed throughout the nineteenth century. During the 1880s and 1890s, however, extracurricular activities proliferated in high schools.* Literary societies, publications, athletics,* and forensics were the most common student activities. Student government, concerned primarily with meting punishments to infractors, and dramatics were conducted relatively sporadically. A variety of special-interest clubs thrived as well. Until about 1910, although faculty participation was common, extracurricular activities were initiated and run by students. "Secret societies," modeled after college fraternities, dominated both the student activity scene and the social life of many high schools. Typically, students organized these exclusive, cliquish social clubs along social-class lines. Rivalries and even hostilities among secret societies were the rule. Social clubs exerted a divisive and disruptive effect on school life, undermining the common school ideal of uniting students of diverse backgrounds through a comprehensive high school experience. With the exception of the social clubs, most student activities typically were poorly managed.

During the early twentieth century, local officials resisted the divisiveness by wresting control of extracurricular activities from students. Increased faculty control of extracurricular activities was typically welcomed by students but resisted by secret societies. Progressive education* theory that conceived of learning as a quality of lived experience legitimized the educative value of student activities. By the 1920s, educators regarded the extracurriculum as a potent force for developing social learnings. The acceptance of the educative value of extracurricular activities was part of the growing recognition in the field of curriculum of the imperative of viewing the educational program of a school as whole rather than as a loose assemblage of disparate parts. Notable advocates included Thomas H. Briggs and Charles R. Foster, who wrote the first book about the topic, *Extra-Curricular Activities* (1925). During the 1920s and 1930s, Elbert K. Fretwell* became the recognized leader of the extracurricular activity movement. By midcentury, extracurricular activities became a fixture of the high school program. Research has demonstrated a correlation between participation in extracurricular activities and outcomes such as academic achievement, self-esteem, school completion, and community participation later in life. Despite such findings, educators and the general public frequently regard extracurricular activities as unrelated to the formal curriculum and as supplemental rather than essential to quality education.

Some early writings on this topic include Foster's book, as well as Elbert K. Fretwell, *Extra-Curricular Activities in Secondary Schools* (1931); V. K. Froula, "Extra-Curricular Activities: Their Relation to the Curricular Work of the School" (1915); Paul W. Terry, "The Origin and Growth of Student Activities" (1930); Paul G. W. Weller, "Open School Organizations" (1905); and Guy M. Whipple, ed., *Extra-Curricular Activities* (1926). More recent work and historical treatments include Laura E. Berk, "The Extracurriculum" (1992); Ronald E. Gholson and Robert L. Buser, *Cocurricular Activity Programs in Secondary Schools* (1983); Thomas W. Gutowski, "Student Initiative and the Origins of the High School Extracurriculum: Chicago, 1880–1915" (1988); Edward A. Krug, *The Shaping of the American High School, 1880–1920* (1964); and Joel Spring, *The American School, 1642–1990* (1994).

William G. Wraga

F

FACULTY PSYCHOLOGY holds that the mind is not unitary, but is composed of a number of discrete mental "faculties," each responsible for performing a separate intellectual function. Although this idea was developed in classical Greece, nineteenth-century American educators were most influenced by the faculty psychology of John Locke and the Scottish Enlightenment. Locke's notion of *tabula rasa* is commonly misunderstood to imply that a child's mental life is shaped entirely by external stimuli; Locke, however, actually held that the mind contains a number of "inborn faculties" capable of translating sense impression into ideas. Locke's followers in the Scottish Enlightenment were more specific about the nature and number of these faculties. Thomas Reid found more than thirty distinct faculties, including not only "intellectual powers" such as "Memory" and "Judgement" but also instinctive ones such as "Lust" and moral faculties such as "Duty."

Nineteenth-century American educators embraced Scottish faculty psychology, disagreeing only on the number of faculties and whether they had a physical existence in the brain or were subdivisions of an immaterial mind. Faculty psychology provided educators with a clear, common-sense map of the mind and a guide for pedagogy. The goal of education, faculty psychology implied, was to strengthen each mental faculty. Using the analogy of physical exercise, educators claimed that through rote exercise, mental faculties could be developed like muscles. Experimental psychologists in the early twentieth century discredited faculty psychology, denying the existence of distinct mental faculties. The brain performs various functions, they argued, but it is illogical to assume that each function must be performed by a discrete faculty. Still, the ideas of faculty psychology linger in our culture, particularly in popular notions about memory as a distinct and trainable mental skill. Recent neurological study of the localization of brain functions has revived interest in the search for the components of mental activity.

For background material, see Thomas H. Leahey, *A History of Modern Psychology* (1991), and Donald Myer, *The Instructed Conscience* (1972).

Ernest Freeberg

FAMILY EDUCATIONAL RIGHTS AND PRIVACY ACT OF 1974 (FERPA). Senator James Buckley (R.-New York) sponsored FERPA, or the Buckley Amendment, to address the right of parents and students to access school records and the necessity of educational institutions to have records. FERPA's main purposes were to prevent school officials from including speculative, derogatory information in student records, to allow parents and guardians to challenge the contents of student records, and to limit the access of outsiders to personal information about students. The legislation requires school systems receiving federal funding to establish written policies to annually inform parents and students of their rights concerning student records and procedures for challenging accuracy of records. Although parents and students must be given access to records, schools may withhold transcripts and report cards for disciplinary reasons. Student records may be released without consent of parents to school officials with "legitimate educational interest," to persons protecting "the health or safety of the individual or others," and for compliance with a judicial order or subpoena.

For information on the application of FERPA, see the Family Educational Rights and Privacy Act in 20 USCS 1232(g).

Deanna Michael

FEDERAL INDIAN BOARDING SCHOOLS. With the creation of the reservation system in the late nineteenth century, the Bureau of Indian Affairs began to erect a three-tier system of federal schools comprised of day schools, reservation boarding schools, and off-reservation boarding schools—the last enrolling the vast majority of students. The off-reservation concept was launched in 1879 when Richard Henry Pratt opened Carlisle Indian School in Carlisle, Pennsylvania. An ardent critic of all reservation schools, Pratt convinced his many supporters that only by removing Indian children from the reservation environment for a period of three to five years could educators hope to accomplish the government's twofold aim: the complete eradication of the child's Indian or tribal identity and his or her assimilation of white cultural ways. After 1880, both reservation and off-reservation boarding schools spread rapidly, amounting to 125 and 25, respectively, by 1900. Indian agents were originally authorized to use force to fill such schools; then in 1893 Congress legislated that students could be sent to off-reservation schools only with parental consent.

Boarding schools were highly regimented institutions, with off-reservation schools being particularly militaristic in atmosphere and operation, complete with school uniforms for boys and matching dresses for girls. All day's activities—bedrise, morning inspection, meals, movement to and between classes, evening programs, and "lights out"—were governed by a system of bugles or bells. Partly to teach students the concept of clocktime and partly to instill obedience, a portion of each day was devoted to marching on the school's drill field. All these activities were supervised by a staff that included, at a bare minimum, the superintendent and at least one teacher, assistant teacher, farmer, cook, seamstress, matron, and disciplinarian.

The curriculum included academics and industrial training,* usually a half-day schedule of each. Most of the time, the former was devoted to instruction in the fundamentals of English, U.S. history and government, and arithmetic, subjects were deemed essential for eventual citizenship and for economic survival. On the industrial side, reservation boarding schools focused their attention on those skills associated with agriculture: plowing, planting, harvesting, stockraising, blacksmithing, and basic carpentry. Depending on location and climate, some school farms produced large quantities of fruits and vegetables, poultry, and dairy products, all of which were used to enhance the school's meager dietary allowance. Off-reservation schools also offered instruction in such areas as tinsmithing, shoemaking, printing, and tailoring. Girls learned an array of domestic skills, emphasizing cooking, cleaning, ironing, and sewing, although by 1910 some off-reservation institutions had normal (see NORMAL SCHOOLS), nursing, and commercial departments. By 1920, only a few off-reservation schools offered the equivalency of a high school* curriculum. Extracurricular activities (see EXTRACURRICULUM) and religious exercises supplemented the regular school program, with church attendance required. Through so-called outing programs, a few of the larger off-reservation schools placed older students with white ''patrons,'' usually during the summer months, where students could not only experience middle-class family life but also earn a small wage, boys by farming and girls through house cleaning.

Native American students and parents responded in various ways. Whereas many parents looked upon white schooling as a necessary means of adaption and survival, others objected strenuously to the forced removal of children and the schools' assimilationist aims. Opposition to off-reservation schools appeared to be especially strong. Boarding school staffs faced considerable resistance from students who frequently ran away, sometimes covering as much as 100 miles in their determination to return home.

A continuing tide of criticism against the boarding school idea—especially the off-reservation variety—took its toll after 1900. In 1928, a comprehensive study of Native American affairs, *The Problem of Indian Administration*, conducted by the Brookings Institute under the direction of Lewis Meriam and funded by Congress, condemned the government's overreliance on the boarding school model of Indian education. After the Meriam report, policymakers demonstrated a renewed interest in day schools and public schools, although the isolation of Native American populations frequently presented difficulties in abandoning the old system. The number of boarding schools has gradually declined and no longer constitutes the mainstay of federal Indian education efforts. The historical significance of the boarding school system cannot be overstated, however. It was one of the primary instruments of federal Indian policy for accomplishing forced acculturation.

The primary location for papers and documents related to federal Indian schools is the National Archives. An important autobiography is Richard H. Pratt, *Battlefield and Classroom: Four Decades with the American Indian, 1867–1904* (1964). For two general treatments of the subject, see David W. Adams, *Education for Extinction: American Indians and the Boarding School Experience, 1875–1928* (1995), and Michael C. Coleman, *American Indian Children at School, 1850–1930* (1993). For institutional studies, see Sally Hyer, *One House, One Voice, One Heart: Native American Education at Santa Fe Indian School* (1990); K. Tsianina Lomawaima, *They Called It Prairie Light: The Story of Chilocco Indian School* (1994); and Robert Trennert, *The Phoenix Indian School: Forced Assimilation in Arizona* (1988).

David W. Adams

FEDERAL OFFICE OF EDUCATION. See UNITED STATES DEPARTMENT OF EDUCATION.

FEMALE SEMINARIES, private and quasi-public institutions established to provide women with an education comparable to that offered to men in colleges, reached a height of popularity between 1830 and 1850. Emma Willard* may have been the first to use the general term "seminary" to distinguish her institution, Troy Female Seminary, from other female schools, which she viewed as academically and morally inadequate. She preferred the term "college," but she dared not appropriate it for fear of ridicule. Other notable female seminaries were Catharine Beecher's* Hartford Female Seminary, established in 1828 in Connecticut, and Zilpah Grant Banister's Ipswich Female Seminary and Mary Lyon's* Mount Holyoke Female Seminary, opened in 1829 and 1837, respectively, in Massachusetts. These northeastern seminaries set a national standard for women's higher education until the founding of the first well-endowed women's colleges in the post–Civil War era.

The leading seminary founders strove to standardize and upgrade women's schools. A few, like Beecher, traveled about the nation, lecturing and establishing schools. Many more inspected each other's institutions, exchanged catalogues, and held elaborate public examinations to demonstrate their pedagogical practices and academic quality. A subject of debate was boarding arrangements. Some administrators clung to the European practice of warehousing students in large dormitory rooms resided over by one or more teachers. Students more often lived in boarding houses and dormitories, where they shared small rooms with one or two others and sometimes a teacher. In an attempt to cut costs, Lyon required all her students to do daily household chores, such as making pies and bread. She further mandated that all students exercise daily. She also established an elaborate list of rules and regulations requiring students to confess their transgressions before the student body. Such practices were followed in many other female seminaries.

Leading seminary founders strove to standardize entrance criteria, which varied widely. For example, Troy's age requirement was twelve, Hartford's was fourteen, and Mount Holyoke's was fifteen. To gain admittance, students generally had to demonstrate mastery of basic studies, sometimes including Latin. The leading seminaries gradually required students to conform to standards similar to those of the male colleges, although most continued to admit students with inadequate academic backgrounds and limited resources, often providing them with scholarships and loans.

The proper seminary curriculum served as a topic of heated debate. The typical program required only three years of study and consisted of three groups of courses. The largest one included subjects generally viewed as appropriate studies for both genders: natural philosophy (the sciences), moral philosophy (ethics), mental philosophy (psychology), biblical literature, geography, history, English literature, pedagogy, composition, and elocution. A second group of subjects consisted of courses considered frivolous, namely, the "feminine" accomplishments: vocal and instrumental music, drawing and painting, embroidery, dancing, and the modern languages (French, German, and Italian). These subjects often attracted the largest number of students, but they were placed on the periphery of the curriculum because of their low academic status. A third group contained traditional college subjects generally considered too rigorous (i.e., "masculine") for female minds: mathematics (geometry, algebra, trigonometry, solid geometry, and astronomy) and ancient Latin and Greek. Only rarely did some subjects, like Greek, appear in early seminary catalogues because of public resistance and inadequately educated teachers. In an effort to gain academic credibility, ambitious seminaries gradually added more "masculine" subjects to their curricula.

After the Civil War, female seminaries faced stiff competition from the newly established women's colleges and tax-funded high schools.* Additional competition came from the colleges and universities that were finally opening their doors to women. A seminary diploma was now viewed as inferior, especially when compared to a degree from a four-year institution. Most seminaries lacked the financial backing to maintain a footing in the new environment. Although they had managed to raise the necessary funds to purchase property and construct buildings, their efforts to raise large endowments usually failed. Most people preferred to invest in male rather than female higher education. Hence, seminary dormitories were usually overcrowded, preparatory departments large, teaching loads heavy, student fees high, faculty salaries low, and scientific laboratories and equipment inadequate. A few, like Troy Female Seminary (renamed Emma Willard School in 1895), maintained a reputation as an exemplary private female secondary school. Others, like Mount Holyoke, gradually transformed themselves into women's colleges. The rest merged with other institutions, became public high schools, or closed.

Female seminaries have sometimes been called the first teachers' institutions. Before Horace Mann* opened the first state normal schools,* seminaries were training students in pedagogy, child development, and classroom management (see CLASSROOM DISCIPLINE AND MANAGEMENT). Seminary teachers conducted hands-on experiments in science laboratories and took their students into the field for specimen collection and identification. Some gifted instructors included their experimental methods in their textbooks, which were subsequently adopted by many school districts. Willard's popular history, geography, astronomy, and physiology textbooks, for example, demonstrated how classroom teachers could use sensory experiences to move their students from concrete to abstract concepts. A more powerful influence than textbooks was that of the hundreds of seminary students who became teachers in the common schools.* Social convention restricted women's teaching after marriage, but a large number of female seminarians had careers as teachers, governesses, school founders, principals, county superintendents, and textbook writers.

No comprehensive collection of the papers of female seminaries exists. However, individual collections are housed in archives of Protestant and Roman Catholic women's schools and religious orders as well as in the special collections of state libraries. See also Emma Willard, *An Address to the Public: Particularly to the Members of the Legislature of New York, Proposing a Plan for Improving Female Education* (1819). The most comprehensive discussion of female seminaries is Thomas Woody's classic, *A History of Women's Education in the United States* (1929). Also useful are Barbara Solomon, *in the Company of Educated Women* (1985), and David B. Tyack and Elisabeth Hansot, *Learning Together: A History of Coeducation in American Schools* (1990). Most discussions of female seminaries are narrow in scope. See David F. Allmendinger, "Mount Holyoke Students Encouner the Need for Life-Planning, 1837–1850" (1979); Anne Firor Scott, "The Ever Widening Circle: The Diffusion of Feminist Values from the Troy Female Seminary, 1822–1872" (1979); and Lucy Townsend, "The Gender Effect: The Early Curricula of Beloit College and Rockford Female Seminary" (1990).

Lucy Forsyth Townsend

FENTON, EDWIN (September 16, 1921–   ), helped to pioneer innovative conceptions of the social studies* in the secondary curriculum from the 1960s to the 1980s. He earned his undergraduate degree in history and political science at the College of Wooster in 1948, and his M.A. (1949) and Ph.D. (1958) degrees in history from Harvard University, where, under Oscar Handlin, he studied American immigrant history. He began his teaching career at Boston's Brimmer and May School in 1951, moving to Carnegie Mellon University (then Carnegie Institute of Technology) three years later; his career now spans four decades. Fenton's *Teaching the New Social Studies: An Inductive Approach* (1966) provided early impetus for a national movement toward ''inquiry method'' teaching that was in turn nurtured by the social and political climate of the period. From 1964 to 1980, he founded and directed the Social Studies Curriculum Center at Carnegie Mellon, in effect a think tank and development center for secondary textbooks and alternative curriculum materials in U.S. and world history, comparative political and economic systems; he also headed an interdisciplinary program entitled *The Humanities in Three Cities* (1969). The books, maps, films, kits, and teacher guides developed by Fenton, his colleagues, and their graduate students and heavily supported by federal and private foundation grants—some eighty works in all—gained wide circulation in American public schools,* promoting analysis and critical thinking among students as alternatives to traditional, memorization-based texts. In the late 1970s, Fenton collaborated with Lawrence Kohlberg* to develop audiovisual kits to address morals and values in American history and government, drawing on Kohlberg's theories of educating students for moral development (see MORAL EDUCATION). Fenton, between 1972 and 1992, served as a consultant to more than 100 American school districts, as well as to UNESCO and the governments of Israel, Philippines, Iceland, and Sweden. He delivered more than 200 addresses in thirty-one states and nine foreign countries, many devoted to the intersections of historical, civic, and moral education.

Principal among Fenton's twenty-two book projects (some as editor or general series editor) and over 100 articles are *The Scott-Foresman Problems in American History*, eleven volumes (1964–1966 and 1971–1975), and *The Holt Social Studies Curriculum*, eleven volumes (1967–1969 and 1974–1976). In the areas of civic and moral education, Fenton coauthored *Leading Dilemma Discussions* (1980, United States; 1983, Israel) and *Improving School Climate through Fairness Meetings* (1983), along with dozens of conference papers on the roles and processes of education for civic values. In the early 1990s, Fenton not only wrote a retrospective paper, "What Happened to the New Social Studies: A Case Study in Curriculum Reform" (1991), but joined several conference panels analyzing why the 1960s–1970s reform movement had a "brief life span" and considering the conditions under which future reforms could potentially achieve deeper and better institutionalization.

Robert A. Levin

FIRST PLENARY COUNCIL. See THIRD PLENARY COUNCIL.

FISHER, DOROTHY CANFIELD (February 17, 1879–November 9, 1958), was a prolific author of fiction and nonfiction, writing for both adult and juvenile audiences. Fisher's work and her life in general espoused a feminist progressivism that urged educated women to pursue public careers in social work while still maintaining strong familial roles as wives and mothers. Although never formally an educator herself, Fisher wrote widely on childrearing, schooling, and educational reform, embracing such diverse topics as early childhood development in *Self-Reliance* (1943), adolescence,* and the transition into adulthood in *Our Young Folks* (1943).

After earning a Ph.D. in French literature from Columbia University in 1904, Fisher served as an administrator-secretary at New York City's experimental Horace Mann School. During a 1911 trip to Europe, she visited Maria Montessori's* innovative school for young children in Rome. Shortly thereafter, in a series of books, she introduced the Montessori method to American audiences for both home and school use.

Fisher lived most of her adult life with her husband and children in Arlington, Vermont. She was the first woman to sit on that state's board of education and was a long-time supporter of Vermont's Children's Aid Society. By the 1930s, Fisher's interests shifted to issues of youth and adolescence, and she served for a time as president of the American Association of Adult Education. In 1936, Fisher was named to the American Youth Commission and subsequently provided the concluding chapter to its 1942 report, *Youth and the Future*. Eleanor Roosevelt later named Fisher one of the ten most influential women in the United States. Fisher's last published work, *Vermont Tradition: The Biography of an Outlook on Life*, appeared in 1953.

Dorothy Canfield Fisher's papers are held by the University of Vermont, Wilbur Archival Collection. This is the most comprehensive collection of Fisher's papers, which includes copies of all her works, in both published and manuscript forms, as well as a good number of her surviving letters. Two published biographies exist: Ida H. Washington, *Dorothy Canfield Fisher: A Biography* (1982), and Elizabeth Yates, *Pebble in a Pool: The Widening Circles of Dorothy Canfield Fisher's Life* (1958), written for juvenile readers.

Jeff Suzik

FORD FOUNDATION. Established by Henry and Edsel Ford from the profits of the Ford Motor Company, it made grants largely to Michigan charitable and educational institutions until its mission was expanded in 1950 to include national and international initiatives. It disbursed $7 billion by 1992 and now represents the largest philanthropic foundation.

Its chief educational objectives have included improvement of teacher preparation and recruitment, as well as better utilization of teaching resources, curriculum improvement, and increased access to educational opportunities. Among its many higher education activities, the Foundation cooperated with the Carnegie Corporation in 1955 to create the National Merit Scholarship Qualifying Test, administered by the National Merit Scholarship Corporation, which identified and provided scholarships to talented students. Together with the Carnegie Foundation and the U.S. Office of Education,* it also established the National Assessment of Educational Progress.* From 1970 to 1976, the Upper Division Scholarship Program funded scholarships to enable minority student graduates of two-year institutions to achieve baccalaureate degrees. It supported studies of social conditions such as Harry S. Ashmore's *The Negro and the Schools* (1955) and Charles E. Silberman's* *Crisis in Black and White* (1964). It invested over $30 million through the subsidiary Fund for the Advancement of Television to develop instructional television in public schools. Finally, the Foundation supported the Holmes Group, a national consortium of research universities dedicated to improving schools through research and development and the preparation of career teaching K–12 professionals.

In addition to its annual reports, information can be found in secondary sources such as William Greenleaf, *From These Beginnings: The Early Philanthropies of Henry and Edsel Ford, 1911–1936* (1964), and Richard Magat, *The Ford Foundation at Work: Philanthropic Choices, Methods, and Styles* (1979). Robert F. Arnove, in *Philanthropy and Cultural Imperialism: The Foundations at Home and Abroad* (1980), maintains a critical perspective.

Jayne R. Beilke

FOSTER HOMES. See REFORM SCHOOLS.

FRANKLIN, BENJAMIN (January 17, 1706–April 17, 1790), was the first American philosopher of education. Printer, postmaster, scientist, and statesman, he taught Americans to take personal responsibility for their education, a lesson he conveyed by word and deed to his own and subsequent generations.

First, Franklin believed in lifelong learning. As a young adult, he developed a plan for moral self-improvement through a regimen of planning, practice, and reflection. It set a course for self-education that guided the rest of his life and that he shared with countless others through his *Autobiography*. Second, utility distinguished the good from the bad in his philosophy of education. No dilettante, Franklin judged knowledge to be valuable when it contributed to the material or moral progress of the individual or society. Reason represented Franklin's third criterion for defining education. Learning, he thought, was a rational process that cultivated the learner's ability to reason. Founder of the Junto (1728), a self-study group composed of aspiring merchants and artisans, and the American Philosophical Society (1743), the first organization devoted to scientific investigation in North America, Franklin practiced what he preached. Less esoteric, *Poor Richard's Almanack* reached a wide audience, giving practical advice in terms easy to understand and certain to please. First published in 1733, it taught the principle that "the doors of wisdom never close."

As a scientist, Franklin put this maxim to the test. He lived his faith in self-education and confirmed his belief in reason and experience as engines of knowledge through dozens of experiments on electricity, magnetism, and meteorology, among others. However, scientific knowledge did not have to be immediately applicable; the promise of usefulness was enough to satisfy him. When it came to schooling, Franklin was more insistent on utility. His *Proposals Relating to the Education of Youth in Pennsylvania* (1749) and *Constitutions of the Publick Academy in the City of Philadelphia . . .* (1749) favored English over classical education. They laid the groundwork for what in 1791 would become the University of Pennsylvania.

Although Franklin had a powerful hand in determining the outcome of the

American Revolution, he is best known for what he said about living and learning, that is, for his philosophy of education.

Franklin's papers can be found in many repositories, especially the American Philosophical Society, the Historical Society of Pennsylvania, and the Archives of the University of Pennsylvania. Yale University Press published thirty volumes of his papers through 1994. Carl Van Doren, *Benjamin Franklin: A Biography* (1938), remains unmatched, as does his edited collection of Franklin's writings, *Benjamin Franklin's Autobiographical Writings* (1945). For a more recent biography, see Esmond Wright, *Franklin of Philadelphia* (1986). Refer to John H. Best, ed., *Benjamin Frankln on Education* (1962), for Franklin's views on education.

William W. Cutler III

FREE KINDERGARTEN ASSOCIATIONS represented a generic name for a private charity organization that sponsored and ran kindergarten* classes for poor children. These associations began in most American cities and large towns during the 1870s, 1880s, and 1890s. Part of the broader Christian, evangelical, and progressive (see PROGRESSIVE EDUCATION) child-saving campaigns of the late nineteenth century and mostly supported by contributions from upper- and middle-class women, free kindergartens maintained long hours and often provided food, clothing, and other social services in addition to running mothers' classes and training classes for teachers. Among the best known were the free kindergartens sponsored by Felix Adler's Ethical Culture Society in New York City; the Louisville Free Kindergarten Association directed by Anna Bryan* and Patty Smith Hill*; the Chicago Froebel Association (see FROEBEL, FRIEDRICH) and Kindergarten Association founded by Alice Putnam;* and Sarah B. Cooper's Golden Gate Kindergarten Association and Kate Douglas Wiggin's Silver Street Kindergarten in San Francisco. Free kindergartens were also associated with settlement houses, such as Jane Addams's* Hull-House in Chicago. By the late 1880s, free kindergartens began petitioning public school boards to adopt kindergartens, and many free kindergarten associations were incorporated whole into the public schools. Leaders of the free kindergarten movement adopted new psychological ideas and child-centered approaches to better meet the needs of poor and immigrant children in American cities and in the process laid the groundwork for modern public kindergartens.

Sources on the free kindergarten movement include Barbara Beatty, *Preschool Education in America: The Culture of Young Children from the Colonial Era to the Present* (1995); Marvin Lazerson, ''Urban Reform and the Schools: Kindergartens in Massachusetts, 1870–1915'' (1971); Elizabeth Dale Ross, *The Kindergarten Crusade: The Establishment of Preschool Education in the United States* (1976); Michael Steven Shapiro, *Child's Garden: The Kindergarten Movement from Froebel to Dewey* (1983); and Nina C. Vandewalker, *The Kindergarten in American Public Education* (1908).

Barbara Beatty

FREE SCHOOL MOVEMENT was a broad-based movement toward the radical redefinition of the structure and purpose of American schooling. It represented the disillusionment with traditional social institutions prevalent during the 1960s and challenged the dominant notion of schooling. Though a national phenomenon, no recognized leadership or standard features existed; students, parents, and teachers, comprising the school community, defined each school. These schools tended to be small, often founded because of grassroots reaction to perceived inequities or inadequacies in the local public school. Free schools emphasized participatory democracy, as the means of school governance, and alternative curricula. Although typically tuition-driven, several schools sought funding from universities or philanthropic foundations in order to defray or eliminate tuition charges.

Influenced by the 1960s counterculture, the free school movement also drew practical and intellectual guidance from the contemporary work of Summerhill's A. S. Neill, child-centered schools of the Progressive Era (see PROGRESSIVE EDUCATION), and anarchist Modern Schools.* Southern freedom schools* too served as a model. Finally, social commentaries by Paul Goodman and Edgar Z. Friedenberg as well as public school critiques by disaffected teachers such as Herb Kohl, Jonathan Kozol, and James Herndon provided inspiration.

National organizations dedicated to free schooling included the American Summerhill Society (1961–1971) and the New Schools Exchange (1969–1978), both of which served primarily as informational clearinghouses. Regional and local free school associations likewise existed.

This movement, like earlier examples of radical experiments, faced internal conflict over the definition of ''radical'' education. One wing charted a utopian course, focused on cultural radicalism and withdrawal from the problems of the larger society; another wing stressed political radicalism, with direct confrontation of social evils. These competing notions led to very different types of radical experimentation, but all received the label of free schools. Such incompatible images of radical education resulted in internecine battles. This conflict and the growing conservatism of the 1970s led to the demise of the movement as a national American phenomenon.

Yale University houses the New Schools Exchange Collection. Allen Graubard's *Free the Children: Radical Reform and the Free School Movement* (1972) serves as the movement's standard reference work. Other useful books include George Dennison, *The Lives of Children* (1969); Jonathan Kozol, *Free Schools* (1972); and Salli Rasberry and Robert Greenway, *Rasberry Exercises* (1970).

Scott Walter

FREE SCHOOL SOCIETY, organized in 1805, provided basic education for the people of New York City for nearly fifty years. Its charity schools* answered the call for low-cost education by employing the monitorial system* developed by the English school reformer Joseph Lancaster. At its demise in 1853, the Society was represented in every section of the city, operating seventy-five primary and grammar schools that enrolled thousands of poor and working-class children.

The Society made a significant contribution to the development of public education in the United States. By obtaining state support for its charity schools as early as 1807, it pushed forward the idea that government should take responsibility for the education of the young. Changing its name to the Public School Society in 1826, it tried to broaden its mission by attracting at least some pupils from middle- and upper-class homes. At the same time, it argued successfully against the use of public money for sectarian schools. But even as the Society retained hegemony over state support for education in New York City, it remained immune from public control, continuing to be a self-perpetuating corporation managed by wealthy and powerful trustees.

The social and cultural distance that separated the Society's leadership from the common people of New York led to its undoing. In the early 1840s, the city's Irish Catholics requested public money for their burgeoning parish schools (see PAROCHIAL SCHOOLS). Led by Archbishop John Hughes,* they claimed that by observing Protestant customs and teaching Protestant values the Society's schools were no less sectarian than their own. The Catholics did not get their funding, but the Society also lost, relinquishing its autonomy in 1842 when the state legislature imposed a complex system of governance by elected ward commissioners and a central board of education on New York City's state-supported schools. Having thus become an anachronism, the Society drifted and eventually disbanded, taking with it the idea that public schools could be privately controlled.

Many historians have written about the Free/Public School Society. William O. Bourne produced the first study, a compendium entitled *History of the Public School Society of the City of New York* (1870). Modern works include William W. Cutler III, "Status, Values and the Education of the Poor: The Trustees of the New York Public School Society, 1805–1853" (1972); Carl F. Kaestle, *The Evolution of an Urban School System: New York City, 1750–1850* (1973); Vincent P. Lannie, *Public Money and Parochial Education* (1968); and Diane Ravitch, *The Great School Wars: New York City, 1805–1973* (1974).

William W. Cutler III

FREEDMEN'S BUREAU. See BUREAU OF REFUGEES, FREEDMEN, AND ABANDONED LANDS.

FREEDMEN'S EDUCATION refers to the efforts by and on behalf of the freed African American slaves of the American South to secure the benefits of formal schooling, and generally covers such efforts from 1861 to the turn of the century. All slave states prohibited schooling for slaves, fearing the effects of literacy. Many proscribed schooling for free people of color as well. Although many southern African Americans were able to obtain the rudiments of literacy under slavery and clandestine schools operated in towns and cities, the effort remained dangerous and difficult. The earliest efforts to provide schools for slaves freed by the American Civil War came from literate African Americans themselves, often teaching openly in the previously secret schools. Northern voluntary aid societies quickly organized to assist in the educational effort as well. The earliest support came from the American Missionary Association, an abolitionist organization founded in 1846. Within months of the beginning of the war, ad hoc voluntary societies formed, collected funds, clothing, medicine, and other supplies, and recruited teachers. By the end of the war, in 1865, over forty organizations were working to provide relief and schooling for the emancipated slaves, including established missionary societies within all the major Protestant denominations and a dozen secular societies, most of which were loosely afiliated with American Freedmen's Union Commission. In their first decade of work, freedmen's aid societies raised over $7 million and recruited over 6,000 teachers to work in the South. The Freedmen's Bureau* provided another $5 million in aid and support. Yet the demand from the freedmen outstripped northern largesse and a paltry governmental response. Northern enthusiasm also waned quickly. By the 1870s, the freedmen had to rely on their own declining resources and the nascent public southern school systems. Freedmen's education, at the end of Reconstruction, depended on the work of a few faithful missionary societies supporting a frail network of secondary schools and colleges, the increasing influence of industrialist-philanthropists, state systems of segregated education, and the independent efforts of southern African American educators.

Several collections of papers related to freedmen's education exist, though the best known is the American Missionary Association Archives, Amistad Research Center, located at Tulane University. For the early years of freedmen's education, see Ronald E. Butchart, *Northern Whites, Southern Blacks, and Reconstruction: Freedmen's Education, 1862–1875* (1980), and Robert C. Morris, *Reading, 'Riting, and Reconstruction: The Education of Freedmen in the South, 1861–1870* (1981). Later developments are covered by James D. Anderson, *The Education of Blacks in the South, 1860–1935* (1988), and Joe M. Richardson, *Christian Reconstruction: The American Missionary Association and Southern Blacks, 1861–1890* (1986), among other many recent studies.

Ronald E. Butchart

FREEDOM SCHOOLS were alternative educational programs created by civil rights movement activists in the 1960s. The best known were a component of the 1964 Mississippi Freedom Summer, when hundreds of northern volunteers, most of them white college students, worked as political organizers and as teachers in forty-one freedom schools.

Activists organized freedom schools both to protest the segregated, unequal, stultifying education imposed on black children and to create a model of meaningful inquiry. Although freedom schools often included remedial instruction, classes focused on social issues. Pedagogy was grounded in the conviction that by examining their own experience, students could understand the American social order and, based on that understanding, transform society.

Freedom schools drew on deep roots in the civil rights movement. Activists committed to nonviolence sought to embody the values of a just society, and education was an essential component of efforts to foster self-directed grassroots activism. Citizenship Schools organized by the Highlander Folk School and the Southern Christian Leadership Conference, for example, prepared adults for voter-registration literacy tests by addressing problems of daily life. Mississippi freedom school planners drew on Highlander's efforts, as well as on freedom schools that had already been created in rural Virginia, Boston, and New York.

Despite their deep roots, freedom schools had a brief existence. Amid the resistence of the U.S. government and the Democratic Party to racial equality, calls for integration and redemptive nonviolence gave way to demands for black power. By the late 1960s, loss of faith in American democracy undermined the progressive pedagogy of questioning and discovery by African American youth. In their short life, freedom schools exerted a wide influence. Their affirmation of the intellectual capacity of African American children refuted deficit-model explanations of student failure. Even after the appeal of the freedom schools had waned, activists sought to recreate their pedagogy in public school open education programs and in feminist consciousness raising.

The entire issue of *Radical Teacher* no. 40 (winter 1991), edited by Paul Lauter and Daniel Perlstein, is devoted the the "Mississippi Freedom Schools." For the impact on white volunteers, see Doug McAdam, *Freedom Summer* (1988). Also, refer to Daniel Perlstein, "Teaching Freedom: SNCC and the Creation of the Mississippi Freedom Schools" (1990).

Daniel Perlstein

FRETWELL, ELBERT KIRTLEY (September 27, 1878–August 22, 1962), led American educators in the establishment of extracurricular activities as a bona fide component of the school program and was active in leadership positions in the Boy Scouts of America* (see EXTRACURRICULUM).

Born in Williamstown, Missouri, he graduated from LaGrange College in 1899 and became principal of Canton High School and commissioner of schools for Lewis County until 1903. He briefly taught English at his alma mater and in 1904 received his M.A. in English from Brown University. After working as vice-principal at the Peddie Institute in Hightstown, New Jersey, Fretwell taught English at the Polytechnic Preparatory School in Brooklyn until 1913. He earned his doctorate in 1917 at Teachers College, Columbia University, and taught that college's first course on extracurricular activities that fall, teaching there until his retirement in 1943. During World War I, under the auspices of the U.S. Surgeon General's Office, he organized recreation and physical education* programs for stateside rehabilitation hospitals. After the war, Fretwell served as national director of recreation for the American Red Cross. In 1920, he organized and directed until 1938 a training course for camp leaders. In 1921, he became director of education and chair of the Boy Scouts' National Committee on Education, served on the executive board of the Boy Scouts' National Council between 1933 and 1943, and held the post of chief scout executive from 1943 until 1948. As the leading advocate of extracurricular activities in his day, Fretwell lectured widely on the topic and compiled extensive bibliographies. He was associate eidtor of *School Activities* from 1934 to 1962. His major work, *Extra-Curricular Activities in the Secondary Schools* (1931), synthesized extracurricular practices from around the country.

Fretwell's other works include "The Place of Extra-Curricular Activities in Education" (1925) and "Extra-Curricular Activities of Secondary Schools IV: Bibliographies of Home Rooms, Pupil Participation in Government, Finances, Assemblies, and Fraternities" (1926). See his biography in the *National Cyclopaedia of American Biography* (1966), as well as John R. Beale, "Elbert K. Fretwell and the Extra-Curricular Activity Movement, 1917–1931" (1983).

William G. Wraga

FREUDIAN PSYCHOLOGY is derived primarily from the work of Sigmund Freud, who in the 1890s began the process that revolutionized the way human beings view themselves. His structural and developmental theories represent the key components of psychoanalytic theory. Freud believed that human behavior is instinctual and driven by unconscious mechanisms. He proposed a structural theory that postulates that the human psyche is divided into three parts: *id, ego,* and *superego*. The id is dominated by the pleasure principle and involves unconscious processes that are revealed through dreams, slips of the tongue, and free associations. The superego is the moral component of the ego and constantly strives for perfection. The ego, governed by the reality principle, functions to mediate the needs of the id, superego, and reality. To avoid the anxiety that results from the pressure of these drives, the ego employs unconscious defense mechanisms. Freud also believed that every child passes through a sequence of biologically driven psychosexual developmental stages, and that personality is formed by the age of six. If the child is under- or overgratified at any given stage, the child becomes fixated at that stage. Freud's developmental theory has been instrumental in the study of personality formation, in that fixation usually leads to the discontinuance of one componenet of personality development. For example, if a baby is not weaned properly from breast feeding, there is a high probability that he or she will become fixated at the oral stage of development; or if a child is adversely potty trained, he or she will become fixated at the anal stage of development. The manner in which needs are met or not met ultimately determines how a child relates to others and feels about itself. Unresolved needs and conflicts in any stage may afflict a person throughout his or her lifetime.

Additional information on psychoanalysis can be found in Ralph R. Greenson, *The Technique and Practice of Psychoanalysis* (1972). For details on Freud's life see Ernest Jones, *The Life and Work of Sigmund Freud* (1953, 1955, 1957), and Peter Gay, *Freud: A Life for Our Time* (1988).

Harriett H. Ford

FROEBEL, FRIEDRICH (April 21, 1782–June 21, 1852), originator of the kindergarten,* was born in Thuringia, in what is now Germany, the son of a Lutheran minister. He attended the University of Jena, where he was introduced to naturalistic philosophy, rationalism, and the work of Romantic writers. He then learned about the ideas of the Swiss educator Pestalozzi,* at whose model school he studied for two years. After some educational experimentation, Froebel opened the first kindergaten, a play school for young children with adjoining classes for mothers and teachers, in 1837 in Blankenburg, Thuringia. Froebel's somewhat mystical philosophy, described in his *Education of Man* (1826), was based on supposedly natural laws of unity, self-activity, connectedness, and opposites. He designed educational materials and activities, called gifts and occupations, based on these laws. As described in his *Pedagogics of the Kindergarten* (1863), the gifts were a sequenced set of planar and solid geometrical shapes such as a ball, cubes, flat parquetry squares, and triangles. The occupations, based on traditional handicrafts, were activities such as sewing, weaving, and cutting intricate designs and patterns. He also developed fingerplays, songs, games, and poetry based on German folklore and children's play. Designed to socialize young children to be cooperative and internalize self-control, these structured play activities formed the core of his kindergarten methods. After his death, his second wife, Luise, his niece, Henrette Schrader-Breygmann, and others carried on his methods in Germany; and Margarethe Meyer Schurz, Elizabeth Peabody,* Maria Kraus-Boelte, Susan Blow,* Lucy Wheelock,* Anna Bryan,* Alice Putnam,* and others introduced the kindergarten to the United States, where it eventually became incorporated into the public education system.

Autobiographical and biographical information include Ann Taylor Allen, *Feminism and Motherhood in Germany* (1991); Robert B. Downs, *Friedrich Froebel* (1978); Emile Michaelis and H. Keatley Moore, trans., *The Autobiography of Froebel* (1886); Denton J. Snider, *The Life of Friedrich Froebel, Founder of the Kindergarten* (1900); and Lucy Wheelock, trans., ''Autobiography in Letter to the Duke of Meiningen'' (1890).

Barbara Beatty

FUTURE FARMERS OF AMERICA (FFA) has been an important part of American public education, growing in its membership and evolving with agriculture and education. Organized in 1928 in Kansas City, Missouri, with Leslie Applegate as its first president, the FFA traces its original purpose, providing courses in agricultural education and leadership training for farm boys, to the Smith-Hughes Act* (1917). The FFA took its name from Henry Glascoe, an agricultural education instructor who started the Future Farmers of Virginia in

Blacksburg in 1920. One of FFA's founders, Glascoe was largely responsible for its by-laws, constitution, and rituals.

Over the years, the FFA became more inclusive and continued to grow as one of the leading agricultural educational organizations in the United States. It became an integral part of public schooling after 1950 when Congress granted it a federal charter under the National Vocational Education Acts. In 1965, the FFA merged with the New Farmers of America, the organization for African American students of agriculture, adding 50,000 new members. In 1969, it admitted girls into its membership. It adopted the National FFA Organization as its official name in 1988. Six years later Corey Flournoy, of Chicago, became the organization's first African American president and urban student leader. The FFA currently claims 444,497 members in 7,264 rural, urban, and suburban chapters representing fifty states, Puerto Rico, the Virgin Islands, and Guam.

The best source of information is the *1994–1995 Official FFA Manual.*

Jeffrey A. Liles

G

GALLAUDET, THOMAS HOPKINS (December 10, 1787–September 10, 1851), co-founded with Laurent Clerc* and Mason Cogswell the first publicly supported institution for deaf students in the United States, the American School for the Deaf (ASD) in Hartford, Connecticut. Principal from 1817 to 1830, Gallaudet argued effectively for public and private support of deaf education and helped secure the financial viability of ASD and succeeding schools. His actions helped determine the institutional characteristics, curriculum, and pedagogical methods that defined nineteenth-century American deaf education, especially use of sign language in the classroom, acceptance of nonpaying students, employment of deaf teachers, and emphasis on moral development and vocational training.

Gallaudet graduated from Yale College in 1805 and 1810 and Andover Theological Seminary in 1814 and then became acquainted with Alice Cogswell, the deaf daughter of Hartford neighbor Mason Cogswell. An evangelical, Gallaudet thought that Christianizing those who are deaf would hasten the new millennium. He traveled to England, Scotland, and France in 1815 and 1816 to study deaf pedagogy and while in Scotland met philosopher Dugald Stewart, whose work convinced him of the centrality of sign language in deaf education. He then studied French Sign Language and deaf education in Paris and brought back to the United States Laurent Clerc, a nonspeaking, signing, deaf teacher, to help organize ASD.

Gallaudet was involved in educational reform causes as well, supporting high schools,* industrial schools (see VOCATIONAL EDUCATION), women's colleges, and the lyceum* movement. He wrote extensively about these issues and about deaf education, particularly in a British journal, the *Christian Observer*, and in the *American Annals of the Deaf* and *American Annals of Education and Instruction*; he also published several children's books for the American Tract

Society. Gallaudet University, in Washington, D.C., founded by his youngest son, Edward Miner Gaullaudet, is named for him.

Gallaudet's papers are in the Thomas Hopkins Gallaudet and Edward Miner Gallaudet Papers, Library of Congress, Manuscript Division, Washington, D.C. There are, in addition to articles in the periodicals listed above, two important sources for understanding Gallaudet's thinking about deaf education: "A Sermon Delivered at the Opening of the Connecticut Asylum for the Education and Instruction of Deaf and Dumb Persons" (1817) and "A Sermon on the Duty and Advantages of Affording Instruction to the Deaf and Dumb" (Concord, NH: Isaac Hill, 1824). These and all other publications and papers of Gallaudet are available at the Gallaudet University Library. Useful biographical studies are James J. Fernandes, "The Gate to Heaven: T. H. Gallaudet and the Rhetoric of the Deaf Education Movement" (1980); Edward Miner Gallaudet, *The Life of Thomas Hopkins Gallaudet* (1888); and Phyllis Klein Valentine, "American Asylum for the Deaf: A First Experiment in Education, 1817–1880" (1993).

John Vickrey Van Cleve

GARY PLAN attracted considerable national and international attention during the early decades of the twentieth century. Developed by William A. Wirt,* Gary, Indiana, school superintendent (1907–1938), the Gary Plan—also known as the Work-Study-Play Plan—because of its broad emphasis maintained two central characteristics that pertained to all elementary grades. First, because of a concern for efficiency, Wirt believed in maximizing school facilities by constant use of all classrooms, including nights (for adults), weekends, and summers. Second, he expanded the curriculum to include manual training, recreation, nature study, daily auditorium activities (including public speaking, music lessons, and movies), and other subjects beyond traditional academic concerns. According to theory, the plan organized students into two platoons. During the morning, platoon A students occupied the specialized academic classrooms (math, science, English, history, etc.), while platoon B students were in the auditorium, shops, gardens, or playground. They switched facilities during the afternoon. The students, busy every day, developed their mental and physical abilities. The Gary Plan attracted considerable publicity, and by 1929, 202 cities had over 1,000 platoon schools. It also generated much controversy, with New York City, for example, rejecting it in 1917 after a three-year experiment. During the 1920s, the Gary Plan was termed the Platoon School Plan and promoted by the National Association for the Study of the Platoon or Work-Study-Play School Organization, formed in 1925. This organization and its quarterly journal, *The Platoon School*, edited by Alice Barrows, promoted the system until the 1930s. The Gary Plan lost favor during the Depression, with Gary phasing it out by the 1950s. Only a vestige remained in Detroit in later decades (also, refer to PROGRESSIVE EDUCATION).

The Gary Plan can be studied in the William A. Wirt Papers, Lilly Library,

Indiana University, Bloomington, and the Wirt Papers in the Calumet Regional Archives, Indiana University Northwest, Gary. Leading secondary studies include Roscoe D. Case, *The Platoon School in America* (1931); Ronald D. Cohen, *Children of the Mill: Schooling and Society in Gary, Indiana, 1906–1960* (1990); and Ronald D. Cohen and Raymond A. Mohl, *The Paradox of Progressive Education: The Gary Plan and Urban Education* (1979).

Ronald D. Cohen

GENERAL EDUCATION BOARD (GEB) was founded in New York by John D. Rockefeller, Sr., in 1902. The GEB spent over $324 million before it disbanded in 1960. Board founders and leaders assumed that education served as the panacea for most human problems, and they supported schooling at all levels: preschool, primary, secondary, adult, undergraduate, graduate, and professional.

Many of the GEB's efforts were directed to the South, almost exclusively before 1920 and after 1940. It was the major financier of the southern educational campaigns that created working public school systems before World War I. The Board financially supported and often had interlocking directorates with other funds and organizations that controlled educational philanthropy in the South, including the Southern Education Board—formed by the GEB to organize and administer the southern educational campaigns of the early twentieth century—and the Peabody,* John F. Slater,* and Jeanes* funds. For much of its history, the GEB strongly supported industrial* and agricultural education as the proper type of schooling for African Americans; it expended about 20 percent of its funds on African American education.

The GEB funded movements usually associated with the "administrative" progressives (see PROGRESSIVE EDUCATION), but it also supported the Progressive Education Association* and subsidized one of the most creative of the progressive schools, the Lincoln School. It helped to finance the Eight-Year Study* of the progressive secondary schools and funded pioneer studies in child development, including the work of Arnold Gesell. In addition, the Board appropriated $90 million to upgrade U.S. medical education, including major grants to traditionally African American Howard and Meharry medical schools.

The GEB's support for industrial and agricultural training for African Americans, rather than general and academic education, has been the source of much historical controversy. Until the revisionist interpretations of the 1970s, historians accepted the contention of the GEB's leaders, and southern progressives generally, that industrial education was the most desirable type of schooling for African Americans. Recent historians have criticized this approach, recognizing that economic and sociopolitical interests as well as humanitarianian motivations drove these early philanthropists.

The GEB's papers, and the related Anna T. Jeanes Foundation and John F. Slater Fund Papers, are at the Rockefeller Archive Center, Pocantico Hills, New York. For general historical background, refer to Abraham Flexner, *Abraham*

Flexner: An Autobiography (1960); Raymond B. Fosdick, *Adventures in Giving: The Story of the General Education Board* (1962); and the General Education Board's *Review and Final Report, 1902–1964* (1964). More recent and critical scholarship includes James D. Anderson, "Northern Foundations and the Shaping of Southern Rural Black Education, 1902–1935" (1978); Henry Snyder Enck, "The Burden Borne: Northern White Philanthropy and Southern Black Industrial Education, 1900–1915" (1971); and James H. Madison, "John D. Rockefeller's General Education Board and the Rural School Problem in the Midwest, 1900–1930" (1984).

Clinton B. Allison

GIRL SCOUTS OF AMERICA (GSA) was founded on March 12, 1912, in Savannah, Georgia, by Juliette Gordon Low as the female counterpart of the Boy Scouts of America (BSA).* In 1911, on a trip to England, Low met British Scouting founder, Robert S. S. Baden-Powell and Agnes Baden-Powell, his sister and founder of the Girl Guides. Upon her return to the states, Low was determined to create a parallel scouting organization for American girls.

Similar to other character-building organizations that enjoyed a resurgence of popularity during the progressive era (see PROGRESSIVE EDUCATION), the Girls Scouts reflected the concern shown by individuals who felt that the growth of modern, urban, industrial society was eroding the ability of communities to inculcate sound character traits. Therefore, efforts were made in a variety of often gender-segregated youth organizations to take over where it was perceived that the community was failing. The Girl Scout Law encompasses the character traits the organization defined as needing reinforcement. Members promise to "do my best: to be honest, to be fair, to help where I am needed, to be cheerful, to be friendly and considerate, . . . to respect authority, . . . to show respect for myself and others through my words and actions." From its founding, the GSA has conducted a wide range of community service functions as a means of putting these values into action. The history of the Girl Scouts has also reflected changing gender roles of women in American society, especially the expanding employment possibilities for women throughout the century, possibilities that have been consistently celebrated and encouraged by the organization.

Like the BSA, the Girl Scouts grew quickly. Between 1912 and 1920, the membership ballooned from eighteen girls in the original Savannah troop to nearly 70,000 girls in over 3,000 troops. A national headquarters in Washington, D.C., was established in 1913 and was moved in 1916 to New York City, where it remains. In 1917, a national monthly publication, *The Rally*, renamed *American Girl* in 1920, was launched to share information within the growing organization. In 1950, the U.S. Congress granted the Girl Scout a federal charter.

The Girl Scouts currently involves approximately 2.5 million girl in various age-based programs. Girls move from the Daisy Girl Scouts for five- to six-year-olds to Brownie Girl Scouts, Junior Girl Scouts, Cadette Girl Scouts, and finally Senior Girl Scouts for fourteen- to seventeen-year-olds. Girl Scout troops are organized by local geographic councils chartered by the national organization.

The GSA papers are housed at its national headquarters, New York City. The GSA has produced two concise overviews of the organization: *75 Years of Girl Scouting* (1987) and *Highlights in Girl Scouting, 1912–1991* (1991).

Alexander Urbiel

GODDARD, HENRY HERBERT (August 14, 1866–June 20, 1957). Although he was the first to translate and publicize the intelligence tests* of Alfred Binet* and Theodore Simon, Goddard may be remembered more for his invention of the term "moron." He earned his B.A. (1887) and M.A. (1889) at Haverford College and his Ph.D. in psychology, under G. Stanley Hall,* at Clark University. Goddard was first an educator and then a psychologist and merged these two disciplines in his studies of the causation, amelioration, and prevention of "feeblemindedness." To his last days, he maintained his belief in heredity as the essential factor in mental deficiency (see HEREDITARIANISM).

In 1906, Goddard left his psychology professorship at what is now West Chester University (Pennsylvania) to establish the first laboratory for the study of mental deficiency at the Vineland, New Jersey, Training School for Feeble-Minded Boys and Girls. There he validated to his own satisfaction the suitability of his translation of the Binet test for the classification of intelligence. He there coined the term "moron" to describe those with mental ages of eight to twelve, who could thus be trained to function in society.

Goddard may be best known for his research of the Kallikak (a pseudonym based on the Greek words for "beauty" and "bad") extended family. In *The Kallikak Family; A Study in the Heredity of Feeble-Mindedness* (1912), he proposed his hypothesis that mental deficiency is transmitted in true Mendelian fashion via a single entity. Goddard's work, including "The Binet Tests in Relation to Immigration," *Journal of Psycho-Asthenics* (1913), and *Psychology of the Normal and Subnormal* (1919), further purported to link mental deficiency with delinquency and immorality; this work was subsequently used to tighten immigration standards based on mental ability—see, for example, "Mental Tests and the Immigrant," *Journal of Delinquency* (1917). In his later years, Goddard conceded that "feeblemindedness" was not incurable and that the mentally deficient need not be confined lest they reproduce.

Goddard's papers are housed in the Archives of the History of Psychology, University of Akron, Ohio. A biography can be found in *American Men of Science* (1933).

Catharine C. Knight

GOETZ V. ANSELL, 477 F.2d. 636 (1973). See PLEDGE OF ALLEGIANCE.

GOGGIN, CATHARINE (September, 1855–January 4, 1916), gained fame as an early leader of the Chicago Teachers Federation (CTF).* Born in Adirondack,

New York, the daughter of Irish immigrants, she moved to Chicago as a girl. In 1872, three months after her graduation from Central High School, she began teaching elementary school in the the working-class immigrant districts of that city. Goggin joined a group fighting for a pension plan for elementary teachers in 1893, three years later earned a seat as trustee on the city pension board, and became a leading member of the CTF, founded in 1897. After she won election as the Federation's second president in 1899, she filed suit against the city public utilities for tax avoidance. The following year she and her colleague, Margaret Haley,* left the classroom to become paid officials and leaders of the CTF. Goggin served as both the Federation's legislative genius and a skilled political mediator. As the cousin of a popular local judge, she used her political connections and warm personality to advance the CTF's goals. Although less nationally renowned than Haley, Goggin won the loyalty of Chicago's teachers and the respect of labor and civic leaders. As Goggin's health declined, she gradually abdicated more responsibility to Haley. She was killed in a street accident on her way home from a Federation meeting. Her body lay in state at Chicago City Hall, honored by the city's teachers as well as city and national labor and government officials.

Goggin left no personal papers. CTF records at the Chicago Historical Society include her professional papers, legal documents, and correspondence.

Kate Rousmaniere

GONG LUM V. RICE, 275 U.S. 78 (1927). Plaintiffs of Chinese descent, residing in Mississippi, sought a writ of mandamus to require school officials to permit their daughter to attend an all-white school in their school district of residence, rather than a school for children of other races in a neighboring district. In affirming the Mississippi Supreme Court's decision denying the writ of mandamus and upholding the state's separate but equal public education system, the U.S. Supreme Court relied on *Plessy v. Ferguson.** The Court held that "a Chinese citizen of the United States is [not] denied equal protection of the laws when [she] is classed among the colored races and furnished facilities for education equal to that offered to all" (p. 85). With regard to the absence of a colored school in plaintiff's own school district in Mississippi, the Court observed that the "system of creating the common school districts for the two races, white and colored, does not require schools for each race as such to be maintained in each district" (p. 84). The effect of denying the writ of mandamus was that the Asian students were required to attend schools for races other than white.

Ralph D. Mawdsley

GOSS V. LOPEZ, 419 U.S. 565 (1975), is the leading case on the due process rights of students in public schools* who may be subject to short-term suspensions because of their misbehavior. Nine high school students in Columbus, Ohio, who were suspended without hearings for a variety of infractions, filed the lawsuit. A three-judge district court panel agreed with the students' assertion that their right to due process was violated by the state law that allowed them to be suspended for up to ten days without a hearing. The U.S. Supreme Court affirmed in favor of the students. The Court held that since the state conferred a property right upon students to receive an education, that right could not be withdrawn on the ground of misconduct unless fundamentally fair procedures were conducted to determine whether the misbehavior had, in fact, taken place. As such, the Court ruled that since a short-term suspension was not a minimal deprivation of their right to an education, students could not be excluded from school for up to ten days unless they received at least notice of the charges against them and had an opportunity to respond. At the same time, aware of educators' need to maintain a safe and orderly environment in the schools, the Court added that there was no reason to delay the time between giving notice and students' responses. The Court also noted that students who pose a continuing danger to persons or property or who disrupt the educational process can be removed immediately, but they must be provided with due process as soon as is practicable.

Charles J. Russo

GRAMMAR SCHOOL. See CLASSICAL CURRICULUM; LATIN GRAMMAR SCHOOL.

GRISCOM, JOHN (September 27, 1774–February 26, 1852), known as the first chemistry teacher in the United States, became one of the most prominent founders of the New York (City) House of Refuge (1825), the first institution of its kind in the United States. Griscom founded the Society for the Prevention of Pauperism in New York in 1817. The following year he toured European charitable institutions and returned convinced that a different approach to pauperism was required. Griscom and other New York philanthropists regarded juvenile delinquency—caused, they believed, by a lack of education and skill on the part of young people—as one of the principal reasons for continued pauperism. Break the cycle of crime and dependency, they asserted, and pauperism—endemic poverty—can be alleviated. In 1823, the Society for the Prevention of Pauperism renamed itself the Society for the Reformation of Juvenile Delinquents and called for the establishment of a house of refuge for juvenile offenders. Griscom, impressed by an institution for juvenile offenders in Hofwyl, Switzerland, took the lead in pushing for a similar institution in New York. The state of New York chartered the New York House of Refuge in 1824, and it opened its doors the next year (see REFORM SCHOOLS).

The records of the New York House of Refuge are housed in the Manuscript Division of the Carnegie Library at Syracuse University. Also see, Joseph M. Hawes, *Children in Urban Society: Juvenile Delinquency in Nineteenth-Century Society* (1971); Robert M. Mennel, *Thorns and Thistles: Juvenile Delinquents in the United States, 1825–1940* (1973); Robert S. Pickett, *House of Refuge:*

Origins of Juvenile Reform in New York State, 1815–1857 (1969); David J. Rothman, *The Discovery of the Asylum: Social Order and Disorder in the New Republic* (1971); Steven L. Schlossman, *Love and the American Delinquent: The Theory and Practice of "Progressive" Juvenile Justice, 1825–1920* (1977).

Joseph M. Hawes

GUIDANCE COUNSELING. The process of guiding a person into a suitable occupation was originally based on the concept of matching an individual's qualifications with specific occupational specifications. During the late nineteenth and early twentieth centuries, several social and psychological instruments, pioneered by early social workers and psychologists, influenced the guidance movement. One such instrument, the community social service surveys, an early attempt at data gathering, reported that students were neither at work nor in the school. Another, the scientific measurement approach, utilized standardized tests to measure innate intelligence to help gauge a person's ability and thus placement in the job market. The development of counseling techniques, pioneered by Frank Parsons* in Boston at the Vocational Bureau, influenced and speeded their adoption by many school systems around the country. Finally, the gathering and dissemination of occupational information was systematized by the development of job descriptions in the 1920s.

Rapid industrialization in the 1880s, the unprecedented numbers of southern and eastern European immigrants, and the education of the newly freed African Americans created a need to integrate, as defined by the experts, millions of individuals into society. The desire to help individuals achieve some success in life may have served as one of the initial impulses for vocational guidance. It began informally in the settlement houses (see ADDAMS, JANE), where workers developed a list of employers who would consider hiring a newly arrived immigrant adult, and if possible, a child. By 1910 or 1911, it was obvious to these early settlement house workers and other progressives that a more effective process would be needed to keep the child in school to receive additional education and that a more systematic and organized process would be necessary to help immigrants and poor people find a job.

During the progressive era (see PROGRESSIVE EDUCATION), the development of the differential curriculum also prompted the need for counseling. The breakdown of the academic curriculum as the common learning experience for all school children and the creation of different educational tracks, such as business, technical, and industrial courses, necessitated guidance counselors in the schools (see TRACKING; VOCATIONAL EDUCATION). The new curriculum, especially vocational in nature, was based on the assumption that not all children were capable of achieving at the highest level and that a person had to find a particular niche; students, in other words, needed help to make proper choices. Consequently, they were not so much placed into the nonacademic curricula, or given a particular track, but to a great extent they self-selected their careers based on the use of the IQ test and "assistance" from guidance counselors (see INTELLIGENCE TESTING). The vocational guidance process became the vehicle for pointing out to students that, based on the results of standardized tests and their defined ability, they were best suited to a range of nonprofessional jobs. The theoretical role of the guidance counselor was to give the student the best opportunity to succeed in the workplace. In reality, students were often given a list of choices based, not on their free choice, but on race, IQ, and gender, as well as counselor biases and industrial needs.

Guidance counseling served as the vanguard of industry, ensuring that skilled workers would be available to fill the blue-collar positions in the factories. Several school systems allowed private organizations, such as local businesses, to have access to student records in order to help students select a job or to persuade a student to remain in school. The concept of efficiency superseded individual choice; that is, the expert used science to create a well-ordered, smooth-running, and rational society that ensured that everyone operated at peak efficiency.

Vocational education was also closely connected to the development of vocational guidance. Schools became a place where a child was prepared for work as opposed to a place where one can acquire knowledge, understand the world, and ultimately make judgments based on one's individual judgments.

Guidance counseling has been an integral part of public education since the 1920s. It served the purposes of the educator as a way to ensure that all children would experience success in the workplace. As long as the objectivity of the various standardized tests administered to the students remained unchallenged, the counselor continued to perform the same role. During the 1960s and 1970s, serious scientific as well as ethical and moral issues were raised regarding the validity of the overwhelming majority of nonacademic noncollege tracks in high schools.* Nevertheless, during the 1980s and 1990s, the guidance counselor's role did not change except in name: career development, not vocational guidance; and technology training, not vocational education (see CAREER EDUCATION).

For general information, see Norton W. Grubb, "Learning to Work: The Case for Reintegrating Job Training and Work" (1996), and Ira S. Steinberg, "On the Justification of Guidance" (1964).

Peter Sola

H

HALEY, MARGARET ANGELA (November 15, 1861–January 5, 1939), was the founding leader of the Chicago Teachers Federation (CTF)* and an activist reformer for elementary teachers' rights within professional associations and school systems. The daughter of Irish immigrants, she taught in Chicago's schools for fifteen years before she joined the newly formed CTF for elementary school teachers. As a paid business representative, she led campaigns against corporate tax exemptions and the centralization of the city school administration, advocated improved teachers' working conditions, a stable pension plan, increased salaries and tenure laws, and enlarged professional status for teachers. She engineered the CTF's affiliation with the Chicago Federation of Labor in 1902 and the newly formed American Federation of Teachers* in 1916.

In 1901, Haley became the first woman and first elementary school teacher to speak from the floor of the National Education Association (NEA).* In her notorious 1904 NEA speech, "Why Teachers Should Organize," she enumerated her reform proposals not only for the organization of protective unions for teachers but also for an expanded notion of teacher professionalism that included the opportunity to develop progressive pedagogy, improve educational practice, and promote the democratic participation of teachers in school management.

Haley, a former student of the Cook County Normal School (see Parker, Francis Wayland), promoted progressive education* and expanded teacher education. She also supported women's suffrage and labor law reform, and she displayed expertise at maneuvering her different supporters on behalf of teachers' rights. Haley lived and worked in a wide circle of female political activists, including Ella Flagg Young,* Jane Addams,* and CTF founder Catharine Goggin.* Highly popular among teachers through the 1920s, she died two years after the CTF amalgamated into the Chicago Teachers Union.

The CTF's papers at the Chicago Historical Society contain a wealth of original material on Haley. Haley's autobiographical account of her CTF work was edited by Robert Reid and published with Haley's *Battleground* (1982). Haley's role as a union leader is analyzed in several studies of American teacher unions, including Marjorie Murphy, *Blackboard Unions: The AFT and the NEA, 1900–1980* (1990), and Wayne J. Urban, *Why Teachers Organized* (1982).

Kate Rousmaniere

HALL, GRANVILLE STANLEY (February 1, 1844–April 24, 1924), was a pioneer in the field of psychology. He received the first doctorate in the United States in 1878 from Harvard University, founded the American Psychological Association in 1892 and served as its first president (1892–1893), created the first psychological laboratory at Johns Hopkins University in 1883, and began the *American Journal of Psychology* in 1887, the first psychology journal in the United States. Hall also served as the first president of Clark University in 1889, where he helped to develop a strong foundation for graduate education and research.

Hall made significant contributions to educational psychology and the study of children by developing questionnaires on child development and applying the principles of evolution to problems of human development. Hall's developmental psychology is elaborated in *Adolescence: Its Psychology, and Its Relations to Physiology, Anthropology, Sociology, Sex, Crime, Religion, and Education* (1904), his most influental work. Hall's later interests included aging, which influenced him to write *Senescence* (1922).

Hall's papers are housed at Clark University. He wrote two autobiographical works: *Recreations of a Psychologist* (1920) and *The Life and Confessions of a Psychologist* (1923). The leading biography is by Dorothy Ross, *G. Stanley Hall: The Psychologist as Prophet* (1972).

Harriett H. Ford

HALL, SAMUEL READ (October 27, 1795–June 26, 1877), was an educator, author, and minister generally credited with establishing the first school for educating teachers in the United States, writing the first American book on teaching, organizing some of the earliest education associations, and introducing new instructional methods and materials. His pioneering efforts contributed toward the professionalization of teaching and the standardization of education.

Hall established his first teacher-training school in Concord, Vermont, in 1823, where he prescribed the curriculum and admitted young children for demonstration and practice purposes, thereby establishing a laboratory school and introducing practice teaching. This model of a common curriculum, professional classes, and practice teaching was later replicated by essentially all normal schools.*

His most important volume was based on his observations as a teacher and was written to explain the task to those preparing to enter the field. Titled *Lectures on School-Keeping* (1829), it was immensely popular and influential and eventually went through five editions through 1852. The last chapter in this book was expanded and published as *Lectures to Female Teachers* (1832). His writings and lectures emphasized the need to know subject matter, the importance of making study pleasant and practical, and the desirability of not limiting instruction to the textbook.

After seven years at the Concord Academy, Hall resigned to become principal of the English Department and head of the new teacher seminary at Phillips Academy in Andover, Massachusetts (1830–1837). During his tenure there, he wrote seven textbooks and helped to organize the American Institute of Instruction,* which successfully prodded the Massachusetts legislature to establish the first publicly supported normal school (Lexington, 1839) and appoint a common school superintendent, Horace Mann.* Failing health and finances led Hall to leave Phillips in 1837. Declining the position of president of the new Oberlin College, he instead went to the Holmes-Plymouth Academy in Plymouth, New Hampshire, where, once again, he established a department for training teachers. In 1840, he became the principal of Craftsbury Academy and pastor of the Craftsbury Congregational Church in Vermont. His chronic poor health forced him to take less burdensome positions, living out his last twenty years writing, lecturing, and ministering in Brownington, Vermont, where he died.

No repository of Hall's papers exists, and surprisingly little remains. Some correspondence relating to his possible appointment as Oberlin president is located in that college's archives, and a few documents about Academy affairs remain at Phillips Academy Archives. Hall's *Lectures* has been reprinted several times; the most useful edition, by Arthur D. Wright and George E. Gardner (1929), includes an account of Hall's life and works. Henry Barnard provides a biographical sketch and discusses Hall's work in the *American Journal of Education* (vol. 5, 1858). A more recent account is Richard Paul Finn, "An Historical Analysis of the Contributions of Samuel Read Hall to Nineteenth-Century Teacher Education" (1970), and Tedd Levy, "First in His Class: The Many Contributions of Samuel Read Hall" (1991).

Tedd Levy

HANNA, PAUL ROBERT (June 21, 1902–April 8, 1988), is widely recognized for his conception of "expanding communities" as a scope and sequence curriculum framework for elementary school social studies.* Born in Sioux City, Iowa, he received a B.A. degree from Hamline College (1924) and a doctorate from Teachers College, Columbia University (1929). He then served as a faculty member at Teachers College for the next five years. From 1935 to 1967, Hanna served as a professor of education at Stanford University, where he headed the elementary education program, retiring as the Lee L. Jacks Professor of Education. In 1954, he founded the Stanford International Development Education Center and was a senior research associate at the Hoover Institution on War, Revolution, and Peace. He was also a consultant to the State Department, the United Nations, the United Nations Educational, Scientific, and Cultural Organization, and many private agencies.

From 1934 to 1947, Hanna and others developed the *Building America* series, which was published and distributed through the Association for Supervision and Curriculum Development. During his career, Hanna also served as editor of the Scott, Foresman social studies textbook series and wrote textbooks, including spellers for children and volumes for educators.

Hanna's papers are housed at the Hoover Institute, Stanford University. For a brief biography of Hanna, see Murry R. Nelson, "Paul Robert Hanna" (1978); also see Murry R. Nelson, "Paul Hanna" (1988). Jane B. Powers treats his contribution in "Paul R. Hanna's Scope and Sequence" (1986).

Chung-Ju Fan

HARRIS, WILLIAM TORREY (September 10, 1835–November 5, 1909), was both an eminently successful school administrator and a respected scholar who was regarded as the leader of the St. Louis movement in philosophy. Born in North Killingly, Connecticut, he studied at Yale University but never completed a degree. He began his career as a teacher in St. Louis and rapidly rose in the ranks of the school system, becoming superintendent in 1868. He actively supported coeducation* and age-grading,* worked toward the consolidation* of rural schools, and during his superintendency introduced the kindergarten.* Harris resigned his superintendency in 1880 to resume his philosophical studies with Amos Bronson Alcott* in Concord, Massachusetts. Having founded the *Journal of Speculative Philosophy* in 1867 as part of an effort to offset the influence of Herbert Spencer in America, Harris became America's leading Hegalian. In 1889, President Benjamin Harrison appointed him as commissioner of education (see UNITED STATES DEPARTMENT OF EDUCATION). He served in that position until 1906; during his tenure, he improved educational recordkeeping and his annual *Reports* became models of their kind.

During his career, Harris became the leading spokesperson for a curriculum drawn from the finest fruits of Western civilization. In the case of young children, he was fond of expressing this in terms of "the five windows of the soul," by which he meant arithmetic and mathematics, geography, history, grammar, and literature and art. For secondary education, he advocated the study of Latin and Greek as well as the classics of literature. Harris was deeply suspicious of manual training as an educational reform, publicly debating Calvin M. Woodward.* He made only grudging concessions to efforts designed to attune the curriculum to the psychological needs and interests of students, confronting disciples of Herbart in a dispute over the report of the Committee of Fifteen on Elementary Education (1895) (see HERBARTARIAN MOVEMENT).

The Harris papers are located in the Library of Congress, and his *Reports* represent an excellent source of his ideas. Henry Ridgely Evans, "A List of the Writing of William Torrey Harris," in the Commissioner's *Report for the Year Ending June 30, 1907*, lists 479 of Harris's articles, addresses, and other publications. Harris's most famous work in education is *Psychologic Foundations of Education* (1898). Two older biographical studies are Kurt Leidecker,

Yankee Teacher: Life of William Torrey Harris (1946), and J. S. Roberts, *William T. Harris: A Critical Study of His Educational and Related Philosphical Views* (1924). Merle Curti, *The Social Ideas of American Educators* (1935), includes an astute assessment of Harris's role in education.

Herbert M. Kliebard

HARVARD DESCRIPTIVE LIST (1887). See SCIENCE EDUCATION.

HAZELWOOD SCHOOL DISTRICT V. KUHLMEIER, 484 U.S. 260 (1988). Former student editors of a high school newspaper unsuccessfully sought declarative and monetary relief after a high school principal had deleted two pages from the newspaper on part of which were two articles on divorce and student pregnancy. The principal found the divorce article objectionable because one of the parents had not had an opportunity to respond, and the student pregnancy article objectionable because the students could be identified. The newspaper operated as part of the school's journalism course and received a significant portion of its funding from the school. In reversing the Eighth Circuit Court of Appeals, which had found that the students' free expression rights had been violated, the U.S. Supreme Court found the principal had not violated the students' constitutional rights where he reasonably believed that the articles could not be modified in time to permit publication prior to the end of the school term. A school newspaper that is part of an academic course for which students receive credit is not a public forum, and therefore school officials could set reasonable restrictions on speech. In this carefully crafted opinion, the Court found no free speech violation as long as editorial control over student expression in school-sponsored expressive activities is reasonably related to legitimate pedagogical concerns.

Ralph D. Mawdsley

HEAD START is a federally funded program administered by the Department of Health and Human Services providing comprehensive developmental services to qualifying preschool children and their families. Initiated in 1965 by the Office of Economic Opportunity under the directorship of Sargent Shriver, it was conceived as a major strategy to fight the War on Poverty. Its conceptual basis includes early intervention through compensatory educational programming. The program's major components include (1) health, nutritional, and social services for children and families utilizing interagency collaboration; (2) parental empowerment through job opportunities, education, support services, and local program planning; (3) developmentally and culturally responsive practice, developmental assessments, and individualized planning; (4) the improvement of parenting skills; (5) parent volunteerism; and, (6) five program options based on community needs. Selection critieria include children age three to school age whose families are at or below the poverty line or are eligible for public assistance. Ten percent of the enrollment may exceed the income guidelines. In addition, 10 percent of the enrollment opportunities in each state must be made available to children with disabilities. The impact of the Head Start program has been widespread, providing comprehensive services to more than 11 million children and their families and serving as a model for many educational innovations. Research has demonstrated long-term positive effects for children and supports the program as an investment rather than an expense. Finally, Head Start has profoundly affected the field of early childhood education in areas of professional development, applied research, and preschool programs (see COMPENSATORY EDUCATION; ELEMENTARY AND SECONDARY EDUCATION ACT).

Refer to the Department of Health and Human Services, "Rules and Regulations of Head Start Program" (1992). Also, see Polly Greenberg, "Before the Beginning: A Participant's View" (1990), and Joan Lombardi, "Head Start: The Nation's Pride, a Nation's Challenge" (1990).

Nancy T. McKnight

HEALTH EDUCATION has functioned as a separate academic discipline for approximately the last sixty years. The modern era of health education in the United States grew out of the child study* movement of the early 1900s, which saw the first of several White House conferences on the health of children beginning in 1901. It was also during this time that Dr. Thomas Denison Wood established the first professional preparation program in hygiene at Columbia University. Known as the "Father of Health Education," Wood also founded the American Child Health Association. In 1910, the American Physical Education Association (see AMERICAN ALLIANCE FOR HEALTH, PHYSICAL EDUCATION, RECREATION, AND DANCE) recognized the distinction between the fields of health education and physical education* by making "School Hygiene and Physical Education" the theme for its seventeenth annual meeting. The founding of the Child Health Organization (CHO) in 1918 as a result of concern over childhood malnutrition is generally recognized as the beginning of the health education movement. To assist in promoting school health practices, the term "hygiene" was replaced with "health education" during the CHO's 1919 conference in New York City.

Until this time, public health educators were primarily writers, journalists, social workers, and nurses (home visits) who focused on sanitation and control of epidemics through quarantine and fumigation. No health education existed in the schools. Health education efforts in this area consisted mostly of lectures, pamphlets, news releases, and exhibits. Around 1917, a new philosophy emerged that emphasized involvement of the learner in the educational process. The principal function of health educators subsequently became the provision of learning experiences related to health as well as direct interaction with people in face-to-face settings in order to bring about these experiences. Program foci also shifted to an emphasis on communicable diseases as well as infant and maternal mortality. By 1929, thirty-six states had laws dealing with health education in the schools.

The 1930s and 1940s saw public health educators begin to adopt community organization principles, using existing community groups, such as parent-teacher associations* and voluntary agencies, and their resources to confront local and regional health problems systematically. By the 1960s, the field of health education entered the "behavioral era" in which public health practice was profoundly influenced by knowledge of determinants of human behavior, application of this knowledge to program planning, incorporation of conceptual models from the psychological and social sciences, and use of rigorous evaluation formats to determine the effectiveness of health education strategies in modifying health practices.

Professional preparation programs in health education follow guidelines set forward by the National Task Force on the Preparation and Practice of Health Educators in *A Competency-Based Framework for Professional Development of Certified Health Education Specialists*. This document culminated a ten-year effort to establish a credentialing process for certifying health educators. Between 1978 and 1985, groups of health educators assembled at the First and Second Bethesda Conferences to determine the competencies of the entry-level health educator in school, community, and medical care settings. In 1988, a national credentialing examination system for becoming a certified health education specialist was established by the National Commission for Health Education Credentialing. National accreditation also exists for many professional preparation programs, including undergraduate community health and school health as well as graduate programs in public health education.

The strength and influence of health education is founded on its broad base of several professional organizations, each with overlapping goals. Together these organizations comprise the Coalition of National Health Education Organizations and include the American Association for Health Education, the American College Health Association, the American School Health Association, the Association of State and Territorial Directors of Health Promotion and Public Health Education, the Society for Public Health Education, and the Society of State Directors of Health, Physical Education, and Recreation (also refer to SEX EDUCATION).

Secondary sources include Thomas J. Butler, *Principles of Health Education and Health Promotion* (1996); Glen G. Gilbert and Robin G. Sawyer, *Health Education: Creating Strategies for School and Community Health* (1995); and Richard K. Means, *A History of Health Education in the United States* (1962).

Michael J. Cleary

HENDRICK HUDSON CENTRAL SCHOOL DISTRICT V. ROWLEY, 458 U.S. 176 (1982), was the first special education case reviewed by the U.S. Supreme Court. The dispute centered around Amy Rowley, a deaf first-grader in New York with excellent lip-reading skills. After Amy's parents and school officials were unable to compromise on the Rowleys' request that Amy be assigned a sign language interpreter during academic classes, administrative review upheld the district's decision to deny the interpreter (see DEAF EDUCATION).

Having exhausted administrative remedies, the Rowleys filed suit. A federal trial court ordered the interpreter. It noted that while her academic performance was above average, Amy would have learned even more had the interpreter been present to assist her in receiving the free appropriate public education to which she was entitled under the Education for All Handicapped Children Act (EHA),* now the Individuals with Disabilities Education Act. The Second Circuit affirmed in favor of the Rowleys.

The Supreme Court reversed this decision. It opined that in determining whether an education is appropriate, the courts cannot substitute their own conceptions of sound educational policy for those of school officials. The Court rejected the notion that the EHA requires services designed to maximize the potential of a child with a disability. It found that since Amy had personalized instruction and related services, earned passing grades in her regular classroom, and advanced from grade to grade, she received an appropriate education. The Court held that instead of the best program available, the EHA mandates that a student with a disability be provided with one that is appropriate. In so doing, the Court interpreted the EHA as a floor of educational opportunity rather than an open-ended ceiling under which students with disabilities can reach their maximum potential.

Charles J. Russo and Debra L. Russo

HERBART, JOHANN FRIEDRICH. See HERBARTARIAN MOVEMENT.

HERBARTARIAN MOVEMENT, a trans-Atlantic educational movement, originated in Germany in the early nineteenth century and was introduced to the United States in the late nineteenth century by Americans, such as Charles De Garmo,* who had been educated in German universities. The movement originated with the educational philosophy of Johann Friedrich Herbart (1776–1841). Herbart, who studied philosophy under Johann Gottlieb Fichte, earned his doctorate at the University of Gottingen in 1802. He developed an interest in education, was a tutor, and visited Pestalozzi's institutes in Switzerland (see PESTALOZZIANISM). Herbart taught at the Universities of Gottingen and Koningsberg, where he conducted seminars on philosophy, psychology, and pedagogy. At Koningsberg, Herbart organized a pedagogical seminar and supervised a demonstration school. Among his books were *General Principles of Pedagogy Deduced from the Aim of Education* and *Outlines of Pedagogical Lectures.* He emphasized moral development as the focus of education, "interests," "apperception," correlation of ideas, and systematization of instruction.

Herbart's leading interpreters were Tuiskon Ziller at the University of Leipzig and Wilhelm Rein at the University of Jena. Ziller and Rein introduced American educators such as Charles De Garmo and Charles and Frank McMurry to Herbart's educational philosophy. Returning to the United States, American Herbartians popularized Herbart's philosophy and pedagogy in the period between 1880 and 1900. For the American Herbartians, Herbart's instructional steps—preparation, presentation, association, and application—were a key phase of the method. The National Herbart Society for the Scientific Study of Teaching was organized in 1885 and reorganized in 1902 as the National Society for the Study of Education.* After enjoying several decades of intense popularity, Herbartianism waned, replaced by John Dewey's* experimentalism and Edward L. Thorndike's* scientific psychology.

For Herbart's theories, see his *Science of Education* (1892) and *Outlines of Educational Doctrine* (1901). Finally, see Henry Felkin and Emmie Felkin, *An Introduction in Herbart's Science and Practice in Education* (1898).

Gerald L. Gutek

HEREDITARIANISM is a theory that looks for genetic causes of such social behaviors or problems as inequality, crime, gender roles, or differences in intellectual ability and educational achievement. Tracing back to the mid-nineteenth century, it reflects the impact of Mendelian genetics and Darwin's evolutionary theory on social philosophy. Herbert Spencer, the influential Social Darwinist, believed that societies evolved like biological organisms, with social improvement resulting from the unrestricted operation of natural selection and the "survival of the fittest." Consequently, he opposed state intervention to ameliorate conditions such as poverty, since it unnaturally aided the unfit against the workings of natural law and evolutionary social progress. Sir Francis Galton, Charles Darwin's cousin, similarly argued in *Hereditary Genius* (1869) that intellectual ability was inherited and that the British elite of his period were innately superior, thereby justifying existing inequalities. Hereditarianism and Social Darwinism have exerted a profound influence on social and education policy in the United States. The turn-of-the-century eugenics movement in the United States was based on the hereditarian assumption that human societies could be improved through the selective breeding of innately superior individuals. The belief that races, nationalities, and classes are inherently unequal supported the immigration restrictions of the 1920s and, in some states, the forced sterilization of the "feeble-minded." In schools, intelligence tests,* believed to be measures of innate ability, were widely adopted and used to help track an increasingly diverse student population (see TRACKING). Some educational historians have argued that hereditarian explanations of social problems gained favor whenever liberal reforms failed, as happened following the common school* movement, the progressive era (see PROGRESSIVE EDUCATION), and the educational and social reforms of the 1960s and early 1970s. Hereditarians argue that the intractability of educational inequality and social problems supports their contentions that many problems have genetic rather than environmental causes. However, critics of the hereditarian position not only dispute its scientific support but also contend that it ignores broader social structural causes for the behaviors in question and provides an ideological rationalization for existing social inequalities.

For one of the earliest "scientific" hereditarian documents, see Sir Francis Galton, *Hereditary Genius* (1869). Richard Hofstadter, *Social Darwinism in American Thought* (1955), provides a good overview of that theory's influence in the late nineteenth and early twentieth centuries. Robert Church, *Education in the United States* (1976), and Michael B. Katz, *The Irony of Early School Reform* (1968), discuss the historical role of hereditarianism in educational theory and practice. Hereditarian arguments on intelligence and educational achievement include Arthur R. Jensen, "How Much Can We Boost IQ and Scholastic Achievement?" (1969), and, more recently, Richard J. Herrnstein and Charles Murray, *The Bell Curve* (1994). For hereditarian explanations of other human behaviors, see E. O. Wilson, *Sociobiology* (1975), or James Q. Wilson and Richard J. Herrnstein, *Crime and Human Nature* (1985). R. C. Lewontin, Steven Rose, and Leon J. Kamin, *Not in Our Genes* (1984), provide a critique of a variety of hereditarian and biological determinist theories, as does Stephen J. Gould, *The Mismeasure of Man* (1981).

Stephen H. Aby

HIGH SCHOOLS. Free public high schools began when Boston opened the English Classical School,* later known as English High, in 1821. It offered a nonclassical, English curriculum to non-college-bound boys only. The first urban high schools along the eastern seaboard, in the South, and in the border states initially excluded girls, though most of these places ultimately built separate "female" high schools. The typical free high school in the North by the midnineteenth century was coeducational, located in a village or small town, and taught by one or two teachers, who mostly offered a nonclassical education to a small number of students. Only about 5 percent of school-aged students attended high schools in the urban North by the 1880s. Girls, many of whom became teachers, comprised the majority of secondary students. Most pupils, both male and female, came from native-born and middle-class families.

Tainted by its association with the education of urban poor, public education gained status during the nineteenth century by building quality secondary schools for largely middle-class youths. Drawing affluent students into the high school system in particular helped to popularize public education in general. High schools offered a rigorous academic education in advanced subjects that before the 1820s had been available only in tuition academies.* Most pupils studied an English curriculum, which emphasized useful subjects, including English grammar, algebra, geography, history, science, and modern language. Critics opposed to public taxation for secondary education often incorrectly called the high school a classical school. Even if they offered a class in Latin, most high schools were oriented toward an English or modern curriculum; instead, they prepared most boys for commercial and mercantile jobs and the professions, and girls for teaching and domestic life.

The fit between credentials and jobs was not as tight in the nineteenth century as later became true. A handful of boys gained an edge for white-collar jobs, and girls had an advantage for teaching posts by merely attending high school. Only a quarter of those admitted to high school before the 1880s graduated, and except for some teacher training (i.e., normal classes), vocationalism per se was absent (see NORMAL SCHOOLS). Vocational education* grew in importance during the twentieth century, profoundly changing the missions and social functions of high schools. With fewer jobs open to school-aged children and tougher and enforcable child labor laws, secondary enrollment dramatically rose, but the high school was still not a mass institution. Growing enrollments transformed its character, however. Although in the 1890s the Committee of Ten* of the National Education Association* recommended against offering students different curricula geared to their future occupations, by the 1920s high schools offered an array of vocational courses, explicitly trying to link schools with a more complex industrial society. High schools gradually became more common in the South, at least for whites, and even rural or county secondary institutions there tried to slow urban migration by offering vocational courses in agricultural science. Guidance counselors became more common throughout the nation's schools during the 1920s, as standardized tests sorted youth for different curricular tracks. Critics of tracking* complained that academic classes served middle- and upper-class students, whereas vocational courses hosted the children of manual workers. The notion that education should be linked with job opportunities nevertheless remained common.

High schools also gave birth to a new student culture in the early twentieth century. Students created literary societies and newspapers in many village and city high schools in the nineteenth century, but teachers and administrators gradually monitored and controlled more aspects of student life. This reflected a growing concern for the social rather than the intellectual goals of high schools. In 1918, a committee of educators issued the *Cardinal Principles Report on the Reorganization of Secondary Education,** which, among other things, emphasized that schools should help youths learn how to spend their leisure time wisely and enhance their social skills (see ADOLESCENCE). By then, more pupils had joined various adult-sponsored clubs and organizations, participated in or cheered for various athletic* teams, and increasingly saw going to high school as a social rather than simply intellectual activity. The division of schooling by age-grading* promoted the formation of stronger peer associations among students. Parents, teachers, and administrators increasingly bemoaned the effects of such peer associations throughout the twentieth century.

High schools nationwide became mass institutions following World War II. While entrance examinations were common in town and city high schools during the nineteenth century, they had disappeared by 1900; in the 1950s, nearly every adolescent attended high school and was expected to graduate or would wear the pejorative label "dropout."* As high schools became mass institutions in the 1950s and 1960s, they lost the privileged status they had once held in American life when only a few youths attended. Vocationalism was reinforced by the life adjustment movement* of the 1940s, which according to many critics made high schools even less academic than in previous decades.

Many critics have decried the lack of serious academic expectations and achievement in America's high schools. James B. Conant* and other educators in the late 1950s and early 1960s called for even more sorting of high school youths, separating the college- from the non-college-bound while keeping everyone under the same roof in the "comprehensive" high school. The Cold War nourished the belief that the education system had failed to produce enough talented individuals to compete with the Soviet Union's technological and strategic advances. In the 1980s and early 1990s, many states raised academic standards, some even mandating exit exams before conferring high school diplomas upon students. Politicians, business representatives, and educators bombarded the public with claims about declining standardized test scores, poor performance in international academic competition, and the general trend toward mediocrity, with students enrolling in undemanding courses taught by marginal teachers. Critics held America's educational system, especially its high schools, accountable for many social ills as well as a declining economy.

Racial segregation has been a persistent problem. Segregated high schools were the norm in the South before the U.S. Supreme Court decision, *Brown v. Board of Education*,* in 1954. Violent resistance by whites to busing* for racial integration occurred by the late 1960s and early 1970s, in the North and in the South. Northern high schools grew more segregated after the 1960s because of a declining industrial economy, the rise of all-white suburbs, and the resurgence of racism. As affluent whites dominated suburbs and the poor and minorities remained in inner cities, "high schools" became profoundly different institutions. Some suburban high schools had facilities rivaling many colleges, with a largely college preparatory orientation, while their inner-city counterparts increasingly seemed like "blackboard jungles" to many critics.

The clientele and social functions of high schools have dramatically changed since their origins in the 1820s. The educational mission and structure of high schools will continue to evolve as teachers, parents, and policymakers face new economic and political challenges in the twenty-first century.

See Edward A. Krug's classics, *The Shaping of the American High School: I, 1880–1920* (1964) and *The Shaping of the American High School: II, 1920–1940* (1972), as well as Robert Hampel's *Last Little Citadel: American High Schools since 1940* (1986). William J. Reese, *The Origins of the American High School* (1995), offers the most recent, comprehensive historical treatment. The leading critics of high schools include Ernest L. Boyer,* *High School* (1983); James B. Conant, *The American High School Today* (1959); and Arthur G. Powell, Eleanor Farrar, and David K. Cohen, *The Shopping Mall High School: Winners and Losers in the Educational Marketplace* (1985).

William J. Reese and Scott Walter

HIGHER HORIZONS PROGRAM was a nationally emulated effort by the New York City Board of Education to increase the academic achievement of minority students. Launched with considerable fanfare in September 1959, the program served more than 100,000 students before it was quietly abandoned in the summer of 1966.

Created in response to civil rights protestors' demands for school integration, Higher Horizons built on the efforts of the Demonstration Guidance Project (DPG). Initiated in 1956, DGP offered intensive compensatory education to students at one junior high school.* The program, which continued when students moved on to high school,* included small classes, remedial instruction, cultural activities, counseling, clinical services, and parental involvement. DGP dramatically raised academic achievement. By offering the components of DGP on a vastly larger scale and extending them to elementary students, education officials hoped to demonstrate that the schools served the educational needs of African American children.

Higher Horizons increased arithmetic achievement and led to some improvement in classroom behavior. Still, it failed to achieve the dramatic results of DGP, and it failed to satisfy the civil rights activists it was meant to mollify. School officials offered Higher Horizons teachers, many of them inexperienced, little training, and they never funded the program at a level that would have allowed the intensive program offered by DGP. Even so, the program served only a fraction of minority students. School officials, moreover, justified Higher Horizons with notions of cultural deprivation; indeed, the program's most publicized component was field trips to museums, the theater, and the opera. In the eyes of civil rights activists, instead of challenging institutionalized racism, such activities stigmatized African American children. Hailed and imitated across the country, Higher Horizons demonstrated the potential of large-scale programs to increase significantly the educational attainment of disadvantaged youth, and exposed the political forces that shape and circumscribe such efforts.

The New York City School Board offers its assessment in Henry T. Hillson and Florence C. Myers, *The Demonstration Guidance Project, 1957–1962* (1963), and J. Wayne Wrightstone, George Forlano, Edward Frankel, Barbara Lewis, Richard Turner, and Philip Bolger, *Evaluation of the Higher Horizons Program for Underprivileged Children: Cooperative Research Project No. 1124* (1964). For a news report at the program's end, see Fred M. Hechinger, "Curtains for Higher Horizons," *New York Times*, 10 July 1966, sec. 4, p. 7. Diane Ravitch, *The Great School Wars: New York City, 1805–1973* (1974), locates the program in its historical context.

Daniel Perlstein

HILL, PATTY SMITH (March 27, 1868–May 25, 1946), kindergarten* and nursery school educator and educational reformer, was the leader of the younger, progressive (see PROGRESSIVE EDUCATION) kindergartners who modernized Froebelianism (see FROEBEL, FRIEDRICH), and she was the head of kindergarten education at Teachers College, Columbia University. The daughter of a Presbyterian minister and women's college president and an educated mother, Hill was inculcated with the values of education and community service. She graduated from Louisville (Kentucky) Collegiate Institute in 1887 and began kindergarten training with Anna Bryan,* who introduced her to innovative, child-centered methods. In 1893, Hill succeeded Bryan as head of the Louisville Free Kindergarten Association, where Hill espoused politically progressive views on the universality of children's development and preschool pedagogy. In 1894 Hill and Bryan attended the Clark University Summer School, where they were introduced to G. Stanley Hall's* child study* movement. In 1904–1905, Hill was invited to lecture at Teachers College, where Susan Blow,* the leading advocate of traditional Froebelianism, also taught. Hill's progressive, experimentally derived approach to kindergartening overshadowed Blow's position, and Hill became a permanent faculty member, joining John Dewey,* Edward L. Thorndike,* William Heard Kilpatrick,* and other psychologists and educators from whom she learned and with whom she worked. She served as president of the International Kindergarten Union* and wrote the "progressive report" published as part of the book *The Kindergarten* (1913). She worked with teachers at the Horace Mann Kindergarten at Teachers College to develop new curriculum methods and edited *A Conduct Curriculum for the Kindergarten and First Grade* (1923), which combined behavioristic (see BEHAVIORISM) and progressive approaches. A strong advocate of public kindergartens, Hill became one of the first to introduce nursery school* methods; in 1925, she helped to found the National Committee on Nursery Schools, now the National Association for the Education of Young Children.* She is popularly known for the introduction of large wooden blocks and rhythm instruments to preschool education and for writing the words to the song "Good Morning to You." An innovator and leader, Hill set the psychologically oriented course of modern American preschool education and influenced and trained generations of preschool teachers.

Her papers and manuscripts are at the Filson Club, Louisville, and in the Patty Smith Hill Collection, Teachers College, Columbia University. There is a biographical essay on Hill by M. Charlotte Jammer, *American Notable Women* (1971). See also Beulah Amidon's interview with Hill, *Survey Graphic* (1927); articles by Benjamin Fine, "American Childhood" (1936), and by Ilse Forest, "Education" (1954). Finally, refer to Barbara Beatty, *Preschool Education in America: The Culture of Young Children from the Colonial Era to the Present* (1995), and Michael Steven Shapiro, *Child's Garden: The Kindergarten Movement from Froebel to Dewey* (1983).

Barbara Beatty

HOBSON V. HANSEN, 269 F. Supp. 401, 1967; aff'd sub nom. *Smuck v. Hobson,* 408 F.2d 175, D.C. Cir. (1969). The trial court opinion in this case is one of the lengthiest and most comprehensive in the history of urban school desegregation. In *Hobson*, which was one of a series of six rulings between 1966 and 1971, a federal trial court in Washington, D.C., held that the public schools in the nation's capitol failed to comply with the Supreme Court's 1954 decision in *Bolling v. Sharp* 347 U.S. 497 (1954), the companion case of *Brown v. Board of Education*.* More specifically, the court ruled that the school district unconstitutionally deprived African American and poor students of their right to equal educational opportunities with white and other more affluent children. As part of its remedy, the court ordered the school system to end racial and economic discrimination in the schools, to stop using ability-group tracking* to place students, to discontinue busing* children to remediate overcrowding, and to integrate its teaching staff. *Hobson* is noteworthy because the court also addressed spending differences between schools for white students and African American students. Rather than pursue equity under the rubric of equal expenditures, the court approached it as an issue of how funding contributes to racial segregation. As such, *Hobson* stands out because it is one of the earliest cases to target financial inequities as an underlying cause in denying equal educational opportunities to students (also see SPECIAL EDUCATION).

Charles J. Russo

HOME ECONOMICS, taught in 90 percent of U.S. secondary schools, focuses on the acquisition of practial skills and knowledge necessary to take care of oneself and one's family. Home economics is the product of the social, political, and technological developments of the second half of the nineteenth century. These influences included Reconstruction, rapid industrialization and urbanization, increasing importance of science and technology in the everyday life of most Americans, and the expanding social and economic roles of women. These developments, according to some observers, threatened traditional family life. From 1899 to 1909, concerned educators conducted ten conferences at Lake Placid, New York, that featured discussion of the use of home economics as a subject to strengthen families. Reformers in the South were also interested in using home economics to improve domestic and social life in rural communities. Some educators also envisioned home economics as a subject that promised greater professional and social importance to women.

In 1913, the U.S. Department of Agriculture established the Bureau of Home Economics. Home economics offerings gradually gained popularity at all levels of American schooling. Federal funding for home economics education was secured through the 1914 Smith-Lever Act and the 1917 Smith-Hughes Act.* Some scholars, citing the heavy emphasis on cooking and sewing in home economics classes in secondary schools, especially at the early part of this century, argued that the new home economics courses turned out to be technical training for future housewives. The high percentage of females enrolled in home economics classes supports this view. Some home economists in the late nineteenth century, such as Catharine E. Beecher* and her sister Harriet Beecher Stowe, advocated the training of young women in home economics so they could be competent housewives. Today, home economics is viewed as valuable to society by providing professionals and paraprofessionals to various service sectors such as child care and dependent care personnel. Home economics is also regarded as helpful to individuals who have to navigate through complex family issues. The most important organization of professional home economists and home economics educators is the American Home Economics Association, which was formed in 1909 at Lake Placid and publishes the *Journal of Home Economics* (also, refer to VOCATIONAL EDUCATION).

For a comprehensive history, see Marjorie East, *Home Economics: Past, Present, and Future* (1980). Other histories include Betty E. Hawthorne, "Echoes of the Past—Voices of the Future" (1983); Mary S. Hoffschwelle, "The Science of Domesticity: Home Economics at George Peabody College for Teachers, 1914–1939" (1991); and Beatrice Paolucci and Twyla Shear, "Home Economics Education—Overview" (1971).

Tsz Ngong Lee

HOME SCHOOLING has been a feature of the American educational landscape since the colonial period. During the 1600s and most of the 1700s, the family was the fundamental religious, educational, and economic unit of society. Parents bore the primary responsibility for teaching their children Christian doctrine, vocational skills, and reading; churches and schools often supplemented parents' instruction. Toward the end of the colonial era the family began to lose its position as society's most important economic and social unit. The slow shift of family functions, including education, to nonfamilial institutions occurred initially in the settled areas of the eastern seaboard. By the end of the period, a variety of schools educated an increasing number of children.

Unlike their colonial counterparts, most nineteenth-century parents relied heavily on schools, the vast majority of which were public by 1875, to teach their children the three R's and morals. A small of number of parents, however, availed themselves of the widely available literature on "domestic" or "fireside" education and taught their children at home. The number of children instructed by their parents at this time is unknown. Several home-schooled children of this period are well known: Thomas Edison, Jane Addams,* and Andrew Still, colleague of abolitionist John Brown and founder of osteopathic medicine.

Though extended, institutional schooling has become the norm for twentieth-century American children, the last two decades of the twentieth century witnessed a revival of home schooling. A small but growing number of families chose to reduce the number of years their children spend in nonfamilial educational institutions. The number of home-schooled children in the United States grew from about 15,000 in the late 1970s to about 1 million in 1997. Although home-schooling parents were primarily evangelical Christians who elected to teach their children for religious reasons, a growing number of parents were also motivated by academic, social, and safety concerns. Home schooling experienced a rebirth in the late twentieth century as a growing number of parents of increasingly diverse persuasions fashioned an educational configuration that bore a resemblance to that of the colonial period.

Useful secondary works include Allan C. Carlson, "From Cottage to Work Station . . . and Back Again: The Family and Home Education" (1996); James C. Carper, "Home Schooling, History, and Historians" (1992); Steven Mintz and Susan Kellogg, *Domestic Revolutions: A Social History of the American Family* (1988); Brian D. Ray, *Strengths of Their Own: Academic Achievement, Family, Characteristics, and Longitudinal Traits* (1997); Jane Van Galen and Mary Anne Pitman, eds., *Home Schooling: Political, Historical, and Pedagogical Perspectives* (1991); and Maris A. Vinovskis, "Family and Schooling in Colonial and Nineteenth-Century America" (1987).

James C. Carper

HONIG V. DOE, 484 U.S. 305 (1988), is the case wherein the U.S. Supreme Court established the parameters for disciplining students with disabilities. Two pupils with emotional disabilities and histories of inappropriate behavior received indefinite suspensions pending their expulsions from the San Francisco Unified School District for violent and disruptive conduct that was disability related.

The federal district court permanently enjoined the school system from indefinitely suspending or expelling any child for disability-related misconduct or for authorizing a unilateral change in placement. The Ninth Circuit affirmed with minor modifications.

The Supreme Court affirmed the ruling of the Ninth Circuit with minor alterations. At the heart of its opinion, the Court reviewed the "stay-put" provision of the Education for All Handicapped Children Act (EHA),* now the Individuals with Disabilities Education Act. It interpreted the language of the EHA, which mandates that a child remain in his or her current setting pending an attempted change in placement, as prohibiting a school from unilaterally excluding a student with a disability for dangerous or disruptive behavior caused by the disability.

Despite its unwillingness to redraft the EHA, the Court did not leave educators powerless. It indicated that educators could continue to employ normal disciplinary procedures when dealing with dangerous students. The Court made specific reference to the use of study carrels, timeouts, detention, and even short-term suspensions of up to ten days. The Court added that educators may promptly remove the most dangerous students (pending administrative review) and can provide a cooling-off period during which a student's Individualized Education Program is reviewed and/or possible changes of placement are negotiated with the child's parents.

Charles J. Russo and Debra L. Russo

HORNBOOKS served as a child's introduction to reading in England and later in America from the late sixteenth to the end of the eighteenth century. Hornbooks have been documented in America as early as 1655 and advertised as late as 1772. American colonial children as young as two years used them in dame schools.* Regularly imported from Britain, hornbooks consisted of a small paddle of wood, usually less than four inches high by three wide, with a single page glued on and covered by a transparent sheet of horn edged by a brass rim.

The hornbook blended reading with religious instruction, presenting Christian prayers along with an abbreviated syllabary that introduced children to short and long vowels. The text's single page typically began with a cross, followed by a capital *A*, then the entire lower-case alphabet, an ampersand, and the five vowels. Two lines of the upper-case alphabet came next. The page was then divided into parallel columns, each headed by the five vowels. Each column contained the first three lines of the syllabary: *ab eb ib ob ub* alongside *ba be bi bo bu*, down to *ad . . .* and *da. . . .* The rest of the page was devoted to the invocation "In the Name of the Father," and the Lord's Prayer. Later hornbooks displayed only an upper-case alphabet.

The classic history of the hornbook can be found in Andrew W. Tuer, *History of the Horn Book* (1897; 1979), supplemented by George A. Plimpton, *The Hornbook and Its Use in America* (1916).

E. Jennifer Monaghan

HUGHES, JOHN JOSEPH (June 24, 1797–January 3, 1864), served as the first archbishop of New York City and as a forceful advocate for the rights of Catholics to a share of state school monies. Failing to achieve his ends, he then devoted much time and energy to establishing an alternate network of parochial schools.* Hughes, born in Ireland, immigrated to the United States in 1817. Ordained as a priest on October 15, 1826, he quickly established a reputation as a fiery controversialist. He was appointed coadjutor bishop of New York City in 1837 and diocesan bishop two years later. His involvement in schooling began with an 1840 campaign to pressure the New York state legislature to grant a share of state school funds to Catholic schools, rather than solely to the Protestant-dominated Public School Society. In 1841, Hughes successfully mobilized Catholic voters in New York City around this issue during local elections. The following year, his support for state legislation providing for local election of school commissioners helped to break the power of the Society. Afterward Hughes turned his efforts to the development of a diocesan parochial school system that enrolled 15,000 students by 1862. Nationally, he also was a highly visible Union supporter during the Civil War and served as an emissary from President Abraham Lincoln to the French bishops.

The archives of the Archdiocese of New York City house Hughes's collected papers. The first biography of Hughes was written by John Rose Greene Hassard, *Life of the Most Reverend John Hughes, D.D.* (1866). Arguably the best is Richard Shaw's *Dagger John: The Unquiet Life and Times of Archbishop*

John Hughes of New York (1977). The conflict with the Public School Society is treated comprehensively in Vincent P. Lannie, *Public Money and Parochial Education* (1968).

F. Michael Perko

HULL-HOUSE. See ADDAMS, JANE.

HUTCHINS, ROBERT M. See *PAIDEIA*.

I

INDEPENDENT SCHOOLS. See NATIONAL ASSOCIATION OF INDEPENDENT SCHOOLS.

INDIAN REORGANIZATION ACT. See COLLIER, JOHN.

INDIAN SELF-DETERMINATION AND EDUCATION ASSISTANCE ACT (1975), also known as P.L. 93-638, represents a major policy change in the battle between the federal government and Native American children. Passed by Congress in 1974 during President Richard Nixon's administration and signed into law by President Gerald Ford on January 4, 1975, the law was intended to facilitate an "orderly transition from federal domination of programs for and services to Indians" and foster "effective and meaningful participation by Indian people in the planning, conduct, and administration of those programs and services." The Act was amended in 1988 in order to further increase tribal participation and help ensure long-term financial stability for tribally run programs. Additional reforms were made with the Indian Self-Determination and Contract Reform Act of 1994 (S. 2036). Designed to eliminate massive bureaucratic regulation, it prescribed the terms and conditions that must be used in any contract between an Indian tribe and the Bureau of Indian Affairs or the Indian Health Service.

P.L. 93-638 allowed tribal governments to take control of reservation schools, boarding schools (see FEDERAL INDIAN BOARDING SCHOOLS), and any other school formally controlled by the federal government expressly for Native American children. The result was the community-controlled contract school. All aspects of these schools are controlled by tribal officials who contract the services of administrators, teachers, curriculum specialists, and other service providers, depending on the desires and needs of respective communities. Tribally controlled schools such as Rough Rock Demonstration School (1966) and Navajo Community College (1969), which predated P.L. 93-638, were important models of success that bolstered support for tribal control of education.

Refer to Hearing before the Subcommittee on Native-American Affairs, House of Representatives, 103rd Congress, 2nd Session, July 29, 1994, *The Implementation of the Indian Self-Determination Act, and Development of Regulations Following Passage of the 1988 Amendments to the Act*, serial no. 103–105. For basic information about P.L. 93-638, see Guy B. Senese, *Self-Determination and the Social Education of Native Americans* (1991). For historical background of the self-determination struggle, see Margaret Szasz, *Education and the American Indian: The Road to Self-Determination, 1928–1973* (1977).

Jeffrey A. Liles

INDUSTRIAL EDUCATION. See VOCATIONAL EDUCATION.

INFANT SCHOOLS served as one component of general social reform during the early 1800s. Robert Owen established the first infant school in New Lanark, Scotland, in 1816. Within ten years, infant school societies were formed in English cities targeting impoverished children eighteen months to six years of age. Public perception was that poverty rendered children useless and potentially harmful to society. The goals were to rescue them from their environment, to effect good character, and to prevent future violence and crime.

In the mid-1820s, American newspapers and magazines disseminated the philosophy of these English schools and advocated their establishment. Infant school societies formed in several urban areas: New York and Philadelphia (1827); Boston, Providence, New Haven, and Hartford (1928); and Newark and Charleston (1829). A product of evangelical concern for charity schooling, the infant school was a sibling of the Sunday school* and the pauper school.* Ministers promoted it through sermons, and churches hosted public exhibitions of the school, where toddlers marched, sang hymns, prayed, recited the multiplication table, and performed other intellectual and moral feats. American infant schools prospered during the late 1820s and early 1830s. By 1840, however, they were nonexistent. Ironically, they disappeared when problems of industrialization were severe. Though short-lived, the movement was significant: It attracted public attention to education, fostered debate over the method and content of early childhood education, served as the forerunner of the kindergarten,* and provided women an opportunity for agency outside the home, as they managed the societies and taught the infants.

See Vera Butler, "The Infant School Movement" (1969); John Jenkins, "Infant Schools and the Development of Public Primary Schooling in Selected American Cities before the Civil War" (1978); Dean May and Maris Vinovskis, "A Ray of Millenial Light: Early Education and Social Reform in the Infant

School Movement in Massachusetts, 1826–1840'' (1977); and Caroline Winterer, "Avoiding a 'Hothouse System of Education': Nineteenth-Century Early Childhood Education from the Infant Schools to the Kindergartens'' (1992).

Ben Burks

INGLIS, ALEXANDER JAMES (November 24, 1879–April 12, 1924), played a definitive role in the transformation of secondary education during the early twentieth century. Born in Middletown, Connecticut, Inglis graduated from Wesleyan University in 1902 and then taught Latin and held administrative positions at several elite college preparatory schools, including the Horace Mann School. His three Latin textbooks established his national reputation. Under the tutelage of Paul Monroe and Junius Sachs, Inglis received his doctorate from Teachers College, Columbia University, in 1911. Inglis's published dissertation, *Rise of the High School in Massachusetts* (1911), became a standard citation for historians of American secondary education. The following year he joined the faculty at Rutgers College, where he directed extension courses and summer session and began to formulate a theory of secondary education in his lectures. In 1914, Inglis moved to Harvard University, where he taught until his death. He collaborated with Walter Dearborn on school surveys and continued to develop his theory of secondary education, which emphasized differentiation and integration as complementary functions of the high school. In 1916, he joined the Commission on the Reorganization of Secondary Education, serving on the Reviewing Committee for the final draft of the *Cardinal Principles of Secondary Education* (1918).* The *Cardinal Principles* report manifested Inglis's theory of secondary education. In 1918, *Principles of Secondary Education*, his most important work, appeared. In it Inglis maintained that differences in intelligence were caused not by race or gender but by environmental factors, that faculty psychology* was invalid, and that the recommendations of the Committee of Ten* were obsolete. He argued in favor of selection of subject matter according to its social utility, of coeducation,* and of the comprehensive high school.* During World War I, Inglis served on the organization committee on education and special training in the war plans division of the army general staff, and following the war he focused on intelligence testing,* generating his *Intelligence Quotient Values* (1921). Upon his death, Harvard established the Inglis Lecture in his memory.

No collected papers and no published biographies exist for Inglis. Refer to his work as well as *In Memoriam: Alexander Inglis, 1879–1924* (1925).

William G. Wraga

INGRAHAM V. WRIGHT, 430 U.S. 651 (1977), is the leading U.S. Supreme Court case on the use of corporal punishment in public schools.* In *Ingraham*, the parents of two high school* students in Florida alleged that administrators violated the Eighth and Fourteenth Amendments by punishing their children without prior notice. The students were paddled so severely that one was out of school for eleven days and the other lost the full use of his arm for a week. After a federal trial court dismissed the complaint, the Fifth (now Eleventh) Circuit initially reversed in favor of the students, but ultimately it upheld the earlier ruling. A closely divided Supreme Court, in a 5 to 4 ruling, affirmed. Writing for the Court, Associate Justice Lewis Powell held that the disciplinary paddling of public school students did not violate the Eighth Amendment. In reviewing the history of corporal punishment in American public schools, Powell reasoned that since the Eighth Amendment was designed to protect individuals who had been convicted of crimes, it did not apply to students. Powell added that although corporal punishment in the case implicated a constitutionally protected liberty interest under the due process clause of the Fourteenth Amendment, it did not require prior notice and a hearing before students could be paddled. Powell found that imposing additional administrative safeguards before permitting paddling would have resulted in a significant intrusion into an area of educational responsibility that lies within the duties of public school officials.

Charles J. Russo

INSTRUMENTALISM in philosophy of science is the idea that scientific laws are not true or false, but are means for predicting observable phenomena; in value theory, the term is used to distinguish between values that are means to an end and those that are intrinsic. John Dewey* used the term more widely as a synonym for pragmatism, which began with Charles Sanders Peirce and William James in the last quarter of the nineteenth century, and particularly to characterize his own version of that philosophy, which he also called experimentalism.

Dewey's instrumentalism began with logical studies and soon extended to social thought, the arts, and education. It holds that ideas are instruments for constructing knowledge, which is not simply discovered, but is "made" by joining tangible material with ideas—interests, hypotheses, distinctions, procedures—in the process of settling a doubtful or problematic situation through inquiry. Ideas are the means by which material is formed for future use.

This view of instrumentalism presumes that change predominates in experience. Thus, the problem of knowledge is not to discover essences (see ESSENTIALISM) but to formulate procedures for inquiry into whatever the present offers as potential for future experience. Knowledge, in both its formulation and use, is hypothetical. Using the educationally equivalent term, subject matter is not inherent; it is, rather, whatever can be used for present and future ends. Problems arise in specific contexts, none of which are exactly alike, so new problems cannot be solved by old solutions. Conclusions from previous inquiry have presumed value, but provide no guarantee, for future success.

Dewey's instrumentalism suggests democracy. Advocates think of instrumentalism, or pragmatism, as the philosophical and educational counterpart of democracy. Further, Dewey's formulation of instrumentalism is a forerunner of the concern with function in social science. It is also a version of behaviorism,* not the simple stimulus-response kind, but in advocating that knowing is doing; inquiry is physical and active; ideas are standpoints, attitudes, and methods for dealing with concrete facts; and verfication requires active experimentation. Finally, because of the belief that every human device and ability should be used intelligently to make life more fruitful and worthwhile, instrumentalism is a form of humanism, which the English philosopher F.C.S. Schiller called his own version of pragmatism.

For general sources, see George Boas, "Instrumentalism and the History of Philosophy" (1950); John Dewey, *Democracy and Education* (1916); John Dewey, *Essays in Experimental Logic* (1916); M. C. Otto, "Instrumentalism" (1928); and Joseph Ratner, ed., *The Philosophy of John Dewey* (1928).

Robert R. Sherman

INTEGRATED CURRICULUM. Although the beginnings of reform emphasizing the integration of curriculum can be traced to the 1800s and the Herbartian movement,* most agree that progressive education* influenced the changes that took place in state and national curricula during the 1930s and 1940s. Certainly John Dewey's* emphasis on meaningful learning led to a student-centered curriculum and an integrated approach to education. At Dewey's laboratory school (see UNIVERSITY OF CHICAGO LABORATORY SCHOOL), "theme activities" wove together language, mathematics, the arts, science, geography, and so on, always with the social motive of learning in mind.

The integrated curriculum grew out of a desire to help students make sense of a school curriculum traditionally fragmented into separate subject areas taught in departmentalized grade levels. To integrate a curriculum, teachers, either as a group or as a school, working together with their students, tied learning experiences together through the employment of a central theme or topic addressed in multiple curricular areas, such as social studies,* language arts,* and arts.*

An integrated curriculum has four attributes. First, it emphasizes authentic, meaningful learning experiences that are closely attuned to the way children and adults learn. Second, such experiences are generative, causing teachers and students to work together seeking answers to real questions. Third, an integrated curriculum, by definition, requires thinking that is critical and an understanding of concepts across disciplines. Finally, the learning is cyclical, involving problem formulation, concept formulation, application, evaluation, reflection, celebration, and modification.

Integrated curriculum, also called thematic teaching and learning, is supported by many contemporary progressive educators. It has been addressed by such professional organizations as the Association for Supervision and Curriculum Development, International Reading Association,* National Council of Teachers of English,* and the National Association of Teachers of Mathematics.* Although the concept of an integrated curriculum has a long legacy and solid support in research, teaching and learning periodically shift from student-centered, authentic learning to subject matter acquisition and back again.

For the quintessential progressive position, see John Dewey, *How We Think* (1933). Lawrence A. Cremin, *The Transformation of the School: Progressivism in American Education, 1876–1957* (1964), places this curriculum emphasis within the historical context of the progressive movement. Gordon F. Vars, "Integrated Curriculum in Historical Perspective" (1991), provides a brief historical overview. Contemporary views include Elliot Eisner, *Cognition and Curriculum: A Basis for Deciding What to Teach* (1982); Robin Fogarty, "Ten Ways to Integrate Curriculum" (1991); Marilyn Hughes, *Curriculum Integration in the Primary Grades: A Framework for Excellence* (1991); and Mary Ann Manning, Gary Manning, and Roberta Long, *Theme Immersion: Inquiry-Based Curriculum in Elementary and Middle Schools* (1994).

Kathleen Strickland

INTELLIGENCE TESTING. Alfred Binet* and Theodore Simon first developed it in France, at the request of the French minister of public instruction, to identify students who were significantly behind in their studies and, therefore, in need of remediation. Binet saw the test as a diagnostic tool and did not assume that it measured the subject's innate ability. The Binet-Simon intelligence scale was introduced into the United States between 1908 and 1920 by Lewis Terman,* Robert Yerkes,* and Henry Goddard,* among others. As eugenicists, these early mental testers believed in the innate superiority of certain racial and ethnic groups and saw the test as a means of "scientifically" verifying this belief and, contrary to Binet's original intent, reinterpreted it as a measure of innate ability. The test's use with immigrants at Ellis Island and with World War I army recruits helped to legitimize it and to establish the field of psychology. Public schools* began adopting the intelligence test as a seemingly scientific means of sorting and selecting an increasingly diverse student population.

The earliest public debate over intelligence testing dates from this period. In a series of popular magazine articles in the 1920s, Walter Lippmann and Terman debated the evidence, validity, and assumptions of intelligence testing, including the interpretation of the data form the army intelligence tests. Research and writing on intelligence continued over the next four decades, but the intelligence testing debate was not rekindled until Arthur Jensen's 1969 article, "How Much Can We Boost IQ and Scholastic Achievement?" He argued that genetics accounted for differences in individual intelligence. Jensen concluded that efforts at compensatory education,* such as Head Start,* were doomed to fail because they were ignoring inherent intellectual inequalities. He generated a storm of protest when he suggested that African Americans were, on average, less intelligent than European Americans and less capable of abstract learning. Jensen's critics accused him of legitimizing racism and educational inequality, ignoring test bias, minimizing environmental causes of unequal test performance, misunderstanding the concept of heritability, and uncritically accepting the basic research on heritability of intelligence (i.e., twin, adoption, and kinship studies) (see HEREDITARIANISM). Jensen and his supporters defended the validity and fairness of intelligence tests, but the debate has raged ever since.

Alternative conceptions of intelligence also flourished. Robert Sternberg's triarchic theory of intelligence and Howard Gardner's theory of multiple intelligence both suggest that intelligence is multifaceted, with individuals having their own distinct pattern of strengths and weaknesses in a broad range of areas. Gary Collier has also reviewed research suggesting that intelligence has many social origins that are unappreciated in more traditional views. These newer theories suggest that intelligence testing has been overly narrow in its assumptions about the nature and origins of intellectual ability and sharply contrast with the earlier, psychometric view that sees intelligence as a biologically fixed, unitary ability.

For a discussion of the development of the first Binet and Simon intelligence scales, see Alfred Binet and Theodore Simon, *The Development of Intelligence in Children (The Binet-Simon Scale)* (1916; 1973). Henry Goddard, *The Kallikak Family: A Study in the Heredity of Feeble-Mindedness* (1912); Carl C. Brigham, *A Study of American Intelligence* (1923); and Clarence S. Yoakum and Robert M. Yerkes, *Army Mental Tests* (1920), give insight into the perspectives of the early mental testers. Raymond Fancher, *The Intelligence Men: Makers of the IQ Controversy* (1985), provides social and intellectual biographies on these and other key figures in the history of the IQ debate. The debates between Terman and Lippman can be found in *The IQ Controversy: Critical Readings* (1976), edited by N. J. Block and Gerald Dworkin. Paul D. Chapman's *Schools as Sorters: Lewis M. Terman, Applied Psychology, and the Intelligence Testing Movement, 1890–1930* (1988) shows how intelligence tests became established and adopted by schools. The resurgence of the IQ debate can be traced to Jensen's article, and more recently to *The Bell Curve* (1994) by Richard J. Herrnstein and Charles Murray. Important critiques of Jensen's position include Jeffrey M. Blum, *Pseudoscience and Mental Ability* (1978); James R. Flynn, *Race, IQ and Jensen* (1980); Leon J. Kamin, *The Science and Politics of IQ* (1974); and William H. Tucker, *The Science and Politics of Racial Research* (1994). For an annotated bibliography on the intelligence testing debate, see Stephen H. Aby, *The IQ Debate: A Selective Guide to the Literature* (1990).

Stephen H. Aby

INTERCULTURAL EDUCATION. See MULTICULTURAL EDUCATION.

INTERNATIONAL EXPOSITIONS provided educators from around the world with a forum where they could exchange ideas, share materials, and observe the educational experiments and advancements of other nations. In doing so, they were achieving the primary purpose intended by the organizers of the expositions—the exchange and advancement of new technical information and knowledge.

The phenomenon of international expositions began with the 1851 London

Palace Exposition. It was not until the 1867 Paris Exposition that education received attention as a special subject of interest at any of the expositions. Assigned to the "Department of Social Science," the educational exhibit included materials from nearly 1,200 different sources and from countries such as France, England, Belgium, Prussia, Sweden, and Denmark. The success of the Paris exhibit encouraged the commissioners of the 1873 Viennese Exposition to make education an important part of their exhibits. Over 5,000 exhibitors submitted materials for display as part of the educational exhibit at Vienna. Twenty different nations were represented.

The expositions are noteworthy because of their role in disseminating educational innovations internationally. The 1876 Philadelphia Centennial Exposition displayed drawings, models, and tools illustrating the work of Victor Della Vos at the Moscow Imperial Technical School. These materials became the basis for manual and industrial training used in American public schools* prior to World War I (see VOCATIONAL EDUCATION). That exhibition also included the first display of kindergarten* education in the United States, as well as the first major introduction of metric education and the Dewey decimal system. Similar innovations were included at other expositions. Of particular interest was the founding of the first audiovisual education department in an American school, which was an outgrowth of the 1904 Louisiana Purchase Exposition in St. Louis, and the introduction of Maria Montessori* to American educators as part of the 1915 Panama-Pacific Exposition, in San Francisco. Each of the major international expositions held in the United States, beginning in 1876 with the Philadelphia Centennial Exhibition and continuing through the World's Columbian Exposition in Chicago in 1893 and the 1904 St. Louis Louisiana Purchase Exposition, included major educational exhibits and congresses.

For background on the international expositions and their role in the development of American education, see Eugene F. Provenzo, Jr., *Culture as Curriculum: Education and the International Expositions, 1876–1904* (forthcoming).

Eugene F. Provenzo, Jr.

INTERNATIONAL KINDERGARTEN UNION (IKU) was founded in 1892 as an organization to promote the kindergarten* cause and provide a forum for debate about kindergarten philosophy and methods. Originating as the Kindergarten Department of the National Education Association* in 1884, with Sarah B. Cooper as its first president and with a membership consisting primarily of free kindergarten associations,* the IKU grew rapidly to become the third largest educational organization in the country. The organization started a child study* committee to discuss the role of G. Stanley Hall's* theories of developmental psychology in Froebelian (see FROEBEL, FRIEDRICH) kindergarten pedagogy. Debates over the modification and modernization of Froebelian pedagogy intensified and in 1903 a Committee of Nineteen, chaired by Lucy Wheelock,* was appointed to resolve the issue. The IKU split into three factions—conservatives led by Susan Blow,* moderates led by Wheelock and Elizabeth Harrison, and progressives (see PROGRESSIVE EDUCATION) led by Patty Smith Hill*—and published *The Kindergarten* (1913) with three separate reports on these opposing views. Arguments over kindergarten pedagogy and other educational methods, such as Maria Montessori's* sensorial preschool pedagogy, continued at meetings and annual conventions. During World War I, the IKU expanded its mission to include organizing kindergartens in European war zones. In 1931, the IKU merged with the National Council of Primary Education and eventually became the Association for Childhood Education International (ACEI). Despite the intense ideological turmoil that was the focus of much of the organization's activity, the IKU served an important training and coordinating function for the kindergarten movement and advanced knowledge of the kindergarten among educators and the general public.

The IKU's *Proceedings*, papers, and reports are held in the ACEI archives at the University of Maryland–College Park Library. See also Evelyn Weber, *The Kindergarten: Its Encounter with Educational Thought in America* (1969), and Michael Steven Shapiro, *Child's Garden: The Kindergarten Movement from Froebel to Dewey* (1983).

Barbara Beatty

INTERNATIONAL READING ASSOCIATION (IRA) was founded in 1956 from the merger of the International Council for the Improvement of Reading Instruction and the National Association for Reading Teaching. William S. Gray was the Association's first president. The IRA's official journal, *The Reading Teacher*, also began publication that year. The Association's headquarters, originally housed at the University of Pittsburgh, moved to Newark, Delaware, in 1962. As part of its goals, the IRA promotes high levels of literacy, endorses equitable access to quality reading instruction,* and actively encourages lifelong reading habits. The Association seeks to accomplish these goals by studying reading processes and teaching techniques and by disseminating reading research and theory through its series of conferences and print and electronic publications. IRA membership, representing ninety-nine countries, includes literacy professionals whose work ranges from classroom practice to basic research.

International Reading Association

IQ. See INTELLIGENCE TESTING; TERMAN, LEWIS M.

ISLAMIC SCHOOLS, as full-time primary and secondary institutions, represent the most recently established form of religious education in the United States. The Clara Muhammad School, founded in Detroit in 1934 as the University of Islam, became the first full-time Islamic school. Forty-nine Islamic schools existed in 1989, enrolling approximately 3,400 students; by 1994, these figures jumped to 108 and 100,000, respectively. The sharp increase in schools and enrollment paralleled the rise of Muslims residing in the United States, as well as the growth of mosques and the creation of Islamic institutions in general. The number of Muslims, both immigrants and U.S. citizens, rose from some 2 million in 1980 to 5–8 million in 1994. During these same years, 80 percent of the U.S. mosques were opened. Most Islamic schools are concentrated in ten states, where 70 percent of Muslims live: California, New York, Illinois, New Jersey, Indiana, Michigan, Virginia, Texas, Ohio, and Maryland.

Full-time Islamic schools reflect the diversity of the American Muslim community, growing from three different educational initiatives: the agenda of the Nation of Islam; the social, cultural, and educational needs of multiethnic Islamic communities throughout the United States; and the mandates of foreign governments. Approximately one-third of Islamic schools are Sister Clara Muhammad Schools, named for the wife of the founder of the Nation of Islam, Elijah Muhammad. They were founded, from the 1930s through the 1960s, as part of the African-American nationalist movement advocated by the Nation of Islam. Over half of Islamic schools, representing the second incentive for the expansion of Islamic institutions, grew out of the multiethnic communities of American Muslims, whose numbers increased because of changes in immigration restrictions in the 1960s. After 1965, the number of American Muslims rose significantly through increased immigration from South Asia, the Arab world, Iran, Turkey, Eastern Europe, and Africa. These Muslims supplemented the growing number of Islamic converts within the African American community. Islamic schools expanded rapidly for twenty years, beginning in the 1970s, in response to changes in the Islamic world, such as the 1967 Arab-Israeli and 1991 Persian Gulf wars, and the perception that American culture was hostile to the values of Islamic culture. The third group of Islamic schools is comprised of government schools, defined by the nation that founded them. For example, the Islamic Saudi Academy in Alexandria, Virginia, receives its funding from and is subject to the government of Saudi Arabia. The Saudi Arabian ambassador to the United States serves as the chairman of the board of trustees, and the top administrators are Saudi educators.

American Islamic schools operate as private schools,* charging tuition; but they rely on a public school* curriculum based on that used by the local community or county. Classes are conducted in English, and Arabic is taught as a foreign language. The study of Islam, particularly the Koran and the life and work of the prophet Muhammad, serves as part of the formal curriculum, while Islamic values are integrated throughout the life of the school. These schools collectively articulate a set of goals that include the need to elevate the importance of Islam in the lives of Muslim children, integrate religious and temporal education in the school curriculum, emulate Islamic character and values, free the public school curriculum of secular and other undesirable elements, and generally Islamicize the education of Muslim children. Most Islamic schools in general lack adequate funding, sufficient numbers of qualified instructors, especially those trained in Arabic and Islamic studies, and uniformity of Islamic education throughout the country. Two national organizations give direction and support for Islamic schools. The Islamic Society of North America (ISNA), founded in 1982, working through its Islamic Schools Department, conducted a field study that resulted in a 1989 report, "In-Depth Study of Full-Time Islamic Schools in North America." ISNA further organized a national conference whose agenda was entitled "Towards an Applied Islamic Educational Model in North America." The Council of Islamic Schools in North America (CISNA) supplies academic, technical, and administrative assistance, providing advice on school accreditation,* teacher certification, school administrator training, and curriculum development. CISNA is a member of the National Private School Leadership Council, a national network of religious and other nonpublic schools, which functions under the auspices of the U.S. Department of Education.*

For background, see Kamal Ali, "Islamic Education in the United States: An Overview of Issues, Problems, and Possible Approaches" (1984); Kamal Ali, "Muslim School Planning in the United States: An Analysis of Issues, Problems and Possible Approaches" (1981); ISNA, *In-Depth Study of Full-Time Islamic Schools in North America: Results and Data Analysis* (1991); and Molook Roghanizad, "Full-Time Muslim Schools in the United States, 1970–1990" (1990).

Alan W. Proctor

J

JEANES FUND, founded in 1907 by Anna T. Jeanes, a Quaker philanthropist, and otherwise known as the Negro Rural School Fund, was established to improve the rural conditions of African Americans through aid to public schools and rural school supervision. James H. Dillard, the Fund's first president and director, modeled it after the Hampton-Tuskegee program of industrial-agricultural training* and the work of Virginia A. Randolph, a Virginia African American teacher. Randolph had taught common industrial arts in her rural schools and mentored other teachers to do the same. Thrilled with the way she integrated industrial arts into the curriculum, Randolph became a model for the Jeanes teachers. The Fund gained approval of and cooperation with local southern public school officials in order to employ supervisors of industrial teachers, who worked under the direction of county superintendents but were paid largely by the Fund. Jeanes teachers taught and supervised elementary industrial work; promoted home improvement work, clubs for pupils and parents, health campaigns, and agricultural leadership; raised money for new schoolhouses and equipment; and attempted to extend the school year. They assumed great latitude in determining neighborhood improvement needs and often used the county training schools established by the Slater Fund* as bases of operation. Their efforts resulted in high school industrial programs in nine southern states. In 1937, the Jeanes Fund was merged into the Southern Education Board* along with the George Peabody Fund,* the John F. Slater Fund, and the Virginia Randolph Fund. By 1950, approximately 500 Jeanes teachers continued to work throughout the South, but with the 1954 U.S. Supreme Court decision *Brown v. Board of Education** and the general desegregation movement, their numbers began to decrease. The program ended in 1968.

Archival materials related to the Fund are included in the holdings of the Southern Education Foundation in Atlanta. Also refer to Henry Allen Bullock, *A History of Negro Education in the South from 1619 to the Present* (1967);

Ambrose Caliver, *Rural Education among the Negroes under Jeanes Supervising Teachers* (1933); and Arthur D. Wright and Edward E. Redcay, *The Negro Rural School Fund, Inc. (Anna T. Jeanes Foundation, 1907–1933)* (1933).

Jayne R. Beilke

JEFFERSON, THOMAS (April 13, 1743–July 4, 1826). Best known for his authorship of the Declaration of Independence and as the third president of the United States, Jefferson holds a place of primary importance in the history of American education. He founded the University of Virginia in 1819, but perhaps of greater importance, Jefferson was the first American statesman to emphasize the vital link between an educated citizenry and self-government in a society based upon the ideals of liberty and equality. Jefferson's educational theory was thus an integral part of his democratic political philosophy.

As a representative from Virginia to the Continental Congress, Jefferson drafted the Declaration of American Independence, the final wording of which was approved on July 4, 1776. Jefferson, "the penman of the Revolution," returned to Virginia and in the fall of 1776 took up his pen once again as chair of a committee appointed to revise the laws of Virginia. His committee presented 126 bills to the Virginia legislature. Among the most important of the proposals was the Bill for the More General Diffusion of Knowledge, authored by Jefferson and submitted in 1779.

Although he had been born into the Virginia gentry and enjoyed the educational privileges reserved for children of fortunate parentage—private tutoring* and boarding schools* and higher education at parental expense at the College of William and Mary—Jefferson's educational bill called for the establishment of tax-supported elementary schools in every county and for the education of "all the free children, male and female," gratis. His plan called also for the creation of district secondary schools to which boys of the greatest ability would be given access without charge. At the top of Jefferson's proposed pyramidal system, the College of William and Mary was to accept each year without fee those scholars who in each district had given evidence of their intellectual superiority. Jefferson based his meritocratic system on the belief that talented and virtuous children occupied every rank of society, and that potential members of this "natural aristocracy" should be given opportunity to prove their worth in competition with members of the existing "artificial aristocracy." This bill, however, as well as later proposals designed to lay the foundation for a statewide system of publicly supported schools, failed to win legislative support.

Jefferson lived to see one part of his general plan become reality. He considered his role as "Father of the University of Virginia" to be one of the three greatest accomplishments of his life, the other two being his authorship of the Declaration of Independence and of the Virginia Statute for Religious Freedom. The underlying principle shaping each of these achievements was freedom—intellectual, political, and religious.

The most important collections of Jefferson's papers are those at the Library of Congress, Massachusetts Historical Society, University of Virginia, Virginia State Library, and Henry E. Huntington Library. Several published editions of Jefferson's papers are available, the most useful of which are Julian P. Boyd, gen. ed., *The Papers of Thomas Jefferson* (1950–   ); Paul Leicester Ford, ed., *The Writings of Thomas Jefferson* (1892–1899); and A. A. Lipscomb and A. E. Bergh, eds., *The Writings of Thomas Jefferson* (1903). Jefferson's only published book is *Notes on the State of Virginia* (1787; 1955), edited by William Peden. The magisterial biography is Dumas Malone, *Jefferson and His Time* (1948–1981). Of many one-volume biographies, among the best is Merrill D. Peterson, *Thomas Jefferson and the New Nation: A Biography* (1970). Frank Shuffelton, *Thomas Jefferson: A Comprehensive, Annotated Bibliography of Writings about Him (1826–1980)* (1983), offers a comprehensive guide to Jeffersonian materials.

Jennings L. Wagoner, Jr.

JEWISH EDUCATION. Since the American Jewish community's establishment, both day and part-time schooling have been part of its tradition. In 1731, Yeshibat Minhat Arab was founded as the day school of Congregation Shearith Israel of New York. Six years later, this institution for New York's Sephardic community became a private school* under the direction of David Mendez Machado. Sketchy records suggest that a poor school was founded in that city in 1758, and attempts were made to establish institutions in the Carolinas; but these efforts were, at best, sporadic.

The massive immigration of central and eastern European Jews beginning in the 1840s profoundly changed the ethos of American Jewry. Large congregations of German Jews frequently founded day schools, such as New York's Talmud Torah and Hebrew Institute (1842). By the 1870s, however, most of these had ceased to exist, victims of poor funding, lack of students, and in some cases, congregational opposition. The second wave of immigration between 1880 and 1920 once again changed the character of the Jewish community, giving it a more pronounced Slavic tone. While the United States had become home to 30 percent of world Jewry by the end of this era, little increase in day schooling occurred because of immigrant preference for public education, their poverty, belief in the "melting pot," and desire for upward mobility.

The post–World War II era marked the next significant growth in day schooling. Most such schools were Conservative or Orthodox in character, emphasizing subjects such as prayer, the Torah and commentary, Hebrew, ethics, and Jewish and Zionist history. Motivated by the general postwar surge of American religious sentiment, focus on the Holocaust and establishment of the State of Israel, and concern about the rate of intermarriage (52 percent according to one 1990 study) and the declining Jewish birth rate, and fueled by the community's prosperity, American Jews founded over 95 percent of the schools presently in existence. The result has been a doubling of enrollment since the late 1960s.

In 1994, some 150,000 children attended 540 Jewish day schools. While Orthodox institutions predominate, over 30 percent of the schools are non-Orthodox, with the Conservative movement enrolling about 17,000 students in its 70 Solomon Schechter schools, and some 2,000 in the 16 schools affiliated with Reformed Judaism.

Although day schools have been an important part of American Jewish education, the majority of instruction has always been carried out on a part-time basis. During the colonial period, preparation for Bar Mitzvahs was generally done by synagogue officials or privately hired tutors.* The formation of the Polonies Talmud Torah in New York in 1808 began the pattern of part-time Jewish education as a supplement to secular day schools. The first major wave of Jewish immigration from central and eastern Europe resulted in a far more culturally heterogenous Jewish community. As a result, institutions besides the synagogue took on an importance in the preservation of Jewish heritage. Sunday and afternoon schools became popular, at least in part as a result of Christian attempts at proselytization.

After the second wave of immigration in the 1880s, Jewish part-time education became even more diverse. The Talmud Torahs, founded by individual congregations and the Young Men's Hebrew Association (YMHA), taught poor boys in the afternoons or on Sundays. The schools run by Jewish charitable agencies had the best attendance records, but some parents remained skeptical because the curriculum emphasized religion over Hebrew and Jewish culture. Schools sponsored by individual congregations, mainly Conservative or Orthodox in character, met several times a week and emphasized the understanding of prayers and Torah. Many Sunday schools were taught by well-meaning public school teachers with little background in Jewish studies. One result of the uneven character of institutions and instructors was minimal attendance. Never in the nineteenth century did more than around 20 percent of Jewish children, even in a city with a large Jewish population like New York, receive any sort of formal Jewish education.

With the founding in 1910 of the Bureau of Education of the Jewish Community of New York City, attention was paid for the first time to the systematic education of American Jewish children. The Bureau, along with comparable institutions in other cities, assisted in the foundation of schools, trained teachers, and published a variety of educational texts. While some cities began central Talmud Torahs, suburbanization asserted itself, with the result that schools sponsored by individual congregations became more and more numerous, enrolling more students in New York state by 1928 than did the central ones.

A feature of Jewish education in the early decades of the twentieth century was the appearance of heretofore unseen types of institutions. Schools oriented toward the teaching of Yiddish began to appear, including national-radical schools that taught religion and socialism, Shalom Aleichem schools that emphasized socialism and Zionism, and largely secular Arbeiter Ring schools sponsored by left-wing workers' organizations.

As in the case with day schools, the experiences of the Holocaust and foundation of the State of Israel, together with concern about the long-term preservation of the Jewish community, fueled rapid expansion of the Jewish part-time education in the years following World War II. By 1994, around 75 percent of Jewish children received some form of Jewish education (mainly associated with study for Bar or Bat Mitzvah), with overwhelming majority (around two-thirds) in part-time programs. These programs increasingly resided in synagogues, a reflection of the rise of the synagogue as a center of American Jewish life and the decline of its home-centered character. The foundation of the State of Israel and resurgence of Hebrew as a living language also motivated the establishment of a small number of institutes specializing in the study of Hebrew language and literature.

Finally, the educational activities of general purpose organizations like the YMHA and Young Women's Hebrew Association (YWHA), as well as the Hillel Foundation, make them significant actors in the history of American Jewish education. The roots of the YMHA can be traced to the literary societies founded by young Jewish men in the 1840s. The first appeared in Baltimore in 1854, followed by one in New York City twenty years later. A women's auxiliary took the YWHA name in 1888 and became independent in 1902. The National Council of Young Men's Hebrew Associations and Kindred Organizations was founded in 1913. The training of religious school teachers became one explicit educational activity. By the late 1980s, the 275 Jewish community centers, YMHAs and YWHAs, and camps served some 1 million members with a variety of activities, including physical and health education, as well as lectures and forums.

The first Hillel Foundation, sponsored by B'nai B'rith, was established at the University of Illinois in 1925. Since then, some 110 official foundations and 300 secondary affiliates have been established on both private and public campuses. These offer 250,000 students a variety of programs, forums, and discussion groups, as well as opportunities to participate in religious and cultural celebrations.

Jewish education has been a widely diverse sector of American education since its inception. Encompassing a variety of schools and alternative educational agencies, it has sought to maintain and strengthen the Jewish identity of its participants.

Among the few historical sources on Jewish education are Lloyd P. Gartner, *Jewish Education in the United States: A Documentary History* (1969), and Judah Pilch, *A History of Jewish Education in America* (1969). A good source on recent trends is J. J. Goldberg, ''U.S. Jewry Pins Its Future on Education'' (1994).

F. Michael Perko

JOB CORPS is a national residential training and employment program administered by the Department of Labor to address the multiple barriers to employment faced by disadvantaged youths throughout the United States. Each year this voluntary program provides opportunities to over 60,000 students, ages sixteen through twenty-four, at 113 Jobs Corps centers nationwide, including the District of Columbia and Puerto Rico. Since its establishment in 1964, the program has served over 1.7 million disadvantaged adults.

Job Corps was originally established by the Economic Opportunity Act of 1964 as part of President Lyndon Johnson's "Great Society" program, with $800 million initial funding. The first Job Corps center opened on January 15, 1965, at Camp Catoctin, Maryland, serving thirty students. Job Corps opened its first women's center in Cleveland, Ohio, in April of that same year. On July 1, 1969, Job Corps was transferred from the Office of Economic Opportunity to the Department of Labor, where it remains today. Current authorization for the program is Title IV-B of the Job Training Partnership Act.

The purpose of Job Corps has been to assist eligible young people who need and can benefit from an intensive program, operated primarily in the residential setting of a Job Corps center, to become more responsible, employable, and productive citizens. Job Corps provides a comprehensive mix of services that address the multiple barriers to employment faced by disadvantaged young adults in an integrated and coordinated manner in each facility. These services include entry diagnostic testing of reading and math levels, occupational exploration and world-of-work training, academic education, competency-based vocational training programs, social skills training, counseling and related support services, health care, and post-program placement and support. All centers enforce a zero tolerance policy for alcohol and drugs.

The residential experience distinguishes Job Corps from other employment and training programs, enabling it to provide the comprehensive array of services in one setting twenty-four hours a day, seven days a week. Centers are located in rural as well as urban areas. Approximately 90 percent of the students reside at the facilities; the remainder are commuters. Enrollment is voluntary, and programs remain open-entry, open-exit, and self-paced to allow students to progress at their own speed.

The Job Corps program has always operated through a partnership by government, labor, and the private sector. The residential nature of the program dictates unique space and facility requirements beyond what is required for classrooms, vocational shops, and administrative offices. The federal government provides the facilities and equipment and relies on contracts for recruiting and screening of new students, center operations, and placement of students upon termination from the centers. Private Job Corps operators assume responsibility for the management and administration of the centers.

Additional information about Job Corps is available on the internet at http://www.jobcorps.org

United States Department of Labor

JOURNAL OF NEGRO EDUCATION (JNE), in continuous publication since 1932, was founded that year at Howard University, Washington, D.C., because existing agencies and publications failed to provide the needed services related to the education of African Americans (called Negroes at that time). Further, the leadership of Negroes was not accepted by the majority group with respect to the investigation of education problems pertaining to the minority subculture.

JNE therefore began with a threefold purpose: ''(1) to stimulate the collection, and facilitate the dissemination, of facts about the education of Negroes; (2) to present discussions involving critical appraisals of the proposals and practices relating to the education of Negroes; and (3) to stimulate and sponsor investigations of problems incident to the education of Negroes.'' That general purpose was refined in 1973, and its current mission is to fulfill its purposes within the research mission and goals of the University and of the School of Education by ''(1) introducing new strategies, proposals, and philosophies for the education of Black people in the United States, as well as those in developing countries; (2) encouraging and stimulating the collection of facts about the education of Black people and facilitating the dissemination of the information; (3) presenting discussions involving critical appraisals of proposals and practices relating to the education of Black people; (4) providing a forum for established scholars, while encouraging the participation of younger developing scholars and students; (5) criticizing anti-egalitarian research and offering counter-proposals; (6) maintaining its reputation and function as a chief repository of scholarly information about every aspect of Black education, and every development of any consequence to the education of Blacks in America and developing countries.''

The School of Education at Howard University serves as *JNE*'s parent unit. As a scholarly refereed journal, published quarterly under the auspices of Howard University Press, it operates under the guidance of a national editorial and advisory board. The *JNE* publishes historical and contemporary articles as well as descriptive-explanatory, ethnographic, and experimental research findings. While its substantive content focuses on professional education, this periodical includes material from the social sciences, physical and natural sciences, the arts, law, and technology as those fields relate to the education of blacks. Maintaining a broad domestic and foreign circulation, the *JNE* functions as a major resource for the educational community, providing reliable peer-reviewed historical and contemporary information about educational problems encountered by blacks in this country and abroad, as well as solutions to those problems.

Faustine C. Jones-Wilson

JUNIOR HIGH SCHOOLS. In 1910, American seventh-, eighth-, and ninth-graders were segregated for the first time in separate schools. Over the decades, the junior high school spread across the United States. Originally conceived to serve the needs of the college bound, the first junior high schools were charged with retaining urban students in school and preparing them for the industrial workplace. The junior high school was also asked to serve the total development needs of the adolescent (see ADOLESCENCE).

At the end of the nineteenth century, college presidents joined school officials to demand more rigorous academic training for the small minority of students destined for higher education. Led by Harvard's Charles Eliot, the National Education Association's (NEA)* Committee of Ten on Secondary School Studies* called for cutting elementary school from eight to six years and introducing younger students to such subjects as Latin and algebra.

At about the same time, changes in the labor market led researchers and school officials to conclude that twelve-, thirteen-, and fourteen-year-olds belonged in school, not in the factory. E. L. Thorndike* and Leonard Ayres, among others, documented huge attrition rates in the eight-year elementary school. Students left school, they argued, not out of economic necessity but because existing schools did not suit them. In 1913, the NEA's Committee on the Economy of Time in Education endorsed the junior high school and urged that it offer vocational training and guidance.

In 1918, the NEA Commission on the Reorganization of Secondary Education issued its *Cardinal Principles** report. Committed to engineering society and to meeting both the varied needs of individual students and the generic "needs of the adolescent," reformers called for the introduction of departmental instruction and for some choice in classes. Junior high schools often developed differentiated academic and vocational tracks (see TRACKING; VOCATIONAL EDUCATION).

Only fifty-five junior high schools existed in 1920, but by 1930 this number had jumped to 1,800. After a period of slow growth in the 1930s and 1940s, the number of junior high schools again mushroomed in the 1950s and 1960s. The persuasiveness of reformers' rationales alone, however, did not lead to the creation of junior high schools. Rather, classroom shortages complemented allegiance to progressive practices (see PROGRESSIVE EDUCATION), and although reformers advocated the seventh- to ninth-grade junior high school, superintendents reorganized schools according to the availability of space.

The junior high school spread even though economic and social changes rendered some of its rationales anachronistic. As child labor laws took hold and the high school became a mass institution, "elimination" ceased to be a junior high school problem. Instead, the developmental needs of adolescents competed with smooth transition to the academic demands of the high school as the institution's justification.

Despite the junior high's more limited mission, by 1970 dissatisfaction with the institution led to the organization of the Midwest Middle School Association, which three years later changed its name to the National Middle School Association (NMSA). Echoing earlier calls for junior high schools, reformers argued that a new, transitional institution was needed to address the unique (and uniquely varied) developmental needs of "in-between-agers." They advocated team teaching, discovery and inquiry methods that allowed learning at individual rates, extended homerooms during which teachers would act as counselors, flexible scheduling, and the fostering of career and life pursuits. At the same time, middle school reformers also claimed that school reorganization could relieve overcrowding, allow the earlier introduction of intensive academic study, and promote desegregation in large cities.

By 1983, the sixth- to eighth-grade middle school replaced the seventh- to ninth-grade junior high school as the most common institution for schooling early adolescents. Nevertheless, the middle school was little more effective than the junior high school in promoting the integration of subjects, joint planning by teachers, active learning, or other practices advocated by reformers.

Recast as middle schools, junior high schools remain a major institution in American education. Like the junior high school, the middle school has fluctuated between elementary and secondary patterns. The very multiplicity of conflicting purposes that facilitated the establishment of junior high and middle schools inevitably limited the institution's ability to establish its own accepted niche.

For a historical account, see Larry Cuban, "What Happens to Reforms That Last? The Case of the Junior High School" (1992). NMSA, *This We Believe: Developmentally Responsive Middle Level Schools* (1995), provides an insider's perspective.

Daniel Perlstein

JUVENILE DELINQUENCY is a term that has included a broad range of youthful misbehaviors since it came into common usage around 200 years ago. At the beginning of the nineteenth century, the term was used rather generally to define the suspicious and occasionally criminal activities of urban lower-class children, some of whom roamed the city streets free of parental supervision. The nation's first reform schools,* such as the New York House of Refuge* (1825), were founded in part to institutionalize and discipline these children. Legitimized by the legal doctrine of *parens patrie* (the right of the state to remove a child from his or her family to protect the child's welfare), these reform schools incarcerated children, both criminal and noncriminal, who were thought likely to benefit from a regimented work and educational environment. Reform schools became increasingly common after the middle of the century, though most delinquent behavior continued to be handled informally by parents or local charitable and law enforcement authorities.

By the turn of the century, growing disenchantment with the failures of reform schools and with the abilities of institutions per se to cope with juvenile delinquency prompted the creation of special juvenile courts. The first juvenile courts opened in Cook County, Illinois, and Denver, Colorado, in 1889. Founders of these courts believed that delinquency was rooted in improper environment and family life. As an alternative to institutional discipline, juvenile courts attempted to rehabilitate delinquents by "individual treatment," focusing less on the children's offenses than on their motivations and family support systems. Informal courtroom procedures and probation (to monitor the juvenile's home life, as well as his or her behavior) were the courts' principal rehabilitative tools, supplemented by use of short-term detention, psychological clinics, and continued recourse to long-term commitment to reform schools.

Children and youth brought before juvenile courts included both criminal and status offenders (the latter accused of incorrigibility, truancy, running away, curfew violations, and—for girls—sex offenses). Most delinquents were between the ages of twelve and sixteen; as in the early nineteenth century, delinquents continued to be urban, lower-class youths, usually from immigrant backgrounds. Police, charitable agencies, schools, parents, and neighbors all referred children to juvenile court. Much delinquency, however, continued to be handled informally as well. During the 1920s and 1930s, schools, police, social scientists, and social workers initiated a variety of experimental community programs (perhaps the most famous was the Chicago Area Project) to prevent and respond to delinquent behavior before children entered juvenile courts.

By the 1940s and 1950s, World War II and the Cold War political climate promoted widespread public fears about the growth of juvenile delinquency. Delinquency seemed to have spread to the middle class, as exemplified by the rebellious suburban youths of the film *Rebel without a Cause* (1954) and as documented by numerous scholarly studies. At the same time, urban lower-class delinquents were perceived to be increasingly dangerous, as represented by the violent teens in the film *Blackboard Jungle* (1955). Throughout the 1950s, juvenile delinquency was seen primarily as a white phenomenon. Only since the mid-1960s has delinquency come to be identified largely with African Ameican and Latino youth.

By the 1980s and 1990s, public sympathy for "juvenile delinquency" gave way to public fear over "juvenile violence." Juvenile courts and reform schools throughout the United State deemphasized rehabilitation and education in favor of punishment. In addition, most states amended laws to facilitate the transfer of juveniles to adult criminal courts at younger and younger ages. The older idea of "juvenile delinquency," which implied that disruptive children could be reformed, fell not merely into disfavor, but increasingly into contempt.

For further reference, see Thomas J. Bernard, *The Cycle of Juvenile Justice* (1992); Donna M. Bishop, Charles E. Frazier, Lonn Lanza-Kaduce, and Lawrence Winner, "The Transfer of Juveniles to Criminal Court" (1996); James Gilbert, *A Cycle of Outrage* (1986); Joseph M. Hawes, *Children in Urban Society* (1971); Michael B. Katz, *The Irony of Early School Reform* (1968); Robert M. Mennel, *Thorns and Thistles* (1973); Mary E. Odem, *Delinquent Daughters* (1995); Anthony Platt, *The Child Savers* (1980); David J. Rothman, *Conscience and Convenience: The Asylum and Its Alternatives in Progressive America* (1980); Wiley Sanders, ed., *Juvenile Offenders for a Thousand Years* (1970); Steven L. Schlossman, *Love and the American Delinquent* (1977); Steven L. Schlossman, "Delinquent Children" (1995); Steven L. Schlossman and Michael Sedlak, "The Chicago Area Project Revisited" (1983); Steven Schlossman and Stephanie Wallach, "The Crime of Precocious Sexuality" (1978); Eric C.

Schneider, *In the Web of Class* (1992); Jennifer Ann Trost, "Gateway to Justice" (1996); and David Wolcott and Steven Schlossman, "A Children's Culture of Casual Crime and Violence" (forthcoming).

David Wolcott and Steven Schlossman

K

KILPATRICK, WILLIAM HEARD (November 20, 1871–February 13, 1965), popularized the project method,* activity movement, and child-centered school. Although Kilpatrick's reputation will always suffer criticism for "misapplying" John Dewey's* and progressive ideals, he did fulfill the important role of a teacher and popularizer for progressive education.* Born in Georgia, he graduated from Mercer University in 1891; after spending a year at Johns Hopkins University, he received a master's degree from Mercer in 1892. For the next twenty years, Kilpatrick taught in the Georgia public schools* and at Mercer while briefly serving as its acting president, though had no wish to become president at the institution. His decision to leave Mercer was precipitated by charges of religious heresy brought forth by certain members of the Mercer University Board of Trustees. In 1912, Kilpatrick completed a Ph.D. at Teachers College, Columbia University, where he became a professor until his retirement in 1937.

The professional watershed for Kilpatrick came with his 1918 *Teachers College Record* essay, "The Project Method: The Use of the Purposeful Act in the Educative Process," later reprinted in monograph form. Although he has been granted no originality in the development of this concept, since it had already been popular in agricultural, architectural, and vocational education,* he did extend it to all subjects of the school curriculum, emphasizing social interaction. This contrasted with Franklin Bobbitt's* social efficiency and scientific management approach. Kilpatrick also became a spokesperson for the child-centered school, blending the importance of student needs and interests with the direction and leadership of the teacher. From this vantage point, with the philosophical underpinnings and endorsement of Dewey, Kilpatrick made his greatest contributions as a teacher and public figure. Kilpatrick also initiated many educational and social projects, including the formation of the John Dewey Society, Bennington College, and *Social Frontier*. The *New York Post* dubbed him the "Million Dollar Professor'' from totaling fees paid by his students at Teachers College. Kilpatrick often coordinated a class numbering in the hundreds—on occasion 650—through a combination of lecture and group discussion. Mercer University maintains Kilpatrick's papers, with his diaries and scrapbooks at Teachers College, Columbia University. The November 1961 issue of *Studies in Philosophy and Education* provides a complete bibliography of his works. Biographies include Samuel Tenebaum, *William Heard Kilpatrick: Trail Blazer in Education* (1951); John Benneke, *William Heard Kilpatrick* (forthcoming); and William Van Til, ''William Heard Kilpatrick: Respector of Individuals and Ideas'' (1996).

Craig Kridel

KINDERGARTEN, a German word meaning ''garden of children'' or ''child's garden,'' was the name given by German educator Friedrich Froebel* to his play-oriented preschool for three- to seven-year-old children. Based on Romantic and naturalistic concepts of organic growth and development, the first kindergarten opened in Blankenburg, Thuringia (Germany), in 1837. Froebel developed carefully sequenced educational materials and activities called ''gifts'' and ''occupations,'' and he structured fingerplays, games, and songs from which children were to learn rather than be taught to read, write, and count. During the 1840s, kindergartens and training schools opened in Frankfurt, Hamburg, and other parts of Germany. Froebel's ideas became associated with German liberalism, and as a result the kindergarten was banned in Prussia following the failure of the 1848 revolution. The diaspora of German ''freethinkers'' after the revolution made the kindergarten an international movement. Froebel died in 1852, but kindergartens spread throughout Europe in the 1850s and were introduced to the United States by Margarethe Meyer Schurz, who opened a small German-speaking kindergarten in her home in Watertown, Wisconsin, in 1856.

Schurz introduced Elizabeth Peabody* to the kindergarten, and she started the first English-speaking kindergarten in America in Boston in 1860. Private kindergartens for upper- and middle-class children were begun in many American cities in the 1870s and 1880s and a public kindergarten experiment was started in the St. Louis schools in 1873 by Susan Blow* and William Torrey Harris.* Kindergarten exhibits at the 1876 Philadelphia Centennial Exposition (see INTERNATIONAL EXPOSITIONS) created more public awareness and interest. Between 1870 and 1900, free kindergarten associations,* churches, clubs, settlement houses,* and other organizations ran charity kindergartens for poor children in most major American cities. Through the work of free kindergartners Alice Putnam* in Chicago, Anna Bryan* in Louisville, and others, Froebel's German methods were modified for American children and made more child-centered and reality-oriented. New concepts in psychology, particularly G. Stanley Hall's* child study movement,* affected the kindergarten as well. Kindergarten training schools such as those founded by Lucy Wheelock* in Boston and Elizabeth Harrison in Chicago produced teachers who used these newer methods. Patty Smith Hill,* head of the Kindergarten Department at Teachers College, Columbia University, led younger, progressive (see PRO-GRESSIVE EDUCATION) kindergartners who favored modernization and adoption by the public schools.*

The National Kindergarten Association, founded in 1909 in New York, helped in the campaign for public kindergartens, which was successful in part because of the kindergarten's potential as an agent of socialization and Americanization for poor and immigrant children. Free kindergarten associations were incorporated into the public schools in 1888 in Boston, and in 1892 in Chicago and in New York City, and by World War I most major American cities and larger towns had public kindergartens. The South and West slowly adopted kindergartens, and few existed for African American children. After the institutionalization in the public schools, home visits and other social welfare functions of charity kindergartening gradually disappeared and double sessions were adopted. The success of the kindergarten in extending public education to five-year-olds is one of the best examples of the maternalist, "social housekeeping" programs of the American women's movement and of progressive, child-centered educational reform (also, refer to BRADLEY, MILTON).

For sources on the history of the kindergarten, see Barbara Beatty, *Preschool Education in America: The Culture of Young Children from the Colonial Era to the Present* (1995); Elizabeth Dale Ross, *The Kindergarten Crusade: The Establishment of Preschool Education in the United States* (1976); Michael Steven Shapiro, *Child's Garden: The Kindergarten Movement from Froebel to Dewey* (1983); Nina C. Vandewalker, *The Kindergarten in American Public Education* (1908); and Evelyn Weber, *The Kindergarten: Its Encounter with Educational Thought in America* (1969).

Barbara Beatty

KINGSLEY, CLARENCE DARWIN. See *CARDINAL PRINCIPLES OF SECONDARY EDUCATION.*

KOHLBERG, LAWRENCE (October 25, 1927–January 17, 1987), a social psychologist at Yale and Harvard universities, was noted for his research and theories about moral development. Born and raised in Bronxville, New York, he attended Phillips Andover Academy and completed his undergraduate studies in 1948 at the University of Chicago, earning his Ph.D. in psychology there in 1958. He began his teaching career at Yale University the following year, becoming a fellow in the Center of Advanced Study of Behavior Science at the university. He served as director of the Child Psychology Program at the University of Chicago between 1963 and 1967, and as director of the Center for Moral Education at Harvard University from 1967 to 1987.

His cognitive moral theory posits six stages at three levels of moral development: (1) *Preconventional Level*: Stage 1, Punishment and Obedience; Stage 2, Individual Instrumental Purpose and Exchange; (2) *Conventional Level*: Stage

3, Mutual Interpersonal Expectations, Relationships, and Conformity; Stage 4, Social System and Conscience Maintenance; (3) *Postconventional and Principled Level*: Stage 5, Prior Rights and Social Contract; Stage 6, Universal Ethical Principles. This schema focuses on reasons for doing what is right, which become more principled and less egocentric as they advance. His early research employed male subjects and led to charges that cognitive moral stages neglected the female perspective. In response to this criticism, Kohlberg significantly modified his theories and research on moral judgment.

He was interested in advancing moral growth by bringing moral education to schools. Kohlberg fostered the Moral Dilemma Discussion approach and Just Community Education. The goal in these efforts was to advance moral reasoning, while avoiding indoctrination, by exposing students to higher stages of moral reasoning and promoting a climate of participatory democracy.

Kohlberg's major work is *The Philosophy of Moral Development: Moral Stages and the Idea of Justice* (1981). The best secondary source about Kohlberg's theories is Brenda Munsey, ed., *Moral Development, Moral Education, and Kohlberg: Basic Issues in Philosophy, Psychology, Religion, and Education* (1980).

Patrick M. Socoski

L

LABORATORY SCHOOLS sit at the intersection of most of the major themes and conflicts in the history of teacher education in American normal schools,* colleges, and universities since the late nineteenth century. In particular, the history of these schools helps to illustrate the struggles of university-based teacher educators and their programs to carve out an identity vis-à-vis the practical worlds of classroom teachers, the research mission and status hierarchy of universities, and the sociopolitical contexts of K–12 schooling.

A laboratory school—whether for primary grades, elementary school, high school,* or K–12—exists as an adjunct department or institution to a school, college, or department of education in a university. Laboratory schools may be public or independent, may be located on or off campus, and may serve a general and nonselective student clientele or one that is distinguished by special need, interest, talent, or university family affiliation. Lab school teachers today typically hold college faculty appointments but, by custom, may or may not attain the formal rank or informal status of a professor's position on campus. Since the establishment of teacher-training normal schools in the mid-nineteenth century, laboratory schools were originally known as model or demonstration schools—a few retain that name today—when they existed to showcase for preservice teachers what the normal school principal considered best practices in the elementary classroom. By the 1890s, teacher-training institutions had begun to view the model school as a prospective site for two other functions: *practice (or student) teaching*, in which teacher candidates would put their pedagogical training to use, and *experimentation*, in which professors and teachers would try out and assess new theories and practices. John Dewey* is credited with creating the first site named and intended to be a laboratory (experimental) school, which he opened at the University of Chicago in 1896. This represented a profound break with the traditional model school because it crafted a research-and-development relationship with two university departments at Chicago and sought to link itself with progressive social philosophies of the time (see PRO-GRESSIVE EDUCATION).

However, both experimentation and practice teaching proved to be problematic roles for laboratory schools—as has their very survival to the present day. State normal schools evolved into teachers' colleges, which then diversified beyond teacher education gradually during the first half of the twentieth century. While some variety of the model school existed at most single-purpose teacher-training institutions, many of these schools lost their academic status and financial clout as the mission and budget priorities of colleges changed. During the same decades, institutions not founded especially to prepare teachers, such as land grant universities and private colleges, also developed teacher certification programs but often had no tradition of a campus lab school. Where lab schools did grow and flourish, pressures from teachers and parents tended to inhibit and often obliterate their experimental function. Parents and school boards often wanted their children exposed to the most tried-and-true practices rather than unproved methodologies. Furthermore, educational research—especially as it evolved prior to the 1980s—tended to exclude classroom practitioners from its design and execution. Accordingly, lab schools were often either left out or dictated to by academic researchers whose training, loyalty, status, and reward structure in the university distanced them from school practitioners. Lab schools' practice-teaching function faced challenges as well, in part because degree programs rapidly grew much too large for labs to accommodate all the field placements, and also because educators debated the appropriateness of training teachers in a perceived hothouse environment rather than in a more typical public school.

By 1964, some 205 of the estimated 1,200 institutions with teacher education programs had a lab school. By the 1990s, only about 100 remained, but many had developed creative ways to address the historical problems that have plagued these schools and now engage in a varied agenda of demonstration, research, development, and practice teaching. As such, their importance in their own local setting, as well as their potential to model important research and practice collaborations in education, may be larger than their numbers suggest. Lab schools also stand as the great-grandparents of more recently conceived campus-affiliated projects, such as professional development schools, professional practice schools, "coalition," "network," or "partnership" schools, and some types of charter schools. Among the lab schools with the longest historical roots in American teacher education are University School (1878), Indiana University of Pennsylvania; Malcolm Price Laboratory School (1883), University of Northern Iowa; Robert Reid Laboratory School (1892), Eastern Washington University; Wheelock School (1909), Keene (NH) State College; University Laboratory School (1915), Louisiana State University; and Edith Bowen Laboratory School (1928), Utah State University. Dewey's school evolved into the present-day Laboratory School of the University of Chicago.

Historical sources about teacher education and laboratory schools include

John I. Goodlad, "How Laboratory Schools Go Awry" (1980); John I. Goodlad, Roger Soder, and Kenneth M. Sirotnik, eds., *Places Where Teachers Are Taught* (1990); Harry Hutton, "Historical Background of the Campus School in America" (1991); Robert A. Levin, *Educating Elementary School Teachers: The Struggle for Coherent Visions, 1909–1978* (1994); Robert A. Levin, "An Unfulfilled Alliance: The Lab School in Teacher Education, Two Case Studies, 1910–1980" (1990); National Society for the Study of Education, "Curriculum Making in Private Laboratory Schools" (1926); and William Van Til, *The Laboratory School: Its Rise and Fall?* (1969).

Robert A. Levin

LANCASTER SYSTEM. First gaining prominence in England and quickly popularized across the globe, the monitorial system of instruction found a receptive audience in early nineteenth-century America. Monitorial instruction, developed by Joseph Lancaster around 1800, proved popular because it addressed concerns about social disorder and embodied the scientific ethos of social reformers of its day. The Lancaster system made a number of innovations that proved to be influential to future schooling efforts: It provided a systematic approach to education that gave priority to efficiency; professionalized pedagogy; popularized nonsectarian, tax-supported, uniform schools; and implemented a system of instruction and discipline based on meritocratic principles.

Although Lancaster seemed to have developed his system independently, he and his organized allies, the British and Foreign School Society, had to answer accusations of forgery and actively compete for students with his rival Andrew Bell, who had developed a similar monitorial system in India. The major difference between the systems was Lancaster's nonsectarian, scriptural approach to moral training; Bell, in contrast, advocated instruction in the doctrines of the Church of England. While this difference proved an impediment to Lancaster at home, it helped him abroad, particularly in the United States.

Conceived as a means to educate and morally train the poor, Lancaster's system proved attractive because it promised to be highly efficient. It was economically efficient because it utilized advanced students, "monitors," to instruct those students beneath them in the educational hierarchy. The system also appeared efficient in performing its instructional goals. Lancasterian schools appeared almost machinelike in operation, with students' motion and speech highly routinized and coordinated. Rejecting the coercive forms of behavior control, such as corporal punishment, that guided previous educational efforts, Lancaster based his system of instruction on "emulation," in essence, competition among peers. By having students compete with one another for positions within the school hierarchy, Lancaster believed he could most effectively guide the behavior and realize the potential of his students.

Lancaster's system gained its most enthusiastic reception where anxieties about the urban poor were highest, in New York and Philadelphia. In New York, the Free School Society* succeeded in gaining control of the city's elementary schools and placing them under the monitorial system. In Philadelphia, Lancasterian advocates, including Roberts Vaux, succeeded in making monitorial education legislatively obligatory for the education of the poor. By midcentury, however, the monitorial system had lost favor, in large part because of Pestalozzian philosophy, which stressed the individuality of children (see PESTALOZZIANISM).

The largest collection of primary materials on Lancaster and the monitorial school movement is the Joseph Lancaster Papers at the American Antiquarian Society in Worcester, Massachusetts. A selection of writings by Lancaster and other commentators on the monitorial system, as well as an interpretive essay on that approach, can be found in Carl F. Kaestle, *Joseph Lancaster and the Monitorial School Movement: A Documentary History* (1973). David J. Hogan, "The Market Revolution and Disciplinary Power: Joseph Lancaster and the Psychology of the Early Classroom System" (1989), provides an excellent evaluation of the monitorial system's significance.

Rodney Hessinger

LANGUAGE ARTS. See ENGLISH LANGUAGE ARTS.

LATHROP, JULIA CLIFFORD (June 29, 1858–April 15, 1932), devoted her professional life to children's welfare and proved instrumental in establishing the Children's Bureau.* In 1890, ten years after attending Rockford College and graduating from Vassar, Lathrop joined fellow Rockford graduates Jane Addams* and Ellen Gates Starr at Hull-House, the recently founded Chicago social settlement. As a Cook County agent visitor and later as a Governor John P. Altgeld appointee to the State Board of Charities in 1893, she investigated the lives of relief applicants within a mile of Hull-House, later publishing her research in *Hull-House Maps and Papers* (1895), and extended her investigations to over 100 county poorfarms and almshouses in Illinois. She lobbied for over a decade to provide separate facilities for children, the sick, the mentally ill, and the elderly. Her work culminated in the establishment of the nation's first juvenile court in Chicago in 1899. Lathrop participated in the first White House Conference on Children in 1901 and was part of a group that included Lillian Wald, founder of Henry Street Settlement, and Florence Kelley, head of the National Consumer's League, who engineered a proposal to found a children's bureau. Three years of reformers' lobbying of Congress ended with President William Howard Taft signing the bill establishing the Children's Bureau on April 9, 1912, and naming Lathrop as its first chief. On a meager appropriation and a hand-picked staff of fifteen, the Bureau under Lathrop's guidance, emphasizing the "whole child" approach to research, managed to produce a birth registration study, a unique infant mortality study based on sociological and graphic anecdotal evidence, published the pamphlet *Prenatal Care* in 1913, and commissioned the pamphlet, *Infant Care*, which shaped the lives of countless children in its various editions from 1914 to the present. One of the reasons for the Bureau's success was a female network of thousands of women belonging to diverse organizations who acted as Bureau adjuncts in distant communities. During Lathrop's tenure of office, until illness forced her to retire in 1921, the Bureau increased its scope, enforcing the first child labor law in 1916 until the act was declared unconstitutional in 1918, administering the Sheppard-Towner Act in 1921 that provided federal aid to the states for the protection of maternity and infancy, and building the scaffolding for children's welfare that became the infrastructure for health and welfare programs under President Franklin D. Roosevelt.

The Rockford College Library hosts the Lathrop Papers. For biographies, see Jane Addams, *My Friend, Julia Lathrop* (1935), and Jacqeline K. Parker and Edward M. Carpenter, "Julia Lathrop and the Children's Bureau: The Emergence of an Institution" (1981). Also, refer to Robyn Muncy, *Creating a Female Dominon in American Reform, 1890–1935* (1991).

Nancy Weiss

LATIN GRAMMAR SCHOOLS in America, like their English prototypes, were established as elite college preparatory institutions to prepare upper-class boys for the religious, governmental, and legal professions. The curriculum focused on the classical humanism (see CLASSICAL CURRICULUM) of the Renaissance, emphasizing Latin, Greek, and sometimes Hebrew languages and literatures. The entire course of study was formidable, with students starting school at age seven or eight and spending the good part of up to six days a week in class year-round for seven years, although they tended to withdraw and return depending on their circumstances. Memorizing texts under a strict discipline was the primary activity. Although in theory grammar schools were distinguished from the more elementary reading and writing schools, in practice most of them became more general institutions with limited students, teachers, and funds. Modes of sponsorship and quality of instruction varied as well. Some distinguished masters, the most notable being Ezekiel Cheever at the Boston Free School, commanded impressive salaries, but most received modest pay. The Massachusetts Law of 1647,* and similar legislation in other New England colonies, initially specified these schools. Around 1700, the law mandating grammar schools in larger towns was more stringently enforced, and the requirement for full-time certified Latinists as teachers was added. The institutions continued into the nineteenth century, being mandatory in Massachusetts until 1827, but ultimately they lost ground to academies* offering a more practical education for the growing middle class.

Secondary sources include Robert Middlekauff, *Ancients and Axioms: Secondary Education in Eighteenth-Century New England* (1963), and Rena Lee Vassar, "Elementary and Latin Grammar School Education in the American Colonies, 1607–1700" (1958).

Eric R. Ebeling

LAU V. NICHOLS, 414 U.S. 563 (1974). This case represented a class action suit by non-English-speaking Chinese students against the San Francisco Unified School District, alleging unequal educational opportunities under the equal protection clause of the Fourteenth Amendment and Title VI of the Civil Rights Act of 1964.* Without reaching the equal protection argument, the Supreme Court found a violation of Title VI in the manner in which California administered its state-mandated education graduation requirements with relationship to non-English-speaking students. Because the state required "the mastery of English by all pupils in the schools," the Court ruled that "there is no equality of treatment merely by providing students with the same facilities, textbooks, teachers, and curriculum" (p. 565). Since plaintiffs had sought no specific remedy, the Court remanded the case to the district court to fashion appropriate relief. (See also BILINGUAL EDUCATION.)

Ralph D. Mawdsley

LEARNING DISABLED. See SPECIAL EDUCATION.

LEE V. WEISMAN, 112 U.S. 2649 (1992), is the U.S. Supreme Court's most recent pronouncement on school-sponsored prayer at public school graduation ceremonies. A middle-school student in Providence, Rhode Island, and her father objected to prayer at her graduation, where school officials had invited a rabbi to deliver the invocation and benediction. The rabbi was asked to follow guidelines outlined in a pamphlet on public prayer in a pluralistic society published by the National Conference on Christians and Jews. After the federal trial court permanently enjoined the prayers, the First Circuit affirmed. The Supreme Court further agreed, holding that prayer at a public school graduation ceremony violates the establishment clause of the First Amendment. Writing for the five-member majority of a bitterly divided Court, Associate Justice Anthony Kennedy eschewed the tripartite *Lemon v. Kurtzman** standard that had been applied by the lower courts in striking down the prayers. He based his argument on two major points. First, he maintained that the state, through the school officials, had a pervasive role not only by selecting who would offer the prayer but also by directing the content of the prayer. Second, he concluded that the role of the school qua government in permitting prayer at the graduation resulted in the possible psychological coercion of the students. He reasoned that arguments to the contrary notwithstanding, the students were a captive audience forced to participate possibly against their wishes because they were not free to absent themselves from their graduation ceremony.

Charles J. Russo and Ralph D. Mawdsley

LEGAL DEFENSE AND EDUCATION FUND (LDF). The National Association for the Advancement of Colored People (NAACP), founded in 1910, made racial integration its central aim. In 1935, Charles Hamilton Houston, the dean of Howard University's law school, became the organization's special counsel. After Houston decided to leave the NAACP in 1939, it created the LDF to undermine, through litigation, the U.S. Supreme Court decision, *Plessy v. Ferguson*,* that allowed states to offer separate but equal facilities for African Americans.

Headed by Thurgood Marshall, the LDF won a Supreme Court decision in *Smith v. Allwright*, 321 U.S. 649 (1944) that ended the Texas Democratic Party's practice of prohibiting African American voters from voting in election primaries. In *Morgan v. Virginia*, 328 U.S. 373 (1946), the LDF unsuccessfully tried to prevent Virginia from requiring African American passengers on interstate buses to sit in the rear seats, leaving the convenient front seats for white passengers. However, the Federal Housing Administration stopped rewarding racial segregation in its appraisals of property following an LDF victory in a federal Supreme Court case, *Shelley v. Kraemer*, 334 U.S. 1 (1948).

The LDF achieved a great deal in education. From 1935 to 1950, it tried many cases to achieve equal pay for African American teachers in southern cities. In mid-1943, LDF had salary cases pending in eleven states. By 1946, these cases proved to be inconsequential because school boards had found another strategy: African American teachers scored lower than white teachers on the National Teacher Examination. Even if LDF won and thereby eliminated racially distinct salary scales in a particular district, that board could use merit pay, based on test scores, to maintain differentiated salaries based on race. The LDF also pursued litigation against segregated universities. Before LDF was officially founded, Marshall won admittance for Donald Murray to the University of Maryland Law School in 1935 because that state lacked a separate law school for African Americans but offered scholarships to African American students to attend a school out of state. In 1938, Houston tried to force Missouri to admit Lloyd Gaines to its state law school. Although the legislature agreed to build a separate school for African Americans, Gaines disappeared. In *McLaurin v. Oklahoma State Regents*, 339 U.S. 637 (1950), and *Sweatt v. Painter*, 339 U.S. 629 (1950), however, the LDF argued that Oklahoma and Texas, respectively, could not segregate African Americans in university graduate schools. While George McLaurin sought a doctoral degree in education, he was forced to sit in a special roped off area at the Oklahoma University. In this case, the Court ruled that these restrictions impeded the educational process by preventing McLaurin from engaging in discussions with other students. In the second case, Texas A & M University had created a new school for African American students in response to *Sweatt*. The Court decided that unequal law schools could not satisfy the "separate but equal" requirements in *Plessy*, since these prevented African American students from gaining the skills essential for their profession.

With these precedents, the LDF directly attacked public school* segregation in *Brown v. Board of Education* (1954).* The Court's justices agreed that segregation harmed the emotional and intellectual development of African American children. A year later the Court charged lower courts to ensure that the local school officials dismantled segregated districts. As a result, the LDF sued recalcitrant school officials, winning a string of victories that expanded the definition of school desegregation. In *Green v. New Kent County*, 391 U.S. 430 (1968), the Court ruled that desegregation plans could not simply exist in policies that had no effect. Later, in *Swann v. Charlotte Mecklenberg* (1971),* the Court approved the use of ratios to measure desegregation and busing to achieve the desired proportion of students. Further, in *Keyes v. School District No. 1 Denver, Colorado*, 413 U.S. 189 (1972), the Court found that district guilty of enacting segregation policies, although the state had not required racially separate schools.

In *Milliken v. Bradley*,* the Supreme Court stopped expanding the definition of desegregation. It decided that white children in suburban Detroit could not be forced to cross district lines to attend predominately African American city schools. While districts such as St. Louis, Missouri, and Wilmington, Delaware, had to create metropolitan desegregation plans after 1974, the Detroit decision ended the hopes of winning cases where the fact of segregation was the compelling issue. At the same time, it silenced a growing movement to adopt an amendment to the U.S. Constitution to prevent busing for school desegregation.

The LDF continued to protect the civil rights of minority groups throughout the 1980s and 1990s by pursuing litigation in such areas as school desegregation, Medicaid rights, and criminal justice. The highest praise for the LDF may be that other groups representing such minorities as women, handicapped children, and linguistic minorities imitated the LDF in their campaigns to secure rights for their constituents (also, refer to SPECIAL EDUCATION).

A variety of secondary sources exist: Scott Baker, "Testing Equality" (1995); Jack Greenberg, *Crusaders in the Courts* (1994); Richard Kluger, *Simple Justice* (1975); Genna Rae McNeil, *Groundwork* (1983); Rosemary Salomone, *Equal Education under the Law* (1986); and Mark Tushnet, *Making Civil Rights Law* (1994).

Joseph Watras

LEMON V. KURTZMAN, 403 U.S. 602 (1971). This U.S. Supreme Court decision ruled on two separate state laws and developed a three-part test to be used to decide future establishment clause cases. A Pennsylvania statute provided reimbursement for teachers' salaries and textbooks for courses taught in sectarian schools, and a Rhode Island law authorized that state to directly supplement teacher salaries in sectarian schools for teaching secular subjects. The *Lemon* text stated that all such laws must maintain a secular purpose, neither promote nor inhibit religion, and avoid fostering "an excessive government entanglement with religion" (pp. 612–613). Using this three-part test, the Court found that both state statutes had a secular purpose because their intent was to enhance the quality of secular education for all children. The Court did not discuss whether the laws had a primary effect of advancing or inhibiting religion, since it regarded the amount of government supervision to assure that parochial school* teachers did not infuse religious material into secular subjects would result in excessive entanglement. Therefore, the statues were ruled as a violation of the establishment clause.

Tony Eastland, ed., *Religious Liberty in the Supreme Court: The Cases That Define the Debate over Church and State* (1993), focuses on legal reasoning and effect; in contrast, David A. J. Richards, *Toleration and the Constitution* (1986), maintains an intellectual-history approach.

Bruce Beezer

LESSINGER, LEON. See ACCOUNTABILITY MOVEMENT.

LEWIS, SAMUEL (March 17, 1799–July 28, 1854), became the first superintendent of Ohio Schools. Born in Falmouth, Massachusetts, Lewis and his family moved to Ohio in 1813. The following year he began working in the office of the clerk of common pleas court and reading law in the evenings. He was admitted to the Ohio Bar in 1822. While residing in Cincinnati, Lewis formed friendships with Nathan Guilford, William Holmes McGuffey,* William Woodward, and Calvin Stowe,* with whom he shared interests in universal education, temperance, and abolitionism. They joined with others to form the Western Literary Institute and College of Professional Teachers in 1829. This group disseminated papers about educational concerns and campaigned for educational reform. Although he never attended more than six or nine months of school in his entire life, Lewis became president of the board of trustees of Woodward High School in 1831. In 1837, the Ohio House of Representative appointed Lewis the first superintendent of Ohio schools for one year. Few other states had such a central office and the bill to create it in Ohio passed by only one vote. In 1838, the House adopted his suggestions, creating a school fund of $200,000, providing state taxes for school support, and making county and township officials superintendents of schools. Opponents decried these increased expenses for schools. Lewis resigned the state superintendency in 1839, and the legislature abolished the office a year later. Lewis devoted his remaining life to politics, running for state senator in 1843 and governor in 1846 and in 1853.

Lewis maintained beliefs about schooling typical among school reformers during the common school* era. More interested in common schools than colleges, he encouraged teachers to stress English grammar, handwriting, arithmetic, geography, and Christian morality. Like Horace Mann,* he thought women's natural fondness for children made them better teachers than men. Lewis also argued that classes number less than forty students. Lewis further asserted that the best way to establish common schools was to furnish instruction to all children rather than to charge them different tuitions based on their abilities to pay. Finally, he thought prospective teachers should pass an examination demonstrating their competency.

Hundreds of Lewis's personal letters are lost, but primary sources include papers he wrote for the journal *Transactions of the Western Literary Institute* (1836, 1837, 1838) and *Annual Reports* (December 1837, December 1838, December 1839). Secondary sources are Allen Oscar Hansen, *Early Educational Leadership in the Ohio Valley* (1923; 1969); William G. W. Lewis, *Biography of Samuel Lewis* (1857); F. Michael Perko, "Educational Biography and the Protestant Paideia" (1991); and Sr. Mary Loretta Petit, O.P., "Samuel Lewis, Educational Reformer Turned Abolitionist" (1966).

Joseph Watras

LIFE ADJUSTMENT EDUCATION FOR YOUTH. The two life adjustment commissions represented the most visible manifestations of an era in American education that culminated in a searing conflict between educationists and academic scholars. That era had its formal inception on the second day of a conference sponsored by the U.S. Office of Education.* On June 1, 1945, Charles A. Prosser,* a long-time leader in the field of vocational education,* having been asked to summarize the proceedings, proposed a resolution declaring that though 20 percent of the high school* population were not being adequately served by college entrance programs and another 20 percent by vocational programs, the remaining 60 percent were not being provided with life adjustment education that was most appropriate for them. He further asked the commissioner of education to initiate a series of conferences.

At the Life Adjustment Conference held in Chicago in 1947, the First Commission on Life Adjustment Education was launched with Benjamin Willis, a Yonkers, New York, superintendent of schools, serving as chair. That Commission devoted itself largely to defining what was meant by life adjustment education, concluding in the end that it was appropriate for all high school students, not simply the 60 percent that Prosser had originally projected. Much of its effort sought to tie the new movement to the *Cardinal Principles** report of 1918. The First Commission ended its work in 1950 with its report *Vitalizing Secondary Education*. The Second Commission published its report in 1954 under the title *A Look Ahead in Secondary Education*.

This movement always suffered from an absence of a precise definition and program, but life adjustment education, in general, became associated with the study of social and personal problems such as personal grooming, dating, and clothing selection rather than academic subjects. Support for these programs came, in large measure, from the National Association of Secondary School Principals, the Sears-Roebuck Foundation, and the U.S. Commissioner of Education, John Studebaker, although little financial backing came from the commissioner's office. In 1952, Arthur E. Bestor, Jr.,* joined by other academicians appalled by life adjustment's anti-academic and anti-intellectual tendencies, launched a major attack on the movement. By the late 1950s, life adjustment education had lost its momentum.

The First Commission of Life Adjustment Education for Youth was published as Bulletin No. 3 by the U.S. Office of Education in 1951. In 1954, the Second

Commission of Life Adjustment Education for Youth issued its report as the U.S. Office of Education's Bulletin No. 4. Some documents pertaining to the two commissions and to life adjustment generally may be found in the National Archives, Record Group 12; the files of the Dunwoody Institute in Minneapolis, Minnesota; and the records of the Sears-Roebuck Foundation in Chicago, Illinois. The best published account of the life adjustment movement appears in Edward A. Krug's *Shaping of the American High School: II, 1920–1940* (1972). Finally, Dorothy Elizabeth Broder, "Life Adjustment Education: An Historical Study of a Program of the United States Office of Education, 1945–1954" (1977), is an excellent source of information on the movement.

Herbert M. Kliebard

LITERACY refers to the comprehension and use of those language skills needed to read and write. Other forms of symbolic communication, such as graphics and scientific notation, may be considered as special types of literacy. Degrees of literacy are usually defined by reading and writing achievement levels and their functional equivalents in settings demanding literacy skills. As historians and sociolinguists have discovered, the terms "literate" and "illiterate" are notoriously vague because the distinction between orality and literacy is not a sharp one and the uses and expectations for literacy vary with different social and historical contexts. The achievement of literacy carries with it a metalinguistic recognition that seeing the world through print is different from other forms of experience, and that there is a culture of print that shapes both public discourse and private imagination.

In seventeenth-century colonial America, the task of transmitting literate culture, including literacy skills, was shared by family, church, and school, usually in that order of importance. To be literate often meant the ability to read (recite) from the Bible and to sign one's name. Bible literacy remained the focus for the development of literacy skills throughout the colonial period. Thus the effect of literacy was essentially conservative. Even with the emergence of a civic, secular model for literacy following the War for Independence, Bible literacy remained important. It was in the common school* that an evangelical Protestant tradition merged with a theory of republican government to form one of the educational building blocks of democracy and self-governance. By the mid-nineteenth century, public common schools had assumed the primary burden for teaching literacy skills.

By 1840, the moral value of literacy was part of a larger set of values associated with nationalism, progress, public enlightenment, and good citizenship. The contribution of literacy to worldly success was also touted by printers, booksellers, authors, and promoters of the common school. By the mid-nineteenth century, educational leaders were convinced that a high literacy rate was an indicator of social well-being. Many believed that the unlettered posed a threat to social stability and were condemned to a life of poverty and possibly crime.

Technological advances in printing and improvements in transportation helped to support new, more sophisticated networks of distribution for books and periodical literature. These, in turn, helped lay the groundwork for rising literacy rates in the mid-nineteenth century. In northern states illiteracy dropped from an average of 25 percent in 1800 to a range of 3 to 9 percent in 1840; in the same period in the South the drop among southern whites was from 40–50 percent illiteracy to approximately 19 percent. Town and city formation and the growth of commercial and manufacturing activity helped support schools and libraries. Literacy levels, however, varied consistently with people's socioeconomic position, ethnicity, nativity, race, and gender. Women, the foreign born, those living in poverty, and nonfarm manual laborers were more likely to be illiterate in the mid-nineteenth century. When these variables combined adversely within families, the probability of intergenerational family illiteracy increased.

The expansion of schooling at the elementary level contributed to increased literacy rates during the first seventy years of the nineteenth century. By 1870, most children ages ten to fourteen were enrolled in common schools. School enrollments, however, were still affected by wealth, ethnicity, nativity, race, and parental occupation. This trend continued in the early twentieth century as educators voiced increasing concern about limited literacy among African Americans and eastern and southern European immigrants. As basic literacy levels rose, educators turned their attention to higher-order cognitive skills associated with literacy. The burden of rising expectations for literacy was then shifted to secondary education (see *CARDINAL PRINCIPLES OF SECONDARY EDUCATION*; HIGH SCHOOLS).

From 1918 to 1982, readership varied proportionately by occupation, wealth, and ethnicity, but over the same period the proportion of total expenditures on print material was about the same across wealth classes. The types of print consumed by different wealth groups, however, did change from 1890 to 1980. In 1890, the working classes mostly bought newspapers, whereas the wealthy dominated the book market. By the mid-twentieth century, wealth was far less a factor in purchasing different types of print material.

The term "functional literacy" came into use in the 1930s. It usually described a level of literacy associated with occupational utility and the ability to read newspapers and other public documents. Army recruitment during World War II brought the problem of functional literacy into focus as the U.S. Army discovered the limited literacy of thousands of recruits. Following the war, government officials and economists focusing on workforce development sought a greater role for the federal government in literacy education. The 1964 Economic Opportunity Act was the first federal program to subsidize literacy education directly. This was followed two years later by the Adult Basic Education Act (ABE). To the dismay of ABE advocates, it was found that most adult illiterates and most of the hard-core poor did not participate in ABE programs. The problem seemed to be intractable as it became clear that the achievement of literacy continued to be mediated by stubborn social, economic, and racial barriers.

To simplify the measurement of functional literacy, educators established grade-level equivalents for specified functional tasks. More recently, direct measures of functional literacy have replaced the surrogate measure of grade level. Direct tests frequently measure survival skills in the workplace and the ability to read public documents, instructions, and questionnaires. In the competition for jobs, it has become clear that formal school credentials and basic literacy are not enough.

The practical, cultural, and moral significance of literacy is linked to the role of the public school in American culture. If the public school has an important role to play in achieving equality of opportunity, social justice, and social progress, then the achievement of literacy is a measure of the success of the public school. If literacy is linked to the distribution of resources and rewards in society, it has a moral significance far beyond its technical and practical merits. Whether literacy is an instrument of liberation or control then becomes a social and moral issue to be resolved by educators and citizens in a public forum.

See William Gilmore, *Reading Becomes a Necessity of Life: Material and Cultural Life in Rural New England, 1780–1835* (1989); Harvey J. Graff, *The Legacies of Literacy: Continuities and Contradictions in Western Culture and Society* (1987); Carl F. Kaestle, Helen Damon-Moore, Lawrence C. Stedman, Katherine Tinsley, and William Vance Trollinger, Jr., *Literacy in the United States: Readers and Reading since 1880* (1991); Jonathan Kozol, *Illiterate America* (1985); Kenneth Lockridge, *Literacy in Colonial New England: An Enquiry into the Social Context of Literacy in the Early Modern West* (1974); Lee Soltow and Edward W. Stevens, Jr., *The Rise of Literacy and the Common School in the United States: A Socioeconomic Analysis to 1870* (1981); Edward W. Stevens, Jr., *The Grammar of the Machine: Technical Literacy and Early Industrial Expansion in the United States* (1995); Edward W. Stevens, Jr., *Literacy, Law, and Social Order* (1988); and Michael Warner, *The Letters of the Republic: Publication and the Public Sphere in Eighteenth-Century America* (1991).

Edward W. Stevens, Jr.

LOCAL CONTROL. See OCEAN HILL–BROWNSVILLE.

LOWELL EXPERIMENT. When the Lowell, Massachusetts, textile mills began to produce cloth in 1823, they hired thousands of young, single women from rural areas at low pay to work sixty or more hours per week. To gain parental approval, as well as to reassure these young women, the mills promised to provide a strict, wholesome environment. Thus, single female workers, some as young as fifteen, lived in company-owned boarding houses that were connected to the mills and cut off from the outside world. Alchohol was prohibited, and church attendance required. The charge of being a gossip brought dismissal from both the boarding house and work. Mill owners defended these restrictions as necessary.

Looking for a more positive way to bring about moral and educational improvement, mill owners supported a magazine, *The Lowell Offering* (1840–1845). Because female workers edited the magazine, it focused on their concerns. The magazine published poetry, moral fiction, and articles on savings accounts, self-improvement, moral reform, worker discipline, how to get along in a boardinghouse, practical tips on buying and selling while in town, and difficulties workers might expect with relatives back home. Matters of love, and especially the need to pick a proper mate wisely, occupied much of the magazine. Women workers generally expected to leave the mills to marry, and most did. The magazine never criticized the mill owners, and much of the content, though useful to workers, was also useful to the mills in shaping a moral, sober, discipline, and nonunion workforce.

Refer to *The Lowell Offering*, available in paperback reprint. Lucy Larcom, *A New England Girlhood: Outlined from Memory* (1889), recalls her years in the Lowell mills. For secondary sources, see Thomas Dublin, *Women at Work: The Transformation of Work and Community in Lowell, Massachusetts, 1826–1860* (1979), and Laurence F. Gross, *The Course of Industrial Decline: The Boott Cotton Mills of Lowell, Massachusetts, 1835–1955* (1993).

W. J. Rorabaugh

LYCEUMS. Josiah Holbrook, a teacher, founded the first lyceum in Millbury, Massachusetts, in 1826. Named for the place where Aristotle lectured in ancient Greece, lyceums were evening public lecture series that emphasized science, moral reform, and philosophy. From the 1830s through the 1860s, lyceums provided both education and entertainment in most towns and cities. Many lyceums developed close ties to adult evening schools and public libraries, and some grew so successful that they built their own halls. By the 1840s, rotating professional speakers traveled regular circuits. New England and the western frontier settled by New Englanders hosted the strongest lyceum movement. Men and women from all social classes attended. The only requirement, other than a small fee, was a thirst for self-improvement. Adolescents (see ADOLESCENCE) liked lyceums because they could go unchaperoned.

Lyceums held a broad appeal through diverse topics and clever, dramatic presentations. Samuel Colt, for example, demonstrated the effects of laughing gas on volunteers from the audience. Other favorites included the exhibition of miniaturized working steam engines and travelogues with lantern slide shows. Susan B. Anthony, Frederick Douglass,* and Henry David Thoreau discussed moral reform. John B. Gough described drunkenness from the viewpoint of a reclaimed alcoholic. His performance included a portrayal of shaking with delirium tremens. The most famous lecturer was Ralph Waldo Emerson, whose poetic talks uplifted audiences toward transcendentalism. Lyceums made Emerson and other leading lecturers rich. After the Civil War, lyceums faded, but many of the same ideas continued in the later Chautauqua movement.

Primary documents include the Concord Lyceum Records, Concord Public Library, Concord, Massachusetts, and the Salem Lyceum Records, Essex Institute, Salem, Massachusetts. Also, refer to the *American Journal of Education* (1826–1830) and the *American Annals of Education* (1831–1839). Finally, see Carl Bode, *The American Lyceum: Town Meeting of the Mind* (1956); Kenneth W. Cameron, *The Massachusetts Lyceum during the American Renaissance* (1969); and Mary K. Cayton, *Emerson's Emergence: Self and Society in the Transformation of New England, 1800–1845* (1989).

                                                                        W. J. Rorabaugh

LYON, MARY (February 28, 1797–March 5, 1849), founded Mount Holyoke Seminary (1837), one of the early schools for the secondary education of young women. Born in Buckland, Massachusetts, she attended one-room schools and started teaching at age seventeen. She alternated periods of studying with periods of teaching until she opened a girls' school in Buckland, which flourished until 1828, when she began teaching at Ipswich (Massachusetts) Female Seminary. In 1833, she decided to found her own seminary for young females. Unlike many such seminaries at this time, Lyon's school would own its own property and be operated on a non-profit basis by a board of trustees. Three Massachusetts towns bid for her school, and Mount Holyoke Female Seminary opened in South Hadley in 1837 with eighty students. Lyon founded her seminary with an education as rigorous as many of that of the men's colleges, to train middle-class females as teachers, missionaries, and wives of missionaries, and to prepare them for self-sufficient lives. She served as its principal as well as chemistry teacher for nearly twelve years. Mount Holyoke's success led to increased acceptance of education for women and paved the way for the founding of women's colleges. Mount Holyoke became a college in 1887 and thus survives as the oldest women's higher education institution in the United States.

The Mount Holyoke College Library Archives houses most of Mary Lyon's papers, including her only book and several pamphlets. Valuable biographies include Elizabeth Alden Green, *Mary Lyon and Mount Holyoke: Opening the Gates* (1979); Edward Hitchcock, *The Power of Christian Benevolence, Illustrated in the Life and Labors of Mary Lyon* (1858); Marion Lansing, *Mary Lyon through Her Letters* (1937); and Sarah D. Stow, *History of Mount Holyoke Seminary: During Its First Half Century* (1887).

                                                                    Carole B. Shmurak

M

MAINSTREAMING. See SPECIAL EDUCATION.

MANAGEMENT BY OBJECTIVES. See ACCOUNTABILITY MOVE-MENT.

MANN, HORACE (May 4, 1796–August 2, 1859), often referred to as the "Father of the Public School" championed the free and universal education for all Massachusetts children, the institutionalization of teacher training, and the construction of well-planned school buildings.

Mann was born in Franklin, Massachusetts, during a time when the United States was in the first stages of industrial development and children learned to read in an array of educational environments—at home, in church, in libraries, and occasionally in schools. He experienced education in all these settings and, through the process, cultivated a concept of education and of childhood that would transform his own views of education, childhood, and ultimately of American children.

Mann emerged from the educational web of Franklin, Massachusetts, with a vision of human environments awash in possibility. The daily routines and experiences of the first dozen years of his life provided a crucible for the forging of a transforming educative sensibility. In an environment where he experienced the rigors of physical labor, moral and psychological instruction, and the loss of a father and brother, he discovered the vulnerability of childhood. In an environment of benevolent nurture and feminine sensibility, he became sensitive to the small spaces and human relationships in which moral and intellectual constructs might develop. Nurtured in the bosom of orthodox Calvinism and the doctrines of predestination, he nonetheless learned to become a devout environmentalist. Through daily acts of piety, prayer, and biblical rote learning, he discovered the power of the word and the liberating possibilities of literacy and schooling.

From the tutelage of his four educational environments, Mann transformed the particularities of his lived experience into new visions of educational possibility. He discovered education as an instrument of moral discipline, intellectual succor, imaginative power, and individual empowerment. He learned to envision a range of educational possibilities.

Through the complexities of his early immersions in the world of books, he was to wed an intense natural love of beauty and nature with a love of words and verbal imagery. Together they would form a foundation for the cultivation of an education rhetoric of uncommon elegance and enormous persuasive power. In the educational environments of Franklin, Massaschusetts, Mann had, by the time he was eighteen, acquired a kind of intellectual, psychological, and rhetorical arsenal with which to build and do battle with a new world emerging in mid-nineteenth-century America.

As a politician, educator, and reformer, Mann worked continuously to provide children with political and educational possibilities and environments denied to him when he was young. A lawyer, he served in the Massachusetts legislature for six years (1827–1833), and in the Senate for four years (1833–1837). Mann earned his greatest notoriety, however, as the first secretary of the Massachusetts Board of Education, serving for twelve years (1837–1848). In his twelve annual reports, numerous articles, lectures, essays, the *Common School Journal*, and his books—*Lectures on Education* (1845), *A Few Thoughts for a Young Man* (1850), and *Powers and Duties of Woman* (1853)—he used his finely tuned rhetorical skills to unfold his convictions about children, education, and the fate of the nation and the world. Mann concluded his productive career by serving in Congress (1848–1853) and as president of Antioch College (1853–1859).

Mann's papers were compiled by Mary P. and George C. Mann, eds., *Life and Works of Horace Mann* (1891). Also see Mary P. Mann, ed., *Life of Horace Mann* (1937). Biographies include Robert Downs, *Horace Mann: Champion of Public Schools* (1974); Barbara Finkelstein, "Perfecting Childhood: Horace Mann and the Origins of Public Education in the United States" (1990); Jonathon Messerli, *Horace Mann: A Biography* (1972); and Louise H. Tharp, *Until Victory: Horace Mann and Mary Peabody* (1953).

Barbara Finkelstein and Hariklia Efthimiou

MANUAL TRAINING. See VOCATIONAL EDUCATION.

MARLAND, SIDNEY. See CAREER EDUCATION.

MASON, LOWELL (January 8, 1792–August 11, 1872), is recognized as a central figure in the founding of public school* music education* in the United States. He served an instrumental role in establishing music in the Boston public schools in 1838 and in publishing special music for children.

Born and reared in Medfield, Massachusetts, he spent his early (1813–1827) professional life in Savannah, Georgia, where he helped to organize one of the earliest missionary societies and the first African American Sunday school* in North America. Returning to Massachusetts in 1827, he organized church music for the famous Lyman Beecher at Hanover Street Church in Boston and taught music in private schools,* most notably Mount Vernon School near Boston (1833–1834). From about 1834, Mason became heavily involved in training music teachers in summer institutes (see TEACHER INSTITUTES), which spread his ideas and influence, especially in New England and western settlements of New Englanders. He knew and corresponded with several educational notables, including Horace Mann,* William Channing Woodbridge, and the writer Jacob Abbott Woodbridge, who introduced Mason to Pestalozzianism,* which influenced his work. His Boston Academy of Music, founded in 1832 and supported largely by conservative Congregationalists, demonstrated the value of teaching music to children in large groups. Mason's *Manual of the Boston Academy of Music* (1834) served as a guide for teaching children for decades, and his *Juvenile Lyre* (1831) was one of the first successful school music collections. Mason is also remembered as the patriarch of the most influential family of music teachers and musical entrepreneurs in nineteenth-century America.

Mason's papers are housed at Yale University Music Library. The leading biography is by Carol A. Pemberton, *Lowell Mason: His Life and Work* (1985). *The Quarterly of Music Teaching and Learning* (vol. 3, no. 3, fall 1992) devoted a whole issue to Mason. Secondary sources that refer to Mason's impact are Edward Bailey Birge, *History of Public School Music in the United States* (1939); James A. Keene, *A History of Music Education in the United States* (1982); and Michael L. Mark and Charles L. Gary, *A History of American Music Education* (1992).

William R. Lee

MASSACHUSETTS COMMISSION ON INDUSTRIAL AND TECHNI-CAL EDUCATION, otherwise known as the Douglas Commission, decisively shaped the discussions of the emerging vocational education* movement, which in 1917 brought about the passage of the Smith-Hughes Act.* In May 1905, the Massachusetts legislature authorized Governor William L. Douglas to appoint a commission "to investigate the needs for education in the different grades of skill and responsibility in the various industries of the Commonwealth." The Commission on Industrial and Technical Education, with Carroll D. Wright as chair, held public hearings and made special investigations; she submitted her report to the general assembly in April 1906. The Commission criticized the traditional curriculum as too "literary" and manual training as too "lifeless." The public schools did not furnish the skills and "industrial intelligence" students needed to participate efficiently in industry and life. Susan Kingsbury, a special investigator, included an addendum that documented the large number of children who had dropped out of school, not because of economic necessity but because they found school unattractive and uninteresting; these children, either employed in low-wage jobs or idle, had no hope—without vocational education—of economic and social advancement. The Commission made two recommendations: First, the elementary schools should provide instruction in the "elements of productive industry," and the high schools* should supply "new elective courses" in agricultural, mechanical, and domestic arts; second, a permanent Commission should be appointed to create and supervise full-time and part-time "industrial schools" for youths and adults that would exist independent of, and parallel to, the traditional public education system. In June 1906, Governor Douglas approved the second recommendation, but in 1909, the work of the Commission became absorbed into the State Board of Education.

The Commission published its report as Commonwealth of Massachusetts, *Report of the Commission on Industrial and Technical Education*. The Commission's work is described and analyzed in length in Herbert M. Kliebard, *The Struggle for the American Curriculum, 1893–1958* (1995); Edward A. Krug, *The Shaping of the American High School: I, 1880–1920* (1964); and Marvin Lazerson, *Origins of the Urban School: Public Education in Massachusetts, 1870–1915* (1971).

Michael Knoll

MASSACHUSETTS EDUCATION ACT OF 1789. The Massachusetts government, one year after achieving statehood, codified into one comprehensive law the educational policies that had become common practice during the colonial period. The 1789 act compelled towns with fifty or more families to offer six months of schooling (distributed among one or more schools) over a year, and towns with 200 or more families to provide a grammar school as well. The legislation also bestowed legal recognition on the town school committee as an agency for controlling and supervising local education, specifically hiring teachers and visiting schools.

More important, the statute, for the first time, acknowledged the district form of school administration (see EDUCATIONAL ADMINISTRATION). During the eighteenth century, that colony's population had dispersed throughout the countryside, and centrally located town schools could no longer serve the needs of rural citizens. District schools* were thus established in the different sections of each township, and the 1789 act encouraged towns that had not previously created districts to do so. In granting towns this authority, this law opened the door to tax support for schools, a principle instituted eleven years later with the assignment of the tax prerogative to the districts.

A source of primary documents is Nathaniel B. Shurtleff, ed., *Records of the Governor and Company of the Massachusetts Bay in New England* (1853–1854). Leading secondary sources that treat this act are Marcus W. Jernegan, *Laboring and Dependent Classes in Colonial America, 1607–1783* (1931; 1980); and Geraldine J. Murphy, "Massachusetts Bay Colony: The Role of Government in Education" (1960).

Eric R. Ebeling

MASSACHUSETTS EDUCATION LAWS OF 1642, 1647, AND 1648. Historians have focused on seventeenth-century Massachusetts in attempts to locate the seeds of American educational development, and with good reason; these laws mark the beginning of state control of education and compulsory schooling in America. One of the most highly literate European groups ever to immigrate on a large scale settled the colony in the 1630s. Educated in some of the best English schools and colleges, many of these colonists took that heritage with them to America. In addition, their Puritan religious beliefs emphasized personal knowledge of the Scriptures as a requirement for temporal living and eternal salvation.

The first law, passed on June 14, 1642, represented the earliest attempt by civil authority to mandate the education of the young. Recognizing "the great neglect in many parents and masters in training up their children in learning, and labor, and other employments," the law empowered the selectmen of each town to assess the education of children in terms of "their ability to read and understand the principles of religion and the capital laws of the country," and it authorized these officials "to put forth apprentices the children of such as shall not be able and fit to employ and bring up." It is significant that this legislation passed soon after the catechism and laws of the colony had been prepared under the auspices of the Massachusetts General Court. Departing from English tradition, the act transferred educational supervision from the clergy of the Tudor era to selectmen.

This law stressed education, not schooling. Five years later, however, the emphasis changed. The Massachusetts School Law of 1647 followed on the heels of voluntary efforts by some of the large towns during the preceding years of settlement to found, operate, and fund schools. These schools served only a small fraction of the population of the colony, which by this time had grown to 21,000 inhabitants. To impel the rest of Massachusetts to attend to the education of its children, the General Court passed legislation on November 11, 1647, which has become know as the Old Deluder Satan Act because of its opening reference to the Devil's efforts "to keep men from the knowledge of the scriptures." This law required towns with fifty or more families to organize a petty schools, that is, to appoint a teacher of writing and reading for children. Towns with 100 or more families were required to establish a grammar school to provide more advanced instruction. Failure to comply with this mandate would result in a fine of £5. In contrast to the 1642 law and probably in consequence of its apparent neglect, this act stipulated the creation of schools under the jurisdiction of towns, establishing a precedent for governmental control in education.

Another piece of educational legislation was passed the following year. The 1648 law represented more of a revision of the initial 1642 law than a new mandate. It proved to be more specific in some ways, stipulating that apprentices as well as children were to be taught reading, the laws, the catechism, and "some honest lawful calling, labor or employment." Parents and masters either taught their charges themselves or had to engage others to fulfill this educational responsibility. The law further authorized selectmen, as supervisors of the population, to conduct examinations and either admonish and fine the guardians or place the young with other masters if their education was neglected. In other matters, the law appeared less specific, omitting language from the previous act regarding reporting and enforcement. This law was subsequently copied in the legislation of other New England colonies and reiterated in the 1660 code in Massachusetts.

It remains difficult to determine the extent to which these laws were followed. During the first decade after the 1647 law was enacted, all eight of the 100-family towns and one-third of the fifty-family towns met the respective grammar and petty school requirements; subsequently, however, new towns often ignored both mandates and instead paid the fine. As other evidence of a lack of compliance, an act was passed in 1668 to enforce the code of 1660, which contained the legislation from 1648. Whatever the initial effect of these laws in seventeenth-century New England, the long-term impact of this early legislation was significant, for the laws established an educational role for government that has grown ever since.

For primary sources, refer to *The Book of the General Lawes and Libertyes Concerning the Inhabitants of the Massachusetts, Collected Out of the Records of the General Court for the Several Years Wherein They Were Made and Established*, published in 1648. Also, see Nathaniel B. Shurtleff, ed., *Records of the Governor and Company of the Massachusetts Bay in New England* (1853–1854). Secondary sources include Marcus W. Jernegan, *Laboring and Dependent Classes in Colonial America, 1607–1783* (1931; 1980), and Geraldine J. Murphy, "Massachusetts Bay Colony: The Role of Government in Education" (1960).

Eric R. Ebeling

MATHEMATICS EDUCATION, until the end of the nineteenth century, lacked curricular coherence, relying on the teacher and the textbook. During the colonial period, mathematics learning was usually drill with no explanations of principles. Masters gave a rule and a problem, which students were expected to practice in their cipher books. A British text, Thomas Dilworth's *School Master's Assistant: Being a Compendium of Arithmetic Both Practical and Theoretical* (first American edition, 1773), became the leading authority of teaching methodology during the eighteenth century. The inception of the common schools* during the early nineteenth century and growing demand for mathematics with the industrial revolution prompted a call for more mathematics education and a more systematic approach. Arithmetic moved from a largely secondary subject to the elementary levels. Warren Colburn's work, partly based on Pestalozzi's earlier ideas (see PESTALOZZIANISM), and Daniel Adams began to place emphasis on concrete experience through many examples leading to an understanding of rules, or inductive discovery. Toward the middle of the nineteenth century, the deductive approach to mathematics began to emerge in textbooks such as Colburn's *Arithmetic on the Plan of Pestalozzi with Some Improvements* (1821) and *Introduction to Algebra on the Inductive Method of Instruction* (1825), and Adams's *Arithmetic in Which the Principles of Operating by Numbers Are Analytically Explained, and Synthetically Applied; Thus Combining the Advantages to Be Derived Both from the Inductive and the Synthetic Mode of Instruction* (1827). Within these texts, general definitions and principles were stated and developed into a deductive system or science.

The Committee of Ten,* convened by the National Education Association* in 1892, became the first national group to consider cognitive goals and a curriculum sequence for mathematics education. During the first thirty years of the twentieth century, elementary school arithmetic pedagogy stressed the science of numbers, from European philosopher Herbert Spencer's "number is relation" concept to John Dewey's* "number is measurement" idea. Algebra was introduced into seventh and eighth grades, along with further number work. At the secondary level, integration and articulation among algebra, geometry, and science were being proposed, as well as more concrete laboratory instruction. In their "1923 Report," the National Commission of Mathematical Requirements formalized this reorganization of the teaching of algebra and geometry, helping to institute a broad-based general mathematics program for grades 7 through 9. It was during this period that the varied needs and abilities of students became a central focus. Two primary questions emerged: What should be the contribution of mathematics to the general education for all students? How can mathematical instruction be redesigned to accommodate individual differences? Over the next twenty years, educational and psychological theorists, such as William Brownell, Edward L. Thorndike,* Jean Piaget, Robert Gagne, Jerome Bruner, David Ausabel, and Dewey, began to have a greater influence on mathematics teaching and sequencing as they attempted to answer these questions.

Mathematics and science became increasingly important, from a national standpoint, with the Cold War and the 1957 launching of the Soviet Union's *Sputnik* satellite. Attention was given to student intrinsic interest, the importance of structure in learning, the role of discovery learning, and the transfer of learning toward generalized problem solving. Great support was given to the development of new and experimental course content materials. The University of Illinois Committee on School Mathematics, School Study Mathematics Group, and University of Maryland Mathematics Project were but a few of the curricular projects sponsored by the National Science Foundation, which led to the "modern mathematics era" of the 1960s and 1970s. In 1980, the National Council of Teachers of Mathematics (NCTM)* published *An Agenda for Action: Recom-*

mendations for School Mathematics of the 1980s, which became a modestly successful thrust focused on problem solving, statistics, calculators, and microcomputers. A more concerted effort by NCTM to change mathematics education began in the 1980s. Centered on a constructivist* perspective, NCTM began a comprehensive attempt to change curriculum, instruction, and assessment. These three elements became the key areas developed in NCTM's *Curriculum and Evaluation Standards for School Mathematics* (1989), followed by *Professional Standards for Teaching Mathematics* (1991) and *Assessment Standards for School Mathematics* (1995). Along with the publication and distribution of these documents, NCTM has integrated other organized activities and publications intended to activate this curriculum movement on a coordinated national scale.

For an overview, see National Council of Teachers of Mathematics, *A History of Mathematics Education in the U.S. and Canada* (1970); Jack Price and J. D. Gawronski, eds., *Changing School Mathematics: A Responsive Process* (1981); and William Wooten, *SMSG: The Making of a Curriculum* (1965). Recent trends are included in Iris M. Carl, ed., *Prospects for School Mathematics* (1995), and Thomas J. Cooney, and Christian R. Hirsch, eds., *Teaching and Learning Mathematics in the 1990s* (1990 NCTM Yearbook).

Thomas Kandl

McGUFFEY, WILLIAM HOLMES (September 28, 1800–May 4, 1873), is best known for compiling a series of popular children's readers. McGuffey began compiling his textbook or reader series in 1836. Subsequent revisions continued through 1901, with the final revised edition being *The New McGuffey Readers*. McGuffey's brother, Alexander, compiled the *Sixth Eclectic Reader* in 1857. These readers proved widely successful, in both sales and influence. According to the American Book Company, McGuffey's publisher, total sales reached 122 million. During the latter half of the nineteenth century, one-half of all public school students, according to estimates, used the *Readers*.

Several factors contributed to the *Readers'* success. They were inexpensive, comprehensive, and conveniently published during a period of rapidly increasing school enrollment. At a time of limited teacher training, the *Readers* included teaching suggestions and developmentally ordered selections that were of high literary quality. Illustrations enhanced the text, and the *First Reader* included an illustrated alphabet. The *Readers* implicitly and explicitly presented widely accepted moral themes; the *Fourth Reader* contained seventeen Biblical passages.

McGuffey became president of Cincinnati College in 1836 and of Ohio University three years later. From 1845 until his death, he served as professor of moral philosophy at the University of Virginia.

With the exception of his *Readers*, McGuffey did not appear to have been a prolific writer. His most significant works are housed in the Special Collections Library at Miami University in Ohio. The leading biography is John H. Westerhoff III, *McGuffey and His Readers: Piety, Morality, and Education in Nineteenth-Century America* (1978).

Thomas Gordon

MENTAL HYGIENE MOVEMENT was the predecessor of a broader concern for mental health in America. Publications under "mental hygiene" were most common in the period from 1908 through World War II, although the term was not completely extinct even late in the century. Likely its heaviest use came during the 1920s. References to "mental hygiene" appeared even before 1850, but the most commonly cited beginning of the movement dates from Clifford Beer's book, *A Mind That Found Itself* (1908). A Yale graduate, Beers had been a patient in both public and private mental hospitals and told of his experiences in those institutions. After being released, he became determined to devote the remainder of his life to arousing interest in the prevention of mental disease. Immediately Beers founded the Connecticut State Committee for Mental Hygiene, and a year later the National Committee for Mental Hygiene was organized. The movement soon spread to other eastern and midwestern states, and by 1917 a quarterly journal, *Mental Hygiene*, was sponsored by the National Committee. No group was more receptive to the movement than educators, albeit in their hands the focus shifted away from the pathology of mental illness to a focus on normalcy. For the next quarter of a century, educators too narrowly focused on the prevention of emotional breakdowns. Their own central interest was for students and teachers to develop and enjoy good mental health so they could achieve their maximum potentialities. A group of mental hygienists, meeting at the Third White House Conference on Child Health and Protection in 1930, attempted to formulate a broad-based concept of mental hygiene, one that centered on the adjustment of individuals to themselves and the world at large. This was still the emphasis in 1955 when Harry Rivlin wrote in the Fifty-Fourth Yearbook, Part 2, of the National Society for the Study of Education* that "mental hygiene has a greater and more positive role to play in the schools than merely attempting to reduce the incidence of mental illness" (p. 7). Such objectives as creating a wholesome emotional climate in the classroom and assuring students of well-adjusted teachers took their place along with providing for the recognition and treatment of emotional difficulty and helping disturbed children. Yet after midcentury a heavy school concern with special education,* more than with mental hygiene, seemed to return the center of gravity back on children who were demonstrating symptoms outside the normal range.

Sources on the subject are numerous, with the major classical work being Clifford W. Beers, *A Mind That Found Itself: An Autobiography* (1953). The most important historical study is Theresa R. Richardson, *The Century of the Child: The Mental Hygiene Movement and Social Policy in the United States and Canada* (1989).

Irving G. Hendrick

MERCER, CHARLES FENTON (June 16, 1778–May 4, 1858), proposed legislation for state-supported schooling in Virginia. Born in Fredericksburg to a prominent family, Mercer was an early opponent of the slave trade. A Federalist who became a Whig, he supported extending the right of suffrage to all men of property and the right of the federal government to be involved in internal improvements. As a member of the Virginia House of Delegates from 1810 to 1817, he authored a report in 1816 that called for the extension of state-supported schooling to all of Virginia's white children. Primary schools were to receive highest priority, followed by academies and universities. The report also called for a supervisory "Board of Public Instruction" to be appointed by the legislature, which would possess real authority. In 1817, he introduced a bill in the legislature to establish a state system of education for all social classes of whites. The bill passed the House of Delegates, but it died in the Senate by virtue of a tie vote. Thomas Jefferson* opposed Mercer's bill for two reasons. First, he feared that its funding emphasis on primary schools would "exhaust" any revenue for a university, which was paramount in his educational plans at the time; second, he favored local support and control of schooling, rather than state control as contained in Mercer's bill. Mercer resigned from his seat in the Virginia legislature later that year to enter Congress as a member of the House of Representatives, where he served until 1839.

Primary documents include *Journal of the House of Delegates of the Commonwealth of Virginia* (December 8, 1816), pp. 65–70; Jefferson's letter to Joseph C. Cabell (October 24, 1816), in Paul B. Barringer, James Mercer Garrett, and Rosewell Page, *University of Virginia* (1904); and Charles Fenton Mercer, *A Discourse on Popular Education* (1826). Also see Mercer's brief biography in *Dictionary of American Biography*, vol. 6 (1933). Finally, refer to James Mercer Garrett, "James Mercer" (1908).

Thomas C. Hunt

MERIAM REPORT. See FEDERAL INDIAN BOARDING SCHOOLS.

MEYER V. NEBRASKA, 262 U.S. 390 (1923). The U.S. Supreme Court in this case decided whether a Nebraska State statute that forbade the teaching of a foreign language to any child who had not completed the fourth grade had unreasonably infringed on the liberty of a religious school teacher guaranteed under the due process clause of the Fourteenth Amendment. Mr. Meyer had taught a ten-year-old child to read German from a book that contained Bible stories; the state prosecuted him for violating the law. The Court first found the statute was a violation of the due process clause because it materially interfered with a foreign language teacher's calling, a student's opportunity for knowledge, and the power of parents' legitimate control of their child's education. The Court next considered the state's justification for the law, which was to promote a child's civic development by inhibiting education in a foreign language before the child had learned English and acquired American ideals. The justification was rejected by the Court, since the state had failed to show an emergency that rendered the knowledge by a child of some foreign language so clearly harmful as to justify infringement of a constitutionally protected right to liberty.

Thomas J. I. Emerson, *The System of Freedom of Expression* (1971), is a standard and reflects a liberal sense of case law; Rodney A. Smolla, *Free Speech in an Open Society* (1992), represents the genre of a growing contemporary conservative approach.

Bruce Beezer

MIDDLE SCHOOL. See JUNIOR HIGH SCHOOL.

MILITARY ACADEMIES. In 1812, just ten years after the U.S. Military Academy at West Point was established, the first military school for boys was founded in Lewisburg, in what is today West Virginia. One of over 650 military secondary schools that have operated in the United States, Greenbriar Military School closed in 1972. Presently twenty-eight military institutes for students in grades K–12 operate, which is just over 2 percent of all independent secondary schools (also, see NATIONAL ASSOCIATION OF INDEPENDENT SCHOOLS; PRIVATE SCHOOLS). At the secondary level, military schools range in size from fewer than 100 cadets to more than 650, although many of the earliest schools opened with only a handful of students, some with just two.

Histories of present-day academies reveal varied origins. Some of the earliest academies (those founded in the early 1800s) began as classical schools for both girls and boys (refer to ACADEMIES; CLASSICAL CURRICULUM). Over time, military programs were added to these schools, and eventually these military programs came to predominate. Other academies were originally founded to provide a religious education. Community townspeople and church members would frequently provide for the establishment and administration of a school with religious and military overtones. In most cases, a former military officer was appointed headmaster. Some other academies were established by retired military men or by their families. These families retained control until well into the twentieth century, when boards of trustees became the most common means of governance.

The preparation of strong, capable citizens through a combination of intellectual, moral, and physical challenges has formed the philosophical foundation of military academies from the beginning. Founders believed that the skills, qualities, and ideals of professional military personnel are worthy of emulation, regardless of students' future career paths. Although some military school graduates have served in the U.S. armed forces, the goal of military academies has not been to create junior officers or future soldiers. Rather, it has been to develop in each cadet a "certain kind of person," someone to participate with confidence, competence, and strength of character as a U.S. citizen.

Because founders of military schools believed that military training integrates moral and intellectual education, military programs are not just present, but prominent, at most military schools. Cadets wear military-style uniforms, are organized into hierarchical units, reside in barracks-style dorms, adhere to rigorous daily schedules, and participate in mandatory physical (and often religious) activities. They are held to challenging academic standards and are charged with fulfilling the leadership responsibilities associated with their ranks and positions. Cadets routinely conduct inspections, hold formations, plan and conduct military training, and handle discipline problems.

As the cadets at Greenbriar did in 1812, cadets at academies have lived and learned under the guiding ideals of military secondary schools, the principles emphasized by the U.S. armed services: development of leaders who are strong in character, loyal, competent, and intellectually, morally, and physically disciplined.

For a historical treatment, see Alvan C. Hadley, Jr., "Military Schools: The Association of Military Colleges and Schools of the United States (AMSCUS) and the Historical Struggle for the Survival of the Military Preparatory Schools in America" (1997). The educational philosophies of specific military academies can be gleaned in Kim Hays, *Practicing Virtues: Moral Traditions at Quaker and Military Boarding Schools* (1994); Willard Pearson, *Valley Forge Military Academy and Junior College: Dedicated to Excellence* (1985); and Winfield W. Scott, Jr., *New Mexico Military Institute: Duty-Honor-Achievement* (1993). For general background, refer to Christopher J. Georges and James A. Messina, *The Harvard Independent: Insider's Guide to Preparatory Schools* (1987); *Handbook of Private Schools* (1996); *Peterson's Annual Guide to Independent Secondary Schools* (1996); *Private Independent Schools* (1995); and Kiliaen V. R. Townsend, *The Boarding School Guide* (1989).

Jennifer Lynn Deets and O. L. Davis, Jr.

MILLIKEN V. BRADLEY, 418 U.S. 717 (1974), 433 U.S. 267 (1977), was perhaps the most important U.S. Supreme Court decision regarding civil rights and education since *Brown v. Board of Education.** In *Milliken I*, the Supreme Court ruled that suburban school districts could *not* be included with the Detroit Public Schools in a busing plan to achieve racial balance. The ruling was the first defeat in a school desegregation case for the National Association for the Advancement of Colored People (NAACP)* in over two decades.

This case arose out of unusual circumstances. From the mid-1950s to 1970, Detroit had the most liberal school board of any big city in the nation. During those years, the Detroit board upgraded schools in African American neighborhoods, introduced multicultural curricula (see MULTICULTURAL EDUCATION), integrated staff throughout the district, and hired more African American teachers and promoted more African American administrators than in any other large American city. Nevertheless, the educational performance of African American students remained stagnant, and the board made no attempt to integrate students who were attending racially segregated schools. Early in 1970, in response to the poor achievement of African American students and demands for greater community control* of the schools, Michigan's Governor William Milliken signed a bill approving the decentalization of the district.

The liberal majority of the Detroit board, however, feared that decentralization would further isolate students by race. The board, while planning for the decentralized districts, introduced a busing plan for high school* students that would have integrated most of the city's high schools. Amid a huge public outcry against the busing plan, the Michigan legislature took the power to create the decentralized districts out of the board's hands and nullified the busing plan. In August 1970, a special election recalled the liberal board members. Two weeks after the recall, the NAACP filed a desegregation suit against the Detroit Board of Education and the state of Michigan.

The NAACP asserted that despite the very positive actions taken by the board in the areas of school construction, curriculum, and staffing, prior to adopting its ill-fated high school busing plan the board had made virtually no effort to desegregate schools. Indeed, the NAACP argued, the board often allowed administrators to assign students to schools or shift attendance boundaries in ways that perpetuated racial isolation. Consequently, the NAACP declared that the Detroit board had adopted a series of policies that kept the city schools segregated. The board responded that it had made every conceivable effort to integrate the district and that segregation persisted largely because of housing patterns.

Federal Judge Stephen J. Roth heard the case and ruled in favor of the NAACP. As a result of the Michigan legislature's nullifying the busing plan, he found the state culpable as well and introduced a remedy that ultimately forced the case to the U.S. Supreme Court. With African American students comprising almost two-thirds of the district's enrollment, Roth realized that busing *within* the city alone would not achieve integration; he ordered a metropolitan plan in which fifty-two suburban school systems would join Detroit in massive cross-district busing. He believed he had the authority to implement a metropolitan busing plan because school districts were creations of the state and the state had played a role in maintaining segregation in Detroit. Suburban school districts immediately appealed Roth's ruling, arguing that they were not responsible for the segregation actions of the Detroit board or those of the state legislature.

The U.S. Supreme Court ruled on the case on July 25, 1974. In a 5 to 4 decision that stunned the NAACP and its allies, the Court majority agreed with the suburban districts and overturned Roth's massive busing plan. The Court argued that the suburban districts had not caused the segregation of the Detroit schools and therefore should not bear the burden of correcting the violation. Consequently, to achieve racial balance only students within Detroit would be bused. At the time, however, fewer than 23 percent of the students in the district were white; within six years, only 12 percent of the students in the Detroit public schools were white.

Rejecting the main thrust of the NAACP's argument, the Court did indicate that it believed the state was indeed culpable for some aspects of the segregation in Detroit. That indication paved the way for *Milliken II*. In this case, the state of Michigan appealed an order by federal judge Robert DeMascio to provide additional funds to the Detroit schools to help improve educational outcomes. The Court repealed its finding that the state was partially responsible for segregation in Detroit and ordered it to provide the additional funds.

The importance of *Millken I* cannot be underestimated. The ruling eliminated cross-district busing as a remedy for segregation in northern school districts.

Refer to Gary Orfield, *Must We Bus? Segregated Schools and National Policy* (1978), and Eleanor P. Wolf, *Trial and Error: The Detroit School Segregation Case* (1981), for specific background on the cases. For a broader perspective, see Jeffrey Mirel, *The Rise and Fall of an Urban School System: Detroit, 1907–81* (1993).

Jeffrey Mirel

MINERSVILLE SCHOOL DISTRICT (PENNSYLVANIA) V. GOBITIS, 310 U.S. 586 (1939). See PLEDGE OF ALLEGIANCE; *WEST VIRGINIA BOARD OF EDUCATION V. BARNETTE*.

MODERN SCHOOL. The Modern Schools of America gained inspiration from the ideas and practices of Francisco Ferrer y Guardia, a Spanish educator who embraced a philosophy of "rational education" to contest the stifling influences of church-dominated schools in his homeland. Ferrer established the Escuela Moderna in Barcelona in 1901 and other similar schools for children throughout Spain. He viewed these schools as having a dual purpose: as instruments of self-development and as levers of social transformation. Ferrer was allied with Spanish anarchist causes in further pursuit of his goals, and in 1909 he was executed by the Spanish government, becoming a martyr to radicals around the world.

The Francisco Ferrer Association in the United States was inaugurated in New York City in 1910. While first a venture involving radicals of different affiliations, the organization quickly became more closely allied with those who identified themselves as anarchists. By World War I, with financial support from several benefactors, a network of Modern Schools for children was established. *The Modern School* magazine, published between 1912 and 1922, enabled schools to keep reasonably informed of each other's activities. Successful day schools that embraced communal living were eventually established in several locales, including Stelton, New Jersey (1915–1953); Lake Mohegan, New York (1924–1941); and Lakewood, New Jersey (1933–1958). Most of the Modern Schools were short-lived, however, and despite intentions to be converted as day schools, they functioned as Sunday schools. In all, about twenty-one Modern (or Ferrer) Schools existed in the United States, as well as a dozen related schools, most of which were no longer in existence by 1930.

Modern School educators attempted to foster a heightened concern for social injustice and inequality and an antagonism for capitalist culture. At the same time, they emphasized creative self-expression and self-realization. In practice, it was not always easy to decide when attention to social causes intruded upon (or should limit) individualism and spontaneity. The Modern Schools tended to resolve this dilemma on the side of a rather extreme form of educational freedom, with a relative absence of external constraints on children as a guiding principle. The curriculum centered on practical knowledge, the arts, theater, music, stories, crafts, hygiene, and other activities and areas of inquiry that would be of direct interest to children.

The *Modern School Collection* is located at Rutgers University, New Brunswick, N.J. Also, see Joseph J. Cohen and Alexis C. Ferm, *The Modern School of Stelton* (1925), published by the Modern School Association. Finally, for a comprehensive historical overview, refer to Paul Avrich, *The Modern School Movement: Anarchism and Education in the United States* (1980).

Kenneth Teitelbaum

MONITORIAL SYSTEM. See LANCASTERIAN SYSTEM.

MONTESSORI, MARIA (August 31, 1870–May 2, 1952), gained international renown for her preschool education approach. Born in Chiaravalle, Italy, she received a medical degree from the University of Rome in 1896 and initially worked with ''feeble-minded'' children, pioneering research in neuropsychiatry. In 1907, Montessori began supervision of the day nursery for a low-income housing project that demonstrated that children have a spontaneous desire to learn. A well-trained ''directress,'' who facilitated their self-initiated ''work'' within a prepared environment, served as the heart of her method.

In 1915, Montessori's demonstration school was a popular exhibit at the Panama-Pacific International Exposition held in San Francisco (see INTERNATIONAL EXPOSITIONS), and she was a controversial speaker at the annual meeting of the National Education Association.* Her ideas were used to challenge the authoritarian stance of American schools and to support the progressive education* movement, but her ''method'' for preschool education was not popularized in the United States until the 1960s. Montessori's ideas were reintroduced by Nancy Rambusch, who had taken a Montessori training class in London. She established the Whitby School in Greenwich, Connecticut, in 1958. It received widespread recognition in the popular press and an American Montessori Society was formed in 1960. This reintroduced educational system was congruent with an emerging national appreciation for children's autonomy and self-expression, and it is estimated that there are now between 5,000 and 6,000 Montessori preschools in the United States.

A distinguishing element of the Montessori curriculum has been the use of standardized ''didactic'' materials. This equipment, designed for children's individual and self-correcting manipulation, has been commercially produced by Albert Nienhuis in Holland since the 1920s. However, self-designated ''Montessori'' preschools may use the apparatus without uniformity of philosophy or methodology. The Association Montessori Internationale, established in 1929, has no enforceable licensing system. Several associations are working toward a process of external peer review and accreditation for the United States.

Accompanied by her son, Mario, Montessori gained international renown as she taught courses and was entertained by heads of state in European, North and South American, and Asian countries. Late in her life, when she told an interviewer that "my country is a star which turns around the Sun and is called Earth," her words reflected her status as an individual who had contributed on a global scale, not just in education but in efforts toward world peace.

Refer to the archives available at the Association Montessori Internationale, Amsterdam, Holland, as well as the Nienhuis Montessori USA Research Center, Mountain View, California. Also, see Dorothy C. Fisher, *A Montessori Mother* (1912); Maria Montessori, *The Montessori Method* (1912; 1964); and Mario M. Montessori, Jr., *Education for Human Development* (1976).

Dorothy W. Hewes

MORAL EDUCATION has marked American education throughout its history. Training in the virtues of the dominant Puritan society dominated New England colonial society; the other colonies also stressed religious morals. The framers of the U.S. Constitution called for the schools to perform a moral function. According to Thomas Jefferson,* schooling prepared people for responsible citizenship in a republic. For Benjamin Rush,* religious and political training went hand in hand. Such a dialogue began a tendency to link the moral ends of education with preparation for life in a republic. Horace Mann* relied on the need to teach religious morals as a rationalization for the common schools.* Moral education as habit formation held sway into the late 1800s, manifested through school texts like those written by William Holmes McGuffey* and through religious rituals like Bible reading* and prayer.

Moral education in the early twentieth century was characterized by the exclusion of religious education, especially denominational indoctrination, from public schools. John Dewey* became one of the strongest advocates of secular moral education. Through the school, students could, in Dewey's view, participate in the social consciousness of society. The function of the school was similar to that of the home environment—it would teach all its members to act civilly toward one another and respect each other's rights. Despite Dewey's proposals for moral education, programs stressing the acquisition of moral character "traits" dominated education efforts. The National Education Association (NEA)* recommended the establishment of a new democratic "ideal" in order to foster individual and social development. The NEA's *Cardinal Principles of Secondary Education** influenced this formative period through its recommendations that instruction methods increase emphasis on moral "traits."

By 1930, research conducted by Hugh Harthshorne and Mark May found programs that stressed the acquisition of moral traits were ineffective and misconceived. They contended that the specific situation or context of a person eclipsed the influence of any instilled "traits," or "virtues," in determining actual behavior. Because character development required the influence of a social group, this research suggested that society and schooling transform themselves into agencies of social adjustment in order to bring about character development. Although these theories and research on moral development were pervasive in scope and unsurpassed in magnitude, their impact on public school moral education was mitigated by the trauma of the onset of the Great Depression.

Since mid-twentieth century, moral education has aimed to achieve one of two major goals: to transmit a preexisting set of values or to help students find their own values. Educators who believed that the family and religion represent the proper agents of moral education subscribed to the first approach. The second approach included several strategies and reflected a belief that the school should make an effort to cause students to adopt desirable values.

Two major strategies achieved notoriety in classrooms: values clarification and cognitive moral education. Both have sought to avoid values transmission through indoctrination of ideas represented as absolutely true or right.

In avoiding indoctrination, values clarification approaches focused on strategies that encourage students to arrive at their own value decisions by clarifying and defending their own values. Beginning in the 1960s, proponents of values clarification, such as Louis Raths, Merrill Harmin, and Sidney B. Simon, in *Values and Teaching* (1966), formulated teaching techniques for obtaining values designed to be positive for students and constructive for a larger social context. Widely adopted by schools, values clarification programs received significant criticism by the late 1970s. Critics charged that this approach contained a relativistic ethical base; they also noted an absence of procedures for the justification of value decisions.

Cognitive moral education has also received widespread attention. Its underlying theory and resultant education programs focus on moral development as growth in moral reasoning or judgment. Its leading proponent, Lawrence Kohlberg,* proposed six stages of moral judgment to explain how moral learning takes place in people. The cognitive moral stages and their assumptions suggested that teachers concern themselves with encouraging students to attain the highest possible stage. To accomplish this, Kohlberg recommended the resolution of particular moral dilemmas through classroom discussion. Additionally, the implementation of cognitive moral education programs aimed toward a school atmosphere in which interpersonal issues were settled on the basis of moral principles, such as justice and fairness. Thus many Kohlbergian moral educators strove to implement programs designed to function as participatory democracies, or "just communities." Major criticism of the cognitive developmental approach included charges that the theory was too wedded to cognitive processes and too narrow in defining morality in terms of reasoning about justice.

The late twentieth century has been marked by schools' continuing efforts to provide moral education by values clarification and cognitive developmental approaches. There have also been efforts to provide specific religious instruction* in schools through school-sanctioned prayer and other religious activities. Furthermore, the last two decades have seen a revival of character education. Schools, in this view, should have an ethos of pride, loyalty, and discipline, where character would develop through habituation. Planned activities would invite students to practice good habits. No large-scale assessment of the effectiveness of these efforts has been undertaken.

For a historical overview, see Lawrence A. Cremin, *Traditions of American Education* (1977). Another source is William K. Kilpatrick, *Why Johnny Can't Tell Right from Wrong* (1992).

Patrick M. Socoski

MORGAN V. KERRIGAN, 509 F.2d 580 (1st Cir. 1950). In an early case testing the limits of *de jure* segregation in an urban school sysem, the First Circuit Court of Appeals, in this appeal from a federal district court where the case was tried as *Morgan v. Hennigan* (379 F. Supp. 410 [D. Mass. 1974]), upheld the district court's order desegregating the Boston school system. The First Circuit determined that even though Boston had never had a statutory dual school system, the school board had nevertheless violated the equal protection clause through a series of affirmative actions, as well as refusals to act. The court cited to such practices as construction of school buildings within one-race housing areas, establishment of feeder systems that funneled black and white students to separate schools, open enrollment and controlled transfer policies along with irregularly drawn school boundaries, and discriminatory hiring and assignment policies. In upholding the district court's finding of segregative intent, the court of appeals concurred in the district court's order to the school district to implement plans that eliminate "every form of racial segregation in the public schools of Boston" (379 F. Supp. at 484).

Ralph D. Mawdsley

MOUNT HOLYOKE FEMALE SEMINARY. See LYON, MARY.

MULTICULTURAL EDUCATION argues that mainstream, or Anglo-American, culture and history is not the only one that should be taught in American public schools.* The fundamental basis of multicultural education rests on the acknowledgment of significant nonmainstream cultural and historical contributions to the fabric of American society.

Most scholars date the emergence of multicultural education to the 1960s civil rights movement, but the general concept first appeared among various groups during the 1920s and 1930s and assumed different forms. Between the mid-1920s and the end of the World War II, a group of white educators at Columbia's Teachers College, New York University, and the Springfield, Massachusetts, public schools formed the Service Bureau for Intercultural Education (SBIE), a think-tank attempting to ease the process of assimilation or "Americanization"* for second-generation Southern and Eastern European immigrants. Three key trends enabled the SBIE's formation: (1) the end of mass immigraton to the United States in the mid-1920s primarily as a result of World War I and anti-immigration quotas passed by the federal government between 1917 and 1924; (2) the poor achievement rates of second-generation European immigrant schoolchildren during the 1920s and 1930s; (3) the rise of Nazi Germany during the 1930s, causing a number of Jewish scholars to support the movement as a way to prevent the rise of American fascism.

Prominent progressive (see PROGRESSIVE EDUCATION) educators, including William Kilpatrick,* became involved in the process of devising curricula that would make public schools accessible to Southern and Eastern Europeans. Rachel Davis-DuBois led the movement to reform the curriculum, and, unlike Kilpatrick and most SBIE scholars, she contended that curricular changes beyond the implementation of "cultural appreciation" and "international" food days in public education systems were necessary. By creating a curriculum that was inclusive rather than exclusive of many cultures, Davis-Dubois argued, more Americans would be able to achieve both in school and in society. African Americans and other groups, however, were omitted from this flurry of SBIE activity to change public education's curricula. Davis-DuBois's voice also went unheard among white scholars, and by the end of World War II, whatever concern there had been over cultural *inclusion* had virtually ended.

A group of African American scholars also discussed issues of "cultural pluralism" within their circles during the interwar period. W.E.B. Du Bois,* Carter G. Woodson,* and Alain LeRoy Locke played major roles in the development of modern multicultural education. These African American scholars responded to trends emerging in their community during the 1920s and 1930s, including the (1) Great Migration of 1.5 million southern African Americans into northern cities; (2) related high educational expectations of these migrants, expectations that went unfulfilled because of discriminatory public school systems throughout the urban North; (3) rise of the Harlem Renaissance and other New Negro movements in African American communities throughout the United States between the mid-1920s and 1940. Du Bois, Woodson, and Locke, by the late 1920s and early 1930s, proposed a curriculum in segregated African American public schools and colleges and universities that taught both African American and mainstream American culture and history. What made the movement toward multicultural education among the African American intelligentsia different from the intercultural education effort was that African American scholars were concerned with *both* the assimilation of the Western cultural canon and the maintenance and re-creation of African American culture and history.

The civil rights movement of the 1960s helped to make multicultural education an implementable concept in American public and higher education institutions. Pressure came from the black studies movement at both African

American and white universities, as well as from similar movements among Chicanos, Asian Americans, and women during the late 1960s. With a variety of nonmainstream constituents, the concept of multicultural education expanded beyond race and ethnicity to include issues of gender, class, religion, and language. Partly in response to this public pressure, and partly in response to the advice of liberal educators, the federal government passed a series of bills designed to give federal monies to aid the implementation of multicultural education and multicultural curriculum on the public school level. Title IV Race Desegregation and Sex Desegregation of the Civil Rights Act of 1964,* the Elementary and Secondary Education Act of 1965,* the Bilingual Education Acts of 1968 and 1974,* and the Ethnic Studies and Heritage Act of 1972 gave the post-1960s multicultural education movement legal and monetary impetus. The contributions of multicultural education theorists James Banks, Christine Sleeter, and Carl Grant have helped tremendously in circulating the concept in academic and public discourse since the late 1960s.

Multicultural education has become controversial because of the rise of derivative concepts like Afrocentricity,* as well as because of the conservative educational response that confuses Afrocentricity with multicultural education. Afrocentrists believe that multicultural education represents a weak alternative for addressing issues of racism and racial pride, whereas conservative scholars and policymakers have attacked it because it has, in their view, the potential consequence of creating "divisiveness" in the curriculum and among American students. Because multicultural education does not give a privileged position to Anglo-American cultural and historical contributions to American society—that is, above other groups—conservatives believe that a unifying cultural theme would be missing. Since the 1980s, the rise of multicultural education has been met with a drive to maintain the mainstream American cultural canon, with study and debate of the concept continuing.

The early history of multicultural education is captured by Rachel Davis-DuBois, *Adventures in Intercultural Education* (1938); Ronald K. Goodenow, "The Southern Progressive Educator on Race and Pluralism: The Case of William Heard Kilpatrick" (1981); and Nicholas V. Montalto, *A History of the Intercultural Education Movement, 1924–1941* (1982). African American perspectives and contributions can be found in W.E.B. Du Bois, *The Education of Black People* (1973); Frederick D. Dunn, "The Educational Philosophies of Washington, Du Bois, and Houston: Laying the Foundations for Afrocentrism and Multiculturalism" (1993); Alain LeRoy Locke, ed., *The New Negro* (1924; 1992); and Carter G. Woodson, *The Mis-education of the Negro* (1933). For more recent trends and definitions, refer to James A. Banks, "African-American Scholarship and the Evolution of Multicultural Education" (1992); James A. Banks, "The Canon Debate, Knowledge Construction, and Multicultural Education" (1993); James A. Banks and Cherry A. McGee, *Multicultural Education* (1989); as well as Christine E. Sleeter, ed., *Empowerment through Multicultural*

Education (1991). Refer to the classic by Horace M. Kallen, *Cultural Pluralism and the American Idea* (1956). Finally, some criticisms include Molefi K. Asante, *The Afrocentric Idea* (1987), as well as liberal and conservative positions and attacks by William J. Bennett, *Our Children and Our Country: Improving America's Schools and Affirming the Common Culture* (1988); Dinesh D'Souza, *Illiberal Education: The Politics of Race and Sex on Campus* (1991); Diane Ravitch, "Diversity and Democracy: Multicultural Education in America" (1990); Arthur Schlesinger, Jr., *The Disuniting of America* (1991); and Thomas Sowell, *Inside American Education: The Decline, the Deception, the Dogmas* (1993).

Donald E. Collins

MURRAY, LINDLEY (June 7, 1745–January 16, 1826), was an important author of literacy textbooks in the United States and Britain. In an era when school texts outsold all books except the Bible, Murray was second only to Noah Webster* as a best-selling author.

Raised in a prominent New York City shipping merchant family, Murray made a fortune trading with the occupying British forces during the Revolution. At war's end, like other Loyalists he left the city and moved to an estate near York, England. He published his first textbook, English Grammar, in 1795. This proved to be successful and was followed in 1797 by two grammar exercise books and a popular abridgement of the grammar. He published the *English Reader* in 1799, a spelling book in 1804, and two French readers. All the titles were quickly issued in the United States and by 1809 were available in all leading U.S. cities and even on the Kentucky frontier. In the United States, sales of Murray's texts totaled some 11 million by midcentury. The *English Reader* alone sold about 6.5 million copies and was probably used, in their school days, by half of all Americans who reached age forty between 1845 and 1865. It dominated the U.S. reading text market until the appearance of the McGuffey (see McGUFFEY, WILLIAM H.) series in 1836. Abraham Lincoln called the *English Reader*, whose selections leaned heavily on the humanitarian ideas of the Scottish Enlightenment, "the best schoolbook ever put in the hands of an American youth." It is credited with contributing to the development of antislavery sentiment in the United States.

Murray's papers were destroyed at his death, but some letters are housed at the Haviland Records Room of the New York Yearly Meeting of the Religious Society of Friends, the New York City Archives, the New York Public Library, and several other research libraries. Murray's *Memoirs* (1826) is the most important source on his life, but the work is self-serving, avoiding any discussion, for instance, of Murray's Loyalist past. A small volume by Stephen Allott, *Lindley Murray, 1745–1826: Quaker Grammarian* (1991), includes a portion of the *Memoirs* and adds other biographical material. The only full-length book on Murray is edited by Ingrid Tieken-Boon van Ostade, *200 Years of Lindley*

Murray's Grammar (1996). Michael Belok devotes an essay to Murray in *Forming the American Mind: Early School-Books and Their Compilers, 1783–1837* (1973).

Charles Monaghan

MUSIC EDUCATION was important to the New England colonists, as evidenced by the publication of the *Bay Psalm Book* (1640). By the early 1700s, singing schools were established in the Northeast for the purpose of improving singing in churches. The southern coastal cities, particularly Charleston and New Orleans, offered a cultural life patterned after the European model with private musical instruction available for the elite. The oral tradition proved strong among African Americans, Native Americans, and settlers of the Appalachian mountain region. In 1838, Lowell Mason* pioneered the introduction of music into the public schools of Boston, advocating the teaching of music to all children through singing experiences. Proponents believed that music provided many extramusical advantages to the individual, such as better citizenship, improved home environments, and a generally more satisfying lifestyle. As music education expanded in the public schools, graded series of music textbooks were introduced after the Civil War, and instrumental music emerged at the turn of the century. This curriculum area, which previously had a vocal emphasis, now extended to instrumental music. School bands grew exponentially during the 1920s. Class instruction in instrumental music was developed, facilitating the instruction of large numbers of students by a single teacher. Early music teachers received their training through singing schools, societies, and conventions. In the late nineteenth century, normal schools* began to offer teacher-training curricula in music; this evolved with teachers' colleges and university teacher education. Most of this training concentrated on musical skills rather than pedagogy. In 1907, music educators held a national meeting in Keokuk, Iowa, and organized the Music Supervisors National Conference, changed in 1934 to the Music Educators National Conference (MENC).* Several influential professional journals have been published, such as *Music Educators Journal* and *Journal of Research in Music Education*. State associations have been formed, and biennial conferences have been established under MENC auspices. MENC has been particularly important and influential in articulating and recommending goals for American music education. By 1970, although extra-musical benefits remained important, philosophies of music education expanded to encompass the learning process and lifelong intrinsic values of music. Performance also remains important in American music education.

The University Libraries, University of Maryland, possesses special music collections for MENC, International Society for Music Education, American Bandmasters Association, and College Band Directors National Association, among others. Leading secondary sources include Edward B. Birge, *History of Public School Music in the United States* (1939); James A. Keene, *A History of Music Education in the United States* (1982); Michael L. Mark and Charles L.

Gary, *A History of American Music Education* (1992); and Lloyd F. Sunderman, *Historical Foundations of Music Education in the United States* (1971).

Hoyt F. LeCroy

MUSIC EDUCATORS NATIONAL CONFERENCE (MENC) was originally established as the Music Supervisors National Conference in 1907 by Philip Hayden, who organized a conference in Iowa to address the concerns of school music education supervisors. In subsequent years the original organization expanded its areas of interest and opened its doors to all music educators. This expansion necessitated a change in the name to Music Educators National Conference in 1934. In 1940, MENC affiliated with the National Education Association,* but it withdrew in 1972.

Through its conferences, annual meetings, and publications, MENC sponsors consideration of a broad range of issues of concern to music educators. It provides an arena for conversations between general music educators and performing artists, for debates regarding the content and focus of elementary and secondary school music curricula, and for explorations in contemporary topics in music. The organization now has a membership of well over 60,000. It sponsors the Contemporary Music Project and the Historical Research Center. It publishes the *Journal of Research in Music Education* and a monthly magazine, the *Music Educators Journal*.

The conference's history is detailed best in Michael L. Mark and Charles L. Gary, *A History of American Music Education* (1992), and Rita H. Mead, ''Music Educators National Conference'' (1980). Also, refer to sources in MUSIC EDUCATION.

Amy F. Rolleri

N

A NATION AT RISK. See ESSENTIALISM; *PAIDEIA*; SCIENCE EDUCA-
TION.

NATIONAL ART EDUCATION ASSOCIATION (NAEA) was created in
Cincinnati in 1947 through the union of four regional associations of art teachers—the Eastern Art Teachers Association, and the Southeastern, Western, and
Pacific Arts Associations—as well as the Art Education Department of the National Education Association.* The regional associations retained their identities
after the merger, meeting in their own conferences in alternating years; the
national organization convened in the off-years. In the late 1960s, the regional
conferences were discontinued; thereafter the national conference began to meet
annually.

The NAEA, which has grown from 3,500 members at its inception to approximately 15,000 members in 1995, provides a forum for debate and discussion regarding art education methods and curriculum; it also lobbies on behalf
of art education* in the schools. It publishes a journal for classroom teachers,
Art Education; a research journal, *Studies in Art Education*; and a newsletter,
NAEA News.

The Association's papers are housed at its headquarters in Reston, Virgina.
Its history is best summarized in Arthur D. Efland, *A History of Art Education*
(1990).

Amy F. Rolleri

NATIONAL ASSESSMENT OF EDUCATIONAL PROGRESS (NAEP).
Originally sponsored through the Carnegie Corporation, the Fund for the Advancement of Education, and the U.S. Office of Education,* NAEP was developed in 1969 as a survey of educational achievement in ten subject areas for a
sample of nine-, thirteen-, and seventeen-year-olds in the United States. In 1983,

the design of NAEP was changed to include a section on school demographics and information about the teachers of the students surveyed. Another addition was the reporting of student performance by scaled proficiency levels. These scales allow policymakers to evaluate student performance with reference to age and proficiency level. Since 1991, NAEP results have been published for individual states. Individual scores are protected by the Family Educational Rights and Privacy Act of 1974,* though the public may have access to all data, questions, and test instruments. The Educational Testing Service (ETS) currently administers the NAEP, which is completely funded by the federal government through the National Institute of Education (NIE).*

For additional information, see the annual publication *NAEP Trends in Academic Progress* (Washington, DC: Office of Educational Research and Improvement, U.S. Department of Education).

Deanna Michael

NATIONAL ASSOCIATION FOR THE ADVANCEMENT OF COLORED PEOPLE (NAACP). See LEGAL DEFENSE AND EDUCATION FUND.

NATIONAL ASSOCIATION FOR THE EDUCATION OF YOUNG CHILDREN (NAEYC) is the primary organization for persons working with preschool children and their families. The National Committee on Nursery Schools, which held its first public conference in Washington, D.C., in 1926, was incorporated as the multidisciplinary National Association of Nursery Education in 1931 (see NURSERY SCHOOLS). Patty Smith Hill,* Mary Dabney Davis, and Arnold Gesell were among its initiators, with Lois Meek (later Stolz) elected first president. The original purposes, continued to the present, were to improve early childhood education through setting standards, providing opportunities for experts to exchange information, and disseminating knowledge about children. Following World War II, as research studies emphasized the importance of early education and mothers of young children expanded their domestic roles, there was increased public demand for preschool education and child care centers. One result was the development of early childhood education as a professional field. Although there were active local and state associations, the national organization had only a few hundred members and no national office until 1958. In 1964, when outside funding became available and a new affiliate structure required payment of both local and national dues, the name was changed to the NAEYC, and Cornelia Goldsmith became its first full-time director. Membership was about 6,000 in 1966, 28,000 in 1976, and above 100,000 in 1997.

About seventy full-time staff members now carry out policies and programs determined by an elected governing board and appointed advisory panels. NAEYC accredits preschools that meet approved standards, credentials Child Development Associates, provides services to affiliate groups, and coordinates public awareness campaigns. NAEYC produces videotapes and publishes books, pamphlets, the bimonthly *Young Children*, and *Early Childhood Research Quarterly*. Annual NAEYC conferences attract about 25,000 people. Regional, state, and local affiliates also schedule conferences and workshops.

See NAEYC Organizational Archives at Cunningham Memorial Library, Indiana State University, as well as the NAEYC Headquarters in Washington, D.C., and the NAEYC Annual Report, *Approaching the New Millennium: Lessons from NAEYC's First 70 Years* (1996). Also refer to Mary D. Davis, "How NANE Began" (1964), and Dorothy W. Hewes, *NAEYC's First Half Century: 1926–1976* (1976; 1996).

Dorothy W. Hewes

NATIONAL ASSOCIATION OF INDEPENDENT SCHOOLS (NAIS) is the largest organization of independent schools in the United States. Founded on March 1, 1962, it was established when delegates from the Independent Schools Education Board (ISEB) and the Council of Independent Schools (NCIS) voted to consolidate their organizations to form a new entity. The ISEB's progenitor was founded in 1923 when representatives of eighteen schools in the New England and Middle Atlantic states met at the Fessenden School (Massachusetts) to consider the standardization of admissions procedures to private secondary schools. As a result, the Secondary Entrance Examination Board was created in 1924. It changed its name to the Secondary Education Board four years later, and it became the ISEB in 1958. It membership reached 500 schools by 1962. The NCIS, the NAIS's other founding organization, was established in 1943 to defend the interests of private schools* in an increasingly hostile public climate. During the 1920s, questions were raised about the legitimacy of education outside of the public system in a democratic society. Although private education had been formally supported in *Pierce v. Society of Sisters** (1925), the legitimacy of private education continued to be questioned through the 1940s. The NCIS, consisting of 234 members, served as a unified and assertive advocate of independent schools, a formal channel of information about private schools, and a centralized forum for collective action. By the early 1960s, concerns about overlapping professional services and the need for a more effective and unified proponent of independent schools prompted the creation of NAIS.

According to the NAIS, independent schools—whether single sex, coeducational, primary or secondary—are distinct from public and other private schools (see PUBLIC SCHOOLS). They are independently governed by a board of trustees and primarily supported by tuition, charitable contributions, and endowment income, rather than by public revenue or church funds. The organization defines independent schools as those that remain autonomous from any religious authority, although 27 percent of its member schools in 1994 claimed religious affiliation; 50 percent of these are Episcopal schools. Of the 110,000 U.S. schools, almost 28,000, or approximately 25 percent, are private schools. Of these, 1,500 are self-designated as independent, of which 912 belong to the NAIS; this includes 387,000 students, 40,000 teachers, and 7,500 administrators.

The decision to relocate NAIS headquarters from Boston to Washington, D.C., in 1993, underscores the rise of private education as a national rather than a regional phenomenon and reflects the organization's interest in working with public and nonpublic agencies, such as the Department of Education and the Council of American Private Education. The Association thus represents independent schools to the national and regional media, to federal agencies, and to congressional committees, monitoring legislation and regulations, and provides a wide variety of professional and technical services to member schools.

For background, see Pearl R. Kane, ed., *Independent Schools, Independent Thinkers* (1992); Otto F. Kraushaar, *American Nonpublic Schools: Patterns of Diversity* (1972); Cary Potter, "NAIS: Twenty-Five or Sixty-Two?" (1987); and Peter D. Relic, "NAIS Goes to Washington" (1993).

Alan W. Proctor

NATIONAL ASSOCIATION OF SECONDARY SCHOOL PRINCIPALS. See EDUCATIONAL ADMINISTRATION.

NATIONAL CAREER DEVELOPMENT ASSOCIATION. See NATIONAL VOCATIONAL GUIDANCE ASSOCIATION.

NATIONAL COUNCIL FOR THE SOCIAL STUDIES (NCSS) is the largest professional organization of social studies* educators in the world. Growing out of interests of former presidents of the regional History Teachers of the Middle States and Maryland (now the Middle States Council for the Social Studies) founded in 1903 and other groups and individuals, NCSS was formally organized in 1921 under the sponsorship of the National Education Association* and the American Historical Association (see RUGG, HAROLD). In 1975, NCSS became wholly independent. With more than 20,000 members, NCSS is the acknowledged leader in the development and dissemination of social studies ideas. The majority of members are secondary social studies teachers; however, the Council also counts significant numbers of supervisors, curriculum specialists, college and university professors, and elementary instructors. The Council publishes three major publications for classroom teachers: *Social Education* (the official NCSS journal); *Social Studies and the Young Learner* (devoted to elementary social studies); and *Theory and Research in Social Education* (the research journal of the NCSS's College University Faculty Assembly). In addition, NCSS publishes a newsletter and bulletins of special interest to teachers as well as sponsors policy statements on any number of concerns of social studies educators. As well as offering awards and recognition for achievement in social studies, NCSS sponsors annual conferences in November that attracts more than 5,000 social studies educators from throughout the world.

Helpful materials include O. L. Davis, Jr., *NCSS in Retrospect* (1995); NCSS, *Curriculum Standards for Social Studies* (1995); Daniel Rosell, ed., *Voices of*

Social Education (1987); and James P. Shaver, ed., *Research on Social Studies Teaching and Learning* (1991).

David Warren Saxe

NATIONAL COUNCIL OF TEACHERS OF ENGLISH (NCTE), as the world's largest subject matter organization, has had considerable impact on English instruction and continues to be a key source of information about theory, research, and practice in the teaching of English and language arts. The purpose of the organization is to improve the teaching of English and language arts at all levels of education to provide a forum for exchange of ideas in the profession.

The Council was established in December 1911 in Chicago. Of the sixty-five persons attending, thirty-five signed the roster of charter members, twenty-one of whom were teachers or administrators from secondary schools, six from normal schools* or teachers' colleges, and eight from other colleges or universities. Their main purpose was to protest domination of the English curriculum in the public secondary schools by colleges, which had effected excessive standardization of the content of precollege English programs. The meeting rapidly expanded from a single-issue event to concern for English language arts* instruction at elementary and college levels as well. This theme of inclusiveness continued to grow and has taken many forms throughout NCTE's history, for example, embracing concern for teaching all students and hearing the voices of underrepresented individuals and groups in the profession.

Currently, NCTE claims 62,000 voting members, including about 39,000 secondary, 12,000 elementary, and 11,000 college members. Three major subgroups—the Conference on College Composition and Communication, the Conference on English Education, and the Conference on English Leadership—constitute part of NCTE's governance structure. The Council also has 130 regional, state, and local affiliates in the United States and Canada and twenty-three interest groups. It publishes a member newsletter, twelve journals, and approximately twenty books each year and also sponsors an annual convention, two spring conventions, and numerous teleconferences and professional development institutes throughout the country. The Council's national headquarters is located in Urbana, Illinois.

Charles Suhor

NATIONAL COUNCIL OF TEACHERS OF MATHEMATICS (NCTM) was founded during the 1920 meeting of the National Education Association (NEA)* to provide an organized voice for teachers of mathematics. The turn of the century had seen a growing number of external reformers speaking out for changes in public school mathematics (see MATHEMATICS EDUCATION). Many of these reforms, in the eyes of teachers of mathematics themselves, seemed not to be in the interest of mathematics or students. The call for reform came to a head during the 1919 NEA meeting in Chicago, when mathematics teachers had no place on the NEA program and no national organization to voice their interests. During a subsequent meeting of the Chicago Mathematics Club, members appointed a committee to conduct a national survey, eliciting teachers' views on forming such an association.

Although NCTM's membership grew steadily, it exerted little national influence until the advent of the "new math" reforms of the 1950s and 1960s. These reforms, begun by university mathematicians as a response to a shortage of mathematically trained personnel in the United States, launched NCTM's first major involvement in national curriculum development. In response to the "back-to-the-basics" movement of the 1970s, NCTM developed its *Agenda for Action* (1980), which rejected the notion of a limited focus on paper-and-pencil computation and called for curricular balance including problem solving, understanding, and application of mathematics to realistic situations. The *Agenda* met with only mild success, and again the call for reform in mathematics education surfaced from many different arenas in both the public and private sectors. This endeavor set the stage for NCTM's more comprehensive attempt to change curriculum, instruction, and assessment. These three elements became the key areas developed in NCTM's *Curriculum and Evaluation Standards for School Mathematics* (1989), the *Professional Standards for Teaching Mathematics* (1991), and the *Assessment Standards for School Mathematics* (1995). Along with the publication and distribution of these documents, NCTM has integrated other organized activities and publications intended to activate this curriculum movement on a coordinated national scale.

Today, with over 117,000 members, NCTM is the largest mathematics education organization in the world. All NCTM members receive one or more of the following publications: *Teaching Children Mathematics, Mathematics Teaching in the Middle School, The Mathematics Teacher*, and the *Journal for Research in Mathematics Education*. Additional NCTM publications include books, videotapes, software, and research reports. In conjunction with one or more of its 270 affiliated local and special interest groups, NCTM sponsors annual conferences at the national and regional levels.

For an overview, see National Council of Teachers of Mathematics, *A History of Mathematics Education in the United States and Canada* (1970), and George Stanic and Jeremy Kilpatrick, "Mathematics Curriculum Reform in the United States: A Historical Perspective" (1992). More recent developments are covered in Iris M. Carl, ed., *Prospects for School Mathematics* (1995), and F. Joe Crosswhite, "National Standards: A New Dimension in Professional Leadership" (1990).

Thomas Kandl

NATIONAL DEFENSE EDUCATION ACT (NDEA). Enacted as emergency education legislation in response to the Soviet Union's launch of the *Sputnik* satellite in 1957, NDEA became a permanent component of the federal government's support of education. House Representative Carl Elliot (D.-Alabama) and Senator Lister Hill (D.-Alabama) pushed this bipartisan Cold War legislation through Congress, and President Dwight D. Eisenhower signed it into law on September 2, 1958. The original NDEA titles were intended to assist American educational institutions from elementary schools to graduate facilities to focus on areas believed to be critical to national defense: science, mathematics, and foreign languages. It enlarged the administrative functions of the U.S. Office of Education* in the U.S. Department of Health, Education, and Welfare* and set the precedent for passage of large educational bills. Through the process of reauthorization, NDEA's titles were expanded to include support of the social sciences and English. Its programs were eventually consolidated with the titles of the Elementary and Secondary Education Act (1965)* and higher education financial legislation. By the 1980s, the strategic and national defense orientation of the original bill was hardly recognizable.

For a thorough analysis of the passage of NDEA legislation and its evolution, refer to Barbara Barksdale Clowse, *Brain Power for the Cold War: The Sputnik Crisis and National Defense Education Act of 1958* (1981).

Deanna Michael

NATIONAL EDUCATION ASSOCIATION (NEA), founded on August 26, 1857, as the National Teachers Association,* has developed along three discrete paths in its almost 150-year history. For its first half century, the NEA functioned mainly as a platform from which the famous educational leaders of the period could propound their educational and social ideas. The roster of NEA speakers and officeholders featured the most notable names in American education, such as James M. Canfield, William T. Harris,* Charles H. Judd, and Edward A. Sheldon. These men were the acknowledged leaders of American education, holding notable positions in the schools and in colleges and universities. At the turn of the twentieth century, however, movement within the NEA began to turn the organization in the direction of becoming an advocacy group for the agenda of various subgroups of public school people (administrators, teacher trainers, and teachers) rather than a group that also spoke to the concerns of colleges and universities.

In 1917, the NEA underwent a series of changes designed to turn itself into a national advocacy group for the educational profession at the K–12 level (including teacher educators). The headquarters, which had previously resided at the home institution of the secretary, was moved to Washington, D.C., in an attempt to pursue a national educational agenda. The secretary also became, for the first time, a full-time worker for the association. The NEA office quickly developed a large staff, with operations in communications, field services, research, and other areas. J. W. Crabtree, the first full-time secretary, also presided over the modernization of the NEA's political and organizational structure. Governed from its beginnings by a town meeting format, the NEA now moved to a representative assembly structure, where delegates from local and state associations were elected to conduct the business at the national meetings. Concomitantly, the state education associations grew as part of the larger NEA and as powerful educational lobbies in their own settings. Teachers, who had exercised some independent influence within the NEA under the town meeting format, found their power diminished somewhat with the change in governance to the Representative Assembly. Thus, the NEA itself developed a hierarchical and complex governance system that mimicked the increasingly complex hierarchy that was manifesting itself in local, state, and national public school governance. The modernized NEA was also composed of a number of "departments" that existed along with the formal governance structure and represented the special interests of different members, such as classroom teachers, teacher educators, and subject matter specialists. This large, diverse, complex, and growing NEA remained intact until the late 1950s.

In 1957, as it celebrated its centennial, the NEA slowly began a transformation that would, by 1973, culminate in its becoming a strong, militant, national teachers' union. In that latter year, a new constitution was adopted whereby classroom teachers, as they organized themselves in strong local associations, became the backbone of NEA membership and the primary focus of its organizational activities. Responding to the development of collective bargaining by the locals of its rival organization, the American Federation of Teachers (AFT),* the NEA moved to develop its own approaches to bargaining, contract negotiations, and other pursuits of teachers' occupational interests, including strikes. In the latter stages of this organizational transformation of the NEA into a teachers' union, various moves toward a merger with the AFT were contemplated, and an actual merger of the two organizations occurred in New York state. From the NEA's point of view, the New York merger proved unsatisfactory, dominated by AFT leaders and policies. In the 1990s, merger has again become a prominent item on the organizational agenda, with movements to merge occurring in several cities, most notably Los Angeles and San Francisco.

The NEA's official papers are housed in the NEA Archives in Washington, D.C. Also, see Maurice R. Berube, *Teacher Politics: The Influence of Unions* (1988); Marjorie Murphy, *Blackboard Unions: The AFT and the NEA, 1900–1980* (1990); Wayne J. Urban, *Why Teachers Organized* (1982); Wayne J. Urban, "The Making of a Teachers' Union: The National Education Association, 1957–1972" (1993); and Edgar B. Wesley, *The National Education Association: The First Hundred Years* (1957).

Wayne J. Urban

NATIONAL INSTITUTE OF EDUCATION. See UNITED STATES DEPARTMENT OF EDUCATION.

NATIONAL SCHOOL BOARDS ASSOCIATION (NSBA) was formed in February 1940 by representatives of several state school boards associations attending the annual convention of the American Association of School Administrators (AASA). Originally called the National Council of State School Boards Association (NCSSBA), the NSBA was the culmination of efforts to establish a national and federal presence on behalf of local school boards that had begun some seventy-five years earlier.

In 1865, the first association of school board members, the National Association of School Superintendents (NASS), was formed in Harrisburg, Pennsylvania. Within five years NASS merged with the National Teachers Association* (1857) and the American Normal School Association* (1858) to form the National Educational Association (NEA),* later chartered by Congress in 1906 as the National Education Association of the United States. Through the merger, NASS became NEA's Department of Superintendence, which evolved into the AASA in 1937.

The NCSSBA formally changed its name to the National School Boards Association in 1948 and, a year later, established itself as a federation of state school boards associations. The Association held its first annual conference apart from AASA in 1958, confirming its independence. In the 1960s, NSBA opened an office in Washington, D.C., and began advocating on behalf of school boards at the national level. Over the last thirty years, NSBA has become the leader in school board advocacy, representing the nation's 95,000 school board members who govern 14,772 local school districts that serve more than 45 million public school* students.

Since its creation in 1940, NSBA has had one mission: to foster excellence and equity in public elementary and secondary education in the United States through local school board leadership. The Association achieves its mission by amplifying the influence of school boards in all public forums relevant to federal and national education issues, by representing the school board perspective before federal government agencies and with national organizations that affect education, and by providing vital information and services to NSBA members and school boards throughout the nation.

See Thomas A. Shannon, *The National School Boards Association: Reflections on the Development of an American Idea* (1997).

Michael Wessely

NATIONAL SCIENCE TEACHERS ASSOCIATION (NSTA). In 1944, two existing national organizations, the American Science Teachers Association, an affiliate of the American Association for the Advancement of Science since the early 1930s, and the National Education Association's* American Council of Science Teachers, which originated in 1895, merged to form the NSTA. Membership grew from 1,745 to 47,930 between 1945 and 1993. In 1950, NSTA purchased and began publishing *The Science Teacher*, a professional journal for secondary science teachers. The Association introduced *Science and Children* in 1963, a publication for elementary teachers, and *Science Scope* in 1983, for middle and junior high* science teachers. In addition to forming position statements on a variety of science education* issues, the Association has been involved in ongoing science curriculum reform. In 1989, NSTA began developing the Scope, Sequence, and Coordination program (SS&C), designed to address the depth, breadth, and sequence of school science instruction. See Robert Carleton, *The NSTA Story, 1944–1974* (1976), for a detailed account of its early history. For recent developments, refer to the NSTA's World Wide Web homepage at http://www.nsta.org.

Jeffrey R. Lehman

NATIONAL SOCIETY FOR THE PROMOTION OF INDUSTRIAL EDUCATION (NSPIE), was founded on November 16, 1906, in New York City, through the initiative of Charles R. Richards, professor of manual training at Teachers College, Columbia University, to unite all people convinced that secondary vocational education* held the key to industrial and social progress. From the beginning, NSPIE served as a forum of discussion for prominent manufacturers, labor unionists, civic leaders, and professional educators such as Jane Addams,* John Mitchell, Henry S. Pritchett, David S. Snedden,* Frank A. Vanderlip, and Mary Schenk Woolman. In 1912, Charles A. Prosser* became the first full-time executive secretary. The Society played an increasingly active role: It published important bulletins on women's education, teacher training, and continuation schools*; it sponsored comprehensive surveys to determine the needs of the shoe and textile industries and of cities like Richmond, Virginia, and Minneapolis, Minnesota; and it pushed for financial aid legislation by building coalitions, advising commissions, and drafting bills at state and national levels. Its greatest success came when it mediated the conflict between the American Federation of Labor and the National Association of Manufacturers over trade schools, independent boards, and civic education* and managed the passage of the 1917 Smith-Hughes Act.* More than half of the members of the Federal Board of Vocational Education were drawn from NSPIE's leadership, and Prosser was appointed as the Board's first executive director. After 1917, the NSPIE became the professional organization of vocational educators and changed its name to National Society for Vocational Education; in 1916, it merged with the Vocational Education Association of the Middle West to create the American Vocational Association, which is still in existence.

The Library of Congress and the American Vocational Association hold rich collections of NSPIE manuscript documents as well as complete sets of the Society's numerous bulletins. Lloyd E. Blauch, *Federal Cooperation in Agricultural Extension Work, Vocational Education, and Vocational Rehabilitation* (1935), represents the best description of the Society. Melvin L. Barlow, *History of Industrial Education in the United States* (1967), presents a sympathetic interpretation, whereas Harvey A. Kantor, *Learning to Earn: School, Work, and Vocational Reform in California, 1880–1930* (1988), maintains a critical view. Of general interest is Elizabeth Fones-Wolf, ''The Politics of Vocationalism: Coalitions and Industrial Education in the Progressive Era'' (1983). Several unpublished dissertations exist, but the most useful is Sheldon J. Lloyd, ''An

Investigation into the Development of the National Society for the Promotion of Industrial Education and Its Role in Promoting Federal Aid for Vocational Education, 1906–1917'' (1979).

Michael Knoll

NATIONAL SOCIETY FOR THE STUDY OF EDUCATION, founded in 1901 as the National Society for the Scientific Study of Education, has been devoted to the investigation and discussion of educational questions and problems. Administrators and teachers in school systems and university-level teacher education programs have constituted this organization since its inception. Although the Society has maintained its scientific emphasis, it dropped that term from its name in 1909 and became the National Society for the Study of Education (NSSE). The latter grew out of the National Herbart Society for the Scientific Study of Teaching, originally founded by Charles and Frank McMurry and Charles De Garmo* at the 1895 National Education Association's* annual meeting in Denver, Colorado. The McMurray brothers and De Garmo had formed the Herbart Club in 1892, the forerunner to the National Herbart Society. American Herbartians, with their theories on teaching and the curriculum, guided NSSE's interests into the practical development of the curriculum. As American Herbartarianism and its emphasis on the teacher and teaching faded from fashion in the early twentieth century, NSSE shifted its focus to the child and learning, reflecting the influence of child study and experimental psychology, both employed in the movement to find a scientific basis for pedagogy. The Society's emphasis on curricular reform attracted support from educators such as John Dewey,* Colonel Francis Parker,* William T. Harris,* and Nicholas Murray Butler.* Since 1902, NSSE has published many influential yearbooks, the two most influential being the twenty-sixth and thirty-ninth. The former, titled *The Foundation and Technique of Curriculum-Construction* (1927), written with a committee including Harold Rugg,* George Counts,* William H. Kilpatrick,* and Franklin Bobbitt,* attempted to construct some consensus on curriculum development between progressive educators (see PROGRESSIVE EDUCATION) and their opponents. Robert L. Thorndike, George Stoddard, and Lewis Terman,* among other contributors to the latter yearbook, *Intelligence: Its Nature and Nurture* (1940), sought to find the limits of environment and heredity on mental growth—a Sisyphean task fraught with contradictory results (see HEREDITARIANISM).

A complete set of NSSE yearbooks and the minutes of the board of directors' meetings are located at the Society's office in Chicago. Leading histories of the Society include Gerald L. Moulton, ''A Limited Historical Review of Sixty-Five Years of Educational Discussion in the Yearbooks of the National Society for the Study of Education'' (1962), and Guy M. Whipple, *Commemorating a Quarter of a Century of Service of the National Society for the Study of Education* (1927).

Laurie Moses Hines

NATIONAL TEACHERS ASSOCIATION (NTA), one of the first national educational organizations and the forerunner to the National Educational Association (NEA),* was founded on August 26, 1857, in Philadelphia by a group of state teacher association presidents. Forty-three educators from twelve states and the District of Columbia comprised the initial membership. Two women, also present, could become honorary and nonvoting members only if recognized by the NTA board of directors; women did not gain full membership status until 1866. Preeminent educators such as Horace Mann* and Henry Barnard* joined the NTA. The Association's goals included the improvement of the schools, the intellectual and social elevation of teachers, and the development of public interest in education. Supporting professionalization of the field, NTA wanted a national teachers' organization to be responsible for teacher certification. Although membership never exceeded 200 active members, the NTA held annual meetings, except in 1861 and 1862 because of the Civil War. The Association actively concerned itself with southern reconstruction following the war. Through NTA efforts, the U.S. Office of Education (see U.S. DEPARTMENT OF EDUCATION) was created in 1867. Three years later the NTA changed its name to NEA and united with the American Normal School Association, National Association of School Superintendents, and Central College Association, which became departments in the NEA along with the newly created Elementary Education Department.

The NEA Archives in Washington, D.C., possesses the NTA's papers. Secondary sources include Mildred Sandison Fenner, *The National Education Association: Its Development and Program* (1950), and the classic by Edgar B. Wesley, *The National Education Association: The First Hundred Years* (1957).

Laurie Moses Hines

NATIONAL VOCATIONAL GUIDANCE ASSOCIATION (NVGA) developed as a natural extension of the National Society for the Promotion of Industrial Education (NSPIE),* since promoting the consummative aspect of vocational education* would of necessity create a mechanism to funnel children into the vocational curriculum. In 1908, NSPIE was organized to install vocational education in elementary and secondary schools. Two days prior to NSPIE's annual meeting in Boston in 1910, a small group of NSPIE members, Bernard Rothwell, David Snedden,* and David Thompson, held the first annual conference on vocational guidance. One of the major addresses focused on students leaving elementary schools without proper training for factory work. The second annual conference on vocational guidance, held in New York City in 1912, discussed the famous Vocational Education Survey (1911–1912) and confirmed the need to organize vocational guidance for vocational training as opposed to use of vocational guidance for finding jobs. Conference attendees appointed a committee of five to further define the vocational guidance concept; the relationship between the NSPIE and the vocational guidance organization was complimentary in nature, and members usually belonged to both organizations. At the sixth annual meeting of NSPIE, held in Philadelphia in 1912, the committee developed the framework of a vocational guidance organization. During the next thirty years, the Association worked with federal and state governments as well as the expanding industries to create a more efficient transition for youth from school to work. This organization, a child of the progressive education* movement, grew to become one of the most critical components of the American public schools.* The development of sophisticated psychological tests and refinement of IQ tests brought guidance counseling to the forefront in the sorting and slotting of high school* graduates (see INTELLIGENCE TESTING; TRACKING). By the 1960s and early 1970s, the federal government promoted career education* to achieve vocational goals. In 1985, the NVGA changed its name to the National Career Development Association and became a division of the American Counseling Association. Its current membership is 5,200, mainly consisting of secondary school counselors.

See Richard W. Stephens, *Social Reform and the Origins of Vocational Guidance* (1970).

Peter Sola

NATIONAL YOUTH ADMINISTRATION (NYA) was established by executive order in 1935 as part of the Works Progress Administration and was terminated in 1943. Sharing with the Civilian Consevation Corps (CCC)* a concern with problems of unemployed youth during the Great Depression, the activities of the NYA, under the leadership of Aubrey Williams, were more variegated, egalitarian, and cost effective than those of the CCC. The primary aim of the NYA was to keep young people out of a labor market that could not absorb them, but it was also engaged in two productive arenas of educational activity. One was a work-study program that provided jobs for high school* and college students. In addition to making possible the completion of school for thousands of students who otherwise could not attend, the NYA, under the tutelage of National Advisory Committee member Mary McCleod Bethune, played an important role in enlarging the pool of African American Ph.D.'s. The second education focus of the NYA included vocational guidance and job training. The latter provided a much greater emphasis on skilled work than did the CCC. Participants were trained in such areas as auto mechanics, cabinetry, electrical work, and welding, often in connection with the paid work they performed. Despite the value of the NYA's educational activities, the agency was always viewed as a relief program. Consequently, when the demand for labor dramatically increased during World War II, Congress disbanded it. The NYA anticipated both the college work-study program and the youth employment and training programs of the Great Society (see JOB CORPS; VOCATIONAL EDUCATION).

The records of the National Youth Administration are housed at the National Archives, Washington, DC. General treatments can be found in Betty Lindley and Earnest K. Lindley, *A New Deal for Youth: The Story of the National Youth*

Administration (1938), and George P. Rawick, "The New Deal and Youth: The Civilian Conservation Corps, the National Youth Administration, and the American Youth Congress" (1957). For a biography, see John Salmond, *A Southern Rebel: The Life and Times of Aubrey Willis Williams, 1890–1965* (1983).

Robert Lowe

NEEF, JOSEPH. See PESTALOZZIANISM.

NEW ENGLAND PRIMER has been called the most important book of the eighteenth-century nursery. This diminutive book (most editions measured around 3 1/4 by 4 1/2 inches), along with the Bible and an occasional almanac, constituted the entire library of many colonial homes. It remained popular until 1830, continued to be published for nearly another fifty years, and profoundly affected the development of American schoolbooks.

"Primer" today refers to an early elementary schoolbook, but originally a "primer" was an adult prayer book, a manual of daily devotion intended for the Roman Catholic laity. When the printing press made books available to the hitherto illiterate, an alphabet was added, intertwining reading and religious instruction. Puritanism, based on the tenet that everyone should read and study the Bible, wanted to ensure that independent reading of the Bible did not lead to independent interpretation. The function of the *New England Primer*, therefore, was to narrowly catechize children. Thus, a tool for teaching intense Protestantism became the most famous primer of all.

In addition to the alphabet, vowels, consonants, syllables, spelling words, and the famous rhyming-couplet alphabet ("In Adam's Fall/We Sinned All"), the *New England Primer* emphasized verses, prayers, and sentences for children to memorize (among them "The Dutiful Child's Promises," lines from the Bible arranged as "An Alphabet of Lessons for Youth," "Duty of Children towards Their Parents," the Lord's Prayer, the Creed, the Ten Commandments, and "Now I Lay Me Down to Sleep"); the woodcut of John Rogers burning at the stake in 1554, followed by his advice to his children—albeit written the following year by another martyr, Robert Smith; and the 107 questions and answers of the Westminister Shorter Catechism, followed sometimes by John Cotton's catechism. "A Dialogue between Christ, Youth and the Devil" was sometimes added, as were, arount the mid-1700s, selected poems by Isaac Watts. Pervading the content of the *New England Primer* was the Puritan's resolve that children would be prepared to die young and live their lives so without sin that they would be ensured a place in Heaven. In spite of its historical importance, the origin of the *Primer* remains shrouded in mystery. It might have been first printed in London in 1683 by John Gaine, or it might have been compiled and printed in Boston between 1687 and 1690 by Benjamin Harris, or John Gaine and Benjamin Harris might have been the same person. (Also, refer to BASAL READERS; READING INSTRUCTION.)

The New York City Public Library possesses the earliest (1727) extant edition

of the *Primer*. Paul L. Ford, ed., *The New England Primer* (1897; 1962), wrote
the first historical and authoritative study. John A. Nietz, *Old Text Books* (1961),
stresses the educational significance of the *Primer* within the colonial context.
Charles F. Heartman's bibliographic checklist, *The New England Primer Issued
Prior to 1830* (1934), represents the basic authority on both the *Primer's* various
editions and the location of extant copies.

Frances Walsh

NEW YORK CHILDREN'S AID SOCIETY, created in 1853 by Charles Loring Brace, specialized in the placing of city children on rural farms, without
using formal indentures. Brace argued that he was taking surplus children from
city streets and placing them with farm families where their labor was in demand. Some critics charged Brace with proselytism, that is, placing children
from Catholic backgrounds into midwestern Protestant homes. Other critics accused the society of failing to supervise the children they had placed.

The Children's Aid Society also established the Newsboys Lodging House in
1854, a place where young street vendors could buy a place to sleep and that
encouraged the boys to maintain a small savings account; and the House was
the source of many of the characters depicted in the rags-to-riches novels of
Horatio Alger. In 1862, the Society added a Girls Lodging House, hoping
thereby to prevent young women from becoming prostitutes. To provide the
children with a decent living, the Society set up industrial schools designed to
teach young people a skill or trade (see VOCATIONAL EDUCATION). These
schools also served as funnels to the placing-out system. Brace claimed that his
system reduced juvenile delinquency* and vagrancy in New York City. Western
opponents claimed he only moved crime to their states. In spite of many criticisms, the New York Children's Aid Society (which still exists) soon had imi-
tators. Children's aid societies were founded in Baltimore in 1860, in Boston in
1864, and in Brooklyn in 1866.

Leading secondary sources include Joseph M. Hawes, *Children in Urban
Society: Juvenile Delinquency in Nineteenth-Century Society* (1971); Marilyn
Irvin Holt, *The Orphan Trains: Placing Out in America* (1992); Miriam Lang-
sam, *Children West: A History of the Placing Out System of the New York
Children's Aid Society, 1853–1890* (1964); Christine Stansell, *City of Women:
Sex and Class in New York, 1789–1860* (1987).

Joseph M. Hawes

NEW YORK HOUSE OF REFUGE. See GRISCOM, JOHN.

NEW YORK JUVENILE ASYLUM was founded in 1853 by the New York
Association for Improving the Condition of the Poor, a private charitable organization headed by Robert M. Hartley that believed individuals could overcome poverty primarily through education. It functioned much like other
nineteenth-century reform schools,* receiving inmates from parents and from

law enforcement authorities and serving destitute children as well as those convicted of minor crimes. As a rule, police magistrates remanded younger or minor offenders to the Juvenile Asylum and sent older or more serious offenders to the publicly financed New York House of Refuge.*

Although the rhetoric of the Juvenile Asylum stressed its commitment to education, religion, and family discipline, the institution's routine emphasized training in mechanical skills for boys and domestic skills for girls. Children were denied permission to play or talk in their work, at meals, or in their rooms. Following at least six months of training, the Juvenile Asylum indentured children with rural families. Like Charles Loring Brace's New York Children's Aid Society (CAS),* managers of the Juvenile Asylum believed that poor and delinquent city children could be reclaimed by country living. However, unlike CAS, which immediately placed juveniles with farmers, the Juvenile Asylum imposed training and discipline before children left its care. Throughout the latter half of the nineteenth century, the Juvenile Asylum placed over 100 children a year with families in Illinois.

For further reference, see New York Juvenile Asylum, *Annual Reports* (1853–1964), housed at the New York Public Library. Also, see Joseph M. Hawes, *Children in Urban Society* (1971); and Robert M. Mennel, *Thorns and Thistles* (1973); David Rothman, *The Discovery of the Asylum* (1971); and Wiley Sanders, ed., *Juvenile Offenders for a Thousand Years* (1970).

David Wolcott and Steven Schlossman

NEWLON, JESSE HOMER (July 16, 1882–September 1, 1941), served as administrator at two important progressive (see PROGRESSIVE EDUCATION) schools—the Denver public schools (1920–1927) and the Lincoln School of Teachers College, Columbia University (1927–1937). Whereas many academics explored the implications of progressive thought at a more conceptual level, Newlon actually became involved with the daily running of the school and, more than any other educator of his generation, proved that an educational administrator could adhere to progressive ideals and involve himself in the community while overseeing the operation of a large school complex (see EDUCATIONAL ADMINISTRATION).

Born in Salem, Indiana, he graduated from Indiana University in 1907 and completed graduate work at Columbia University, receiving a master's degree in 1914. In 1920, after serving as a teacher, principal, and superintendent in Indiana, Illinois, and Nebraska schools, Newlon became superintendent of the Denver schools, where he had the opportunity to further develop his ideas of progressive education and administration.

Newlon's most profound role in the history of educational administration came in Denver, where he implemented his belief that teachers, not school boards, should be involved in curriculum development. He appointed teacher committees to revise curricula and courses of study and scheduled time for them during the school week, thereby consigning such responsibility as a legitimate part of a teacher's work. Newlon's conception of school administration also attracted national attention by establishing an equal salary schedule, developing an exceptional school library system, and organizing a permanent curriculum department, all during a period that saw the construction of fifteen schools. Newlon's influence continued long after his departure in 1927; the Denver schools not only became a part of the Progressive Education Association's* Eight-Year Study* (1934–1942), but Newlon's foundational work was viewed by many as a reason for the schools to be selected as one of the six most experiential and successful schools in the project. During that same period, he also was elected president of the National Education Association* (1924–1925). From 1927 to 1941, Newlon served as professor of education at Teachers College, Columbia University and, until 1934, as director of the Lincoln Experimental School, which also participated in the Eight-Year Study. He became director of the division of instruction (1934–1938) and division of foundations of education (1938–1941), where he participated in the Teachers College discussion group *The Social Frontier*, the American Historical Association's Commission on Social Studies, and the Committee for Academic Freedom of the American Civil Liberties Union. Newlon visited the Soviet Union in 1937 and became increasingly fearful of rising fascism abroad; upon his return to the States, he further underscored progressive education's faith in the values of democracy and the school's role in the preservation of freedom. He became so distraught over loyalty oaths and authoritarian conditions he witnessed in the schools that his health seemed to adversely and permanently affected.

The Archives and Special Collections at the University of Denver's library possesses Newlon's papers. Newlon wrote *Educational Administration as Social Policy* (1934) and *Education for Democracy in Our Time* (1939). For a biography, see Gary L. Peltier, "Jesse L. Newlon as Superintendent of the Denver Public Schools, 1920–1927" (1965). Lawrence A. Cremin, *The Transformation of the School* (1961), gives Newlon extensive treatment.

Craig Kridel

NORMAL SCHOOLS. Early-nineteenth-century educators like Horace Mann* believed that in order for mass public schooling* to succeed, the United States needed to establish teacher-training institutions. Ministers and statesmen rallied legislative support for and served as prinicpals of early normal schools. Normal school founders looked to the Prussian teacher seminary and the French *ecole normale* as examples, but they designed American institutions dedicated to creating a corps of teachers who could cultivate moral, obedient, and efficient young citizens.

A variety of normal schools existed in the nineteenth century. The earliest, founded in 1823 by Reverend Samuel Hall* in Concord, Vermont, was privately owned. Private academies,* public high schools,* colleges, and universities increasingly included a normal course of study in their curricula for students interested in becoming teachers. During the middle decades of the nineteenth century, some states, including New York and Wisconsin, subsidized private academies' normal programs. By the century's final decades, public normal schools were opened in growing cities and in rural counties to prepare teachers for local schools. Private normal schools, normal departments, and municipal and county normals did not last far into the twentieth century. Most early teacher preparation programs closed, but some normal schools developed into multipurpose colleges, and normal courses often became departments of education.

The state-supported normal school, however, became the most widespread and enduring model. The first opened in Lexington, Massachusetts, in 1839, and within a decade three state normal schools operated in Massachusetts and one each in New York and Connecticut. By 1870, forty state normal schools existed in the East, Midwest, and California. Some of these focused on elementary teaching; others stressed educational administration or offered extensive liberal arts instruction. In the postwar South, normal schools trained African American instructors to teach African American children an industrial-vocational curriculum (see VOCATIONAL EDUCATION).

Although normal schools differed, they also maintained many consistent elements. They were generally coeducational, though mostly attended by women. Faculties included both male and female instructors; some possessed college degrees, and others had a normal school education and teaching experience. Normal faculty often held teacher institutes* and were actively involved with state boards of education and teachers' associations.

Founded to prepare teachers, early state normal schools usually offered a two- or three-year program. An average normal school student brushed up on her general subjects, learned about daily classroom instruction and management in a demonstration or training school, and secured a teaching position, having attended normal school for less than a year. Not all normal students intended to be teachers, however. Because opportunities for advanced study in recently settled western areas were few, many students saw the emerging normal schools as an inexpensive means for continued education.

At the end of the nineteenth century, when well over 100 state normal schools existed throughout the United States, increasing numbers of high school graduates attended. They often took the full normal school course of study and became educators or entered other professions. The normal school curriculum gradually began to resemble that of colleges rather than academies, and normal schools increasingly offered collegiate extracurricula, such as literary societies and competitive sports.

Developing an *esprit de corps* among normal students and kindling an enthusiasm for teaching were part of the normal school mission, but advocates also hoped these institutions would set professional teaching standards. The American Normal School Association (ANSA), formed in 1855, held its first annual convention in 1859. Participants focused on defining a science of education, a conversation that continues to this day. In 1870, the ANSA became the National Educational Association's* Department of Normal Schools. It remained active until the 1920s, when the ANSA merged with the newly formed American Association of Teachers Colleges and became the Department of Teachers Colleges.

By the early twentieth century, most prospective teachers were high school graduates, and some even had college degrees. Normal schools upgraded their curricula and began to offer bachelor's degrees. During the 1920s and 1930s, most normal schools changed their names to "teachers colleges," and in the 1960s they dropped "teachers" from their names, officially becoming state colleges and universities. Although the term "normal school" has disappeared, these institutions pioneered teacher education and expanded the concept of and access to higher education.

Primary sources can be found in Merle L. Borrowman, ed., *Teacher Education in America: A Documentary History* (1965). Also refer to the classic by Charles A. Harper, *A Century of Public Teacher Education: The Story of the State Teachers Colleges as They Evolved from the Normal Schools* (1939). A variety of secondary sources include John I. Goodlad, Roger Soder, and Kenneth M. Sirotnik, eds., *Places Where Teachers Are Taught* (1990); Jurgen Herbst "Nineteenth-Century Normal Schools in the United States: A Fresh Look" (1980); Jurgen Herbst, *And Sadly Teach: Teacher Education and Professionalization in American Culture* (1989); Paul H. Mattingly, *The Classless Profession: American Schoolmen in the Nineteenth Century* (1975); Christine A. Ogren, "Where Coeds Were Coeducated: Normal Schools in Wisconsin, 1870–1920" (1995); and assorted articles in Donald R. Warren, ed., *American Teachers: Histories of a Profession at Work* (1989).

Laura Docter Thornburg and Christine A. Ogren

NORTHWEST ORDINANCE OF 1787 created the fiscal mechanism and the principle of federal support to public education in the United States. The legislation represented one of the most significant actions of the American states under the Articles of Confederation. Its original intent was to prescribe the means for admitting new states out of the Northwest Territory and joining them to the original thirteen states with equal power and standing. The 1787 Ordinance anticipated three to five new states out of the land east of the Mississippi and north of the Ohio River to the Canadian border. The 1787 Ordinance encompassed the earlier stipulations of the Ordinance of 1785, which had specified that the sixteenth lot of every township be committed to support public schools.

The precise mechanism for land distribution depended on the definition of a township, which the Ordinance declared to be six miles square divided into thirty-six sections of 640 acres. In every township one of these 640-acre sections was to be dedicated via lease or sale to provide for the education of town children. Ever after, the Ordinance not only would represent this specific mechanism of distribution but would enshrine the principle of government-supported public education. In spite of flagging public support during the ensuing generation, the Ordinance would be reactivated to create tax-supported elementary schools in the antebellum period (see COMMON SCHOOLS). In addition, in 1862 it would serve as the precedent for the Morrill Land Grant Act, which opened the way to a state-supported university in every state of the nation. Within the aegis of the Ordinance of 1787, the federal government ultimately distributed some 80 million acres of land for the support of American public education; indeed, before the Morrill Act, the federal government had used the Ordinance to distribute more than 4 million acres for higher education.

Refer to Paul H. Mattingly and Edward W. Stevens, Jr., eds., *"Schools and the Means of Education Shall Forever Be Encouraged": A History of Education in the Old Northwest, 1781–1880* (1987). Also see Peter S. Onuf, *Statehood and Nation: A History of the Northwest Ordinance* (1987).

Paul H. Mattingly

NURSERY SCHOOLS are usually part-day enrichment programs for children prior to kindergarten* entrance, although some have extended hours to accommodate working parents. Teachers traditionally emphasize the acquisition of cognitive skills through self-choice activities and materials, the social knowledge gained through group interaction, and an understanding of the natural world through investigation. Nursery schools may be sponsored by universities for research and teacher training, by high schools* or community colleges as parent education classes, by religious denominations as community outreach, or as prekindergarten classes in public schools.* Others are operated by individuals or as parent-initiated nonprofit cooperatives.

Rachel and Margaret McMillan opened the first nursery school near London in 1911 with a strong focus on ''nurturing'' low-income children (not ''nursing'' them). It was based upon the Froebelian kindergarten belief that young children learn best through self-initiated activities in a supportive environment (see FROEBEL, FRIEDRICH). The concept was brought to the United States by Abigail Eliot, a Bostonian who had studied with Margaret McMillan in 1921. Eliot trained teachers at the Ruggles Street Nursery, near Boston, and helped Patty Smith Hill* arrange the first demonstration classes at Teachers College, Columbia University. In 1925, Hill was a founding member of the National Committee on Nursery Schools, now the National Association for the Education of Young Children.* The American Association of University Women also established child study* groups in 1925 and began to provide publications to help them start nursery schools. About 1,700 Works Project Administration nursery schools were federally funded during the Great Depression, which gave further recognition to this ''first step on the educational ladder.'' The great impetus for the movement came between 1950 and 1960. As more mothers took full-time employment, full-day care became necessary. In the mid-1990s, it is estimated that about 1 million prekindergarten children in the Unites States are enrolled in nursery schools.

Refer to the Wolman Archives, Pacific Oaks College, Pasadena, California, and Margaret McMillan, ''The Nursery School'' (1996). Also, see Elizabeth

O

OBJECT TEACHING dominated normal school* practice during the second half of the nineteenth century. This method of teaching was an expression of Pestalozzi's educational theory (see PESTALOZZIANISM). Pestalozzi's ideas influenced the method of object teaching adopted at the Home and Colonial School Society in London, which, in turn, was the prototype for Edward Sheldon's* work in Oswego, New York (see OSWEGO MOVEMENT). The framework of theoretical and philosophical principles of object teaching was based on Pestalozzi's sense of realism and his ideal of the symmetric cultivation of moral, physical, and mental abilities. Object teaching was considered part of the systematic attention by educators to create methods, list principles, and systematize rules in order to establish the science of teaching. Oswego's Sheldon tried to institutionalize object teaching as a complete system of teaching methodology and foundational theory. Object teaching aimed at understanding, linking knowledge of objects to the development of the child's perception and the growth of reasoning power. Lessons presented according to stages in children's mental growth were designed to cultivate writing and oral and linguistic skills. The standard practice of instruction was to use objects and have children name the qualities of the objects used. Furthermore, the Oswego teaching methodology involved a revolt against the reliance upon textbooks. After 1895, the Herbartarian movement* and its five steps of instruction became the dominant teaching paradigm.

A variety of secondary sources exist. See, for example, Merle L. Borrowman, *The Liberal and Technical in Teacher Education: A Historical Survey of American Thought* (1956); Ned Dearborn, *The Oswego Movement in American Education* (1925); Barbara Finkelstein, *Governing the Young: Teacher Behavior in Popular Primary Schools in Nineteenth-Century United States* (1989); Jurgen Herbst, *And Sadly Teach: Teacher Education and Professionalization in American Culture* (1989); and Dorothy Rogers, *Oswego: Fountainhead of Teacher Education* (1961).

Hariklia Efthimiou

OCEAN HILL–BROWNSVILLE. The battle for community control was a significant movement in urban education, raising important questions about the meaning of community participation and the nature of power in the American educational system. The demand for community control in the late 1960s came from disenfranchised African American and Puerto Rican parents, community leaders, and educational activists seeking substantial change in New York City's public school system. Community members were distrustful of the city's school system, which was severely overpopulated, antagonistic to parental concerns, slow to integrate, rife with student failure and discipline problems, and suffering from poor community relations.

Champions of community control viewed it as a means to make the school system, in general, and school personnel, in particular, accountable to the community. Activists also saw in community control a path toward empowerment for low-income communities of color by arming community members with decision-making authority and making accessible teaching and administrative job opportunities previously closed to people of color in that city's educational system.

At the institutional level, the concept of community control received support from several city agencies and sectors. The New York City Board of Education acknowledged the need for systemic reform and, lacking creative ideas of its own, did not oppose community control. The mayor's office regarded the experiment as an opportunity to give urban communities the same voice in local educational matters as their suburban counterparts. The Ford Foundation* embraced the community-based vehicle and funded the creation of experimental districts in Harlem, the Two Bridges community on the lower East Side of Manhattan, and the Ocean Hill–Brownsville section of Brooklyn.

The experiment exploded in Ocean Hill–Brownsville when the personnel committee of the predominantly African American local governing board, consisting of elected parents and community members, sought to transfer out of the district school personnel they believed to be uncooperative with the goals of community control. Nineteen school professionals, most of whom were Jewish, were given transfer orders. The predominantly Jewish United Federation of Teachers* viewed the transfers as outright dismissals, even though at the time such personnel moves were a common policy in that school system. The union viewed the transfers as a threat to teacher unionization and demanded that the governing board allow those transferred to return to their teaching duties in the district. The local board members defended their decision and refused to readmit the transferred teachers. In support of their colleagues, the teachers' union conducted a dramatic citywide strike, which effectively shut down the New York City school system for more than five weeks. However, schools in the Ocean Hill–Brownsville district remained open through the efforts of community members and concerned teachers who disagreed with the strike. Symbolically, the strike and ensuing charges of African American anti-Semitism pitted the African American and Latino community against the predominantly white teaching corps and created enduring social and political cleavages along racial, ethnic, and social-class lines. Officially, community control came to an abrupt end in April 1969 when the New York state legislature passed decentralization legislation that stripped the local governing boards of their power.

For primary sources, see Clayborne Carson, David J. Garrow, Gerald Gill, Vincent Harding, and Darlene Clark Hine, *Eyes on the Prize, Civil Rights Reader: Documents, Speeches, and First Hand Accounts from the Black Freedom Struggle, 1954–1990* (1991), and New York Civil Liberties Union, "The Burden of Blame: A Report on the Ocean Hill–Brownsville School Controversy" (1968). For secondary sources, refer to Maurice R. Berube, "Community Control Revisited" (1994); Maurice R. Berube and Marilyn Gittell, eds., *Confrontation at Ocean Hill–Brownsville: The New York School Strikes of 1968* (1969); Daniel H. Perlstein, "The 1968 New York City School Crisis: Teacher Politics, Racial Politics, and the Decline of Liberalism" (1994); Diane Ravitch, *The Great School Wars, New York City, 1805–1973: A History of the Public Schools as Battlefield of Social Change* (1974); and Carol A. Wielk, "The Ocean Hill–Brownsville School Project: A Profile" (1969).

D. Crystal Byndloss

OLD FIELD SCHOOLS. These rural schools received their name from their location, as they were established on fallow or worn-out tracts of land. They were common during the colonial and antebellum periods, especially in the South. Like the district school,* they were initiated and operated by local communities: Neighboring families or farms banded together to construct the school, to hire a teacher, to set the teacher's salary and the school's subsequent tuition, and to specify the curriculum and the length of the local sessions. Often the school year was determined by agricultural seasons, by when the children's labor was not needed for planting and harvesting. Textbooks consisted of books owned by parents and were thus quite diverse. Children were grouped according to ability rather than age; instruction was frequently tailored to the individual. Itinerant teachers, ministers, and local parents taught boys and girls between the approximate ages of four and fourteen. The subject matter and quality of this instruction varied according to the teacher's experience, education, and temperament. Education in the old field schools rarely transcended rudimentary instruction in reading, writing, and arithmetic.

See Sheldon Cohen, *A History of Colonial Education, 1607–1776* (1974); Carl F. Kaestle, *Pillars of the Republic: Common Schools and American Society, 1780–1860* (1983); and Wayne J. Urban and Jennings Wagoner, Jr., *American Education: A History* (1996).

Ben Burks

ONE-ROOM SCHOOLHOUSES dominated the American educational scene until the nation ceased to be predominantly rural. The number of one-room schools peaked at 196,037 during the 1917–1918 school year and thereafter began a continuous and sometimes rapid decline. By 1958–1959, the number had decreased to 23,695. Just twenty years later the number was down to about 1,000. The decline of the one-room schoolhouse can be attributed to the radical drop in the number of farms during the same period and to an increasingly popular cultural assumption that equated school consolidation* with school improvement.

The one-room schoolhouse had been used to symbolize both the best and the worst aspects of American public education. On the one hand, some argue that it functioned as a kind of community center positively binding neighbors together. Also, so the argument goes, it made use of inexpensive pedagogical techniques, things like peer tutoring and multiage grouping, that are currently regaining popularity. On the other hand, some argue that it was a narrow and provincial experience taught by the procession of young, undereducated, underpaid teachers who taught didactically and maintained order through the heavy use of corporal punishment.* As is quite frequently the case, the reality probably lies somewhere between these extremes.

One-room schools were generally built out of materials near at hand. Logs, boards, stone, brick, and prairie grass represent the range of construction types. Log and prairie grass and schools were usually replaced by framed lumber structures as more financial resources became available in a given vicinity. Fuel for warming the schoolhouse also depended on what was available in the immediate area. Wood, coal, twisted prairie grass, and even dried buffalo manure were used to heat the one-room schools across the country. In later years, oil-burning furnaces were sometimes installed.

One-room schoolhouses did not generally sit on prime agricultural land. They tended to be built on less productive high or low ground, or on a triangular patch formed at the intersection of a road, railroad, marsh, or some other natural or humanmade obstacle. Since one-room schools were frequently built on less-productive ground, they tended to be surrounded by pasture, and thus it was necessary to fence the schoolyard. During the first few decades of the twentieth century, playground equipment, like swing sets and teeter-totters, began to appear within these yards (see PLAY MOVEMENT). Also, depending on how wealthy the district was or on how much the community members were willing to tax themselves, two outhouses were built behind the school. Nevertheless, many districts neglected to construct these facilities, expecting the students and teacher to use the trees or surrounding high grasses instead. By the 1910s, companies began to advertise that they could convert cloakrooms or schoolhouse antechambers into "water closets." These remained scarce until the 1940s and 1950s, however. (Also, refer to DISTRICT SCHOOLS; SCHOOLHOUSES AND SCHOOL ARCHITECTURE.)

Refer to Wayne E. Fuller, *The Old Country School: The Story of Rural Education in the Middle West* (1982); Paul Theobald, "Country School Curriculum and Governance: The One-Room School Experience in the Nineteenth-Century Midwest" (1993); and Paul Theobald, *Call School: Rural Education in the Midwest to 1918* (1995).

Paul Theobald

OPEN CLASSROOM. See SILBERMAN, CHARLES E.

OSWEGO MOVEMENT represented the formal organization of general rules of teaching and the development of a systematic training curriculum in normal schools* during the nineteenth century. In 1859, Edward Sheldon* organized his first classes for teachers in Oswego, New York. This became the Oswego Primary Teachers Training School in 1861, with Margaret Jones in charge, a Pestalozzian (see PESTALOZZIANISM) expert from the London Home and Colonial School Society—a training school for teachers that fostered a formalized adaptation of Pestalozzian object teaching.* Sheldon himself became a student at the Training School, as he believed in "a great and important revolution" in teaching through the new method he labeled "object teaching." In 1862, Sheldon assumed full control of the school; and in 1865, after three years of debate, the school became the Oswego State Normal and Training School, under the auspices of the state school superintendent.

Within a decade, Oswego became well known, attracting students from many parts of the country. It was during the first twenty-five years (1861–1886) of its existence that the institution enjoyed its greatest prominence. Characterized as the "Oswego movement," or "Oswego Plan," Sheldon cultivated Pestalozzian principles, the object teaching doctrine, an emphasis on sense perception, and the administrative organization of the school. By 1890, however, the Herbartarian movement* had replaced object teaching. Oswego, nonetheless, remained in the forefront, testing Herbart's theory, although the Illinois State Normal University housed and spread that movement. During the twentieth century, Oswego Normal, like most normal schools, became a teachers' college. Indeed, in 1948, the State University of New York (SUNY) was created, with Oswego one of the units designed to prepare school teachers. It became a College of Education in 1959, part of the SUNY system.

For sources, refer to OBJECT TEACHING.

Hariklia Efthimiou

OWEN, ROBERT DALE (November 9, 1801–June 24, 1877), an Owenite communitarian, a social reformer, and a politician during various phases of his life, favored tax-supported free schools and was involved in numerous educational experiments. He supported innovative pedagogy and, rejecting the notion that educating the poor invited revolution, favored education for the poor and females.

Owen's early educational experiences in Europe shaped his ideas about pedagogy, the curriculum, and the social purposes of education. Born in Scotland, he attended Philip Emanuel von Fellenberg's school at Hofwyl, Switzerland, at age sixteen. This provided Owen with his first experience with Pestalozzian pedagogy (see PESTALOZZIANISM), of which he became a lifelong supporter. By 1822, he worked with his father, Robert Owen, at the elder Owen's New Lanark schools for children of mill workers, and wrote *An Outline of the System of Education of New Lanark* (1823), describing the curriculum and pedagogical principles of the school. The Owens abhorred coercion in the formation of character, eliminated all punishments and rewards in the school, and provided a cheerful and stimulating environment for learning. Teachers proceeded from concrete facts to more abstract ideas; depended upon lectures; utilized charts, maps, and objects; and emphasized practical subjects—all Pestalozzian pedagogical principles. The younger Owen began to diverge from his father's educational notions to support strongly the exclusion of child labor from the mills and to develop his ideas about state-supported boarding schools* for all children.

Owen left Scotland in 1826 to join his father at the New Harmony, Indiana, communitarian experiment. He became involved with the Society for Mutual Instruction, an education society whose members included William Maclure, Joseph Neef, and Marie Fretageot, all Pestalozzian reformers. At New Harmony, Owen took charge of the boys over age twelve in the adult school. Relying on Pestalozzian priniciples, he taught with kindness, organized the curriculum around the students' interests, and developed their minds and bodies.

After New Harmony failed, Owen joined Frances Wright in New York City to open the Hall of Science, a lyceum* for freethinkers that also offered workingmen a chance to gain practical knowledge. Owen's venture with the Hall of Science (1829–1833) most clearly displayed his social concerns for avoiding class disparity by providing improved educational facilities as a prerequisite to all reforms. He encouraged New York's Working Men's Party to favor tax-supported free schools and fully developed his state guardianship plan, which eventually caused a schism within the ranks of the labor party.

In 1830, Owen published his proposed system of education, called the National Republican or State Guardianship Education. In a measure to create a truly equal society, the state would become the guardian of all children—both male and female beween the ages of two and sixteen—and provide them with equal food, clothing, instruction, and lodgings at public expense. Equality in education, especially in the curriculum, was key; every child would receive instruction in reading, writing, arithmetic, history, modern languages, chemistry, drawing, and music. Each child would also learn a useful trade and be trained in agriculture. Owen believed such a literary and manual education would inculcate an appreciation of the dignity of labor and therefore eliminate class stratification in American society. The American public, however, rejected this radical scheme, and Owen abandoned his guardianship concept.

Owen returned to New Harmony in 1833, formed a village lyceum, served as its first president, and donated a building for use by its members. The lyceum, the New Harmony Institute, valued cooperative study but suffered a decline in membership in 1836. The Institute was eventually revived under William Maclure as the Workingman's Institute.

In 1836, Owen won election to Indiana's General Assembly. Serving on the Committee of Education, he diverted extra monies into the State Common School Fund. He returned to the state legislature, after a brief hiatus in Congress, and in 1852 supported and defended Indiana's new common school law, which taxed citizens for common school funds. Owen's attitudes toward the actual practices in the Hoosier state are ambivalent, however. Although he supported the common school law, he declined to run as the Democratic candidate for the position of state superintendent of public instruction in 1851, despite widespread support for him. He eventually left Indiana in 1853 for a political appointment in Europe.

Owen's papers appear to be scattered. Manuscript materials for New Harmony are at the New Harmony Workingmen's Institute, New Harmony, Indiana. For biographical background on Owen and his influence, see Arthur Bestor, *Backwoods Utopias: The Sectarian Origins and the Owenite Phase of Communitarian Socialism in America, 1663–1829* (1970); John F. C. Harrison, ed., *Utopianism and Education: Robert Owen and the Owenites* (1968); Richard Leopold, *Robert Dale Owen: A Biography* (1969); Harlow Lindley, ed., "Robert Dale Owen and Indiana's Common School Fund" (1929); and Elinor Pancoast and Anne E. Lincoln, *The Incorrigible Idealist: Robert Dale Owen in America* (1940).

Laurie Moses Hines

P

PAIDEIA, from the Greek, is commonly taken to mean "education." Werner Jaeger, who has written the definitive account of *Paideia* (3 vols., 1939–1944), includes civilization, tradition, culture, and literature in the concept. *Paideia* is the interaction between historical events and the development of intellect and is known most directly through the study of literature.

Mortimer J. Adler has used the idea in *The Paideia Proposal: An Educational Manifesto* (1982), where he defined *paideia* as the upbringing of a child, thus relating to pedagogy and pediatrics, and asserted its equvalency to the Roman idea of *humanitas*, a general learning that all humans should possess. Adler worked with Robert M. Hutchins, president of the University of Chicago (1929–1945), who believed that "all education must be the same." Hutchins elminated diverse undergraduate programs and activities that detracted from intellectual development and focused the university curriculum on the study of classic Western literature. Adler, in turn, developed the study of the "great books," which was most successful as a publishing venture by the *Encyclopedia Britannica*, in adult education study groups, and in the formation of St. John's College in Maryland. Adler's *Paideia Proposal* capitalized on the widespread criticism of elementary and secondary education, symbolized by the National Commission on Excellence in Education report, *A Nation at Risk** (1983).

Adler believed that universal suffrage and universal schooling have been the two great accomplishments of American culture. The next effort must be to provide the same quality of education for all students. To do so, all students must follow the same course of study. The three objectives of education should be to prepare students for lifetime learning, for participation in democratic society, and to earn a living. Elementary schooling must be concerned with providing organized knowledge through didactic instruction in language, literature, the arts, sciences, and social studies. A second kind of learning must develop "intellectual skills" (reading, writing, computation, speaking, problem solving, and critical judgment) through coaching and practice. The highest kind of learning, in advanced high school and colleges and universities, is "enlarged understanding of ideas and values" and is accomplished through Socratic dialogue and the discussion of books.

Adler's *Paideia Proposal* and the "great books" curriculum represented a form of educational *perennialism*. Derived from the philosophies of Aristotle and Thomas Aquinas, it held that present problems in sociey and education result from a drift away from "everlasting" or perennial truths, embodied in literature, that give meaning to all experience. The central problems of life, really moral problems such as good and evil and war and peace, are always the same, whether in modern America or ancient times. Environmental influences are largely irrelevant. Consequently, the educational task is to seek this truth and make it the foundation of conduct.

For further details on the *Paideia* concept, refer to Adler's *Paideia Proposal* (1982), *Paideia Problems and Possibilities* (1983), and *The Paideia Program: An Educational Syllabus* (1984). Also see Robert M. Hutchins, *The Higher Learning In America* (1936). Finally, for perennialism, see Theodore Brameld's treatment in *Philosophies of Education in Cultural Perspective* (1955).

Robert R. Sherman

PARENT-TEACHER ASSOCIATIONS (PTA). Introduced in the United States in the 1880s, home-and-school, or parent-teacher, associations were expected to improve education by building bridges of understanding and respect between the home and school. However, PTAs have always been political organizations. They offer educators the opportunity to influence the home environment and co-opt parents before they turn into critics. Parents join PTAs not only to meet one another but to exercise some control over the schooling of their children.

Women formed mothers' clubs, at first, to engage in child study.* As more and more children began to spend many years in school, such clubs gradually turned into PTAs, especially at the kindergarten and elementary levels. Representatives of the home and school came together in both rural and urban America at the end of the nineteenth century, but parents in cities led the way. In Boston and Philadelphia, so many schools had PTAs by 1907 that leagues appeared to enhance parental communication, collaboration, and, ultimately, clout.

At the same time, parents and teachers joined forces on a national scale. The National Congress of Mothers, formed in 1897, became the National Congress of Mothers and Parent-Teacher Associations in 1908 and, simply, the National Congress of Parents and Teachers (NCPT) in 1924. Separate if not equal, the National Congress of Colored Parent-Teacher Associations, representing African Americans in states like Georgia, Florida, Alabama, and Delaware, began in 1926. The NCPT, led by club women and reformers, built a vast network of state, regional, and local PTAs. By 1944, its membership exceeded 2.5 million in more than 28,000 dues-paying affiliates. Ten years later total membership had more than tripled, with California, Ohio, and Illinois themselves accounting for more than 2.4 million members, but thereafter growth slowed. The NCPT maintained Protestant values and stood for moral reform. In the 1920s, it backed the peace movement, social hygiene, and the maintenance of Prohibition; in the 1940s, it stressed citizenship education and world understanding. The NCPT, also committed to child welfare reform, supported many measures for wholesome recreation, parent education, juvenile justice, and the regulation of child labor. Begun in 1925, its Summer Roundup of preschoolers for health examinations became in time a sustained but limited program for the medical and dental supervision of children of all ages.

For most Americans, the PTA was not a national or even a reform organization. It called to mind those women who met once a month to help the local school. They came together to socialize, perform community service, and learn from one another. It was a forum for exchange between the home and school. Educators hoped that it would be a powerful advocate for public education. Short of that, it could be the school's most effective outlet for good public relations. Men attended PTA meetings too; in some boys' schools, fathers organized their own associations. In most schools, however, the PTA was and remains a women's organization.

The conventional wisdom among educators dictates that volunteers should outrank the professionals in the PTA. The president should always be a mother. Parents must be made to feel that they are in control. Such views are not new; they originated with the first formal efforts to coordinate home and school. But even as educators today lament the indifference of parents and condemn the family for its failure to prepare children for school, it remains open to debate just how welcome parents really are at school.

No modern history of parent-teacher associations in the United States exists. *The Parent-Teacher Organization: Its Origins and Development* (1944), by the National Congress of Parents and Teachers, is perhaps the most comprehensive. *Child Welfare Magazine*, first published in 1906, remains a useful source on PTA policy and practice. Originally called the *National Congress of Mothers Magazine*, it became the *National Parent-Teacher: The P.T.A. Magazine* in 1934 and *The P.T.A. Magazine* in 1960 before ceasing publication altogether in 1974. Also valuable are Julian Butterworth, *The Parent-Teacher Association and Its Work* (1929), and Martha Sprague Mason, ed., *Parents and Teachers: A Survey of Organized Cooperation of Home, School, and Community* (1928).

William W. Cutler III

PARKER, FRANCIS WAYLAND (October 9, 1837–March 2, 1902), the "Father of American Progressive Education,"* criticized traditional teaching methods and advocated child-centered classrooms. His ideas influenced philosophers such as John Dewey* and for over a century the theory and practice of education. Born in the village of Piscatauquog, town of Bedford, New Hampshire, he began his teaching career in Corser Hill, New Hampshire, at age sixteen, and in 1859 accepted a principalship in Carrolton, Illinois. He attained the rank of lieutenant colonel in the Union Army during the Civil War. Following the war, he was hired to restructure the schools in Dayton, Ohio. Parker went to Germany in 1872 for three years to study at the University of Berlin and familiarize himself with European pedagogics. His own educational perspectives, that teaching must be relevant to personal experience, were reinforced by the work of Friedrich Froebel* and Johann Friedrich Herbart (see HERBARTARIAN MOVEMENT). Parker held that quality education, based on the needs of the child, was superior to rigid rote methods and essential for the preservation of a democratic society. The national reputation he gained as school superintendent (1875–1880) in Quincy, Massachusetts, led him to Boston and then to the Cook County School in 1883. He promoted experiential learning opportunities, such as field trips, which motivated students to explore underlying rules and generalizations. He grouped students according to ability and introduced science and the arts into the curriculum. He developed methods of teacher training that emphasized carefully planned yet flexible lessons, stressing that teachers must understand not only the subject matter but also the minds of their pupils. Parker believed that skills should be taught in conjunction with content and criticized the isolation of subject matter, citing the uselessness of teaching "geography without history." Colonel Parker was both idealistic and pragmatic; he taught "pupils rather than subjects" and respected individual learning styles. His controversial ideas often embroiled him in debates with school boards and traditional educators. To gain support for his methods, he formed one of the first parent-teacher associations* in the Midwest after arriving in Chicago. Shortly before his death, he established the Chicago Institute, a private school that became the University of Chicago's School of Education. His lifelong fight for "new education," which personalized the curriculum for each child instead of forcing children to conform to a preordained academic structure, brought him international acclaim.

Parker's papers are available at the Chicago Historical Society. Some of his letters are stored at the University Chicago Library, Special Collections. For Parker's philosophy of education, see his *Talks on Pedagogics* (1894). Jack K. Campbell, *Colonel Francis W. Parker: The Children's Crusader* (1967), is a reliable biography. David B. Tyack, *The One Best System: A History of American Urban Education* (1974), treats Parker within the context of the progressive education movement.

Yvette C. Rosser

PAROCHIAL SCHOOLS are day schools attached to local parishes or congregations of a particular group or denomination. The term is most frequently applied to Roman Catholic institutions, which constitute the largest element of this sector, but it also encompasses other Christian sects.

Catholic parochial education began during the colonial era with sporadic foundations. Only in Pennsylvania did such schools take genuine root, with the formation of institutions by German Jesuits in 1743 and 1752. During the early national period, Catholic schooling remained a small-scale enterprise, despite the establishment of several American communities of religious sisters and the importation of others from Europe. As a result of the poverty of a sparse and scattered Catholic population, as well as the lack of teachers, only about 200 schools had been established by 1840. Significant parochial school development began with the rapid growth of the Catholic population after 1830, with an increase from 500,000 in 1829 to 8 million by 1884. Church hierarchs initially sought to co-opt state common school funds for Catholic schools, such as Massachusetts's Lowell Plan (1831–1852) and New York's Poughkeepsie Plan (1873–1898).

After state revenues began to be channeled exclusively to developing common schools* that were pan-Protestant in character, Catholic bishops became more strenuous in their insistence on a separate network of schools to support Catholic and ethnic culture. Beginnning with mild exhortations by the First Plenary Council* of Baltimore in 1829, they placed increasing pressure on parents and pastors to establish separate schools. The late nineteenth and early twentieth centuries witnessed even greater attention to parochial school development as the Catholic population grew from 9 million in the 1890s to 20 million by the 1920s. Child labor legislation, releasing children from the rigors of work, promoted Catholic school development, as did the increasingly shrill calls by Church leaders to promote Catholic schools and eschew "godless" public education. This reached a high point at the 1884 Third Plenary Council* of Baltimore, which mandated the establishment of a school in each parish within two years.

Nevertheless, variations existed within the Catholic community. In Boston, where co-optation of the public schools had been successful, the percentage of Catholic children enrolled in parochial schools was less than half that of Chicago. Archbishop John Ireland, of St. Paul, Minnesota, favored attendance at public schools, and in 1891 he approved a compromise whereby the local board absorbed two parochial schools, which retained their Catholic teachers. Objections by other bishops caused the Vatican to allow Ireland's experiment, but forbid its replication, blunting whatever Catholic enthusiasm for compromise with public school authorities still existed.

By the 1920s, parochial schooling was well established with over 1.7 million pupils as a result of the increasing prosperity and size of the Catholic community. Administration became more structured with the establishment of the first diocesan school board in New York in 1886 and the Catholic Educational Association in 1908. High school* education, begun in Philadelphia in 1890, also grew. The number of Catholic schools doubled and pupils tripled between World War I and the 1960s. During the peak "baby boom" years, between 1950 and 1960, elementary parochial enrollment outstripped public education, 171 to 142 percent respectively. A marked decline followed, however. Lower birth rates and Catholic assimilation sharply reduced parochial school enrollment, dropping as much as 25,000 in New York state in 1969 alone. A decreasing supply of religious sisters threatened the financial well-being of these schools as well. The nuns represented 48.9 percent of the teaching force in 1968, but only 21.9 percent by 1981. Lay teachers replaced them, which greatly increased the cost of parochial schools. Parochial schools have slightly expanded their enrollments in recent years. A growing Hispanic population has increased demand, but given the absence of priests and religious sisters from these ethnic communities, whether this will compare with earlier immigrant growth remains unclear. Since the 1960s, African American parents have used urban parochial schools as alternative settings, yet severe financial constraints make significant growth in this direction unlikely.

Although Catholics have dominated parochial schooling, various Protestant denominations have also become involved. A disproportionate number have come from the conservative sector. The Lutheran Church, Missouri Synod, has supported the largest number of schools. After its foundation in 1847, the synod usually established a school in every congregation. These schools were modeled on the German *Volkschule*, transmitting conservative Lutheran doctrine as well as German language and culture. Passage of the restrictive Bennett and Edwards laws in Wisconsin and Illinois in the 1890s forced the Lutheran Church to reassess its educational mission and resulted in the use of more English as the instructional language. These schools declined as a result of improvements in public education as well as anti-German sentiment during World War I. By 1936, however, with the waning of the Great Depression, they experienced a resurgence, and by 1961 the Lutheran Church sponsored 1,323 schools enrolling over 150,000 students. These schools continue to be popular, attracting an increasing proportion of non-Lutheran students.

Likewise, the Seventh Day Adventists maintain a significant commitment to parochial schooling. Beginning in the 1840s, this denomination established schools oriented toward the classics and, more radically, toward manual labor. The Adventists moved into the educational mainstream during World War II, and their educational system experienced significant growth. By the 1980s, that church operated over 1,000 elementary and 80 secondary schools with over 68,000 students.

The Christian day school represents the newest arrival on the parochial school scene. Since the 1960s, evangelicals and others outside the religious mainstream have established schools, according to some observers, at the rate of two per day. Between 9,000 and 11,000 such schools have been founded, with an estimated enrollment of over 1 million. Individual local churches sponsor about 70 percent of these schools. Like their earlier Catholic counterparts, their founders frequently first sought to co-opt local public institutions and ended by establishing their own, with curricula and discipline tailored to their particular beliefs. Parochial schooling thus continues as it began, an alternative educational arrangement serving the needs of various communities to preserve their own unique religious cultures.

Reliable secondary sources include Harold A. Buetow, *Of Singular Benefit*

(1970); Robert D. Cross, "Origins of Catholic Parochial Schools in America" (1965); and Marvin Lazerson, "Understanding American Catholic Educational History" (1977). Also see an edited collection by James C. Carper and Thomas C. Hunt, *Religious Schooling in America* (1984).

F. Michael Perko

PARSONS, FRANK (November 14, 1854–September 2, 1908), is called the "Father of Vocational Guidance." Born in Mount Holly, New Jersey, he graduated from Cornell University in 1873 with a degree in math and engineering. He studied law, was admitted to the Massachusetts bar, and became chief clerk in a Boston law firm. He also lectured at Boston University. In 1895, as the candidate of the Prohibition, Populist, and Socialist parties, he ran for mayor of Boston. Two years later he took a leave of absence from Boston University and took a position as a lecturer in economics and sociology and as a professor of history and political science at the Kansas Agricultural College. Parsons organized the Ruskin College of Social Science in Trenton, Missouri, a school dedicated to the study of economics and social studies in 1899.

This sojourn to the Midwest proved to be unsuccessful, and Parsons returned to Boston to resume his position at Boston University. In 1905, he resigned from the university and became associated with Myer Bloomfield. Like most reformers of the Progressive Era, Parsons began his work in Boston's settlement houses (see ADDAMS, JANE; PROGRESSIVE EDUCATION). He and Ralph Albertson also co-founded Bread Winners College.

In 1907, Parsons sought and received financial support from Mrs. Quincy A. Shaw to establish the Boston Vocational Bureau. As its first director, he pioneered the field of vocational guidance (see GUIDANCE COUNSELING). His method included short, intensive counseling sessions coupled with tests to help define a person's aptitude. Based on the student's performance, Parsons would then fit him or her to a specific occupation. Social class and race represented some of the criteria used to help select the correct job for a student. Part of Parsons's approach necessitated the development of a complete and detailed personal history. This student record would follow the young person through the school experience and help place him or her into a proper job. Parsons's *Choosing a Vocation* (1909), published posthumously, summarizes his vocational methods.

For a biographical source, see Howard Vaughn Davis, *Frank Parsons: Prophet, Innovator, Counselor* (1969). Another useful source is Arnold R. Spokane and Ian T. Glickman, "Light, Information, Inspiration, and Cooperation: Origins of the Clinical Science of Career Intervention" (1994).

Peter Sola

PATRI, ANGELO (November 7, 1876–September 13, 1965), was a leading public school* progressive (see PROGRESSIVE EDUCATION), school administrator, and parent educator during the first half of the twentieth century. He was born in Italy and came to New York City with his family in 1881. He grew up in an Italian American neighborhood and earned a B.A. from City College of New York in 1897. He taught school and then studied at Teachers College, Columbia University, where he received his M.A. in 1904. At Teachers College, he became a Deweyan (see DEWEY, JOHN) progressive, learning theories and practices that he was to use as principal of PS No. 4 from 1908 to 1913. He was New York's first Italian American school administrator. Patri wrote about his work at that school in a widely read book, *Schoolmaster of the Great City* (1917).

In 1913, Patri became principal of PS No. 45, where he successfully used progressive approaches with a diverse student population until his retirement in 1944. In 1915, PS No. 45 was the first New York school to experiment with the Gary Plan.* Patri worked closely with parents and neighborhood residents, turning PS No. 45 into one of New York's first community-oriented (see COMMUNITY CONTROL) schools. He also became an early and eloquent supporter of multicultural education,* which respected the heritage of students and families while helping them to integrate into American society.

Patri wrote several books for children. His interest in parent education led to his writing columns for newspapers and magazines that reached millions of readers. He integrated these articles into twelve popular books for parents published between 1922 and 1948.

Patri's papers are in the Manuscript Division, Library of Congress, and his master's thesis is in the Special Collections, Milbank Library, Teachers College, Columbia University. The best source of his early life is in Angelo Patri, *Schoolmaster of the Great City* (1917).

James M. Wallace

PAUPER SCHOOLS. Charitable education in the United States was based on English models and encompassed a variety of institutions and practices: missionary instruction of slaves, Native Americans, and German immigrants; apprenticeships* of poor children and orphans; and Sunday schools,* pauper schools, and infant schools.* Unlike in England, charitable education gained wide acceptance in the United States during the colonial and early national periods. Through such outreach, numerous American boys and girls of different races were taught Christian morals and basic reading and writing. Regardless of its form, the goals of charitable education were fixed: the salvation of souls, social control, acculturation, and moderate literacy. Social mobility of those allegedly in need was of incidental concern.

During the last quarter of the eighteenth century and the first quarter of the nineteenth century, pauper, or charity, schools flourished primarily, though not exclusively, in northern and southern urban centers. Originally, these were denominational schools opened for congregational members who could not afford to pay for their child's education. As apprenticeships declined and the ills of industrialization spread, pauper schools increasingly welcomed children outside of the sponsoring congregation. Quakers, in particular, were notable for reaching beyond their own ranks. The denominational pauper schools eventually evolved into pan-Protestant institutions open to white children of all classes and capable of uniform and efficient management. The network of pauper schools garnered local and state financial support and formed the basis for the common schools.*

See Lawrence A. Cremin, *American Education: The Colonial Experience, 1607–1783* (1970); Lawrence A. Cremin, *American Education: The National Experience, 1783–1876* (1980); Carl F. Kaestle, "Common Schools before 'The Common School Revival'" (1972); Carl F. Kaestle, *Pillars of the Republic: Common Schools and American Society, 1780–1860* (1983); William Kemp, *Support of Schools in Colonial New York by the Society for the Propagation of the Gospel* (1913; 1969); A. J. Morrison, *The Beginnings of Public Education in Virginia, 1776–1860* (1917); and Samuel Weber, *The Charity School Movement in Colonial Pennsylvania* (1905; 1969).

Ben Burks

PEABODY, ELIZABETH PALMER (May 16, 1804–January 3, 1894). Educational reformer, early leader of the American kindergarten* movement, Transcendentalist, and teacher, Elizabeth Palmer Peabody was one of the first nationally prominent schoolwomen of the nineteenth century. Her long career in education began in the mid-1820s when she taught the daughters of renowned Unitarian minister William Ellery Channing and became involved with the influential group of Boston intellectuals known as Transcendentalists. In the mid-1830s, she collaborated with the radical Romantic educator Amos Bronson Alcott* and taught at his short-lived Temple School. Her *Record of a School* (1835) described Alcott's Socratic educational methods and showed Peabody's own insight into experimental pedagogy. In 1840, Peabody opened the West Street Bookstore in Boston, which became a center for Transcendentalist discussion and publishing. She first heard about the kindergarten in the mid-1850s from Henry Barnard* and in 1859 was introduced to Friedrich Froebel's* naturalistic German educational philosophy and methods by Margarethe Meyer Schurz. An enthusiastic Peabody opened the first English-speaking kindergarten in the United States in Boston in 1860 and wrote *Kindergarten Guide*, which was published in 1863 with *Moral Culture of Infancy*, by her sister, Mary Peabody Mann. Peabody traveled through Europe in 1867 visiting kindergartens, and she returned more knowledgeable about Froebelianism and dedicated to the kindergarten cause. In 1873, she started and edited a journal, *The Kindergarten Messenger*, and in 1877 she founded the American Froebel Union. Peabody brought German kindergartners to this country and became extensively involved in kindergarten training. Her *Lectures in the Training Schools for Kindergartners* (1886) documented her maternalistic educational philosophy and views on the importance of the "mother spirit" in teaching and education. She was one of the first to emphasize the critical role of caring and play as opposed to didactic instruction for young children. Peabody's indefatigable advocacy and extensive writings were a major factor in the eventual successful universalization of the kindergarten in American public schools. (Also, refer to WINNEMUCCA, SARAH.)

Many of Peabody's letters have been collected and edited by Bruce Allen Ronda, *Letters of Elizabeth Palmer Peabody: American Renaissance Woman* (1984). Sources on Peabody's life and work include Ruth M. Baylor, *Elizabeth Palmer Peabody: Kindergarten Pioneer* (1965), and Hersha S. Fisher, "The Education of Elizabeth Peabody" (1980). See, also, biographical essays in International Kindergarten Union,* *Pioneers of the Kindergarten in America* (1924), and Edward T. James, ed., *Notable American Women, 1607–1950* (1971).

Barbara Beatty

PEABODY, ENDICOTT (May 30, 1857–November 17, 1944), founded Groton School, where he served as headmaster for fifty-six years. That school, located in Groton, Massachusetts, functioned as a private Episcopalian, secondary boarding school* for boys. Peabody also actively participated on civic committees and belonged to over thirty associations, ranging from the New England Association of Colleges and Church Schools to the Boston Children's Aid Society. He attended Trinity College, Cambridge, and the Episcopal Theological School in Cambridge, Massachusetts, where he was ordained in 1884. That same year, Peabody, committed to the education of patrician youth, secured a gift of land in Groton and opened his school with twenty-three students and two other masters. Far from being an innovator, he made no significant contributions to educational theory. Groton functioned as a church school, and Peabody saw his mission as cultivating manly Christian character. He embraced the concept of "in loco parentis," maintaining that a pupil's education must be linked with moral discipline, even at the expense of intellectual development. Fearing idleness, he subjected students to a highly structured daily routine consisting of mandatory chapel services, lessons from a classical curriculum, rigorous athletic activities, and a supervised study hall. Peabody preached about the values of public service and used the ideas of muscular Christianity to educate a new generation of socially responsible aristocratic gentlemen, including Franklin D. Roosevelt and Dean Acheson.

The Groton School library possesses about 160 boxes of Peabody's correspondence and speeches, including the Atwood Papers, a collection of numerous letters between the rector and his friend Bishop Julius Atwood. Also located in the archives are *The Grotonian* and *Groton School Quarterly*, both school publications that contain a plethora of indispensable information regarding Peabody and Groton. Peabody expressed his educational approaches in two articles: "The Continuous Moral Influence of the School through College and through Life" (1899) and "The Aims, Duties, and Opportunities of the HeadMaster of an Endowed Secondary School" (1901). Finally, Frank D. Ashburn, *Peabody of Groton: A Portrait* (1967), and a collection of essays written by Groton graduates, *Views from the Circle; Seventy-Five Years of Groton School* (1960), remain the definitive publications about Peabody's life and educational philosophy.

Mark Desjardins

PEABODY EDUCATION FUND was the first of several funds set up by northern philanthropists to promote education in the post–Civil War South. George Peabody, a native of Massachusetts and a long-time resident of England, established the $2 million fund in 1867. Key individuals proposed and implemented the Fund's policy. Robert Winthrop, former congressman from Massachusetts, served as the first chair of the Fund's board of trustees; Barnas Sears, president of Brown University, and Jabez L. M. Curry,* a former member of the U.S. and the Confederate congresses, operated as general agents. Under Sears's leadership, the Fund sought to revitalize southern education by assisting local public schools* and strengthening state systems of education. Curry redirected the fund's efforts to promote teacher education in state normal schools and universities and establish the George Peabody College for Teachers, jointly sponsor state supervisors of rural schools with the Southern Education Board,* and assist the Slater Fund* in promoting industrial training* for southern African Americans. Although modest, distributing $3.6 million between 1867 and 1914, the Fund proved to have considerable influence. It sought to build up tax support for public schools and teacher education in the South and expand state-level influence and control. It assumed that the education of African American and white children and the solution for the "Negro problem" should be on terms acceptable to the southern white community. Its opposition to the original proposals for integrated schools in the Civil Rights Act of 1875 (see CIVIL RIGHTS ACTS) and its discriminatory funding in favor of white schools and colleges assumed the subordinate status of African Americans and defined as misguided the more radical proposals of the Reconstruction governments and abolitionist educators.

Vanderbilt University, George Peabody College Library, houses the Peabody Fund Papers, and the six volumes of the *Proceedings of the Trustees of the Peabody Education Fund: From the Original Organization of the 8th of February 1967*. The J.L.M. Curry Papers can be found in the Library of Congress. The traditional interpretation set by Curry, in his *History of the Peabody Fund* (1898), and reconfirmed by Charles William Dabney, *Universal Education in the South* (1936), dominated most accounts until the 1960s. Franklin Parker, *George Peabody: A Biography* (1971), devotes one chapter to the Fund. Critics of the Fund have focused on its role in promoting public education within a white supremacist society. One of the earliest critics, Horace Mann Bond,* in *Negro Education in Alabama* (1939; 1969), underscored its discriminatory funding practices based on race. James D. Anderson, *The Education of the Blacks in the South, 1860–1935* (1988), and Louis R. Harlan, *Separate and Unequal* (1958), both allude to the Fund's role in promoting industrial education for

African Americans. More comprehensive studies of the Fund's activities in promoting African American education are Henry Allen Bullock, *A History of Negro Education in the South* (1967); William P. Vaughn, "Partners in Segregration: Barnas Sears and the Peabody Fund" (1964); William P. Vaughn, *Schools for All: The Blacks and Public Education in the South* (1974); Earl H. West, "The Life and Educational Contributions of Barnas Sears" (1961); and Earl H. West, "The Peabody Education Fund and Negro Education" (1966). Finally, the Fund's role in promoting state-level interest in control of and funding for schools is briefly treated in William Link, *The Paradox of Southern Progressivism, 1880–1930* (1992).

Harvey G. Neufeldt

PEIRCE, CYRUS (August 15, 1790–April 5, 1860), was America's first public teacher educator. After graduation from Harvard College in 1810 and from Harvard Divinity School in 1815, he became a successful pastor and teacher. Horace Mann,* first secretary of the Massachusetts Board of Education, visited Peirce's school on Nantucket Island in 1837 and recognized Peirce as an outstanding instructor. In 1839, Mann persuaded the Massachusetts Board of Education to appoint Peirce principal of the Lexington Normal School, the first public normal school* in the United States. Lexington Normal School opened in 1839 with only three students, but enrollment soon grew, and in spite of financial and political difficulties, the school survived. It later moved to West Newton and then to Framingham. Peirce's school and others that soon opened in Massachusetts enrolled mostly young women and taught them both subject matter and methods of teaching. They were successful enough so that as other states established common schools,* they also created normal schools to help provide trained instructors. Peirce shared Mann's commitment to free, nondenominational, universal public education. While teaching on Nantucket, Peirce insisted that his school be open to African American students, and when an African American woman applied for admission to his normal school, Peirce admitted her despite of local opposition. He retired in 1849.

For primary documents, see Eleanor Craven Fishburn, ed., *The First State Normal School in America—The Journals of Cyrus Peirce and Mary Swift* (1926). Biographical material includes Benjamin W. Frazier, "The First State Normal School" (1939); John Hillison, "Cyrus Peirce: First Public Teacher Educator" (1984); Samuel J. May, "Memoir of Cyrus Peirce" (1857); and Kathleen O'Leary, "Cyrus Peirce: Educator of the Nineteenth Century" (1950). Finally, refer to the *Dictionary of American Biography*, pp. 403–404.

James M. Wallace

PENMANSHIP. The petty, or dame,* schools of the colonial period did not teach writing because literacy* then entailed only reading. Children who desired to learn to write attended writing schools after completing their petty schooling. Early guides established forms of penmanship that were highly ornate. They were also difficult to learn and execute, given the crude and unstable nature of the goose-feather quill (which was in ordinary use), and the undeveloped small-muscle coordination of young children. Following the American Revolution, the gradual creation of tax-supported public education districts led to schools with grades 1 to 8, where penmanship was taught as a regular part of the curriculum. Younger children were taught to print their letters on slates until they developed the dexterity required to use the quills and the mental acuity required to memorize the forms of cursive writing. Teachers taught writing by first emphasizing practice and drill on the letter forms. When these were mastered, the teacher wrote aphorisms on a small slate board. This was referred to as "setting the copy." Short aphorisms were written for the beginners, with long aphorisms reserved for the more proficient students. The selection of these aphorisms, often taken from the Bible or from classical authors, became a form of moral instruction as well as an exercise in directed practice. The definition of literacy was, by then, expanded to include both reading and writing skills.

Advances in technology led to improvements in penmanship (also, see EDUCATIONAL TECHNOLOGY). In the 1830s, blackboards and chalk were increasingly used in schools. This provided a means for children to practice penmanship without the use of expensive paper. By the 1840s, the manufactured steel nib was introduced to replace the quill pen. The nib was fitted into a wooden holder. It held more ink than the quill and did not require the frequent reshaping that the quill had demanded. The "pen knife" was no longer a necessary school implement and its mastery a pedagogical requirement. The development of the fountain pen, at the turn of the century, led to the eventual banishment of inkwells. By the 1950s, the newly invented ballpoint pen replaced the fountain pen.

Technological improvements in penmanship were accompanied by changes in the letter forms. Emphasis was placed on making the forms simpler, which would allow the learner to memorize them more quickly and to write them faster. This was in keeping with the nation's infatuation with the industrial revolution and its attendant interest in speed and efficiency. Platt Rogers Spencer, usually referred to as "Father Spencer," or the "Father of American School Penmanship," led the movement to create simpler forms. His work, which began in the 1840s, was continued beyond his death by his sons until the 1880s. His method placed great emphasis upon posture, the placement of the paper in order to create the standard slant, and frequent practice in forming lines and circles to develop muscle coordination. In the early 1900s, Spencerian forms and their competitors were replaced by an even simpler script developed by A. N. Palmer. Palmer's system of cursive writing created letter forms keyed to a ruled line either one or two spaces in height. Above the regular line was a line indicated by dashes. Below the regular line was a similar broken line. The lower-case *a*, as an example, was placed on the line and extended to the broken line above it, making it one space high. The lower-case *l* was placed on the line and extended upward beyond the broken line to the regular line above it, making it two spaces high.

The lower-case q was also two units, but was one space above the line and one space below the line. The Palmer method was in ordinary use in American schools until the 1950s. The Palmer Company sold copybooks, special ruled writing tablets, oversized pencils designed for use by the younger children learning to print, and wall charts that showed the forms of the manuscript style in both lower and upper case; the charts were placed over the chalkboard in the front of the class. Children who demonstrated good penmanship were awarded certificates and premiums. Examples of the students' penmanship were often exhibited and frequently displayed for visiting parents to view.

Penmanship declined after the 1950s. The widespread use of the typewriter and later the word processor relegated penmanship into a private rather than public form of communication. Efforts to revive penmanship in the contemporary elementary school to the level of former glory have been largely unrealized.

For general historical background, refer to Carroll Gard, *Writing Past and Present: The Story of Writing and Writing Tools* (1937), and Ray Nash, *American Penmanship, 1800–1850: A History of Writing and a Bibliography of Copybooks from Jenkins to Spencer* (1969).

William E. Eaton

PERENNIALISM. See *PAIDEIA*.

PERRY, WILLIAM FLAKE (1823–December 18, 1901), as the first state superintendent of education in Alabama, worked to establish a statewide common school* system during the 1850s. His goals of extending schooling to all white children and improving teaching, buildings, and the curriculum were virtually identical to those of other state school reformers, North and South. Perry made modest progress toward the goals by circumventing some of the political, administrative, and financial problems that blocked antebellum school reform throughout much of his region.

Born in Jackson County, Georgia, and largely self-educated, Perry taught school and read law in Alabama before gaining admission to the bar in 1854. That same year, friends in the Alabama legislature, including Jabez L. M. Curry* of Talladega, persuaded Perry to accept the superintendency of the newly chartered state school system. The difficulties of the job took him by surprise. Some local officials simply ignored him when he ordered the election of school trustees in each township; other officials informed him that townships were meaningless political jurisdictions in rural Alabama. He traveled throughout the state in 1855, learning valuable political lessons. The next year he persuaded the legislature to establish the office of county superintendent, which gave Perry a cadre of local administrators who reported to him. This strategy proved to be the key to organizing township schools and maintaining trustee involvement. As Perry grew adept at handling the sensitive issue of centralized control, he learned to offer constant reassurances to local people that his role was limited to advocacy, guidance, and record keeping. His emphasis on local responsibility played well in the Alabama legislature, even if conservatives foresaw the day when state recommendations would become state regulations. Because the state provided no more than $1.50 annually per student throughout his administration, Perry advised local trustees to use public funds to start the school term and then, if necessary, ask teachers to collect tuition to finish the year. This practice, burdensome to teachers, sometimes resulted in the exclusion of poor students. Perry maintained a strong egalitarian streak, however, and over the protests of affluent Alabamians, he devised a funding formula that channeled more state money to poor townships than to wealthy ones. The system Perry turned over to his successor in 1858 provided state-subsidized schooling to about half of Alabama's white children, making the state one of the more successful in the region in antebellum school reform.

Perry gives valuable insight into the development of Alabama's public education system in his article "The Genesis of Public Education in Alabama" (1898). Important secondary sources include Charles William Dabney, *Universal Education in the South* (1936); Forrest David Mathews, "The Politics of Education in the Deep South: Georgia and Alabama, 1830–1860" (1965); and Stephen B. Weeks, *History of Public School Education in Alabama* (1915).

Joseph W. Newman

PESTALOZZI, JOHANN HEINRICH. See PESTALOZZIANISM.

PESTALOZZIANISM. The educational ideas and methods of Swiss educator Johann Heinrich Pestalozzi exerted some influence on education in the United States since their introduction in the nineteenth century. Many of Pestalozzi's basic educational notions became, at some time or another, characteristics of American education, such as the child-centered curriculum, a utilitarian education according to the child's natural development, the humane treatment of students, a balanced development of the child's intellectual, moral, and physical abilities, experimentation in education, and teacher professionalization.

Pestalozzianism, which appealed to the romanticism of the late eighteenth and early nineteenth centuries, believed that society could be reformed by educating all children, developing their innate moral and mental abilities. Pestalozzi first opened a school at Stantz in 1798, only to move it to Burgdorf in 1801. Four years later, after his unsuccessful attempt to work with educator Emanuel von Fellenberg, Pestalozzi transferred the school to Yverdon. The Institute at Yverdon remained open until 1825, attracting the attention of educators worldwide. Visitors included William Maclure in 1805 and Robert Dale Owen* in 1818, both later associated with Indiana's New Harmony community.

Maclure introduced Pestalozzianism to the United States at the beginning of the nineteenth century. During his visit to Yverdon, Maclure asked Pestalozzi to come to the United States. He declined the offer, in his place recommending Joesph Neef, one of his disciples at the Burgdorf school, for the appointment. In 1808, Neef published in English *Sketch of a Plan and Method of Education*, which not only outlined his proposal for a U.S. Pestalozzian school but also introduced Pestalozzian ideas to an American audience. The next year, Neef and Maclure opened the first U.S. Pestalozzian school in Philadelphia. In 1812, Neef moved the school to Village Green, Pennsylvania, and then eventually to Louisville, Kentucky, in 1815, where the school failed financially. Neef moved to New Harmony in 1826, at Maclure's invitation, and directed that community's schools. Although the New Harmony experiment ended in 1827, the schools successfully used Pestalozzian principles. They taught all children a trade and, thus, became the first to include industrial education* as part of the public school* system. Two other New Harmony teachers, Marie Fretageot and Phiquepal d'Arusmont, who taught the infant school and trade school respectively, were also Pestalozzian proponents.

The failure of Pestalozzianism to gain widespread attention in early nineteenth-century America can be attributed to a number of reasons. Neef moved his schools too frequently for the ideas to catch on, and, because Neef was a proclaimed atheist, his attitude toward religion proved to be unacceptable to some people. Neef's brand of Pestalozzianism may also have arrived too early, since the monitorial system* was popular in the 1820s. He also did not prepare teachers to use Pestalozzian techniques, as his mentor did. Therefore, followers failed to emerge until the 1860s and the Oswego movement.*

Pestalozzianism gained widespread attention in the 1840s with Horace Mann.* In 1843, he visited the Prussian schools where many Pestalozzi-trained teachers taught. Teacher preparation institutions appealed to Mann, who also agreed with Pestalozzi's reformist ideas. Mann's *Seventh Annual Report* (1843) to the Massachusetts Board of Education promoted the Pestalozzian notions of moral character development, the child's innate goodness, parental love as the basis for the operation of a school, and teacher preparation. Pestalozzianism blossomed during the third quarter of that century. Henry Barnard* promoted Pestalozzianism in *Pestalozzi and Pestalozzianism* (1862) and in his *American Journal of Education*. In 1859, Edward A. Sheldon,* superintendent of the Oswego, New York, schools, visited the Toronto schools, which used the Pestalozzian object lesson method of instruction (see OBJECT TEACHING). Sheldon became an advocate of this method and in 1861 contacted the Home and Colonial School Society in London for assistance on how to implement object lesson teaching. Margaret Jones from the Society spent a year at Oswego teaching Sheldon and his instructors. However, the Society had formalized the object lesson and, in so doing, lost touch with the spirit of Pestalozzianism. It was this type of Pestalozzianism that formed the basis of the Oswego movement and became associated with Pestalozzianism in the United States. Many U.S. teachers used the (Oswego) object lesson after the Oswego School was made a state normal school in 1865 and became the model upon which six other normal schools* were designed. Sheldon and Oswego teachers believed that teachers must be intellectually, emotionally, psychologically, and spiritually prepared to work with children. Pestalozzianism too surfaced in both higher and teacher education through the efforts of Louis Agassi. Lowell Mason* popularized Pestalozzian techniques specifically in music education,* whereas Amos Bronson Alcott* supported Pestalozzianism in schools in general. Other American proponents of Pestalozzianism included George Bancroft,* William Russell, James G. Carter,* and Charles Brooks. In the twentieth century, Pestalozzian principles, such as the child-centered curriculum, gained suppport from progressive educators (see PROGRESSIVE EDUCATION), although direct links to Pestalozzi were not acknowledged.

For biographies of Pestalozzi and analyses of the impact of his theories, see Thomas A. Barlow, *Pestalozzi and American Education* (1977), and Rick E. Heironimus, "Johann Heinrich Pestalozzi: A Study of His Influence on American Sunday Schools" (1977). Also refer to William S. Monroe, *History of the Pestalozzian Movement in the United States* (1969), and Gerald L. Gutek, *Joesph Neef: The Americanization of Pestalozzianism* (1978).

Laurie Moses Hines

PHELPS-STOKES FUND was incorporated in 1911 to administer an $800,000 bequest from Carolyn Phelps Stokes (1854–1909), granddaughter of Anson Greene Phelps, a successful New York merchant, manufacturer, and philanthropist. Her deep religious convictions motivated a lifetime of concern for the less fortunate. Her will directed the Fund to provide "housing for the poor families of New York City, for the education of Negroes in Africa and the United States, North American Indians, and needy white students." The early policies were influenced by Thomas Jesse Jones, educational director from 1913 to 1946.

The Fund's policies emphasized agricultural, industrial, and health and hygiene education for southern blacks (see VOCATIONAL EDUCATION). Transplanted to Africa, these policies influenced the work of missionaries and the colonial powers. Limited resources meant few direct grants. Jones believed the Fund could most improve education and race relations by the collection and dissemination of information. The work of public officials and private philanthropies was influenced by this small Fund through survey reports on black colleges (1928), education in Africa (1922, 1925), American Indian education (1928), and the Caribbean (1978). These policies were criticized by Carter G. Woodson,* W.E.B. Du Bois,* and some African leaders. The Fund helped found the Commission on Interracial Cooperation (1919), established the "Improved Instruction Program" (1954), and the Education Policy and School Reform Program (1991). In collaboration with public and private agencies, the Fund sponsors the Africa Forum, the Center for Human Development, the African Student Advisory Program, an African visitors' program, and a program for internationalizing the curriculum of historically black colleges and universities.

Primary sources include the Phelps-Stokes Archives, New York City; the Anson Phelps Stokes Papers, Yale University Library; and the Dillard family papers, University of Virginia Library. Also, see Toni Trent Parker, *Annotated Bibliography of the Books, Reports, and Papers Published, Written, or Spon-*

sored by the Phelps-Stokes Fund (1976). Other sources are Edward Henry Berman, "Education in Africa and America: A History of the Phelps-Stokes Fund, 1911–1945" (1970); Stephen Taylor Correia, "For Their Own Good: An Historical Analysis of the Educational Thought of Thomas Jesse Jones" (1993); and Kenneth J. King, "The American Negro Background of the Phelps-Stokes Commission and Their Influence on Education in East Africa, Especially in Kenya" (1968).

Earle H. West

PHILADELPHIA HOUSE OF REFUGE. In Philadelphia, during the 1820s, the Society for Alleviating the Miseries of Public Prisons began to investigate conditions in the prisons of the city. The Society found that juvenile vagrants and youthful offenders were confined in that city's Walnut Street Jail along with adult criminals. The investigators recommended that separate quarters be found for juvenile vagrants and that a separate institution, a house of refuge for juvenile offenders, be established. Inspired by the opening of the New York House of Refuge in 1825 (see GRISCOM, JOHN), Philadelphia opened its own institution in 1826. Like the New York institution the Philadelphia House of Refuge used a combination of work, basic education, and moral instructions. House administrators also placed their well-behaved inmates with foster families (see REFORM SCHOOLS).

The Philadelphia House of Refuge was the subject of two legal challenges. The first, *Commonwealth v. M'Keagy*, 1 Ashmead (PA) 248 (1831), resulted in the release of one inmate on a writ of *habeas corpus*, the court finding that the institution could not act in loco parentis for a child who was neither a criminal nor a vagrant. In the other case, *Ex parte Crouse*, 4 Wharton (PA) 9 (1839), the court found that the state, using its power of *parens patriae*, could retain an inmate in order to provide an education. *Ex parte Crouse* confirmed the exercise of parental power by the Philadelphia House of Refuge and overturned the restrictions set in *Commonwealth v. M'Keagy*.

Joseph M. Hawes, *Children in Urban Society: Juvenile Delinquency in Nineteenth-Century Society* (1971); Robert M. Mennel, *Thorns and Thistles: Juvenile Delinquents in the United States, 1825–1940* (1973); David J. Rothman, *The Discovery of the Asylum: Social Order and Disorder in the New Republic* (1971); Steven L. Schlossman, *Love and the American Delinquent: The Theory and Practice of "Progressive" Juvenile Justice, 1825–1920* (1977).

Joseph M. Hawes

PHONICS. See READING INSTRUCTION.

PHRENOLOGY, though now discredited as a pseudoscience, served as an influential theory of human nature, the inspiration for a range of educational and social reform movements in the early nineteenth century. Franz Joseph Gall, a French anatomist, conceived of phrenology in the 1820s. Comparing skull shape with personality traits, Gall claimed that the brain was composed of more than twenty smaller organs. Gall's new science was popularized in the United States by the Scottish philosopher George Combe, whose *Constitution of Man* interested many American educators.

Phrenologists claimed that the brain was the physical seat of the mind. They further held that the brain was actually a collection of smaller organs, each performing a distinct mental function. Most controversial, they believed that the size, and therefore the relative strength, of these organs affected the shape of the cranium, making the bumps on the skull a sign of individual character. Their practice of "reading skulls" has received the most attention and ridicule. Although phrenology linked individual character to skull size and shape, phrenologists avoided biological determinism by claiming that proper education and exercise could improve brain capacity and alter character, at least to some degree. English and American phrenologists often championed liberal educational reforms, arguing that their science vindicated the importance of universal education and of treating each child individually. They urged teachers and parents to avoid harsh discipline and rote memorization and to study and nurture each child's innate capacities. Believing that all "organs" of the brain required development, they also called for a curriculum that balanced physical, intellectual, and moral training (see MORAL EDUCATION; PHYSICAL EDUCATION). Horace Mann* became a friend and disciple of George Combe and as a result made phrenology required reading in his state's normal schools.* Most American intellectuals abandoned phrenology by mid-nineteenth century. In recent years, however, the phrenologists have been given credit for anticipating the study of the localization of brain function.

For historical background, refer to John Davies, *Phrenology: Fad and Science* (1955); David DeGiustino, *Conquest of Mind: Phrenology and Victorian Social Thought* (1975); and Thomas H. Leahey and Grace E. Leahey, *Psychology's Occult Doubles: Psychology and the Problem of Pseudoscience* (1983).

                                                                            Ernest Freeberg

PHYSICAL EDUCATION. In 1825, Dr. Charles Beck, a German immigrant who was a member of Friedrich Jahn's gymnastics-based Turner movement of physical training, became instructor of gymnastics at the Round Hill School* in Massachusetts. The subsequent influx of other "Turners" into the United States ensured the central role of gymnastics in school curricula through the 1840s and 1850s. Another crusader for better health in the schools was Catharine Beecher,* who is generally credited with developing the first American system of gymnastics as well as being recognized as the first female physical education leader in the United States. The Association for the Advancement of Physical Education was founded in 1885 (see AMERICAN ALLLIANCE FOR HEALTH, PHYSICAL EDUCATION, RECREATION, AND DANCE), and by 1899 both Ohio and North Dakota had passed legislation requiring physical education in the public schools.* The curricular emphasis at this time was based on the German and Swedish models of disciplinary mastery.

The influence of John Dewey* and the progressive education* movement ushered in a school curriculum that was more concerned with child development. The 1920s and 1930s subsequently witnessed a shift in the physical education orientation from disciplinary mastery in gymnastics to a more diverse format that included a variety of sports and recreational activities as the center of the curriculum. With the onset of World War II, physical education teachers initially focused on military-style fitness activities such as rope climbing, circuit training, and obstacle course running, as well as team sports. The decade ended, however, with a renewed commitment to individual development through lifetime fitness.

The disciplinary mastery emphasis of the 1950s saw the knowledge base of physical education expand to include the new subdisciplines of biomechanics, kinesiology, and exercise physiology as well as the establishment of the necessary research facilities. In response to civil unrest, poverty, and other social problems, the goal of teaching children social responsibility assumed a prominent role in curricular planning in the 1960s. Physical educators systematically investigated child growth and development in relation to the acquisition of motor skills. Movement education for elementary students and lifetime sports for secondary students increased greatly in popularity as physical educators emphasized the goals of individualization and self-actualization. Skill development relative to competitive athletics, however, continued to define life in the gymnasium for most school-aged students.

The social reconstruction* paradigm of the 1970s envisioned the schools as a focal point to enhance the worth of each individual by advancing the goals of affirmative action, bilingual education.* mainstreaming,* and improved educational services to special populations. The physical education curriculum attempted to respond to these goals through cooperative movement activities and an increased emphasis on creativity; at the same time, the need to develop and refine sports-related skills (disciplinary mastery) to ensure competitive interscholastic athletic teams continued to frame the curricular agenda of contemporary physical education programs.

See Ann E. Jewett and Linda L. Bain, *The Curriculum Process in Physical Education* (1985).

Michael J. Cleary

PIAGET, JEAN. See CONSTRUCTIVISM.

PICKET, ALBERT (April 15, 1771–August 30, 1850), published a variety of school books and became a leading common school* advocate. He was born in Connecticut, and although he studied there with Noah Webster* in 1782, Picket was largely self-educated. He moved to New York City in 1794, started the Manhattan School, offering advanced instruction for young women, and helped to found the Incorporated Society of Teachers.

Picket began his publishing career in 1804, when he published *The Union Spelling Book*. In 1819, he produced a sequence of seven textbooks and a dictionary entitled *American School Class Books*. From 1818 until 1820, Picket and his eldest son, John, wrote a semimonthly educational periodical, *The Academician*, that discussed the philosophic outlines of education based on analyses of the human mind.

Picket moved to Cincinnati, Ohio, in 1826, establishing another school for young women. Three years later he helped to form the Western Literary Institute and College of Professional Teachers, serving as the Institute's only president throughout its existence. In his presidential address of 1834, Picket explained that the aim of the Institute was to advance instruction by encouraging teachers to talk with each other. At other meetings, he noted that the most important function of schools was to shape the feelings and dispositions of the students. These sentiments supported the Institute's aim of cultivating an American system of education to shape a distinctly American citizen. From 1829 until 1845, this organization spread a network of auxiliary and local organizations through the western and southern states, extending the influence of the central convention in Cincinnati.

Picket worked to advance schools of all sorts, serving on Cincinnati's board of education and as a trustee of Cincinnati College. Thus, throughout his career, Picket sought to replace haphazard instruction with the reasonable and ordered curricula he lacked as a child.

The records of the Western Literary Institute include various papers and addresses by Picket. Eight volumes are available that begin with the third annual meeting in 1834 and extending to the eleventh in 1842. *The Academician* is available on University Microfilms. Refer to "Albert Picket" in *Dictionary of American Biography*, vol. 14 (1937). Also, see Allen Oscar Hansen, *Early Educational Leadership in the Ohio Valley* (1969).

Joseph Watras

PIERCE, JOHN DAVIS (February 18, 1797–April 5, 1882), served as Michigan's first superintendent of public instruction. He planned the state's common school* system and was a leader in the establishment of the University of Michigan.

Born in Chesterfield, New Hampshire, he taught school three months each year to maintain himself before graduating from Brown University in 1822. Pierce served as principal of Wrentham Academy (Massachusetts), spent a year at Princeton Theological Seminary, receiving a license from the Congregational Association, served as a pastor in Oneida County (New York), and in 1831 settled as a missionary in Marshall, Michigan. Pierce became friends with Isaac Crary,* and together they read and were influenced by Victor Cousin's report on the Prussian system of education.

In 1836, Crary recommended Pierce for superintendent of public instruction; Pierce was unanimously approved. Pierce traveled east and consulted with prominent educators and statesmen before proposing an educational plan for Michigan, which assumed state status in 1837. He organized the common school system, which divided the state into school districts and provided for a public library in each district. As superintendent, Pierce also began the publication of the *Journal of Education* (1838–1840), the first educational journal in the Great Lakes region. He arranged for the sale of public lands to support the schools, helped to establish early qualifications for teachers, and prepared a plan for the new state's university. Pierce was elected to the state legislature in 1847. In 1850, he was elected to the convention for framing a new state constitution, and in this capacity he was instrumental in securing the provision for free public schools.

Pierce, an advocate of state-sponsored teacher preparation, delivered the leading address at the opening of the Michigan State Normal School (see NORMAL SCHOOLS) in 1852. He briefly served as the county superintendent of schools in Washtenaw County (1867–1868). He remained in Ypsilanti, actively engaged in ministry and educational debate until his death.

Pierce's correspondence and photograph series is housed at the Bentley Historical Library, University of Michigan. For his biography, see Charles O. Hoyt and R. Clyde Ford, *John D. Pierce, Founder of the Michigan School System: A Study of Education in the Northwest* (1905). Also, see James Bartlett Edmunson, *The Legal and Constitutional Basis of a State School System* (1926); George L. Jackson, *Development of State Control of Public Instruction in Michigan* (1926); Daniel Putnam, *The Development of Primary and Secondary Public Education in Michigan* (1904); and W. L. Smith, *Education in Michigan* (1881). Finally, refer to the sources for CRARY, ISAAC.

Laura Docter Thornburg

PIERCE V. SOCIETY OF SISTERS, 268 U.S. 510 (1925). This U.S. Supreme Court case established the constitutionality of nonpublic education. In 1922, Oregon voters passed an initiative, promoted by the Ku Klux Klan and Scottish Rite Masons, which required children between the ages of eight and sixteen to attend public school.* The Sisters of the Holy Names of Jesus and Mary, who staffed a number of Oregon schools, and Hill Military Academy challenged the law in the federal district court in 1923, although the law was not scheduled to become effective until 1926. That court imposed a restraining injunction in March 1924, and the Oregon attorney general appealed to the U.S. Supreme Court. The following year the Court upheld the district court's decision, rejecting Oregon's contention that the law was necessary regulation to ensure Americanization and to prevent the destruction of the public school system. The Supreme Court found that the Oregon law represented undue interference. It further affirmed the rights of parents to select the appropriate educational setting for their children and denied that the child is the creature of the state. This decision established the rights of nonpublic elementary and secondary education in the United States and indirectly fueled the growth of parochial schooling* throughout the country (also, refer to PRIVATE SCHOOLS).

For analyses of the context and consequences of this decision, see Lloyd P. Jorgenson, ''The Oregon School Law of 1922: Passage and Sequel'' (1968), and David B. Tyack, "The Perils of Pluralism: The Background of the Pierce Case" (1969).

F. Michael Perko

PLATOON PLAN. See GARY PLAN.

PLAY MOVEMENT, in addition to having a lasting material effect on American public education, provides a look into the assumptions, aims, and methods of urban educational reformers during the Progressive Era (see PROGRESSIVE EDUCATION). The play movement was a response to the material and social effects of urbanization and industrialization. The play time lost to organized schooling, the loss of open spaces for play, the disappearance of child labor, and the congested, closed-in nature of city life were cited as the material reasons for the play movement. Socially, educational reformers were trying to protect the children from the streets and the streets from the children. The movement reflects the sense of social responsibility among reformers of the period as well as the emerging view of the teacher as social worker and the "child rather than the course of study as the center of educational interest." Scholars of the period argue that the movement's leaders also intended to socialize and train children into attitudes, values, and skills suitable for an industrialized society.

With influential roots in Germany and England, the play movement in the United States was pioneered in Boston in the late nineteenth century. That city opened an organized playground as early as 1868, but Boston's sand gardens, opened in 1885 and 1886, marked the official inauguration of the play movement. After reading a report on public parks in Berlin written by Dr. Marie E. Zakrsewska, the Massachusetts Emergency and Hygiene Association placed large piles of sand in the yards of a chapel and a nursery during the summer of 1885 (see NURSERY SCHOOLS). Sand was placed in three more locations the following summer. These efforts are considered the beginning of the movement because of their organization and influence on other cities. The play areas were supervised by neighborhood women and hired "matrons" until 1893, when a superintendent, with assistants, was hired for the sand gardens. With the new staff in place, digging tools and building blocks were furnished, organized games were played, and "occupation work" was encouraged. Nine other cities opened sand gardens between 1886 and 1887. The connection with public schooling occurred when the New York City Board of Education opened thirty-one playgrounds in 1898.

Playgrounds were generally built by private organizations, usually a playground committee of a women's or civic club. Some cities organized playground and recreation associations. Most efforts were funded by a combination of city appropriations and private philanthropic sources. The movement eventually split into two divisions. One was concerned with establishing municipal parks and playgrounds under the supervision of a parks board or recreation commission. The other advocated placing playgrounds with play equipment in schoolyards under the supervision of boards of education.

The movement established stability and momentum with the founding of the Playground and Recreation Association of America in 1906. Behind the leadership of its first president, Luther Gulick Jr., the Association furnished information and guidance to cities interested in establishing playgrounds and recreation programs. The Association's second president, Joseph Lee, and Henry S. Curtis are generally considered the most influential men in the play movement because of their long-standing public advocacy of the movement as well as their published works on it.

For a firsthand view of this movement, see Henry S. Curtis, *The Play Movement and Its Significance* (1917), and Henry S. Curtis, *Education through Play* (1930). Also refer to Clarence E. Rainwater, *The Play Movement in the United States: A Study of Community Recreation* (1922), and Paul C. Violas, The Training of the Urban Working Class: A History of Twentieth-Century American Education (1978).

Jeffrey A. Liles

PLEDGE OF ALLEGIANCE has its origins in the early 1890s, when James Upham, circulation head of the popular children's magazine *Youth's Companion*, developed a plan to encourage patriotism among America's school students. In a series of articles in the *Youth's Companion*, Upham encouraged thousands of children across the country to raise money to buy flags for their classrooms. Over 30,000 flags were eventually purchased for classrooms.

Spurred on by the success of the flag purchasing-program, Upham decided to create a pledge of allegiance that students would recite each morning as the flags in their classrooms were raised. Francis J. Bellamy, one of the editors of the *Youth's Companion*, wrote the Pledge and devised a plan that would include schoolchildren across the nation in the Columbus celebrations. He urged that the dedication day of the World's Columbian Exposition, October 12, 1892, be set aside as a national holiday. In order to make the Columbus Day celebrations truly national in character, copies of the Pledge were circulated to teachers throughout the country by the U.S. Bureau of Education.*

The use of the Pledge as part of the daily routine of the public schools* became widespread following its introduction in 1892. Controversy over who actually wrote the Pledge arose among the descendants of Upham and Bellamy. In 1939, the issue was settled by a committee made up of two historians and a political scientist—credit for authorship being given to Bellamy. Alterations were made to Bellamy's original version of the Pledge in 1923 and 1924 by the National Flag Conferences. In 1954 the words "under God" were added, and President Dwight D. Eisenhower signed a resolution approving the change.

Considerable controversy has surrounded the Pledge. State laws mandate that the Pledge be recited daily in public schools. In 1940 the Supreme Court ruled in *Minersville School District v. Gobitis** that two children who refused to salute the flag as part of a daily exercise could be required to do so. This decision was overturned in 1942 in the case of *West Virginia State Board of Education v.*

*Barnette.** In *Barnette*, Justice Robert Jackson argued that "no official, high or petty, can prescribe what shall be orthodox in politics, nationalism, religion, or other matters of opinion or force citizens to confess by word or act their faith therein." The *Barnette* ruling was generally understood as maintaining the religious rights of individuals who chose not to salute or pledge to the flag—in this case a principle rejected by Jehovah's Witnesses who were plaintiffs in the case. In the late 1960s an important test case came to light after two students in High School 217 in Briarwood, New York, refused to say the Pledge of Allegiance and stand for the salute to the flag. Under New York State Education Law, students were required to participate in the Pledge. In this case, the students' actions were motivated by their political convictions and dissatisfaction with the government's pursuit of the war in Vietnam. In May 1970, Governor Marvin Mandel of Maryland signed a bill requiring teachers to lead their classes in the Pledge. Implementation of this law was delayed by the circuit court until pending legal cases were decided. Clarification of the controversies surrounding the Pledge of Allegiance occurred in 1973 with the case of *Goetz v. Ansell*. Building on *Barnette*, this decision assured teachers and students the right to remain silent and seated, without having to leave the room, while the Pledge was being recited by other students.

A comprehensive history can be synthesized from Scot M. Guenter, *The American Flag, 1777–1924: Cultural Shifts from Creation to Codification* (1990), and Eugene F. Provenzo, Jr., and Asterie Baker Provenzo, "Columbus and the Pledge" (1991).

                                        Eugene F. Provenzo, Jr., and Asterie Baker Provenzo

PLESSY V. FERGUSON, 163 U.S. 537 (1896), introduced the pernicious doctrine of separate but equal on the basis of race into the national lexicon of the U.S. judicial system.

In June 1892, Homer Adolph Plessy, a passenger on a railroad train in Louisiana, who was seven-eighths Caucasian and one-eighth African American, was forcibly removed and jailed for purposely sitting in a first-class coach reserved for whites. Plessy challenged the state's Jim Crow criminal law on the basis that requiring railway companies to provide "equal but separate accommodations" (p. 540) for whites and African Americans violated the Fourteenth Amendment by distinguishing citizens according to race. Criminal court judge John H. Ferguson, whose name was thus linked to the case, rejected Plessy's argument and found him guilty. The Supreme Court of Louisiana affirmed.

The U.S. Supreme Court, on May 18, 1896, upheld the constitutionality of the statute. In reaching its decision, the Court relied partly on *Roberts v. City of Boston,** an earlier Massachusetts case, which permitted separate schools for African American and white children. The Court reasoned not only that laws requiring racial separation did not imply the inferiority of either group, but also that social prejudice could not be overcome by law. Consequently, in deferring to the discretion of the legislature, the Court affirmed the law as a reasonable exercise of the state's police power. *Plessy*, although technically limited to transportation, was subsequently applied to uphold segregation in public schools* and other state institutions.

Justice Harlan's lone dissent, which provided the basis for *Brown v. Board of Education*,* argued that since the Constitution was "color blind" (p. 559), the government should not have been able to determine a person's rights on the basis of race.

Charles J. Russo

PORT ROYAL EXPERIMENT influenced federal Reconstruction policy, especially educational programs for freed slaves. At the start of the Civil War, on November 7, 1861, the U.S. Navy seized the islands in Port Royal Sound, off the South Carolina coast, which hosted some 10,000 slaves. Secretary Salmon P. Chase, of the U.S. Treasury Department, assumed responsibility and decided to use this opportunity to test the notion that former slaves could become free laborers. In March 1862, the first band of fifty-three missionaries from New York City and Boston arrived at the Sea Islands; several hundred more followed by the end of the war. These missionaries organized the abandoned cotton plantations, encouraged the former slaves to continue production, and started schools.

The results were mixed. The most successful aspect of the experiment was the educational component. By 1863, approximately 2,500 African American children attended schools and even more adults participated in formally organized classes or received private instruction. Agricultural production, however, proved to be disappointing. Federal troops stole livestock, crops, and farm materials from the former slaves. Further, in May 1862, the U.S. Army drafted hundreds of former slaves, who were tending the cotton crops, to form the First Regiment of South Carolina Volunteers. Finally, in February 1865, occupation troops either returned parcels of the Sea Islands to the former owners or auctioned them for taxes, causing the former slaves to lose the small farms they had carved from the large plantations.

Nonetheless, members of such societies as the New England Freedman's Aid Society, the American Missionary Society, and the New York Freedman's Aid Society cited the Port Royal Experiment as having demonstrated that former slaves could sustain themselves as free people. In 1866, the U.S. Congress accepted these arguments and passed the Freedman's Bureau Bill over President Andrew Johnson's veto. (Also, refer to BUREAU OF REFUGEES, FREEDMEN, AND ABANDONED LANDS; FREEDMEN'S EDUCATION.)

See *First Annual Report* (1863), Port Royal Relief Committee, which is available on microfiche. Also, refer to Elizabeth Hyde Botume, *First Days among the Contrabands* (1893; 1968), and Charles Nordoff, *The Freedmen of South Carolina: Some Account of Their Appearance, Character, Condition, and Peculiar Customs* (1863). For secondary sources, refer to Guion Griffis Johnson, *A Social History of the Sea Islands with Special Reference to St. Helena Island,*

298   PRAGMATISM

South Carolina (1969), also see Willie Lee Rose, *Rehearsal for Reconstruction:*
The Port Royal Experiment (1964).

                                                              Joseph Watras

PRAGMATISM. See INSTRUMENTALISM.

PRIMERS. See *NEW ENGLAND PRIMER.*

PRIVATE SCHOOLS as well as public schools* have been affected by eras
of reform that have moved across the American educational landscape altering
institutional arrangements, programs, and beliefs. Mid-nineteenth-century common school reform contributed significantly to the development of modern concepts of private and public education. Prior to this time, institutional diversity
dominated, and blurred lines existed between private schools and public schools.
Colonial education consisted of an incredible variety of institutions, largely following regional lines: town and dame schools* in New England; denominational, charity,* and pay schools in the Middle Colonies; old field schools* in
the South; and academies* throughout the provinces during the 1700s. Southern
landowners established old field schools in fallow fields for the benefit of their
children; these schools sometimes received state funds for charity cases.
Therefore, classifying any of these schools as purely private and public proves
to be problematic from a historical perspective. To most colonials, a school was
public if it served a public purpose. Schools administered by public officials
charged tuition to students able to pay, whereas institutions controlled by boards
of trustees or religious bodies received public funds or land grants, frequently
for providing charity education for the poor, and were often perceived as public
schools. Thus, public education did not require public support and control.
   This broad concept of education persisted without major modification
throughout the Early National Period. Almost every state provided land grants
or financial aid to academies. Primary religious and private schools also received
public aid in many states, including Connecticut, Pennsylvania, Georgia, Tennessee, and Ohio. Even privately organized Sunday schools* received public
funds from at least three states—Delaware, Virginia, and Maryland.
   Intense debate and reform, during the mid-nineteenth century, led to profound
changes in educational arrangements inherited from the colonial period, namely,
the gradual emergence of the modern concept and practice of public schooling.
Common schools, proponents argued, would create a moral, disciplined, and
unified population prepared to participate in American political, social, and economic life. They cast private schools as divisive, undemocratic, and inimical
to the public interest. With few exceptions, notably several Lutheran and Calvinist bodies, which opted for schools designed to preserve cultural and/or con-
fessional purity, Protestants generally supported the common school movement.
Rather than share funds with Roman Catholic schools, as Bishop John Hughes*
proposed, they united behind the ''nonsectarian''—in reality pan-Protestant—

common school as the sole recipient of government funds for education. Parochial schools* were denied tax dollars as well as legitimacy. Common school reform led to a clear line of demarcation between private education and public education as states eliminated tax support for private schools, increased expenditures for public schools, and experienced a marked expansion in enrollment in the public sector. This trend accelerated in the late 1800s as the modern definition of "public" extended to secondary education, and many academies were incorporated into expanding public systems (see FEMALE SEMINARIES). Academies that were not transformed into public high schools* or state normal schools* either went defunct or redefined themselves as colleges or elite boarding schools.* Ninety-two percent of America's schoolchildren were enrolled in the public sector by 1900. Sixty-five percent of the remainder attended the burgeoning, ethnically diverse Roman Catholic schools, with most of the rest in Lutheran, Reformed, Episcopal, or independent institutions.

Multifaceted educational reform in the progressive era (see PROGRESSIVE EDUCATION) shaped private as well as public schools. While pedagogical progressives stimulated the creation of independent schools devoted to active, child-centered learning—such as Marietta Johnson's School of Organic Education (1907) and Caroline Pratt's Play School (1914)—administrative progressives influenced state efforts either to regulate private schools into conformity with the public school pattern or simply to abolish them. Lutheran and Catholic schools bore the brunt of these efforts during the last decade of the nineteenth century and the first quarter of the twentieth century. Following the *Pierce** decision, disputes between the state and private and schools declined, and major private school groups accepted the public school model and associated accreditation and certification standards.

Both the two-decade-long period of school reform that commenced in the 1950s and the era of reform that began in the mid-1980s have had an impact on private and public institutions. Equality concerns of the earlier period certainly affected private education. The federal government both provided funds for services for disadvantaged students in private schools and threatened them—especially "segregation academies" founded in the South between the mid-1960s and early 1970s—with the loss of their tax exempt status and federal funds for failure to conform to civil rights regulations (see CIVIL RIGHTS ACTS). At the same time, many private institutions opened their doors to minorities. By 1995, minority enrollment in Catholic schools and member institutions of the National Association of Independent Schools* reached 24 (8.4 African American) and 17 (5.5 African American) percent, respectively. Even a majority of the evangelical Christian schools also had integrated to some extent.

The private sector has been shaped by three additional trends since the mid-1960s. First, overall enrollments have declined. Catholic enrollments have fallen, with the exception of slight increases in the mid-1990s, but those in Protestant (excepting those in Seventh Day Adventist), Jewish, and nonreligious schools have risen. Second, many evangelical Protestants and their churches have forsaken their historic commitment to public education and founded about 10,000 independent Christian day schools, including a small but growing number established by and for African Americans. By the mid-1990s, enrollment in all these schools topped 1 million, about 20 percent of all private school students, who account for about 11 percent of all precollegiate enrollments. Third, since the early 1980s, a growing number of evangelical Protestants have chosen to teach their children at home (see HOME SCHOOLING) for many of the same reasons that gave birth to the Christian day school movement, the alternative schools,* and the free schools (see FREE SCHOOL MOVEMENT) of the late 1960s.

Although the 1980s "state mandates" phase of that reform movement had little direct impact on nonpublic schools, the 1990s "restructuring" phase may have a profound effect on private as well as public schools. Parental choice (see VOUCHERS) and private operation of public schools may once again blur the line between these two sectors.

Useful secondary works include James C. Carper and Jack Layman, "Black-Flight Academies: The New Christian Day Schools" (1997); Francis X. Curran, *The Churches and the Schools: American Protestantism and Popular Elementary Education* (1954); Richard J. Gabel, "Public Funds for Church and Private Schools" (1937); Thomas C. Hunt and James C. Carper, eds., *Religious Schools in the United States, K–12: A Source Book* (1993); Lloyd P. Jorgenson, *The State and the Non-Public School, 1825–1925* (1987); Pearl R. Kane, ed., *Independent Schools, Independent Thinkers* (1992); Otto F. Kraushaar, *American Nonpublic Schools: Patterns of Diversity* (1972); James M. McLachlan, *American Boarding Schools: A Historical Study* (1970); and E. Vance Randall, *Public Schools and Public Power: A Case for Pluralism* (1994).

James C. Carper

PROGRESSIVE EDUCATION is a term used both narrowly and broadly. Narrowly, it refers to the educational movement associated with pre–World War I American political progressivism, which lasted until the mid-1950s. Broadly, progressive education describes a range of innovative movements that promote educational and social reform; this larger movement has found expression throughout the modern history of schooling and continues into the present.

Progressive educators trace their intellectual ancestry back to John Comenius, Jean-Jacques Rousseau, Johann Heinrich Pestalozzi,* Friedrich Froebel,* and other thinkers. Progressive education in the United States had its antecedents in the work of Horace Mann* and other reformers of the common school* era. The specific movement can be traced to the work of educators like Francis W. Parker,* superintendent of the Quincy, Massachusetts, schools in the 1870s, who developed a variety of innovative practices in that system. Parker continued his work at the Cook County Normal School in Chicago during the 1880s and 1890s. There his work paralleled and reinforced that of John Dewey,* who, with his wife Alice, conducted, between 1896 and 1904, the most significant educational experiment in progressive educational history at the University of Chicago Laboratory School.* Generally acknowledged as the chief figure in progressive education, Dewey described Parker as the "Father of Progressive Education."

Progressive education was an effort by educators to respond to the growth of cities, industrialization, and the massive immigration flowing into the country. Philosophers like Dewey proposed and experimented with schooling that began with the needs and interests of children, engaged them in discovery activities, and prepared them to participate in social change.

Scholars identify several strands among progressive educators. One group followed the lead of psychologists like G. Stanley Hall* in focusing on children's needs and interests. A second, inspired by psychologists such as Edward L. Thorndike,* emphasized the utility of intelligence testing* and other purportedly scientific approaches to education. This group overlapped with one that was bringing business efficiency practices into the schools; some of these have been described as "administrative progressives" (see EDUCATIONAL ADMINISTRATION). A third group, led at various times by men like George Counts,* emphasized the importance of preparing students to be active, knowledgeable participants in social change (see SOCIAL RECONSTRUCTIONISM). During the 1930s, some groups in this last strand established links with radical organizations that sought the fundamental restructuring of American society.

The Progressive Education Association (PEA),* founded in 1921, was led, during the 1920s, by child-centered educators associated with private schools.* By the 1930s, public school educators became more involved in its activities, and schools and entire districts experimented with progressive approaches. This movement declined during World War II, and the organization disbanded in 1955, weakened by internal dissent, lack of public support, and pressure from American conservatives who linked it with radical causes.

In spite of traditionalist accusations that progressivism had taken over and destroyed education, it had a limited impact on classroom practice. Teacher education institutions, most notably Teachers College, Columbia University, disseminated progressivism, and it had, for varying periods, some influence in districts like Gary, Indiana; Winnetka, Illinois; and Pasadena, California (see GARY PLAN; WINNETKA PLAN). But most public school classrooms retained formal, traditional practices, and progressive education never became the threat imagined by conservatives nor the success claimed by its enthusiasts.

Progressive ideas and practices, nevertheless, recurred at various times and places. A neoprogressive movement flourished in the 1960s and 1970s and resulted in the establishment of alternative schools,* free schools,* and experimental colleges, some of which survive today (see SILBERMAN, CHARLES). Progressive educators in the 1980s and 1990s have been inspired by Brazilian educator Paolo Freire; Eliot Wigginton, founder of the Foxfire movement; and Myles Horton, director of Highlander Folk School; as well as by other innovators.

The challenges that led to the founding of the political progressive movement and to the creation of progressive education still exist; thus educational progressivism may well continue into the forseeable future. One advantage the current movement has over earlier ones is that much educational research now provides a sound basis for progressive experiments. Research in such areas as learning styles, multiple intelligences, and constructivist psychology supports the value of further implementation of progressive theories and methods (see CONSTRUCTIONISM).

Although no single coherent group of educational progressives now exists, reformist educators currently participate in such organizations as the Coalition of Essential Schools, the Institute for Democratic Education, the Coalition of Educational Activists, the Foxfire network, and the Rethinking Schools group. They also work within the teacher unions, the National Education Association* and the American Federation of Teachers* to promote a progressive political and educational agenda through coalitions with feminists, minorities, civil libertarians, and like-minded groups.

The progressive education movement remains significant in part because some of the recurrent controversies in education—particularly in the United States—center around it. Since its inception in the late nineteenth century, political liberals generally supported it as an instrument of social progress, whereas conservatives often attacked it as a force undermining traditional social values.

Dewey, in *Democracy and Education* (1916), formalized the philosophical framework of progressivism. Scholarly and popular interpretations of progressivism have followed political trends. From the early 1900s through the 1960s, writers like Sol Cohen, *Progressives and Urban School Reform* (1964); Lawrence A. Cremin, *The Transformation of the School* (1961); and Agnes de Lima,* *Our Enemy the Child* (1925) saw the movement as a generally promising and effective one that made positive changes in education. Beginning as early as the 1930s, conservatives, like William Randolph Hearst, attacked progressive education as an effort to radicalize students and undermine existing institutions. Traditionalists, like Mortimer Smith* and Arthur Bestor,* blamed progressive education for vocationalizing schooling and for promoting anti-intellectualism. Revisionist scholars, like Samuel Bowles and Herbert Gintis, in *Schooling in Capitalist America* (1976), have, since the 1960s, interpreted progressive education as part of a broader corporate liberalism that failed to implement radical reforms in society and the schools. Other historians, like Larry Cuban, *How Teachers Taught* (1993), and Arthur Zilversmit, *Changing Schools* (1993), have provided substantial evidence that progressivism did not represent a threat to the established order simply because it did not have widespread influence in the schools. Recently, some scholars have emphasized the continuities between the earlier progressive education movement and current reform efforts. See, for example, Kathe Jervis and Carol Montag, eds., *Progressive Education for the 1990s* (1991); Patrick Shannon, *The Struggle to Continue: Progressive Reading Instruction in the United States* (1990); and Kathe Jervis and Arthur Tobier, eds., *Education for Democracy* (1988). Various scholarly perspectives on progressivism, in addition to those noted above, have been provided during the past three decades by C. A. Bowers, *The Progressive Educator and the Depression: The Radical Years* (1969); Patricia A. Graham, *Progressive Education: From Arcady to Academe* (1967); William J. Reese, *Power and the Promise of School Reform: Grassroots Movements during the Progressive Era* (1986); David B. Tyack, *The One Best System: A History of American Urban Education* (1974); and James M. Wallace, *Liberal Journalism and American Education, 1914–1941* (1991).

James M. Wallace

PROGRESSIVE EDUCATION ASSOCIATION (PEA). Founded in 1919 as the Association for the Advancement of Progressive Education, this organization adopted the PEA name from 1931 until 1947, when it became the American Education Fellowship (AEF). The AEF returned to its previous PEA title in 1953 and maintained this name until its dissolution two years later. Stanwood Cobb, joined by Marietta Johnson of the Fairhope School and others affiliated with the Lincoln School of Teachers College, the Washington Montessori School, and the Park School of Baltimore, organized the first meeting in Washington, D.C. The Association published *Progressive Education*, a quarterly journal, from 1924 to 1957. From 1934 to 1943, the PEA also sponsored *The Social Frontier*, retitled *Frontiers of Democracy* in 1939. The John Dewey Society supported the PEA during its last two years.

A group of headmasters, primarily from small private schools* serving-upper- and upper-middle-class clienteles, guided the Association during its first ten years and emphasized elementary education. Harvard's retired president, Charles W. Eliot,* and not John Dewey,* as is commonly believed, served as PEA's first honorary president. "Freedom" and "creative opportunity" served as conference topics and guided discussions, and the project method* and the child-centered school represented common membership interests. In order to provide focus and build membership, in 1920 the Association adopted the Seven Principles of Progressive Education (see PROGRESSIVE EDUCATION). Between 1924 and 1929, these seven principles appeared in each issue of *Progressive Education*, and included phrases such as "freedom to develop naturally"; "interest, the motive of all work"; "the teacher as guide, not as task-master"; "scientific study of pupil development"; "greater attention to all that affects the child's physical development"; "cooperation between school and home to meet the needs of child-life"; and "the progressive school as leader in educational movements."

In the late 1920s, the Assocation directed its attention to the public schools.* Public school administrators and professors of education, many of whom were affiliated with Teachers College, supplanted the leadership provided by private school headmasters, thus shifting the focus from pedagogy to political and social issues. This striking contrast in PEA ideology, from its first to its second decade, was reflected in the titles of conference speeches—from honorary president John Dewey's scholarly 1928 talk, "Progressive Education and the Science of Education," to George Counts's* dramatic 1932 polemic, "Dare Progressive Education Be Progressive?" This change in focus caused the Association to grow. From 1924 to 1930, PEA membership increased over fourfold, to 7,600 members, and by the late 1930s membership grew to 10,000.

During this period, the PEA initiated three commissions whose work redefined the nature of scholarship in American education. The Commission on the Relation of School and College (Wilford Aikin, chair; 1930–1942) became known as the Thirty-School Study or the Eight-Year Study.* Its five-volume report described the curricular experimentation of thirty diverse schools in the United States and concluded that college-bound students from these progressive schools did as well in a college structured-setting as their counterparts who attended conventional college preparatory secondary schools. The Commission on the Secondary School Curriculum (V. T. Thayer, chair; 1933–1940) grew out of the Thirty-School Study and released a series of publications that displayed ways in which curriculum could attend to the ideals of democracy and needs of students. Finally, the Commission on Human Relations (Alice V. Keliher, chair; 1935–1942, the "Hanover Group") released a six-volume report that attended to the development of teaching materials oriented toward the psychological needs of youth. Unfortunately, a variety of cultural factors deterred the impact of these commissions.

The post–World War II years of PEA represented a continuation of internal strife. Leaders of progressive education were not as active in the PEA. The name change to AEF sought to strengthen its international dimension and to expand its general aim and purpose. Yet tension between those supporting radical social change and those involved in practical school reform caused further dissipation of the organization's ideological focus.

The cause of the PEA's demise will always be a disputed topic. Membership declined to an estimated 600 individuals by the mid-1950s. Post–World War II cultural forces of political conservatism, anti-intellectualism, and narrowly conceived vocationalism (see VOCATIONAL EDUCATION) all served to combat the ideals of the PEA/AEF, while the then-current educational trends of standardization and centralization lessened the perceived importance of progressive school reform.

No PEA archives exist. Leading secondary sources include Lawrence A. Cremin, *The Transformation of the School* (1964); Patricia A. Graham, *Progressive Education: From Arcady to Academe* (1967); and Harold O. Rugg, *Foundations for American Education* (1947).

Craig Kridel

PROJECT METHOD represents an enterprise in which children solve a practical problem over a period of several days or weeks. It may involve building a rocket, designing a playground, or publishing a class newspaper. The projects may be suggested by the teacher, but as far as possible they should be planned and executed by the students themselves, either individually or in groups. The goal of the project work focuses less on imparting specific knowledge or skills, and more on motivation and attitude in order to foster self-confidence, judgment, and responsibility.

According to traditional historiography, the project idea first developed in American agricultural education, during the late nineteenth and early twentieth centuries. William Heard Kilpatrick* popularized it in his famous article "The Project Method" (1918). More recent historiography traces the concept of learning through projects to the teaching of architecture in sixteenth-century Italy; this 400-year history includes five phases: In phase 1, 1590–1765, advanced students executed a "project," for example, designing a monument, palace, or church, once a year at the academies of architecture in Rome and Paris. In phase 2, 1765–1880, newly established schools of engineering adopted the project idea, and the Massachusetts Institute of Technology introduced it into the United States. In phase 3, 1880–1915, Calvin M. Woodward* adapted the project concept to the school; students actually produced the projects they designed in the workshops at his Manual Training School. In phase 4, 1915–1965, the project idea spread from manual training to academic subjects, when Kilpatrick defined it broadly as "hearty purposeful activity." Boyd H. Bode and John Dewey,* leading American progressive educators (see PROGRESSIVE EDUCATION), criticized Kilpatrick's concept, yet it received general approval in England, India, and the Soviet Union. Since the mid-1960s, phase 5, Germany, Netherlands, and other European countries have rediscovered Kilpatrick's project method. Under the influence of British primary school education, some U.S. educators have attempted to redefine the project, seeing it as an alternative to the traditional teacher-centered curriculum.

For the traditional view of the project method, see Herbert M. Kliebard, *The Struggle for the American Curriculum, 1893–1958* (1995); for its early history, refer to Richard Chafee, "The Teaching of Architecture at the Ecole des Beaux-Arts" (1977), and John H. Weiss, *The Making of Technological Man* (1982). The reintroduction of the project method in the United States is treated by Lillian G. Katz and Sylvia C. Chard, *Engaging Children's Minds: The Project Approach* (1989). Michael Knoll presents an overview of the most recent research in "The Project Method: Its Origin and International Dissemination" (1995). An indispensible tool is Ulrich Schafer's *International Bibliography of the Project Method in Education, 1895–1982* (1988).

Michael Knoll

PROSSER, CHARLES ALLEN (September 20, 1871–November 26, 1952), represented an important figure in the vocational education* movement and was particularly known for his links to the passage of the 1917 Smith-Hughes Act* and his association with life adjustment education* during the 1940s. He received B.A. (1897) and M.A. (1906) degrees from DePauw University, the LL.B. (1898) from the University of Louisville, and a Ph.D. (1915) from Teachers College, Columbia University. He served as a teacher, principal, and superintendent in Indiana for fifteen years, became Massachusetts's assistant commissioner of education in 1910; he acted as executive secretary of the National Society for the Promotion of Industrial Education* in 1912. From 1915 to 1945, the rest of his professional life, he served as director of the William H. Dunwoody Institute in Minneapolis, interrupted only by the period when he acted as the first executive director of the Federal Board for Vocational Education (1917–1919).

Beginning in 1903, Prosser, like David S. Snedden,* criticized the high school* curriculum for its traditional emphasis on scholarship and college preparation, and in 1911 he began campaigning for federal funds to provide social and economic opportunities for practically inclined children through the creation of specific vocational schools and programs. In the 1945 "Prosser Resolution," he accused secondary schools of failing to prepare the great majority of children to take their place in adult society. These "sixty percent of youth"—served neither by vocational study nor by college preparatory courses—desperately needed "life adjustment education"; that is, they needed practical training that included personality, etiquette, health, home, and family living.

Prosser wrote numerous articles. His most important books are Charles A. Prosser, *Secondary Education and Life* (1939); Charles A. Prosser and Charles A. Allen, *Vocational Education in a Democracy* (1925); Charles A. Prosser and Charles A. Allen, *Have We Kept the Faith?* (1929); and Charles A. Prosser, Layton S. Hawkins, and John C. Wright, *Development of Vocational Education* (1951). Also refer to John Gadell's biography, "Charles Allen Prosser: His Work in Vocational and General Education" (1972). Critical interpretations of Prosser's work appear in Herbert M. Kliebard, *The Struggle for the American Curriculum, 1893–1958* (1986), and Arthur G. Wirth, *Education in the Technological Society: The Vocational-Liberal Studies Controversy in the Early Twentieth Century* (1972); Katy L. B. Greenwood, "A Philosophical Rationale for Vocational Education: Contributions of Charles A. Prosser and His Contempories, 1900–1917" (1978), provides a more sympathetic analysis.

Michael Knoll

PUBLIC SCHOOLS. See COMMON SCHOOLS.

PUTNAM, ALICE HARVEY WHITING (January 18, 1841–January 19, 1919). Kindergarten* advocate and trainer, Alice Harvey Whiting Putnam was one of the moving figures behind the establishment of public kindergartens in Chicago. Daughter of the founder of the Chicago Board of Trade, she was devoted to civic improvement and to children's education. Putnam became interested in the kindergarten when her own children were young, and in 1874, responding to a public call from Elizabeth Peabody,* began a parents class to discuss Friedrich Froebel's* ideas. In 1880, she helped form the Chicago Free Kindergarten Association and the Chicago Froebel Association, which sponsored a kindergarten training school that she directed until 1910. Putnam herself trained with noted kindergartners Susan Blow,* in St. Louis, and Maria Kraus-Boelte, in New York City, and with the progressive (see PROGRESSIVE ED-UCATION) educator Colonel Francis W. Parker,* whom she was instrumental in bringing to head the Cook County Normal School. Putnam taught kindergarten training classes at Cook County Normal School, at Hull-House, and at the University of Chicago; and she worked with Jane Addams,* John Dewey,* and Chicago's other progressive reformers. In 1883, she founded the Chicago Kindergarten Club with kindergarten leader Elizabeth Harrison and was active in the International Kindergarten Union.* Putnam trained many kindergarten teachers who became influential, including Anna Bryan,* who pioneered curriculum reforms in free kindergartens in Louisville, and Annie Howe, who brought kindergartens to Japan. Some of the free kindergartens sponsored by the Chicago Free Kindergarten Association were located in public schools, and in 1892 the Chicago Board of Education incorporated them into the city system. A model of maternalist educational and civic activities, Putnam was known for her child-centered approach to kindergartening; her pragmatic, nondogmatic ideas were important in leavening the rigidity of Froebelianism and in adapting kindergarten pedagogy to American schools and culture.

Many of Putnam's writings appeared in *Kindergarten Review* (vols. 8, 9, 12, 14, 16) and the National Education Association's* *Journal of Proceedings and Addresses* (1889, 1893, 1901, 1902, 1908). Biographies can be found in International Kindergarten Union, *Pioneers of the Kindergarten in America* (1924); *Kindergarten Magazine* (1893); and Edward T. James, ed., *Notable American Women, 1607–1950* (1971). See also Barbara Beatty, *Preschool Education in America: The Culture of Young Children from the Colonial Era to the Present* (1995) and Michael Steven Shapiro, *Child's Garden: The Kindergarten Movement from Froebel to Dewey* (1983).

Barbara Beatty

R

READING INSTRUCTION has been historically divorced from, and preceded, writing instruction. The alphabet method (spelling and prounouncing syllables aloud, "A B ab, E B eb") was the only method known in both Britain and America until the 1820s. It was the methodology presupposed by spelling books. The alphabet method assumed that learning proceeded from part to whole, from the unit of the letter to that of the syllable, the word, and the sentence. Words for spelling and reading were organized in lists of increasing syllabic length. It was thought that children, naturally sinful, had to be drilled in learning. English and American women introduced children to reading in dame schools.*

Shifts in the view of the child led to new approaches to instruction. In the 1820s, American educational reformers adopted the views of Johann Heinrich Pestalozzi,* who held that learning proceeded from the whole to the part, from concrete to abstract, and that children should understand what they read. These reformers attacked spelling books for their meaningless columns of words. Their proposed solutions included a whole word approach (learning words as units, at sight, without regard to the relationship of letters to phonemes), what would later be called "systematic phonics" (treating letters as sounds and blending the isolated sounds into a whole word), and a sentence approach (learning to memorize entire sentences before dividing them into their component words and sounds). By 1910, teacher trainers advocated a "judicious blending" of the alphabet, word, phonic, and sentence methods.

Although reading series increasingly included hints for teachers, one of the earliest being Samuel Worcester's *Primer* (1826), the first books published separately as teacher manuals date from Rebecca Pollard's *Synthetic Method* (1889), an accompaniment to her reading series, and Sarah Louise Arnold's *Reading, How to Teach It* (1899). Over the course of the twentieth century, the length of teacher manuals increased even while teachers received ever more training.

Broader educational movements often influenced reading instruction. The progressive education* movement, dating from 1870, fostered the use of the word method as it sought to avoid the drill associated with phonic instruction. The movement toward teaching "good literature," a feature of the 1910s, also favored the word method, as it freed authors of basal readers from vocabulary restrictions based on phonic principles. When silent reading replaced oral reading as the standard classroom procedure during the first quarter of the twentieth century, it increased opportunities for teachers to assign "seat work." The scientific movement of the 1930s emphasized sequential skills in teaching reading.

Parental dissatisfaction with the readers that embodied the methods used between the 1930s and 1950s (see BASAL READERS) found a spokesperson in 1955. Rudolf Flesch, in *Why Johnny Can't Read*, attacked the reading profession for teaching children by the "whole word" method and "analytic phonics" rather than by synthetic phonics. Both he and Jeanne Chall, in her *Learning to Read: The Great Debate* (1967), charged the reading profession with ignoring the results of its own research. Defenders of the status quo responded that synthetic phonics produced "word callers," children who could pronounce words without understanding them. As the beleaguered reading profession closed ranks and merged two organizations to found the International Reading Association* in 1956, teaching letters as "isolated sounds" became taboo in many teacher-training institutions. It took many years for the prohibition to be relaxed.

A concurrent revival of behaviorism* in the 1960s led to the creation of systems that presupposed reading acquisition to be the mastery of a conglomeration of discrete skills, in which the teacher's role was reduced to that of a systems manager. The skills to be taught were, in the 1940s and 1950s, described as word attack, comprehension, vocabulary, and study skills.

When Noam Chomsky reintroduced mentalism to language and cognitive psychology began to supplant behaviorism in the 1960s, reading researchers proposed new theoretical models for the reading process, now envisioned as a complex interactional whole. The focus moved from the presumed defects of the child and the difficulty of the text to the gaps in the child's own experiential background. Teachers were encouraged to help students use story grammars and schemata and to identify textual cohesion. An interest in teaching comprehension, already present in the preceding century, increased. The gulf between research and classroom practice remained wide, however.

Dating from the early 1970s but achieving broad popularity in the 1990s, a "whole language" movement, associated with the writings of Frank Smith, Kenneth Goodman, and Donald Graves, aroused teacher interest (see INTEGRATED CURRICULUM). The movement attacked basal readers. For almost the first time, pedagogy stressed the importance of children's writing as well as reading and advocated teaching children to read from their own compositions, using invented spelling, and children's books. The movement had much in common with the progressive movement, though the methodology was reminiscent of the "sentence" method. Learning to read was viewed as just as natural as learning to speak. Children were said not to make oral reading errors but "miscues," which could be used to identify their misconceptions about print.

Phonics continued to be a flashpoint of controversy among reading teachers, researchers, and parents. Researchers such as Marilyn Jager Adams, in *Beginning to Read: Thinking and Learning about Print* (1995), pointed to the demonstrated importance of phonemic segmentation in reading acquisition. Some dissatisfied parents promoted the teaching of systematic, explicit phonics in the public schools by persuading their state legislatures (e.g., Ohio, Alabama, and California) to mandate it. The current consensus is "balanced reading instruction."

Public School Methods (1908) serves as a primary source on reading instruction trends. For secondary historical sources on reading instruction, refer to Miriam Balmuth, *The Roots of Phonics: A Historical Introduction* (1982); Richard L. Bvenezky, "A History of the American Reading Textbook" (1987); Jeanne S. Chall, *Learning to Read: The Great Debate* (1967); Rudolph Flesch, *Why Johnny Can't Read and What You Can Do about It* (1955); Kenneth S. Goodman, "Reading: A Psycholinguistic Guessing Game" (1976); William S. Gray, *On Their Own in Reading: How to Give Children Independence in Attacking New Words* (1948); E. Jennifer Monaghan and E. Wendy Saul, "The Reader, the Scribe, the Thinker: A Critical Look at the History of American Reading and Writing Instruction" (1987); H. Alan Robinson, Vincent Faraone, Daniel R. Hittleman, and Elizabeth Unruh, *Reading Comprehension Instruction, 1783–1987: A Review of Trends and Research* (1990); Frank Smith, *Understanding Reading* (1971); and Nila B. Smith, *American Reading Instruction* (1986).

E. Jennifer Monaghan

RECITATION as a teaching and learning practice refers to the public display of reading ability, speech-making, and rote reproduction of facts. As old as literacy and the written word itself, the recitation constituted a major educational means to link the oral and written word. With the institutionalization and universalization of group learning settings over the course of the nineteenth century, individual and simultaneous recitations became standard forms of daily classroom practice, so standard that district school* classrooms were named "recitation rooms." As fearsome for students as they were delightful for parents, recitations constituted an important form of educational communication.

Toward the end of the nineteenth century, educators formulated more systematic and elaborated pedagogical theories that brought the recitation method under close scrutiny. Emerson White, in *Elements of Pedagogy* (1886), treated the term "recitation" as a systematic part of instructional activities, distinguishing it from the lesson, "an exercise combining both instruction and drill . . . in which the test is the chief element." By the turn of the century, Charles and Frank McMurry, in *The Method of Recitation* (1897), treated it as part of lesson presentation by the teacher. Influenced by the teachings of Johann Friedrich

Herbart (see HERBARTARIAN MOVEMENT), the McMurrays suggested that the teaching of subject matter, rather than the cultivation of recitation, should form the guiding purpose of the method of teaching. The Herbartarian five-step taxonomy—preparation, presentation, comparison, generalization, and application—broadened the concept of recitation to include teacher-organized practice rather than public displays by students. In general, the Herbartarians rejected recitation as a learning exercise, a controversial position that produced strong criticism. For example, W. Charters, in *Methods of Teaching* (1912), asserted a need for "memorization and drill." During most of the twentieth century, the recitation method, as learning and teaching practice, became synonymous with a mechanical approach to education as opposed to a more critical, dynamic, and creative approach that became the theme of continuous educational reform efforts.

Refer to Barbara Finkelstein, *Governing the Young: Teacher Behavior in Popular Primary Schools in Nineteenth-Century United States* (1989), and Walter S. Monroe, *Teaching-Learning Theory and Teacher Education, 1890 to 1950* (1952).

Hariklia Efthimiou

REEL, ESTELLE (November 26, 1862–August 2, 1959), became the first woman to be elected to a state office, as superintendent of public instruction in Wyoming in 1894, and appointed as U.S. superintendent of Indian schools (1898–1910). Born in Pittsfield, Illinois, Reel began her teaching career in Cheyenne, Wyoming, where her brother was mayor in the early 1880s. She was elected as Laramie County superintendent of schools between 1886 and 1888, before becoming the Wyoming state superintendent of public instruction. As state superintendent, she also served as registrar of the Land Board and secretary of charities and reforms, which included oversight of the state's penitentiaries and insane asylums. As registrar, she introduced many innovations, some of which resulted in increased revenues for the schools. Her work in prison reform earned her a medal for outstanding service by the Prison Congress in New York City. Her appointment as U.S. superintendent of Indian schools, the highest political office held by a woman to that time, was directed by Republican politicians and a coalition of women's clubs and national educational leaders who championed the distinction for a woman from one of only four states that had granted women suffrage.

Reel attributed her interest in the Indian Service to missionary relatives, though she was quick to point out that she had no ambitions toward evangelism. Activities during Reel's term as U.S. superintendent corresponded to her highly practical style and prejudices. Deeming the American Indian incapable of more than manual training, she refocused the Indian Service's pedagogical and curricular reform efforts. She sought to upgrade the training and respect received by Indian school teachers and administrators through the development of summer institutes and the Department of Indian Education within the National Ed-

REFORM SCHOOLS

ucation Association.* Despite a strong lobby on her behalf, Congress discontinued funding for her office, preferring to divide the tasks among six district supervisors. She left office in 1910.

Her reports as the superintendent of Indian schools are included in the *Annual Reports of the Commissioner of Indian Affairs*. Reports of the Department of Indian Education are included in annual volumes of the *Journal of the Proceedings and Addresses of the National Education Association* from 1900 to 1908. A volume of copies of correspondence concerning Reel and relating to possible violations of civil service regulations (1902) is available among the Records of the Office of the Commissioner of Indian Affairs in the National Archives; see *Guide to Records in the National Archives of the United States Relating to American Indians*. The Museum of Native American Culture in Spokane, Washington, holds her papers. Materials related to her position as Wyoming state superintendent of public instruction are available at the Wyoming State Archives and Historical Department in Cheyenne. For biographies and biographical material, see Maurine Carley, ''Estelle Reel Meyer,'' *Let Your Light Shine: Pioneer Women Educators of Wyoming* (1965); Isabel Gordon Curtis, ''The Housekeeper at Large: The People and the Problems She Meets'' (1910); and Francis Paul Prucha, *The Great Father: The United States Government and the American Indians* (1984).

Patricia Anne Carter

REFORM SCHOOLS operated on the fundamental concept of a ''reformation'' of the character of youthful offenders. The New York House of Refuge,* founded in 1825, became the first reform school, quickly followed by two similar institutions, the Boston House of Reformation* and the Philadelphia House of Refuge,* both opened in 1826. They received state charters but depended on private funds. The principal idea behind these early schools was that if youthful offenders were incarcerated early, offered a basic education, and taught a trade, they could become responsible adult citizens. These institutions followed a combined regimen of kindness and continuous activity, including morning prayers, schooling, and work. Inmates worked for outside contractors, who were supposed to teach the inmates skills, while agents of the institution maintained discipline; constant disputes occurred over whether contractors actually taught the skills or merely exploited inmate labor. Reformed boys and girls under the age of majority (twenty-one for boys; eighteen for girls) were indentured. Some of the boys became sailors, and others were apprenticed* to farmers; most girls became household servants.

As early houses of refuge dealt primarily with convicted youth, some reformers worked to create institutions that would catch children and youth at a predelinquent stage. This was the intent of the founders of the Boston Asylum and Farm School created in 1832. The farm school was for vagrant or homeless boys and taught farming skills and basic education. The New York Juvenile Asylum, a similar institution, opened in 1853.

Massachusetts established the first state-supported reform school at Westborough in 1847. Eight years later Massachusetts created the first state reform school based on a family or cottage plan, the State Reform School for Girls at Lancaster. Ohio followed in 1857, opening its state-run reform school for boys organized on the family system. Inmates in these institutions were organized into small groupings or families. In Ohio, families numbered forty boys.

Indeterminate sentence, that is, the notion that well-behaved inmates left early, represented another nineteenth-century innovation. The New York State Reformatory at Elmira pioneered this feature in 1876. Virtually all states established some sort of reform school during the nineteenth century, although internal structure, methods of discipline, and the use of indentures varied.

In the twentieth century, comprehensive reform schools of the type founded throughout nineteenth-century America fell out of favor. The institutions remained and became, for all practical purposes, juvenile prisons. A few states such as Massachusetts closed their juvenile reform schools and relied on other programs such as probation for juvenile correction. By the late twentieth century, juvenile corrections in most states had become a statewide system of varying levels of supervision and punishment for youthful offenders. These systems were large bureaucratic agencies; reformers' zeal and idealism had long since vanished from the field of juvenile corrections.

Refer to Barbara M. Brenzel, *Daughters of the State: A Social Portrait of the First Reform School for Girls in North America* (1983); Joseph M. Hawes, *Children in Urban Society: Juvenile Delinquency in Nineteenth-Century Society* (1971); Joseph M. Hawes, *The Children's Rights Movement: A History of Advocacy and Reform* (1991); Michael B. Katz, *The Irony of Early School Reform: Educational Innovation in Mid-Nineteenth-Century Massachusetts* (1968); Robert M. Mennel, *Thorns and Thistles: Juvenile Delinquents in the United States, 1825–1940* (1973); Robert S. Pickett, *House of Refuge: Origins of Juvenile Reform in New York State, 1815–1857* (1969); David J. Rothman, *The Discovery of the Asylum: Social Order and Disorder in the New Republic* (1971); and Steven L. Schlossman, *Love and the American Delinquent: The Theory and Practice of "Progressive" Juvenile Justice, 1825–1920* (1977).

Joseph M. Hawes

REHABILITATION ACT OF 1973. See SPECIAL EDUCATION.

RELIGIOUS INSTRUCTION. See BIBLE READING; BOARDING SCHOOLS; ISLAMIC SCHOOLS; PAROCHIAL SCHOOLS; PRIVATE SCHOOLS; SUNDAY SCHOOLS.

REPORT OF THE COMMISSION ON THE REFORM OF SECONDARY EDUCATION. See CARDINAL PRINCIPLES OF SECONDARY EDUCATION.

RICE, JOSEPH MAYER (May 20, 1857–June 24, 1934), is best known for a series of nine articles published between 1892 and 1893 in the *Forum*, where he reported on the deplorable conditions, inept administration, and tedious teaching practices of schools. These articles established Rice's reputation as a writer who brought the topic of schooling to the public's attention and, in so doing, introduced "muckraking" to the field of education.

Although born in Philadelphia, Rice attended City College of New York City and, in 1881, received a degree in medicine from the College of Physicians and Surgeons, Columbia University. In 1888, he abandoned his New York City medical practice and journeyed to Germany, where for the next two years he studied psychology and pedagogy, and traveled throughout Europe to observe school systems and pedagogical practices. Rice visited the first laboratory of experimental psychology, directed by William Wundt, and was introduced to Herbartarianism as it was taught at the University of Jena and its laboratory school (see HERBARTARIAN MOVEMENT). Rice returned to the United States with strong beliefs for the improvement of elementary education.

In 1891, he first presented his views in an article for the *Forum*, a New York monthly magazine owned by Rice's brother, Isaac Leopold Rice. Joseph Mayer Rice's critique was clear: The scientific management of education would occur with better training of teachers and with a curriculum based upon sound psychological principles. Rice conducted a school study tour for the magazine, beginning in January 1892. During the next six months, he traveled to thirty-six cities, visiting six to eight schools in each city. He focused on the juxtaposition of traditional schools and their narrow curricula and recitation with that of the "new pedagogy," that is, progressive education,* of modern schools and their integrated approach to curriculum and instruction (see INTEGRATED CURRICULUM). The *Forum* exposé created an electrifying reaction among the American public, who had previously linked good education with national progress. Rice's articles reported actual dialogue and exchanges of the most tedious, pedantic teaching imaginable; he described the deplorable conditions of the schools and the thoughtlessness and ineptness of educational practices. As the general public became outraged at educators with each succeeding *Forum* essay, professional educators' reaction to and criticism of Rice grew sharper, if not hysterical.

Rice began another *Forum*-sponsored tour of classrooms in 1895. This time he conducted a sixteen-month survey of nearly 33,000 students—what is often considered the first comparative test ever used in American education. One aspect of the test results involved spelling pedagogy, deemed by Rice as the "futility of the spelling grind," whereby he concluded that there was no correlation between the amount of spelling drill and success in the actual act of spelling (see SPELLING BEES). This comparative test was widely applauded, and though the results were not universally supported, Rice received acknowledgment for initiating the modern movement for objective study of education. Two years later he became the *Forum*'s editor, serving in that role until 1908. Rice retired to private life in Philadelphia in 1915, devoting the remainder of his life to writing.

Rice's unpublished manuscripts are located at Special Collections, Milbank Memorial Library, Teachers College, Columbia University. General descriptions of Rice's *Forum* articles can be found in Lawrence A. Cremin, *The Transformation of the School* (1964), and Herbert M. Kliebard, *The Struggle for the American Curriculum, 1893–1958* (1986).

Craig Kridel

RICKOVER, HYMAN GEORGE (January 27, 1900–July 8, 1986), often characterized for his outspoken nature and unconventional methods, sharply criticized the American educational system. Born in Russia, he immigrated to the United States, trained as an engineer at the U.S. Naval Academy (1922), and gained fame as an officer in the U.S. Navy for over sixty years. He attained the rank of admiral and is credited with founding America's nuclear navy.

In *Education and Freedom* (1959), *Swiss Schools and Ours: Why Theirs Are Better* (1962), and *American Education: A National Failure* (1963), Rickover argued that American education was falling behind that of Europe and the Soviet Union. This criticism was based on his belief that the school curriculum should be narrowed, focused on math and the hard sciences, and expectations of students increased. As a result, after his retirement from the U.S. Navy in 1982, he founded the Center for Excellence in Education. Dedicated to the improvement of American education, the Center continues to promote competitiveness in science and technology and focuses on America's finest students and teachers and their improved training. The foundation supports the integration of science, technology, and math. Through its Role Models and Leaders Project, the Center attempts to address the underrepresentation of minorities in science, technology, and business. This project currently operates in Washington, D.C., Los Angeles, and Chicago. Finally, the Research Science Institute, a part of the Center, sponsors a six-week summer research internship for America's most talented students in science and math.

Rickover's papers are scattered, with some at the Naval Academy, the Naval War College, and the Army War College. The leading biography is by Norman Polmar and Thomas Allen, *Rickover* (1982).

Charles E. Jenks

ROBERTS V. CITY OF BOSTON, 5 Cush. 198 (1849), represented the American judicial precedent involving separate but equal on the basis of race in public education, and was referred to in *Plessy v. Ferguson,** the U.S Supreme Court's decision upholding segregation in public transportation.

Benjamin F. Roberts, acting on behalf of his five-year-old daughter, Sara, challenged the authority of Boston's General School Committee to enact a resolution calling for the education of African American children in schools segregated on the basis of race. Roberts based his suit on an 1845 statute that provided that any child unlawfully excluded from public school in Massachusetts was entitled to damages. The legal issue was whether Sara Roberts was unlawfully excluded from public instruction by being denied admission to the school nearest her home because it was for whites.

The Supreme Judicial Court of Massachusetts upheld the law. It reasoned that insofar as the statute did not mention any restrictions based on race, mandating only that a child attend school, she could be required to enroll in a school for African American children because it was, in all other respects, equal. The court held that since the School Committee had the power to exercise reasonable control over the schools, it had the authority to develop a system under which children of different races could be compelled to attend separate schools. The court concluded by providing a basis for *Plessy* when it noted that while separate schools may foster prejudice, it is a condition that is neither created, nor can be remedied, by the law.

Charles J. Russo

RODMAN (DE FREMERY), HENRIETTA (1878–March 21, 1923). Feminist reformer, high school English teacher, and lifelong activist for teacher rights, she achieved national attention for her leadership in the campaign for maternity leave for teachers. As a result of her work, New York became the fourth big city school system to grant maternity leaves. A founding member of the New York City Feminist Alliance, president of the League for Civic Service for Women, and member of the Greenwich Village feminist community during the 1910s, Rodman participated in other campaigns, including birth control education, the election of socialist-feminist political candidates, pacifism during World War I, and the building of a feminist apartment house inspired by the writings of philosopher-economist Charlotte Perkins Gilman. In the schools, she helped develop a home economics curriculum, worked for the institutionalization of the Montessori* method, and campaigned vigorously for non-gender-biased schooling. Her suspension during the maternity leave campaign in 1914 inspired her commitment to building a teachers' union, serving on the executive committee and as vice-president. Before her death, Rodman focused on defeating the Lusk bill, which required teacher loyalty oaths. Her career was defined by antipathy to what she perceived as state repression of teachers.

Some information is provided on her in Dolores Hayden, *The Grand Domestic Revolution: A History of Feminist Designs for American Homes, Neighborhoods, and Cities* (1981), and June Sochen, *Movers and Shakers: American Women Thinkers and Activitists, 1900–1970* (1973).

Patricia Anne Carter

ROSENWALD, JULIUS (August 12, 1862–January 6, 1932), descended from a family of clothing merchants, became president of Sears, Roebuck and Company in 1909. In 1917, he established the Julius Rosenwald Fund, a broad-based philanthropic organization dedicated to the "well-being of mankind." The Fund became incorporated in 1928, and Edwin R. Embree was named president and served until its demise in 1948. The Fund concentrated its activities in four areas: education, health, race relations, and individual support of creative endeavors. Influenced by Booker T. Washington's* autobiography *Up from Slavery*, Rosenwald directed a substantial portion of the Fund's assets toward the improvement of southern economic conditions by providing educational opportunities for African Americans. The most notable initiative was the rural school-building program that coordinated the construction of 5,357 public schools, shops, and teachers' houses for African Americans throughout fifteen southern states before it ended in 1932. Other educational ventures included the provision of libraries for African American and white schools and colleges; the institution of a county library demonstration program and branch libraries in schools, churches, and stores; the support of teacher-training colleges; and a fellowship program for graduate and professional training for southern African Americans and whites. Consistent with Washington's philosophy of self-help, the Rosenwald Fund stipulated that recipients provide "matching" funds in some amount. Another unique feature of the Fund was its founder's insistence that capital as well as interest be expended, thereby limiting its influence.

Rosenwald's papers are housed at the University of Chicago Archives; the Fund's papers can be found in Special Collections, Fisk University. Rosenwald's own views on philanthropy can be found in two of his articles: "Principles of Public Giving" (1929) and "The Trend Away from Perpetuities" (1930). Also, see biographies by Edwin R. Embree and Julia Waxman, *Investment in People: The Story of the Julius Rosenwald Fund* (1949), and Morris Robert Werner, *Julius Rosenwald: The Life of a Practical Humanitarian* (1939).

Jayne R. Beilke

ROUND HILL SCHOOL. See BANCROFT, GEORGE.

RUFFNER, HENRY (January 16, 1790–December 17, 1861), an ordained Presbyterian minister, an educator, and a Virginian, was a strong advocate of public education and an outspoken proponent of emancipation.

Ruffner graduated from Washington College (now Washington and Lee University) in 1813. He studied theology, traveled, and taught at an academy before he was licensed to preach and appointed to a professorship at his alma mater in 1819. He was pastor of the Timber Ridge Church during much of the period he served as a college professor. Ruffner was elected president of Washington College in 1836, and he served in that capacity until poor health compelled him to resign in 1848. He then moved to the Kanawha Mountains in what is now West Virginia; there, he continued to preach and write, as his health permitted, until his death.

At an educational convention held in Clarksburg (now West Virginia) in 1841, Ruffner submitted a plan for the organization of a complete system of public education. A second convention held in Lexington in 1842 recommended the adoption of Ruffner's plan by the state legislature. Although heralded as "the most valuable document on general education issued in Virginia since the early days of Thomas Jefferson,"* Ruffner's pleas on behalf of public education in this and other writings and speeches failed to sway state lawmakers. His anti-slavery stance also challenged the dominant views at that time. An 1847 essay in which Ruffner proposed the gradual abolition of slavery caused considerable debate in the state and contributed to the eventual separation of the two Virginias during the Civil War.

Ruffner's son, William Henry,* wrote the 1869 law that established Virginia's public school* system and served as that state's first superintendent of public instruction.

Refer to Henry Ruffner's "Plan for Schools in Virginia," in *Report of the United States Commissioner of Education, 1899–1900*, vol. 1, pp. 381–397. For secondary sources, see Charles H. Ambler, *History of Education in West Virginia* (1951); Charles H. Ambler, *Sectionalism in Virginia from 1776–1861* (1910); Sadie Bell, *The Church, the State, and Education in Virginia* (1930); and Charles William Dabney, *Universal Education in the South* (1936).

Jennings L. Wagoner, Jr.

RUFFNER, WILLIAM HENRY (February 11, 1824–November 24, 1908), an ordained Presbyterian minister, farmer, geologist, and educator, was the author of influential public school* law and was Viginia's first superintendent of public instruction.

The son of Henry Ruffner,* William Henry graduated from Washington College (now Washington and Lee University) in 1842 and completed his M.A. there in 1845. He studied theology at Union Theological Seminary in Virginia (1845–1846) and at Princeton Theological Seminary (1846–1847). From 1849 to 1851, he served as the chaplain of the University of Virginia. An active social reformer, he denounced slavery, preached temperance, participated in the lyceum* movement, peddled religious literature, established and taught Sunday schools* for the spiritual and intellectual uplift of African Americans, served as an agent of the African Colonization Society, and was a member of the American Peace Society.

Following the Civil War, Ruffner became Virginia's first superintendent of public instruction. During his twelve-year tenure (1870–1882), he penned Virginia's school law, which became a model for other southern states; urged the coeducation* of sexes; fashioned the public school as a nonsectarian moral agent (see MORAL EDUCATION); and championed education for all races. The survival of tax-supported education remained tenuous in a state with strong individualistic beliefs. When a national civil rights bill (see CIVIL RIGHTS ACTS) mandating racial integration in education was being considered in 1874–1875, Ruffner, along with other educational reformers like Barnas Sears, lobbied against its passage. Ruffner, believing that racial integration would politically kill Virginia's public schools, implemented a dual system for African Americans and European Americans. During the tumultuous era of Reconstruction and Restoration, he established a school system that not only survived but markedly increased the educational opportunities for both races. Following his administration as superintendent, he served as the first president of the State Female

Normal School (now Longwood College) from 1884 to 1887 (see NORMAL SCHOOLS); he also conducted numerous geological surveys.

Ruffner's papers are located at the Historical Foundation of the Presbyterian and Reformed Churches, Montreat, North Carolina. For biographical background, see Walter Fraser, Jr., "William Henry Ruffner: A Liberal in the Old and New South" (1970); Walter Fraser, Jr., "William Henry Ruffner and the Establishment of Virginia's Public School System, 1870–1874" (1971); and Thomas C. Hunt and Jennings Wagoner, Jr., "Race, Religion, and Redemption: William Henry Ruffner and the Moral Foundations of Education in Virginia" (1988).

Ben Burks

RUGG, HAROLD ORDWAY (January 17, 1886–May 17, 1960), was the most influential social studies* educator of his time and perhaps of the twentieth century. He was one of the first curriculum theorists who successfully articulated the role of education as a means toward social change.

Born in Fitchburg, Massachusetts, and educated in local public schools,* he received his B.S. in civil engineering from Dartmouth College (1908). He taught engineering at Millikin University, in Illinois, in 1909 and taught courses in drafting and general engineering at the University of Illinois from 1911 to 1915. He earned his Ph.D. in education from the University of Illinois in 1915 and then taught at the University of Chicago between 1915 and 1920. He joined John Dewey,* William H. Kilpatrick,* and other nationally known educators at Teachers College, Columbia University, in 1920, teaching there until his retirement in 1951. Between 1921 and 1936, Rugg and his Columbia associates developed social studies materials for the public schools. He and his brother, Earle, were in part responsible for the National Council for the Social Studies.* He became the single most effective social studies author of the 1920s and 1930s, and at the height of his popularity in the late 1930s, Rugg's materials were reported to be in use with over 5 million children. His social studies program was designed as the first scientifically derived curriculum in the United States, rooted in "child-centeredness." As the Great Depression worsened, however, this theory became suspect. As George Counts,* Rugg, and others articulated the need for a "new social order" through such publications as *The Social Frontier* and *Progressive Education*, Rugg's social studies evolved into a social reconstructive (see SOCIAL RECONSTRUCTIONISM) curriculum that appeared to place blame for social problems squarely on the shoulders of industrialists and Wall Street financiers. Rugg's work came under savage criticism in the late 1930s and, despite the support of teachers and parents, he was labeled a communist; consequently, his books became targeted as un- and anti-American. By 1940, several school districts banned his textbooks, and one city actually burned them. Given the enormous pressure of public opinion running against Rugg amid the wartime need for unconditional patriotism, his textbooks were abandoned and virtually disappeared from the schools by 1945. A prolific author, Rugg counted among his principal works *The Child-Centered School* (1928), *The Great Technology* (1931), and *Culture and Education in America* (1931). A complete collection of Rugg's social studies textbooks published by Ginn, as well as early publications in mimeographed form, are located at Milburn Library, Teachers College, Columbia University. Personal letters and other material related to Rugg can be found at Teachers College as well as in other library collections at Columbia and the Library of Congress. His autobiography, *That Men May Understand* (1941), is most helpful. Biographies include Peter Carbone, Jr., *The Social and Educational Thought of Harold Rugg* (1977), and Elmer A. Winters, "Harold Rugg and Educaton for Social Reconstruction" (1968).

David Warren Saxe

RUSH, BENJAMIN (December 24, 1745–April 19, 1813), infamous for the medical treatment he used during Philadelphia's 1793 yellow fever epidemic, is remembered more favorably as a signer of the Declaration of Independence and for advocating a wide range of social reforms, including abolition, temperance, care for the mentally ill, penal reform, and education. Born in Byberry Township, Pennsylvania, Rush studied at Samuel Finley's academy in Nottingham, Maryland, and then earned a degree at the College of New Jersey. At the age of fifteen, Rush apprenticed himself to Dr. John Redman of Philadelphia to train as a physician, staying with him for five and a half years. Rush completed his medical instruction with Dr. William Cullen in Edinburgh, Scotland, studying from fall 1766 to June 1768.

Rush pursued diverse educational interests. He promoted curricular reform, such as the study and teaching of chemistry, the founding of Dickinson College, and the establishment of America's first free, nonsectarian Sunday school.* Rush was most influential, however, as a supporter of women's education (see CO-EDUCATION) and common schools.*

During the Federalist period Rush strongly advocated schooling for girls and women. In "Thoughts on Female Education" (1787), he argued that schooling for women was needed to preserve republican government. Educated women would infuse the home with republican virtue, passing it along to America's future leaders, their sons. Exemplifying this vision, Rush helped to establish the Young Ladies Academy in 1787, serving as an instructor as well.

Rush actively pursued the establishment of tax-supported, free public schools. He did not live to see this vision realized, but his ideas proved influential during the antebellum period. He defended common schools by arguing that they protected individual liberty, encouraged cultural homogeneity, and taught respect for the country and its laws. He stated these ideas most clearly in *A Plan for Establishing Public Schools in Pennsylvania, and for Conducting Education Agreeably to a Republican Form of Government* (1786). In many other essays, he considered related topics such as the curriculum of common schools, the Bible as a tool of instruction, methods of discipline in common schools, and the establishment of a national university to teach future civil servants.

The bulk of Rush's papers are held for the Library Company of Philadelphia at the Historical Society of Pennsylvania. A copy of *A Plan for Establishing Public Schools*, as well as other educational essays, is contained in Rush's recently reprinted *Essays: Literary, Moral, and Philosophical* (1988). The most relevant biographies are Harry G. Good, *Benjamin Rush and His Services to American Education* (1918), and Nathan G. Goodman, *Benjamin Rush, Physician and Citizen, 1746–1813* (1934); the latter provides an excellent bibliography of Rush's published and unpublished writings.

Rodney Hessinger

S

SAN ANTONIO INDEPENDENT SCHOOL DISTRICT V. RODRIQUEZ,
411 U.S. 1 (1973), was the first and only equal protection suit on school finance examined by the U.S. Supreme Court. Parents of Mexican American children filed a class action suit on behalf of their own and other minority and poor students in Texas, alleging that the state's system of funding, based on the value of taxable property in local school districts, was unconstitutional. They claimed that the funding scheme violated the equal protection clause of the Fourteenth Amendment to the U.S. Constitution, since it resulted in disparities in per pupil expenditures based on wealth. A federal trial court in Texas ruled in favor of the parents, but a closely divided Supreme Court, in a 5 to 4 decision, reversed in favor of the state. The Court held that Texas's system neither discriminated against a definable class of poor people on the basis of wealth nor impermissibly interfered with a ''fundamental'' right or liberty. In fact, in rejecting the equal protection claim, the Court unambiguously posited that ''[e]ducation, of course, is not among the rights afforded explicit protection under our Federal Constitution. Nor do we find any basis for saying it is implicitly so protected'' (p. 35). As significant as *Rodriquez* was in eliminating the federal courts as a venue for school finance litigation, it has had little direct impact on cases filed in state courts because these actions typically are based on state constitutional provisions.

Charles J. Russo

SANCHEZ, GEORGE ISIDORE (1906–1972), is recognized as the pioneer in the struggle for equity in education for Mexican American children through laws and the courts. He began his education career as a sixteen-year-old principal-teacher at a rancheria in rural New Mexico. He graduated from the University of New Mexico in 1930 and received a General Education Board (GEB)* grant for graduate studies at the University of Texas and the University of California, Berkeley, where he earned an Ed.D. In New Mexico, during the 1930s, Sanchez received grants from the GEB, the Julius Rosenwald* Foundation, and the Carnegie Foundation; the second subsidized fieldwork for his study, *Mexico: A Revolution by Education* (1936), while the third financed a survey of Taos County, resulting in his book *Forgotten People: A Study of New Mexicans* (1940). From 1931 to 1935, he directed the New Mexico State Department of Education's Division of Information and Statistics, also funded by the GEB. As an associate with the Rosenwald Fund, Sanchez conducted fieldwork in to rural education in Mexico, from 1935 to 1936, and rural and African American education in the South the following year. Between 1937 to 1938, he worked in the Venezuelan Ministry of Education and served as the director of the Instituto Pedagogica Nacional, a normal school. He taught at the University of New Mexico for two years, accepting a professorship in Latin American studies at the University of Texas, Austin, in 1940. He served as chair of the History and Philosophy of Education Department, from 1951 to 1959, director of the Center for International Affairs, and member of the Executive Committee of the Institute of Latin American Studies.

In Texas, Sanchez continued his fight for equal educational opportunities for Mexican American children through organizations and the courts. He selected cases and lawyers, planned the strategies, and assisted in fund raising. His master's thesis, which examined the inequity of using IQ tests (see INTELLIGENCE TESTING) developed for English-speaking children for placement of Spanish-speaking children, was frequently cited in cases, and Sanchez was often called as an expert witness regarding the segregation of Mexican American children. *Delgado v. Gracy et al.* (1948), which ended in an agreed judgment, resulted in a formal policy by the Texas State Board of Education opposing the segregation of Mexican American school children; the Board cited Sanchez and Gus Garcia, an attorney, in its decision. The U.S. Supreme Court ruled favorably on *Hernandez v. Texas* (1954), a jury selection case, two weeks before *Brown v. Board of Education* (Topeka),* basing its argument on Sanchez's "class apart" theory; that is, the Court agreed that surnames or ethnicity should not result in separate treatment.

Sanchez achieved a national reputation, serving as a consultant and board member for numerous government bureaus and private organizations, such as President John F. Kennedy's Committee of Fifty on New Frontier Policy in the Americas, the Migrant Children's Fund, and the Mexican American Legal Defense and Education Fund, among others. In 1941, he was national president of the League of Latin American Citizens (LULAC). He also maintained membership in a variety of scholarly associations. He founded the American Council of Spanish-Speaking People, which helped fund many Texas court cases involving Mexican Americans through national foundation grants that Sanchez wrote and administered. He was recognized as the leader in laws affecting Mexican Americans by a retrospective honoring him by the University of California School of Law in 1984.

The Benson Latin American Collection, University of Texas, Austin, houses Sanchez's papers. Ricardo Romo, in "George I. Sanchez and the Civil Rights Movement: 1940–1960" (1986), provides a biographical glimpse. Leading secondary sources include John R. Chavez, *The Lost Land: The Chicano Image of the Southwest* (1984); David Montejano, *Anglos and Mexicans in the Making of Texas, 1836–1986* (1987); Americo Paredes, ed., *Humanidad: Essays in Honor of George I. Sanchez* (1977); Guadalupe San Miguel, Jr., *Let All of Them Take Heed: Mexican Americans and the Campaign for Educational Equality in Texas, 1910–1981* (1987); L. Glenn Smith and Joan K. Smith, *Lives in Education: A Narrative of People and Ideas* (1994); Tom Wiley, *Politics and Purse Strings in New Mexico* (1965); and Tom Wiley, *Public School Education in New Mexico* (1965).

Martha Tevis

SCHOLASTIC APTITUDE TEST (SAT). See BRIGHAM, CARL CAMPBELL.

SCHOOL CHOICE. See VOUCHERS.

SCHOOL DISTRICT OF ABINGTON V. SCHEMPP. See BIBLE READING.

SCHOOL LIBRARIES. Libraries have been a part of schools and colleges since the seventeenth century, and private libraries, or collections of books, have been known to exist since early times. In the age of multimedia centers, we are hard pressed to imagine an era when libraries were not an important part of educating the young; and yet this is a contemporary movement. Colleges early in the antebellum period of the nineteenth century took great pride in the existence of book collections at their institutions. These libraries were often run by student societies and were not used for instruction. In the waning years of the 1890s, a collaboration between school principals and public librarians began the formation of school libraries.

College libraries were found on campuses long before the first high school libraries existed in any schools. The college libraries contained print material that was collected in a variety of ways. The earliest library of record was the Bodleian at Oxford University in 1602, but surely the most memorable in America was the Harvard College library, a gift from John Harvard that is recorded for posterity in *New England First Fruits*. Student societies managed to provide libraries larger than those of the colleges themselves. The books often duplicated those held by the college because they were random gifts as well as selected purchases. Records of the circulation of these volumes are extant, but there are no personal records of the use of the library holdings as a part of the curriculum. Use for instruction came with the formation of the research university toward the end of the century. Once established, research library collections doubled in size every sixteen years from 1876 to 1938. The data collection has been questioned in recent years, but the rapid growth pattern has not. This has led to some curiosity about the lack of similar library growth in America's schools. In the last decade of the nineteenth century, isolated school libraries began to appear, and by 1930 each high school had usually allocated a space for books. As late as 1961, however, only 25 percent of the elementary schools had adequate media centers, and 25 percent still had none. In a survey completed by the National Center for Education Statistics in 1974, it was found that 84 percent of all schools in the United States had library or media centers that served 43.9 million students and their teachers.

In Brooklyn, New York, Mary Kingsbury became the first high school librarian in 1900. This appointment had the full support of such groups as the National Education Association (NEA)* Library Department, the Library Section of the National Council of Teachers of English,* and the American Library Association. With this level of support, it is not surprising that libraries in high schools grew to become a permanent part of the educational enterprise. The teacher librarian, with totally different functions, headed the new organization, and interested groups began to develop standards to assist in the operation.

The secondary school library became entrenched with a clearly defined role as the place to gather information and the place for reference and reading in history and English. Elementary school libraries, though finding support from various groups in the early twentieth century, did not develop; the public libraries continued to provide for these needs. One group that met this description was the NEA Department of Elementary Principals. In 1925 and 1933, it published yearbooks expressing its ideas on the introduction of elementary libraries, but it was not until the federal government became involved in 1958 through the National Defense Education Act* that there was a marked growth in school libraries.

The 1950s marked a key change with two concurrent events. The technology explosion began along with the demand for more science education.* Federal funding expanded to meet the need for moving the library from being the repository for books to becoming a media center that is now a vital tool for education. The library media specialist remains a teacher but now has the broader role of filling the multimedia needs of the students the center serves. Many view the new media center concept as one that will pass, but there is little or no evidence of this as librarians continue to expand their part as motivators and instructors in the use of the multitude of information services.

For sources on the history of school libraries and their functions, see D. Philip Baker, *The Library Media Program and the School* (1984); Kathleen W. Craver, *School Library Media Centers in the Twenty-First Century: Changes and Challenges* (1994); C. Dyer, R. Brown, and E. D. Goldstein, *The Role of School Libraries in Education* (1970); Rita S. Saslaw, "Student Societies: A Nineteenth-Century Establishment" (1971); Helen E. Saunders, *The Modern School Library: Its Administration as a Materials Center* (1968); and Robert

Wedgeworth, ed., *ALA World Encyclopedia of Library and Information Services* (1980).

Rita S. Saslaw

SCHOOL NURSES owe their historical roots to early public health efforts in England and the United States. The first school nurse was employed in 1892 in London, England, to give nutrition education. School health services began in the United States with medical inspections in 1894 with the goal of excluding children with communicable diseases, such as measles, scarlet fever, and impetigo, from the schools. There was no followup on those excluded, and truancy was rampant. In New York City, Lillian Wald, who had established the first public health nursing center, the Henry Street Settlement, sought permission to place a public health nurse in the schools experimentally. The goal was to increase school attendance by educating students, parents, and school officials regarding disease control and by home-visit followup. The first school nurse, Lina Rogers, was placed in four New York City schools in 1902. The school nurse's efforts remarkably decreased the length and the number of student absences.

School nurses' roles paralleled the expansion of the school health program as they worked cooperatively with physicians in the health inspections and examinations of students to exlude the ill, especially those with communicable diseases, to follow up in the homes, and to return students to school. The nurses' health education* efforts became important in the schools, as specific lessons were given and an integrated health education program was implemented. By the 1930s, school nurses were overextended, and studies showed that school nurses needed specialized training in the practice of public health.

When healthy young men were needed for the military draft during World War II, one-quarter were rejected for physical defects. National concern grew over the health of schoolchildren, which greatly augmented interest in the school nurse role. The school nurse became an advisor to school administrators and teachers, identified the integration of school and community resources, interpreted test results for parents and secured needed followup, and made home visits to interpret issues for parents and to foster school-home efforts for meeting health needs. Mandated screenings for physical problems started at this time and continue in many school settings to this day.

In the next two decades, the school health program endeavored to develop optimum health for each student, with the school nurse acting as facilitator and health educator. A teamwork concept unfolded, with the nurse serving as an active participant with administrators and teachers. The active role of the school nurse on interdisciplinary teams today owes its roots to this time period.

Recent decades have been marked by several trends. Special education* greatly expanded the school nurse role and the need for additional education in the management of medically fragile school students. Complicated case management activities, primary care, and services to students with special health care needs are all part of the role of the school nurse in health services. School nurses also have responsibility for health education and the maintenance of a healthy school environment. The school nurse practitioner, with additional preparation in assessments and physical examinations, has been an effective addition to the school health program in many states since the 1970s.

Budgetary cutbacks have eliminated the school nurse in some settings. In other areas, there have been demands for expanding roles, better educational preparation, and increased community health involvement for the school nurse. Controversies over the need for delegation of some duties led to the addition of health assistants as a recent development.

Educational preparation and certification required for school nurses varies throughout the United States. Furthermore, the ratio of nurse to student ranges from 1:500 to 1:800. This variability relates to the financial support from the state and local districts.

The National Association of School Nurses (NASN), the official organization for school nurses, was organized in 1969. Its mission is to "advance the practice of school nursing and provide leadership in the delivery of quality health programs to the school community." Two of its publications include the *Journal of School Nursing* and the *NASN Newsletter*.

Refer to NASN, which is located in Scarborough, Maine. Also, see Judith B. Igoe, "School Nursing" (1975); NASN, "National Association of School Nursing Newsletter" (1997); Judith S. Palfrey, *Community Child Health: An Action Plan for Today* (1994); PSEA, *Pennsylvania State Education Association School Nurse Section, Executive Board Position Paper* (1997); and Susan J. Wold, *School Nursing: A Framework for Practice* (1981).

Ruth E. Leo

SCHOOLHOUSES AND SCHOOL ARCHITECTURE. The schoolhouse represents one of the most distinctive buildings in America. Found in every community, schools stand out as specialized structures, giving form to their function by design. School buildings in the United States were not always so recognizable, however. Before 1820, the place called school provided shelter, little more. It was not until the early nineteenth century that Americans erected buildings for the express purpose of schooling. Both the external appearance and internal layout of school buildings then began to support the mission and methods of formal instruction. Schoolhouses also became more than an extension of the curriculum. As community property and symbols of civic pride and public virtue, they turned out to be no less political in their own way than the function they performed.

American common school* reformers did not invent the idea that the schoolhouse should be a planned environment. English and Prussian educators thought about the design of school buildings before Horace Mann* and Henry Barnard.* The English school reformer Joseph Lancaster had a clear vision of the architectural layout that would complement his monitorial system.* But Mann and

Barnard were the first Americans to believe that good schoolhouses meant good schools. Mann, in a supplement to his initial report as secretary to the Massachusetts Board of Education, equated the deplorable condition of schoolhouses with the neglect of public education in his state. Barnard's *School Architecture* (1848) gave explicit advice on what and how to do better. It included model schoolhouses for both rural and urban school districts and stressed the importance of architectural symbolism; as "temples" of education, Greek Revival school buildings conveyed the message that the future of American republicanism and capitalism depended upon education.

The expansion of schooling in America in the nineteenth century forced educators and school reformers to pay close attention to the school's layout. Pioneered in Boston in the 1840s, the so-called eggcrate schoolhouse featured many self-contained classrooms, facilitating efficient management by segregating pupils according to their age and level of achievement. Urban educators quickly recognized the advantages of such a floor plan, but the standardization and differentiation of educational space was only just beginning. In rural areas, the one-room schoolhouse* persisted until after World War II. Its shortcomings became the subject of countless jeremiads as educators and reformers called for modern buildings with specialized classrooms and up-to-date systems of heating, lighting, and ventilation.

The curriculum of the American school became more diversified and extensive at the beginning of the twentieth century. The introduction of kindergartens,* laboratory science, and manual training* required many different kinds of dedicated space. Educators and reformers, at the same time, insisted that no school was complete without facilities specifically for physical training and moral education.* Elizabeth Peabody* and Lucy Wheelock* believed that kindergarten classrooms should support the focus of their teachers on the child. Although school apparatus for the outdoors first attracted the attention of educators before 1850, it was not until the progressive era (see PROGRESSIVE EDUCATION) that the work of reformers like Luther H. Gulick, Jr., and Joseph Lee made the case for physical education* in schools (also, see PLAY MOVEMENT). Playing fields, swimming pools, and gymnasiums now appeared on school grounds to teach teamwork and self-discipline. The auditorium best embodied the relationship between the school plant and moral education. First installed in grammar* and high schools,* it became the premier place for group activities and inspirational events, celebrating school, community, and national life.

The school plant has often represented the largest capital asset of an American town or city. Accordingly, educators have long believed that schoolhouses should be built to last. University professors of school administration (see EDUCATIONAL ADMINISTRATION), working with school architects like C.B.J. Snyder of New York City and superintendents like William A. Wirt* of Gary, Indiana, developed detailed standards for school design, construction, and maintenance at the beginning of the twentieth century. George B. Strayer, Nicholas L. Engelhardt, and Arthur B. Moehlman taught these standards to students at Teachers College, Columbia University, and University of Michigan. They urged them upon state and local authorities through the medium of the school district survey. Regulations pertaining to school construction became integral to state school codes. Nevertheless, well-built schools and well-groomed grounds meant more than safety and operational efficiency; they served as a district's best advertisement—a bonanza of good public relations.

Since the nineteenth century, schoolhouses have shared in the politics of American education. Their cost alone made certain that they would be the subject of conflict. In the 1920s and 1950s, enrollments grew so rapidly in many communities that financing new school buildings had political implications at the local, state, and even federal level. The school building referendum became a political test for many school administrators. The schoolhouse itself participated in the politics of American education. Before the centralization of school policymaking and administration, its custodian, the school janitor, was a patronage appointee. Even after school bureaucratization, political neutrality remained an illusion. School naming represents a case in point. Introduced in New York City before the Civil War, calling schools by number really functioned as a political act, designed to disassociate schools from their neighborhoods. In many towns and cities, schoolhouse names served the cause of cultural assimilation (see AMERICANIZATION). First named for their geographic location, after 1860 public elementary schools in Boston and Philadelphia increasingly assumed the identity of national heroes or local elites. The same trend overtook twentieth-century comprehensive high schools, obscuring their neghborhood connection behind the names of famous people like George Washington, Abraham Lincoln, and Benjamin Franklin.* Since the 1960s, building names in some cities have begun to reflect the culture of all patrons. Schools named after Roberto Clemente and Frederick Douglass* have appeared, but in the absence of large school building programs, the politics of pluralism has made but modest headway in the field of school naming.

The schoolhouse is a powerful symbol in American culture. From the little red schoolhouse to the shopping mall high school, its representation evokes strong feelings in almost everyone. Yet like any public building, the schoolhouse derives its meaning from what goes on inside. It stands for both the myths and the realities of American education.

For historical background on the development of schoolhouses and school architecture, see William W. Cutler III, "A Preliminary Look at the Schoolhouse: The Philadelphia Story, 1870–1920" (1974); William W. Cutler III, "Cathedral of Culture: The Schoolhouse in American Educational Thought and Practice since 1820" (1989); and William W. Cutler III, "Symbol of Paradox in the New Republic: Classicism in the Design of Schoolhouses and Other Public Buildings in the United States, 1800–1860" (1992). Also refer to Andrew

Gulliford, *America's Country Schools* (1984), and Jean and Robert McClintock, eds., *Henry Barnard's "School Architecture"* (1970).

William W. Cutler, III

SCHURZ, MARGARETHE MEYER. See KINDERGARTEN.

SCIENCE EDUCATION. The origins of science as a school subject can be traced to the academy* era of the late 1700s and early 1800s. Natural philosophy, a forerunner of physics, served as the first recognizable science course. As the high school* developed in the 1800s, chemistry and natural history, which later became biology, became part of the curriculum. The method of science instruction during this time focused on learning about objects rather than with them; thus recitation* and sometimes discussion dominated instruction.

During the second half of the nineteenth century, the encyclopedic and classification approach to science began to give way to the study of natural objects and the conceptual understanding of content within the disciplines. Object teaching* and the laboratory became more important in instruction. In 1872, Harvard University announced that work in high school physics and other science courses would be accepted for college entrance requirements. Other colleges followed Harvard's lead, and college domination of secondary school science began. As college teachers prepared outlines of high school science study and authored high school science textbooks, Harvard published the Harvard Descriptive List in 1887, identifying forty-six physics experiments acceptable for college entrance; this accelerated the shift toward more laboratory work in science.

By the early 1900s, high schools offered a number of short courses in astronomy, biology, chemistry, geology, physics, physiology, and zoology. The National Education Association's (NEA)* *Report of the Committee of Ten on Secondary School Studies* (1894) (see COMMITTEE OF TEN) did not support this practice, recommending a fewer number of sequential, full-year courses. Consequently, the sequence of physical geography, biology, physics, and chemistry became common in high schools. By 1920, during the junior high school* movement, general science, which found its way into the seventh and eighth grades, replaced physical geography.

A philosophical shift also occurred. Science at the elementary level remained limited to nature study, if it existed at all. From the mid- to late 1800s, science was purported to develop high school students' intellectual skills. During the first decades of the twentieth century, however, several reports altered the justification for school science, focusing on developing students who would contribute to society. The NEA's 1920 subcommittee report on the reorganization of science in secondary schools represented the first comprehensive document dealing exclusively with the teaching of science in schools and outlined ways that science teaching could meet six of the seven cardinal principles of secondary education (see CARDINAL PRINCIPLES OF SECONDARY EDUCATION). In 1932, the National Society for the Study of Education (NSSE),* in its thirty-first yearbook, recommended for the first time a twelve-year sequence in science. Additional reports on science study during this time were issued by the Commission on Secondary School Curriculum (1938), NEA's National Committee on Science Teaching (1942), and NSSE (1947).

World War II and the launching of the Soviet Union's *Sputnik* in 1957 generated rapid curricular change. Congress established the National Science Foundation (NSF) in 1950 to promote science, and the National Defense Education Act of 1958* to provide funding to agencies like NSF to support curriculum development in the sciences. The high school science curriculum took precedence, followed by the junior high and elementary levels, respectively. These projects were often referred to as alphabet or alphabet soup curricula because they became widely known by three or four letters, often the first initials of each word in the project's name. Projects at the high school level encompassed the Physical Science Study Committee (PSSC), the Chemical Educaton Materials Study (CHEM), the Chemical Bond Approach (CBA), and the Biological Science Curriculum Study (BSCS). The junior high curriculum claimed Introductory Physical Science (IPS), with Science, A Process Approach (SAPA), Elementary Science Study (ESS), and Science Curriculum Improvement Study (SCIS) serving as the elementary science projects. They all maintained common attributes: (1) an emphasis on pure versus applied science; (2) in-depth treatment of selected topics instead of an encyclopedic approach; (3) courses centered around a few unifying themes; (4) a laboratory base; (5) emphases on both processes and products of science; and (6) a total package approach including materials and teacher training.

With the technological growth of the 1970s and early 1980s, science curriculum issues tended to emphasize the interface between science, technology, and society. Several reports critical of education, such as *A Nation at Risk** (1983), were also published, stimulating school reform. One of the most ambitious efforts, since the 1960s, to effect curricular and instructional change has been the American Association for the Advancement of Science's (AAAS) *Project 2061* (1989). This project, scheduled to continue well into the twenty-first century, is directed at reforming science, mathematics, and technology education. Among its basic tenets is the need for all students to be scientifically and technologically literate. The National Science Teachers Association's* Scope, Sequence, and Coordination Program (1989) represents another ongoing initiative designed to examine the depth and breadth of the school science curriculum.

For a comprehensive overview, see George E. DeBoer, *A History of Ideas in Science Education: Implications for Practice* (1991). Paul DeHart Hurd, *New Directions in Teaching Secondary School Science* (1969) and *New Curriculum Perspectives for Junior High School Science* (1970), treats the alphabet experience. More recent trends can be found in Rodger W. Bybee, *Science/Technology/Society* (1985), and AAAS's *Project 2061*.

Jeffrey R. Lehman

SCOPES V. STATE, 289 S.W. 363 (Tenn. 1927). This case was more famous for the prominent attorneys representing both sides than for its legal pecedent. Representing the defendant, John Scopes, was Clarence Darrow; assisting the prosecution as witness and attorney was William Jennings Bryan. A public high school* biology teacher in Dayton, Tennessee, Scopes was charged with violating the state's anti-evolution statute as a result of teaching his tenth-grade students "a certain theory that denied the story of the divine creation of man, as taught in the Bible" (p. 363). A jury found John Scopes guilty, and the trial judge imposed a $100 fine. On appeal to the Tennessee Supreme Court, the court found the anti-evolution statute constitutional but nonetheless reversed the conviction because fines in excess of $50 in the state of Tennessee could be imposed only by a jury and not by a judge. Although the jury had found Scopes guilty of violating the Act, the judge, rather than the jury, had imposed the $100 fine. Since Scopes was no longer employed by the state, the court, in recommending to the attorney general that no further legal proceedings against Scopes be undertaken, observed, in conclusion, that "[w]e see nothing to be gained by prolonging the life of this bizarre case" (p. 367).

Ralph D. Mawdsley

SECOND PLENARY COUNCIL. See THIRD PLENARY COUNCIL.

SECONDARY SCHOOL STUDY FOR NEGROES was a project of the Commission on Secondary Schools of the Association of Colleges and Secondary Schools for Negroes (ACSSN) and was very much within the experimental tradition of the Progressive Education Association's* Eight-Year Study* and the Southern Association's Study (see SOUTHERN STUDY). The Secondary School Study (1940–1947) involved the participation of sixteen high schools* from each of the eleven Southern Association states and was supported by a grant from the General Education Board.* The Study served as an effort to determine clearer insights for African American schools, in part, because the ACSSN felt southern African American practitioners were not involved in the larger "stream of educational ideas" and, thus, were placing too much emphasis on existing, conservative practices. Similar to the Eight-Year Study and the Southern Study, the participating school staffs of the Secondary School Study were free to explore ways to develop school policy, curriculum, data-gathering methods, and pupil-community involvement during the first three years of the project. In keeping with basic progressive (see PROGRESSIVE EDUCATION) school beliefs of the time, the school staffs attended to aspects of "democratic practices in the school," core curriculum, pupil-teacher planning, and student government. Participating schools were visited by consultants and staffs from the other schools and engaged in regional summer workshops for curriculum development.

The second three-year period involved a vigorous effort to broaden the experimental aspects to other southern African American secondary schools in the South. In addition, staff development activities were developed with regional colleges. The project, officially ending in 1947, served as an incentive for more southern African American high schools to become regionally accredited.

Refer to the Secondary School Study Archival Project, Museum of Education, University of South Carolina. Also see Verner M. Sims, Eugene A. Waters, and W. A. Robinson, "Experimental Programs in the Southern Association" (1946).

Anthony Edwards and Craig Kridel

SERRANO V. PRIEST I, 487 P.2d 1241 (Cal. 1971), is perhaps the leading state case in the wave of school finance litigation that began in the early 1970s. In *SERRANO I* the Supreme Court of California held that a system of financing that relies heavily upon local property taxes and results in substantial disparities among individual school districts in the amount of revenues available to be spent per pupil invidiously discriminates against the poor in violation of the equal protection clause of the Fourteenth Amendment to the U.S. Constitution. The court reached this conclusion based on its assertion that education is a "fundamental interest." The court further ruled that since the equal protection language in the California constitution could be construed as substantially equivalent to the Fourteenth Amendment, its analysis was also applicable under the state provision. The U.S. Supreme Court's subsequent repudiation of education as a "fundamental" right entitled to equal protection under the Fourteenth Amendment in *San Antonio Independent School District v. Rodriquez,** 411 U.S. 1 (1973), notwithstanding, *Serrano I* continued to exert considerable influence in school finance litigation. Perhaps the most important aspect of *Serrano I* was its creation of the standard of fiscal neutrality, employed in later finance cases, under which the court reasoned that the quality of a child's education should be based on the wealth of the state as a whole rather than on that of a local school district.

Following the U.S. Supreme Court's ruling in *Rodriquez*, in *Serrano v. Priest II*, 557 P.2d 929 (Cal. 1976), *cert. denied sub nom. Clowes v. Serrano*, 432 U.S. 907 (1977), the California Supreme Court affirmed that the state's system of financing public education violated the equal protection provision of the state constitution. In *Serrano v. Priest III*, 226 Cal. Rptr. 584 (Cal. Ct. App. 1986), an intermediate appellate court relinquished jurisdiction over the dispute when it found that wealth-related disparities were reduced to insignificance and that any remaining differences were justified by legitimate state interests.

Charles J. Russo

SERVICE BUREAU FOR INTERCULTURAL EDUCATION (SBIE). See MULTICULTURAL EDUCATION.

SETTLEMENT HOUSE MOVEMENT. See ADDAMS, JANE.

SEX EDUCATION refers to a comprehensive plan of instruction that includes sexual anatomy and physiology, reproduction, contraception, sexually transmitted diseases (STDs), and related topics. It also addresses sexual decision making, social skills, communication in relationships, and development of a personal value system.

In the early 1900s, sex education efforts in the United States focused on pregnancy prevention for unwed mothers, birth control information for married couples, and prevention of venereal (sexually transmitted) diseases. Curricula were subsequently oriented toward biology and emphasized basic factual information about reproduction, with occasional coverage given to contraceptive practices as well as how to avoid infection with syphilis and gonorrhea. According to some researchers, the underlying theme pervading these sex education programs was one of antagonism toward sexual activity.

An increased understanding about human sexual behavior led, beginning in the 1940s, to curricula that fostered an appreciation of an individual's sexuality. With greater knowledge of childhood psychosexual development, more organizations, such as schools, public health clinics, and voluntary health organizations, became involved in sex education initiatives. Formal instruction at this time, in addition to the usual factual information about contraceptive practices and disease prevention, consistently stressed a respect for traditional values and beliefs regarding the roles of men and women in contemporary American society. By the 1970s and 1980s, while still retaining a focus on family planning and STD prevention, sex education programs shifted toward a less moralistic and judgmental tone relative to an individual's sexual behavior. Also, during this period, sex education became more universal, since an increasing number of sex education programs were adapted for special populations, including the mentally retarded, physically handicapped, and elderly.

Thus, throughout this century, sex education assumed broader instructional goals with more school-aged children exposed to systematic instruction in multiple settings and the development of programs that address the emotional elements of sexual maturation as well as the biological components. Only a few states required sex education in 1980, but by 1995 forty-seven states required or recommended sex education; over half of all states require HIV-AIDS education. However, although it is estimated that between 25 percent and 75 percent of all American adolescents receive some formal sex education coursework, experts believe that no more than 15 percent of these programs are sufficient in terms of breadth or depth (see ADOLESCENCE).

Many myths surround sex education. Contrary to claims that sex education promotes sexual activity and increases pregnancy rates, no scientific study to date supports this hypothesis. Empirical evidence instead strongly suggests that sex education not only increases young people's knowledge but also raises the likelihood that they will use contraception while delaying the onset of initial sexual intercourse. Gallop, Harris, and Roper polls consistently report that over 85 percent of Americans favor sex education in the public schools.

Developments in learning theory and educational psychology have greatly influenced the manner in which sex education is delivered today. Multifaceted approaches are believed to be the most effective educational strategy to help teenagers from all backgrounds acquire accurate content knowledge, change attitudes, and increase motivation to modify risky sexual behaviors. Comprehensive programming subsequently includes interactive video, role play, simulation exercises, assertiveness training, active listening, debate panels, peer-educators, guest speakers, and field trips.

See the Guttmacher Institute, *Teenage Pregnancy: The Problem That Hasn't Gone Away* (1981); Douglas Kirby and Pamela M. Wilson, *Sexuality Education* (1984); and SIECUS Fact Sheet, *SIECUS Report* (1992).

Michael J. Cleary

SHELDON, EDWARD AUSTIN (October 4, 1823–August 26, 1897), reconstructed nineteenth-century teacher education and teaching methods through the Oswego movement.* He was born and raised in a period during which political reformers, educators, philanthropists, and an array of social feminists discovered a common interest in the child and worked to create new educational environments. He was educated in district schools* and attended Hamilton College (1844–1847) in Clinton, New York. Like many of these middle-class educational reformers, Sheldon possessed a strong missionary spirit and, after failing in business pursuits, turned to education. In 1848 in Oswego, New York, he organized and taught in ''The Orphan and Free School Association'' for the ''intellectual and moral education* and improvement of poor and orphan children.'' Three years later he was appointed superintendent of public schools in Syracuse, a position he left in 1853 to become secretary of the Oswego Board of Education. His educational visions became reality as he organized the Oswego public school system, creating ''arithmetic schools'' for boys and girls, and an ''Unclassified School'' for those ''with particular problems who wish to pursue some special subjects.''

Aware of the need for new and qualified teachers for that area's school system, Sheldon championed the establishment of a teacher-training school in Oswego. Over the next quarter century, he transformed a small teacher-training school into a pioneering institution for the preparation of teachers. From a modest beginning in 1859 as classes for teachers, the institution was transformed by Sheldon into a full-blown state normal school* by 1865. There, he introduced Pestalozzian (see PESTALOZZIANISM) object teaching* methodologies in the United States. His pedagogical beliefs about teaching-learning theories were reflected in his books: *A Manual of Elementary Instruction* (1862); *Lessons on Objects* (1863); *First Reading Book and Phonic Cards* (1863); and *Teachers' Manual of Instruction in Reading* (1875). He also wrote a reading series (1872–1875) (see READING INSTRUCTION) and primary and graded spellers (1875–1876).

His daughter, Mary Downing Sheldon-Barnes, edited and published the *Au-*

tobiography of Edward Austin Sheldon (1911). For additional sources, refer to OBJECT TEACHING.

Hariklia Efthimiou and Barbara Finkelstein

SIGHTLESS AND SIGHT IMPAIRED EDUCATION. During the 1830s, some of the most popular tourist attractions in the United States were the nation's new schools for blind children. Thousands flocked to see blind students demonstrate their ability to read raised-letter books, play music, and make mathematical calculations on special metal types. Many commentators considered the education of the blind to be one ot the most profound humanitarian acts in an age noted for social reform. Until that time, those with visual impairments were generally considered uneducatable and often doomed to a life of poverty and marginalization. Since those exciting first days, the visually handicapped have continued to look to education as a key to realizing the goal of full integration into a society controlled by the sighted.

In 1831, Boston reformer Samuel Gridley Howe accepted the job as director of the first school for the blind in America. He immediately sailed to Europe, which was a half-century ahead in the development of schools for the blind. Interest in the subject began with the French philosopher Denis Diderot. In his influential *Letter on the Blind* (1749), Diderot profiled several blind people, including the famous Cambridge mathematician Nicholas Saunderson (1682–1739), who had overcome their handicap to become masters of their fields. He argued that these cases proved that when sight is lost, other senses can serve equally well as sources of information. Diderot urged more attention to the plight of the blind.

Diderot's challenge was answered in 1784 when Valentin Hauy founded the world's first school for blind children in Paris. Hauy, a humanitarian, was moved to action by the sight of blind beggars on French streets. His school combined basic academic and musical instruction with simple craft training designed to give his students a chance to earn financial independence. Other European countries soon followed France's lead. England founded its first school for the blind in 1791, and by 1820 every European nation had at least one school, widely varying in quality.

Howe toured these schools in 1831 and returned to Boston convinced that American schools could improve on Old World models. He urged Americans to grant their blind children a full common school* education, using raised-letter books and other materials adapted to their needs. A well-rounded education, he argued, was not only their democratic birthright but also the best way to ensure that they would be able to support themselves upon graduation. A practical educator as well as a democratic idealist, Howe created a number of educational tools for the blind, including embossed maps and a new, more efficient form of raised-letter printing. Boston represented the first American city to charter a school in 1829. Howe opened its doors in 1832, naming it the Perkins School for the Blind to honor a Boston merchant who donated his mansion to house the new school. The New York Institution for the Blind opened in 1832, under the direction of Dr. John Russ. The Philadelphia School began in 1833, led by Julius Friedlander, a German immigrant who had trained in European schools. Led by the energetic Howe, these schools spread the gospel of education for the blind. Howe visited capitals around the country, demonstrating the accomplishments of his blind students and urging legislators to found their own schools. By the time of Howe's death in 1876, there were thirty public and private schools* for the blind around the country. These new schools often recruited teachers and directors from among the graduates of the older schools. Howe also presided over the first organization for teachers of the blind, the American Association for Instructors of the Blind, established in 1853.

Howe claimed that education would allow the blind to become financially self-sufficient. Many graduates did succeed in fields once closed to the blind, working as teachers, musicians, writers, and skilled artists. By the 1850s, however, school directors found that a growing number of graduates struggled to support themselves by their own effort, unable to compete effectively with the sighted, particularly in manual labor. In the second half of the nineteenth century, American schools responded by developing sheltered workshops, which provided students with manual training and subsidized graduates with employment in trades such as broom-making and mattress sewing. In the twentieth century, most of these workshops were disassociated from schools, and many have been abandoned in favor of direct financial support for the blind.

These schools also led in developing libraries for the blind. Progress in this area was slowed by a chronic shortage of funds and disagreements over which raised-letter system should be used. In 1879, Congress created the American Printing House for the Blind in Kentucky to support the creation of reading materials for the blind. In 1932, Standard English Braille was adopted as a uniform standard in England and the United States.

Howe always insisted that institutions for blind children operate as part of a state's educational system, not charity organizations. He grew increasingly concerned that separate residential schools for the blind stigmatized them, and he argued that institutional living was unhealthy for any child. He urged educators to find ways to better integrate blind children into their communities. In 1870, Howe initiated the first step in this process by creating a ''noncongregate'' living system at the Perkins School, which housed students in cottages that recreated some of the intimacy of family life. A similar plan was used for the first kindergarten* for the blind in the world, established by Howe's successor at Perkins, Michael Anagnos, in 1887.

In 1900, the Chicago school system became the first to provide day classes for blind children in schools for the sighted, supported by special instruction in braille. Other city school systems soon followed, experimenting with various ways to integrate blind children into their regular public schools. While residential schools continue to serve blind students around the country, they now concentrate much of their effort on serving multiple-handicapped children. Most

visually impaired children now attend conventional public schools, where they
are supported by special education* teachers.

For Howe's biography, see Harold Schwartz, *Samuel Gridley Howe: Social
Reformer, 1801–1876* (1956). Broader background can be found in Gabriel Far-
rell, *The Story of Blindness* (1956), and Ferne K. Roberts, "Education of the
Visually Handicapped: A Social and Educational History" (1986).

Ernest Freeberg

SILBERMAN, CHARLES E. (January 31, 1925–   ), with his wife and research associate, Arlene Silberman, brought the fledgling open classroom movement in American education to national prominence and debate with the
publication of his landmark work *Crisis in the Classroom* (1970). He was born
in Des Moines, Iowa, and earned his bachelor's degree from Columbia College
in 1946, majoring in economics. He tutored and taught in the economics departments of City College of New York and Columbia University while attending graduate school, and he completed all doctoral requirements except the
dissertation at Columbia by 1953. For the next eighteen years, Siberman worked
at *Fortune* magazine, first as associate editor and later as a member of that
magazine's board of editors. During a leave of absence from *Fortune*, Silberman
embarked upon a career as an investigative journalist-scholar, supported by various foundation grants, culminating in three national award-winning books: *Crisis in Black and White* (1964), which addressed race relations at the height of
America's civil rights movement; *The Myths of Automation* (1966), which examined the nation's economy in transition; and *Crisis in the Classroom* (1970),
which received six national awards for its contribution to the national dialogue
about schooling. It is generally considered to have been the most widely read
and discussed single work about American education during a revival of John
Dewey's* progressive education* ideals. Initially funded by a Carnegie Foundation grant (see CARNEGIE UNIT) focusing on the education of educators,
the completed study embraced a range of problems regarding equality of educational opportunity. It used examples, based on field research, of neoprogressive school reform projects designed to address this dilemma in urban and rural
America. This book also included a section on the open classroom and infant
school movements in England. Silberman edited a subsequent resource book,
The Open Classroom Reader (1973), which provided additional documentary
information about various school sites and programs. The National Society for
the Study of Education* commissioned a volume of critical essays, edited by
A. Harry Passow (1971), in response to Silberman's findings and to his advocacy
of neoprogressive school reform.

Silberman wrote three other multiyear studies about the criminal justice system (1978), Jewish life in America (1985), and the nation's health care system
(1994). Active in the Judaic Reconstructionist movement, Silberman serves on
the board of governors of the Reconstructionist Rabbinical College and as a
contributing editor of *Reconstructionist* magazine.

Robert A. Levin

SMITH, MORTIMER B.   339

SKINNER, B. F. See BEHAVIORISM.

SLATER, JOHN F. (SLATER FUND). John F. Slater, a New England textile manufacturer, established the first philanthropic fund exclusively for African American education in 1882. From 1882 to 1891, Atticus Green Haygood was the general agent of the Fund. A Methodist minister and president of Emory College, he argued that blacks and whites had similar intellectual capacities, and he supported academic curricula as well as industrial training (see VOCATIONAL EDUCATION). During the southern educational campaigns of the early twentieth century, the Slater Fund became closely allied with other philanthropic funds. Former Confederate congressman Jabez L. M. Curry* was general agent from 1891 to 1903; he also served as general agent of the Peabody Education Fund* and as a member of the Southern Education Board.* Curry was more opposed to academic education for African Americans than Haygood, and, while he controlled the Fund, more than half of the income went to Hampton Institute or Tuskegee Institute (see WASHINGTON, BOOKER T.). At Curry's death in 1903, Wallace Buttrick, agent of the General Education Board,* also became agent of the Slater Fund, and support from the Fund increasingly went to African American public industrial schools, despite the indifference and sometimes hostility of members of the African American community who often preferred more traditional curricula. James H. Dillard, president of Tulane University, became general agent in 1911. He used the Fund to support a network of public county industrial, agricultural, and homemaking training schools for African Americans throughout the South. A normal course was offered in the final year to train industrial teachers for rural African American common schools* (also, see NORMAL SCHOOLS). The number of training schools increased from 4 in 1911 to 356 by 1933. In the 1930s, the training schools became part of the public school system in the southern states, and in 1937 the residue of the money in the Slater Fund was granted to the Southern Education Foundation.

See James D. Anderson, ''Northern Foundations and the Shaping of Southern Black Rural Education, 1902–1935'' (1978); James D. Anderson, *The Education of Blacks in the South, 1860–1935* (1988); Roy E. Finkenbine, ''A Little Circle: White Philanthropists and Black Industrial Education in the Postbellum South'' (1982); John E. Fisher, *The John F. Slater Fund: A Nineteenth-Century Affirmative Action for Negro Education* (1988); and Harold W. Mann, *Atticus Greene Haywood: Methodist Bishop, Editor and Educator* (1965).

Clinton B. Allison

SMALL-GROUP LEARNING. See COOPERATIVE LEARNING.

SMITH, MORTIMER B. (February 17, 1906–April 26, 1981), critical of the public schools,* co-founded, with Arthur Bestor,* the Council for Basic Education in 1956. Born in Mt. Vernon, New York, he left a brief career in business to became a self-employed writer in 1933. The primary focus of his writing was education and applied psychology. His polemic work, *And Madly Teach: A*

Layman Looks at Public School Education (1949), attacked the principles and practices of modern education. The writings of John Dewey* and the work of Teachers College were the targets of his criticism, which echoed the work of Bernard Bell.* Smith and other critics asserted that schools had failed to teach basic skills and that they divested themselves of moral and intellectual content. After writing *The Diminished Mind: A Study of Planned Mediocrity in Our Public Schools* (1954), Smith worked with Bestor on the Council for Basic Education. The Council's mission was based on the belief "that there is an inalienable relationship between a healthy democracy and excellence in education." The Council's mission was to strengthen teaching and learning of the basic subjects, English, history, government, geography, mathematics, the sciences, foreign languages, and the arts to foster lifelong learning and responsible citizenship. Smith edited the *Council for Basic Education Bulletin* from 1957 until 1974. He also served on the White House Conference on Education in 1965 and on the White House Conference on Children in 1970. He wrote *My School, My City* (1980) one year before his death to further promote the place of a basic core curriculum in public education.

His educational views are encapsulated in his edited piece *A Decade of Comment on Education, 1956–1966: Selections from the Bulletin of the Council of Basic Education* (1966).

Charles E. Jenks

SMITH-HUGHES ACT marked the beginning of federal involvement in non-college education after more than a decade of public debate and legislative action by the vocational education* movement, spearheaded by individuals like Congressmen Charles R. Davis, Jonathan P. Dolliver, and Carroll S. Page and organizations such as the National Society for the Promotion of Industrial Education.* Led by Senator Hoke Smith and Representative Dudley M. Hughes, both of Georgia, Congress created the Commission on National Aid to Vocational Education in January 1914. That Commission, with Charles A. Prosser* as dominant noncongressional member, drafted a bill that President Woodrow Wilson supported as part of his "national preparedness" program and signed with few modifications on February 23, 1917. The Smith-Hughes Act mandated that $7 million of federal money be provided each year for training and salaries for teachers and supervisors of agricultural, trade, industrial, and home economics education to fit youths for "useful employment." These funds, which states had to match, went to full-time day trade and high schools* that devoted half their teaching time to these vocational subjects, and also to part-time evening schools for adult workers. The Act designated at least one-third of the total budget for working children between fourteen and eighteen years of age who attended part-time continuation schools* to further their "civic or vocational intelligence" during a school session of "not less than 144 hours classroom instruction per year." The Federal Board for Vocational Education, which administered the Act, consisted of the secretaries of agriculture, commerce, and labor and the commissioner of education; three other members, representing various interests, were presidential appointees who received Senate confirmation. Within a year, all states submitted plans and began to establish vocational boards, either affiliated with or autonomous from the state boards of education. Several times, Congress supplemented the Act by new laws: the George-Reed (1929), George-Ellzey (1934), George-Deen (1938), George-Bardeen (1946). In 1933, an executive order transferred the functions of the federal board to the commissioner of education. A general policy reorientation did not occur until the second Vocational Education Act of 1963.

Lloyd E. Blauch, *Federal Cooperation in Agricultural Extension Work, Vocational Education, and Vocational Rehabilitation* (1935), provides a comprehensive history, including a reprint of the Act. Layton S. Hawkins, Charles A. Prosser, and John C. Wright, *Development of Vocational Education* (1951), give a description from the view of participants; Harvey A. Kantor, *Learning to Earn: School, Work, and Vocational Reform in California, 1880–1930* (1988), and various contributors to *Work, Youth, and Schooling: Historical Perspectives on Vocationalism in American Education* (1982), edited by Harvey A. Kantor and David B. Tyack, present a critical perspective.

Michael Knoll

SNEDDEN, DAVID SAMUEL (November 19, 1868–December 1, 1951), a prominent educator in progressive education,* advocated a "social efficiency" approach, which reconciled the demands of industrial society with the capabilities and interests of children. He received his A.B. from Stanford University (1897) and his M.A. from Teachers College, Columbia University (1901). From 1897 to 1900, he served as teacher, principal, and superintendent in California's schools and taught as an assistant professor at Stanford between 1901 and 1905 and as an adjunct professor at Teachers College, Columbia University, from 1905 to 1909. In his dissertation on reform schools,* he presented practical and useful education for delinquents as a model for the improvement of the public school* system. With Samuel T. Dutton, he coauthored the first school administration textbook, *The Administration of Public Education in the United States* (1908). From 1909 to 1916, Snedden served as Massachusetts's state commissioner of education, promoting vocational education,* industrial arts, and the project method* as means to secure, through differentiation and learning by doing, equality of opportunity for the "rank and file." Between 1916 and 1935, he returned to Teachers College, where he applied his concept of social efficiency to curriculum construction and civic education.* His book *Educational Sociology* (1922) became a standard in the field. Although like other progressive educators Snedden opposed traditional ways of abstract, unreal, and bookish instruction, he criticized these same colleagues for an overemphasis on growth, creativity, and self-realization. His debates with Boyd H. Bode and John Dewey* about vocational education, democracy, and social predestination demonstrated his belief in the value of specific objectives and scientific methods.

Some of Snedden's most important works include *Administration of Education for Juvenile Delinquents* (1906), *The Problem of Vocational Education* (1910), *Problems of Educational Readjustment* (1913), and *Sociological Determination of Objectives in Education* (1921). Boyd H. Bode, *Modern Educational Theories* (1927), gives a contemporary critique of Snedden's views. Walter H. Drost, *David Snedden and Education for Social Efficiency* (1967), offers a biography; Herbert M. Kliebard, *The Struggle for the American Curriculum, 1893–1958* (1986) places Snedden in the context of the progressive education movement; and Arthur G. Wirth, *Education in the Technological Society: The Vocational-Liberal Studies Controversy in the Early Twentieth Century* (1972), documents the philosophical debates between Dewey and Snedden.

Michael Knoll

SOCIAL RECONSTRUCTIONISM represents the most radical contingent of the progressive education* movement and is best portrayed through the work of George S. Counts,* Harold Rugg,* John Childs, and a group of academics from the University of Illinois, including B. O. Smith, William Stanley, Kenneth Benne, Archibald Anderson, and Harlen Shores. Social reconstructionists, greatly influenced by the Great Depression, were primarily concerned with domestic socioeconomic ills and the ways in which education might help. These tenets were much in keeping with progressivism; however, while progressive education constituted the *means*, social reconstructionism proposed *ends*, namely, a "genuinely democratic" social order, a socieconomic planned society, and a future-centered orientation. In response to the question "What is the role of the school in the social order?" social reconstructionist believed that teachers and schools must be actively involved in shaping the values of students. Progressive educators cried "indoctrination" at this ideological stance and believed that educators should never impose values on students; social reconstructionists, though, viewed America's crisis as being so serious that educators could not stand by and watch the destruction of society.

Although Theodore Brameld* is often associated with this group, he distinguished his work, reconstructionism, from social reconstructionism in that he viewed the adjective "social" as being too restrictive. Brameld stressed the "world situation" and the "ever-shrinking planet" over domestic issues and saw the community for reconstruction as encompassing the entire world. Brameld attempted to diffuse criticisms of "indoctrination" by establishing the doctrine of defensible partiality. Though this served as a conceptual reconciliation for the reconstructionists, the imposition of values remained a dilemma for social reconstructionism efforts. Brameld attempted to resurrect the movement in the 1970s with the Society for Educational Reconstructionism, but that organization did not develop a substantial enough following. Although no distinct movement exists today, the works of Michael Apple, William Ayers, Henry Giroux, and Alex Molnar appear to be very much within the social reconstructionist tradition.

For the basic tenets of this movement, refer to Theodore Brameld, *Ends and*

Means in Education (1950); George S. Counts, *Dare the School Build a New Social Order?* (1932); and Harold Rugg, *Foundations for American Education* (1947).

Craig Kridel

SOCIAL STUDIES is a subject taught in elementary, middle or junior high,* and high schools.* It was conceived as an educational idea in the late 1880s and emerged as an important progressive pedagogical answer (see PROGRESSIVE EDUCATION) for urban and rural problems in the 1910s. Drawing upon the social theories of Frank Lester Ward, Albion Small, John Dewey,* and others, Arthur William Dunn developed one of the first social studies curricula for students in Galesburg, Illinois, and later Indianapolis, Indiana, in the early 1900s. Dunn's initial conception of social studies was as a broad-based subject area completely devoted to the practice and learning of competent citizenship. Later, as a secretary of the seminal 1916 Social Studies Committee sponsored by the U.S. Bureau of Education* and the National Education Association,* Dunn was instrumental in merging the concept of social studies as a problem-solving development subject with the learning of discrete content in history, geography, and civics. Since the 1920s, social studies as an integrated subject area for competent citizenship has vacillated, often used as an umbrella term for the teaching of history, geography, and the other social sciences. Despite the initial rejection by the history establishment, whose leaders thought of social studies as ''history with all of the history taken out,'' social studies soon became a fixture in American schools through course offerings in life adjustment* and expanding environment courses in the elementary grades and community civics and problems of American democracy in high schools.

Social studies may be defined in any number of ways depending on the teacher's focus. The lack of a single definition of the field has been both a strength and a weakness. Since the beginning of the century, when social studies entered schools, supporters claimed a variety of purposes for the field. Three of the most common definitions, or purposes, are social studies as content transmission, citizenship education (see CIVIC EDUCATION), and cultivation of critical-thinking skills and dispositions. For those interested in teachers and students as the center of curricular activities, this loose definition is generally applied. For those interested in a carefully designed content-centered approach, a more fixed curriculum is suggested. As a loosely constructed field of study, social studies may be defined by educators in terms of differing combinations of content, skills, and dispositons. According to the largest social studies organization, the National Council for the Social Studies,* established in 1921, social studies is ''the integrated study of the social sciences and humanities to promote civic competence. Within the school program, social studies provides coordinated, systemic study drawing upon such disciplines as anthropology, archeology, economics, geography, history, law, philosophy, political science, psychology, religion, and sociology, as well as appropriate content from the humanities, mathematics, and natural sciences. The primary purpose of social studies is to help young people develop the ability to make informed and reasoned decisions for the public good as citizens of a culturally diverse, democratic society in an interdependent world.''

The social studies curriculum at the elementary levels is typically offered in thematic units such as pioneers, medieval times, and Africa. Other elementary teachers present social studies as part of the "expanding environments curricula," where children begin with study of self in kindergarten, progress through the grades with studies of family, community, state, and region, and conclude with studies of other parts of the world in sixth grade. Social studies in middle and junior high schools may be offered as either discrete courses in history, geography, and civics or as multidisciplinary and interdisciplinary courses that draw upon content from history, geography, and civics as well as other humanities, physical sciences, and mathematics. As found in high schools, social studies is usually offered as subject-centered courses entitled among other variations as U.S. history, world history, global affairs, geography, civics, and economics (also, see FENTON, EDWIN; TABA, HILDA).

Sources include O. L. Davis, Jr., *National Council for the Social Studies in Retrospect* (1995); David Jenness, *Making Sense of Social Studies* (1990); National Council for the Social Studies, *Curriculum Standards for Social Studies* (1994); David Warren Saxe, *Social Studies in Schools: A History of the Early Years* (1991); and James P. Shaver, ed., *Handbook of Research on Social Studies Teaching and Learning* (1991).

David Warren Saxe

SOCIALIST SUNDAY SCHOOLS were established by German, Finnish, and other radical immigrant groups during the late nineteenth and early twentieth centuries as weekend schools for working-class children. They were marked by a blend of ethnic traditions (language, stories, songs, etc.), working-class themes, and radical theory. The more extensive Socialist Sunday school movement was organized by grassroots (often female) supporters of the Socialist Party of America from 1900 to 1920, with a few schools in New York City continuing into the mid-1930s. The Socialist Sunday schools were typically English speaking, eschewed any ethnic or religious identification, and met on Sundays because it was the one day off for most laborers.

At least 100 Socialist Sunday schools for children were organized in sixty-four cities and towns in twenty states and the District of Columbia. Enrollments ranged from a dozen to several hundred, with the average enrollment less than 100 students. The most prominent schools existed in New York City (which had fourteen schools in 1912), Rochester, Buffalo (two in 1918), Philadelphia (two in 1912), Washington, D.C., Pittsburgh (two in 1916), Cleveland (three in 1912), Chicago (eight in 1919), Milwaukee (three in 1915), and Los Angeles. Although some schools lasted for ten years or more, most of the schools were short-lived.

The two-hour morning sessions usually consisted of age-divided classes and general assemblies. Socialist Sunday school teaching focused primarily on the character of working-class life, the nature of the capitalist system and how it results in serious social problems, and the value of cooperative industrial and personal relations. The schools were intended to supplement, not substitute for, the public school experience, and in particular to counteract the overly individualistic, competitive, nationalistic, militaristic, and anti-working-class themes that seemed prevalent in the weekday schools and other segments of American culture. They were never expected to provide a complete socialist education for youth, only a more formal, systematic one (albeit only two hours a week) than they received at home, at rallies, and in youth clubs. Although some staff members tended to rely too heavily on the adaptation of adult-oriented reading materials for lessons, the Socialist Sunday school movement as a whole did include a variety of teaching methods and materials, including question-and-answer discussion formats, socialist and nonsocialist children's readers and magazines, songs, plays, pageants, games, field trips, and guest speakers.

Refer to the *Kendrick Philander Shedd Papers*, located at the Rush Rhees Library, Rare Books Department, Special Collections, University of Rochester. The most comprehenisve history is Kenneth Teitelbaum, *Schooling for "Good Rebels": Socialism, American Education, and the Search for Radical Curriculum* (1995).

Kenneth Teitelbaum

SOCIETY FOR THE PROPAGATION OF THE GOSPEL IN FOREIGN PARTS. The Church of England organized the Society by a charter issued June 16, 1701. Designed to establish and maintain ministers leading to an Anglican episcopacy in the New World, the Society also took on one of the most ambitious educational efforts of the eighteenth century in founding charity schools* for poor children, supporting college and parish libraries (see SCHOOL LIBRARIES), and providing religious instruction* for Native Americans and African Americans, especially in the southern and middle colonies. It established at least 169 missionary stations from New Hampshire to Georgia, employed more than eighty schoolmasters and some eighteen catechists, and distributed thousands of Bibles and other works printed in English and other languages, including Native American dialects. Reverend Thomas Bray, who labored primarily in Maryland and Virginia, became its most notable champion. Despite obstacles, the Society achieved relative success in its mission to Anglicize colonists and Christianize Native Americans, particularly in New York with the chartering of King's College in 1754. After the Revolution, however, its enterprises were either dissolved or transformed, and its missionaries suppressed. In 1783, the Society ended its activities in the independent colonies, but it pursued its work elsewhere in the world.

The Society's archives in England contain its manuscript collections. In addition, most of the public documents of the Society are available at the Missionary Research Library of Union Theological Seminary and the New York

Public Library. Also, see John Calam, "Parsons and Pedagogues: The S.P.G. Adventure in American Education" (1969); John Kendall Nelson, "Anglican Missions in America, 1701–1725: A Study of the Society for the Propagation of the Gospel in Foreign Parts" (1962); and Henry P. Thompson, *Into All Lands: The History of the Society for the Propagation of the Gospel in Foreign Parts, 1701–1950* (1951).

Eric R. Ebeling

SOUTHERN EDUCATION BOARD (SEB). In 1901, philanthropists who financed the early twenthieth-century southern education campaigns established the SEB to administer those efforts and to direct propaganda for free, tax-supported systems of schools in southern states. The Board also campaigned for graded schools, school consolidation,* state financial aid for equalization, establishment of county high schools,* improved teacher training, and industrial and agricultural education (see AGE-GRADING; SMITH-HUGHES ACT; VOCATIONAL EDUCATION). The SEB established its Bureau of Information and Investigation in Knoxville, under supervision of University of Tennessee president Charles Dabney. Philander Priestley Claxton was appointed administrator of the Bureau and editor of its journal, *Southern Education*, which flooded the South with thousands of pieces of literature decrying the woeful state of southern schools and propagandizing for tax increases to support education. Until it disbanded in 1914, the SEB controlled educational philanthropy in the South. It was responsible for dispersing large sums (primarily Rockefeller money) raised by the interlocking General Education Board (GEB).* Because the two boards were so closely allied, it is difficult to separate their responsibilities and activities. Robert C. Ogden of the Wanamaker Department Stores of Philadelphia and New York was the first president of both the GEB and the SEB, and ten other men (there were no female members) served on the SEB and the GEB at the same time. By appointing the general agents of the Peabody Education Fund* and the John F. Slater Fund* to the SEB, a "community of interests" with other major southern education philanthropies was established. Created during a time of African American disfranchisement, the SEB has been criticized for its timid approach to race and education and for its acceptance of white supremacy. The northern members who dominated the SEB developed a policy that permitted only southern members to speak publicly on race issues.

The Special Collections Library, University of Tennessee, Knoxville, includes a large collection of SEB papers. The University of North Carolina, Chapel Hill, possesses a smaller collection. Most of Robert C. Ogden's papers are in the Library of Congress, with another collection at the University of North Carolina. The University of North Carolina houses the Charles W. Dabney Papers, and the University of Tennessee hosts the Philander Priestley Papers. Also, see Charles William Dabney, *Universal Education in the South* (1936); Louis R. Harlan, *Separate and Unequal: Public School Campaigns and Racism in the Southern Seaboard States, 1901–1915* (1958); James L. Leloudis, *Schooling in the New South: Pedagogy, Self, and Society* (1996); and Charles Lee Lewis, *Philander Priestley Claxton: Crusader for Public Education* (1948).

Clinton B. Allison

SOUTHERN STUDY was a curriculum project of the Commission on Curricular Problems and Research of the Southern Association of Colleges and Schools. The Study (1938–1943) involved the participation of thirty-three high schools,* three from each of the eleven Southern Association states, and was primarily supported by more than $200,000 worth of grants from the General Education Board.* The Study confronted each participating school's faculty with one central underlying problem: "What adjustments in our education program will better meet the needs of the youth in our community?"

General topics addressed in the study included successful teaching and learning methodologies, short- and long-term outcomes of these methodologies in the schools, and specific achievements of pupils as they were graduated from high school and entered higher education or the workforce. The fundamental concern of the Commission and four-member Southern Study staff was to focus attention on the improvement of the local school by providing appropriate learning formats and encouraging general use of a sound method for addressing local problems. Multiple Study projects included regional summer teacher conferences, local and state conferences and meetings, in-school visits and workdays by Southern Association administrators and Southern Study staff members, and comparisions of existing test score results between Study schools and nonparticipating schools.

See the Southern Study Archival Project, Museum of Education, University of South Carolina. The Study staff report was first published in the *Southern Association Quarterly* 10 (February 1946 and August 1946). The official report was prepared by Frank C. Jenkins, Druzilla C. Kent, Verner M. Sims, and Eugene A. Waters, *The Southern Study: Cooperative Study for the Improvement of Education* (1947).

Bruce E. Konkle

SPALDING, JOHN LANCASTER (1840–1916), can be called the "Horace Mann"* of American Catholic education, a lifelong advocate of the Catholic schools. While serving as the first Catholic bishop of the Peoria (Illinois) Diocese, he represented a major force in establishing and rationalizing a system of Catholic education, which extended from elementary through higher education. He wrote twenty books and numerous articles, most of them on the subject of education. He authored the *Baltimore Catechism* (1885), which became the primary religious textbook used in Catholic schools, as well as a series of readers. Spalding led the movement at the Third Plenary Council of Baltimore* to have every parish establish its own elementary school. He worked to ensure a system of grades, examinations, teacher qualifications, and superintendence in parochial schools.* In Peoria, in 1899, Spalding built one of the first central Catholic high schools* in the United States. He founded Catholic University in Washington, D.C., in 1887, and fifteen years later supported the first American Catholic normal school,* which Catholic University later established in New York City. Spalding, the only university-educated American bishop of his era, fervently believed and argued that "American" and "Catholic" were not antithetical terms. He fought against the 1889 Illinois Edwards Law, which required that parochial schools be subject to public school board approval, but did so on constitutional rather than sectarian grounds. Although public school educators treated their Catholic counterparts with suspicion, Spalding served as a respected member of the National Education Association.* He received further recognition from William T. Harris* and Nicholas Murray Butler.* His fellow bishops also selected him as president of the Catholic educational exhibition at the Chicago World's Columbian Exposition of 1893 (see INTERNATIONAL EXPOSITIONS).

The archives of the University of Notre Dame and Catholic University of America possess what remains of Spalding's papers. Biographies include Robert N. Barger, *John Lancaster Spalding: Catholic Educator and Social Emissary* (1988), and David F. Sweeney, *The Life of John Lancaster Spalding* (1965).

Robert N. Barger

SPECIAL EDUCATION. Social actions and cultural developments, even in antiquity, served as precursors to safeguarding the interests of special children. Second-century Rome forbade the right of *paterfamilias* to expose children and later, under Constantine, offered financial assistance to families who might otherwise abandon their children. However, the history of special education in the West is usually identified with the cultural framework of the Enlightenment and expressed in the work of select continental Europeans; in particular, the work of Jacob Rodrigue Pereire (1715–1780), Abbe Charles Micel de l'Eppee (1712–1769), and Samuel Heinicke (1772–1790) with the deaf, Valentin Hauy (1745–1822) with the blind, Philippe Penel (1745–1826) with the mentally ill, and Jean Marc Gaspard Itard (1775–1838) and Edouard Seguin (1812–1880) with the mentally retarded.

Only one public special facility existed in the United States in 1816, located in Virginia and dedicated to the insane. The number of special institutions expanded throughout the nineteenth century, with the exception of the Civil War period. Through reformers such as Horace Mann,* Henry Barnard,* and Egerton Ryerson advanced rhetoric for the education of disabled populations, the latter were accommodated in the nineteenth century by public charity institutions, not the common schools.* Amidst the general prejudice, incredulity, and indifference that prevailed, these largely custodial and isolated institutions for the disabled were enabled through philanthropy, donations of public lands, and linkages between their boards of directors and state legislatures. By the early twentieth century, the custodial mode of these special institutions was replaced with educational goals.

An increasing pressure to handle unruly, disabled, low-functioning, and immigrant children came to bear on the public schools by the latter part of the nineteenth century. Ungraded classes and classrooms for the unruly were created in the 1870s before the use of the term "special education," which did not emerge until 1884. These classes enabled the segregation of special populations within the common schools, which became an organizational option to isolation in special institutions. These classes were the means for dealing with special populations before statutes for the mandatory or permissive education of handicapped children, which commenced in New Jersey in 1911.

An elaboration of classes, such as "Open Air," "Crippled," "Deaf," "Subnormal," and "Disciplinary," emerged for a range of special student populations in the 1920s. During that same period, the term "exceptional children" was employed and in 1922 the International Association for the Education of Exceptional Children founded. This term has since come to denote children at both extremes of various scales. By the 1930s, with a lack of resources, many of the classrooms, especially those dedicated to the segregation of behavioral and academic problems, seemed to serve more administrative than pedagogical ends. After World War II, with positive changes in perceptions of the disabled, their care, and treatment and with technological and medical advances in prevention and intervention, support for segregated classrooms grew through the early 1960s. In the 1960s, however, conflict and controversy occurred when the use of these special classes and programs were viewed as bureaucratic "dumping grounds" for minority and poor children.

Citizen-parent groups, court decisions, and legislative action challenged these practices through the 1970s. The interrelated factors of disproportionate enrollment of minority students in segregated special classrooms or programs, issues of legal rights, and litigation effectively confronted the institutional segregation of special education students. Court decisions eliminated programs based on their large and disproportionate enrollment of minority students, illustrated in *Hobson v. Hansen** (1967), which affected the District of Columbia public schools. Changes in ideas about the character of the learning of special students compared to the "normal"—a matter of degree, not kind—as well as the mobilization of citizens, shaped policy vis-à-vis special students. "Normalization" advocates changed understandings about the place of segregated special classrooms and argued for "mainstreaming," that is, placing special students in classrooms with "normal" students.

These many pressures for change, in addition to the view that many handicapped youngsters were not receiving adequate services and that such services were not mandatory, resulted in the Rehabilitation Act of 1973, Section 504, which was, in large part, a consequence of the lobbying of organized groups of parents of handicapped children, as was, more importantly, P.L. 94-142, the Education for All Handicapped Children Act, now known as the Individuals with Disabilities Education Act. Signed into law in November 1975, P.L. 94-142 supported principles of normalization and the "least restrictive environment" for handicapped children. Because of this act, school systems could no longer exclude students on the basis of physical or intellectual handicaps;

due process and confidentiality were afforded parents and guardians, and a range of educational services was mandated with, concomitantly, a greater share of fiscal and human resources dedicated to handicapped children.

Federal funds, which supported the classification and education of special students, produced wide variations among states and school districts in the proportions of students within the various special student classifications. This has led to recent changes to put downward pressure on the "labeling" of special populations within the schools. (Also, refer to DEAF EDUCATION; SIGHTLESS AND SIGHT IMPAIRED EDUCATION.)

See John W. Melcher, "Law, Litigation, and Handicapped Children" (1976); Edward L. Meyen, *Exceptional Children and Youth* (1982); Nancy L. Quisenberry, *Resources for Understanding P.L. 94-142 and Classroom Management and Behavior* (1981); Marvin Rosen, Gerald R. Clark, and Marvin S. Kivitz, eds., *The History of Mental Retardation: Collected Papers* (1976); William Paul Sosnowsky, Paula Wood, and Asa J. Brown, *Inclusive Education: Toward the Maximum Potential* (1990); Joseph L. Tropea, "Structuring Risks: The Making of Urban School Order" (1992); and Margaret A. Winzer, *The History of Special Education: From Isolation to Integration* (1993).

Joseph L. Tropea

SPELLING BEE, or spelldown, although still practiced in today's schools, was one of the most interesting technologies of the early-nineteenth-century American school. With the emergence of large-group learning, an array of pedagogical forms supplemented spelling bees as important forms of instruction. Consistent with the principles dictated in Noah Webster's* *American Spelling Book* (1783), the subject of spelling emerged as the intellectual foundation for reading instruction* and along with it the "spelling bee," a spelling competition that pitted one student against another, defined winners and losers, and otherwise publicized the forms that reading instruction took. Spelling bees also took the form of a group activity; that is, two students chose teams from their classmates, and the master called out the words to be spelled. When a student on one team failed to spell a word correctly, he or she was eliminated from the competition and the other team was given the chance to spell a word correctly. Becoming standard practice in rural and urban district schools* and surviving to this day, spelling bees both reflected and organized commitments to competitive modes of teaching and learning and, as observers then and now have noted, served theatrical and public purposes as well. In addition, people used them as a standard of educational achievement and educational status. Indeed, spelling bees have evolved from a localized tradition to a national ritual for Americans.

See Barbara Finkelstein, *Governing the Young: Teacher Behavior in Popular Primary Schools in Nineteenth-Century United States* (1989).

Barbara Finkelstein and Hariklia Efthimiou

STEVENS, THADDEUS (April 4, 1792–August 11, 1868), is best known for his political abolitionism and his push for "radical" Reconstruction; but he also deserves attention as an important architect of common school* reform. Born in Danville, Vermont, he received his early education at Peacham Academy, which he followed with collegiate training at the University of Vermont and at Dartmouth College, receiving his degree from the latter. Arriving in York, Pennsylvania, and initially working as an instructor in 1815, Stevens moved to Gettysburg to practice law the following year. In 1833, he won election to the Pennsylvania House, where he remained until 1841. During his tenure there, he proved to be an advocate of public schooling.

Stevens's defense of Pennsylvania's Free Public School Act of 1834, in the face of imminent repeal, proved crucial in saving the bill. It also exemplified common themes of discourse that surrounded debates of public schooling at that time, assigning public schools the role of providing children both equality of opportunity and moral guidance. Stevens's widely published address suggested that the popular alternative to public schooling, charity schooling* for poor children, was undesirable because it stigmatized those children who attended, and thus parents avoided it. He also argued that public education would discourage future social unrest and stated that on those grounds, it was in the interest of all taxpayers to support schooling. Reflecting a paternalism common to antebellum school reformers, he portrayed those parents who would deprive their children of education by having them work as selfish and in need of enlightened guidance. This speech before the Pennsylvania legislature transcended local importance by articulating an emerging bourgeois ideology shared by educators across America.

The Library of Congress houses the largest collection of Stevens's papers and letters. The *Journal of the Lancaster County Historical Society* (October 1958) includes a copy of his Public School Act speech. The best treatment of Stevens's contributions to and ideas about education is by Ralph Korngold, *Thaddeus Stevens: A Being Darkly Wise and Rudely Great* (1955). The fullest bibliography of Stevens's published and unpublished materials is in Alphonse B. Miller, *Thaddeus Stevens* (1939).

Rodney Hessinger

STOWE, CALVIN ELLIS (April 26, 1802–August 22, 1886), advanced the cause of public schooling in Ohio. Born in Natick, Massachusetts, he earned enough as an apprentice papermaker to attend Bowdoin College and Andover Theological Seminary. In 1833, he moved to Cincinnati to teach biblical literature at Lane Theological Seminary. Three years later he married his second wife, Harriet E. Beecher, author of *Uncle Tom's Cabin*. While in Cincinnati, he joined Samuel Lewis* and others to present papers to the Western Literary Institute and College of Professional Teachers. In 1835, Stowe reported on the "Education of Immigrants," describing efforts of a group of students from Lane Seminary. He claimed that a system of public schools* would augment the salutary effects of churches, newspapers, and Sunday schools.* Stowe traveled to Europe in 1836 to purchase a library for Lane Seminary. Ohio's governor and legislature asked him to survey the condition of schools there. On his return,

Stowe delivered an extensive report, "On the Course of Instruction in the Common Schools of Prussia and Wirtemberg," to the Ohio legislature in 1837. He urged the people of Ohio to imitate Prussians in using schools to develop the intellectual and moral powers of all children in all parts of the country. When that report circulated through the legislatures of Pennsylvania, Michigan, Massachusetts, North Carolina, and Virginia, Stowe rose to national prominence.

In 1850, Stowe returned to Bowdoin College to teach religion. He retired in 1863, and in 1867 he published *Origins and History of the Books of the Bible.*

See the Harriet Beecher Stowe Collection, Henry E. Huntington Library, San Marino, California. The University of Cincinnati library contains the complete records of the Western Literary Institute and College of Professional Teachers. Also refer to Edgar W. Knight, ed., *Reports on European Education* (1930). For biographies, refer to John Stanley Harker, "The Life and Contributions of Calvin Ellis Stowe" (1951), and F. Michael Perko, "Educational Biography and the Protestant Paideia" (1991).

Joseph Watras

STRACHAN (FORSYTHE), GRACE CHARLOTTE (1863–July 21, 1922), served as president of the 14,000-member Interborough Association of Women Teachers (IAWT) in New York City from 1907 to 1921. She led that organization's successful fight to gain equal pay for women teachers. The organization and its campaign inspired similar activities across the country and asserted the importance of grassroots activity among female teachers in coalition with other women's rights groups. Strachan, born in Buffalo and educated in the parochial schools,* graduated from the New York State Normal School in that city. She taught at Buffalo High School between 1879 and 1882, moving to a similar position at P.S. 11 in Brooklyn for a year. The following two years she taught at the city's Training School for Teachers before becoming principal of P.S. 42. She served as vice-president of the Brooklyn Teachers' Association, helped to organize the local branch of the Principals' Association, and was elected as chair of the Women's Civic Committee in 1921. Strachan became IAWT president during that organization's second year; she continued to be reelected until her death. As a tireless defender of teachers' rights, she campaigned for equal pay, for women teachers' right to marry, and against New York's Lusk bill, which required loyalty oaths for teachers. Strachan served as district superintendent of schools from 1904 to 1921, became the first female associate superintendent of schools in 1921, and unsuccessfully ran twice for president of the National Education Association.*

Strachan recounts many of the early details of the highly politicized equal pay campaign in her book *Equal Pay for Equal Work: The Story of the Struggle for Justice Being Made by the Women Teachers of the City of New York City* (1910). She also wrote "Salaries Based on Position and Not on the Sex of Incumbent" (1914) and "Teachers and Woman Suffrage" (1915).

Patricia Anne Carter

CHARLES E. STUART & OTHERS V. SCHOOL DISTRICT NO. 1 OF THE VILLAGE OF KALAMAZOO & OTHERS, (30 Mich. [69 1874]), was the first case to test the legality of the public high school* before a state supreme court. Indicative of a longstanding controversy over the place of "higher learning" in the publicly supported common school* system, the Kalamazoo case was one of nine such cases heard at this level in the late nineteenth century. The resolution of the case in favor of the school district set an important precedent by which the local district was confirmed in its power to expand the definition of "common schooling" by supplementing the minimum course of study required by state authorities.

Following the 1851 consolidation of the Kalamazoo district schools into a town system and the 1857 appointment of Daniel Putnam as the first local superintendent, a "high school department" was added to the newly erected Union School building in 1858 to stand at the apex of the newly "graded" school system. The addition of the high school department to the Kalamazoo common schools foreshadowed the Michigan legislature's passage of a law allowing publicly supported high schools the following year.

Charles E. Stuart first lodged a complaint against the high school at an 1867 town meeting. In the formal complaint filed at the district court in 1873, he claimed that any taxes supporting that portion of the school budget allotted to the high school were illegally assessed because the state constitution allowed public support only for schools that taught the "primary English branches." He further claimed that the 1859 law allowing the creation of public high schools was unconstitutional, and that regardless of the constitutionality of the 1859 law, the Kalamazoo high school department had still been created illegally both because it was created prior to 1859 and because the Kalamazoo School Board failed to affirm its decision to create a high school through a district vote (as was mandated by the 1859 law). Finally, Stuart claimed that no law authorized a local school board to hire a superintendent.

The Kalamazoo case was dismissed by the district court in February 1874, and this decision was affirmed by the Michigan Supreme Court that July. Justice Thomas Cooley delivered the court's opinion. Citing both the Northwest Ordinance of 1787* and the state constitution, he concluded that state support for education was to be broadly defined and not limited to the elementary subjects. Cooley's decision to look beyond the particulars of the Kalamazoo case and to render a broader judgment concerning the legality of the high school as a public institution contributed to the historical evaluation of this case as a landmark decision.

Representative analyses of the Kalamazoo case can be found in Archie P. Nevins, "The Kalamazoo Case" (1960), and William J. Reese, *The Origins of the American High School* (1995).

Scott Walter and William J. Reese

STUDENT GOVERNMENT. Since the nineteenth century, many schools have promoted the creation of student organizations that would contribute in varying degrees to individual school governance while at the same time inculcate qualities of leadership, cooperation, and greater civic consciousness and skills. The particular forms student governments took in individual schools have been remarkably varied. From bodies that consciously mirror the organization of national, state, or local governments to unique arrangements that provide representation of students by grade level, homerooms, or other school divisions, student governments have fulfilled a variety of functions in American schools.

Beginning in the progressive era (see PROGRESSIVE EDUCATION), the push for student government organizations became closely linked with new forms of civic education* and the growth of the extracurriculum.* Civic education courses, beginning in the first decade of the twentieth century, began to emphasize developing greater understandings of how governments and communities actually function. Instead of promoting mythical heroes, reflexive patriotism, and pristine governmental theories, civic education in the progressive period promoted involvement in local affairs and a commitment to re-creating a sense of community on local, state, and national levels that was eroded by the modern forces of industrialization, immigration, and urbanization.

Student governments were often linked to civic education efforts as practical ways to become involved in school and community activities. As schools specialized their offerings to attract an increasingly diverse student body, the importance of extracurricular organizations such as student government was elevated as a means by which students would learn cooperative living and democratic processes regardless of their eventual occupation or educational achievement. The *Cardinal Principles of Secondary Education,* sponsored by the National Education Association* (1916), often viewed as a highpoint in progressive curriculum development, recommended the use of student governments in fostering a democratic school environment that would translate into more adults able and willing to participate actively in civic life.

In actual practice, the theory behind student government has often diverged from its intent. Historical studies that examine the day-to-day life of schools often point out how extracurricular activities such as student government reflect larger existing social fault lines such as class, gender, and race. Student government participants have often come from backgrounds that correspond with greater amounts of social, economic, and political power outside of schools. Still, the idea and practice of getting students involved in activities, however limited, that contribute to participating in decision making over school matters continues to be appealing to most educators and is evidenced by the continued widespread existence of student government organizations in all types and levels of schools.

The best description of the rationale behind student governments during the progressive era can be found in the Commission on the Reorganization of Secondary Education, *Cardinal Principles of Secondary Education* (1918). For an example of how extracurricular activities mirror societal divisions, see Paula

Fass, *Outside In: Minorities and the Transformation of American Education* (1989).

Alexander Urbiel

SUMNER, CHARLES. See CIVIL RIGHTS ACTS OF 1866, 1875, 1957, 1964.

SUNDAY SCHOOLS. A decade after Robert Raikes started the first Sunday school in England (c. 1780), Sunday schools were established in Philadelphia, New York City, and other eastern cities by philanthropic men and women. These charity schools* were not under church auspices, and their primary focus was providing literacy for children unable to attend weekday schools. The emphasis in Sunday (or Sabbath) schools began shifting to religious education in the 1820s as public schools* expanded. Teaching reading continued to be important in Sunday schools on the expanding western frontier and in schools serving African Americans.

Protestant laypersons organized the American Sunday School Union in Philadelphia in 1824 to help establish Sunday schools and provide publications for them. The Union published and distributed primers, spellers, catechisms, Bible manuals, moral and religious books, and sets of Sunday school libraries. As editorial secretary from 1828 to 1867, Frederick A. Packard wrote more than forty books and edited some 2,000 for the Union. When Packard tried to get Horace Mann* to accept a Sunday School Union book for the Massachusetts school libraries* in 1838, a well-publicized battle ensued. Sunday school libraries were the majority of "public" libraries in the country in 1859, and in the nineteenth century the Union was one of the major publishers of children's literature.

Some denominations were wary of an organization operated by laypersons, not under ecclesiastical and clerical control, and felt the Union's publications were not sectarian enough to ensure their children's religious education. The denominations began to form their own Sunday school societies in the mid-1820s. During the nineteenth century, however, most of the denominational boards had limited resources, and none could rival the Sunday School Union's publishing program.

In 1830, the Union pledged to establish "a Sunday school in every destitute place" in the Mississippi Valley, and this campaign, conducted with other national voluntary benevolent societies, spread education and evangelical Protestantism. Sunday schools played an important role as an "agency of cultural transmission" and, historian Anne M. Boylan maintains, were almost rivaled as important schools in the nineteenth century. In 1865, Henry Barnard* noted that in the West and cities, the Sunday school "oftentimes becomes the precursor and pioneer both of the district school and of the church." Eventually, most Protestant denominations accepted the dual pattern of nondenominational public schools (though often pervaded by Protestantism) and Sunday schools under church auspices.

Like the public schools, most Sunday schools in the nineteenth century stressed memorization, especially of Bible verses. Teachers were relatively young, predominantly women, and volunteers, though in the early "mission school" years, some were paid. Classes were small (six to fifteen students) and typically met for two to three hours, before and sometimes after worship services.

Sunday school conventions became increasingly important. Beginning on local and state levels, there was an International Sunday School Convention by 1869. Loosely organized, these conventions provided teacher training, adopting policies from the teacher institutes common for public schools of the time. Leaders in this movement included businessman Benjamin F. Jacobs, author Edward Eggleston, evangelist Dwight Moody, and clergyman John Vincent (who later organized the Chautauqua Assembly as a "National Sabbath School University"). The major innovation of the conventions was the Uniform Lessons Series adopted in 1872. This six-year cycle of selected Bible verses gained wide popularity; even secular newspapers devoted coverage to the weekly lessons.

The Sunday school continued to evolve in the twentieth century. Protestant ministers, led by George Albert Coe, organized the interdenominational Religious Education Association in 1903. One thrust of this movement was to incorporate the insights of John Dewey* and progressive education* into Sunday schools. With professionalization, a new vocation developed in churches: the director of religious or Christian education. The American Sunday School Union was most influential in the antebellum years; it still exists, renamed the American Missionary Fellowship in 1974. After World War II, many denominations developed new Sunday school curricula. Independent companies also provide Sunday school materials, and the Uniform Series is still widely used in Bible study.

Catholic and Jewish congregations have adapted the Sunday school, although it is still preeminently a Protestant institution. Sunday (or church) schools enroll primarily children, but in some denominations and regions, adult classes are quite important. Sunday schools continue to be the main source of new members for most churches, though they have a smaller role in religious education and in the total configuration of American education than in the nineteenth century.

The American Sunday School Society's papers are at the Presbyterian Historical Society, Philadelphia. Also, see Anne M. Boylan, *Sunday School: The Formation of an American Institution, 1790–1880* (1988); William Bean Kennedy, *The Shaping of Protestant Education: An Interpretation of the Sunday School and the Development of Protestant Educational Strategy in the United States, 1789–1860* (1966); Robert W. Lynn and Elliott Wright, *The Big Little School: Sunday Child of American Protestantism* (1971); and Edwin W. Rice, *The Sunday-School Movement, 1780–1917, and the American Sunday-School Union, 1817–1917* (1917; 1972).

Natalie A. Naylor

SWANN V. CHARLOTTE-MECKLENBURG BOARD OF EDUCATION, 402

U.S. 1 (1971), marked the entry of busing into the national debate on school desegregation. *Swann* is also noteworthy as the first significant school desegregation case decided on its merits under the leadership of Warren Burger, the recently appointed chief justice who authored the opinion, and the U.S. Supreme Court's last unanimous ruling in a major school desegregation suit.

Swann arose in the Charlotte-Mecklenburg, North Carolina, school system, an urban area inhabited mostly by minorities that was surrounded by largely white suburbs. The federal trial court approved a plan, later modified by the Fourth Circuit, which used busing to restructure school attendance zones as a means of bringing about greater racial balance throughout the system. The Supreme Court affirmed the decision of the trial court, reasoning that while the Constitution does not require a specific degree of racial integration in public schools, numerical ratios and quotas can be used as a starting point. Acknowledging that it could not establish rigid guidelines on student transportation, the Court concluded that where the assignment of children to neighborhood schools did not effectively dismantle a dual system, a federal trial court could order busing to help eradicate segregation.

Charles J. Russo

SWETT, JOHN (July 31, 1830–August 12, 1913), California's fourth superintendent of public instruction, between 1863 and 1867, is generally regarded as the "father" of free, or tax-supported, schooling in that state. The son of a school master, he was born near Pittsfield, New Hampshire, attended a village school for eight years, and spent three years at Pittsfield Academy. Swett moved to California in 1854, seeking a more healthful living environment. He spent more than fifty years in education, most of it as a teacher, principal, deputy superintendent, superintendent, and school board member in northern California communities, mainly San Francisco. As California's superintendent of public instruction, he rewrote the *School Code*, secured a state school tax and a minimum rate for county school taxes, developed a system of teacher institutes,* organized a professional teachers' association, edited a school journal, and generally inspired the citizens of his adopted state to support a common school* system to a degree previously unheard of. The school year ending June 30, 1867, marked the transition in California from rate bill common schools to a "free" school system. Although Swett was himself nonpartisan in advocating public education, he was elected and defeated as a Union Republican.

By far the longer portion of Swett's life and career occurred after he left the state superintendency. In addition to holding various teaching and administrative positions, he authored a popular textbook and numerous articles on education, developed San Francisco's evening schools, and published the first history of California education, *Public Education in California* (1911). He died at his Hills-Girt farm in the Alhambra Valley, near Martinez, California.

Swett's papers are housed at the Bancroft Library, University of California, Berkeley. His biographies include William G. Carr, *John Swett: The Biography of an Educational Pioneer* (1933), and William G. Carr, *John Swett: California's Frontier Schoolmaster* (1978).

Irving G. Hendrick

T

TABA, HILDA (December 7, 1902–July 6, 1967), was one of the most important curriculum theorists and social studies* educators in the mid-twentieth century. A university professor for more than thirty years, she had a career that spanned a number of fields, including student evaluation, human relations, and teacher training, as well as curriculum development. Born in Estonia, where she received her B.A. (1926), she earned an M.A. from Bryn Mawr College (1927) and her Ph.D. (1933) from Teachers College, Columbia University, where she studied under William Heard Kilpatrick* and John Dewey.*

Taba worked with Ralph Tyler* in the Progressive Education Association's* Eight-Year Study* as an evaluation consultant in the 1930s, taught at the University of Chicago (1939–1945), and directed the American Council on Education's intergroup education project (1945–1948) and the University of Chicago's Center for Intergroup Education (1948–1951), before becoming professor of education at San Francisco State College, where she taught for the rest of her life.

Taba always worked closely with teachers, especially in social studies projects with Contra Costa County teachers in California in the 1950s and 1960s. She was convinced that teachers at the classroom level needed to participate in curriculum development, and her own ideas were influenced by their experiences. Taba's contributions included analyses of the structure of content, concept development, processes for inductive learning, and teaching strategies to promote critical thinking. Her most important book, *Curriculum Development: Theory and Practice* (1962), has become a classic in the field. The culmination of her professional career was a social studies textbook series for grades 1 to 8 that implemented her ideas and work. Posthumously named the Taba Social Science Program, the collaborative project was completed by her colleagues and published by Addison-Wesley in the 1970s. Her ideas continue to influence curriculum development and social studies education.

For a sense of Taba's contributions to curriculum development and social studies teaching, see Hilda Taba *Curriculum Development: Theory and Practice* (1962), and Hilda Taba, Mary C. Durkin, Jack R. Fraenkel, and Anthony H. McNaughton, *Teacher's Handbook for Elementary Social Studies* (1969). Also refer to Jack R. Fraenkel, "The Evolution of the Taba Curriculum Development Project" (1994); Mark M. Isham, "Hilda Taba, 1904–1967: Pioneer in Social Studies Curriculum and Teaching" (1982); and Mark M. Isham, "Hilda Taba: Pioneer in Curriculum Development" (1984).

Natalie A. Naylor

TAYLOR, JOHN ORVILLE (1807–January 18, 1890), was one of a number of reformers during the 1830s and 1840s who argued for the role that tax-supported common schools* could play in a democracy, referring to each school as a "Sentinel of Liberty, a Light House of Freedom." Along with other writers and state leaders, he emphasized that such public school teaching could also foster among the next generations a respect for private property, good work habits, and deference to authority.

Taylor graduated from Union College in 1830 and taught school in Philadelphia for two years. During the next two decades, he authored *District School or National Freedom* (1835), which went through three editions and had a first printing that sold over 5,000 copies; was a professor of popular education at the University of the City of New York (New York University); edited a short-lived but influential journal, *Common School Assistant* (1836–1840); lectured widely about the need for the expansion and reform of common schools; and wrote several other books, including *The Farmer's School Book* (1837), *Satirical Hits on the People's Education* (1839), and three *Lectures on Popular Education* (n.d.), which were published by the American Common School Society.

Taylor was one of the first American educators to focus attention on the Prussian system of education, which was known at the time for its excellent common, normal, and higher schools (see HIGH SCHOOLS; NORMAL SCHOOLS). He wrote and spoke about all aspects of the common schools, including the role to be played by parents and community leaders; the need to upgrade the profession of teaching; the importance of normal schools; the content of the elementary curriculum; the organization, management, and conditions of schools; and the effects of good schools on colleges, religion, a free press, crime, and other aspects of American life. He left the educational field in 1852 for business ventures in New York City, which he continued to be involved in until his retirement in 1879.

Taylor's views can be found in his *The First/Second/Third Public Lectures on Popular Education* (n.d.), published by the American Common School Society. For a biography, see Paul D. Travers, "John Orville Taylor: A Forgotten Educator" (1969). Carl F. Kaestle, *Pillars of the Republic: Common Schools and American Society, 1780–1860* (1983), provides a contextual backdrop for Taylor's life.

Kenneth Teitelbaum

TEACHER INSTITUTES. Before the establishment of the normal school,* the most deliberate training for the work of pedagogy was the teacher institute. Many of its features—its short-term program from several days to several weeks, its inspirational efforts to "awaken" or "quicken" moral character, its graphic and practical application of instructional techniques—derived from older evangelical procedures of religious revivals. During the antebellum period, particularly, it was no accident that many of the institute "conductors" were themselves ministers and their students were poor but worthy aspirants, if not to the ministry itself, then to surrogate work like teaching. Hymns and devotional songs were often part of their proceedings, which were often housed in churches. Henry Barnard,* the first U.S. commissioner of education, is generally credited with organizing the first institute in Hartford, Connecticut, in 1839. Twenty years later he pronounced the teacher institute an "educational revival agency, of the most extensive, permanent, and unobjectionable character."

The antebellum teacher institute thus engrafted itself onto an indigenous tradition rather than modeling itself on European practices or educational theories. Even after the Civil War, when normal schools began to produce an effective corps of professional teachers, teacher institutes continued to serve an in-service training function, inspirational and practical, even into the twentieth century. They never became certificate or degree-granting agencies; rather, they converted the once generic pre-bureaucratic term "institute," which referred to any practical instruction in basic skills, into a more specialized connotation of short-term, supplementary, technical training for immediate application.

See Paul H. Mattingly, *The Classless Profession: American Schoolmen in the Nineteenth Century* (1975).

Paul H. Mattingly

TEACHER RIGHTS. See ACADEMIC FREEDOM.

TENURE. See ACADEMIC FREEDOM.

TERMAN, LEWIS MADISON (January 15, 1877–December 21, 1956), represented a leading figure in the study of individual differences and the psychological testing movement. He earned his doctorate from Clark University in 1905. Terman spent the majority of his academic career at Stanford University in the College of Education (1910–1922) and then as head of the Psychology Department (1922–1942).

Terman was instrumental in developing group intelligence tests to classify U.S. Army recruits during World War I; subsequently, he helped to transform the army tests into the *National Intelligence Tests* for schoolchildren, which were used to sort and classify students by academic ability. Terman is also noted for his role in modifying the 1908 Binet-Simon (see BINET, ALFRED; INTELLIGENCE TESTING) Scales of Intelligence, which led to the 1916 version of the *Stanford-Binet Intelligence Scales.* Terman and his associates introduced the term "intelligence quotient" (IQ) and incorporated it into the 1916 Stanford-Binet. Terman also began a longitudinal study of gifted children (see SPECIAL EDUCATION) in 1921, which is ongoing. His interests in giftedness inspired his five-volume series *Genetic Studies of Genius* (1959).

The Stanford University Archives houses the Terman Papers. See Henry L. Minton's excellent biography, *Lewis M. Terman, Pioneer in Psychological Testing* (1988). Paul D. Chapman, *Schools as Sorters* (1988), focuses on Terman's role in the schools' adoption of intelligence tests to classify students into ability groups.

Harriett H. Ford and Mary Nesbit

TEXTBOOK ADOPTION practices are remarkably similar despite the differences that exist among schools and the variety of religious, economic, and political interests competing for control of those schools. Although public schools* in various states designate different selection agencies, in each case the final decison rests with local school people. Most state governments do not play strong roles in selecting texts, but many have laws reinforcing statewide approval of textbooks. Nearly all the states with such adoption policies are in the South and West. These state-regulated systems developed during the late nineteenth and early twentieth centuries out of a fear that eastern publishing houses would use unethical practices or charge too much for texts. By 1930, however, only Indiana, California, and Kansas tried to publish texts for their local schools. These efforts proved impractical.

As textbook publishing tried to satisfy a mass market, authors sought to satisfy diverse political or social interests in three general ways. First, the authors stressed technical aspects such as readability or adequate coverage of a vast amount of information. Second, they divided the work of writing among several authors to provide an overview of the subject. Third, they avoided making interpretations. The resulting texts were often dull and uninteresting, for livelier texts that advanced viewpoints could alienate an interest group. This happened, in the 1930s, to Harold Rugg,* who wrote a popular social studies* textbook series. Although the texts made only a few references to the social and economic difficulties of the time, the National Association of Manufacturers, the American Legion, and the Advertising Federation of America attacked those books as favoring socialist or anti-American ideas. School districts stopped using them as a result. Rugg withdrew from textbook authorship by the 1950s.

In the 1970s, educators again faced nationwide campaigns of textbook censorship. In 1974, conservative parents in Charleston, West Virginia, complained about the English language arts textbooks selected by the Kanawha County school board from a state approved list. They argued that the books threatened belief in God, made patriotism appear foolish, portrayed ethical norms as dependent on the situation, made slang appear as acceptable as standard English, and encouraged students to discuss family matters openly. These parents filed suit in U.S. District Court and had the books removed from the school. As in other cases, such as *President's Council, Dist. 25 v. Community School Board No. 25*, 457 F.2d 292 (2nd Cir. 1972), the court acknowledged the responsibility of locally elected or appointed authorities to select textbooks. Fearing the Kanawha County protest would inspire other campaigns of textbook censorship, public school educators recommended that all local districts use procedures similar to those followed in Michigan, Iowa, or Wisconsin. These policies set up steps for any resident or employee to follow in challenging the selections. They recommended that professionally certified staff form textbook selection committees and make recommendations to send to the superintendent, who would present them to the board. Although this model remains popular, studies in several states found that districts do not train the members of textbook selection committees nor give them ample information or time to make intelligent decisions.

Furthermore, school districts generally have limited freedom. By 1990, twenty-two states reimbursed local districts if their school boards selected texts from approved lists. The remaining twenty-eight states left local districts free to make their own choices. Since two large states, California and Texas, used approved lists, their decisions loomed large in the minds of publishers.

The textbook publishing industry also influences selection policies, particularly with its emphasis on uniformity. First, the production of any basal reading text or mathematics series includes the complex development of supplementary materials and teacher guides. Second, schools adopt new texts every five or six years. To take advantage of the brief time before the text falls out of date, publishers must have inventories, marketing research, and sales strategies on hand. As a result, by 1990, seven major publishers controlled 80 percent of this nation's textbook industry.

This uniformity has produced blandness in textbooks, which political conservatives and liberals alike have criticized. In 1986, Paul Vitz reported, in *Censorship: Evidence of Bias in Our Children's Textbooks*, that religion, traditional family values, and conservative positions did not appear in social studies texts or anthologies or literature published for elementary and secondary school children. Vitz, a conservative, thought that tax credits and vouchers* that direct state money to private schools* would cause publishers to address specialized interests. The next year, the Association of Supervision and Curriculum Development (ASCD), reflecting largely a liberal perspective, sponsored a panel study, *Religion in the Curriculum*. Agreeing in part with Vitz, panel members concluded that textbook publishers avoided mention of religion to the extent that the books distorted history and science. Instead of supporting private schools, that ASCD panel advised school boards to draft policies encouraging the adoption of texts that describe the place of religion in society.

As in any politically controversial process, judicial appeal has played a role in textbook adoption. Since state statute governed the approval of texts, many people turned to several state courts contesting textbook selection. By 1930, various state courts established several times that unless a board of education had violated its legal authority, no remedy was available. Similarly, federal courts refused to contradict local control of textbook selection unless those decisions intruded on some constitutional rights. In *Abington v. Schempp*, 374 U.S. 203 (1963), the U.S. Supreme Court found nothing wrong with a study of the Bible for literary and historic purposes (also, see BIBLE READING). However, in *Edwards v. Aguillard*, 107 S. Ct. 2573 (1987), the justices struck down a Louisiana statute mandating the teaching of both creation science and evolutionary science because that requirement imposed religion.

Finally, private schools follow procedures similar to those in public schools. Some Catholic dioceses (see PAROCHIAL SCHOOLS) allow local parishes or schools to form their own textbook selection committees. The committees can choose from a list of books approved by diocesan officials and the state department of education. In contrast, in other dioceses the central office makes the decisions for the parish schools. Although Catholic schools buy some texts from the same large firms that serve public schools, they are careful not to include things offensive to their religion. In addition, several small publishers serve religious schools such as Catholic or nondenominational Christian schools. Like Catholic school teachers, nondenominational Christian educators seek books with lessons that correspond to their religious views.

Secondary sources include Philip G. Altbach, Gail P. Kelly, Hugh G. Petrie, and Lois Weis, *Textbooks in American Society* (1991); Michael W. Apple and Linda K. Christian-Smith, *The Politics of the Textbook* (1991); David L. Elliott and Arthur Woodward, *Textbooks and Schooling in the United States* (1990); Edward B. Jenkinson, *The Schoolbook Protest Movement* (1986); Connaught Coyne Marshner, *Blackboard Tyranny* (1978); James Moffett, *Storm in the Mountains* (1988); and Guy M. Whipple, *The Textbook in American Education* (1931).

Joseph Watras

THIRD PLENARY COUNCIL OF BALTIMORE, a legislative meeting of all U.S. Roman Catholic bishops, met between November 9 and December 7, 1884, in Baltimore to stress the establishment of Catholic elementary schools (see PAROCHIAL SCHOOLS). Whereas the First Plenary Council of Baltimore (1852) had issued a decree that a Catholic school should, "if possible," be established beside every church and the Second Plenary Council of Baltimore (1866) had again commanded that Catholic schools should, "where possible," be built, the Third Plenary Council went farther. It adopted a standard catechism, *The Baltimore Catechism*, and decreed that profits from its sale should be used for the maintenance of Catholic schools. Bishop John Lancaster Spalding,* in a sermon at the Council, emphasized the necessity of parochial schools. He further enunciated the Council's position on public education, supporting the spread of literacy and secular knowledge, but stressing the primacy of religious knowledge. The Third Plenary Council's Catholic school policy guided the American Catholic Church until the Second Vatican Council's 1965 ''Declaration on Christian Education.''

The primary source document for the Third Plenary Council is *The Memorial Volume: A History of the Third Plenary Council of Baltimore* (1885). John T. Ellis's biography, *The Life of James Cardinal Gibbons* (1952), is considered the best secondary analysis of the Third Plenary Council.

Robert N. Barger

THORNDIKE, EDWARD LEE (August 31, 1874–August 9, 1949), psychologist, teacher educator, was the founder of educational psychology. Born in Williamsburg, Massachusetts, the son of a Methodist minister, Thorndike attended Wesleyan University, in Middletown, Connecticut, from which he graduated in 1895 with an A.B. in English. After receiving a second A.B. in English from Harvard University in 1896, he began studying psychology under William James and doing research on chickens, which he kept in the basement of James's house. Thorndike received an M.A. in psychology from Harvard in 1897; he then went to Columbia University in New York City, where he completed his doctorate in psychology in 1898 under James McKeen Cattell. An instant classic, his dissertation, *Animal Intelligence* (1898), set the direction of behavioristic (see BEHAVIORISM) experimental psychology for years to come.

In 1899, Thorndike began teaching at Teachers College, Columbia University, and remained there for the rest of his long career. He combined learning theory derived from his animal research with measurement of individual difference in humans and other school-related research to form educational psychology. His findings on the lack of transfer training from one subject to another, the result of a famous experiment done in 1901 with Robert S. Woodworth, refuted the worth of studying classical subjects like Latin and Greek to strengthen the mind generally and pointed to the need for more specific studies of human learning. Thorndike founded the *Journal of Educational Psychology* in 1910. In his three-volume text *Educational Psychology* (1913, 1914), he formalized his well-known Laws of Readiness, Exercise, and Effect and explained learning as a series of incremental connections influenced by genetic and environmental factors.

During World War I, Thorndike worked on the development and analysis of standardized intelligence tests* for the U.S. Army. The first psychologist to theorize about multiple intelligences, he rejected the idea of general intelligence. In the 1920s, Thorndike helped expand psychometrics into a full-scale testing industry and published many popular achievement tests and textbooks. His best-selling dictionaries for teachers and *Thorndike Arithmetics* had a lasting influence on school curriculum practice. In the 1930s, Thorndike did research on vocational guidance (see GUIDANCE COUNSELING), applied psychology to many fields, and proposed a natural science of values. Having written more than 500 publications, he retired from Teachers College in 1940. His behavioristic learning theory, standardized tests and measurements, and attempt to turn education into a science had an enormous impact on teacher education and schooling throughout the twentieth century.

Thorndike's papers and letters are held in the Teachers College Archives, Columbia University, and in the collections of other psychologists at Cornell and Harvard universities. Geraldine Joncich, *The Sane Positivist* (1968), is the definitive biography. Additional biographical information can be found in Carl Murchison, ed., *A History of Psychology in Autobiography* (1936). See also Barbara Beatty, "From Laws of Learning to a Science of Values: Efficiency and Morality in Thorndike's Educational Psychology" (1998).

Barbara Beatty

TINKER V. DES MOINES INDEPENDENT COMMUNITY SCHOOL DISTRICT, 393 U.S. 503 (1969), is the seminal case addressing the First Amendment free speech rights of students in public schools.* Three junior and senior high school students were suspended and sent home from classes for refusing to remove the black armbands they wore to protest American involvement in Vietnam. The students were disciplined pursuant to a two-day-old policy that the local school board adopted in anticipation of the protest. After the students' request to prevent the school from enforcing the policy was dismissed by the federal district court in Iowa on the ground that the board acted within the scope of its authority, an equally divided Eighth Circuit affirmed. The U.S. Supreme Court reversed in favor of the students. The Court began by noting that wearing armbands as a form of passive, nondisruptive protest was the type of symbolic act that placed the students' actions within the free speech clause of the First Amendment. As such, the Court reasoned that since school officials did not possess absolute power and that pupils do not "shed their constitutional rights to freedom of speech or expression at the schoolhouse gate" (p. 506), limits can be placed on the extent to which educators may regulate student speech. The Court concluded that absent a reasonable "forecast [of] substantial disruption of or material interference with school activities" (p. 514), school officials could not infringe upon students' constitutional right to freedom of expression.

Charles J. Russo

TRACKING is a generic term used to describe the processes of sorting students based on future vocation, family income, and notions of intelligence, race, and gender. The idea of tracking has evolved to encompass two general notions of sorting. There is a general notion that sorts according to ability at the secondary level. Traditionally, this has meant the dividing of high school students into three categories: college preparation, vocational, and general. The second notion of tracking has been developed by Jeannie Oakes, a leading opponent of the idea. Oakes sees tracking as a systematic and institutional way to nurture inequality among students.

Tracking is a term with no one point of origin. Instead, there are numerous starting points from which we can chart the rise of tracking within public education, including the postcolonial era, late-nineteenth-century industrialization, and the rise of the intelligent quotient (IQ) as a sorting mechanism (see INTELLIGENCE TESTING). As the United States emerged from the Revolution, the idea of public education had to be invented. In this debate over the meaning(s) and purpose(s) of public education, Thomas Jefferson* proposed the creation of a two-tiered system to educate the children of the young nation. This tracking system would, in his words, rake "a few geniuses from the rubbish," whereby the geniuses, or learned class, would be provided an education up through the completion of university training, whereas the laboring class would receive three years of primary education. Of course, women and Native Americans were for the most part excluded even from the three years of primary education, and African Americans with few exceptions were not included in any concept of public education. We can also trace the concept of tracking to late-nineteenth-century industrialization. Tracking became a way of funneling urban youth from public schools,* where they were inculcated with the ideals of punctuality, obedience, and repetition, to the urban factories, where they lived out these ideals (see VOCATIONAL EDUCATION). Finally, we can trace tracking to the rise of the notion of a fixed or hereditary intelligence. Whereas in England the notion of a fixed IQ was used to sort working-class students from the upper and middle classes, in America IQs were used to sort according to ethnicity and race. Led by Henry H. Goddard,* Lewis Terman,* and eugenicists, school officials in America reacted to the shifting trends of immigration by justifying tracking based on hereditary notions of IQ (see HEREDITARIANISM). This justification began to end officially with the rise of Nazism and its adoption of eugenic notions and practices. Tracking in schools nevertheless continued unabated until the 1960s. Since then, critics and activists have challenged tracking, claiming that it is a form of institutional racism and sexism. However, tracking continues as a practice in many contemporary schools.

As a result of court cases, curricula reforms (thematic units), pedagogical innovations (cooperative learning),* and social movements (multiculturalism), alternatives to tracking have emerged (see MULTICULTURAL EDUCATION). These include inclusion that seeks to join with "mainstream" groups those school populations that have been traditionally separated from others because of learning and physical disabilities (see SPECIAL EDUCATION).

For historical background, see Michael B. Katz, "The Origins of Public Education: A Reassessment" (1986); Joel H. Spring, *The Sorting Machine* (1976); and David B. Tyack, *Turning Points in American Educational History* (1967). Jeannie Oakes, *Keeping Track: How Schools Structure Inequality* (1985); Jeannie Oakes, *Multiplying Inequalities: The Effects of Race, Social Class, and Tracking on Opportunities to Learn Mathematics and Science* (1990); and Jeannie Oakes and Martin Lipton, *Making the Best of Schools: A Handbook for Parents, Teachers, and Policymakers* (1990), provides the most comprehensive contemporary overview. More recent treatments can be found in Anne Turnbaugh Lockwood, *Tracking: Conflicts and Resolutions* (1996), and Anne Whee-lock, *Crossing the Tracks: How "Untracking" Can Save America's Schools* (1992).

John A. Weaver

TRIBAL SCHOOLS. The tribal public school systems of the Cherokee, Choc-taw, Chickasaw, Creek, and Seminole tribes offers important insight into Native American culture and raises significant questions regarding schooling as a de-culturalizing force. Each of the five tribes organized these comprehensive public school* systems in Indian Territory shortly after they were removed from the eastern states by the terms of the Indian Removal Act of 1830. The National Councils of the Cherokees and the Choctaws legislated the creation of the first systems in 1841 and 1842, respectively. The school systems of the Creek, Chick-asaw, and Seminole tribes developed in the 1850s. The systems evolved from schools established by missionaries before and after removal. While they dif-fered slightly from nation to nation, they shared some fundamental organiza-tional characteristics: supervision by tribal boards of trustees and school superintendents, funding from tribal revenues, tuition arrangements for white noncitizens, and separate schools for freed slaves after the Civil War. The sys-tems consisted of "day" or "neighborhood" schools for the younger children and seminaries and academies* for young men and women. By 1906, 995 day and thirty-eight boarding schools existed among the five tribes.

The curricula varied widely. Subject matters included the "three R's," man-ual and vocational training, and in some academies European languages (see VOCATIONAL EDUCATION). The nations provided free textbooks for stu-dents. McGuffey's *Readers** and Noah Webster's* spelling book were used for lessons in English. Lessons were also taught using native languages; Cherokees used Sequoyah's alphabet and the Choctaws used the *Choctaw Definer*. Most of the teachers in the schools were Native Americans, but some were white.

The demise of the tribal public schools began in 1898 as part of a larger government effort to dissolve the tribal nations and take back Indian Territory. The secretary of the interior ruled that his control over the Choctaw-Chickasaw coal and asphalt royalties and all Cherokee and Creek revenues used to support the schools, established by the terms of the Atoka Agreement and the Curtis Act, invested him with management of the schools. On February 19, 1898, he appointed a white school superintendent for the Indian Territory and a supervisor for each of the tribes, except the Seminole. The superintendent, in a series of reports, berated tribal leaders for their inefficient, corrupt, and wholly inadequate guardianship of the schools. These reports along with agitation by white non-citizens in Indian Territory who did not have access to schools, led Congress in 1904 to appropriate money from the federal treasury for the support of a territorial school system for all children in Indian Territory. The Five Tribes Act of 1906 was the deathknell of the tribal public school systems. It strengthened the federal government's management and control of the tribal schools, absorbing them into the federally supported territorial school system. With Oklahoma's statehood in 1907, all schools in Indian Territory became part of the Oklahoma state school system.

For primary sources, see the Duke Oral History Collection, the Gilbert W. Dukes Manuscript Collection, the Indian Pioneer Papers, and Works Progress Administration Historic Sites and Federal Writers Project Manuscript Collection in the Western History Collections at the University of Oklahoma, Norman. Government documents include Alice C. Fletcher, *Indian Education and Civilization: A Report Prepared in Answer to Senate Resolution of February 23, 1885* (1888); "Report of the Superintendent of Schools for Indian Territory with Annual Report of the Commissioner of Indian Affairs" (1907); and U.S. Congress, House, Secretary of the Interior (1899, 1907).

Jeffrey A. Liles

TUTORS, most extensively used in colonial and antebellum families and colleges, were an informal source of education often used to provide education where more permanent institutions or funds were lacking. Reflecting and reinforcing the transient nature of the tutorial position was its source of labor, generally young men and women in transitional stages in training and life.

Along with the education that parents provided their children and that masters were expected to bestow upon apprentices (see APPRENTICESHIP) and servants, tutorial instruction helped make the family a central educational institution during the colonial period. Genteel families of the colonial and antebellum South relied most heavily on tutors. The scattered pattern of settlement in the South may have been instrumental in shaping such educational arrangements. Tutors' roles within the family extended beyond teaching subjects and skills. Southern patriarchs frequently relied upon them to provide discipline, enabling parents to maintain more tender relationships with their children.

Tutorial instruction within the family had important gender dimensions, especially when a family reached such a level of wealth that a woman's labor could be dispensed with. Whereas boys were expected to concentrate on subjects that were considered practical, such as Latin and mathematics, girls were often geared toward more ornamental subjects suited for entertainment, such as dancing, music, and French, in the great plantation houses.

Hunter Dickenson Farish's edited collection, *Journal and Letters of Philip Vickers Fithian* (1943), gives a vivid firsthand account of tutoring from the perspective of a tutor. Daniel Blake Smith, *Inside the Great House* (1980), provides a fine discussion of the role tutors played in southern planter families. See Thomas Woody, *A History of Women's Education in the United States* (1929), for useful detail on the tutorial experiences of young women and girls.

Rodney Hessinger

UNITED STATES DEPARTMENT OF EDUCATION (ED), created by an act of Congress in 1979, became the first cabinet-level education agency of the federal government, superseding the U.S. Office of Education (USOE) and the National Institute of Education (NIE). The former was established in 1867 as a subcabinet department to encourage educational improvements through the nationwide collection and dissemination of statistics and information. Congress established NIE in 1972 to support research and development that would advance teaching, learning, and equal educational opportunity.

Originally proposed during the antebellum period by Henry Barnard* and leaders of the National Teachers Association* (later renamed the National Education Association*), the idea of a federal education bureau eventually won congressional approval in the aftermath of the Civil War. Advocates expected the new agency to promote the spread of public education, particularly in the South and the western territories, and to provide practical advice to educators (see PUBLIC SCHOOLS) in much the same way the new Department of Agriculture was to help farmers. Critics argued it would centralize control over schools, thus infringing on local and state prerogatives. Such hopes and fears aside, the new department's clearest mandate was to gather data and publish reports. Barnard served as the first commissioner of education, resigning when Congress shifted the agency to bureau status in the Department of Interior. Among his prominent successors were John Eaton, William T. Harris,* Philander P. Claxton, and John W. Studebaker, each of whom served terms of ten years or longer. Eaton, who served between 1870 and 1886, defended the Bureau of Education against attempts in Congress to abolish it and gradually secured increased appropriations. Under his leadership, the Bureau established routines and protocols for the collection of educational statistics, producing comprehensive biennial reports that in most years arrived on schedule. Beyond topics related to elementary and secondary schools, Bureau interests gradually encompassed higher, vocational,* early childhood,* and international education and the educational roles of families, libraries, world fairs, and museums. From the 1890s through the 1920s, it administered schools, medical services, and economic development initiatives in the Alaskan Territory. Although detractors at the turn of the twentieth century worried that it had become merely a "bureau of information," the agency lacked any authority, beyond its Alaskan responsibilities, to redirect educational operations at state or local levels.

Shifted to the new Department of Health, Education, and Welfare (HEW) in 1953, USOE experienced significant growth in terms of budget, staff, and authority between 1953 and 1979. New assignments included specified duties related to impact aid (i.e., federal monies made available to school districts whose student populations were "impacted" by the children of personnel at federal installations and facilities, like military bases), the National Defense Education Act* in the 1950s, and during President Lyndon Johnson's administration, the Elementary and Secondary Education Act,* several pieces of Great Society legislation, and enforcement of civil rights regulations (see CIVIL RIGHTS ACTS).

The last proved controversial. The Office of Education's scope ranged across international, bilingual,* special,* postsecondary, private,* and vocational education, in addition to elementary and secondary schools. Prominent educators who served as USOE's commissioner during this period included Francis Keppel, Harold Howe II, James Allen, and Ernest Boyer*; few remained in office longer than three years, a turnover rate that weakened the agency's stability and influence. Despite the growth, USOE remained only one of the federal agencies having education-related assignments, including the Departments of Defense, Labor, Commerce, and HEW, the National Science Foundation, and the National Endowment for the Humanities. The overlapping programs gave ammunition to advocates of departmental status for USOE, which sought ways of making federal involvement in education more focused and efficient.

Proponents expected ED to continue in the reformist tradition envisioned for USOE and NIE and to represent education more clearly as a national priority. The Department of Education Reorganization Act won bipartisan support in Congress and endorsements from a wide variety of professional and scholarly associations. Emphasizing the absence of specific references to education in the U.S. Constitution, opponents feared the creation of a cabinet-level agency would encourage political responses to educational problems and federal intrusions upon a policy area traditionally left to the states. President Jimmy Carter appointed federal appeals judge Shirley Hofstedler as the first secretary of education. In 1981, President Ronald Reagan announced his intention to abolish ED, but Secretary of Education Terrel Bell advised against taking such a step. Confronted with congressional support for the department among both liberals and conservatives, President Reagan abandoned his plan as public debate over school reform intensified during the 1980s. Issues encompassed declines in measured student achievement, international comparisons that showed U.S. students faring poorly, roles education might play in strengthening the U.S. economy relative to that of other countries, uses of standardized tests to ascertain educational results, the introduction of vouchers* to permit parental choice in the selection of public or private schools for their children, and proposed systemic reorganization of public education. Various states initiated reforms to address these concerns in the early 1980s, efforts eclipsed by the widely noted 1983 publication *A Nation at Risk,** compiled by ED's National Commission on Excellence in Education. Fueled by numerous other reports equally critical of public schools and measured student achievement, a national debate ensued in which ED and subsequent department secretaries played leading roles. Throughout the 1990s, the department remained at the forefront of campaigns to introduce national curriculum and assessment standards that would hold students, teachers, and schools accountable for higher levels of academic attainment.

While committed to high achievement standards, President Bill Clinton, with Secretary of Education Richard Riley, also directed ED to strengthen the learning opportunities available to all age groups. The Educate America Act of 1994 established national educational goals for the first time in U.S. history. Other legislation sought more effective transitions from schooling to workplace and job retraining programs for adults. In addition to carrying out its new responsibilities, the department administered previously mandated activities, including data gathering and dissemination, research and development, enforcement of civil rights statutes, and programs in elementary, secondary, postsecondary, vocational, bilingual, and special education. It fulfilled limited responsibilities for four federally supported institutions, the American Printing House for the Blind, Gallaudet University, Howard University, and the National Technical Institute for the Deaf. Like USOE, ED must coordinate its efforts with several other federal agencies that have education-related assignments. In 1995, the Republican majorities in both houses of the 104th Congress targeted ED as a likely prospect for budget cuts and an easing of government regulation, specifically with regard to national educational goals.

For historical background, refer to Beryl A. Radin and Willis D. Hawley, *The Politics of Federal Reorganization: Creating the U.S. Department of Education* (1988), and Donald R. Warren, *To Enforce Education: A History of the Founding Years of the U.S. Office of Education* (1974).

Donald R. Warren

UNITED STATES DEPARTMENT OF HEALTH, EDUCATION, AND WELFARE. See UNITED STATES DEPARTMENT OF EDUCATION.

UNITED STATES OFFICE OF EDUCATION. See UNITED STATES DEPARTMENT OF EDUCATION.

UNIVERSITY OF CHICAGO LABORATORY SCHOOL. Founded by John Dewey* in January 1896, it served as an experimental setting for his philosophy of education. The "Dewey School" enrolled thirty-six students between the ages of six and twelve and employed two teachers and one manual training instructor during its first year. By October 1897, enrollment had grown to sixty pupils and sixteen teachers. Located in the Hyde Park–Kenwood area of Chicago, adjacent to the university, it became the University Elementary School in 1900. The next year Colonel Francis W. Parker* left as director of the Chicago City (formerly Cook County) Normal School to assume that post at the elementary school, bringing faculty and students with him. This arrangement led to the university overseeing two elementary schools—Parker's practice school for the training of teachers and Dewey's laboratory of the Department of Pedagogy. The university also opened the University Secondary School that same year with Dewey as director. It later merged with the Chicago Manual Training School and the South Side Academy to become the University High School. Parker died in 1902, and in 1904 Dewey resigned in protest at the termination of Alice Dewey, his wife, as elementary school principal. By 1905, while under new leadership, the University schools maintained little of the Deweyan tradition. When Charles Judd arrived at the university to head the Department of Education in 1909, he brought new faculty, Franklin Bobbitt* and then Henry Morrison, and a new perspective of testing, efficiency, organized course of study, and systematic and sequential perspective to the overall direction of the laboratory school. Judd and Morrison fundamentally altered the educational direction of the school, moving from a progressive (see PROGRESSIVE EDUCATION) approach to the academically oriented, college preparatory tradition that still dominates.

The Laboratory School participated with other schools in the Progressive Education Association's* Eight-Year Study* (c. 1932–1940) but never became as progressive as its northside counterpart, the Francis Parker School, which was considered to be one of the most progressive schools in the country. Although the Laboratory School abandoned Dewey's philosophy, it did maintain its experimental tradition. It also received notoriety for its attempt to embody university president Robert M. Hutchins's "great books" (see *PAIDEIA*) program at the secondary school level. The Lab School also provided a laboratory setting for the study of students who gained early admission to the University of Chicago and entered the undergraduate college after only two years of high school.

The exact locations of the Dewey School were West of Washington Park, January 1896; 5714 South Kimbark Avenue, October 1896; 5412 Ellis Avenue, October 1898; Emmons Laine Hall, University of Chicago, October 1903. The Laboratory School archives are housed at the Special Collections, University of Chicago. School descriptions include Ida DePencier, *The History of the Laboratory Schools: The University of Chicago* (1967), and Katherine Camp Mayhew and Anna Camp Edwards, *The Dewey School* (1936).

Craig Kridel

V

VOCATIONAL EDUCATION involves school training in a specific job such as agriculture, trade, and industry, usually done through a combination of theoretical and practical experience. Vocational education in the United States began informally, experiencing historical permutations as manual training, industrial education, and cooperative education.

This attempt at nonacademic education began as a response to the urbanized and industrialized society that emerged after the Civil War. Germany and Russia began to train workers formally in the latter half of the nineteenth century. Influenced by these European examples, American business leaders and sympathetic educators believed that a new curriculum, which allowed students to begin to acquire workplace skills, was needed to integrate schooling with the needs of a rapidly changing society. The early manual arts movement attempted to synthesize academic and practical skills in one program. Johann Heinrich Pestalozzi, the father of manual training, had already successfully combined manual work with general education in Europe (see PESTALOZZIANISM). The1876 Philadelphia Exposition exhibited training technology pioneered by the Moscow Imperial Technical School (see INTERNATIONAL EXPOSITIONS). This training represented a break from the traditional apprenticeship* model; the Moscow Imperial Technical School separated technical instruction from production. This exhibit greatly influenced John D. Runkle and Calvin M. Woodward,* both of whom pioneered manual education in the United States. Finally, some isolated schools began to experiment with a utilitarian educational approach. In the 1880s, Chicago's Crane Technical High School began to teach college-bound engineers the practical side of the profession.

The initial pedagogical thrust of manual arts was perceived as a part of a broad and general education program that would balance theoretical and abstract knowledge with a hands-on approach. From a labor market perspective, it would also create a cadre of skilled workers able to meet the demands of the emerging complex industrial workplace of the 1880–1920 era. Furthermore, some educators argued that manual education recreated agrarian values of work satisfaction, with individual workers gaining the ability to see how their small piece of the finished product represented a part of the whole production process. They saw manual arts education as a countervailing force to the separation of work and life caused by industrialization. These educators perceived manual training as a process to preserve traditional values and facilitate industrial progress.

Proponents strongly promoted the moral aspect of manual arts in the South among newly freed slaves. Industrial education served as the curriculum at African American institutions like Hampton and Tuskegee. Booker T. Washington* supported the concept of an education experience that combined schooling and actual workplace training, and many of the early buildings at Tuskegee were constructed by the students.

A clear notion of vocational education emerged during the early 1900s when some industrial and public school leaders no longer wanted to link the teaching of theory with practice. Many interest groups accepted vocational education as a part of a new and separate curriculum for the rapidly growing high schools.* The business community became its most vocal and visible booster, joined by like-minded educators. Supporters founded the National Association for the Promotion of Industrial Education in 1907 and embraced the view that a differentiated curriculum, suitable to students from various social classes, would democratize mass education. The labor movement opposed the concept of differentiated education at first, since it would exacerbate social class conflict by prescribing separate schools for academic work and vocational training. By 1908, however, business leaders had co-opted labor, and the American Federation of Labor lent its support to vocational education. Unions saw truncated schooling, through dropping out (see DROPOUTS), as detrimental to gaining skills for higher-paid jobs; vocational education, in this perspective, retained students by addressing their job needs. Labor leaders also accepted vocational education as part of a comprehensive high school curriculum, which would theoretically facilitate the mingling of students from different social classes. Becoming institutionalized, vocational education received federal support with the passage of the Smith-Hughes Act of 1917.*

The rise of distributive education can also be traced to the earliest years of vocational education. In the early 1900s, private business schools effectively trained students for the needs of the business office and the retail store (also, refer to BUSINESS EDUCATION). By the 1920s, Frederick G. Nichols was championing retail sales training in the emerging comprehensive public high school.

By the 1920s, vocational guidance (see GUIDANCE COUNSELING) and its "scientific methods," including the extensive use of intelligence testing,* was in full use to separate students into the various curriculum tracks that had emerged in the comprehensive high school. Choices offered to students were not necessarily based on the individual's choice but, rather, on the bias of the selector. Such sorting, for critics, redefined democracy as well as the equality of education and educational opportunity. The development of the comprehensive high school muted the class education argument, and vocational education became an integral part of the public school system.

The biggest challenge to vocational education arose with the attack on segregated education, since many of the nonacademic curricula were populated by poor whites and people of color. This tracking* system was challenged in the 1960s. By the 1970s, the federal government promoted career education.* The concept of technology training represents the latest permutation of the concept of vocational education. (Also, refer to MASSACHUSETTS COMMISSION ON INDUSTRIAL AND TECHNICAL EDUCATION; NATIONAL VOCATIONAL GUIDANCE ASSOCIATION.)

For historical background information, see Lawrence A. Cremin, *The Transformation of the School: Progressivism in American Education, 1876–1957* (1964); Clarence J. Karier, *Shaping the American Educational State: 1900 to the Present* (1975); and Edward A. Krug, *The Shaping of the American High School* (1964); and Marvin Lazerson, *Origins of the Urban School: Public Education in Massachusetts* (1971). Contemporary views can found in G. Bottoms and D. Sharpe, *Teaching for Understanding through Integration of Academic and Technical Education* (1996); Norton W. Grubb, "The Integrated Curriculum: A Reality Check" (1996); Theodore Lewis, "Toward a New Paradigm for Vocational Educational Research" (1990); and Cathleen Stasz, T. Kaganoff, and R. A. Eden, "Integrating Academic and Vocational Education: A Review of the Literature, 1987–1992" (1994).

Peter Sola

VOUCHERS. As originally proposed in 1955 by Milton Friedman, a University of Chicago economist, states would guarantee each child a minimum level of education by giving parents vouchers each year redeemable for a certain sum of money toward tuition at any "approved" school. Schools participating, both public* and private,* would have to meet minimum government standards in their educational programs in order to be "approved" and to be eligible to receive payment for their vouchers. Parents would be free to choose the school best suited to their child's needs and to supplement the voucher amount with additional money if they so desired. Other sources of the voucher concept have existed. After the 1954 *Brown v. Board of Education** decision, southern communities used vouchers to support segregated schools, but the courts declared these unconstitutional. Some states have attempted to use a voucher system for supporting parochial schools,* and cases are still pending on their legal status.

During the late 1960s and early 1970s, the idea gained popularity in the United States. A large-scale experiment involving some 4,600 students was conducted in the early 1970s in the Alum Rock School District in San Jose, California. Other less ambitious voucher-type schools were established in Berkeley and Pasadena, California; East Lansing, Michigan; and Minneapolis, Minnesota.

These experiments never created a free market in schooling in the sense that a wide range of market alternatives became available to parents. Selection was limited, since only public schools participated in the experiments. Regardless of their perceived success or failure, these experiments did not attract much attention. Strong opposition from many sources continued, and only a few school districts expressed interest in emulating the early experiments. Although proponents deemed these schools successful, many of these programs closed because of lack of interest, and only a few remained in operation by the late 1970s.

The idea of vouchers persisted among advocates of private education. Roman Catholics saw the possibility for direct public support for their parochial schools. Evangelical Christians supported vouchers to subsidize their private sectarian schools. Free market advocates wanted vouchers in order to reduce the cost of schooling. Proponents generally claim that it is unfair for public schools to exist as a tax-supported monopoly. The voucher system would increase competition in the educational arena because of the greater freedom achieved through educational choice. Public schools would have to compete with private schools, raising the quality of education in both sectors by forcing mediocre schools out of the education business.

Many public school people and organizations, such as the American Federation of Teachers,* generally opposed the concept. These critics contended that vouchers would weaken and perhaps destroy the public schools as a common school system. Public schools would become the refuge of the economically disadvantaged and minority students as affluent groups abandoned them for private schools. They further charged that vouchers would encourage racial segregation and encourage expensive duplication of schools and lead to many of marginal quality. Aid to parochial schools would also violate the principle of the separation of church and state. Finally, competition between schools would foster publicity seeking, and teachers would try to be popular rather than professional.

A specific secondary source is Peter W. Cookson, Jr., ed., *The Choice Controversy* (1992). Also, refer to general sources such as Jack L. Nelson, Kenneth Carlson, and Stuart B. Palonsky, *Critical Issues in Education: A Dialectic Approach* (1996), and Joseph W. Newman, *America's Teachers: An Introduction to Education* (1998).

Don T. Martin

W

WASHBURNE, CARLETON WOLSEY (December 2, 1889–November 27, 1968), as the charismatic superintendent of schools in the affluent Chicago suburb of Winnetka from 1919 to 1943, served as a leader in the progressive education* movement. His "Winnetka plan"* attracted international attention, and his extensive writings were translated into several foreign languages.

Washburne was deeply influenced by his mother, who had worked with two well-known pioneers of progressive education, Colonel Francis W. Parker* and John Dewey.* After graduating from Stanford University in 1912, the newly married Washburne, looking for any kind of employment, became a teacher in a rural California school. This experience convinced him that the curriculum had to be individualized to meet the widely differing needs of his pupils. This led him to San Francisco State College, in 1914, where he worked with Frederic Burk, a pioneer in individualized education. Burk recommended Washburne for a superintendency, assuring him that "Winnetka is a very small place; so if you fail, it won't make a very big splash."

Washburne worked closely with Winnetka's teachers and developed a curriculum based on a form of programmed learning. In addition, as the Winnetka plan evolved, children spent half of each day in "group and creative activities," based on progressive ideas. Washburne, at the same time, was deeply concerned with developing ways of making schooling more efficient.

In 1943, Washburne joined the U.S. Army and was assigned the task of reopening Italian schools after purging them of their fascist ideology. Six years later he became director of Teacher Education at Brooklyn College. Washburne retired from that position in 1960.

For Washburne's educational views, see *A Living Philosophy of Education* (1953) and a book he coauthored with Sidney P. Marland, Jr., *Winnetka: The History and Significance of an Educational Experiment* (1963). Washburne also wrote an autobiography, "An Autobiographical Sketch" (1971). Finally, see

Patricia A. Graham, "Carleton Wolsey Washburne: A Biographical Essay" (1971).

Arthur Zilversmit

WASHINGTON, BOOKER TALIAFERRO (April 5, 1856–November 14, 1915), the founder of Tuskegee Institute and "Wizard of Tuskegee," became known for his educational philosophy of industrial education.* His first experience with industrial (or vocational) education came as a student at Hampton Institute in the 1870s under General Samuel Chapman Armstrong. Attributing the "Tuskegee idea" to Armstong, Washington founded and began to build Tuskegee Institute in Alabama in 1881 to provide a way for African Americans to achieve economic success. By the 1890s, he espoused a philosophy that suggested political enfranchisement could be achieved through educational and economic attainment, and his 1895 Atlanta address explicated how he saw industrial education as part of a process of racial uplift for African Americans. His autobiographical polemic *Up from Slavery* (1901) also stressed industrial education as the key to success in the African American community.

In addition to speaking and writing, Washington used his influence to obtain philanthropic contributions from Andrew Carnegie, John D. Rockefeller, and the General Education Board* to fund his and other Southern black industrial education programs. These professional activities—as his well as his personal difficulties—led to a serious debate between Washington and W.E.B. Du Bois* about the direction industrial education was taking the African American community. Du Bois and other African American leaders suggested that northern white philanthropists controlled Tuskegee Institute and the industrial education movement in southern black public schools, colleges, and universities. Despite opposition from other black leaders, Washington and the "Tuskegee Machine" led the dominant educational strategy of industrial education until his death.

Louis R. Harlan edited *The Booker T. Washington Papers* (1972–1984) and wrote two biographies, *Booker T. Washington: The Making of a Black Leader, 1865–1901* (1972) and *Booker T. Washington: The Wizard of Tuskegee, 1901–1915* (1983). Also see Washington's autobiography as well as the book he coauthored with W.E.B. Du Bois, *The Negro in the South: His Economic Progress in Relation to His Moral and Religious Development* (1907). Biographical and philosophical studies include Frederick D. Dunn, "The Educational Philosophies of Washington, Du Bois, and Houston: Laying the Foundations for Afrocentrism and Multiculturalism" (1993); August Meier, *Negro Thought in America, 1880–1915: Racial Ideologies in the Age of Booker T. Washington* (1963); and Raymond Smock, ed., *Booker T. Washington in Perspective: Essays of Louis R. Harlan* (1988).

Donald E. Collins

WEBSTER, NOAH (October 16, 1758–May 28, 1843), published the most popular introductory reading text, *The American Spelling Book*, in the United

States, selling nearly 9 million copies by 1832. This and Webster's 1829 revision, *The Elementary Spelling Book*, totaled at least 70 million copies, and the *Elementary* became the arbiter of American spelling.

Born in West Hartford, Connecticut, Webster graduated from Yale College in 1778 and began a long publishing career. He composed a spelling book, *A Grammatical Institute of the English Language, Part I* (1783), while teaching at a classical school in Goshen, New York. He published *Part II* (a grammar) and *Part III* (a reader) in 1784 and 1785, respectively. In 1787, Webster revised his speller as *The American Spelling Book*. He published the *American Magazine* from 1787 to 1788 in New York City. Then in 1789 moved to Hartford, but returned to New York, editing that city's first daily newspaper, the pro-federalist *American Minerva* (1793–1798). Disenchanted with politics, Webster relocated to New Haven to work on his dictionary, issuing a stopgap work, *The Compendious Dictionary*, in 1806. He published his masterpiece, *An American Dictionary of the English Language*, in 1828. Aided by Aaron Ely, a New York educator, Webster revised his speller as *The Elementary Spelling Book* the following year.

Although he published on diverse subjects, including epidemics and a bowdlerized Bible, Webster's primary interest was education. He envisaged a whole system, "beginning with *children* & ending with *men*." His other publications include four volumes of the *Elements of Useful Knowledge* (1802, 1804, 1806, 1812), covering geography, history, the climate, and a history of animals; *History of the United States* (1832); *A Manual of Useful Studies* (1839); and several school dictionaries (also, see SPELLING BEE).

Webster's spelling books and dictionary became his most enduring contributions to education. The *Elementary*, dubbed the "blue-back speller" or just "ole blue-back" because of its blue covers, was reprinted—not long after Webster's death—at the rate of a million copies a year. The *Elementary* brought the alphabet method of reading instruction to its most perfect form. Used after the 1830s mainly as a book to teach spelling, it still taught reading to some; in 1866, its sales leaped by half a million copies, purchased by the newly emancipated slaves in order to learn how to read. Webster's lexicographical work, culminating in the over 70,000 entries of the *American Dictionary*, secured his long-lasting fame and made "Webster" a synonym for dictionary.

Altering American orthography represented Webster's other major contribution. Webster abandoned his early and radical attempts at reform (*nabor*), but he succeeded in more modest changes. Basing his decisions on principles of uniformity and consistency, Webster created all the differences that exist today between American and British spellings (i.e., classes of words like *center/centre*, *honor/honour*, and *defense/defence*, as well as individual words like *jail/gaol* and *plow/plough*). He introduced them in his spelling books and dictionaries and popularized them through his spellers.

The New York Public Library is the largest repository of Webster's textbooks and papers. The Connecticut Historical Society has the business correspondence of his last years. For a complete bibliography, see Emily Ellsworth Ford Skeel, comp., *A Bibliography of the Writings of Noah Webster* (1958; 1971). For autobiographies, consult Richard M. Rollins, ed., *The Autobiographies of Noah Webster from the Letters and Essays, Memoir, and Diary* (1989). Biographies include Richard M. Rollins, *The Long Journey of Noah Webster* (1980), and Harry Warfel, *Noah Webster: Schoolmaster to America* (1936; 1964). See also E. Jennifer Monaghan, *A Common Heritage: Noah Webster's Blue-Back Speller* (1983).

E. Jennifer Monaghan

WEST VIRGINIA STATE BOARD OF EDUCATION V. BARNETTE, 319 U.S. 624 (1942). The U.S. Supreme Court in this case reconsidered its decision in *Minersville School District (Pennsylvania) v. Gobitis,* 310 U.S. 586 (1939). The West Virginia Board of Education had adopted a resolution that ordered a mandatory flag salute for the schools (see PLEDGE OF ALLEGIANCE). The Barnette children, members of the Jehovah's Witnesses sect, refused on religious grounds to salute the flag and were expelled from school. The Court's decision framed the issue as a conflict between state authority and individual rights. In ruling against the West Virginia Board of Education resolution, and overruling the three-year-old *Gobitis* decision, the Court stated a frequently quoted position on individual rights under the Constitution: "If there is any fixed star in our constitutional constellation, it is that no official, high or petty, can prescribe what shall be orthodox in politics, religion, nationalism, religion, or other matters of opinion, or force citizens to confess by word or act their faith therein" (p. 642).

Thomas J. I. Emerson, *The System of Freedom of Expression* (1971), is a standard and reflects a liberal sense of case law, whereas Rodney A. Smolla, *Free Speech in an Open Society* (1992), reflects the genre of a growing contemporary, conservative approach.

Bruce Beezer

WESTMINISTER SCHOOL DISTRICT OF ORANGE COUNTY V. MEN-DEZ, 161 F.2d 774 (9th Cir. 1947). This case represented an early challenge to a state practice of segregating Mexican school-aged children in separate schools and featured Thurgood Marshall as the lead attorney for plaintiffs, Mexican parents of school-aged children. Plaintiffs, in this case, challenged, under the equal protection and due process clauses of the Fourteenth Amendment, a California common school plan, adopted pursuant to state rules and regulations, that required children of Mexican and Latin descent to be taught in separate schools. The Sixth Circuit Court found such segregative practice to violate not only the Fourteenth Amendment but also state statutes that authorized admission to its schools of "children of a foreign country, living across the border" (p. 780). Although segregation in this case could have been resolved at the state level by a state appeals court interpreting its own state law, the federal court assumed jurisdiction and took the occasion to rule that the segregative plan was "void on its face" (p. 781).

Ralph D. Mawdsley

WHEELOCK, LUCY (February 1, 1857–October 2, 1946), kindergarten* educator and leader, was the founder of Wheelock College in Boston. The daughter of a Congregational minister, school superintendent, and Vermont state representative, she moved to Boston to attend the Chauncy Hall School, where she first saw a kindergarten. Immediately impressed, Wheelock sought advice and training from Elizabeth Peabody* and others, and she first taught kindergarten at Chauncy Hall in 1879. An effective teacher, she began adapting Friedrich Froebel's* methods and trained with psychologist G. Stanley Hall* at the Clark University Summer School. In 1888, the year public kindergartens were instituted in Boston, she inaugurated a training class at Chauncy Hall, which in 1896 became the Wheelock Kindergarten Training School. Primary education courses were added in 1899, and soon after Wheelock's retirement in 1939 the school became a chartered college. Active in the international and national kindergarten movement, Wheelock served as president of the International Kindergarten Union* from 1895 to 1899 and, with Elizabeth Harrison, she coauthored the "liberal conservative" report, which attempted to reconcile Froebelianism with experimental psychology. Wheelock also advocated education for motherhood and in 1899 was appointed to the Committee on Education of the National Congress of Mothers, forerunner of the Parent-Teacher Association.* Fluent in German, she translated some of Froebel's works into English, as well as those of Swiss author Johanna Spyri; wrote children's stories and columns for Sunday school* teachers; and was the principal author, with Elizabeth Colson, of a popular advice book, *Talks to Mothers* (1920). A moderating force within the kindergarten movement, Wheelock demonstrated organizational ability and eclecticism important in maintaining and modifying the Froebelian kindergarten in America and in establishing institutions that made the kindergarten a permanent part of American education.

Wheelock's papers and her unpublished autobiography, "My Life Story," are in the Wheelock College Archives. Biographical information appears in Winifred D. Bain, *Leadership in Childhood Education, Images, and Realities: A History of Wheelock College, 1888–89 to 1963–64* (1964); Edward T. James, ed., *Notable American Women, 1607–1950* (1971); and Elizabeth Ann Liddle, ed., *Wheelock College, 100 Years* (1988). See also Barbara Beatty, " 'The Kind of Knowledge of Most Worth to Young Women': Post-Secondary Vocational Training for Teaching and Motherhood at the Wheelock School, 1888–1914" (1986).

Barbara Beatty

WHOLE LANGUAGE. See INTEGRATED CURRICULUM; READING INSTRUCTION.

WIEMAN V. UPDEGRAFF, 344 U.S. 183 (1952). This case represents a landmark decision protecting public school teachers from government loyalty oaths. Plaintiffs, members of the faculty and staff at Oklahoma Agricultural and Mechanical College, a public institution in Oklahoma, had refused to sign a loyalty oath required by the state for all state officers and employees. Among the prohibited activities in the oath was membership in "subversive" organizations. Invalidating the loyalty oath, the U.S. Supreme Court found that "exclud[ing] persons solely on the basis of organizational membership" violated the due process clause of the Fourteenth Amendment (p. 190). Though the Court remained careful not to disturb its earlier rulings—*Adler v. Board of Education,* 342 U.S. 485 (1952), and *United Public Workers v. Mitchell,* 330 U.S. 75 (1947), namely, that individuals do not have a constitutionally protected right to public employment—the ruling found this statute an exercise of arbitrary power because it included "[i]ndiscriminate classification of innocent with knowing activity" (p. 191).

Ralph D. Mawdsley

WILEY, CALVIN HENDERSON (February 3, 1819–January 11, 1887), as the first superintendent of public education in North Carolina, led the South's most successful state common school* campaign during the 1850s. In part as a result of his leadership and in part because of the political and economic circumstances of his state, Wiley was able to build sustained support for universal schooling for white children and higher standards for teachers, buildings, and curricula.

Born in Guiford County, North Carolina, Wiley attended local schools and graduated from the state university in 1840. Later he studied law, gained admission to the bar, and launched parallel careers in law and journalism. Serving in the state house of representatives from 1850 to 1852, Wiley took up the cause of school reform, and in 1853 his legislative colleagues elected him state superintendent. Whereas other southern state school reformers found it necessary to organize from the ground up, struggling first to get district trustees and county officials into place, Wiley went to work in a state that already had a bureaucratic school structure—albeit a very loose and decentralized one. He also faced less financial opposition because North Carolina had a fairly stable economy and a tradition of state and local taxation for education. In the South, his work appeared most similar to that of Massachusetts's Horace Mann* and Connecticut's Henry Barnard,* northern reformers who maintained contact with Wiley and supported his efforts. Nevertheless, his accomplishments as state superintendent, from 1853 to 1866, were limited. He persuaded county school boards to submit more complete annual reports, but those boards jealously guarded their freedom to allocate school funds as they saw fit. Although Wiley promoted teacher training and boosted teacher salaries to the best in that region, county examining committees retained the right to issue teaching certificates to virtually anyone they deemed qualified. It remained standard practice in North Carolina and other southern states—and, less often, in states outside the region—for local officials to divide public money among independent, tuition-charging schools. These quasi-public schools operated as key components of the North Carolina education system, and they symbolized the incomplete transition to state-regulated schools open to all children. Wiley's achievement was a state-*subsidized* system that enrolled about two-thirds of the white school-aged population—the largest proportion in the antebellum South.

Wiley's papers are housed in the Southern Historical Collection, North Carolina University–Chapel Hill Library. Leading secondary sources include Charles William Dabney, *Universal Education in the South* (1936); Edgar W. Knight, *Public School Education in North Carolina* (1916); and Marcus Cicero Stephens Noble, *A History of Public Schools in North Carolina* (1930). Also see Carl F. Kaestle, *Pillars of the Republic: Common Schools and American Society, 1780–1860* (1983).

Joseph W. Newman

WILLARD, EMMA HART (February 23, 1787–April 15, 1870), profoundly influenced nineteenth-century women's higher education and the common school* movement. She used two primary means to effect reform: her numerous publications, which described both her vision and the innovative methods she was using to reach them; and her institutional experiments, which informed and substantiated a number of her claims.

Many leading nineteenth-century educators shared Willard's optimistic faith in the power of educational institutions to transform American society. More than most, however, she viewed the disparities between male and female schooling as both unjust and imprudent. Her carefully reasoned *Plan for Improving Female Education* (1819) set the terms of the debate on women's education for the next half-century. Willard argued that the nation would ensure its longevity only if it invested in the neglected half of the population, namely, women. The state should take the first step toward larger reforms in women's education by endowing a rigorous female seminary, the contours of which she described and then transformed into reality in her noted school, Troy Female Seminary, in Troy, New York. Established in 1821, the school became an internationally recognized model of advanced female education and the site for many successful experiments in boarding school* arrangements, teacher training, and instructional methodologies.

Willard's influence on the common school movement grew out of her classroom experiences in Troy and in the common schools of Connecticut. Apart from the Bible, schoolbooks represented the most widely read books during the nineteenth century. She was one of a handful of New England writers who dominated that market. Willard, especially in her frequently reprinted geography and history texts, articulated her belief that homes and schools could transform the American Republic into a prosperous, industrial world power that would lead the rest of the nations to universal peace. Common school teachers had the responsibility of protecting the Republic from moral corruption by inculcating Christian piety in the young. Willard urged teachers to work diligently to become effective classroom practitioners. Her texts demonstrated how they could use students' sensory experiences, particularly sight, moving them from concrete to abstract concepts. She pioneered the use of maps in her history texts, and her textbooks contributed significantly to the view, so pervasive during the nineteenth century, that nonsectarian Protestantism should be the cornerstone of American public schools. Many of her teaching methods, especially in geography, remain in use.

The two largest collections of her papers are stored at Emma Willard School, Troy, New York, and Amherst College, Amherst, Massachusetts. Three of Willard's numerous textbooks are *Geography for Beginners; or, The Instructor's Assistant, in Giving First Lessons from Maps, in the Style of Familiar Conversation* (1826); *History of the United States or Republic of America* (1830); and *Morals for the Young; or, Good Principles Instilling Wisdom* (1857). The definitive biography is Alma Lutz, *Emma Willard, Daughter of Democracy* (1929). Also see Nina Baym, "Women and the Republic: Emma Willard's Rhetoric of History" (1991); Murray R. Nelson, "Emma Willard: Pioneer of Social Science Education" (1987); Anne Firor Scott, "The Ever Widening Circle: The Diffusion of Feminist Values from the Troy Female Seminary: 1822–1872" (1979) and "What, Then, Is the American: The New Woman?" (1978); and Claire Diane Wood, "The Cultural and Intellectual Origins of Emma Willard's Educational Philosophy" (1991).

Lucy Forsyth Townsend

WINNEMUCCA, SARAH (Thoc-me-tony) (c. 1844–October 16, 1891), a Piute, founded the first Native American–managed boarding school (see BOARDING SCHOOLS; FEDERAL INDIAN BOARDING SCHOOLS) for Piutes in 1884; providing children with an alternative to Eurocentric pedagogy and assimilationist goals of the Bureau of Indian Affairs schools.

Winnemucca, born at the Sink of the Humboldt River in what is now western Nevada, received her formal education at a Sisters of Charity convent school in San Jose, California, between 1860 and 1863. The second daughter of Winnemucca II and the granddaughter of Winnemucca I, who advocated peaceful coexistence with the encroaching white population, Sarah saw their cooperative spirit shaken by incidents in which Piutes were murdered by whites or mistreated by the Indian Service. As an interpreter at Fort McDermott and Camp Harney, she learned how corruption within the U.S. Indian Services resulted in inadequate supplies for her people forced to live on a reservation. On an eastern seaboard lecture tour (1883–1884), she exposed this inequity and corruption and advocated the passage of a bill to restore land to the Piutes. While on that tour she met and became close friends with Elizabeth Palmer Peabody,* noted kindergarten advocate, and her sister, Mary Tyler Mann, widow of Horace Mann.*

With the financial support and guidance of Peabody, Winnemucca returned home in 1884 to establish the first known Native American–managed boarding school at Lovelock, Nevada. The tuition-free school began with twenty-five children, ranging in age from six to sixteen. Parents were pleased that the school provided a notable contrast with the Bureau of Indian Affairs reservation schools in which their children were treated harshly and deprived of their native language and culture. Before the year ended, over 400 students waited to enroll. Peabody claimed that Winnemucca based her methods on Friedrich Froebel's* principle of a balance between thinking and doing. Ever conscious of the students' need to retain their own culture while surviving among the whites, she taught in both languages. The children participated in housekeeping and agricultural lessons, which also helped to support the school. Increasingly dependent on Peabody, Winnemucca named the school the Peabody Institute in her honor.

White neighbors attacked the school throughout its existence. The town's water company refused Sarah and her brother, Natches, the water rights necessary for their wheat crop. Indian agents promised to aid the school if Natches would surrender his 160-acre farm and Sarah give up the school's direction. As a result of this harassment and Sarah's declining health, the school closed in 1887, at which time she moved to Idaho, where she died. The demise of the school curtailed the Piute people's access to self-determined education and Sarah's dream of starting a normal school* for American Indian women teachers.

See the U.S. Bureau of Indian Affairs, "The Case of Sarah Winnemucca," in *Special Files of the Office of Indian Affairs, 1807–1904, National Archive Publication No. 547.* Also refer to Elizabeth Peabody's writings, "Letter to the Commissioner of Indian Affairs," April 10, 1884 (National Archives, RG-75, Washington, DC); and *Sarah Winnemucca's Practical Solution to the Indian Problem: A Letter to Dr. Lyman Abbott of the "Christian Union"* (1886), a typical nineteenth-century tract defending Winnemucca's activism and politics. Biographies include George F. Brimlow, "The Life of Sarah Winnemucca: The Formative Years" (1952); Catherine S. Fowler, "Sarah Winnemucca, Northern Piute ca. 1844–1891" (1978); Sarah Winnemucca Hopkins, *Life among the Piutes: Their Wrongs and Claims* (1883; 1969); and Patricia Stewart, "Sarah Winnemucca" (1971).

Patricia Anne Carter

WINNETKA PLAN, developed by Carleton Washburne,* the superintendent, and the teachers of the Winnetka, Illinois, public schools, attracted international attention to this affluent Chicago suburb in the interwar period. Through an individualized approach to learning the "common essentials," the plan aimed for 100 percent mastery of a series of goals in the "tool" subjects. The rate at which children completed the goals varied tremendously. Within one classroom, some pupils might be doing second-grade arithmetic, whereas others might be engaged in sixth-grade work. After learning a specific task from a self-instructive text, students took a self-corrective, diagnostic test. If there were errors, the pupil was directed by the text to do an exercise that stressed the kind of problem that had not been solved correctly. When the student completed an error-free test, the child could go on to the next task. Although Washburne's first priority was to individualize instruction, this represented only part of the Winnetka plan. Individualized instruction took up about half of the school day, making it possible to devote equal time to "group and creative activities," including art, music, discussions of current events, student self-government, and field trips. By the 1930s, these activities represented a highly sophisticated program, most fully developed in the junior high school's miniature community. Students participated in self-government and organized clubs, corporations, and even labor unions, leading to an examination of the institutions and problems of the larger society. Although Washburne regarded the group and creative activities as crucial, it was the individualized instruction that attracted the most attention among educators (also refer to PROGRESSIVE EDUCATION).

Refer to Carleton Washburne and Sidney P. Marland, Jr., *Winnetka: The History and Significance of an Educational Experiment* (1963), for a primary retrospective. For historical analyses, see John L. Tewksbury, "An Historical Study of the Winnetka Public Schools from 1919 to 1946" (1962), and Arthur Zilversmit, *Changing Schools: Progressive Education Theory and Practice, 1930–1960* (1993).

Arthur Zilversmit

WIRT, WILLIAM ALBERT (January 21, 1874–March 11, 1938), served as superintendent of the Gary, Indiana, public schools* from 1907 to 1938, where he developed the Gary or Platoon or Work-Study-Play Plan for the elementary grades. Designed to offer a broad as well as efficient school program, the Gary Plan,* although controversial, was copied by over 200 public school systems by 1929.

Born in Markle, Indiana, and a graduate of DePauw University (1898), Wirt had a rural, Protestant, Republican background that strongly influenced his educational ideas. He believed in maximizing school facilities by using all the classrooms all the time, including nights (for adults), weekends, and summers. He also expanded the curriculum to include manual training, recreation, nature study, daily auditorium activities, and other subjects beyond traditional primary school concerns. Moreover, the larger schools, starting in 1909, were organized as unit schools, containing all grades from kindergarten through grade 12. Gary's elementary students each day continually moved about their schools, from specialized classrooms (English, math, history), to the auditorium for public speaking and music lessons, to the gym or swimming pool for recreation, to the shops for manual training, and to the outdoor gardens or zoos for nature study. Wirt's educational activities and national fame declined during the 1930s when he generated much controversy because of his anti–New Deal rhetoric. Nevertheless, in 1937, he published a pamphlet, *The Great Lockout in America's Citizenship Plants*, summarizing his educational views; he believed the Gary Plan, consciously developed in a rapidly expanding multiethnic and multiracial indus-

WISCONSIN V. YODER

trial city, would benefit children and community alike. A longtime member of that city's elite, he died suddenly in office, as his authority was being challenged by a revived teachers' union and city Democratic Party.

The bulk of Wirt's papers are in the Lilly Library, Indiana University, Bloomington, with a somewhat smaller collection and allied sources in the Calumet Regional Archives, Indiana University–Northwest, Gary. Wirt's life is covered in Ronald D. Cohen and Raymond A. Mohl, *The Paradox of Progressive Education: The Gary Plan and Urban Education* (1979), and more fully in Ronald D. Cohen, *Children of the Mill: Schooling and Society in Gary, Indiana, 1906–1960* (1990).

Ronald D. Cohen

WISCONSIN V. YODER, 406, U.S. 205 (1972). The U.S. Supreme Court considered whether Amish parents' conviction of opposing Wisconsin's compulsory education* law infringed on their rights protected by the free exercise clause of the First Amendment. The parents, members of the Old Order Amish, did not believe in public school* education beyond the eighth grade because it violated their beliefs and way of life; they believed they would endanger their own and their children's salvation by complying with the law. The Court held that the Wisconsin regulation requiring the Amish to send their children to high school* contravened their free exercise of rights. The Court expressly utilized a balancing test in which government interests were weighed against the limitations on the free exercise of religion. In balancing the merits of each side's argument, the Court found that the Amish way of life and religion were inseparable and that thus the Amish children's attendance at high school would likely destroy their religious beliefs. The *Yoder* decision established that government action placing an additional burden on a religion violates the free exercise clause when the religious practice outweighs government interests.

Tony Eastland, ed., *Religious Liberty in the Supreme Court: The Cases That Define the Debate over Church and State* (1993), focuses on legal reasoning and effect; whereas David A. J. Richards, *Toleration and the Constitution* (1986), maintains an intellectual history approach.

Bruce Beezer

WOOD V. STRICKLAND, 420 U.S. 308 (1975), is the leading case on the immunity of school board members who have allegedly violated the civil rights of students. In *Wood,* a board expelled three high school* students in Arkansas for disobeying its regulation against the use or possession of intoxicating beverages at school activities. The students filed suit under 42 U.S.C. § 1983, claiming that the board violated their constitutional rights to due process by acting with apparent state authority in expelling them from school. A federal trial court entered a directed verdict in favor of the board members, reasoning that they were immune from liability absent proof of malice or ill-will toward the students. The Eighth Circuit Court reversed in favor of the students; it found that since the board violated the substantive due process rights of the students, the pupils were entitled to a new trial on the question of damages. The U.S. Supreme Court vacated and remanded. The Court observed that while common law and public policy entitled board members to qualified good faith immunity for damages under 42 U.S.C. § 1983, they are not free from liability if they knew or reasonably should have known that their official duties violated the constitutional rights of students or if they acted with malicious intent to do so. The Court ruled that insofar as the students broke the school's rule on alcoholic beverages, their substantive due process rights were not violated. The Court remanded on the matter of procedural due process; it decided that since the Eighth Circuit did not address this question, the trial court was the appropriate forum for the resolution of this new issue.

Charles J. Russo

WOODSON, CARTER GOODWIN (December 19, 1875–April 3, 1950), the "Father of Black History," dedicated his life to the study and teaching of African American history and culture for the purposes of "reeducating" African Americans. Scholars have also recognized his role in laying part of the foundation for multicultural education,* black studies, and Afrocentricity.* Among Woodson's accomplishments were his first book, *Education of the Negro Prior to 1861* (1915), his establishment of the Association for the Study of Negro Life and History and the *Journal of Negro History* in 1916, and the promotion of a black history course at Howard University beginning in the late 1910s. Woodson also implemented Negro History Week in black Washingtonian schools and the *Negro History Bulletin* in 1937, in both promoting "black pride" and diminishing "white prejudice." At this point, however, he had not yet made the intellectual leap from viewing African American history as a base of knowledge merely to teach and preserve to a strategy for empowerment through education.

Specifically addressing the issue of curriculum, Woodson contended in *Mis-Education of the Negro* (1933) that African Americans should concentrate their studies on both African-related history and culture and Western culture. At the same time, Woodson declared that the controversy between Booker T. Washington* and W.E.B. Du Bois* had polarized African American intellectuals and leaders, and this splintering contributed little to African American education efforts. He further argued that industrial education* and classical education (see CLASSICAL CURRICULUM) alike were inadequate for obtaining the highly technical, industrialized jobs that existed in the United States in the 1930s, and that liberal arts training did not necessarily lead to African American success. Woodson thus pioneered a plan that sought to uplift African Americans through an education oriented toward the African American experience.

Woodson's papers are available at the Library of Congress Manuscript Division; the Moorland-Springarn Research Center, Howard University; and the Carter G. Woodson Institute, University of Virginia. Biographies and historical treatments include Jacqueline Goggin, *Carter G. Woodson: A Life in Black History* (1993); August Meier and Elliot Rudwick, "Carter G. Woodson as Entrepreneur: Laying the Foundation of a Historical Specialty" (1986); Samuel A. Hay, "Carter G. Woodson's *Mis-Education of the Negro*: A Re-Visit" (1975); and James Turner and C. Steven McGann, "Black Studies as an Integral Tradition in African-American Intellectual History" (1980).

Donald E. Collins

WOODWARD, CALVIN MILTON (August 25, 1834–June 12, 1915), became an influential proponent of manual education. Born in Fitchburg, Massachusetts, he graduated from Harvard University in 1860 and began his professional education career as a high school* principal of Brown High School in New Berryport, Massachusetts. After the Civil War, he moved to St. Louis, where he became vice-Principal of Smith Academy (1865–1870). In 1870, he became professor of descriptive geology at Washington University, the following year becoming dean of the polytechnic faculty of Washington University (1871–1896, 1901–1910). His role as high school principal and dean helped him to see the relationship between manual training and academic training.

Believing that manual training was to be part of a general education curriculum, Woodward wrote a series of books: *Manual Education* (1878), *The Manual Training School* (1887), and *Manual Training in Education* (1890). He saw the inclusion of hands-on training as a means to comprehend the theory that undergirded practical applications, and he opposed using nonacademic education to serve social-class, economic, and social ends. As the organizer and director of the St. Louis Manual Training School, he exemplified and put his ideas into practice. Rather than track a person into a narrow job for life, the school's curriculum gave the student life choices. The school taught the student a complete traditional academic high school education as part of the manual arts curriculum. Woodward argued against specialization in elementary school; he would enroll only students over fourteen years of age in his manual training school. His school flourished until 1915, when a local public school system co-opted the training school as part of vocational education.*

For a useful biography, see Donald A. Yoder, "Calvin's Crusade: A Reassessment of Calvin Milton Woodward's Social and Educational Ideas for School Reform in the United States" (1994).

Peter Sola

WORK-STUDY-PLAY PLAN. See GARY PLAN.

WRITING INSTRUCTION. See ENGLISH LANGUAGE ARTS.

Y

YERKES, ROBERT MEARNS (May 26, 1876–February 3, 1956), a comparative psychologist, renowned for his studies in animal psychology and primate behavior, was a central figure in the establishment and dissemination of intelligence testing* in America. Educated at Ursinus College, receiving a Ph.D. in psychology from Harvard in 1902, he taught at both Harvard and Yale and served as president of the American Psychological Association (1916–1917) and the American Society of Naturalists (1938). During World War I, he led the effort to use intelligence tests to assess army recruits. Two versions of the test were used, one for literates (Alpha) and another for illiterates (Beta); the tests sorted recruits into five categories ranging from A (officer material) to E (unqualified for army service). This massive testing effort helped to legitimize intelligence tests, which soon thereafter were adopted by public schools for testing and tracking students. The findings from the army tests generated controversy almost from the beginning. Data suggested not only that the average mental age of recruits was thirteen years, but also that recruits with southern and eastern European ancestry were less intelligent than those from northern Europe and Nordic countries. These data provided support to eugenicists who wanted to limit immigration from those countries with lower average scores; the Immigration Restriction Act of 1924 reflected the eugenic viewpoint.

Yerkes's papers are located primarily at the Yale University Library, American Psychological Association Archives of the Library of Congress, New Haven Medical Library, and Psychology Archives of the University of Akron. His main works on the World War I army intelligence tests are Clarence S. Yoakum and Robert M. Yerkes, *Army Mental Tests* (1920), and Robert M. Yerkes, *Psychological Examining in the United States Army* (1921). An important biography is Ernest R. Hilgard, *Robert Mearns Yerkes, 1876–1956* (1965). His autobiography, ''Robert Mearns Yerkes, Psychobiologist,'' can be found in volume 2 of *A History of Psychology in Autobiography* (1932), edited by Carl

Murchison. Raymond Fancher, *The Intelligence Men: Makers of the IQ Controversy* (1985), provides a good discussion of Yerkes's role in the U.S. Army intelligence tests and, more generally, the IQ debate. For the importance of the early mental tests and their adoption by schools, see Paul D. Chapman, *Schools as Sorters: Lewis M. Terman, Applied Psychology, and the Intelligence Testing Movement, 1890–1930* (1988).

Stephen H. Aby

YOUNG, ELLA FLAGG (January 15, 1845–October 26, 1918), became the first woman to head a large, urban school system, serving as superintendent of the Chicago public schools during a turbulent era, 1909–1915.

After graduating from Chicago Normal School in 1862, Young demonstrated intelligence and teaching ability that brought her rapid advancement. In 1865, after only a short stint teaching primary school, she became the principal of the Chicago Normal School's practice school. Appointed assistant superintendent in 1887, she resigned in 1899 to take a position as associate professor of pedagogy at the University of Chicago, where she became a close associate of John Dewey* and supervised the instruction in his well-known University of Chicago Laboratory School.*

Dewey came to regard her as the "the wisest person in school matters" that he knew. She received her doctorate from Chicago in 1900. Young collaborated with Dewey in writing the University of Chicago Contributions to Education series. The first volume, her doctoral dissertation, *Isolation in the Schools* (1901), strenuously argued against the policy of "close supervision" of teachers—only if teachers were given a great deal of freedom could schools become progressive and democratic.

Young left the university when Dewey resigned, and in 1909 she was appointed superintendent of the Chicago schools. A year later she became the first woman to head the National Education Association.* As superintendent, she directed a program of extensive curricular revision, introducing vocational courses (see VOCATIONAL EDUCATION), physical education,* and even sex education.* She resisted the school board's efforts to centralize control over the schools and argued for greater teacher participation in school governance. Her support of the Chicago Teacher's Federation* led to confrontations with the board and ultimately her resignation in 1915.

Young's papers are at Illinois State University. Judy Suratt, "Young, Ella Flagg" (1971), provides a brief biography. For an institutional history and an analysis of that historical context, refer to Mary J. Herrick, *The Chicago Schools: A Social and Political History* (1971), and David J. Hogan, *Class and Reform: School and Society in Chicago, 1880–1930* (1985).

Arthur Zilversmit

SELECTED
BIBLIOGRAPHY

Abbott, Martin. *The Freedmen's Bureau in South Carolina, 1865–1872.* Chapel Hill: University of North Carolina Press, 1967.

Aby, Stephen H., with the assistance of Martha J. McNamara, comps. *The IQ Debate: A Selective Guide to the Literature.* Westport, CT: Greenwood Press, 1990.

Adams, David W. *Education for Extinction: American Indians and the Boarding School Experience, 1875–1928.* Lawrence: University Press of Kansas, 1995.

Adams, David W., and Victor Edmonds. "Making Your Move: The Educational Significance of the American Board Game, 1832 to 1904." *History of Education Quarterly* 17 (winter 1977): 359–384.

Addams, Jane. *My Friend, Julia Lathrop.* New York: Macmillan, 1935.

Addams, Jane. *Twenty Years at Hull-House with Autobiographical Notes.* 1910. Reprint, Urbana: University of Illinois Press, 1990.

Adler, Mortimer J. *Paideia Problems and Possibilities.* New York: Macmillan, 1983.

Adler, Mortimer J. *The Paideia Program: An Educational Syllabus.* New York: Macmillan, 1984.

Adler, Mortimer J. *The Paideia Proposal: An Educational Manifesto.* New York: Macmillan, 1982.

Aikin, Wilford M. *The Story of the Eight-Year Study.* New York: Harper and Brothers, 1942.

Alberty, Harold. *Reorganizing the High School Curriculum.* 2nd ed. New York: Macmillan, 1957.

Alderman, Edwin A., and Armisted C. Gordon. *J.L.M. Curry—A Biography.* New York: Macmillan, 1911.

Ali, Kamal. *In-Depth Study of Full-Time Islamic Schools in North America: Results and Data Analysis.* Plainfield, IN: Islamic Society of North America, 1991.

Ali, Kamal. "Islamic Education in the United States: An Overview of Issues, Problems, and Possible Approaches." *American Journal of Islamic Studies* 1 (spring 1984): 128–132.

Ali, Kamal. "Muslim School Planning in the United States: An Analysis of Issues, Problems and Possible Approaches.'' Ed.D. diss., University of Massachusetts–Amherst, 1981.

Allen, Ann Taylor. *Feminism and Motherhood in Germany*. New Brunswick, NJ: Rutgers University Press, 1991.

Allen, Charles A., and Charles A. Prosser. *Have We Kept the Faith?* New York: Century, 1929.

Allen, Charles A., and Charles A. Prosser. *Vocational Education in a Democracy*. New York: Century, 1925.

Alexander, William M. ''Schools for the Middle School Years.'' *Educational Leadership* 23 (December 1965): 217–223.

Alexander, William M. ''What Educational Plan for the In-Between-Ager?'' *NEA Journal* 55 (March 1966): 30–32.

Allis, Frederick S., Jr. *Youth from Every Quarter: A Bicentennial History of Phillips Academy, Andover*. Hanover, NH: University Press of New England, 1979.

Allmendinger, David F. ''Mount Holyoke Students Encounter the Need for Life-Planning, 1837–1850.'' *History of Education Quarterly* 19 (spring 1979): 3–25.

Allmendinger, David F. ''The Strangeness of the American Education Society: Indigent Students and the New Charity, 1815–1840.'' *History of Education Quarterly* 11 (spring 1971): 3–22.

Allott, Stephen. *Lindley Murray, 1745–1826: Quaker Grammarian*. York, England: Sessions Book Trust, 1991.

Altbach, Philip G., Gail P. Kelly, Hugh G. Petrie, and Lois Weis. *Textbooks in American Society*. Albany: State University of New York Press, 1991.

Ambler, Charles H. *History of Education in West Virginia*. Huntington, WV: Standard Printing and Publishing, 1951.

Ambler, Charles H. *Sectionalism in Virgina from 1776–1861*. Chicago: University of Chicago Press, 1910.

American Alliance for Health, Physical Education, Recreation, and Dance. *The Shape of a Nation: A Survey of State Physical Education Requirements*. Reston, VA: AAHPERD, 1987.

American Association for the Advancement of Science. *Project 2061: Science for All Americans*. Washington, DC: American Association for the Advancement of Science, 1989.

American Association of School Administrators. *Religion in the Public Schools*. Washington, DC: AASA, 1964.

American Journal of Education. ''James Carter.'' 5 (September 1858): 407–416.

Anderson, James D. *The Education of Blacks in the South, 1860–1935*. Chapel Hill: University of North Carolina Press, 1988.

Anderson, James D. ''Northern Foundations and the Shaping of Southern Rural Black Education, 1902–1935.'' *History of Education Quarterly* 18 (winter 1978): 371–396.

Anderson, Lorin W. ''Benjamin Bloom: His Research and Influence on Education.'' *Teaching Education* 2 (spring 1988): 54–58.

Anderson, Olive O. ''The Chicago Teachers' Federation.'' Ph.D. diss., University of Chicago, 1908.

Andrews, William L., ed. *Critical Essays on Frederick Douglass*. Boston: G. K. Hall, 1991.

Angus, David, Jeffrey E. Mirel, and Maris A. Vinovskis. "Historical Development of Age Stratification in Schooling." In *Education, Society, and Economic Opportunity*, 171–193. Edited by Maris A. Vinovskis. New Haven, CT: Yale University Press, 1995.

Apple, Michael W., and Linda K. Christian-Smith. *The Politics of the Textbook*. New York: Routledge, 1991.

Applebee, Arthur. *Tradition and Reform in the Teaching of English*. Urbana, IL: National Council of Teachers of English, 1974.

Arnove, Robert F., ed. *Philanthropy and Cultural Imperialism: The Foundations at Home and Abroad*. Boston: G. K. Hall, 1980.

Asante, Molefi K. *The Afrocentric Idea*. Philadelphia: Temple University Press, 1987.

Asante, Molefi K. *Malcolm X as Cultural Hero: And Other Afrocentric Essays*. Trenton, NJ: Africa World Press, 1993.

Ashburn, Frank D. *Peabody of Groton: A Portrait*. Cambridge, MA: Riverside Press, 1967.

Atkinson, Nancy Bates. *Biography of Rev. George G. H. Atkinson, D.D.* Portland: F. W. Baltes, 1893.

Avrich, Paul. *The Modern School Movement: Anarchism and Education in the United States*. Princeton, NJ: Princeton University Press, 1980.

Baer, Helene G. *The Heart Is Like Heaven*. Philadelphia: University of Pennsylvania Press, 1964.

Bagley, William C. *Education and the Emergent Man*. New York: Ronald Press, 1934.

Bagley, William C. "An Essentialist's Platform for the Advancement of American Education." *Educational Administration and Supervision* 24 (April 1938): 241–256.

Bailyn, Bernard. *Education in the Forming of American Society: Needs and Opportunities for Study*. Chapel Hill: University of North Carolina Press, 1960.

Bain, Winifred E. *Leadership in Childhood Education, Images, and Realities: A History of Wheelock College, 1888–89 to 1963–64*. Boston: Wheelock College, 1964.

Bakan, David. "Adolescence in America: From Idea to Social Fact." *Daedalus* 4 (fall 1971): 979–995.

Baker, D. Philip. *The Library Media Program and the School*. Littleton, CO: Libraries Unlimited, 1984.

Baker, Scott. "Testing Equality." *History of Education Quarterly* 35 (spring 1995): 49–64.

Baker, William J., and John M. Carrol, eds. *Sports in Modern America*. Saint Louis, MO: River City Publishers, 1981.

Balmuth, Miriam. *The Roots of Phonics: A Historical Introduction*. New York: McGraw-Hill, 1982.

Banks, James A. "African-American Scholarship and the Evolution of Multicultural Education." *Journal of Negro Education* 61 (summer 1992): 273–286.

Banks, James A. "The Canon Debate, Knowledge Construction, and Multicultural Education." *Educational Researcher* 22 (June/July 1993): 4–14.

Banks, James A., and Cherry A. McGee. *Multicultural Education: Issues and Perspectives*. Boston: Allyn and Bacon, 1989.

Barger, Robert N. *John Lancaster Spalding: Catholic Educator and Social Emissary*. New York: Garland Publishing, 1988.

Barlow, Melvin. *History of Industrial Education in the United States*. Peoria, IL: Charles Bennett, 1967.

Barlow, Thomas A. *Pestalozzi and American Education*. Boulder, CO: Este Es Press, 1977.

Barnard, Henry. "The American Education Society." *American Journal of Education* 14 (1864): 367–382.

Barnard, Henry, ed. *American Journal of Education*. Vol. 5. Hartford, CT: F. C. Brownell, 1858.

Barringer, Paul, B., James Mercer Garrett, and Rosewell Page. *University of Virginia*. New York: Lewis Publishing Co., 1904.

Baylor, Ruth M. *Elizabeth Palmer Peabody: Kindergarten Pioneer*. Philadelphia: University of Pennsylvania Press, 1965.

Baym, Nina. "Women and the Republic: Emma Willard's Rhetoric of History." *American Quarterly* 43 (March 1991): 1–23.

Baynton, Douglas C. *Forbidden Signs: American Culture and the Campaign against Sign Language*. Chicago: University of Chicago Press, 1996.

Beale, Howard K. *A History of Freedom of Teaching in American Schools*. New York: Scribner, 1941.

Beale, John R. "Elbert K. Fretwell and the Extra-Curricular Activity Movement, 1917–1931." Ph.D. diss., Kent State University, 1983.

Beatty, Barbara. " 'The Kind of Knowledge of Most Worth to Young Women': Post-Secondary Vocational Training for Teaching and Motherhood at the Wheelock School, 1888–1914." *History of Higher Education Annual* 6 (1986): 29–50.

Beatty, Barbara. "From Laws of Learning to a Science of Values: Efficiency and Morality in Thorndike's Educational Psychology." *American Psychologist* 53 (October 1998): 1145–1152.

Beatty, Barbara. *Preschool Education in America: The Culture of Young Children from the Colonial Era to the Present*. New Haven, CT: Yale University Press, 1995.

Beatty, Willard W. *Education for Cultural Change*. Washington, DC: U.S. Bureau of Indian Affairs, 1953.

Beatty, Willard W., and Associates. *Education for Action: Selected Articles from "Indian Education," 1936–1943*. Chilocco, OK: Chilocco Agricultural School, 1944.

Beaumont, Gustave de, and Alexis de Tocqueville. *Penitentiary System in the United States and Its Application in France*. Paris: Fournier, 1833. Reprint, Carbondale: Southern Illinois University Press, 1964.

Beck, Lynn G., and Joseph Murphy. *Understanding the Principalship: Metaphorical Themes, 1920s–1990s*. New York: Teachers College Press, 1993.

Beers, Clifford W. *A Mind That Found Itself: An Autobiography*. Garden City, NY: Doubleday, 1953.

Bell, Bernard. *Crisis in Education: A Challenge to American Complacency*. New York: Whittlesey House, 1949.

Bell, Sadie. *The Church, the State, and Education in Virginia*. Philadelphia: Science Press, 1930.

Belok, Michael. *Forming the American Mind: Early School-Books and Their Compilers, 1783–1837*. Moti Katra, India: Agra V-P, 1973.

Bender, John. *The Functions of Courts in Enforcing School Attendance Laws*. New York: AMS Press, 1972.

Benneke, John. *William Heard Kilpatrick*. New York: Peter Lang, forthcoming.

Bennett, William J. *Our Children and Our Country: Improving America's Schools and Affirming the Common Culture.* New York: Simon and Schuster, 1988.

Bentley, George R. *A History of the Freedmen's Bureau.* 1955. Reprint, New York: Octagon, 1970.

Bereiter, Carl, and Siegfried Englemann. *Teaching Disadvantaged Children in the Preschool.* Englewood Cliffs, NJ: Prentice-Hall, 1966.

Berk, Laura E. "The Extracurriculum." In *Handbook of Research on Curriculum,* 1002–1043. Edited by Philip W. Jackson. New York: Macmillan, 1992.

Berman, Edward Henry. "Education in Africa and America: A History of the Phelps-Stokes Fund, 1911–1945." Ed.D. diss., Columbia University, 1970.

Bernard, Thomas J. *The Cycle of Juvenile Justice.* New York: Oxford University Press, 1992.

Bernstein, Richard. *John Dewey.* New York: Washington Square Press, 1966.

Berube, Maurice R. "Community Control Revisited." Chapter 5 in *American School Reform: Progressive, Equity, and Excellence Movements, 1883–1993.* Westport, CT: Praeger, 1994.

Berube, Maurice R. *Teacher Politics: The Influence of Unions.* Westport, CT: Greenwood Press, 1988.

Berube, Maurice R., and Marilyn Gittell, eds. *Confrontation at Ocean Hill–Brownsville: The New York Strikes of 1968.* New York: Praeger, 1969.

Best, John H., ed. *Benjamin Franklin on Education.* New York: Teachers College Press, 1962.

Best, John H., ed. *Historical Inquiry in Education: A Research Agenda.* Washington, DC: American Educational Research Association, 1983.

Bestor, Arthur. *Backwoods Utopias: The Sectarian Origins and the Owenite Phase of Communitarian Socialism in America, 1663–1829.* Philadelphia: University of Pennsylvania Press, 1970.

Bestor, Arthur. *Educational Wastelands: The Retreat from Learning in Our Public Schools.* Urbana: University of Illinois Press, 1953, 1985.

Bestor, Arthur. *The Restoration of Learning.* New York: Knopf, 1955.

Binder, Frederick M. *The Age of the Common School, 1830–1865.* New York: Wiley, 1974.

Binet, Alfred. *L'Etude experimentale de L'Intelligence.* Paris: Schleicher Freres, 1903.

Binet, Alfred, and Theodore Simon. *The Development of Intelligence in Children (The Binet-Simon Scale).* Baltimore: Williams and Wilkins, 1916. Reprint, New York: Arno Press, 1973.

Binet, Alfred, and Theodore Simon. *Les enfants anormaux.* Paris: Armand Colin, 1907.

Birge, Edward B. *History of Public School Music in the United States.* New York: Oliver Ditson Co., 1939.

Bishop, Donna M., Charles E. Frazier, Lonn Lanza-Kaduce, and Lawrence Winner. "The Transfer of Juveniles to Criminal Court: Does It Make a Difference?" *Crime and Delinquency* 42 (April 1996): 171–191.

Bissinger, H. G. *Friday Night Lights: A Town, a Team, and a Dream.* New York: Harper-Collins, 1990.

Blassingame, John W., and John R. McKivigan, eds. *The Frederick Douglass Papers, Series One: Speeches, Debates, and Interviews.* 5 vols. New Haven, CT: Yale University Press, 1979–1985.

Blauch, Lloyd E. *Federal Cooperation in Agricultural Extension Work, Vocational Ed-*

ucation, and Vocational Rehabilitation. U.S. Office of Education, Bulletin 1933, No. 15. Washington, DC: U.S. Government Printing Office, 1935.

Bleier, Ruth. *Science and Gender: A Critique of Biology and Its Theories on Women.* New York: Pergamon Press, 1983.

Block, N. J., and Gerald Dworkin, eds. *The IQ Controversy: Critical Readings.* New York: Pantheon, 1976.

Bloom, Benjamin S., Allison Davis, and Robert D. Hess. *Compensatory Education for Cultural Deprivation.* New York: Holt, Rinehart & Winston, 1965.

Blum, Jeffrey M. *Pseudoscience and Mental Ability: The Origins and Fallacies of the IQ Controversy.* New York: Monthly Review Press, 1978.

Boas, George. "Instrumentalism and the History of Philosophy." In *John Dewey: Philosopher of Science and Freedom,* 66–87. Edited by Sidney Hook. New York: Dial Press, 1950.

Bobbitt, John F. *The Curriculum.* Boston: Houghton Mifflin, 1918.

Bobbitt, John F. *The Curriculum of Modern Education.* New York: McGraw-Hill, 1941.

Bobbitt, John F. *Curriculum Making in Los Angeles.* Chicago: University of Chicago Press, 1922.

Bobbitt, John F. "The Elimination of Waste in Education." *The Elementary Teacher* 12 (February 1912): 259–271.

Bobbitt, John F. *How to Make a Curriculum.* Boston: Houghton Mifflin, 1918.

Bobbitt, John F. "Orientation of the Curriculum-Maker." In *The Foundations of Curriculum Making: Twenty-Sixth Annual Yearbook of the National Society for the Study of Education,* 41–55. Bloomington, IL: Public School Publishing, 1926.

Bode, Boyd H. *Modern Education Theories.* New York: Macmillan, 1927.

Bode, Carl. *The American Lyceum: Town Meeting of the Mind.* New York: Oxford University Press, 1956.

Bond, Horace Mann. *Education for Freedom: A History of Lincoln University.* Princeton, NJ: Princeton University Press, 1976.

Bond, Horace Mann. *The Education of the Negro in the American Social Order.* Washington, DC: Associated Publishers, 1939.

Bond, Horace Mann. *Education for Production.* Athens: University of Georgia Press, 1944.

Bond, Horace Mann. *Negro Education in Alabama: A Study in Cotton and Steel.* New York: Octagon Books, 1939. Reprint, New York: Atheneum, 1969.

Bond, Horace Mann. *The Search for Talent.* Cambridge, MA: Harvard University Press, 1959.

Borrowman, Merle L. *The Liberal and Technical in Teacher Education: A Historical Survey of American Thought.* New York: Teachers College Press, 1956.

Borrowman, Merle L., ed. *Teacher Education in America: A Documentary History.* New York: Teachers College Press, 1965.

Bottoms, G., and D. Sharpe. *Teaching for Understanding through Integration of Academic and Technical Education.* Atlanta, GA: Southern Regional Education Board, 1996.

Botume, Elizabeth Hyde. *First Days among the Contrabands.* Boston: Lee and Shepard Publishers, 1893. Reprint, New York: Arno Press, 1968.

Bourne, William O. *History of the Public School Society of the City of New York.* New York: William Wood & Co., 1870.

Bowers, C. A. *The Progressive Educator and the Depression: The Radical Years.* New York: Random House, 1969.

Bowers, William L. *The Country Life Movement in America, 1900–1920.* Port Washington, NY: Kennikat Press, 1974.

Bowles, Samuel, and Herbert Gintis. *Schooling in Capitalist America: Educational Reform and the Contradictions of Economic Life.* New York: Basic Books, 1976.

Boy Scouts of America. *Historical Highlights: A Year-by-Year Summary of the Major Events in the History of the Boy Scouts of America.* Irving, TX: BSA External Communications Office, 1995.

Boyce, George A. *When Navajos Had Too Many Sheep: The 1940s.* San Francisco: Indian Historian Press, 1974.

Boyd, Julian P., gen. ed. *The Papers of Thomas Jefferson.* 25 vols. Princeton, NJ: Princeton University Press, 1950.

Boydston, Jo Ann, and Robert L. Andresen, eds. *John Dewey: A Checklist of Translations, 1900–1967.* Carbondale: Southern Illinois Press, 1969.

Boydston, Jo Ann, and Kathleen Poulos, eds. *A Checklist of Writings about John Dewey.* Carbondale: Southern Illinois Press, 1974.

Boyer, Ernest L. *High School: A Report on Secondary Education in America.* New York: Harper & Row, 1983.

Boylan, Anne M. *Sunday School: The Formation of an American Institution, 1790–1880.* New Haven, CT: Yale University Press, 1988.

Bradburn, Elizabeth. *Margaret McMillan: Portrait of a Pioneer.* London: Routledge, 1989.

Brameld, Theodore. *Ends and Means in Education.* New York: Harper & Brothers, 1950.

Brameld, Theodore. *Philosophies of Education in Cultural Perspective.* New York: Dryden Press, 1955.

Braun, Samuel J., and Elizabeth P. Edwards. *History and Theory of Early Childhood Education.* Worthington, OH: Charles E. Jones Publisher, 1972.

Brenzel, Barbara M. *Daughters of the State: A Social Portrait of the First Reform School for Girls in North America.* Cambridge: Massachusetts Institute of Technology, 1983.

Brigham, Carl C. *A Study of American Intelligence.* Princeton, NJ: Princeton University Press, 1923.

Brimlow, George F. "The Life of Sarah Winnemucca: The Formative Years." *Oregon Historical Quarterly* 53 (June 1952): 103–134.

Broder, Dorothy Elizabeth. "Life Adjustment Education: An Historical Study of a Program of the United States Office of Education, 1945–1954." Ed.D. diss., Teachers College, Columbia University, 1977.

Brown, Alan S. "The Northwest Ordinance and Michigan Education." *Michigan History* 71 (November/December 1987): 24–31.

Brown, Elmer E. *The Making of Our Middle Schools.* London: Longmans, Green & Company, 1905.

Brown, Grace Taylor. "The Importance and Influence of James Gordon Carter, Pioneer Educator in Massachusetts, 1795–1849." Ph.D. diss., Boston University, 1957.

Brown, Richard D. *The Strength of a People: The Idea of an Informed Citizenry in America, 1650–1870.* Chapel Hill: University of North Carolina Press, 1996.

Bruner, Jerome S. *Acts of Meaning.* Cambridge, MA: Harvard University Press, 1990.

Bruner, Jerome S. *The Relevance of Education.* New York: W. W. Norton, 1971.

Bruner, Jerome S. *Toward a Theory of Instruction.* Cambridge, MA: Harvard University Press, 1966.

Bryan, Anna E. "The Letter Killeth." In *National Education Association Journal of Proceedings and Addresses,* 573–581. Washington, DC: National Education Association, 1890.

Buchanan, Robert M. "Deaf Students and Workers in the United States: 1800–1950." Ph.D. diss., University of Wisconsin, 1995.

Bullock, Henry Allen. *A History of Negro Education in the South, from 1619 to the Present.* Cambridge, MA: Harvard University Press, 1967.

Butchart, Ronald E. *Northern Whites, Southern Blacks, and Reconstruction: Freedmen's Education, 1862–1875.* Westport, CT: Greenwood Press, 1980.

Butchart, Ronald E. "Punishments, Penalties, Prizes, and Procedures: A History of Discipline in U.S. Schools." In *Classroom Discipline in American Schools: The Political and Ethical Dimensions of Managing Student Behavior.* Edited by Ronald E. Butchart and Barbara McEwan. Albany: State University of New York Press, 1996.

Butler, J. Thomas. *Principles of Health Education and Health Promotion.* Englewood, CO: Morton Publishing Co., 1996.

Butler, Nicholas Murray. *Across the Busy Years: Recollections and Reflections.* 2 vols. New York: Charles Scribner's Sons, 1939, 1940.

Butler, Vera. "The Infant School Movement." In *Education as Revealed by New England Newspapers Prior to 1850,* 258–269. 1935. Reprint, New York: Arno Press, 1969.

Butterworth, Julian. *The Parent-Teacher Association and Its Work.* New York: Macmillan, 1929.

Butts, R. Freeman, and Lawrence A. Cremin. *A History of Education in American Culture.* New York: Holt, Rinehart and Winston, 1953.

Bybee, Rodger W. *Science/Technology/Society.* Washington, DC: National Science Teachers Association, 1985.

Calam, John. "Parsons and Pedagogues: The S.P.G. Adventure in American Education." Ph.D. diss., Columbia University, 1969.

Caliver, Ambrose. *Rural Education among Negroes under Jeanes Supervising Teachers.* Washington, DC: U.S. Government Printing Office, 1933.

Callahan, Raymond E. *Education and the Cult of Efficiency: A Study of the Social Forces That Have Shaped the Administration of the Public Schools.* Chicago: University of Chicago Press, 1962.

Cameron, Kenneth W. *The Massachusetts Lyceum during the American Renaissance.* Hartford, CT: Transcendental Books, 1969.

Campbell, Jack K. *Colonel Francis W. Parker: The Children's Crusader.* New York: Teachers College Press, 1967.

Canter, Lee, and Marilyn Canter. *Assertive Discipline: Positive Behavior Management for Today's Classroom.* Santa Monica, CA: Lee Canter and Associates, 1991.

Carbone, Peter, Jr. *The Social and Educational Thought of Harold Rugg.* Durham, NC: Duke University Press, 1977.

Carl, Iris M., ed. *Prospects for School Mathematics.* Reston, VA: National Council of Teachers of Mathematics, 1995.

Carleton, Robert. *The NSTA Story, 1944–1974.* Washington, DC: National Science Teachers Association, 1976.

Carley, Maurine. *Let Your Light Shine: Pioneer Women Educators of Wyoming.* Sheridan, WY: Alpha Xi State Delta Kappa Gamma, 1965.

Carlson, Allan C. "From Cottage to Work Station . . . and Back Again: The Family and Home Education." *Family in America* 11 (February 1996): 1–8.

Carlson, Robert A. *The Quest for Conformity: Americanization through Education.* New York: John Wiley, 1975.

Carnegie Foundation for the Advancement of Teaching. Concord, NH: Rumford Press, 1919.

Carnoy, Martin, and Henry Levin. *Schooling and Work in the Democratic State.* Palo Alto, CA: Stanford University Press, 1985.

Carper, James C. "Home Schooling, History, and Historians: The Past as Present." *High School Journal* 75 (April/May 1992): 252–257.

Carper, James C., and Jack Layman. "Black-Flight Academies: The New Christian Day Schools." *Educational Forum* 61 (winter 1997): 114–121.

Carr, William G. *John Swett: The Biography of an Educational Pioneer.* Santa Ana, CA: Fine Arts Press, 1933.

Carr, William G. *John Swett: California's Frontier Schoolmaster.* Washington, DC: University Press of America, 1978.

Carson, Clayborne, David J. Garrow, Gerald Gill, Vincent Harding, Darlene Clark Hine. *Eyes on the Prize, Civil Rights Reader: Documents, Speeches, and First Hand Accounts from the Black Freedom Struggle, 1954–1990.* New York: Penguin Books, 1991.

Carter, Patricia A. "Becoming 'New Women': The Equal Rights Campaigns of New York City Schoolteachers, 1900–1920." In *The Teacher's Voice: A Social History of Teaching in Twentieth Century America,* 40–58. Edited by Richard J. Altenbaugh. London: Falmer Press, 1992.

Carter, Patricia A. "A Coalition between Women Teachers and Feminists in New York City, 1900–1920." Ph.D. diss., University of Cincinnati, 1985.

Carter, Stephen L. *The Culture of Disbelief: How American Law and Politics Trivialize Religious Devotion.* New York: Basic Books, 1993.

Case, Roscoe D. *The Platoon School in America.* Stanford, CA: Stanford University Press, 1931.

Cayton, Mary K. *Emerson's Emergence: Self and Society in the Transformation of New England, 1800–1845.* Chapel Hill: University of North Carolina Press, 1989.

Center for National Policy Review. *Justice Delayed and Denied: HEW and Northern School Desegregation.* Washington, DC: School of Law, Catholic University, September 1974.

Chafee, Richard. "The Teaching of Architecture at the Ecole des Beaux-Arts." In *The Architecture of the Ecole des Beaux-Arts,* 61–110. Edited by Arthur Drexler. New York: Metropolitan Museum, 1977.

Chall, Jeanne S. *Learning to Read: The Great Debate.* New York: McGraw-Hill, 1967.

Chamberlin, Dean, E. S. Chamberlin, N. E. Draught, and William E. Schott. *Did They Succeed in College?* New York: Harper and Brothers, 1942.

Chapman, Paul D. *Schools as Sorters: Lewis M. Terman, Applied Psychology, and the Intelligence Testing Movement, 1890–1930.* New York: New York University Press, 1988.

Child, Julia. "Caught between Common Sense and Science: The Cornell Child Study Clubs, 1925–1945." *History of Education Quarterly* 34 (winter 1994): 433–452.

Child, Lydia Maria. *An Appeal in Favor of Americans Called Africans.* 1836. Reprint, New York: Arno Press, 1968.

Child, Lydia Maria. *The Mother's Book.* 1831. Reprint, New York: Arno Press, 1972.

Chudacoff, Howard. *How Old Are You? Age Consciousness in American Culture.* Princeton, NJ: Princeton University Press, 1989.

Church, Robert. *Education in the United States: An Interpretive History.* New York: Free Press, 1976.

Clarke, John Henrik. *African People in World History.* Baltimore: Black Classic Press, 1993.

Clarke, John Henrik. *Christopher Columbus and the African Holocaust: Slavery and the Rise of European Capitalism.* Brooklyn, NY: A & B Books, 1992.

Clayton, Bruce. *Forgotten Prophet: The Life of Randolph Bourne.* Baton Rouge: Louisiana State University Press, 1984.

Clowse, Barbara Barksdale. *Brain Power for the Cold War: The Sputnik Crisis and National Defense Act of 1958.* Westport, CT: Greenwood Press, 1981.

Cohen, Joseph J., and Alexis C. Ferm. *The Modern School of Stelton.* Stelton, NJ: Modern School Association of North America, 1925.

Cohen, Ronald D. *Children of the Mill: Schooling and Society in Gary, Indiana, 1906–1960.* Bloomington: Indiana University Press, 1990.

Cohen, Ronald D., and Raymond A. Mohl. *The Paradox of Progressive Education: The Gary Plan and Urban Education.* Port Washington, NY: Kennikat Press, 1979.

Cohen, Sheldon. *A History of Colonial Education, 1607–1776.* New York: John Wiley & Sons, 1974.

Cohen, Sol. "The History of the History of American Education, 1900–1976: The Uses of the Past." *Harvard Educational Review* 46 (August 1976): 298–330.

Cohen, Sol. *Progressives and Urban School Reform: The Public Education Association of New York City, 1895–1954.* New York: Teachers College Press, 1964.

Cohen, Sol, ed. *Education in the United States: A Documentary History.* New York: Random House, 1974.

Coleman, James S., E. Q. Campbell, C. J. Hobson, J. McPartland, A. M. Mood, F. D. Weinfeld, and R. L. York. *Equality of Educational Opportunity.* Washington, DC: U.S. Office of Education, 1966.

Coleman, Michael C. *American Indian Children at School, 1850–1930.* Jackson: University Press of Mississippi, 1993.

Collier, Gary. *Social Origins of Mental Ability.* New York: John Wiley & Sons, 1994.

Collier, John. *From Every Zenith: A Memoir and Some Essays on Life and Thought.* Denver: Sage Books, 1963.

Commission on the Reorganization of Secondary Education. *Cardinal Principles of Secondary Education.* U.S. Bureau of Education Bulletin No. 35. Washington, DC: U.S. Government Printing Office, 1918.

Committee of Nineteen. *Pioneers of the Kindergarten in America.* New York: Century, 1913.

Commonwealth of Massachusetts. *Report of the Commission on Industrial and Technical Education.* Boston: Wright and Potter, 1906.

Conant, James B. *The American High School Today.* New York: McGraw-Hill, 1959.

Conant, James B. *The Child, the Parent, and the State.* Cambridge, MA: Harvard University Press, 1959.

Conant, James B. *The Citadel of Learning.* New Haven, CT: Yale University Press, 1956.

Conant, James B. *Education and Liberty: The Role of Schools in a Modern Democracy.* Cambridge, MA: Harvard University Press, 1953.

Conant, James B. *My Several Lives: Memoirs of a Social Inventor.* New York: Harper, 1970.

Conant, James B. *The Revolutionary Transformation of the American High School.* Cambridge, MA: Harvard University Press, 1959.

Conant, James B. *Slums and Suburbs: A Commentary on Schools in Metropolitan Areas.* New York: McGraw-Hill, 1961.

Cookson, Peter W., Jr., ed. *The Choice Controversy.* Newbury Park, CA: Corwin Press, 1992.

Cookson, Peter, and Caroline Hodges Persell. *Preparing for Power: America's Elite Boarding Schools.* New York: Basic Books, 1985.

Cooley, Thomas McIntyre. *Michigan: A History of Governments.* Boston: Houghton Mifflin, 1889.

Cooney, Thomas J., and Christian R. Hirsch, eds. *Teaching and Learning Mathematics in the 1990s.* Reston, VA: National Council of Teachers of Mathematics, 1990.

Correia, Stephen Taylor. "For Their Own Good: An Historical Analysis of the Educational Thought of Thomas Jesse Jones." Ph.D. diss., Pennsylvania State University, 1993.

Coughlin, Neil. *Young John Dewey: An Essay in American Intellectual History.* Chicago: University of Chicago Press, 1975.

Counts, George S. *Dare the School Build a New Social Order?* New York: John Day, 1932.

Counts, George S. "A Humble Autobiography." In *Leaders in American Education: The Seventieth Yearbook of the National Society for the Study of Education,* 151–176. Edited by Robert J. Havighurst. Chicago: University of Chicago Press, 1971.

Cox, Charlotte H. "Basic Skills through Mastery Learning: An Interview with Benjamin S. Bloom." Part One. *Curriculum Review* 18 (December 1979): 362–365. Part Two. *Curriculum Review* 19 (February 1980): 10–14.

Coy, Michael W., ed. *Apprenticeship: From Theory to Method and Back Again.* Albany: State University of New York Press, 1989.

Craver, Kathleen W. *School Library Media Centers in the Twenty-First Century: Changes and Challenges.* Westport, CT: Greenwood Press, 1994.

Crawford, James. *Hold Your Tongue: Bilingualism and the Politics of "English Only."* Reading, MA: Addison-Wesley, 1992.

Crawford, James. *Language Loyalties: A Source Book on the Official English Controversy.* Chicago: University of Chicago Press, 1992.

Cremin, Lawrence A. *The American Common School: An Historic Conception.* New York: Teachers College Press, 1951.

Cremin, Lawrence A. *American Education: The Colonial Experience, 1607–1783.* New York: Harper and Row, 1970.

Cremin, Lawrence A. *American Education: The Metropolitan Experience, 1876–1980.* New York: Harper and Row, 1988.

Cremin, Lawrence A. *American Education: The National Experience, 1783–1876.* New York: Harper and Row, 1980.

Cremin, Lawrence A. "The Revolution in American Secondary Education, 1893–1913." *Teachers College Record* 26 (March 1955): 295–308.

Cremin, Lawrence A. *Traditions of American Education.* New York: Basic Books, 1977.

Cremin, Lawrence A. *The Transformation of the School: Progressivism in American Education, 1876–1957.* New York: Knopf, 1961.

Cremin, Lawrence A. *The Wonderful World of Ellwood Patterson Cubberley: An Essay on the Historiography of American Education.* New York: Teachers College Press, 1965.

Cronbach, Leon. "Five Decades of Public Controversy over Mental Testing." *American Psychologist* 30 (1975): 1–14.

Crosswhite, F. Joe. "National Standards: A New Dimension in Professional Leadership." *School Science and Mathematics* 90 (1990): 454–466.

Cuban, Larry. *How Teachers Taught: Constancy and Change in American Classrooms, 1890–1980.* New York: Teachers College Press, 1993.

Cuban, Larry. *Teachers and Machines: The Classroom Use of Technology since 1920.* New York: Teachers College Press, 1986.

Cuban, Larry. "What Happens to Reforms That Last? The Case of the Junior High School." *American Educational Research Journal* 29 (summer 1992): 227–251.

Cubberley, Ellwood P. *Public Education in the United States: A Study and Interpretation of American Educational History.* Boston: Houghton Mifflin, 1919.

Cubberley, Ellwood P. *Public School Administration.* Boston: Houghton Mifflin, 1916.

Curran, Francis X. *The Churches and the Schools: American Protestantism and Popular Elementary Education.* Chicago: Loyola University Press, 1954.

Curry, Jabez L. M. *A Brief Sketch of George Peabody, and a History of the Peabody Education Fund.* Cambridge, MA: John Wilson and Son, 1898.

Curti, Merle. *The Social Ideas of American Educators.* 1935. Reprint, Paterson, NJ: Pageant Books, 1959.

Curtis, Henry S. *Education through Play.* New York: Macmillan, 1930.

Curtis, Henry S. *The Play Movement and Its Significance.* New York: Macmillan, 1917.

Curtis, Isabel Gordon. "The Housekeeper at Large: The People and the Problems She Meets." *Good Housekeeping Magazine* 50 (April 1910): 477–481.

Cutler, William W., III. "Cathedral of Culture: The Schoolhouse in American Educational Thought and Practice since 1820." *History of Education Quarterly* 29 (spring 1989): 1–40.

Cutler, William W., III. "A Preliminary Look at the Schoolhouse: The Philadelphia Story, 1870–1920." *Urban Education* 8 (January 1974): 381–399.

Cutler, William W., III. "Status, Values and the Education of the Poor: The Trustees of the New York Public School Society, 1805–1853." *American Quarterly* 24 (March 1972): 69–85.

Cutler, William W., III. "Symbol of Paradox in the New Republic: Classicism in the Design of Schoolhouses and Other Public Buildings in the United States, 1800–1860." In *Aspects of Antiquity in the History of Education,* 163–176. Edited by F. P. Hager, Marc Depaepe, Manfred Heinemann, Jurgen Herbst, and Roy Lowe. International Series for the History of Education. Vol. 3. Hildesheim, Germany: Verlag August Lax, 1992.

Dabney, Charles William. *Universal Education in the South.* Vol. 1. Chapel Hill: University of North Carolina Press, 1936.

Dahlstrand, Frederick C. *Amos Bronson Alcott: An Intellectual Biography.* East Brunswick, NJ: Associated University Press, 1982.

Dain, Floyd, R. *Education in the Wilderness.* Lansing: Michigan Historical Commission, 1968.

Danbom, David B. *The Resisted Revolution: Urban America and the Industrialization of Agriculture, 1900–1930*. Ames: Iowa State University Press, 1979.

David, Howard V. *Frank Parsons: Prophet, Innovator, Counselor*. Carbondale: Southern Illinois University Press, 1969.

Davies, John. *Phrenology: Fad and Science*. New Haven, CT: Yale University Press, 1955.

Davis, Allen F. *American Heroine: The Life and Legend of Jane Addams*. New York: Oxford University Press, 1973.

Davis, Allen F. *Spearheads for Reform: The Social Settlements and the Progressive Movement, 1890–1914*. New York: Oxford University Press, 1967.

Davis, Howard Vaughn. *Frank Parsons: Prophet, Innovator, Counselor*. Carbondale: Southern Illinois University Press, 1969.

Davis, Mary D. "How NANE Began." *Young Children* 20 (November 1964): 106–109.

Davis, Mary D. *Nursery Schools: Their Development and Current Practices in the United States*. Bulletin No. 9. Washington, DC: U.S. Office of Education, 1932.

Davis, O. L., Jr. *National Council for the Social Studies in Retrospect*. Bulletin No. 92. Washington, DC: National Council for the Social Studies, 1995.

Davis, Robert B., Carolyn A. Maher, and Nel Noddings, eds., *Constructivist Views on the Teaching and Learning of Mathematics*. Reston, VA: National Council of Teachers of Mathematics, 1990.

Davis-DuBois, Rachel. *Adventures in Intercultural Education: A Manual for Secondary School Teachers*. New York: Progressive Education Association, 1938.

de Lima, Agnes. *Our Enemy the Child*. New York: New Republic, 1925.

Dearborn, Ned. *The Oswego Movement in American Education*. New York: Teachers College Press, 1925.

DeBoer, George E. *A History of Ideas in Science Education: Implications for Practice*. New York: Teachers College Press, 1991.

DeGiustino, David. *Conquest of Mind: Phrenology and Victorian Social Thought*. London: Croom Helm, 1975.

Demos, John. "The Rise and Fall of Adolescence." In *Past, Present and Personal*, 92–113. New York: Oxford University Press, 1986.

Dennis, Lawrence J., and William E. Eaton. *George S. Counts: Educator for a New Age*. Carbondale: Southern Illinois University Press, 1980.

Dennison, George. *The Lives of Children: The Story of the First Street School*. New York: Random House, 1969.

Dewey, John. *Democracy and Education: An Introduction to the Philosophy of Education*. New York: Macmillan, 1916.

Dewey, John. *Essays in Experimental Logic*. Chicago: University of Chicago Press, 1916.

Dewey, John. *Experience and Education*. New York: Macmillan, 1938.

Dewey, John. *How We Think*. Boston: Heath, 1933.

DeWulf, B. G. "The Educational Ideas of John Franklin Bobbitt." Ph.D. diss., Washington University, 1962.

Diop, Cheikh Anta. *The African Origins of Civilization: Myth or Reality*. Westport, CT: Lawrence Hill, 1974.

Dixon, John. "Historical Considerations: An International Perspective." In *Handbook of Research on Teaching the English Language Arts*, 18–23. Edited by James Flood, Julie N. Jensen, Diane Lapp, and James R. Squire. New York: Collier Macmillan, 1991.

Doll, William, Jr. *A Post-Modern Perspective on Curriculum Development.* New York: Teachers College Press, 1993.

Donlon, Thomas F. "Brigham's Book." *College Board Review* 113 (1979): 24–30.

Dorn, Sherman. *Creating the Dropout: An Institutional and Social History of School Failure.* Westport, CT: Greenwood Press, 1996.

Douglas, Paul H. *American Apprenticeship and Industrial Education.* New York: Columbia University, 1921.

Douglass, Frederick. *Life and Times of Frederick Douglass: His Early Life as a Slave, His Escape from Bondage, and His Complete History.* Hartford, CT: Park Publishing Co., 1881.

Douglass, Frederick. *My Bondage and My Freedom.* New York: Miller, Orton & Mulligan, 1855.

Douglass, Frederick. *Narrative of the Life of Frederick Douglass, an American Slave, Written by Himself.* Boston: Anti-Slavery Office, 1845.

Downey, Matthew T. *Carl Campbell Brigham: Scientist and Educator.* Princeton, NJ: Educational Testing Service, 1961.

Downs, Robert B. *Friedrich Froebel.* Boston: Twayne Publishing, 1978.

Downs, Robert B. *Horace Mann: Champion of Public Schools.* New York: Twayne Publishers, 1974.

Dreikurs, Rudolph. *Maintaining Sanity in the Classroom: Classroom Management Techniques.* New York: Harper and Row, 1982.

Droat, Walter H. *David Snedden and Education for Social Efficiency.* Madison: University of Wisconsin Press, 1967.

D'Souza, Dinesh. *Illiberal Education: The Politics of Race and Sex on Campus.* New York: Free Press, 1991.

Du Bois, W.E.B. *The Autobiography of W.E.B. Du Bois: A Soliloquy on Viewing My Life from the Last Decade of Its First Century.* New York: International Publishers, 1968.

Du Bois, W.E.B. *The Education of Black People: Ten Critiques, 1906–1960.* New York: Monthly Review Press, 1973.

Du Bois, W.E.B. *The Philadelphia Negro: A Social Study.* New York: University of Pennsylvania, 1899.

Du Bois, W.E.B. *The Souls of Black Folk.* Chicago: University of Chicago, 1903.

Dublin, Thomas. *Women at Work: The Transformation of Work and Community in Lowell, Massachusetts, 1826–1860.* New York: Columbia University Press, 1979.

Dunbar, Willis F. *The Michigan Record in Higher Education.* Detroit: Wayne State University Press, 1963.

Dunkel, Harold B. *Herbart and Education.* New York: Random House, 1969.

Dunkel, Harold B. *Herbart and Herbartianism.* Chicago: University of Chicago Press, 1970.

Dunn, Frederick D. "The Educational Philosophies of Washington, Du Bois, and Houston: Laying the Foundations for Afrocentrism and Multiculturalism." *Journal of Negro Education* 62 (winter 1993): 24–34.

Dutton, Wilbur H. "The Child Study Movement in American Education from Its Origin (1880) to the Organization of the Progressive Education Association (1920)." Ph.D. diss., Stanford University, 1945.

Dyer, C., R. Brown, and E. D. Goldstein. *The Role of School Libraries in Education.* Hamden, CT: Shoestring Press, 1970.

Dykhuizen, George. *The Life and Mind of John Dewey.* Carbondale: Southern Illinois University Press, 1973.

Earle, Alice M. *Child Life in Colonial Days.* 1899. Reprint, Williamstown, MA: Corner House, 1975.

East, Marjorie. *Home Economics: Past, Present, and Future.* Boston: Allyn and Bacon, 1980.

Eastland, Tony, ed. *Religious Liberty and the Supreme Court: The Cases That Define the Debate over Church and State.* Washington, DC: Ethics and Public Policy Center, 1993.

Eaton, William E. *The American Federation of Teachers, 1916–1961: A History of the Movement.* Carbondale: Southern Illinois University Press, 1975.

Eaton, William E. "American School Penmanship: From Craft to Process." *American Journal of Education* 93 (February 1985): 252–267.

Edmunson, James Bartlett. *The Legal and Constitutional Basis of a State School System.* Bloomington, IL: Public School Publishing Company, 1926.

Edwards, Newton, and Herman G. Richey. *The School in the American Social Order.* Boston: Houghton Mifflin, 1963.

Efland, Arthur D. *A History of Art Education.* New York: Teachers College Press, 1990.

Eisner, Elliot. *Cognition and Curriculum: A Basis for Deciding What to Teach.* New York: Teachers College Press, 1982.

Elliott, David L., and Arthur Woodward. *Textbooks and Schooling in the United States.* Chicago: National Society for the Study of Education, 1990.

Embree, Edwin R., and Julia Waxman. *Investment in People: The Story of the Julius Rosenwald Fund.* New York: Harper and Brothers, 1949.

Emerson, George B. *History and Design of the American Institute of Instruction.* Boston: Ticknor, Reed, and Fields, 1849.

Emerson, Thomas J. I. *The System of Freedom of Expression.* New York: Vintage Books, 1971.

Enck, Henry Snyder. "The Burden Borne: Northern White Philanthropy and Southern Black Industrial Education, 1900–1915." Ph.D. diss., University of Cincinnati, 1971.

Evans, M. Stanton. *The Theme Is Freedom.* Washington, DC: Regnery Publications, 1994.

Fancher, Raymond. *The Intelligence Men: Makers of the IQ Controversy.* New York: W. W. Norton, 1985.

Farish, Hunter Dickinson, ed. *Journal and Letters of Philip Vickers Fithian: A Plantation Tutor of the Old Dominion, 1773–1774.* Williamsburg, VA: Colonial Williamsburg, 1943.

Farrell, Gabriel. *The Story of Blindness.* Cambridge, MA: Harvard University Press, 1956.

Fass, Paula. *Outside In: Minorities and the Transformation of American Education.* New York: Oxford University Press, 1989.

Felkin, Henry, and Emmie Felkin. *An Introduction in Herbart's Science and Practice in Education.* Boston: D. C. Heath, 1898.

Fenner, Mildred Sandison. *The National Education Association: Its Development and Program.* Washington, DC: National Education Association, 1950.

Fenton, Christi. "Cooperative Learning: A View from the Inside." *Contemporary Education* 63 (1992): 207–209.

Fenton, Edwin. *The Humanities in Three Cities.* New York: Holt, Rinehart, and Winston, 1969.

Fenton, Edwin. *Teaching the New Social Studies in Secondary Schools: An Inductive Approach.* New York: Holt, Rinehart, and Winston, 1966.

Fenton, Edwin. "What Happened to the New Social Studies: A Case Study in Curriculum Reform." Pittsburgh: Center for University Outreach, Carnegie Mellon University, 1991.

Fenton, Edwin, gen. ed. *The Holt Social Studies Curriculum.* 11 vols. New York: Holt, Rinehart, and Winston, 1st ed. 1967–1969, 2nd ed. 1974–1976.

Fenton, Edwin, and David Fowler, gen. eds. *The Scott-Foresman Problems in American History.* 11 vols. Chicago: Scott, Foresman, 1st ed. 1964–1966, 2nd ed. 1971–1975.

Fenton, Edwin, S. Gomberg, J. Furtek, and C. Hill. *Leading Dilemma Discussions: A Workshop Manual.* Pittsburgh: Carnegie Mellon University, 1980.

Fenton, Edwin, and Elsa Wasserman. *Improving School Climate through Fairness Meetings.* Cambridge, MA: Center for Moral Education, 1983.

Fernandes, James J. "The Gate to Heaven: T. H. Gallaudet and the Rhetoric of the Deaf Education Movement." Ph.D. diss., University of Michigan, 1980.

Filler, Louis, ed. *Horace Mann on the Crisis in Education.* Yellow Springs, OH: Antioch Press, 1965.

Findley, Warren G. "Carl C. Brigham Revisited." *College Board Review* 119 (1981): 6–9.

Fine, Michelle. *Framing Dropouts: Notes on the Politics of an Urban High School.* Albany: State University of New York Press, 1991.

Finkelstein, Barbara. *Governing the Young: Teacher Behavior in Popular Primary Schools in Nineteenth-Century United States.* London: Falmer Press, 1989.

Finkelstein, Barbara. "Perfecting Childhood: Horace Mann and the Origins of Public Education in the United States." *Biography* 13 (winter 1990): 6–21.

Finkenbine, Roy E. "A Little Circle: White Philanthropists and Black Industrial Education in the Postbellum South." Ph.D. diss., Bowling Green State University, 1982.

Finn, Mason. "An Historical Analysis of the Contributions of Samuel Read Hall to Nineteenth-Century Teacher Education." Ph.D. diss., Boston College, 1970.

First State Normal School in America—The Journals of Cyrus Peirce and Mary Swift. Cambridge, MA: Harvard University Press, 1926.

Fishburn, Eleanor Craven, ed. *The First State Normal School in America—The Journals of Cyrus Peirce and Mary Swift.* Cambridge: Harvard University Press, 1926.

Fisher, Dorothy C. *A Montessori Mother.* New York: Henry Holt, 1912.

Fisher, Hersha S. "The Education of Elizabeth Peabody." Ph.D. diss., Harvard University, 1980.

Fisher, John E. *The John F. Slater Fund: A Nineteenth-Century Affirmative Action for Negro Education.* Lanham, MD: University Press of America, 1988.

Fixico, Donald. *Termination and Relocation in Federal Indian Policy, 1945–1960.* Albuquerque: University of New Mexico Press, 1986.

Flaherty, Thomas F., and John J. Flaherty. "James Carter: Champion of the Normal School Movement." 1974. ERIC document ED 087747.

Flesch, Rudolph. *Why Johnny Can't Read and What You Can Do about It.* New York: Harper and Row, 1955.

Fletcher, Alice C. *Indian Education and Civilization: A Report Prepared in Answer to Senate Resolution of February 23, 1885.* Washington, DC: U.S. Government Printing Office, 1888.

Flexner, Abraham. *Abraham Flexner: An Autobiography.* New York: Simon and Schuster, 1960.

Flynn, James R. *Race, IQ and Jensen.* London: Routledge & Kegan Paul, 1980.

Fogarty, Robin. "Ten Ways to Integrate Curriculum." *Educational Leadership* 49 (1991): 61–65.

Fones-Wolf, Elizabeth. "The Politics of Vocationalism: Coalitions and Industrial Education in the Progressive Era." *Historian* 46 (January 1983): 39–55.

Ford, Paul L., ed. *The New-England Primer: A History of Its Origin and Development with a Reprint of the Unique Copy of the Earliest Known Edition and Many Facsimile Illustrations and Reproductions.* 1897. Reprint, New York: Teachers College Press, 1962.

Ford, Paul L., ed. *The Writings of Thomas Jefferson.* 10 vols. New York: G. P. Putnam's Sons, 1892–1899.

Fosdick, Raymond B. *Adventures in Giving: The Story of the General Education Board.* New York: Harper and Row, 1962.

Foster, Charles R. *Extra-Curricular Activities.* Richmond, VA: Johnson Publishing, 1925.

Fowler, Catherine S. "Sarah Winnemucca, Northern Piute ca. 1844–1891." In *American Indian Intellectuals: 1976 Proceedings of the American Ethnological Society,* 32–42. Edited by Margot Liberty. St. Paul, MN: West Publishing, 1978.

Fraenkel, Jack R. "The Evolution of the Taba Curriculum Development Project." *Social Studies* 85 (July/August 1994): 149–159.

Franklin, Barry M. *From "Backwardness" to "At-Risk": Childhood Learning Difficulties and the Contradictions of School Reform.* Albany: State University of New York Press, 1994.

Fraser, Walter, Jr. "William Henry Ruffner: A Liberal in the Old and New South." Ph.D. diss., University of Tennessee, 1970.

Fraser, Walter, Jr. "William Henry Ruffner and the Establishment of Virginia's Public School System, 1870–1874." *Virginia Magazine of History and Biography* 79 (July 1971): 259–279.

Frazier, Benjamin W. "The First State Normal School." *School Life* 24 (February 1939): 131–132.

Fretwell, Elbert K. *Extra-Curricular Activities in Secondary Schools.* Boston: Houghton Mifflin, 1931.

Fretwell, Elbert K. "Extra-Curricular Activities of Secondary Schools IV: Bibliographies of Home Rooms, Pupil Participation in Government, Finances, Assemblies, and Fraternities." *Teachers College Record* 27 (January 1926): 901–929.

Fretwell, Elbert K. "The Place of Extra-Curricular Activities in Education." *School and Society* 21 (May 1925): 633–639.

"Fretwell, Elbert K." *National Cyclopaedia of American Biography.* Vol. 49, p. 370. New York: James T. White & Co., 1966.

Froula, V. K. "Extra-Curricular Activities: Their Relation to the Curricular Work of the School." *Journal of Proceedings and Addresses of the National Education Association.* 53rd Annual Meeting. Ann Arbor, MI: National Education Association, 1915, pp. 737–742.

Gabel, Richard J. "Public Funds for Church and Private Schools." Ph.D. diss., Catholic University of America, 1937.

Gadell, John. "Charles Allen Prosser: His Work in Vocational and General Education." Ph.D. diss., Washington University, 1972.

Gallaudet, Edward Miner. *The Life of Thomas Hopkins Gallaudet*. New York: Henry Holt, 1888.

Galton, Sir Francis, F.R.S. *Hereditary Genius: An Inquiry into Its Laws and Consequences*. London: Macmillan, 1869.

Gard, Carroll. *Writing Past and Present: The Story of Writing and Writing Tools*. New York: A. N. Palmer, 1937.

Gardner, Howard. *Frames of Mind: The Theory of Multiple Intelligences*. New York: Basic Books, 1983.

Garrett, James Mercer. "James Mercer." *William and Mary Quarterly* XVII, No.2 (October 1908): 85–99.

Gartner, Lloyd P., ed. *Jewish Education in the United States: A Documentary History*. New York: Teachers College Press, 1969.

Gathercoal, Forrest. *Judicious Discipline*. San Francisco: Caddo Gap Press, 1993.

Gay, Peter. *Freud: A Life for Our Time*. New York: W. W. Norton, 1988.

General Education Board. *Review and Final Report, 1902–1964*. New York: General Education Board, 1964.

General Education in School and College. Cambridge, MA: Harvard University Press, 1952.

Georges, Christopher J., and James A. Messina. *The Harvard Independent: Insider's Guide to Preparatory Schools*. New York: Plume, 1987.

Gholson, Ronald E., and Robert L. Buser. *Cocurricular Activity Programs in Secondary Schools*. Reston, VA: National Association of Secondary School Principals, 1983.

Gilbert, James. *A Cycle of Outrage: America's Reaction to the Juvenile Delinquent in the 1950s*. New York: Oxford University Press, 1986.

Giles, H., H. P. McCutchen, and A. N. Zechiel. *Exploring the Curriculum*. New York: Harper and Brothers, 1942.

Gilmore, William. *Reading Becomes a Necessity of Life: Material and Cultural Life in Rural New England, 1780–1835*. Knoxville: University of Tennessee Press, 1989.

Glanz, J. *Bureaucracy and Professionalism: The Evolution of Public School Supervision*. Cranbury, NJ: Fairleigh Dickinson University Press, 1991.

Glasser, William. *Schools without Failure*. New York: Harper and Row, 1969.

Glenn, Charles Leslie, Jr. *The Myth of the Common School*. Amherst: University of Massachusetts Press, 1988.

Goddard, H. H. *The Kallikak Family: A Study in the Heredity of Feeble-Mindedness*. New York: Macmillan, 1912.

Goggin, Jacqueline. *Carter G. Woodson: A Life in Black History*. Baton Rouge: Louisiana State University Press, 1993.

Going, Allen J. "The South and the Blair Education Bill." *Mississippi Valley Historical Review* 44 (September 1957): 267–290.

Goldberg, J. J. "U.S. Jewry Pins Its Future on Education." *Jerusalem Report* 5 (October 1994): 26–31.

Good, Harry G. *Benjamin Rush and His Services to American Education*. Berne, IN: Witness Press, 1918.

Goodenow, Ronald K. "The Southern Progressive Educator on Race and Pluralism: The

SELECTED BIBLIOGRAPHY   411

Case of William Heard Kilpatrick.'' *History of Education Quarterly* 21 (summer 1981): 147–170.
Goodlad, John I. ''How Laboratory Schools Go Awry.'' *UCLA Educator* 21 (1980): 46–53.
Goodlad, John I. *The Non-Graded Elementary School.* New York: Teachers College Press, 1987.
Goodlad, John I., Roger Soder, and Kenneth M. Sirotnik, eds. *Places Where Teachers Are Taught.* San Francisco: Jossey-Bass, 1990.
Goodman, Kenneth S. ''Reading: A Psycholinguistic Guessing Game.'' In *Theoretical Models and Processes of Reading,* 259–272. Edited by Harry Singer and Robert B. Ruddell. Newark, DE: International Reading Association, 1976.
Goodman, Nathan G. *Benjamin Rush, Physician and Citizen, 1746–1813.* Philadelphia: University of Pennsylvania Press, 1934.
Goor, Mark, and John Schwenn. ''Accommodating Diversity and Disability with Cooperative Learning.'' *Intervention in School and Clinic* 29 (1993): 6–16.
Gould, Stephen J. *The Mismeasure of Man.* New York: W. W. Norton, 1981.
Graff, Harvey J. *Conflicting Paths: Growing up in America.* Cambridge, MA: Harvard University Press, 1995.
Graff, Harvey J. *The Legacies of Literacy: Continuities and Contradictions in Western Culture and Society.* Bloomington: Indiana University Press, 1987.
Graham, Patricia A. ''Carleton Wolsey Washburne: A Biographical Essay.'' In *Leaders in American Education,* 487–494. Seventieth Yearbook of the National Society for the Study of Education, Part II. Edited by Robert J. Havighurst. Chicago: National Society for the Study of Education, 1971.
Graham, Patricia A. *Progressive Education: From Arcady to Academe.* New York: Teachers College Press, 1967.
Graubard, Allen. *Free the Children: Radical Reform and the Free School Movement.* New York: Random House, 1972.
Gray, James. *The Bay Area Writing Project Model of University-School Collaboration.* Berkeley: University of California Press, 1987.
Gray, William S. *On Their Own in Reading: How to Give Children Independence in Attacking New Words.* Chicago: Scott, Foresman, 1948.
Green, Elizabeth Alden. *Mary Lyon and Mount Holyoke: Opening the Gates.* Hanover, NH: University Press of New England, 1979.
Greenberg, Jack. *Crusaders in the Courts.* New York: Basic Books, 1994.
Greenberg, Polly. ''Before the Beginning: A Participant's View.'' *Children* 45 (1990): 41–52.
Greenleaf, William. *From These Beginnings: The Early Philanthropies of Henry and Edsel Ford, 1911–1936.* Detroit: Wayne State University Press, 1964.
Greenson, Ralph R. *The Technique and Practice of Psychoanalysis.* New York: International Universities Press, 1972.
Greenwood, Katy L. B. ''A Philosophical Rationale for Vocational Education: Contributions of Charles A. Prosser and His Contemporaries, 1900–1917.'' Ph.D. diss., University of Minnesota, 1978.
Griffiths, Daniel E., Robert T. Stout, and Patricia B. Forsyth, eds. *Leaders for America's Schools.* Berkeley, CA: McCutchan Publishing, 1988.
Grizzell, Emit Duncan. *Origin and Development of the High School in New England before 1865.* New York: Macmillan, 1923.

412 SELECTED BIBLIOGRAPHY

Gross, Laurence F. *The Course of Industrial Decline: The Boott Cotton Mills of Lowell, Massachusetts, 1835–1955*. Baltimore: Johns Hopkins University Press, 1993.

Grubb, Norton W. "The Integrated Curriculum: A Reality Check." *Middle School Journal* 29 (1996): 12–19.

Guenter, Scot M. *The American Flag, 1777–1924: Cultural Shifts from Creation to Codification*. Cranbury, NJ: Farleigh Dickinson Press, 1990.

Gulliford, Andrew. *America's Country Schools*. Washington, DC: Preservation Press, 1984.

Gutek, Gerald L. *The Educational Theory of George S. Counts*. Columbus: Ohio State University Press, 1970.

Gutek, Gerald L. *George S. Counts and American Civilization: The Educator as Social Theorist*. Macon, GA: Mercer University Press, 1984.

Gutek, Gerald L. "Geoge Sylvester Counts (1880–1974): A Biographical Memoir." *Proceedings of the National Academy of Education* 3 (Stanford, CA: National Academy of Education, 1976): 333–353.

Gutek, Gerald L. *Joseph Neef: The Americanization of Pestalozzianism*. Tuscaloosa, AL: University of Alabama Press, 1978.

Gutkowski, Thomas W. "Student Initiative and the Origins of the High School Extracurriculum: Chicago, 1880–1915." *History of Education Quarterly* 28 (spring 1988): 49–72.

Gutmann, Amy. *Democratic Education*. Princeton, NJ: Princeton University Press, 1987.

Guttmacher Institute. *Teenage Pregnancy: The Problem That Hasn't Gone Away*. New York: Planned Parenthood of America, 1981.

Hadley, Alvan C., Jr. "Military Schools: The Association of Military Colleges and Schools of the United States (AMSCUS) and the Historical Struggle for the Survival of the Military Preparatory Schools in America." Ed.D. diss., University of Kentucky, 1997.

Hall, Granville Stanley. *Adolescence: Its Psychology and Its Relations to Physiology, Anthropology, Sociology, Sex, Crime, Religion, and Education*. 2 vols. New York: Appleton-Century-Crofts, 1904.

Hall, Granville Stanley. *The Life and Confessions of a Psychologist*. New York: Appleton-Century-Crofts, 1923.

Hall, Granville Stanley. *Recreations of a Psychologist*. New York: Appleton, 1920.

Hall, Granville Stanley. *Senescence: The Last Half of Life*. New York: Appleton, 1922.

Hallinger, Phillip, Keith Leithwood, and Joseph Murphy, eds. *Cognitive Perspectives on Educational Leadership*. New York: Teachers College Press, 1993.

Hamilton, Steven F. *Apprenticeship for Adulthood: Preparing Youth for the Future*. New York: Free Press, 1990.

Hampel, Robert. *The Last Little Citadel: American High Schools since 1940*. Boston: Houghton Mifflin, 1986.

Handbook of Private Schools. Boston: Porter Sargent, 1996.

Hansen, Allen Oscar. *Early Educational Leadership in the Ohio Valley*. Bloomington, IL: Public School Publishing, 1923. Reprint, New York: Arno Press, 1969.

Harker, John Stanley. "The Life and Contributions of Calvin Ellis Stowe." Ph.D. diss., University of Pittsburgh, 1951.

Harlan, Louis R. *Booker T. Washington: The Making of a Black Leader, 1865–1901*. New York: Oxford University Press, 1972.

Harlan, Louis R. *Booker T. Washington: The Wizard of Tuskegee, 1901–1915.* New York: Oxford University Press, 1983.

Harlan, Louis R. *Separate and Unequal: Public School Campaigns and Racism in the Southern Seaboard States, 1901–1915.* Chapel Hill: University of North Carolina Press, 1958.

Harlan, Louis R., ed. *The Booker T. Washington Papers.* Urbana: University of Illinois Press, 1972–1984.

Harper, Charles A. *A Century of Public Teacher Education: The Story of the State Teachers Colleges as They Evolved from the Normal Schools.* Washington, DC: American Association of Teachers Colleges, 1939.

Harris, William T. *Psychologic Foundations of Education.* New York: D. Appleton & Co., 1898.

Harrison, John F. C., ed. *Utopianism and Education: Robert Owen and the Owenites.* New York: Teachers College Press, 1968.

Hartness, Robert W. "The Education Work of Robert Jefferson Breckinridge." Ph.D. diss., Yale University, 1936.

Harveson, Mae Elizabeth. *Catharine Esther Beecher, Pioneer Educator.* Philadelphia: University of Pennsylvania, 1932.

Hassard, John Rose Greene. *Life of the Most Reverend John Hughes, D.D.* New York: D. Appleton and Company, 1866.

Hatfield, Wilbur. *The Experience Curriculum in English.* New York: D. Appleton Century, 1935.

Hawes, Joseph M. *American Childhood: A Research Guide and Historical Handbook.* Westport, CT: Greenwood Press, 1985.

Hawes, Joseph M. *Children in Urban Society: Juvenile Delinquency in Nineteenth-Century Society.* New York: Oxford University Press, 1971.

Hawes, Joseph M. *The Children's Rights Movement: A History of Advocacy and Reform.* Boston: Twayne Publishers, 1991.

Hawkins, Layton S., Charles A. Prosser, and John C. Wright. *Development of Vocational Education.* Chicago: American Technological Society, 1951.

Hawthorne, Betty E. "Echoes of the Past—Voice of the Future." *Journal of Home Economics* 75 (winter 1983): 36–45.

Hay, Samuel A. "Carter G. Woodson's *Mis-Education of the Negro*: A Re-Visit." *Negro History Bulltein* 38 (August-September 1975): 436–439.

Hayden, Dolores. *The Grand Domestic Revolution: A History of Feminist Designs for American Homes, Neighborhoods, and Cities.* Cambridge: Massachusetts Institute of Technology Press, 1981.

Hays, Kim. *Practicing Virtues: Moral Traditions at Quaker and Military Boarding Schools.* Berkeley: University of California Press, 1994.

Heartman. Charles, F. *The New England Primer Issued Prior to 1830.* New York: R. R. Bowker, 1934.

Heckscher, August. *St. Paul's: The Life of a New England School.* New York: Charles Scribner's Sons, 1980.

Heironimus, Rick E. "Johann Heinrich Pestalozzi: A Study of His Influence on American Sunday Schools." Ed.D. thesis, Southern Baptist Theological Seminary, 1977.

Hendricks, James D. "The Child Study Movement in American Education, 1880–1910." Ph.D. diss., Indiana University, 1968.

Henry, Nelson B., ed. *Adolescence*. Forty-Third Yearbook of the National Society for the Study of Education, Part I. Chicago: University of Chicago Press, 1944.

Hentoff, Nat. *The First Freedom: The Tumultuous History of Free Speech in America*. New York: Delacorte Press, 1980.

Herbart, Johann F. *Outlines of Educational Doctrine*. Translated by A. E. Lange. Annotated by Charles De Garmo. New York: Macmillan, 1901.

Herbart, Johann F. *The Science of Education*. Translated by Henry Felkin and Emmie Felkin. Boston: D. C. Heath, 1892.

Herbst, Jurgen. "Nineteenth-Century Normal Schools in the United States: A Fresh Look." *History of Education* 9 (September 1980): 219–227.

Herbst, Jurgen. *And Sadly Teach: Teacher Education and Professionalization in American Culture*. Madison: University of Wisconsin Press, 1989.

Herrick, Mary J. *The Chicago Schools: A Social and Political History*. Beverly Hills, CA: Sage Publications, 1971.

Herrnstein, Richard J., and Charles Murray. *The Bell Curve: Intelligence and Class Structure in American Life*. New York: Free Press, 1994.

Hershberg, James G. *Conant: Harvard to Hiroshima and the Making of the Nuclear Age*. New York: Knopf, 1995.

Hewes, Dorothy W. *NAEYC's First Half Century: 1926–1976*. 1976. Reprint, Washington, DC: National Association of the Education of Young Children, 1996.

Hewes, Dorothy W. "Patty Smith Hill: Pioneer for Young Children." *Young Children* 31 (May 1976): 297–306.

Hewett, Nancy. *Women, Families, and Communities*. New York: Scott, Foresman, 1990.

Higham, John. *Send These to Me: Immigrants in Urban America*. Baltimore: Johns Hopkins University Press, 1984.

Higham, John. *Strangers in the Land*. New Brunswick, NJ: Rutgers University Press, 1955.

Hilgard, Ernest R. *Robert Mearns Yerkes, 1876–1956: A Biographical Memoir*. New York: Columbia University Press, 1965.

Hilliard, Asa G., III. *50 Plus: Essential References on the History of African People*. Baltimore: Black Classic Press, 1993.

Hilliard, Asa G., III. "Why We Must Pluralize the Curriculum." *Educational Leadership* 49 (December 1991–January 1992): 12–16.

Hillison, John. "Cyrus Peirce: First Public Teacher Educator." *Journal of Teacher Education* 35 (July-August 1984): 55–56.

Hillson, Henry T., and Florence C. Myers. *The Demonstration Guidance Project, 1957–1962*. New York: Board of Education of the City of New York, 1963.

Hiner, N. Ray, and Joseph M. Hawes, eds. *Growing up in America: Children in Historical Perspective*. Urbana: University of Illinois Press, 1985.

Hitchcock, Edward. *The Power of Christian Benevolence, Illustrated in the Life and Labors of Mary Lyon*. New York: American Tract Society, 1858.

Hoffschwelle, Mary S. "The Science of Domesticity: Home Economics at George Peabody College for Teachers, 1914–1939." *Journal of Southern History* 57 (November 1991): 658–680.

Hofstadter, Richard. *Social Darwinism in American Thought*. Boston: Beacon Press, 1955.

Hofstadter, Richard, and Walter P. Metzger. *The Development of Academic Freedom in the United States*. New York: Columbia University, 1955.

Hogan, David J. *Class and Reform: School and Society in Chicago, 1880–1930.* Philadelphia: University of Pennsylvania Press, 1985.

Hogan, David J. "The Market Revolution and Disciplinary Power: Joseph Lancaster and the Psychology of the Early Classroom System." *History of Education Quarterly* 29 (fall 1989): 381–418.

Holland, Kenneth, and Frank E. Hill. *Youth in the CCC.* Washington, DC: American Council on Education, 1942.

Holmes, Pauline. *A Tercentenary History of the Boston Public Latin School, 1635–1935.* Cambridge, MA: Harvard University Press, 1935.

Holt, Marilyn Irvin. *The Orphan Trains: Placing Out in America.* Lincoln: University of Nebraska Press, 1992.

Hook, J. N. *A Long Way Together.* Urbana, IL: National Council of Teachers of English, 1979.

Hopkins, Sarah Winnemucca. *Life among the Piutes: Their Wrongs and Claims.* Edited by Mrs. Horace Mann. Boston: Cupples, Upham & Co., 1883. Reprint, Chalfant Press, 1969.

Howe, M. A. DeWolfe. *The Life and Letters of George Bancroft.* 2 vols. New York: Charles Scribner's Sons, 1908.

Hoyt, Charles O., and R. Clyde Ford. *John D. Pierce, Founder of the Michigan School System: A Study of Education in the Northwest.* Ypsilanti, MI: Scharf Tag, Label and Box Co., 1905.

Huggins, Nathan I. *Slave and Citizen: The Life of Frederick Douglass.* Boston: Little, Brown, 1980.

Hughes, Marilyn. *Curriculum Integration in the Primary Grades: A Framework for Excellence.* Alexandria, VA: Association of Supervision and Curriculum Development, 1991.

Hunt, Thomas C. "The Supreme Court, Religion, and the Temper of the Times." *Momentum* 17 (May 1986): 28–31.

Hunt, Thomas C., and James C. Carper, eds., *Religious Schools in the United States, K–12: A Source Book.* New York: Garland, 1993.

Hunt, Thomas C., and James G. Silliman, Jr., eds. *The American School in Its Social Setting.* Dubuque, IA: Kendall-Hunt, 1975.

Hunt, Thomas C., and Jennings Wagoner, Jr. "Race, Religion, and Redemption: William Henry Ruffner and the Moral Foundations of Education in Virginia." *American Presbyterians* 66 (spring 1988): 1–9.

Hurd, Paul DeHart. *New Curriculum Perspectives for Junior High School Science.* Belmont, CA: Wadsworth, 1970.

Hurd, Paul DeHart. *New Directions in Teaching Secondary School Science.* Chicago: Rand McNally, 1969.

Hutchins, Robert M. *The Higher Learning in America.* New Haven, CT: Yale University Press, 1936.

Hutton, Harry. "Historical Background of the Campus School in America." In *Laboratory Schools: An Educational Resource,* 143–158. National Association of Laboratory Schools. Honolulu: Curriculum Research and Development Group, University of Hawaii, 1991.

Hyer, Sally. *One House, One Voice, One Heart: Native American Education at Santa Fe Indian School.* Santa Fe: Museum of New Mexico Press, 1990.

Igoe, Judith B. "School Nursing." *Nursing Clinics of North America* 29 (1975): 443–458.

In Memoriam: Alexander Inglis, 1879–1924. Cambridge, MA: Graduate School of Education, Harvard University, 1925.

Isham, Mark M. "Hilda Taba: Pioneer in Curriculum Development." Ph.D. diss., University of Texas at Austin, 1984.

Isham, Mark M. "Hilda Taba, 1904–1967: Pioneer in Social Studies Curriculum and Teaching." *Journal of Thought* 17 (fall 1982): 108–124.

Jable, J. Thomas. "The Public Schools Athletic League of New York City: Organized Athletics for City Schoolchildren, 1903–1914." In *Sport in American Education: History and Perspective*, 1–18. Edited by Wayne M. Ladd and Angela Lumpkin. Proceedings of the National Association for Sport and Physical Education, 1978.

Jackson, George L. *Development of State Control of Public Instruction in Michigan.* Lansing: Michigan Historical Commission, 1926.

Jacoby, Daniel. "The Transformation of Industrial Apprenticeship in the United States." *Journal of Economic History* 51 (December 1991): 887–910.

James, Edward T., ed. *Notable American Women, 1607–1950.* Vol. 3. Cambridge, MA: Belknap Press of Harvard University Press, 1971.

James, Thomas. "Rhetoric and Resistance: Social Science and Community Schools for Navajos in the 1930s." *History of Education Quarterly* 28 (winter 1988): 599–626.

Jefferson, Thomas. *Notes on the State of Virginia.* Edited by William Peden. Chapel Hill: University of North Carolina Press (1787), 1955.

Jeffrey, Julie Roy. *Education for Children of the Poor: A Study of the Origins and Implementation of the Elementary and Secondary Education Act of 1965.* Columbus: Ohio State University Press, 1978.

Jenkins, Frank C., Druzilla C. Kent, Verner M. Sims, and Eugene A. Waters. *The Southern Study: Cooperative Study for the Improvement of Education.* Durham, NC: Duke University Press, 1947.

Jenkins, John. "Infant Schools and the Development of Public Primary Schooling in Selected American Cities before the Civil War." Ph.D. diss., University of Wisconsin, 1978.

Jenkinson, Edward B. *The Schoolbook Protest Movement.* Bloomington, IN: Phi Delta Kappa, 1986.

Jenness, David. *Making Sense of Social Studies.* New York: Macmillan, 1990.

Jennings, John F., ed. *National Issues in Education: ESEA.* Bloomington, IN: Phi Delta Kappa Educational Foundation, 1995.

Jensen, Arthur R. *Bias in Mental Testing.* New York: Free Press, 1980.

Jensen, Arthur R. "How Much Can We Boost IQ and Scholastic Achievement?" *Harvard Educational Review* 39 (February 1969): 1–123.

Jernegan, Marcus W. *Laboring and Dependent Classes in Colonial America, 1607–1783.* 1931; reprint, Westport, CT: Greenwood Press, 1980.

Jervis, Kathe, and Carol Montag, eds. *Progressive Education for the 1990s.* New York: Teachers College Press, 1991.

Jervis, Kathe, and Arthur Tobier, eds. *Education for Democracy.* Weston, MA: The Cambridge School, 1988.

Jewett, Ann E., and Linda L. Bain. *The Curriculum Process in Physical Education.* Dubuque, IA: Wm. C. Brown Pub., 1985.

Johnson, David, Roger Johnson, Edythe Holubec, and Patricia Roy. *Circles of Learning: Cooperation in the Classroom*. Alexandria, VA: Association for Supervision and Curriculum Development, 1984.

Johnson, Guion Griffis. *A Social History of the Sea Islands with Special Reference to St. Helena Island, South Carolina*. New York: Greenwood Press, 1969.

Joncich, Geraldine. *The Sane Positivist*. Middletown, CT: Wesleyan University Press, 1968.

Jones, Ernest. *The Life and Work of Sigmund Freud*. Vols. 1–3. New York: Basic Books, 1953, 1955, 1957.

Jones, Mary Cover. "Adolescence." In *Encyclopedia of Educational Research*, 18–22. Edited by Ed Walter. New York: Macmillan, 1950.

Jones, Vernon, and Louise Jones. *Comprehensive Classroom Management: Creating Positive Learning Environments for All Students*. Needham Heights, MA: Allyn and Bacon, 1995.

Jorgenson, Lloyd M. *The State and the Non-Public School, 1825–1925*. Columbia: University of Missouri Press, 1987.

Jorgenson, Lloyd P. "The Oregon School Law of 1922: Passage and Sequel." *Catholic Historical Review* 54 (1968): 455–466.

Kaestle, Carl F. "Common Schools before 'The Common School Revival.' " *History of Education Quarterly* 12 (1972): 465–500.

Kaestle, Carl F. "Conflict and Consensus Revisited: Notes toward a Reinterpretaton of American Educational History." *Harvard Educational Review* 46 (August 1976): 390–396.

Kaestle, Carl F. *The Evolution of an Urban School System: New York City, 1750–1850*. Cambridge, MA: Harvard University Press, 1973.

Kaestle, Carl F. *Joseph Lancaster and the Monitorial School Movement: A Documentary History*. New York: Teachers College Press, 1973.

Kaestle, Carl F. *Pillars of the Republic: Common Schools and American Society, 1780–1860*. New York: Hill and Wang, 1983.

Kaestle, Carl F., Helen Damon-Moore, Lawrence C. Stedman, Katherine Tinsley, and William Vance Trollinger, Jr. *Literacy in the United States: Readers and Reading since 1880*. New Haven, CT: Yale University Press, 1991.

Kaestle, Carl F., and Marshall S. Smith. "The Federal Role in Elementary and Secondary Education, 1940–1980." *Harvard Educational Review* 52 (November 1982): 384–418.

Kagan, Spencer. *Cooperative Learning*. San Juan Capistrano, CA: Resources for Teachers, 1992.

Kakebrink, Joan M., ed. *Children at Risk*. Springfield, IL: Charles C. Thomas, 1989.

Kallen, Horace M. *Cultural Pluralism and the American Idea*. Philadelphia: University of Pennsylvania Press, 1956.

Kamin, Leon J. *The Science and Politics of IQ*. Harmondsworth, England: Penguin, 1974.

Kaminsky, James S. *A New History of Educational Philosophy*. Westport, CT: Greewood Press, 1993.

Kandel, I. L. *William Chandler Bagley*. New York: Teachers College Press, 1961.

Kane, Pearl R., ed. *Independent Schools, Independent Thinkers*. San Francisco: Jossey-Bass, 1992.

Kantor, Harvey A. *Learning to Earn: School, Work, and Vocational Reform in California, 1880–1930*. Madison: University of Wisconsin Press, 1988.

Kantor, Harvey A., and David B. Tyack, eds. *Work, Youth, and Schooling: Historical Perspectives on Vocationalism in American Education.* Stanford, CA: Stanford University Press, 1982.

Karenga, Maulana R. *The African-American Holiday of Kwanzaa: A Celebration of Family, Community and Culture.* Los Angeles: University of Sankore Press, 1988.

Karenga, Maulana R. *Introduction to Black Studies.* Los Angeles: University of Sankore Press, 1993.

Karenga, Maulana R., ed. *Reconstructing Kemetic Culture: Papers, Perspectives, Projects.* Los Angeles: University of Sankore Press, 1990.

Karier, Clarence J. *Shaping the American Educational State: 1900 to the Present.* New York: Free Press, 1975.

Katz, Lillian G., and Sylvia C. Chard. *Engaging Children's Minds: The Project Approach.* Norwood, NJ: Ablex Publishing, 1968.

Katz, Michael, B. *The Irony of Early School Reform: Educational Innovation in Mid-Nineteenth-Century Massachusetts.* Boston: Beacon Press, 1968.

Katz, Michael B. "The Origins of Public Education: A Reassessment." In *The Social History of American Education,* 91–118. Edited by B. Edward McClellan and William J. Reese. Urbana: University of Illinois Press, 1986.

Kaufman, Polly Welts. *Women Teachers on the Frontier.* New Haven, CT: Yale University Press, 1984.

Keene, James A. *A History of Music Education in the United States.* Hanover, NH: University Press of New England, 1982.

Keller, Franklin J. *Day Schools for Young Workers: The Organization and Management of Part-Time and Continuation Schools.* New York: Century Company, 1924.

Kelly, Deirdre M. *Last Chance High: How Girls and Boys Drop in and out of Alternative Schools.* New Haven, CT: Yale University Press, 1993.

Kelly, Deirdre M., and Jane Gaskell. *Debating Dropouts: Critical Policy and Research Perspectives on School Leaving.* New York: Teachers College Press, 1996.

Kelly, Lawrence C. *The Assault on Assimilation: John Collier and the Origins of Indian Policy Reform.* Albuquerque: University of New Mexico Press, 1983.

Kemp, William. *Support of Schools in Colonial New York by the Society for the Propagation of the Gospel.* 1913. Reprint, New York: Arno Press, 1969.

Kennedy, William Bean. *The Shaping of Protestant Education: An Interpretation of the Sunday School and the Development of Protestant Educational Strategy in the United States, 1789–1860.* New York: Association Press, 1966.

Keppel, Francis. *The Necessary Revolution in American Education.* New York: Harper and Row, 1966.

Kerber, Linda. "The Republican Mother: Women and the Enlightened—An American Perspective." *American Quarterly* 28 (summer 1976): 187–205.

Kerschensteiner, Georg. *Three Lectures on Vocational Training.* Chicago: Commercial Club of Chicago, 1911.

Kett, Joseph F. "On Revisionism." *History of Education Quarterly* 19 (summer 1979): 229–236.

Kett, Joseph F. *Rites of Passage: Adolescence in America, 1790 to the Present.* New York: Basic Books, 1977.

Kilpatrick, William H. "The Project Method." *Teachers College Record* 19 (September 1918): 319–335.

Kilpatrick, William K. *Why Johnny Can't Tell Right from Wrong.* New York: Simon and Schuster, 1992.

King, Kenneth J. "The American Negro Background of the Phelps-Stokes Commission and Their Influence on Education in East Africa, Especially in Kenya." Ph.D. diss., University of Edinburgh, 1968.

Kirby, Douglas, and Pamela M. Wilson. *Sexuality Education.* Santa Cruz, CA: Norwork Publications, 1984.

Kirst, Michael, and Richard Jung. "The Utility of a Longitudinal Approach in Assessing Implementation: A Thirteen-Year View of Title I, ESEA." In *Studying Implementation: Methodological and Administrative Issues*, 119–148. Edited by Walter Williams et al. Chatham, NJ: Chatham House, 1982.

Kliebard, Herbert M. "Constructing a History of the American Curriculum." In *Handbook of Research on Curriculum*, 157–184. Edited by Philip Jackson. New York: Macmillan, 1992.

Kliebard, Herbert M. *The Struggle for the American Curriculum, 1893–1958.* Boston: Routledge & Kegan Paul, 1986.

Klotter, James C. *The Breckinridges of Kentucky, 1760–1981.* Lexington: University Press of Kentucky, 1986.

Kluger, Richard. *Simple Justice.* New York: Vintage Books, 1975.

Kneller, George F. *Existentialism and Education.* New York: Philosophical Library, 1958.

Knight, Edgar W. *Fifty Years of American Education: A Historical Review and Critical Appraisal.* New York: Ronald Press, 1952.

Knight, Edgar W. *Public School Education in North Carolina.* Boston: Houghton Mifflin, 1916.

Knight, Edgar W., ed. *Reports on European Education.* New York: McGraw-Hill, 1930.

Knoll, Michael. "The Project Method: Its Origin and International Dissemination." In *Progressive Education across the Continents: A Handbook*, 307–318. Edited by Hermann Rohrs and Volker Lenhart. New York: Lang, 1995.

Kohlberg, Lawrence. *The Philosophy of Moral Development: Moral Stages and the Idea of Justice.* San Francisco: Harper and Row, 1981.

Kohn, Alfie. *Punished by Rewards.* Boston: Houghton Mifflin, 1993.

Korngold, Ralph. *Thaddeus Stevens: A Being Darkly Wise and Rudely Great.* New York: Harcourt, Brace, and Company, 1955.

Kotin, Laurence. *Legal Foundations of Compulsory School Attendance.* Port Washington, NY: Kennikat Press, 1980.

Kozol, Jonathan. *Free Schools.* New York: Bantam Books, 1972.

Kozol, Jonathan. *Illiterate America.* New York: Anchor Doubleday, 1985.

Kraushaar, Otto F. *American Nonpublic Schools: Patterns of Diversity.* Baltimore: Johns Hopkins Press, 1972.

Kridel, Craig. "The Eight-Year Study Reconsidered." *Educational Studies* 23 (summer 1994): 101–114.

Krug, Edward A. *The Shaping of the American High School: I, 1880–1920.* New York: Harper & Row, 1964.

Krug, Edward A. *The Shaping of the American High School: II, 1920–1940.* Madison: University of Wisconsin Press, 1972.

Ladd-Taylor, Molly. *Raising a Baby the Government Way: Mothers' Letters to the Children's Bureau, 1915–1932.* New Brunswick, NJ: Rutgers University Press, 1986.

Ladson-Billings, Gloria. *The Dreamkeepers: Successful Teachers of African-American Children.* San Francisco: Jossey-Bass, 1994.

Lagemann, Ellen Condliffe. "Contested Terrain: A History of Education Research in the United States, 1890–1990." *Educational Researcher* 26 (December 1997): 12.

Lagemann, Ellen Condliffe. *Private Power for the Public Good: A History of the Carnegie Foundation for the Advancement of Teaching.* Middletown, CT: Wesleyan University Press, 1983.

Lamberton, Bernice. "A Biography of Lydia Maria Child." Ph.D. diss., University of Maryland, 1953.

LaMorte, Michael. *School Law: Cases and Concepts.* Englewood Cliffs, NJ: Prentice Hall, 1992.

Lane, Harlan. *The Mask of Benevolence: Disabling the Deaf Community.* New York: Knopf, 1992.

Lane, Harlan. *When the Mind Hears: A History of the Deaf.* New York: Random House, 1984.

Langsam, Miriam. *Children West: A History of the Placing Out System of the New York Children's Aid Society, 1853–1890.* Madison: State Historical Society of Wisconsin, 1964.

Lanier, Vincent. *The World of Art Education.* Ruston, VA: National Art Education Association, 1991.

Lannie, Vincent P. *Public Money and Parochial Education.* Cleveland: Case Western Reserve University Press, 1968.

Lansing, Marion. *Mary Lyon through Her Letters.* Boston: Books, 1937.

Larcom, Lucy. *A New England Girlhood: Outlined from Memory.* Boston: Houghton Mifflin, 1889.

Lasch, Christopher. "Jane Addams: The College Woman and the Family Claim." In *The New Radicalism in America, 1889–1963: The Intellectual as Social Type,* 3–37. Edited by Christopher Lasch. New York: Alfred A. Knopf, 1965.

Lasch, Christopher, ed. *The Social Thought of Jane Addams.* Indianapolis: Bobbs-Merrill Company, 1965.

Lattal, Kennon A., ed. "Reflections on B. F. Skinner and Psychology." *American Psychologist* 47 (November 1992): 1265–1560.

Lazerson, Marvin. *Origins of the Urban School: Public Education in Massachusetts, 1870–1915.* Cambridge, MA: Harvard University Press, 1971.

Lazerson, Marvin. "Urban Reform and the Schools: Kindergartens in Massachusetts, 1870–1915." *History of Education Quarterly* 11 (summer 1971): 115–142.

Leahey, Thomas H. *A History of Modern Psychology.* Englewood Cliffs, NJ: Prentice Hall, 1991.

Leahey, Thomas H., and Grace E. Leahey. *Psychology's Occult Doubles: Psychology and the Problem of Pseudoscience.* Chicago: Nelson-Hall, 1983.

Lee, Gordon Canfield. *The Struggle for Federal Aid: First Phase, a History of the Attempts to Obtain Federal Aid for the Common Schools, 1870–1890.* New York: Teachers College Press, 1949.

Leidecker, Kurt. *Yankee Teacher: Life of William Torrey Harris.* New York: Philosophical Library, 1946.

Leloudis, James L. *Schooling in the New South: Pedagogy, Self, and Society.* Chapel Hill: University of North Carolina Press, 1996.

Leopold, Richard. *Robert Dale Owen: A Biography.* New York: Octagon Books, 1969.

Lessinger, Leon. *Every Kid a Winner: Accountability in Education*. New York: Simon and Schuster, 1970.

Levin, Robert A. *Educating Elementary School Teachers: The Struggle for Coherent Visions, 1909–1978*. Landover, MD: University Press of America, 1994.

Levin, Robert A. "An Unfulfilled Alliance: The Lab School in Teacher Education, Two Case Studies, 1910–1980." Paper presented at the Annual Meeting of the History of Education Society, Atlanta, GA, 2 November 1990. ERIC document ED 327487.

Levy, Tedd. "First in His Class: The Many Contributions of Samuel Read Hall." *OAH Magazine of History* 6 (fall 1991): 38–41.

Lewis, Charles Lee. *Philander Priestley Claxton: Crusader for Public Education*. Knoxville: University of Tennessee Press, 1948.

Lewis, David Levering. *W.E.B. Du Bois: Biography of a Race, 1868–1919*. New York: H. Holt and Company, 1993.

Lewis, Theodore. "Toward a New Paradigm for Vocational Educational Research." *Journal of Vocational Educational Research* 15 (spring 1990): 1–30.

Lewis, William G. W. *Biography of Samuel Lewis*. Cincinnati: Methodist Book Concern, 1857.

Lewontin, R. C., Steven Rose, and Leon J. Kamin. *Not in Our Genes: Biology, Ideology, and Human Nature*. New York: Pantheon Books, 1984.

Liddle, Elizabeth Ann, ed. *Wheelock College, 100 Years*. Boston: Wheelock College, 1988.

Lindenmeyer, Kriste. *A Right to Childhood: The U.S. Children's Bureau and Child Welfare, 1912–1946*. Urbana: University of Illinois Press, 1997.

Lindley, Betty, and Earnest K. Lindley. *A New Deal for Youth: The Story of the National Youth Administration*. New York: Viking, 1938.

Lindley, Harlow, ed. "Robert Dale Owen and Indiana's Common School Fund." *Indiana Magazine of History* 25 (March 1929): 52–60.

Link, William. *The Paradox of Southern Progressivism, 1880–1930*. Chapel Hill: University of North Carolina Press, 1992.

Lipscomb, A. A., and A. E. Bergh, eds. *The Writings of Thomas Jefferson*. 20 vols. Washington, DC: Thomas Jefferson Memorial Association, 1903.

Lipsitz, Lawrence, ed. "Behaviorism Today." *Educational Technology* 33 (October 1993): 5–77.

Lloyd, Sheldon J. "An Investigation into the Development of the National Society for the Promotion of Industrial Education and Its Role in Promoting Federal Aid for Vocational Education, 1906–1917." Ph.D. diss., University of Maryland, 1979.

Locke, Alain LeRoy, ed. *The New Negro: An Interpretation*. New York: Atheneum, 1924; reprint, New York: Atheneum, 1992.

Lockridge, Kenneth. *Literacy in Colonial New England: An Enquiry into the Social Context of Literacy in the Early Modern West*. New York: W. W. Norton, 1974.

Lockwood, Anne Turnbaugh. *Tracking: Conflicts and Resolutions*. Thousand Oaks, CA: Corwin Press, 1996.

Lomawaima, K. Tsianina. *They Called It Prairie Light: The Story of Chilocco Indian School*. Lincoln: University of Nebraska Press, 1994.

Lombardi, Joan. "Head Start: The Nation's Pride, a Nation's Challenge." *Young Children* 45 (1990): 22–29.

Lomotey, Kofi, ed. *Going to School: The African-American Experience.* Albany, NY: State University of New York Press, 1990.

Long, Adelbert. "A Study of Three Contemporary Educational Critics." Ed.D. diss., University of Oklahoma, 1967.

Lutz, Alma. *Emma Willard, Daughter of Democracy.* Boston: Houghton Mifflin, 1929.

Lynn, Robert W., and Elliott Wright. *The Big Little School: Sunday Child of American Protestantism.* New York: Harper & Row, 1971.

Macleod, David I. *Building Character in the American Boy: The Boy Scouts, YMCA, and Their Forerunners, 1870–1920.* Madison: University of Wisconsin Press, 1983.

MacMullen, Edith Nye. *In the Cause of True Education: Henry Barnard and Nineteenth-Century School Reform.* New Haven, CT: Yale University Press, 1991.

Madison, James H. "John D. Rockefeller's General Education Board and the Rural School Problem in the Midwest, 1900–1930." *History of Education Quarterly* 24 (summer 1984): 181–99.

Magat, Richard. *The Ford Foundation at Work: Philanthropic Choices, Methods, and Styles.* New York: Plenum Press, 1979.

Malone, Dumas. *Jefferson and His Time.* 6 vols. Boston: Little, Brown, 1948–1981.

Mann, Harold W. *Atticus Green Haywood: Methodist Bishop, Editor and Educator.* Athens: University of Georgia Press, 1965.

Mann, Horace. "Twelfth Annual Report (1848)." In *The Republic and the School: Horace Mann on the Education of Free Men,* 79–112. Edited by Lawrence A. Cremin. New York: Teachers College Press, 1957.

Mann, Mary P., ed. *Life of Horace Mann.* Washington, DC: National Education Association, 1937.

Mann, Mary P., and George C. Mann, eds. *Life and Works of Horace Mann.* Boston: Marsh and Capen, 1891.

Manning, Mary Ann, Gary Manning, and Roberta Long. *Theme Immersion: Inquiry-Based Curriculum in Elementary and Middle Schools.* Portsmouth, NH: Heinemann, 1994.

Mark, Michael L., and Charles L. Gary. *A History of American Music Education.* New York: Schirmer Books, 1992.

Marris, Albert. *Nicholas Murray Butler.* Boston: Twayne Publishers, 1976.

Marshner, Connaught Coyne. *Blackboard Tyranny.* New York: Arlington House, 1978.

Martin, Waldo E., Jr. "Freuerick Douglass: Humanist as Race Leader." In *Black Leaders of the Nineteenth Century,* 59–86. Edited by Leon Litwack and August Meier. Urbana: University of Illinois Press, 1988.

Martin, Waldo E., Jr. *The Mind of Frederick Douglass.* Chapel Hill: University of North Carolina Press, 1984.

Mason, Martha Sprague, ed. *Parents and Teachers: A Survey of Organized Cooperation of Home, School, and Community.* New York: Ginn & Co., 1928.

Mathews, Forrest David. "The Politics of Education in the Deep South: Georgia and Alabama, 1830–1860." Ph.D. diss., Columbia University, 1965.

Mathews, Glenna. *Just a Housewife: The Rise and Fall of Domesticity.* New York: Oxford University Press, 1987.

Mattingly, Paul H. *The Classless Profession: American Schoolmen in the Nineteenth Century.* New York: New York University, 1975.

Mattingly, Paul H., and Edward W. Stevens, Jr., eds. *"Schools and the Means of Edu-*

cation Shall Forever Be Encouraged'': A History of Education in the Old Northwest, 1787–1880. Athens: Ohio University Libraries, 1987.

May, Dean, and Maris Vinovskis. ''A Ray of Millenial Light: Early Education and Social Reform in the Infant School Movement in Massachusetts, 1826–1840.'' In *Family and Kin in Urban Communities, 1700–1930,* 62–99. Edited by Tamara Hareven. New York: New Viewpoints, 1977.

May, Samuel J. ''Memoir of Cyrus Peirce.'' *American Journal of Education* 4 (December 1857): 275–308.

McAdam, Doug. *Freedom Summer.* New York: Oxford University Press, 1988.

McClintock, Jean, and Robert McClintock, eds. *Henry Barnard's ''School Architecture.''* New York: Teachers College Press, 1970.

McCuskey, Dorothy. *Bronson Alcott: Teacher.* New York: Macmillan, 1940.

McEwan, Barbara, ed. *Practicing Judicious Discipline: An Educator's Guide to a Democratic Classroom.* San Francisco: Caddo Gap Press, 1994.

McEwin, C. Kenneth. ''William M. Alexander: Father of the American Middle School.'' *Middle School Journal* 23 (May 1992): 33–38.

McEwin, C. Kenneth. ''William M. Alexander: 1912–1996.'' *Middle School Journal* 27 (November 1996): 2.

McFeely, William S. *Yankee Stepfather: General O. O. Howard and the Freedmen.* New Haven, CT: Yale University Press, 1968.

McLachlin, James. *American Boarding Schools: A Historical Study.* New York: Charles Scribner's Sons, 1970.

McLaughlin, Milbrey Wallin. *Evaluation and Reform: The Elementary and Secondary Education Act of 1965/Title I.* A Rand Educational Policy Study. Cambridge, MA: Ballinger, 1975.

McMillan, Margaret. ''The Nursery School.'' In *Early Childhood Education.* Edited by Karen M. Paciorek and Joyce H. Munro. Guilford, CT: Dushkin, 1996.

McNeil, Genna Rae. *Groundwork: Charles Hamilton Houston and the Struggle for Civl Rights.* Philadelphia: University of Pennsylvania Press, 1983.

McPherson, James M. ''Abolitionists and the Civil Rights Act of 1875.'' *Journal of American History* 52 (December 1965): 493–510.

Mead, Rita H. ''Music Educators National Conference.'' In *New Grove Dictionary of Music and Musicians,* 831. Edited by Stanley Sadie. Washington, DC: Grove's Dictionary of Music, 1980.

Means, Richard K. *A History of Health Education in the United States.* Philadelphia: Lea Febiger, 1962.

Meier, August. *Negro Thought in America, 1880–1915: Racial Ideologies in the Age of Booker T. Washington.* Ann Arbor: University of Michigan Press, 1963.

Meier, August, and Elliot Rudwick. ''Carter G. Woodson as Entrepreneur: Laying the Foundation of a Historical Specialty.'' In *Black History and the Historical Profession, 1915–1980,* 1–73. Edited by August Meier and Elliott Rudwick. Urbana: University of Illinois Press, 1986.

Melcher, John W. ''Law, Litigation, and Handicapped Children.'' *Exceptional Children* 43, no. 3 (1976): 126–130.

The Memorial Volume of the Third Plenary Council of Baltimore. Baltimore: Baltimore Publishing Company, 1885.

Mennel, Robert M. *Thorns and Thistles: Juvenile Delinquents in the United States, 1825–1940.* Hanover, NH: University Press of New England, 1973.

Mensh, Elaine, and Harry Mensh. *The IQ Mythology: Class, Race, Gender, and Inequality.* Carbondale: Southern Illinois University Press, 1991.

Mercer, Charles Fenton. *A Discourse on Popular Education.* Princeton, NJ: Princeton University Press, 1826.

Messerli, Jonathon. *Horace Mann: A Biography.* New York: Alfred A. Knopf, 1972.

Meyen, Edward L. *Exceptional Children and Youth.* Chicago: Love Publishing Co., 1982.

Michael, Ian. *The Teaching of English from the Sixteenth Century to 1870.* New York: Cambridge University Press, 1987.

Michaelis, Emile, and H. Keatley Moore, trans. *The Autobiography of Froebel.* London: Swan Sonneschein & Co., 1886.

Michener, James A. *Sports in America.* New York: Random House, 1976.

Middlekauff, Robert. *Ancients and Axioms: Secondary Education in Eighteenth-Century New England.* New Haven, CT: Yale University Press, 1963.

Miller, Alphonse B. *Thaddeus Stevens.* New York: Harper and Brothers, 1939.

Miller, S. H., Betty Saleem, and Herrington Bryce. *School Dropouts.* Syracuse, NY: Syracuse University Press, 1964.

Milton Bradley Company. *Milton Bradley, a Successful Man: A Brief Sketch of His Career and the Growth of the Institution Which He Founded, Published by Milton Bradley Company in Commemoration of Their Fiftieth Anniversary.* Springfield, MA: Milton Bradley Company, 1910.

Minton, Henry L. *Lewis M. Terman: Pioneer in Psychological Testing.* New York: New York University Press, 1988.

Mintz, Steven, and Susan Kellogg. *Domestic Revolutions: A Social History of the American Family.* New York: Free Press, 1988.

Mirel, Jeffrey. "From Student Control to Institutional Control of High School Athletics: Three Michigan Cities, 1883–1905." *Journal of Social History* 16 (winter 1982): 83–100.

Mirel, Jeffrey. *The Rise and Fall of an Urban School System: Detroit, 1907–81.* Ann Arbor: University of Michigan Press, 1993.

Moffett, James. *Storm in the Mountains: A Case Study of Censorship, Conflict, and Consciousness.* Carbondale: Southern Illinois University Press, 1988.

Monaghan, E. Jennifer. *A Common Heritage: Noah Webster's Blue-Back Speller.* Hamden, CT: Archon Books, 1983.

Monaghan, E. Jennifer. "Gender and Textbooks: Women Writers of Elementary Readers, 1880–1950." *Publishing Research Quarterly* 10 (spring 1994): 28–46.

Monaghan, E. Jennifer, and E. Wendy Saul. "The Reader, the Scribe, the Thinker: A Critical Look at the History of American Reading and Writing Instruction." In *The Formation of School Subjects: The Struggle for Creating an American Institution,* 85–122. Edited by Thomas S. Popkewitz. Philadelphia: Falmer Press, 1987.

Monroe, Walter S. *Teaching-Learning Theory and Teacher Education, 1890 to 1950.* New York: Greenwood Press, 1952.

Monroe, William S. *History of the Pestalozzian Movement in the United States.* New York: Arno Press, 1969.

Montalto, Nicholas V. *A History of the Intercultural Education Movement, 1924–1941.* New York: Garland Publishing, 1982.

Montessori, Maria. *The Montessori Method.* 1912. Reprint, New York: Schocken, 1964.

Montessori, Mario M., Jr. *Education for Human Development*. New York: Schocken, 1976.

Montgomery, James A. "The Growth of the Interscholastic Athletics Movement in the United States, 1890–1940." In *A History of Physical Education and Sport in the United States and Canada*, 217–224. Edited by Erle F. Zeigler. Champaign, IL: Stipes, 1975.

Moores, Donald F. *Educating the Deaf: Psychology, Principles, and Practices*. Boston: Houghton Mifflin, 1996.

Morris, Robert C. *Reading, 'Riting, and Reconstruction: The Education of Freedmen in the South, 1861–1870*. Chicago: University of Chicago Press, 1981.

Morris, Van Cleve. *Existentialism in Education: What It Means*. New York: Harper & Row, 1966.

Morrison, A. J. *The Beginnings of Public Education in Virginia, 1776–1860*. Richmond: Superintendent of Public Printing, 1917.

Mosteller, Frederick, and Daniel P. Moynihan, eds. *On Equality of Educational Opportunity*. New York: Random House, 1972.

Moulton, Gerald L. "A Limited Historical Review of Sixty-Five Years of Educational Discussion in the Yearbooks of the National Society for the Study of Education." Ph.D. diss., University of Oregon, 1962.

Muncy, Robyn. *Creating a Female Dominion in American Reform, 1890–1935*. New York: Oxford University Press, 1991.

Munsey, Brenda, ed. *Moral Development, Moral Education, and Kohlberg: Basic Issues in Philosophy, Psychology, Religion, and Education*. Birmingham, AL: Religious Education Press, 1980.

Munsterberg, Hugo. *The Principles of Art Education*. New York: Prang Educational Company, 1905.

Murchison, Carl, ed. *A History of Psychology in Autobiography*. Worcester, MA: Clark University Press, 1936.

Murphy, Geraldine J. "Massachusetts Bay Colony: The Role of Government in Education." Ph.D. diss., Radcliffe College, 1960.

Murphy, Marjorie. *Blackboard Unions: The AFT and the NEA, 1900–1980*. Ithaca, NY: Cornell University Press, 1990.

Murphy, Marjorie. "From Artisan to Semi-Professional: White Collar Unionism among Chicago Public School Teachers, 1870–1930." Ph.D. diss., University of California, 1981.

Murray, Lindley. *Memoirs of the Life and Writings of Lindley Murray in a Series of Letters Written by Himself, with a Preface and Continuation of the Memoirs by Elizabeth Frank*. York, England: Longman, Rees, Orme, Browne and Green, 1826.

Myer, Donald. *The Instructed Conscience*. Philadelphia: University of Pennsylvania Press, 1972.

Myrdal, Gunnar. *An American Dilemma: The Negro Problem and Modern Democracy*. New York: Harper and Row, 1944.

Nash, Ray. *American Penmanship, 1800–1850: A History of Writing and a Bibliography of Copybooks from Jenkins to Spencer*. Worchester, MA: American Antiquarian Association, 1969.

National Association of Education of Young Children. *Annual Report: Approaching the*

New Millennium: Lessons from NAEYC's First 70 years. Washington, DC: NAEYC, 1996.

National Association of School Nursing. "NASN Newsletter." 12, no. 1 (1997): 20.

National Council for the Social Studies. *Curriculum Standards for Social Studies.* Washington, DC: National Council for the Social Studies, 1995.

National Council of Teachers of Mathematics. *The Agenda in Action.* Reston, VA: National Council of Teachers of Mathematics, 1983.

National Council of Teachers of Mathematics. *Curriculum and Evaluation Standards for School Mathematics.* Reston, VA: National Council of Teachers of Mathematics, 1990.

National Council of Teachers of Mathematics. *A History of Mathematics Education in the United States and Canada.* Reston, VA: National Council of Teachers of Mathematics, 1970.

National Council of Teachers of Mathematics. *The Secondary School Mathematics Curriculum.* Reston, VA: National Council of Teachers of Mathematics, 1985.

National Education Association. *Report of the Committee on College Entrance Requirements.* Washington, DC: NEA, 1899.

National Society for the Study of Education. "Curriculum Making in Private Laboratory Schools." In Twenty-Sixth Yearbook, Part 1, *Curriculum Making, Past and Present,* sec. 4. Bloomington, IL: Public School Publishing Co., 1926

National Society for the Study of Education. Twenty-Fourth Yearbook, Part 2. *Adapting the School to Individual Differences.* Edited by Guy Montrose Whipple. Bloomington, IL: Public School Publishing Co., 1925.

Natriello, Gary, ed. *School Dropouts: Patterns and Policies.* New York: Teachers College Press, 1986.

Naylor, Natalie A. "Holding High the Standard: The Influence of the American Education Society in Ante-Bellum Education." *History of Education Quarterly* 24 (winter 1984): 479–497.

Naylor, Natalie A. "Raising a Learned Ministry: The American Education Society, 1815–1860." Ed.D. diss., Teachers College, Columbia University, 1971.

Nelson, Jack L., Kenneth Carlson, and Stuart B. Palonsky. *Critical Issues in Education: A Dialectic Approach.* New York: McGraw-Hill, 1996.

Nelson, John Kendall. "Anglican Missions in America, 1701–1725: A Study of the Society for the Propagation of the Gospel in Foreign Parts." Ph.D. diss., Northwestern University, 1962.

Nelson, Murry R. "Emma Willard: Pioneer of Social Science Education." *Theory and Research in Social Education* 15 (fall 1987): 245–256.

Nelson, Murry R. "Paul Hanna: 1902–1988." *Social Education* 52 (October 1988): 413.

Nelson, Murry R. "Paul Robert Hanna." In *Biographical Dictionary of American Education,* 595–596. Edited by J. F. Ohles. Westport, CT: Greenwood Press, 1978.

Nevins, Archie P. "The Kalamazoo Case." *Michigan History* 44 (March 1960): 91–100.

"New Alternative Schools." *Educational Leadership* 52 (September 1994).

New York Civil Liberties Union. "The Burden of Blame: A Report on the Ocean Hill–Brownsville School Controversy." New York, October 9, 1968.

Newlon, Jesse. *Educational Administration as Social Policy.* New York: Scribners & Sons, 1934.

Newlon, Jesse. *Education for Democracy in Our Time.* New York: McGraw-Hill, 1939.

Newman, Joseph W. *America's Teachers: An Introduction to Education*. White Plains, NY: Longman Press, 1998.

Newman, Joseph W. "Ellwood P. Cubberley: Architect of the New Educational Hierarchy." *Teaching Education* 4 (spring 1992): 161–168.

Nieman, Donald G. *To Set the Law in Motion: The Freedmen's Bureau and the Legal Rights of Blacks, 1865–1868*. Millwood, NY: KTO Press, 1979.

Nietz, John A. *Old Textbooks*. Pittsburgh: University of Pittsburgh Press, 1961.

Noble, Marcus Cicero Stephens. *A History of Public Schools in North Carolina*. Chapel Hill: University of North Carolina Press, 1930.

Nordoff, Charles. *The Freedmen of South Carolina: Some Account of Their Appearance, Character, Condition, and Peculiar Customs*. New York: C. T. Evans, 1863.

Nye, Russel B. *George Bancroft, Brahmin Rebel*. New York: A. A. Knopf, 1944; reprint, New York: Octagon Books, 1972.

Oakes, Jeannie. *Keeping Track: How Schools Structure Inequality*. New Haven, CT: Yale University Press, 1985.

Oakes, Jeannie. *Multiplying Inequalities: The Effects of Race, Social Class, and Tracking on Opportunities to Learn Mathematics and Science*. Santa Monica, CA: Rand Corporation, 1990.

Oakes, Jeannie, and Martin Lipton. *Making the Best of Schools: A Handbook for Parents, Teachers, and Policymakers*. New Haven, CT: Yale University Press, 1990.

Odem, Mary E. *Delinquent Daughters: Protecting and Policing Adolescent Female Sexuality in the United States, 1885–1920*. Chapel Hill: University of North Carolina Press, 1995.

Ogren, Christine A. "Where Coeds Were Coeducated: Normal Schools in Wisconsin, 1870–1920." *History of Education Quarterly* 35 (spring 1995): 1–26.

O'Leary, Kathleen L. "Cyrus Peirce: Educator of the Nineteenth Century." M.A. thesis, University of Massachusetts–Amherst, 1950.

Olson, David R., ed. *The Social Foundations of Language and Thought: Essays in Honor of Jerome S. Bruner*. New York: W. W. Norton, 1980.

Olson, Robert G. *An Introduction to Existentialism*. New York: Dover, 1962.

Onuf, Peter S. *Statehood and Nation: A History of the Northwest Ordinance*. Bloomington: Indiana University Press, 1987.

Orfield, Gary. *Must We Bus? Segregated Schools and National Policy*. Washington, DC: Brookings Institute, 1978.

Osborn, D. Keith. *Early Childhood Education in Historical Perspective*. Athens, GA: Daye Press, 1991.

Osborne, William S. *Lydia Maria Child*. Boston: Twayne, 1980.

Otto, M. C. "Instrumentalism." In *Philosophy Today*, 37–53. Edited by Edward L. Schaub. Chicago: Open Court, 1928.

Owen, Thomas McAdory. "A Bibliography of Alabama." In *Annual Report of the American Historical Association, 1897*, 886–891. Washington, DC: U.S. Government Printing Office, 1898.

Palfrey, Judith S. *Community Child Health: An Action Plan for Today*. Westport, CT: Praeger, 1994.

Pancoast, Elinor, and Anne E. Lincoln. *The Incorrigible Idealist: Robert Dale Owen in America*. Bloomington, IN: Principia Press, 1940.

Paolucci, Beatrice, and Twyla Shear. "Home Economics Education—Overview." In *En-*

cylcopedia of Education, 447–451. Edited by L. C. Deighton. New York: Macmillan, 1971.

Parker, Francis W. *Talks on Pedagogics*. New York: E. L. Kellogg & Co., 1894.

Parker, Franklin. *George Peabody: A Biography*. Nashville: Vanderbilt University, 1971.

Parker, Jacqueline K. "Women at the Helm: Succession Politics at the Children's Bureau, 1913–1968." *Social Work* 39 (September 1994): 551–559.

Parker, Jacqueline K., and Edward M. Carpenter. "Julia Lathrop and the Children's Bureau: The Emergence of an Institution." *Social Science Review* 53 (March 1981): 60–77.

Parker, Toni Trent. *Annotated Bibliography of the Books, Reports, and Papers Published, Written, or Sponsored by the Phelps-Stokes Fund*. New York: Phelps-Stokes Fund, 1976.

Parman, Donald L. *The Navajos and the New Deal*. New Haven, CT: Yale University Press, 1976.

Passow, A. Harry, ed. *Reactions to Silberman's Crisis in the Classroom*. Chicago: National Society for the Study of Education, 1971.

Patri, Angelo. *Schoolmaster of the Great City*. New York: Macmillan, 1917.

Peabody, Endicott. "The Aims, Duties, and Opportunities of the HeadMaster of an Endowed Secondary School." *School Review* (October 1901): 521–528.

Peabody, Endicott. "The Continuous Moral Influence of the School through College and through Life." *Social Review* (October 1899): 620–632.

Pearson, P. David, and Rebecca Barr, Michael Kamil, and Peter Mosenthal, eds. *Handbook of Research on Reading*. New York: Longman, 1984.

Pearson, Willard. *Valley Forge Military Academy and Junior College: Dedicated to Excellence*. New York: Newcomen Society of the United States, 1985.

Peltier, Gary L. "Jesse L. Newlon as Superintendent of the Denver Public Schools, 1920–1927." Ph.D. diss., University of Denver, 1965.

Pennsylvania State Education Association. *Pennsylvania State Education Association School Nurse Section, Executive Board Position Paper*. Harrisburg, PA: PSEA, 1997.

Perko, F. Michael. "Educational Biography and the Protestant Paideia." *Vita Scholasticae* 10 (1991): 159–182.

Perlstein, Daniel. "The 1968 New York City School Crisis: Teacher Politics, Racial Politics, and the Decline of Liberalism." Ph.D. diss., Stanford University, 1994.

Perlstein, Daniel. "Teaching Freedom: SNCC and the Creation of the Mississippi Freedom Schools." *History of Education Quarterly* 30 (fall 1990): 297–324.

Perry, William F. "The Genesis of Public Education in Alabama." In *Transactions of the Alabama Historical Society*. Vol. 2, pp. 214–227. Tuscaloosa, AL: The Society, 1898.

Peterson, Merrill D. *Thomas Jefferson and the New Nation: A Biography*. New York: Oxford University Press, 1970.

Peterson's Annual Guide to Independent Secondary Schools. Princeton, NJ: Peterson's, 1996.

Petit, Mary Loretta. "Samuel Lewis, Educational Reformer Turned Abolitionist." Ph.D. diss., Case Western Reserve University, 1966.

Pfeffer, Leo. "The *Schempp-Murray* Decision on School Prayers and Bible-Reading." *Journal of Church and State* 5 (November 1963): 165–175.

Philip, Kenneth R. *John Collier's Crusade for Indian Reform, 1920–1954.* Tucson: University of Arizona Press, 1977.

"Picket, Albert." In *Dictionary of American Biography.* Vol. 14, pp. 568–569. Edited by Allen Johnson and Dumas Malone. New York: Charles Scribner's Sons, 1937.

Pickett, Robert S. *House of Refuge: Origins of Juvenile Reform in New York State, 1815–1857.* Syracuse, NY: Syracuse University Press, 1969.

Pierce, Paul R. *The Origin and Development of the Public School Principalship.* Chicago: University of Chicago Press, 1935.

Pilch, Judah, ed. *A History of Jewish Education in America.* New York: American Association for Jewish Education, 1969.

Platt, Anthony. *The Child Savers: The Invention of Delinquency.* Chicago: University of Chicago Press, 1980.

Plimpton, George A. *The Hornbook and Its Use in America.* Worcester, MA: American Antiquarian Society, 1916.

Polmar, Norman, and Thomas Allen. *Rickover: Controversy and Genius.* New York: Simon & Schuster, 1982.

Porter, Rosalie Pedalino. *Forked Tongue: The Politics of Bilingual Education.* New York: Basic Books, 1990.

Potter, Cary. "NAIS: Twenty-Five or Sixty-Two?" *Independent School* 47 (fall 1987): 57–63.

Powell, Arthur G., Eleanor Farrar, and David K. Cohen. *The Shopping Mall High School: Winners and Losers in the Educational Marketplace.* Boston: Houghton Mifflin, 1985.

Powers, Jane B. "Paul R. Hanna's Scope and Sequence." *Social Education* 50 (November/December 1986): 542.

Pratt, Richard H. *Battlefield and Classroom: Four Decades with the American Indian, 1867–1904.* New Haven, CT: Yale University Press, 1964.

Price, Jack, and J. D. Gawronski, eds. *Changing School Mathematics: A Responsive Process.* Reston, VA: National Council of Teachers of Mathematics, 1981.

Private Independent Schools. Wallingford, CT: Bunting and Lyon, 1995.

Prosser, Charles A. *Secondary Education and Life.* Cambridge, MA: Harvard University Press, 1939.

Provenzo, Eugene F., Jr. *Culture as Curriculum: Education and the International Expositions, 1876–1904.* New York: Peter Lang, in press.

Provenzo, Eugene F., Jr., and Arlene Brett. *The Complete Block Book.* Syracuse, NY: Syracuse University Press, 1983.

Provenzo, Eugene F., Jr., and Asterie Baker Provenzo. "Columbus and the Pledge." *American School Board Journal* 178 (October 1991): 24–25.

Prucha, Francis Paul. *The Great Father: The United States Government and the American Indians.* Lincoln: University of Nebraska Press, 1984.

Public School Methods. Vol. 1. Chicago: School Methods, 1908.

Putnam, Daniel. *The Development of Primary and Secondary Public Education in Michigan.* Ann Arbor, MI: George Wahr, 1904.

Quarles, Benjamin. *Frederick Douglass.* Washington, DC: Associated Publishers, 1948.

Quigley, Charles N., and John H. Buchanan, Jr. *A Framework for Civic Education.* Calabasas, CA: Center for Civic Education, 1991.

Quigley, Charles N., and John H. Buchanan, Jr. *National Standards for Civics and Government.* Calabasas, CA: Center for Civic Education, 1995.

Quimby, Ian M. G. *Apprenticeship in Colonial Philadelphia.* New York: Garland Publishers, 1985.

Quisenberry, Nancy L. *Resources for Understanding P.L. 94-142 and Classroom Management and Behavior.* Carbondale: Southern Illinois University Office of Special Education and Department of Education, 1981.

Radin, Beryl A., and Willis D. Hawley. *The Politics of Federal Reorganization: Creating the U.S. Department of Education.* New York: Pergamon Press, 1988.

Ragan, Patricia E. "Cooperative Learning Can Work in Residential Care Settings." *Teaching Exceptional Children* 25 (1993): 48–51.

Rainwater, Clarence E. *The Play Movement in the United States: A Study of Community Recreation.* Chicago: University of Chicago Press, 1922.

Randall, E. Vance. *Private Schools and Public Power: A Case for Pluralism.* New York: Teachers College Press, 1994.

Rasberry, Salli, and Robert Greenway. *Rasberry Exercises: How to Start Your Own School . . . and . . . Make a Book.* Sebastopol, CA: Freestone Publishing Company, 1970.

Ratner, Joseph, ed. *The Philosophy of John Dewey.* New York: Holt, 1928.

Ravitch, Diane. "Diversity and Democracy: Multicultural Education in America." *American Scholar* 14 (spring 1990): 10–14.

Ravitch, Diane. *The Great School Wars, New York City, 1805–1973: A History of the Public Schools as Battleground of Social Change.* New York: Basic Books, 1974.

Ravitch, Diane. "Multiculturalism: E Pluribus Plures." *American Scholar* 59 (summer 1990): 337–354.

Ravitch, Diane. *Revisionists Revisited: A Critique of the Radical Attack on the Schools.* New York: Basic Books, 1978.

Ravitch, Diane. *The Troubled Crusade: American Education, 1945–1980.* New York: Basic Books, 1983.

Rawick, George P. "The New Deal and Youth: The Civilian Conservation Corps, the National Youth Adminstration, and the American Youth Congress." Ph.D. diss., University of Wisconsin, 1957.

Ray, Brian D. *Strengths of Their Own: Academic Achievement, Family Characteristics, and Longitudinal Traits.* Salem, OR: National Home Education Research Institute, 1997.

Reese, William J. *The Origins of the American High School.* New Haven, CT: Yale University Press, 1995.

Reese, William J. *Power and the Promise of School Reform: Grassroots Movements during the Progressive Era.* Boston: Routledge & Kegan Paul, 1986.

Reid, Robert L. "The Professionalization of the Public School Teachers: The Chicago Experience, 1895–1920." Ph.D. diss., Northwestern University, 1968.

Reid, Robert L., ed. *Battleground: The Autobiography of Margaret Haley.* Chicago: University of Illinois Press, 1982.

Reissman, Frank. *The Culturally Deprived Child.* New York: Harper and Row, 1962.

Relic, Peter D. "NAIS Goes to Washington." *Independent School* 51 (fall 1993): 11–13.

Report of the Committee of Ten on Secondary School Studies. Education Report, 1892–1893. Washington, DC: U.S. Government Printing Office, 1893.

"Report of the Superintendent of Schools for Indian Territory with Annual Report of the Commissioner of Indian Affairs." In *Reports of the Department of Interior.* Washington, DC: U.S. Government Printing Office, 1907.

Rice, Edwin W. *The Sunday-School Movement, 1780–1917, and the American Sunday-School Union, 1817–1917.* 1917. Reprint, New York: Arno Press, 1972.

Rice, Jessie Pearl. *J.L.M. Curry: Southerner, Statesman and Educator.* New York: King's Crown Press, Columbia University, 1949.

Rich, John Martin. *Innovations in Education: Reformers and Their Critics.* Newton, MA: Allyn and Bacon, 1988.

Richards, David A. J. *Toleration and the Constitution.* New York: Oxford University Press, 1986.

Richardson, Joe M. *Christian Reconstruction: The American Missionary Association and Southern Blacks, 1861–1890.* Athens: University of Georgia Press, 1986.

Richardson, Theresa R. *The Century of the Child: The Mental Hygiene Movement and Social Policy in the United States and Canada.* Albany: State University of New York Press, 1989.

Richter, William L. *Overreached on All Sides: The Freedmen's Bureau Adminstrators in Texas, 1865–1868.* College Station, TX: Texas A & M University Press, 1991.

Rickover, Hyman G. *American Education: A National Failure.* New York: Dutton, 1963.

Rickover, Hyman G. *Education and Freedom.* New York: Dutton, 1959.

Rickover, Hyman G. *Swiss Schools and Ours: Why Theirs Are Better.* Boston: Little, Brown, 1962.

Riley, Richard W. "The Improving of America's Schools Act and Elementary and Secondary Education Reform." *Journal of Law and Education* 24 (fall 1995): 513–566.

Roberts, Ferne K. "Education of the Visually Handicapped: A Social and Educational History." In *Foundations of Education for Blind and Visually Handicapped Children and Youth: Theory and Practice,* 1–18. Edited by Geraldine Scholl. New York: American Federation for the Blind, 1986.

Roberts, J. S. *William T. Harris: A Critical Study of His Educational and Related Philosophical Views.* Washington, DC: National Education Association, 1924.

Robinson, H. Alan, Vincent Faraone, Daniel R. Hittleman, and Elizabeth Unruh. *Reading Comprehension Instruction, 1783–1987: A Review of Trends and Research.* Newark, DE: International Reading Association, 1990.

Rockefeller, Steven. *John Dewey: Religious Faith and Democratic Humanism.* New York: Columbia University Press, 1991.

Rogers, Dorothy. *Oswego: Fountainhead of Teacher Education.* New York: Appleton-Century-Crofts, 1961.

Roghanizad, Molook. "Full-Time Muslim Schools in the United States, 1970–1990." Ph.D. diss., University of Maryland, 1990.

Rollins, Richard M. *The Long Journey of Noah Webster.* Philadelphia: University of Pennsylvania Press, 1980.

Rollins, Richard M., ed. *The Autobiographies of Noah Webster from the Letters and Essays, Memoir, and Diary.* Columbia: University of South Carolina Press, 1989.

Rorabaugh, W. J. *The Craft Apprentice: From Franklin to the Machine Age in America.* New York: Oxford University Press, 1986.

Rose, Willie Lee. *Rehearsal for Reconstruction: The Port Royal Experiment.* New York: Bobbs-Merrill 1964.

Roselle, Daniel, ed. *Voices of Social Education.* New York: Macmillan, 1987.

Rosen, Marvin, Gerald R. Clark, and Marvin S. Kivitz, eds. *The History of Mental Retardation: Collected Papers*. Baltimore: University Park Press, 1976.

Rosenwald, Julius. "Principles of Public Giving." *Atlantic Monthly* 143 (May 1929): 599–606.

Rosenwald, Julius. "The Trend Away from Perpetuities." *Atlantic Monthly* 146 (December 1930): 741–749.

Ross, Dorothy. *G. Stanley Hall: The Psychologist as Prophet*. Chicago: University of Chicago Press, 1972.

Ross, Elizabeth Dale. *The Kindergarten Crusade: The Establishment of Preschool Education in the United States*. Athens: Ohio University Press, 1976.

Rothman, David J. *Conscience and Convenience: The Asylum and Its Alternatives in Progressive America*. Boston: Little, Brown, 1980.

Rothman, David J. *The Discovery of the Asylum: Social Order and Disorder in the New Republic*. Boston: Little, Brown, 1971.

Roush, Robert E. "The Carnegie Unit—How Did We Get It?" *Educational Forum* 35 (November 1970): 71–74.

Rousmaniere, Kate. *City Teachers: Teaching and School Reform in Historical Prespective*. New York: Teachers College Press, 1997.

Rubin, David. *The Rights of Teachers*. New York: Bantam, 1984.

Rudolph, Frederick, ed. *Essays on Education in the Early Republic*. Cambridge, MA: Harvard University Press, 1965.

Ruffner, Henry. "Plan for Schools in Virginia." In *Report of the United States Commissioner of Education, 1899–1900*. Vol. 1, pp. 381–97. Washington, DC: U.S. Government Printing Office, 1900.

Rugg, Harold O. *Foundations for American Education*. New York: World Book Co., 1947.

Rugg, Harold O. *That Men May Understand*. New York: Doubleday, 1941.

Rush, Benjamin. *Essays: Literary, Moral, and Philosophical*. Philadelphia: T. and S. F. Bradford, 1798. Reprint, Schenectady, NY: Union College Press, 1988.

Russett, Cynthia Eagle. *Sexual Science: The Victorian Construction of Womanhood*. Cambridge, MA: Harvard University Press, 1989.

Ryan, Alan. *John Dewey and the High Tide of American Liberalism*. New York: W. W. Norton, 1995.

Salmond, John. *The Civilian Conservation Corps: A New Deal Case Study*. Durham, NC: Duke University Press, 1967.

Salmond, John. *A Southern Rebel: The Life and Times of Aubrey Willis Williams, 1890–1965*. Chapel Hill: University of North Carolina Press, 1983.

Salomone, Rosemary. *Equal Education under the Law: Legal Rights and Federal Policy*. New York: St. Martin's Press, 1986.

Sanborn, F. B. *Bronson Alcott: At Alcott House, England, and Fruitlands, New England (1842–1844)*. Cedar Rapids, IA: Torch Press, 1908.

Sanchez, George I. *Forgotten People: A Study of New Mexicans*. Albuquerque: University of New Mexico Press, 1940.

Sanchez, George I. *A Revolution by Education*. New York: Viking Press, 1936.

Sanders, Wiley, ed. *Juvenile Offenders for a Thousand Years: Selected Readings from Anglo-Saxon Times to 1900*. Chapel Hill: University of North Carolina Press, 1970.

Sartre, Jean-Paul. *Existentialism*. New York: Philosophical Library, 1957.

Saslaw, Rita S. "Student Societies: A Nineteenth-Century Establishment." Ph.D. diss., Case Western Reserve University, 1971.

Saunders, Helen E. *The Modern School Library: Its Administration as a Materials Center.* Metuchen, NJ: Scarecrow Press, 1968.

Savage, Howard J. "The Carnegie Foundation and the Rise of the Unit." *Forty-Third Annual Report of the Carnegie Foundation for the Advancement of Teaching,* 13–30. Boston: Merrymount Press, 1948.

Saxe, David Warren. *Social Studies in Schools: A History of the Early Years.* Albany: State University of New York Press, 1991.

Schafer, Ulrich. *International Bibliography of the Project Method in Education, 1895–1982.* 2 Vols. Berlin: Verlag Fuer Wissenschaft und Bildung, 1988.

Schlesinger, Arthur, Jr. *The Disuniting of America: Reflections on a Multicultural Society.* New York: W. W. Norton, 1991.

Schlossman, Steven L. "Delinquent Children: The Juvenile Reform School." In *The Oxford History of the Prison: The Practice of Punishment in Western Society,* 363–389. Edited by Norval Morris and David J. Rothman, New York: Oxford University Press, 1995.

Schlossman, Steven L. *Love and the American Delinquent: The Theory and Practice of "Progressive" Juvenile Justice, 1825–1920.* Chicago: University of Chicago Press, 1977.

Schlossman, Steven L., and Michael Sedlak. "The Chicago Area Project Revisited." *Crime and Delinquency* 29 (July 1983): 398–462.

Schlossman, Steven L., and Stephanie Wallach. "The Crime of Precocious Sexuality: Female Juvenile Delinquency in the Progressive Era." *Harvard Education Review* 48 (February 1978): 65–93.

Schneider, Eric C. *In the Web of Class: Delinquents and Reformers in Boston, 1810s–1930s.* New York: New York University Press, 1992.

Schwager, Sally. "Educating Women in America." *Signs* 12 (winter 1987): 333–372.

Schwartz, Harold. *Samuel Gridley Howe: Social Reformer, 1801–1876.* Cambridge, MA: Harvard University Press, 1956.

Scott, Anne Firor. "The Ever Widening Circle: The Diffusion of Feminist Values from the Troy Female Seminary: 1822–1872." *History of Education Quarterly* 19 (spring 1979): 3–25.

Scott, Anne Firor. "Jane Addams." In *Notable Women: A Biographical Dictionary.* Vol. 1, pp. 16–22. Edited by Edward T. James. Cambridge, MA: Belknap Press of Harvard University Press, 1971.

Scott, Anne Firor. "What, Then, Is the American: This New Woman?" *Journal of American History* 65 (December 1978): 679–703.

Scott, Winfield W., Jr. *New Mexico Military Institute: Duty-Honor-Achievement.* New York: Newcomen Society of the United States, 1993.

Seabury, Samuel. *Moneygripe's Apprentice: The Personal Narrative of Samuel Seabury III.* Edited by Robert B. Mullin. New Haven, CT: Yale University Press, 1989.

Sears, Jesse B., and Adin D. Henderson. *Cubberley of Stanford and His Contribution to American Education.* Stanford, CA: Stanford University Press, 1957.

Sellars, Etta. "A Historical Comparative Analysis of the Ideology of Selected Educational Reformers." Ph.D. diss., Indiana University, 1994.

Senese, G. B. *Self-Determination and the Social Education of Native Americans.* New York: Praeger, 1991.

Sex Information and Education Council of the United States. *SIECUS Report*. New York: SIECUS, 1992.

Shakeshaft, Charol. *Women in Educational Administration*. Newbury Park, CA: Corwin Press, 1989.

Shannon, Patrick. *The Struggle to Continue: Progressive Reading Instruction in the United States*. Portsmouth, NH: Heinemann, 1990.

Shannon, Thomas A. *The National School Boards Association: Reflections on the Development of an American Idea*. Alexandria, VA: NSBA, 1997.

Shapiro, Michael Steven. *Child's Garden: The Kindergarten Movement from Froebel to Dewey*. University Park: Pennsylvania State University Press, 1983.

Shaver, James P., ed. *Research on Social Studies Teaching and Learning*. New York: Macmillan, 1991.

Shaw, Richard. *Dagger John: The Unique Life and Times of Archbishop John Hughes of New York*. New York: Paulist Press, 1977.

Shearer, William J. *The Grading of Schools*. New York: H. P. Smith, 1899.

Shepard, Odell. *Pedler's Progress: The Life of Bronson Alcott*. Boston: Little, Brown, 1937.

Shuffleton, Frank. *Thomas Jefferson: A Comprehensive, Annotated Bibliography of Writings about Him (1826–1980)*. New York: Garland Publishing, 1983.

Shurtleff, Nathaniel B., ed. *Records of the Governor and Company of the Massachusetts Bay in New England*. 5 vols. Boston: William White, 1853–1854.

Silberman, Charles E. *Crisis in Black and White*. New York: Random House, 1964.

Silberman, Charles E. *Crisis in the Classroom: The Remaking of American Education*. New York: Random House, 1970.

Silberman, Charles E. *The Myths of Automation*. New York: Harper and Row, 1966.

Silberman, Charles E., ed. *The Open Classroom Reader*. New York: Random House, 1973.

Sims, Verner M., Eugene A.Waters, and W. A. Robinson "Experimental Programs in the Southern Association." In *Secondary Education in the South*, 140–166. Ed. by W. Carson Ryan, J. Minor Gwynn, and Arnold K. King. Chapel Hill: University of North Carolina Press, 1946.

Sizer, Theodore R. *Secondary Schools at the Turn of the Century*. New Haven, CT: Yale University Press, 1964.

Skeel, Emily Ellsworth Ford, comp. *A Bibliography of the Writings of Noah Webster*. Edited by Edwin H. Carpenter, Jr. New York: New York Public LIbrary, 1958. Reprint, New York: New York Public Library & Arno Press, 1971.

Sklar, Kathryn Kish. *Catharine Beecher: A Study in American Domesticity*. New Haven, CT: Yale University Press, 1974.

Slattery, Patrick. *Curriculum Development in the Postmodern Era*. New York: Garland Press, 1995.

Sleeter, Christine E., ed. *Empowerment through Multicultural Education*. Albany, NY: State University of New York Press, 1991.

Smith, Daniel Blake. *Inside the Great House: Planter Family Life in Eighteenth-Century Chesapeake Society*. Ithaca, NY: Cornell University Press, 1980.

Smith, Dora V., ed. *The English Language Arts*. New York: Appleton-Century-Crofts, 1952.

Smith, Eugene R., Ralph W. Tyler, and the Evaluation Staff. *Appraising and Recording Student Progress*. New York: Harper and Brothers, 1942.

Smith, Frank. *Understanding Reading.* New York: Holt, Rinehart and Winston, 1971.

Smith, Mortimer B. *And Madly Teach: A Layman Looks at Public School Education.* Chicago: Regnery Press, 1949.

Smith, Mortimer B. *The Diminished Mind: A Study of Planned Mediocrity in Our Public Schools.* Chicago: Regnery Press, 1954.

Smith, Mortimer B., ed. *A Decade of Comment on Education, 1956–1966: Selections from the Bulletin of the Council for Basic Education.* Washington, DC: Council for Basic Education, 1966.

Smith, Mortimer B., ed. *The Public Schools in Crisis: Some Critical Essays.* Chicago: Regnery Press, 1956.

Smith, Nila B. *American Reading Instruction.* 1934. Reprint, Newark, DE: International Reading Association, 1986.

Smith, W. L. *Education in Michigan.* Lansing, MI: W. S. George & Co., State Printers and Binders, 1881.

Smock, Raymond, ed. *Booker T. Washington in Perspective: Essays of Louis R. Harlan.* Jackson: University Press of Mississippi, 1988.

Smolla, Rodney A. *Free Speech in an Open Society.* New York: Alfred A. Knopf, 1992.

Snedden, David S. *Administration of Education for Juvenile Delinquents.* New York: Teachers College, Columbia University, 1906.

Snedden, David S. *Educational Sociology.* New York: Macmillan, 1922.

Snedden, David S. *Problems of Educational Readjustment.* Boston: Houghton Mifflin, 1913.

Snedden, David S. *The Problem of Vocational Education.* Boston: Houghton Mifflin, 1910.

Snedden, David S. *Sociological Determination of Objectives in Education.* Phildadelphia: Lippincott, 1921.

Snider, Denton J. *The Life of Friedrich Froebel, Founder of the Kindergarten.* Chicago: Sigma Publishing Co., 1900.

Snyder, Agnes. *Dauntless Women in Early Childhood Education.* Wheaton, MD: Association for Childhood Education International, 1972.

Sochen, June. *Movers and Shakers: American Women Thinkers and Activitists, 1900–1970.* New York: Quadrangle, 1973.

Solomon, Barbara. *In the Company of Educated Women.* New Haven, CT: Yale University Press, 1985.

Soltis, Jonas F. *Philosophy of Education since Mid-Century.* New York: Teachers College Press, 1981.

Soltow, Lee, and Edward W. Stevens, Jr. *The Rise of Literacy and the Common School in the United States: A Socioeconomic Analysis to 1870.* Chicago: University of Chicago Press, 1981.

Sosnowsky, William Paul, Paula Wood, and Asa J. Brown. *Inclusive Education: Toward the Maximum Potential.* 1990. ERIC document ED 319172.

Sowell, Thomas. *Inside American Education: The Decline, the Deception, the Dogmas.* New York: Free Press, 1993.

Spokane, Arnold R., and Ian T. Glickman. "Light, Information, Inspiration, and Cooperation: Origins of the Clinical Science of Career Intervention." *Journal of Career Development* 20 (summer 1994): 295–304.

Spring, Joel H. *American Education.* New York: McGraw-Hill, 1994.

Spring, Joel H. *The American School, 1642–1993.* New York: Longman Press, 1994.

Spring, Joel H. *Education and the Rise of the Corporate State*. Boston: Beacon Press, 1972.

Spring, Joel H. *The Sorting Machine Revisited: National Educational Policy since 1945*. New York: Longman Press, 1989.

Squire, James R. "The History of the Profession." In *Handbook of Research on Teaching the English Language Arts*, 3–17. Edited by James Flood, Julie N. Jenson, D. Lapp, and James R. Squire. New York: Longman, 1991.

Squire, James R., and Robert Applebee. *High School English Instruction Today*. New York: Appleton Century, 1969.

Stanic, George, and Jeremy Kilpatrick. "Mathematics Curriculum Reform in the United States: A Historical Perspective." *International Journal of Educational Research* 5 (1992): 407–417.

Stansell, Christine. *City of Women: Sex and Class in New York, 1789–1860*. Urbana: University of Illinois Press, 1987.

Stasz, Cathleen, T. Kaganoff, and R. A. Eden. "Integrating Academic and Vocational Education: A Review of the Literature, 1987–1992." *Journal of Vocational Educational Research* 19 (1994): 25–72.

Steinberg, Ira S. "On the Justification of Guidance." *Educational Theory* 14 (July 1964): 216–223.

Stephens, Richard W. *Social Reform and the Origins of Vocational Guidance*. Washington, DC: National Vocational Guidance Association, 1970.

Sternberg, Robert J. *The Triarchic Mind: A New Theory of Human Intelligence*. New York: Viking, 1988.

Stevens, Edward W., Jr., *The Grammar of the Machine: Technical Literacy and Early Industrial Expansion in the United States*. New Haven, CT: Yale University Press, 1995.

Stevens, Edward W., Jr., *Literacy, Law, and Social Order*. DeKalb: Northern Illinois University Press, 1988.

Stewart, Patricia. "Sarah Winnemucca." *Nevada Historical Quarterly* 14 (winter 1971): 23–38.

Stickney, Benjamin, and Virginia Plunkett. "Closing the Gap: A Historical Perspective on the Effectiveness of Compensatory Education." *Phi Delta Kappan* 64 (December 1983): 287–290.

Stone, Mason. "The First Normal School in America." *Teachers College Press* 24 (May 1923): 263–271.

Storr, Richard J. "The Role of Education in American History: A Memorandum for the Committee Advising the Fund for the Advancement of Education in Regard to This Subject." *Harvard Educational Review* 46 (August 1976): 331–354.

Stow, Sarah D. *History of Mount Holyoke Seminary: During Its First Half Century*. South Hadley, MA: Mount Holyoke Seminary, 1887.

Strachan, Grace C. *Equal Pay for Equal Work: The Story of the Struggle for Justice Being Made by the Women Teachers of the City of New York*. New York: B. F. Buck and Company, 1910.

Strachan, Grace C. "Salaries Based on Position and Not on the Sex of Incumbent." *National Education Association Proceedings and Addresses*. Washington, DC: National Education Associaton, 1914.

Strachan, Grace C. "Teachers and Woman Suffrage." *Journal of Education* 81 (May 1915): 577–578.

Sunderman, Lloyd F. *Historical Foundations of Music Education in the United States.* Metuchen, NJ: Scarecrow Press, 1971.

Suratt, Judy. "Young, Ella Flagg." In *Notable American Women: A Biographical Dictionary*, 697–699. Edited by James T. Edward, Janet Wilson James, and S. Boyer Paul. Cambridge, MA: Harvard University Press, 1971.

Sweeney, David F. *The Life of John Lancaster Spalding, First Bishop of Peoria, 1840–1916.* New York: Herder and Herder, 1965.

Szasz, Margaret. *Education and the American Indian: The Road to Self-Determination, 1928–1973.* Albuquerque: University of New Mexico Press, 1977.

Taba, Hilda. *Curriculum Development: Theory and Practice.* New York: Harcourt, Brace & World, 1962.

Taba, Hilda, Mary C. Durkin, Jack R. Fraenkel, and Anthony H. McNaughton. *Teachers' Handbook for Elementary Social Studies.* Reading, MA: Addison-Wesley, 1969.

Tanner, Daniel, and Laurel Tanner. *History of the School Curriculum.* New York: Macmillan, 1990.

Teitelbaum, Kenneth. *Schooling for "Good Rebels": Socialism, American Education, and the Search for Radical Curriculum.* New York: Teachers College Press, 1995.

Tenebaum, Samuel. *William Heard Kilpatrick: Trail Blazer in Education.* New York: Harper & Brothers, 1951.

Terry, Paul W. "The Origin and Growth of Student Activities." In *Supervising Extra-Curricular Activities in the American Secondary School.* New York: McGraw-Hill, 1930.

Tewksbury, John L. "An Historical Study of the Winnetka Public Schools from 1919 to 1946." Ph.D. diss., Northwestern University, 1962.

Tharp, Louise H. *Until Victory: Horace Mann and Mary Peabody.* Boston: Little, Brown, 1953.

Theobald, Paul. *Call School: Rural Education in the Midwest to 1918.* Carbondale: Southern Illinois University Press, 1995.

Theobald, Paul. "Country School Curriculum and Governance: The One-Room School Experience in the Nineteenth-Century Midwest." *American Journal of Education* 101 (February 1993): 116–139.

Theobald, Paul. "Democracy and the Origins of Rural Midwest Education: A Retrospective Essay." *Educational Theory* 38 (summer 1988): 363–367.

Thernstrom, Stephan, ed. *Harvard Encyclopedia of American Ethnic Groups.* Cambridge, MA: Harvard University Press, 1980.

Thirty Schools Tell Their Story. New York: Harper and Brothers, 1942.

Thomas, Milton Halsey. *John Dewey.* Chicago: University of Chicago Press, 1962.

Thompkins, Ellsworth, and Walter H. Gaumintz. *The Carnegie Unit: Its Origins, Status, and Trends.* Bulletin 1954, No. 7. U.S. Department of Health, Education, and Welfare, Office of Education. Washington, DC: U.S. Government Printing Office, 1954.

Thompson, Henry P. *Into All Lands: The History of the Society for the Propagation of the Gospel in Foreign Parts, 1701–1950.* London: Society for Promoting Christian Knowledge, 1951.

Thompson, Kathleen. "Charlotte Hawkins Brown." In *Black Women in America: An Historical Encyclopedia.* Edited by Darlene Clark Hine. Brooklyn, NY: Carlson Publication, 1993.

Thursfield, Richard Emmon. *Henry Barnard's "American Journal of Education."* Baltimore: Johns Hopkins University Press, 1945.

Tieken-Boon van Ostade, Ingrid, ed. *200 Years of Lindley Murray's Grammar.* Munster, Germany: Nodus Publikationen, for the Henry Sweet Society for the History of Linguistic Ideas, 1996.

Townsend, Kiliaen V. R. *The Boarding School Guide.* Athens, GA: Agee, 1989.

Townsend, Lucy. "The Gender Effect: The Early Curricula of Beloit College and Rockford Female Seminary." *History of Higher Education Annual* 10 (1990): 69–90.

Traver, Paul D. "John Orville Taylor: A Forgotten Educator." *History of Education Quarterly* 9 (spring 1969): 57–63.

Trennert, Robert. *The Phoenix Indian School: Forced Assmilation in Arizona.* Norman: University of Oklahoma Press, 1988.

Tropea, Joseph L. "Structuring Risks: The Making of Urban School Order." In *Children at Risk in America,* 58–88. Edited by Roberta Wollons. Albany: State University of New York Press, 1992.

Trost, Jennifer Ann. "Gateway to Justice: A Social History of Juvenile Court and Child Welfare Network in Memphis, Tennessee, 1910–1929." Ph.D. diss., Carnegie Mellon University, 1996.

Trustees of Groton School. *Views from the Circle: Seventy-Five Years of Groton School.* Groton, MA: Groton School Press, 1960.

Tucker, William H. *The Science and Politics of Racial Research.* Urbana: University of Illinois Press, 1994.

Tuer, Andrew W. *History of the Horn Book.* London: Leadenhall Press, 1897. Reprint, New York: Arno Press, 1979.

Turner, James, and C. Steven McGann. "Black Studies as an Integral Tradition in African-American Intellectual History." *Journal of Negro Education* 49 (winter 1980): 52–59.

Tushnet, Mark. *Making Civil Rights Law: Thurgood Marshal and the Supreme Court, 1956–1961.* New York: Oxford University Press, 1994.

Tushnet, Mark, and Katya Lezin. "What Really Happened in *Brown v. Board of Education.*" *Columbia Law Review* 91 (December 1991): 1867–1930.

Tyack, David B. "Bureaucracy and the Common School: The Example of Portland, Oregon, 1851–1913." *American Quarterly* 19 (fall 1967): 475–498.

Tyack, David B. "The Kingdom of God and the Common School." *Harvard Educational Review* 36 (fall 1966): 447–469.

Tyack, David B. *The One Best System: A History of American Urban Education.* Cambridge, MA: Harvard University Press, 1974.

Tyack, David B. "The Perils of Pluralism: The Background of the Pierce Case." *American Historical Review* 74 (October 1969): 74–98.

Tyack, David B. "The Tribe and the Common School: Community Control in Rural Education." *American Quarterly* 24 (March 1972): 3–19.

Tyack, David B. *Turning Points in American Educational History.* New York: Wiley & Sons, 1967.

Tyack, David B., and Larry Cuban. *Tinkering toward Utopia: A Century of Public School Reform.* Cambridge, MA: Harvard University Press, 1995.

Tyack, David B., and Elisabeth Hansot. *Learning Together: A History of Coeducation in American Public Schools.* New Haven, CT: Yale University Press, 1990.

Tyack, David B., and Elisabeth Hansot. *Managers of Virtue: Public School Leadership in America, 1820–1980*. New York: Basic Books, 1982.

United States Congress. House. Secretary of the Interior. *Free Schools in Indian Territory*. Report prepared by Frank C. Churchill. 57th Cong., 1st sess., 1902.

United States Congress. House. Secretary of the Interior. *Letter from the Acting Secretary of the Interior Transmitting Certain Petitions and Communciations, with Recommendations in Regard to the Education of White and Negro Children in the Indian Territory*. 55th Cong., 2nd sess., 1899.

United States Department of Health and Human Services. "Rules and Regulations of the Head Start Program." *Federal Register* 57 (1992): 236. FR document 92–29520.

United States Department of Labor. Employment and Training Administration. Bureau of Apprenticeship and Training. *Apprenticeship*. Washington, DC: Department of Labor, 1992.

United States Office of Education. *A Look Ahead in Secondary Education: Report of the Second Commission on Life Adjustment Education for Youth*. Bulletin No. 4. Washington, DC: U.S. Government Printing Office, 1954.

United States Office of Education. *Vitalizing Secondary Education: Report of the First Commission on Life Adjustment Education for Youth*. Bulletin No. 3. Washington, DC: U.S. Government Printing Office, 1951.

Unks, Gerald. "Conversation: A Talk with Dr. James S. Coleman." *High School Journal* 63 (November 1979): 48–53.

Urban, Wayne J. *Black Scholar: Horace Mann Bond, 1904–1972*. Athens: University of Georgia Press, 1992.

Urban, Wayne J. "The Making of a Teachers' Union: The National Education Association, 1957–1972." *Historical Studies in Education* 5 (spring 1993): 33–53.

Urban, Wayne J. *Why Teachers Organized*. Detroit: Wayne State University Press, 1982.

Urban, Wayne J., and Jennings Wagoner, Jr. *American Education: A History*. New York: McGraw-Hill, 1996.

Valentine, Phyllis Klein. "American Asylum for the Deaf: A First Experiment in Education, 1817–1880." Ph.D. diss., University of Connecticut, 1993.

Van Cleve, John Vickrey, and Barry A. Crouch. *A Place of Their Own: Creating the Deaf Community in America*. Washington, DC: Gallaudet University, 1989.

Van Doren, Carl. *Benjamin Franklin: A Biography*. New York: Viking Press, 1938.

Van Doren, Carl. *Benjamin Franklin's Autobiographical Writings*. New York: Viking Press, 1945.

Van Galen, Jane, and Mary Anne Pitman, eds. *Home Schooling: Political, Historical, and Pedagogical Perspectives*. Norwood, NJ: Ablex, 1991.

Vanderpoel, Emily Nayes. *Chronicles of a Pioneer School from 1792 to 1833. . . .* Cambridge, MA: Harvard University Press, 1903.

Vandewalker, Nina C. *The Kindergarten in American Public Education*. New York: Macmillan, 1908.

Van Til, William. *The Laboratory School: Its Rise and Fall?* Terre Haute: Indiana State University and Laboratory School Administrators Association, 1969.

Van Til, William. "William Heard Kilpatrick: Respector of Individuals and Ideas." In *Teachers and Mentors*, 217–224. Edited by C. Kridel, R. V. Bullough, and P. Shaker. New York: Garland Press, 1996.

Vars, Gordon F. "Integrated Curriculum in Historical Perspective." *Educational Leadership* 49 (1991): 14–15.

Vassar, Rena Lee. "Elementary and Latin Grammar School Education in the American Colonies, 1607–1700." Ph.D. diss., University of California–Berkeley, 1958.

Vaughn, William H. *Robert Jefferson Breckinridge as an Educational Administrator.* Nashville: George Peabody College, 1937.

Vaughn, William P. "Partners in Segregation: Barnas Sears and the Peabody Fund." *Civil War History* 10 (September 1964): 261–274.

Vaughn, William P. *Schools for All: The Blacks and Public Education in the South, 1865–1877.* Lexington: University of Kentucky Press, 1974.

Vaughn, William P. "Separate and Unequal: The Civil Rights Act of 1875 and Defeat of the School Integration Clause." *Southwestern Social Science Quarterly* 48 (September 1967): 146–154.

Venezky, Richard L. "American Primers: Guide to the Microfiche Collection." *American Primers.* Bethesda, MD: University Publications of America, 1990.

Venezky, Richard L. "A History of the American Reading Textbook." *Elementary School Journal* 87, no. 3 (1987): 247–265.

Violas, Paul C. *The Training of the Urban Working Class: A History of Twentieth-Century American Education.* Chicago: Rand McNally, 1978.

von Glaserfeld, Ernst. *The Construction of Knowledge.* Seaside, CA: Intersystem, 1987.

Wadelington, Charles W. "Charlotte Hawkins Brown." In *Encyclopedia of African-American Education,* 63–65. Edited by Faustine C. Jones-Wilson, Charles A. Asbury, Margo Okazawa-Rey, D. Kamili Anderson, Sylvia M. Jacobs, and Michael Fultz. Westport, CT: Greenwood Press, 1996.

Wahl, Jean. *A Short History of Existentialism.* New York: Philosophical Library, 1949.

Wallace, James M. *Liberal Journalism and American Education, 1914–1941.* New Brunswick, NJ: Rutgers University Press, 1991.

Warfel, Harry. *Noah Webster: Schoolmaster to America.* New York: Macmillan, 1936. Reprint, New York: Octagon Books, 1964.

Warner, Michael. *The Letters of the Republic: Publication and the Public Sphere in Eighteenth-Century America.* Cambridge, MA: Harvard University Press, 1991.

Warren, Donald R. *To Enforce Education: A History of the Founding Years of the U.S. Office of Education.* Detroit: Wayne State University, 1974.

Warren, Donald R., ed. *American Teachers: Histories of a Profession at Work.* New York: Macmillan, 1989.

Washburne, Carleton. "An Autobiographical Sketch." In *Leaders in American Education,* 457–481. Seventieth Yearbook of the National Society for the Study of Education, Part II. Edited by Robert J. Havighurst. Chicago: National Society for the Study of Education, 1971.

Washburne, Carleton. *A Living Philosophy of Education.* New York: John Day Company, 1953.

Washburne, Carleton, and Sidney P. Marland, Jr. *Winnetka: The History and Significance of an Educational Experiment.* Englewood Cliffs, NJ: Prentice-Hall, 1963.

Washington, Booker T. *Up from Slavery: An Autobiography.* New York: A. L. Burt Company, 1901.

Washington, Booker T., and W.E.B. Du Bois. *The Negro in the South: His Economic Progress in Relation to His Moral and Religious Development.* Philadelphia: George W. Jacobs & Co., 1907.

Washington, Ida H. *Dorothy Canfield Fisher: A Biography.* Shelburne, VT: New England Press, 1982.

Washington, Valora. "Reducing the Risks to Young Black Learners: An Examination of Race and Educational Policy." In *Risk Makers, Risk Takers, Risk Breakers: Reducing the Risks for Young Literacy Learners*, 281–314. Edited by JoBeth Allen and Jana M. Mason. Portsmouth, NH: Heinemann Educational Books, 1989.

Weber, Evelyn. *The Kindergarten: Its Encounter with Educational Thought in America.* New York: Teachers College Press, 1969.

Weber, Samuel. *The Charity School Movement in Colonial Pennsylvania.* 1905. Reprint, New York: Arno Press, 1969.

Wedgeworth, Robert, ed. *ALA World Encyclopedia of Library and Information Services.* Chicago: American Library Assocation, 1980.

Weeks, Stephen B. *History of Public School Education in Alabama.* United States Bureau of Education Bulletin No. 12. Washington, DC: U.S. Government Printing Office, 1915.

Weiss, John H. *The Making of Technological Man: The Social Origins of French Engineering Education.* Cambridge, MA: MIT Press, 1982.

Weiss, Nancy. "Save the Children: A History of the Children's Bureau, 1903–1918." Ph.D. diss., University of California–Los Angeles, 1974.

Weller, Paul G. W. "Open School Organizations." *The School Review* 13 (January 1905): 10–14.

Wentworth, Marlene. "Attitudes towards Learning: An Examination of Arthur Bestor's Educational Wastelands." M.A. thesis, University of Illinois at Urbana–Champaign, 1986.

Werner, Morris Robert. *Julius Rosenwald: The Life of a Practical Humanitarian.* New York: Harper and Brothers, 1939.

Wesley, Edgar B. *The National Education Association: The First Hundred Years; The Building of a Teaching Profession.* New York: Harper and Brothers, 1957.

West, Earl H. "The Life and Educational Contributions of Barnas Sears." Ph.D. diss., George Peabody College for Teachers, 1961.

West, Earl H. "The Peabody Education Fund and Negro Education." *History of Education Quarterly* 6 (summer 1966): 3–21.

Westbrook, Robert. *John Dewey and American Democracy.* Ithaca, NY: Cornell University Press, 1991.

Westerhoff, John H., III. *McGuffey and His Readers: Piety, Morality, and Education in Nineteenth-Century America.* Nashville: Abingdon Press, 1978.

Westinghouse Learning Corporation. *The Impact of Head Start: An Evaluation of Effects of Head Start on Children's Cognitive and Affective Development. Executive Summary.* Ohio University Report to the Office of Economic Opportunity. Washington, DC: Clearinghouse for Federal Scientific and Technical Information, 1969.

Wheelock, Anne. *Crossing the Tracks: How "Untracking" Can Save America's Schools.* New York: New Press, 1992.

Wheelock, Lucy, trans. "Autobiography in Letter to the Duke of Meiningen." In *Kindergarten and Child Culture Papers: Papers on Froebel's Kindergarten, with Suggestions on Principles and Methods of Child Culture in Different Countries*, 21–48. Edited by Henry Barnard. Hartford, CT: Office of *Barnard's American Journal of Education*, 1890.

Whipple, Guy M. *Commemorating a Quarter of a Century of Service of the National Society for the Study of Education.* Bloomington, IL: Public School Publishing Co., 1926.

Whipple, Guy M. *The Textbook in American Education*. Bloomington, IL: Public School Publishing Co., 1931.

Whipple, Guy M., ed. *Extra-Curricular Activities*. Twenty-Fifth Yearbook of the National Society for the Study of Education, Part 2. Bloomington, IL: Public School Publishing Co., 1927.

White, Howard Ashley. *The Freedmen's Bureau in Louisiana*. Baton Rouge: Louisiana State University Press, 1970.

Wielk, Carol A. "The Ocean Hill–Brownsville School Project." *Community Issues* 1 (February 1969): 1–16.

Willard, Emma. *An Address to the Public: Particularly to the Members of the Legislature of New York, Proposing a Plan for Improving Female Education*. Middlebury, VT: J. W. Copeland, 1819.

Willard, Emma. *Geography for Beginners; or, The Instructor's Assistant, in Giving First Lessons from Maps, in the Style of Familiar Conversation*. Hartford, CT: Oliver D. Cooke & Co., 1826.

Willard, Emma. *History of the United States or Republic of America*. New York: White, Gallaher & White, 1830.

Willard, Emma. *Morals for the Young; or, Good Principles Instilling Wisdom*. New York: A. S. Barnes and Co., 1857.

Wilson, E. O. *Sociobiology: The New Synthesis*. Cambridge, MA: Harvard University, 1975.

Wilson, James Q., and Richard J. Herrnstein. *Crime and Human Nature*. New York: Simon and Schuster, 1985.

Winefield, Richard. *Never the Twain Shall Meet: Bell, Gallaudet, and the Communications Debate*. Washington, DC: Gallaudet University Press, 1987.

Winterer, Caroline. "Avoiding a 'Hothouse System of Education': Nineteenth-Century Early Childhood Education from the Infant Schools to the Kindergartens." *History of Education Quarterly* 32 (fall 1992): 288–314.

Winters, Elmer A. "Harold Rugg and Education for Social Reconstruction." Ph.D. diss., University of Wisconsin, 1968.

Winzer, Margaret A. *The History of Special Education: From Isolation to Integration*. Washington, DC: Gallaudet University Press, 1993.

Wirth, Arthur G. *Education in the Technological Society: The Vocational-Liberal Studies Controversy in the Early Twentieth Century*. Scranton, PA: Intext, 1972.

Wolcott, David, and Steven Schlossman. "A Children's Culture of Casual Crime and Violence." In *Children Harmed and Harmful: Risks and Risk-Taking among Ten to Fifteen Year Olds*. Edited by Margaret K. Rosenheim and Mark Testa. Forthcoming.

Wold, Susan J. *School Nursing: A Framework for Practice*. St. Louis: C. V. Mosby 1981.

Wolf, Eleanor P. *Trial and Error: The Detroit School Segregation Case*. Detroit: Wayne State University, 1981.

Wolfe, Deborah P. "Curriculum Adaptations for the Culturally Deprived." *Journal of Negro Education* 31, no. 2 (spring 1962): 139–151.

Wolfe, Theta H. *Alfred Binet*. Chicago: University of Chicago Press, 1973.

Wollons, Roberta, ed. *Children at Risk in America: History, Concepts, and Public Policy*. Albany: State University of New York Press, 1993.

Wong, Kenneth K., and Margaret C. Wang, eds. *Rethinking Policy for At-Risk Students*. Berkeley, CA: McCutchan, 1994.

Wood, Claire Diane. "The Cultural and Intellectual Origins of Emma Willard's Educational Philosophy." M.A. thesis, San Jose State University, 1991.

Woodson, Carter G. *The Education of the Negro Prior to 1861: A History of the Education of the Colored People of the United States from the Beginning of Slavery to the Civil War.* Washington, DC: Association for the Study of Negro Life and History, 1915.

Woodson, Carter G. *The Mis-education of the Negro.* Washington, DC: Associated Publishers, 1933.

Woody, Thomas. *A History of Women's Education in the United States.* 2 vols. New York: Science Press, 1929.

Wooten, William. *SMSG: The Making of a Curriculum.* New Haven, CT: Yale University Press, 1965.

Wortham, Sue C. *Childhood, 1892–1992.* Wheaton, MD: Association for Childhood Education International, 1992.

Wright, Arthur D., and George E. Gardner. *Hall's Lectures on School-Keeping; An Exact Reproduction of the First (1829) Edition of This Work, to Which Is Appended an Account of the Life and Works of the Author, Samuel Read Hall, with a Bibliography of His Writings.* Hanover, NH: Dartmouth Press, 1929.

Wright, Arthur D., and Edward E. Redcay. *The Negro Rural School Fund, Inc. (Anna T. Jeanes Foundation, 1907–1933).* Washington, DC: Rural School Fund, 1933.

Wright, Esmond. *Franklin of Philadelphia.* Cambridge, MA: Harvard University Press, 1986.

Wright, Nathaniel. "The Life and Educational Thought of Bernard Iddings Bell (1886–1958)." Ed.D. diss., Harvard University, 1964.

Wrightstone, J. Wayne, George Forlano, Edward Frankel, Barbara Lewis, Richard Turner, and Philip Bolger. *Evaluation of the Higher Horizons Program for Underprivileged Children: Cooperative Research Project No. 1124.* New York: Bureau of Education Research, Board of Education of New York, 1964.

Wrigley, Julia. *Class, Politics and Public Schools: Chicago, 1900–1950.* New Brunswick, NJ: Rutgers University Press, 1982.

Wyman, Andrea. "The Earliest Early Childhood Teachers: Women Teachers of America's Dame Schools." *Young Children* 50 (January 1995): 29–32.

Yates, Elizabeth. *Pebble in a Pool: The Widening Circles of Dorothy Canfield Fisher's Life.* New York: Dutton, 1958.

Yerkes, Robert M. "Robert Mearns Yerkes, Psychobiologist." In *A History of Psychology in Autobiography.* Vol 2, pp. 381–407. Edited by Carl Murchison. Worcester: Clark University Press, 1932.

Yerkes, Robert M., ed. *Psychological Examining in the United State Army.* Washington, DC: U.S. Government Printing Office, 1921.

Yoakum, Clarence S., and Robert M. Yerkes. *Army Mental Tests.* New York: Henry Holt, 1920.

Yoder, Donald A. "Calvin's Crusade: A Reassessment of Calvin Milton Woodward's Social and Educational Ideas for School Reform in the United States." Ph.D. diss., University of Hawaii, 1994.

Young, Timothy W. *Public Alternative Education: Options and Choice for Today's Schools.* New York: Teachers College Press, 1990.

INDEX

Page numbers in **boldface** type refer to main entries in the dictionary.

ABOUT THE EDITOR AND CONTRIBUTORS

ROSA MARIA ABREO, a doctoral student in curriculum and instruction, University of Texas–Austin, has been in education for twenty-three years, eighteen of which were spent teaching in bilingual/ESL classrooms.

STEPHEN H. ABY, Associate Professor and Education Biographer at the University of Akron, has written *The IQ Debate: A Selective Guide to the Literature* (1990), as well as recent contributions to *Educational Studies* and *Discourse: Studies in the Cultural Politics of Education.*

DAVID W. ADAMS, Associate Professor of Education at Cleveland State University, has written *Education for Extinction: American Indians and the Boarding School Experience, 1875–1928* (1995), as well as published articles in *Harvard Educational Review* and *Pacific Historical Review.*

REENE A. ALLEY is Associate Professor in the Department of Educational Administration, Foundations, and Research, Youngstown University. Her research interests focus on career development within educational administration and educational information management system implementation, as well as the historical emergence of leadership roles within the principalship.

CLINTON B. ALLISON is Professor in Cultural Studies in Education, University of Tennessee, Knoxville. He is a specialist in the history of southern education. His most recent book is *Present and Past: Essays in the History of Education.*

RICHARD J. ALTENBAUGH is Associate Professor of Education at Slippery Rock University, where he specializes in the history of education. He is the author of three books, and his articles have appeared in such journals as *History of Education Quarterly*, *Urban Education*, and *Cambridge Journal of Education*.

ROBERT N. BARGER, retired Professor of Education at Eastern Illinois University, earned his Ph.D. in history of education at the University of Illinois in 1976. An Educational Foundations scholar, he has authored nearly 100 books, chapters, and articles, including the authoritative biography of John Lancaster Spalding.

BARBARA BEATTY, Associate Professor of Education, Wellesley College, completed her Ph.D. at the Harvard Graduate School of Education and taught in public schools at the kindergarten level. She is the author of articles and chapters on the history of the kindergarten and on teacher education, and of *Preschool Education in America: The Culture of Young Children from the Colonial Era to the Present* (1995).

BRUCE BEEZER is Professor Emeritus and former Associate Dean of Academic Affairs in the College of Education and Psychology at North Carolina State University. He taught courses in education law and history of education. He has published in the *Journal of Law and Education* and *West's Education Law Reporter*.

JAYNE R. BEILKE, an Assistant Professor of Education at Ball State University, received her Ph.D. from Indiana University–Bloomington. Her dissertation is entitled "To Render Better Service: The Role of the Julius Rosenwald Fund Fellowship Program in the Development of Graduate and Professional Educational Opportunities for African Americans" (1994).

BEN BURKS, Ph.D. candidate at the University of Virginia, is concentrating research on religion and education. He is an ordained United Methodist minister and works as a campus minister at James Madison University.

RONALD E. BUTCHART, Professor and Program Director of the Education Program, University of Washington–Tacoma, has written extensively on freedmen's education, the social history of teachers and teaching, and other issues in the history of U.S. education. He currently directs the Freedmen's Teacher Project.

D. CRYSTAL BYNDLOSS, Ph.D. candidate, Department of Sociology, Harvard University, is writing her dissertation on African American community-based educational movements and has presented her preliminary findings at the annual meeting of the American Sociological Association and the American Educational Research Association.

JAMES C. CARPER, Associate Professor of Foundations of Education, University of South Carolina, has coedited reference volumes on religious schools and contributed essays on related topics to *Educational Forum, Journal of Church and State*, and *History of Education Quarterly*. His research focuses on private education and church-state issues.

PATRICIA ANNE CARTER is a faculty member and administrator for the women's studies program at the University of Connecticut. Her research on Grace Strachan began with her dissertation, "A Coalition between Women Teachers and Feminists in New York City, 1900–1920" (1985), and continued with "Becoming 'New Women': The Equal Rights Campaigns of New York City Schoolteachers, 1900–1920" (1992).

MICHAEL J. CLEARY, Professor and Graduate Program Coordinator, has written work on professional preparation issues and performance-based assessments. He is a Division Board Director in the National Commission for Health Education Credentialing, Inc.

RONALD D. COHEN, Professor of History at Indiana University–Northwest, Gary, Indiana, has written (with Raymond A. Mohl) *The Paradox of Progressive Education: The Gary Plan and Urban Education* (1979) and *Children of the Mill: Schooling and Society in Gary, Indiana, 1906–1960* (1990). He has also served as Associate Editor of the *History of Education Quarterly*.

DONALD E. COLLINS earned his Ph.D. in history at Carnegie Mellon University and specializes in twentieth-century American and African American social history. His dissertation focused on multiculturalism's development in black Washington, D.C., from 1930 to 1960. He has presented and published material on multicultural education, including an article, "Afrocentricity," in *Black Issues in Higher Education*.

WILLIAM W. CUTLER III is a member of the Department of History and the Department of Educational Leadership and Policy Studies at Temple University. He has published widely on oral history, urban history, and the history of education. His special interests include the material culture of education and the history of the home-school relationship in America.

O. L. DAVIS, JR., is Professor of Curriculum and Instruction, University of Texas–Austin. A former President of the Association for Supervision and Curriculum Development, Kappa Delta Pi, and the Society for the Study of Curriculum History, he has focused on curriculum practice, theory, and history and on social studies education, as well as the history of American education.

JENNIFER LYNN DEETS is a doctoral candidate in the Department of Curriculum and Instruction at the University of Texas–Austin.

MARK DESJARDINS received a B.A. in history from Bates College (1988) and an M.Ed. from the University of Virginia (1992). He is a doctoral candidate in the history of American education at the University of Virginia, where he is completing his dissertation on Endicott Peabody and Groton School.

WILLIAM E. EATON has taught, published, and administered at Southern Illinois University–Carbondale for twenty-seven years, following three years of public school teaching. His fields of interest are the history of American education and public policy formation.

ERIC R. EBELING, Assistant Professor of Education at Texas Tech University, teaches graduate courses in the history and philosophy of education. His dissertation explored the educational role of the government in seventeenth-century Maryland, and his research interests include education in early America and public and private issues in education.

ANTHONY EDWARDS, a program administrator, Graduate School, University of South Carolina, is a doctoral student in educational foundations and holds a research associate appointment in the McKissick Museum of Education. He is completing a dissertation on the Booker T. Washington School of Columbia, S.C.

HARIKLIA EFTHIMIOU is a doctoral candidate in the Department of Education Policy, Planning, and Administration at the University of Maryland, College Park. Her work focuses on teacher education in the United States and Europe.

CHUNG-JU FAN is a graduate student in curriculum studies at the University of Texas–Austin.

BARBARA FINKELSTEIN, Professor in the Department of Education Policy, Planning, and Administration, University of Maryland, College Park, is a historian who links the evolution of education with history of childhood and classroom practice. She is also Director of the International Center for the Study of Education Policy and Human Values at the University of Maryland.

HARRIETT H. FORD, Assistant Professor in the school psychology training program at the University of Kentucky, received her doctorate in school psychology from the University of South Carolina, and completed a postdoctoral fellowship in pediatric psychology at Brown University. Her research interests are childhood sexual maltreatment and HIV in adolescents.

ERNEST FREEBERG is an Assistant Professor of Humanities at Colby-Sawyer

College, New Hampshire. His work in nineteenth-century intellectual history includes research on the origins of special education in America, with particular interest in the education of Laura Bridgman, the first deaf and blind person to be taught language.

THOMAS GORDON, Associate Professor, Elementary Education/Early Childhood, Slippery Rock University, earned his doctorate at the University of North Carolina–Greensboro in child development and family relations. His area of expertise is early childhood education.

ELAINE CLIFT GORE, a doctoral student in curriculum and instruction, University of Texas–Austin, has taught music and worked as an educational writer.

GERALD L. GUTEK, Professor of Educational Leadership and Policy Studies, Loyola University–Chicago, teaches history of education, philosophy of education, and comparative education. He has written articles and books in these areas, with *American Education in a Global Society: Internationalizing Teacher Education* (1993) as his most recent.

JOSEPH M. HAWES is Professor of History at the University of Memphis, where he teaches courses in the history of American children. He is the author of *Children in Urban Society: Juvenile Delinquency in Nineteenth-Century America* (1971) and *The Children's Rights Movement: A History of Advocacy and Protection* (1991).

IRVING G. HENDRICK is Professor and Dean of the School of Education, University of California–Riverside. His scholarly work in the history of education has centered regionally on California and topically on teacher preparation, minority group experiences, and special education. He is author of *California Education: A Brief History* (1980).

RODNEY HESSINGER is a doctoral candidate at Temple University and has studied education history with William Cutler. His dissertation will concern the experience of youths in early nineteenth-century America, with special emphasis on religious, family, and school life. He has published "Problems and Promises: Colonial American Childrearing and Modernization Theory," *Journal of Family History* (April 1996).

DOROTHY W. HEWES, Professor Emeritus, San Diego State University, has presented and published on the history of educational philosophies and the administration of early childhood centers. Her most recent work is *It's the Camaraderie: A History of Parent Cooperative Preschools* (1998). She is active in the National Association for the Education of Young Children, International

Standing Committee for the History of Education, and Organisation Mondiale pour l'Education Prescolaire.

LAURIE MOSES HINES is a doctoral student in history of education and in American Studies at Indiana University, Bloomington.

THOMAS C. HUNT is Professor of Educational Foundations at Virginia Tech. His major field is the history of American schooling, with a speciality in religion and education.

CHARLES E. JENKS, Assistant Professor, Pennsylvania State University, received his degree in social science education from the University of Georgia in 1994.

FAUSTINE C. JONES-WILSON is Professor Emeritus at Howard University, Washington, D.C. Prior to her retirement, she served as Professor of Education, Graduate Professor, and Editor of the *Journal of Negro Education*. She authored two books, over twenty book chapters, more than forty articles, and numerous book reviews and editorials—all related to education.

THOMAS KANDL, Professor in the Elementary and Early Childhood Education Department at Slippery Rock University, received his Ph.D. from Michigan State University in Mathematics Education. He has published articles and reviews in *The Arithmetic Teacher, Teaching Children Mathematics*, and *Science and Children*.

POLLY WELTS KAUFMAN, Visiting Associate Professor of History at the University of Southern Maine, has also taught at the University of Massachusetts–Boston and Bowdoin College. Among her books are *Women Teachers on the Frontier* (1984) and *National Parks and the Woman's Voice: A History* (1996). She also edited *The Search for Equity: Women at Brown University, 1891–1991* (1991).

HERBERT M. KLIEBARD has been Professor of Curriculum and Instruction and Educational Policy Studies for the past thirty-five years. His most recent books are *Forging the American Curriculum* (1993), *Struggle of the American Curriculum* (second edition, 1995), and *The Vocationalization of the American Curriculum: The Construction of an Educational Ideal* (1999).

JAMES C. KLOTTER received his Ph.D. from the University of Kentucky and currently serves as the Executive Director and State Historian at the Kentucky Historical Society. He is the author, editor, or coauthor of nearly a dozen books, including *Our Kentucky: A Study of the Bluegrass State* (1992) and *The Breckinridges of Kentucky* (1986).

CATHARINE C. KNIGHT, Assistant Professor, College of Education, University of Akron, focuses her research and publications on cognitive developmental theory. She is active in professional organizations, including the American Educational Research Association and Phi Delta Kappa.

MICHAEL KNOLL, a Research Fellow at the Swiss Institute of Technology, Zurich, and Visiting Assistant Professor in the College of Education, University of South Carolina, has published numerous articles and books on comparative education and the philosophy and history of education.

BRUCE E. KONKLE, Associate Professor of Journalism, University of South Carolina, holds a research associate appointment at the McKissick Museum of Education. He has completed historical research on the Southern Study.

CRAIG KRIDEL, Professor of Education and Curator of the McKissick Museum of Education, University of South Carolina, has edited *Curriculum History: The American Curriculum, Teachers and Mentors* and coedited *Writing Educational Biography*. He is currently completing a history of the Eight-Year Study.

HOYT F. LECROY, National Vice-Chair, History Special Research Interest Group of the Music Educators National Conference, served as Coordinator of Instrumental Music Education for the DeKalb County school system in metropolitan Atlanta. His research, presentations, and publications include history of music education and current issues in music education.

TSZ NGONG LEE is a doctoral student in curriculum studies at the University of Texas–Austin.

WILLIAM R. LEE, Associate Professor of Music at the University of Tennessee–Chattanooga, specializes in the history of music teaching and learning. He has published articles and papers on Lowell Mason, Charles Farnsworth, Max Schoen, rural reform and music education, and music learning among antebellum African Americans and upland southern whites.

JEFFREY R. LEHMAN, Associate Professor of Science Education, Slippery Rock University, has coauthored a secondary science teaching methods textbook and published over thirty-five articles in science education journals. His interests include the integration of science and mathematics and the use of technology in teaching science.

RUTH E. LEO chairs the Department of Nursing, Slippery Rock University, and directs the school nurse program, preparing students for eligibility as school nurses. She has conducted workshops on the care of students with spina bifida in the school setting and authored a chapter on the school nurse role in *Teaching the Student with Spina Bifida* (1993).

ROBERT A. LEVIN, Assistant Professor, Foundations of Education, Youngstown State University, holds his doctorate in history from Carnegie Mellon. He has taught and worked as a school administrator in Brookline (Massachusetts), Montgomery County (Maryland), and Gorham (Maine), and served as secretary of Division F (History/Historiography) of the American Educational Research Association.

TEDD LEVY teaches at Nathan Hale Middle School, Norwalk, Connecticut, and is interested in early U.S. education. A former NEH Teacher-Scholar, he authored "First in His Class: The Many Contributions of Samuel Read Hall," *OAH Magazine of History* (fall 1991).

JEFFREY A. LILES, Visiting Lecturer, Eastern Michigan University, teaches courses in social foundations of education and supervises student teachers. His research focuses on rural public education during the Progressive Era, schools in Indian Territory, and the lives of turn-of-the-century male educators. He is currently researching teacher education and student teaching.

VALINDA W. LITTLEFIELD is the Staff Associate/Editor for the Afro-American Studies and Research Program and an ABD candidate in the Department of History at the University of Illinois–Urbana. Her dissertation is entitled " 'I Am Only One, But I'm One': Southern African-American Female School-teachers, 1884–1954."

ROBERT LOWE, Professor of Education at National-Louis University and Senior Researcher at the Institute for the Transformation of Learning, Marquette University, coauthored, with David Tyack and Elisabeth Hansot, *Public Schools in Hard Times: The Great Depression and Recent Years* (1984), and with Harvey Kantor, "Class, Race, and the Emergence of Federal Education Policy: From the New Deal to the Great Society," *Educational Researcher* 24 (April 1995).

EDITH NYE MacMULLEN has been the Director of the Teacher Preparation Program and a member of the History Department at Yale University. She has written *In the Cause of True Education: Henry Barnard and Nineteenth-Century Reform* (1991).

DON T. MARTIN, Associate Professor, Administrative and Policy Studies, University of Pittsburgh, received his Ph.D. in Social Foundations of Education from Ohio State University in 1970. His teaching and research focus on the social foundations of education, the politics of education, and the history of education. He has authored numerous articles and coauthored two books.

PAUL H. MATTINGLY, Professor, Department of History, New York University, earned his doctorate at the University of Wisconsin under Merle Curti. His principle publications in educational history include *The Classless Profession: American Schoolmen in the Nineteenth Century* (1975); with Michael B. Katz, *Education and Social Change: Themes from Ontario's Past* (1975); and with Edward W. Stevens, Jr., *"Schools and the Means of Education Shall Forever Be Encouraged": A History of Education in the Old Northwest, 1781–1880* (1987). He also served as Editor of the *History of Education Quarterly* for twelve years.

RALPH D. MAWDSLEY, Professor and Chair, Department of Counseling, Administration, Supervision, and Adult Learning at Cleveland State University, holds a J.D. from the University of Illiniois and a Ph.D. from the University of Minnesota. He has published over 160 articles and books in the field of education law.

BARBARA McEWAN, Associate Professor of Education and Coordinator of the Elementary Education Master of Arts in Teaching Program at Oregon State University, teaches and writes about classroom management and educational law. She has edited *Practicing Judicious Discipline* (1993), coauthored *On Being the Boss* (1995), and coedited *The Theory and Practice of Classroom Management* (1997).

NANCY T. McKNIGHT is Associate Professor in the Elementary and Early Childhood Department, Slippery Rock University. She teaches graduate and undergraduate courses in early childhood education, including historical and psychological foundations as well as curriculum.

DEANNA MICHAEL received her Ph.D. from Georgia State University in 1997. The title of her dissertation was "Jimmy Carter and Educational Policy: From the School Board to the White House." She serves as Visiting Assistant Professor at Georgia State.

JEFFREY MIREL is Professor of Educational Studies and Director of the Division of Educational Studies at Emory University. He received his Ph.D. from the University of Michigan, and specializes in the history of urban education, the history of high school curriculum, and the history of civic education.

CHARLES MONAGHAN, an independent scholar and book collector, specializes in early American textbooks. His essay "Lindley Murray, American," appears in Ingrid Tieken-Boon van Ostade, ed., *200 Years of Lindley Murray* (1995).

E. JENNIFER MONAGHAN, Professor, English Department, Brooklyn College–CUNY, has written *A Common Heritage: Noah Webster's Blue-Back Speller* (1993) and has received "best article" awards from the American Studies Association and the History of Education Society. She also founded the History of Reading Special Interest Group of the International Reading Association.

NATALIE A. NAYLOR, Professor of Foundations of Education and Teaching Fellow, New College, Hofstra University, is coauthor of *Teaching Today and Tomorrow* (1981) and *Long Island's History and Cultural Heritage* (1992). She has also edited several books on local history and published articles on educational and local history.

MARY NESBIT is a doctoral candidate in the educational psychology graduate program at the University of Kentucky.

HARVEY G. NEUFELDT is Professor of Educational Foundations at Tennessee Technological University. He received his Ph.D. in 1971 from Michigan State University. His publications in southern and adult education include *Education of the African American Adult* (Greenwood Press, 1990), as well as numerous articles.

JOSEPH W. NEWMAN is Professor of Educational Foundations at the University of South Alabama, where he was named Scholar of the Year in 1991. Focusing his research on teachers and on the history of education in the South, he has written *America's Teachers: An Introduction to Education* (1998).

JO BETH OESTREICH, a graduate student in curriculum and instruction at the University of Texas–Austin, is focusing her research on social studies education. She has served as President of the Texas Council for the Social Studies.

CHRISTINE A. OGREN is Assistant Professor of Social Foundations of Education, University of South Florida. Her 1996 dissertation, "Education for Women in the United States: The Normal School Experience," focuses on seven different normal schools in the late nineteenth and early twentieth centuries.

ALLAN G. OSBORNE, Jr., is Assistant Principal of Snug Harbor Elementary School, Quincy, Massachusetts.

The REVEREND F. MICHAEL PERKO, S.J., received his doctorate from Stanford University, is currently Professor of Education and History at Loyola University of Chicago. He has written or edited four books and over seventy articles and papers dealing with education, religion, and culture in America.

DANIEL PERLSTEIN teaches at the Graduate School of Education at the University of California–Berkeley. His research examines progressive education, the civil rights movement, and twentieth-century urban schooling. A forthcoming book, *Justice, Justice: The 1968 New York City School Crisis and the Eclipse of Liberalism*, focuses on the way urban school politics has shaped and been shaped by race and class relations.

ALAN W. PROCTOR earned his Ph.D. at Boston University, has taught at Milton Academy (1971–1992), and is presently teaching at the Hotchkiss School, where he serves as Director of the Middle East Study Center. He has written a secondary level textbook on the history of the Middle East.

ASTERIE BAKER PROVENZO is a freelance writer and editor.

EUGENE F. PROVENZO, JR., is Professor in the Social and Cultural Foundations of Education at the University of Miami.

WILLIAM J. REESE is Professor of Educational Policy Studies and of History at the University of Wisconsin–Madison. His most recent book is *The Origins of the American High School* (1995), a social history of secondary schools before the 1880s. He also served as Editor of the *History of Education Quarterly*.

MARK J. REID is pursuing a doctoral degree in curriculum studies at the University of Texas–Austin.

JON REYHNER, Associate Professor and Coordinator of the Bilingual Multicultural Education Program at Northern Arizona University, edited *Teaching American Indian Students* (1992) and coauthored *A History of Indian Education* (1989).

MAUREEN A. REYNOLDS received her bachelor's degree in history from Notre Dame University and her law degree from Northwestern University. She is a doctoral student in the history of education at Indiana University. She wrote a chapter on school desegregation in Indiana for *Hoosier Schools: Past and Present* (1998).

DAVID B. RIPLEY received his Ph.D. in History and Philosophy of Education from the University of Iowa. He has taught history of education at Northern Illinois University since 1971.

AMY F. ROLLERI teaches in the Tacoma Public Schools (Washington) and holds a graduate degree in reading education and certification as a school administrator from SUNY College at Cortland, though her first love is art education.

W. J. RORABAUGH, Professor of History, University of Washington, has written *The Alcoholic Republic* (1979), *The Craft Apprentice: From Franklin to the Machine Age in America* (1986), and *Berkeley at War: The 1960s* (1989).

YVETTE C. ROSSER, a doctoral student in curriculum studies at the University of Texas–Austin, is specializing in global education. She has organized numerous workshops for secondary teachers offering strategies for infusing Asian topics in the classroom. She has also developed several programs promoting nonviolence and conflict resolution in the schools.

ERIC ROTHSCHILD has taught for thirty-five years and has been Chair of the Social Studies Department at Scarsdale High School since 1973. He has served on the Executive Board of the Organization of American Historians, been appointed Question Leader of the AP examination in U.S. history, and authored *The Teacher's Guide to Advanced Placement: United States History.*

KATE ROUSMANIERE, Assistant Professor in Educational Leadership at Miami University in Oxford, Ohio, has written *City Teachers: Teaching in New York City Schools in the 1920s* (1996). She is currently writing a biography of Margaret Haley.

CHARLES J. RUSSO, Professor and Chair, Department of Educational Administration, University of Dayton, received his J.D. and Ed.D in Educational Administration and Supervision from St. John's University in New York City. His teaching and research areas are educational law and policy.

DEBRA L. RUSSO, who earned both bachelor's and master's degrees in special education from C. W. Post College, has worked as an educator and social worker in New York, Kentucky, and Ohio. She is currently working in early childhood education.

RITA S. SASLAW, Professor of Education, University of Akron, received her Ph.D. from Case Western University in the history of education with special interest in antebellum education. She has authored numerous articles on educational history and is conducting research on Oberlin female students.

DAVID WARREN SAXE, Associate Professor and Professor In-Charge, Social Studies Education, Pennsylvania State University, specializes in the foundations of social studies. He has written *Social Studies in Schools: A History of the Early Years* (1991), among many articles and book chapters.

STEVEN SCHLOSSMAN, Professor of History and Head of the History Department, Carnegie Mellon University, focuses his research on a variety of topics in the history of education, criminal justice, and military personnel policy. Recent publications include *Foxholes and Color Lines: Desegregating the U.S. Armed Forces* (1998), with Sherie Mershon, and "A Sin against Childhood: Progressive Education and the Crusade to Abolish Homework, 1897–1941," *American Journal of Education* (1996).

GUY SENESE, Associate Professor, Educational Foundations and Leadership, Center for Excellence in Education, Northern Arizona University, received his Ph.D. in educational policy studies from the University of Illinois-Urbana in 1985. His research interests center on critical historical and cultural studies of education and on Native American education policy studies. He has published *Self-Determination and the Social Education of Native Americans* (1991).

ROBERT R. SHERMAN, Professor of Foundations of Education, University of Florida, has written about democracy, stoicism, academic freedom and tenure, history of education, and qualitative research in education. He has taught at numerous institutions in the United States and has lectured in Taiwan and Hong Kong.

CAROLE B. SHMURAK is Assistant Professor of Teacher Education at Central Connecticut State University. Her publications include "Mary Lyon and Science Education," *Teaching Education* (winter/spring 1991), and " 'Castle of Science': Mount Holyoke College and the Preparation of Women in Chemistry, 1837–1941," *History of Education Quarterly* (fall 1992).

PATRICK M. SOCOSKI teaches historical, philosophical, and sociological foundations of education at West Chester State University. He has held professorships at Pennsylvania State University and West Virginia University and published in *Educational Studies, Journal of Moral Education, National Forum of Educational Administration and Supervision Journal, Social Studies,* and *Teaching Education.*

PETER SOLA is Graduate Professor at Howard University. His research includes books on ethics and educational decision making, as well as critiques on school reform and model teacher education programs. He is currently editing a book on health ethics.

JAMES R. SQUIRE, currently retired, serves as an Executive Consultant and teaches part time at Harvard Graduate School of Education and Boston University. He is a former Executive Director of the National Council of Teachers of English and Professor of English at the University of Illinois, as well as a retired publisher.

EDWARD W. STEVENS, JR., Ohio University, has authored numerous books, chapters, and essays on the history of illiteracy and education and directed major grants in adult literacy education.

KATHLEEN STRICKLAND, Associate Professor in Elementary and Early Childhood Education at Slippery Rock University, has published *Literacy Not Labels: Celebrating Students' Strengths through Whole Language* (1995), and coauthored, with James Strickland, *Uncovering the Curriculum: Whole Language in Secondary and Postsecondary Classrooms* (1993).

CHARLES SUHOR has served as Deputy Executive Director, National Council of Teachers of English, between 1977 and 1997. He is currently a freelance writer and consultant, writing over 250 articles and book chapters on English education, censorship, jazz, and interdisciplinary topics. He also authored a process-based composition series (grades 7–12) and literature texts (grades 9 and 11).

JEFF SUZIK, Ph.D. candidate in social history at Carnegie Mellon University, is currently researching the transition of American youth into adulthood in the interwar period, with a particular emphasis on the Civilian Conservation Corps program.

KENNETH TEITELBAUM, Associate Professor in the School of Education and Human Development, Binghamton University, State University of New York, is the author of *School for "Good Rebels": Socialism, American Education, and the Search for Radical Curriculum* (1995) and other publications dealing with the history of education, curriculum studies, and teacher education.

MARTHA TEVIS is Professor of Education and Secondary Program Coordinator at the University of Texas, Pan American. She is writing a biography of George I. Sanchez and has contributed sections on Mexican American education and Sanchez in *Lives in Education: A Narrative of People and Ideas* (1994).

JOHN R. THELIN is Professor of the History of Higher Education and Philanthropy at Indiana University. He received his M.A. in history from Brown University, and his Ph.D. in Educational Studies from the University of California, Berkeley. He was Chancellor Professor of Higher Education at The College of William and Mary from 1981 to 1993.

PAUL THEOBALD, Professor of Education Policy and Practice, Associate Dean of the College of Liberal Studies, and Director of the School of Education at the University of Wisconsin–LaCrosse, has published work in many professional journals. His books include *Call School: Rural Education in the Midwest to 1918* (1995), *Rekindling Community: Place, Pride, and the Renewal of Local and Rural Schooling* (1997).

LAURA DOCTER THORNBURG is Assistant Professor of Education, University of Puget Sound. Her dissertation, "Pedagogy and Professionalism: A History of the Michigan State Normal School through the Life-Work of Julia Anne King, 1838–1919," explores the development of Michigan's first normal school and the career of a woman educator.

LUCY FORSYTH TOWNSEND, Associate Professor of Foundations of Education at Northern Illinois University, specializes in the history of women's higher education and has published the biography *Anna Peck Still and the Struggle for Women's Education* (1988). She and Barbara Wiley, Librarian of Emma Willard School, are collecting documents for a microfilm edition of the Emma Willard Papers.

JOSEPH L. TROPEA is Professor and Chair, Department of Sociology, George Washington University. He has researched the history of special education and has published in refereed journals and book chapters, written reviews, and delivered papers on education and special populations throughout Europe as well as Canada and the United States.

WAYNE J. URBAN, Regents' Professor at Georgia State University, where he has taught since 1971, has written *Why Teachers Organized* (1982) and *Black Scholar: Horace Mann Bond, 1904–1972* (1992). He has served as President of the American Educational Studies Assocation (1995) and the History of Education Society (1980).

ALEXANDER URBIEL, Assistant Professor of History, Ramapo College of New Jersey, received his degree from Indiana University. He teaches courses in U.S. social history and history of education. His research examines the history of civic education during the twentieth century.

JOHN VICKREY VAN CLEVE, Professor of History, Gallaudet University, is Editor-in-chief of the *Gallaudet Encyclopedia of Deaf People and Deafness* (1987). He coauthored of *A Place of Their Own: Creating the Deaf Community in America* (1989), and edited *Deaf History Unveiled: Interpretations from the New Scholarship* (1993).

JENNINGS L. WAGONER, JR., is Professor of History of Education in the Curry School of Education, University of Virginia. He has published numerous chapters, journal articles, and reviews. He is the author or coauthor of four books, of which the most recent is *American Education: A History* (with Wayne J. Urban, 1996).

JAMES M. WALLACE is Professor of Education at Lewis and Clark College, Portland, Oregon. His degrees are from Earlham College, Haverford College, and Harvard University. He has published widely on progressive education, including his book *Liberal Journalism and American Education, 1914–1941* (1991).

FRANCES WALSH, Professor Emeritus, Slippery Rock University, taught children's, young adult, and folk literature for twenty-eight years. She earned her Ph.D. in 1987 from the University of Pittsburgh, School of Library and Information Sciences, is noted for her Irish folklore and culture study tours and works in literary analysis and literature for preschool children.

SCOTT WALTER, a doctoral student in history of education and American studies and Associate Instructor in the Department of Educational Leadership at Indiana University–Bloomington, is researching the history of radicalism and American education.

DONALD WARREN, Professor of Education and University Dean of the Indiana University School of Education, writes on topics related to the history of federal involvement in U.S. education, teacher education, and other education policy issues.

JOSEPH WATRAS, Professor of Historical and Social Foundations of Education, University of Dayton, studied with Victor Kobayashi at the University of Hawaii and with Bernard Mehl at Ohio State University. Watras published *Politics, Race, and Schools* (1997).

JOHN A. WEAVER, Assistant Professor in Educational Foundations and Leadership at the University of Akron, has published articles and book chapters on issues pertaining to popular culture and critical pedagogy, academic politics, museums and memories, the Holocaust and peace education, literacy and race, and postmodernism and technology.

NANCY WEISS, Associate Professor, Social Science and Humanities, Toyo Eiwa Women's University, Yokahama, Japan, wrote her dissertation on the Children's Bureau. She published the prize-winning article ''Mother: The Invention of Necessity, Dr. Benjamin Spock's *Baby and Child Care*,'' *American Quarterly*, as well as ''The Mother-Child Dyad Revisited: Perceptions of Mothers and Children in Twentieth-Century Childrearing Manuals,'' *Journal of Social Issues*.

DEBORAH WELLS, Associate Professor, Elementary/Early Childhood Department, Slippery Rock University, is interested in language and education, which has resulted in several research projects designed to examine how children use language to construct meaning in their lives. She has published in *Research in the Teaching of English* as well as written a book chapter in an edited collection.

MICHAEL WESSELY is Manager of the National School Boards Association

National Education Policy Network and Editor of "Updating School Board Policies," the Network's bimonthly education policy newsletter.

EARLE H. WEST, Professor of Education Emeritus, Howard University, earned his Ph.D. in History and Philosophy of Education, George Peabody College. He served as Professor and Associate Dean, School of Education, at Howard and has written *The Black American and Education*, as well as published articles on black education in *History of Education Quarterly* and *Journal of Negro Education*.

DAVID WOLCOTT, a Ph.D. candidate in social history at Carnegie Mellon University, is currently writing a dissertation on the history of interactions between police and juveniles in American cities.

WILLIAM G. WRAGA, Assistant Professor, Department of Educational Leadership, University of Georgia, is author of *Democracy's High School: The Comprehensive High School and Educational Reform in the United States* (1994) and coauthor of the *Annual Review of Research for School Leaders*.

ARTHUR ZILVERSMIT, Distinguished Service Professor of History, has taught at Lake Forest College since 1966. One of the fields in which he has done both research and teaching is the history of American education. He wrote *Changing Schools: Progressive Education Theory and Practice, 1930–1960* (1993).

ISBN 0-313-28590-X

90000>

9 780313 285905

EAN

HARDCOVER BAR CODE